COLLECTED WORKS OF ERASMUS

VOLUME 7

THE CORRESPONDENCE OF
ERASMUS

v. 7

LETTERS 993 TO 1121

1519 TO 1520

translated by R.A.B. Mynors

annotated by Peter G. Bietenholz

University of Toronto Press

Toronto / Buffalo / London

The research and publication costs of the
Collected Works of Erasmus are supported by the
Social Sciences and Humanities Research Council of Canada.
The publication costs are also assisted by
University of Toronto Press.

Printed on acid free paper

Canadian Cataloguing in Publication Data

Erasmus, Desiderius, d. 1536.
[Works]
Collected works of Erasmus

Includes index.
Partial contents: v. 7. The correspondence of Erasmus:
letters 993 to 1121, 1519 to 1520 / translated by R.A.B. Mynors;
annotated by Peter G. Bietenholz.
ISBN 0-8020-5607-5

1. Erasmus, Desiderius, d. 1536. I. Title.

PA8500 1974   876'.04   C74-6326-x rev

Collected Works of Erasmus

The aim of the Collected Works of Erasmus
is to make available an accurate, readable English text
of Erasmus' correspondence and his
other principal writings. The edition is planned
and directed by an Editorial Board, an Executive Committee,
and an Advisory Committee.

Contents

Illustrations

Preface

On 1 July 1519, when Erasmus wrote the first letter published in this volume, he had lived for two years in Louvain. All things considered, it had been a most agreeable time, productive and carefree. He continued to occupy his rooms at the College of the Lily for almost as long again, but if we can believe the surviving letters, his last two years in Louvain turned out to be very different. Mutual recognition of scholarly achievement which led initially to Erasmus' co-option into Louvain's renowned faculty of theology was giving way to bitter conflict and controversy. In this respect Louvain was a microcosm of Erasmus' world, which was undergoing deep strain. Exuberant expectation of a golden age of civilized Christianity was giving way to helpless apprehension at the progress of what Erasmus often called the 'Lutherana tragoedia,' a play that was to end in catastrophe.[1] Erasmus was, above all, a writer and scholar; in the second half of his stay in Louvain, however, his literary and scholarly output fell notably short of the preceding period. In 1517 he had given the reading public two of the finest of his shorter treatises, the *Querela pacis* and the *Ratio verae theologiae*.[2] After that he published some essays originally composed decades earlier,[3] but no really new literary work was launched until the *Colloquia* of March 1522.[4] The monumental scholarly achievement of the first half of his stay in Louvain was of course the second edition of the New Testament,[5] while his edition of Cyprian was a remarkable pioneering effort.[6] Neither had an immediate sequel in the second half, although before Erasmus left the Netherlands for good – and especially during the carefree summer of 1521 spent at Anderlecht[7] – he must have drafted a good deal of the new *Colloquia* and also done some preliminary work on other new publications that appeared during the early months of his stay at Basel.[8] At least the paraphrases to the New Testament, a highly influential enterprise grounded on Erasmus' *philosophia Christi* and based on his preceding labours in the treadmill of the New Testament edition, continued to appear steadily throughout the four years he spent in Louvain and subsequently during the early years in Basel.[9]

It is true that Erasmus' surviving letters reveal some redeeming features of his later years at Louvain. He continued to acquire new friends and admirers and even his contacts with the remote kingdoms of east central Europe showed a gratifying growth,[10] while in Louvain such men as Maarten van Dorp and Maarten Lips stood by him in his troubles with endearing loyalty. Proudly the Netherlanders rejoiced at the election of their own prince Charles to succeed Maximilian I as emperor, and Erasmus was by no means immune against this upsurge of national sentiment. He now tended to expect of Germany as much and perhaps more than he had ever hoped of England or France,[11] but at the same time the election campaign reminded him poignantly of the greed and the injustice associated with political power.[12] In one respect, at least, the surviving correspondence seems misleadingly gloomy. In 1517 Erasmus' letters had shown his profound satisfaction at the establishment of Louvain's new, humanistic Collegium Trilingue,[13] but throughout 1519 and 1520 he cites many specific examples of hostility towards the new foundation and alleges a general conspiracy among its conservative critics.[14] What his extant letters fail to reflect, however, is the joy he must have experienced in seeing the Trilingue finally obtain a safe and autonomous status within the university (13 March 1520) and move into its own, newly built premises (18 October 1520).[15] At least he never lost faith, and just when things were going badly for the Trilingue, he emphasized that the scholastic tradition of the Middle Ages and the new learning of Renaissance humanism could flourish side by side in universities and schools.[16]

Often, indeed too often, the reader of this volume will encounter a troubled Erasmus, unhappily fighting back against both innuendo and open attacks. While some of his woes are set forth in great and perhaps unexciting detail, others remain for the most part untold, usually for good reason. In the early months of 1519 the first collection of Latin writings by Martin Luther had begun to circulate in Louvain and was eagerly examined by groups of hostile theologians. They may have realized that the anonymously printed volume came from the presses of Erasmus' principal publisher, Johann Froben at Basel[17]; at any rate they harboured grave suspicions about their famous colleague and evidently accused him of connivance with Luther.[18] The agitation against him calmed down around May 1519, and on 1 July, in the very first letter of this volume, he could categorically deny that the faculty of theology was preparing to censure his writings.[19] But the rumour which had prompted that denial[20] was not without foundation. Erasmus was very discreet about the matter; not until August 1521 did he recall in a letter composed for immediate publication that after the appearance of the Luther volume, 'because two or three of the [editorial] prefaces were in rather better

Latin' and hence attributed to himself, 'the bachelors [of theology] were given the task of collecting my errors.'[21] In 1525 he revealed another detail: supposedly the incriminating passages had been sent, he claimed, to Cardinal Adrian of Utrecht, who thought nothing of them, although he was at that time critical of Erasmus[22] and on other occasions endorsed the faculty's condemnations of Reuchlin and Luther. In December 1519 Erasmus merely gave some hints about this investigation in another letter written for swift publication,[23] but at about the same time Caspar Hedio at Basel sent word of the undertaking to Huldrych Zwingli.[24]

The theologians were no less discreet about their investigation than its subject was. The surviving records in the archives of the university apparently fail to shed any light on it, while Erasmus kept complaining of a conspiracy and cabal afoot against himself and the humanities.[25] These machinations become more tangible to us in the actions of two theologians who actually put their complaints against Erasmus into writing: Jacobus Latomus and especially Edward Lee. Both were aspiring to a doctorate in divinity; Erasmus concluded that both were henchmen and tools of other and perhaps more senior theologians.[26] He broadly hinted that none other than Jan Briart of Ath, the venerable head of the theological establishment and 'vice-chancellor' of the university, was the cause of his afflictions.[27] There is reason to think that Erasmus was being unfair; he himself later insisted that Briart had 'approved of everything' in his New Testament[28] and it is clear, moreover, that the 'vice-chancellor' was instrumental in bringing about, on 13 September 1519, a formal truce between Erasmus and his academic opponents.[29] The truce was short-lived, however. Before long printed copies of Erasmus' letter to Luther were gleefully passed around,[30] and, after an official condemnation of Luther on 7 November and the death of Briart on 8 January 1520, the investigation of Erasmus' books apparently was resumed.[31] By then, however, all attention seems to have been focused on the single contest between Erasmus and Edward Lee, which was approaching its climax.

The conflict with Lee comes into view on all but a few pages of this volume. One would like to think that for some reason the letters exaggerate the extent of Erasmus' preoccupation with it, but the slowdown in his scholarly production does not encourage such an assumption. By the summer of 1519 Lee had assembled several hundred notes levelling criticisms at Erasmus' New Testament. Erasmus desperately wanted to see and refute them, so he continued his policy of provocation, as was stated briefly in the preface to CWE 6. Tension continued at fever pitch until Lee's book was eventually published in February 1520.[32] Erasmus lost no time in producing his reply,[33] and in July, when the two protagonists shook hands at an encounter of their respective monarchs,[34] the volcano had finally calmed, except for a carefully orchestrated campaign of support among Erasmus' friends, who kept the presses running for a few months longer.[35] There is little doubt that by overreacting Erasmus was his own worst enemy. Whatever Lee's motives for launching his attack, he was not the villain Erasmus made him out to be. He had taken on a formidable opponent and never regained the offensive once he had lost it; on the other hand, as late as February 1520 he believed that his earlier criticisms had been of real value to Erasmus when he revised the New Testament for the edition of 1518–19.[36] This was probably not the case; but Lee's claim cannot now be disproved. This volume provides detailed information on the progress of the dispute in a series of letters. When the two opponents present conflicting accounts of the same incidents – and they often do – Lee's may possess a marginally higher credibility. On the other hand, Lee had been the one to launch upon Erasmus an attack that was both unjustified and unprofitable.

The view that Lee had failed to make a constructive contribution was advanced by a contemporary observer of remarkable insight and objectivity.[37] Thomas More was a personal friend of both opponents and the genuine affection he felt for each, admiring in the case of Erasmus, almost paternal in that of Lee, is impressively demonstrated in the advice he gave them. More's letters, which take up some of the finest pages in this volume, testify to his rare integrity and clear-sightedness. Even when dealing with his own controversy with the French humanist Germain de Brie,[38] – a controversy capable of arousing initial impulses of passion and scorn in More – his words and actions ultimately reveal a capacity for sober self-assessment and restraint combined with charity that seem almost unprecedented in the turbulent days of the early sixteenth century. As it happened, More's literary joust with Brie reached its climax at the same time as did Erasmus' confrontation with Lee, and each friend did the other a valuable service in counselling moderation. Erasmus' friendship with More inspired the most famous letter to appear in this volume, Ep 999, which will always rank among his finest writing and the great accomplishments of Renaissance literature. The outstanding success of this subtle and sparkling pen portrait of More, the man and the Christian, must have been evident to its author, who in letters to be included in the next volume of this correspondence returned to the formidable challenge of doing justice to More[39] and also attempted similar profiles of two other friends, in this case recently deceased.[40]

Of the 130 letters contained in this volume the great majority were printed in Erasmus' own collections of his correspondence. Sixteen appeared in the *Farrago*[41] of October 1519 and were reprinted in the *Epistolae ad diversos* dated 31 August 1521 on the title-page. That collection included another sixty-three letters found in this volume. Only nineteen letters failed to find their way to print during Erasmus' lifetime, and only Ep 1033 was published at first by others against his wishes, prompting him to include a revised version in the *Epistolae ad diversos*. Thus the modern reader is not substantially better informed than a contemporary of Erasmus studying the *Epistolae ad diversos*. Allen's Epp 660 and 1035–6 have been assigned new dates and appear in this volume as Epp 1013A and 1000A–B. As for letters lacking addresses, Henry de Vocht's hypothesis for the addressee of Ep 1041 has been tentatively accepted, while Allen's identification of the addressee of Ep 1051 has been rejected. Some letters had to be assigned conjectural dates, but alternative hypotheses are normally confined to a narrow span of time.

As in the preceding CWE volumes the introduction to each letter informs the reader of the date by which it became available to the public. For letters published in contemporary collections of Erasmus' correspondence the introduction cites the earliest such collection to print the letter in question. For letters published elsewhere in Erasmus' lifetime the first edition is cited as well. Where manuscript sources exist these are also cited provided they carry any weight. For fuller biographical information on the contemporaries and near-contemporaries of Erasmus whose names may be encountered in this volume, the reader is referred to *Contemporaries of Erasmus: A Biographical Register of the Renaissance and Reformation* (CEBR), published as an ancillary part of the CWE.

The translation of the letters is the work of R.A.B. Mynors, who wishes to acknowledge the stimulus and assistance supplied by his colleagues in the enterprise; the *Dialogus bilinguium ac trilinguium* was translated by Paul Pascal. The annotation of this volume has been greatly facilitated by the unfailing assistance provided by the staff of the University of Saskatchewan Library, the Öffentliche Bibliothek of the University of Basel, the British Library, and the Warburg Institute, University of London. Some of Erasmus' references to classical authors have been identified by Erika Rummel and Alexander Dalzell, and some notes dealing with currency have been supplied by John H. Munro. The index was prepared by Howard Hotson. The manuscript was copyedited by Mary Baldwin. Finally, it should be recalled that the Collected Works of Erasmus could not have been undertaken without the continued support of the Social Sciences and Humanities Research Council of Canada, its generous patron.

PGB

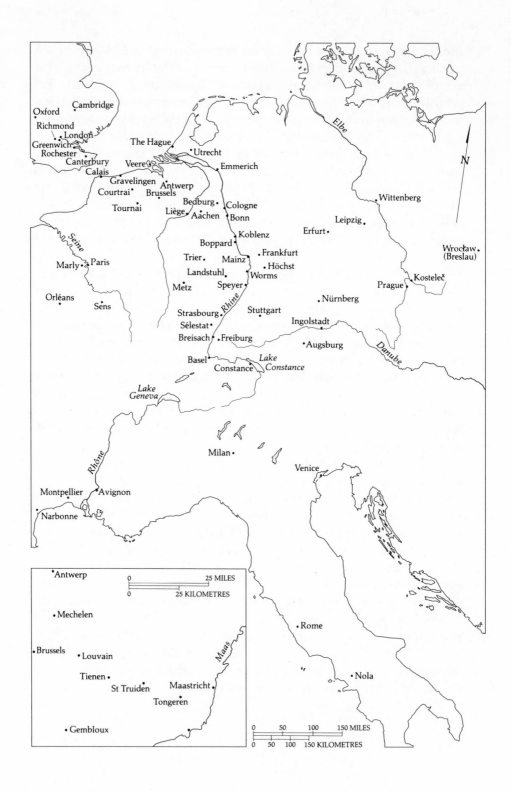

Oxford
Cambridge
Richmond
London
Greenwich
Rochester
Canterbury
Calais
Gravelingen
Courtrai
Tournai
The Hague
Utrecht
Veere
Emmerich
Antwerp
Brussels
Bedburg
Cologne
Liège
Aachen
Bonn
Koblenz
Boppard
Frankfurt
Trier
Mainz
Höchst
Landstuhl
Worms
Metz
Speyer
Strasbourg
Stuttgart
Sélestat
Breisach
Freiburg
Augsburg
Basel
Ingolstadt
Constance
Lake Constance
Nürnberg
Erfurt
Leipzig
Wittenberg
Wrocław (Breslau)
Prague
Kosteleč
Seine
Marly
Paris
Orléans
Sens
Rhine
Danube
Elbe
Lake Geneva
Rhône
Milan
Venice
Montpellier
Avignon
Narbonne

N

Antwerp
Mechelen
Brussels
Louvain
Tienen
St Truiden
Maastricht
Tongeren
Gembloux
Maas

0   25 MILES
0   25 KILOMETRES

Rome
Nola

0   50   100   150 MILES
0   50   100   150 KILOMETRES

THE CORRESPONDENCE OF ERASMUS

LETTERS 993 TO 1121

993 / To Leonardus Priccardus   Louvain, 1 July 1519

At the beginning of his third year of residence in Louvain Erasmus answers an affectionate letter (Ep 972) addressed to him by Priccardus, a canon at Aachen. His answer reflects the accumulation of troubles and worries experienced during the spring months (cf Ep 930: 12n and the preface of this volume) and above all the continuing conflict with Edward Lee. This letter was first printed in the *Farrago*; cf Ep 1009 introduction.

ERASMUS OF ROTTERDAM TO LEONARDUS PRICCARDUS,
CANON OF AACHEN, GREETING

I know quite well, my learned friend Leonardus, that men of this kidney are never idle; their chief resource lies in fluent falsehoods and brazen innuendo. For my part, I am already hardened to all that; I can only marvel 5
that persons who are distinguished by their profession of the religious life should feel themselves free to do something which conflicts above all with true religion. They wish it to be thought an unpardonable sin if they eat meat; and yet it is virtuous to rain the poisoned arrows of their hellish language[1] on a fellow Christian, even on one who has done them some 10
service, although no sort of venom could be more utterly abominable. Really, they seem to have forfeited their souls on oath unto the gods below (forgive my poetic language), unless they extinguish sound learning root and branch. As long as sound learning is secure, they know there is no security for them, and they are convinced that I am one of its main supporters. Yet 15
none of them talk more offensive nonsense than those who have not read a word I ever wrote. Inexperience and ignorance I could forgive, if it were not monstrous in itself to make these wild attacks on another man's reputation without finding out the facts. Nor do I see how they can have the face to use their ignorance as an excuse and yet wish to pass for teachers of the rest of 20
the world.

As for your English (perhaps I may say 'Scotish'?[2]) man, there is a lot of truth in the story. He is a youngster[3] who both by age and disposition has a great desire to shine; and this was, he thought, the perfect short-cut to a reputation. All the same, although his generosity where he himself is 25
concerned is inexhaustible, he is not brazen enough to say he knows more Greek than your humble servant. He talks a great deal about some small book he has written, but gives no one a copy except such as he knows are my ill-wishers. One can get anything out of him, rather than that I should be given the chance to look at it – and I am the one person against whom it is 30
directed. Such is his confidence in this piece of his! – and yet he advertises it all over the place. Be that as it may, he has made himself into a perfect tool for

certain theologians who have long been planning mischief and were simply
biding their time, as the Greek proverb[4] has it. Some say it is not his own
work; it is just a rag-bag, a patchwork of all the scandals, but that this magpie   35
will get the credit for the whole thing; and this seems to me likely enough for
many reasons. It is just what we saw happen not long ago with Latomus'
dialogue:[5] one man's name in the title, and everyone, or at least a good many
people, with a finger in the pie.

Our English friend, who had almost calmed down, had been roused to   40
fresh fury by my statement,[6] at the end of my *Apologia* against Latomus, that
there exists a certain individual compounded of falsehood and lies who is
beside himself with ambition and will stop at nothing where I am concerned;
nor do I add any suggestion that might make suspicion fall on anyone. My
sole object in using that phrase was to frighten off a number of people who   45
knew that the cap fitted them; but this man has now started to behave as
though he were jealous of all other claimants to that proud position. The
fellow has not yet entered the arena, and my more intelligent friends advise
me not to use my claws on such an unworthy object, if he does come; they say
that if I keep quiet there are plenty of people[7] who will deal with the young   50
man and his headlong passion for applause.

Apart from that, if some of the divines are ill-disposed in my direction,
this arises from the most groundless suspicions. They have got it into their
heads that I am the champion and mainstay of Luther's ideas,[8] although I do
not know the man and have never read anything of his. At long last they are   55
perceiving their mistake, but are ashamed to acknowledge it; they set such a
value on consistency that even on the wrong road they will not turn back. All
the same, one man[9] is the principal source for all this flood of venom, and
unless he lays off, he will soon be pilloried in all the writings of the learned
and 'famed in song the wide world o'er.'[10]   60

Up to now, I have restrained many people from writing, but I fear I
cannot do so indefinitely. It seems to me a sort of fatal disease, and the
infection is gradually spreading to more people. So we suffer from the
plague[11] twice over, in spirit as well as in body. Yet a certain number are
seeing the light, especially those who have read what I write with some   65
attention; and I hope that Truth[12] will in the end arise victorious, for
storm-tossed as she often is, she never goes down.

For my own part, I am less affected by all this, either because I have
grown deaf to these monstrosities like Balaam[13] of old, or because my own
conscience is clear and I hope that my unsleeping efforts may be found   70
acceptable with Christ, for whom I labour with such powers as I have, or
because I see that all the best judges approve my zeal. What does distress me
is the way humane studies are being infected with this litigious spirit, while I

am compelled to spend a good part of my precious time in listening to this
kind of nonsense or refuting it. I often feel shame on account of these people, 75
who would like to pass for demigods in public and yet clamour like
fishwives, not to put it too harshly. My own nature finds strife of this sort
utterly revolting, and I try my hardest not to prove the old saw[14] right:
'Oft-wounded patience will to madness turn.' I can see how their active
malevolence deserves to be dealt with; but I am restrained by the mildness of 80
a Christian and by respect for honourable men, whom I should hate to be
thought to cast a slur on while I give the dishonourable the treatment they
deserve. You know how readily the public see a discreditable sense in
everything; and there is a risk that anything said about a few theologians
who are unworthy of the name will be distorted to cover the whole order; 85
that words directed, and rightly directed, against a few who are Black
Friars[15] by name and blackmailers by nature will bring discredit on the order
as a whole, which contains a great many men as far removed from them as
possible in their actions and their character.

It is said that the theologians have decided to smite me with an official 90
resolution.[16] Nothing could be further from the truth. Best wishes, my
valued friend, and pray commend me warmly to your reverend and learned
colleagues.

Louvain, 1 July 1519

994 / From Nicolas Bérault   Paris, 1 July [1519]

Bérault was an old friend, who was now living in Paris (cf Ep 925 introduction).
His letter was published in the *Farrago* and was written evidently after his
patron, Etienne Poncher, had been appointed archbishop of Sens on 14 March
1519. Erasmus answered with Ep 1002.

NICOLAS BÉRAULT TO ERASMUS OF ROTTERDAM, GREETING
I have always had other reasons to think well of Wilhelm Nesen,[1] but this in
particular earns my affection and approval, that I have always found him so
devoted to you. He shares this, of course, with many other men, but yet I
think it important, and not a little in his favour. As he was setting out to visit 5
you at Louvain, I could not let him leave here without a letter from me, partly
because he asked for it so eagerly, and partly to provoke you to a reply; for
three letters from me, two of them[2] sent by Francesco Calvo and the most
recent[3] brought to you in Louvain by Nesen himself, have so far had no
answer. 10

The archbishop of Sens, Etienne Poncher, will shortly be writing to you
with an important proposition,[4] and I will make sure that you get his letter by

a safe hand or will bring it myself. I have written to Dorp[5] on your behalf in the name of a certain theological circle; but what I said you had better learn from Nesen rather than from a letter. The New Testament[6] with your 15 versions and your brilliant and learned annotations, is now in the hands of numerous scholars here, among them some theologians of repute who now (if I may say so) are as excessively devoted to you, thanks to this book, as they were most unfairly hostile before. Certainly this new edition has already won many people over to your side; and a certain number who had 20 long been obstinately opposed to you, and were virtually given up for lost, had already been shaken by your defences.[7]

Best wishes, and greetings from François Deloynes and Louis Ruzé.[8]

Paris, 1 July

995 / From Lorenzo Campeggi   London, 4 July 1519

The papal nuncio to the English court wrote this letter in answer to Ep 961. Erasmus replied with Ep 996 and published the exchange in the *Farrago*. Even before it appeared in print the two men had actually met; see Ep 1025:6.

CARDINAL LORENZO CAMPEGGI TO THE REVEREND DOCTOR
DESIDERIUS ERASMUS OF ROTTERDAM, MOST ERUDITE OF
THEOLOGIANS, AS TO OUR DEAREST BROTHER
Reverend and learned sir, greeting and so forth. Your learning, like a sweet savour, pervades all Italy and the whole western world, and I too have long 5 been under the spell of its fragrance, which grows upon me day by day. Thus I have felt a very great desire to make the acquaintance of a man who radiates such great knowledge and scholarship; the wandering life[1] and wide-ranging journeys which have been my weary lot now for many years seemed to me valueless, and I bore them an unceasing grudge, because after all that 10 voyaging I still found I had never met Erasmus. In compensation, since I was not given the chance to enjoy your society, I did all I could to achieve what many lovers do, who, when they have no access to the loved one, seek passionately from her picture such comfort as they can. And so, finding it impossible to satisfy my wishes by your presence and your conversation, I 15 seized every opportunity to acquire your image,[2] which I found reflected first in what you have written on Jerome, secondly in the *Apologia* in which you justify your treatment of that verse in the Psalms[3] 'Thou madest him a little lower than the angels,' and most recently in your sermon-paraphrase on the Pauline Epistles. 20

As by these steps I came to know you better, and my desire increased, for it was only a partial and imperfect picture of you that I had before me, I

became very anxious to fill out the missing parts; and then by some good
fortune an elegant and learned letter reached me from yourself, from which it
appeared that you suffered from the same desire of making my acquaintance,   25
and this news I received with such delight, that I would set less store by the
rich gifts of princes. My own studies,[4] which have occupied me from
boyhood to the present day, differ by the whole gamut[5] from your own
studies in Holy Scripture, but the encouragement of your researches, and
others like them, has always been so near my heart, that since my early years   30
nothing has given me greater pleasure and delight than to hear or read some
exposition of the Scriptures; to speak or write myself, as a mere tyro, I would
never dare.

Naturally therefore, since I was already eagerly on the look-out for
works by you or by certain ancient theologians, almost as part of my official   35
duties, the receipt of your letter gave me all the more pleasure, because it was
what I most longed for and had no reason to expect. By sending with it the
first and second[6] of your publications on the New Covenant, I feel that you
have offered me the missing portions of that picture of yourself I so much
wanted, so that I can support more patiently and more agreeably my longing   40
for your company and conversation; and this you will undoubtedly achieve,
at any rate for such time as this fruit of all your labours is in my hands – as
often, that is, as I am allowed to take refuge from my public duties in these
private compensations. And if their novelty is more than some people can
stomach, the fault lies in their queasy digestions and not in any poisonous   45
quality in what they have eaten or what is set before them; so that this
disposition of theirs will cause you all the less surprise and resentment, the
more you realize that to a disordered appetite the most health-giving food is
unpalatable.

I am so far from feeling such qualms myself, that very soon I shall   50
greedily devour this same New Covenant of yours that you have sent me; for
I think your orthodoxy at least equal to your learning. This is why you can
safely disregard the bad name which some people, in their folly or malice, are
trying to thrust upon you, making you responsible for the wilder utterances
of others. What you publish openly over your own name is enough to   55
establish your integrity, which, great as it is, cannot hope to escape what
great minds often have not escaped, the perversity of men's judgments and
their ill will and spite. As for the dialogue,[7] I beg you to believe me when I say
that I never said or suggested, or left the suspicion in other people's minds,
that you were the author. The thought may perhaps have crossed my mind,   60
following the opinion of which you speak, which fathers on you every
pamphlet that comes out nowadays with any wit or point to it; but who can

see into the thoughts of men or sit in judgment on them, except him who sees
all things, and reproves what falls below his standard?

Of one thing therefore you can be quite sure: I am not the man to think   65
ill, much less to speak ill, of you or of anyone else. For all scholars, and
yourself especially, I offer gladly and sincerely to do all in my power, and
shall always strive to the uttermost, to encourage their gifts and their
reputation; I do what I can to win glory for you and recognition for your
scholarship, and so I always shall. Henceforward therefore you will count   70
me among your friends, united with you by this exchange of letters, and a
devoted admirer of your learning. When the moment comes that I can do
anything to help you or your reputation, my assistance shall not willingly be
found wanting in any respect. If, when the occasion arises, you tell me of
your needs, my zeal and diligence in promoting your interests will surpass   75
all other men's, and my good will towards you will be delightfully rewarded
if, while I am here, which cannot be much longer,[8] you sometimes give me the
pleasure of one of your charming letters.

In any case, it seems to me a waste of time to express my thanks for the
present you have sent me, for no words, however eloquent, could be   80
adequate to the most welcome service you have rendered me. Instead of
expressions of gratitude, accept the assurance of my attachment and at the
same time, as an earnest of it, the diamond ring[9] enclosed with this letter,
which I wish you to keep as a reminder of myself. The man[10] who brought me
your book has been given ten gold pieces towards his expenses. And so   85
farewell.

London, 4 July 1519

996 / To Lorenzo Campeggi   Louvain, 14 July 1519

This answer to Ep 995 was published in the *Farrago*.

TO THE RIGHT REVEREND CARDINAL LORENZO CAMPEGGI
FROM ERASMUS OF ROTTERDAM, GREETING
My right reverend Lord, what limit shall I set to my audacity in future, now
that this first rash approach has had such a happy outcome? My hope was
merely to secure a measure of respect for a work of mine which was already   5
unpopular in certain quarters for its novelty, if it should have the good
fortune to find a place in your library, much as in the olden days books which
were thought to deserve the attention of posterity were laid up in the temple
of Apollo.[1] This would show, I thought, how learned cardinals endorse the
solemn pronouncement[2] of our Holy Father Leo. No cedar-oil[3] preserves the   10
works of scholars from decay and the assaults of time like the authority of

Lorenzo Campeggi
Courtesy of the Trustees of the British Museum, London

princes such as these. Of one thing, you may be sure, I had very little fear –
that a capital marriage of learning and wisdom such as yours would be
affected by the shameless calumnies of certain persons, which rouse the
scornful laughter of men of moderate intelligence even among ordinary   15
people.

This being my only purpose, think what a windfall came to me
unexpectedly, what an immense fish I drew in with this net! First, it was my
good fortune to get to know much better a leading champion and pillar of the
church of Christ. And then I acquired such a distinguished patron and even,   20
if I may really accept what you offer, such a friend. I had of course a certain
image of you, drawn by popular report; but a much fuller picture of your
mind was given me in conversation by Richard Pace,[4] his Majesty's principal
secretary. Not only had he surveyed your distinguished gifts at closer
quarters, but he is no mean artist in description, being a man as ready of   25
speech as he is well read. However, your letter gave me so full a vision of the
writer that I seemed to myself to have known hitherto only a shadowy
outline of your qualities.

It was a great man, a distinguished man, that he described to me; but
you appear immensely greater in your letter, which breathes not only   30
learning worthy of a papal legate and a generosity of spirit to match that
learning, but a rare nobility of life and a loving zeal for the Scriptures. It was
an almost excessive generosity to give the man who brought those books so
many gold pieces, so that no doubt, passionate devotee of Bacchus[5] as he is,
he could drink even deeper than usual, I having given the fellow all he   35
needed for his journey. As for the ring, which you took from your own finger
and sent me as a sacred token of our friendship, or rather, if I may use your
own words,[6] as a pledge of brotherly love, I am so grateful for it, from the
bottom of my heart, that I would not exchange this one ring for all the
treasure of Attalus.[7] The gold with its glowing brilliance will always be for   40
me a symbol of your wisdom, so worthy of a cardinal, and the enchanting
lustre of the diamond will stand for the unfading glory of your name. In a
word, were it possible that I could ever forget such a patron, it will refresh
my memory, and remind me of what the name Campeggi means to me.

About my gifts (but I am a true Dutch dumpling)[8] and what I have   45
written, you are wrong, of course, wrong in the kindness of your heart, and I
am grateful. Surely these are the eyes of a pure heart, as the Gospel[9] has it,
one that puts the gifts of others on a par with its own, while to the infected
purblind eye even the noblest things are evil. 'What is this?' you will say, 'is
my praise wasted?' Not altogether, for it has at least spurred me on, and after   50
this I shall strive with more energy to become what you maintain I am; for I
believe one is never too old for self-improvement. For those most generous

promises of your kind help towards the advancement of our best minds I
thank you on behalf of all, and will do everything I can to make them
understand what they owe to your Eminence. In the promotion and   55
assistance of my humble self, no one, you say, shall be allowed to seem your
rival; and your intention, of course, I gratefully acknowledge, and think
myself outstandingly fortunate in this respect.

I have dashed off this hasty scribble, for it is not really a letter, for fear
that a letter might not reach your Eminence, since you say that you must soon   60
be on the move. But I cannot rest content with this as a memorial of your
kindness to me and of my feelings towards yourself; and very soon, I hope,
they shall be made known to the world in some work[10] of greater scope and
longer life. My best wishes for your Lordship's welfare, to whom I offer my
humble self as your obedient servant.   65

Louvain, 14 July 1519

997 / To the Chapter of Metz Cathedral   Louvain, 14 July 1519

During his last visit to Basel Erasmus had most likely met Claudius Cantiuncula, a promising young scholar from Metz (cf Ep 852:82–91), who may have
told Erasmus about the treasures of the chapter library there. In 1521
Cantiuncula used, and shared with his lawyer friends at Basel, some
manuscripts obtained from Metz (cf AK II Ep 810). At Metz he had good friends
who were at this time admirers of Erasmus, in particular Henricus Cornelius
Agrippa of Nettesheim and Claude Dieudonné (cf P. Zambelli in *Rinascimento*,
2nd ser 10, 1970, 48–50, 69). Erasmus, who was then putting the finishing
touches on his edition of Cyprian (cf Ep 1000), had recently obtained
manuscripts from the abbey of Gembloux on the basis of a list similar to the one
here requested (Epp 975, 984).

At Metz, as in other dioceses of Lorraine, the cathedral chapter was headed
by a *primicerius* who ranked above the dean. Nicolas Toussain (Tussanus),
whose nephew Pierre was later to become a friend and companion of Erasmus
(cf Ep 1559) had been *primicerius* since 1505. (He died on 5 August 1520 in
Rome.) Ulric des Hazards (d 17 June 1527) had been dean since 1514. Since 1518
the see of Metz had been occupied by the young cardinal Jean de Lorraine
(1498–1550), patron of poets and scholars. The cardinal also appreciated the
treasures of the chapter library; on 29 November 1520 he borrowed 'un
excellent manuscrit en velin des chroniques de Metz,' without keeping his
promise of returning it promptly; see Martin Meurisse *Histoire des évêques de
l'église de Metz* (Metz 1634) 603.

Erasmus published this letter in the *Farrago*. Nothing is known about the
success of his approach.

TO THEIR EXCELLENCIES THE PRIMICERIUS OF THE CATHEDRAL
CHURCH OF METZ, THE DEAN, AND THE WHOLE CHAPTER,
FROM ERASMUS OF ROTTERDAM, GREETING

Honourable and reverend sirs, every man pursues the thing he loves, and in
this way I have learnt from several informants that you possess a library filled   5
not with ordinary books, but with valuable manuscripts of great antiquity.
The gospel precept[1] bids everyone to put his talent out to use for the general
good, in such a way that he who provided the capital may approve the return
upon it; and in this spirit I have devoted my own efforts to the bringing of
ancient authors into the light of day and defending them against moth and   10
worm or to emending their corruptions. It is a serious loss if something
produced with so much effort by the great men of the past is to perish
altogether; but a text can hardly be said to survive which survives so much
befouled in all its parts with error that it can be neither read nor understood.
I have no doubt that as religious men you also wish to forward the public   15
good and cordially disapprove of the dog in the manger of whom Greek
proverbs[2] tell, all the more so since you can share this advantage with other
men with no loss to yourselves.

I beg you therefore of your kindness to send me a list of your library,
recording especially such texts as are not commonly to be found or are only to   20
be found in a corrupt state, as happens usually in most books of a certain age.
From such a list I will choose those which seem most likely to be useful. If you
in Christian charity assist my efforts in this matter, you will be doing that
which in the first place is most pleasing to Christ, and also redounds highly
to the credit of your most distinguished body; for I shall not suffer your   25
kindness to remain unknown to posterity. May Christ Almighty preserve
you in all health and wealth, my most respected lords in Christ.

Louvain, 14 July 1519

998 / To Edward Lee   Louvain, 15 July 1519

This letter marks a new phase in the escalating conflict with Edward Lee (cf CWE
6 preface). Evidently written for immediate publication in the *Farrago* (cf Ep
1009 introduction) and perhaps not even communicated to Lee right away (cf
the beginning of his answer, Ep 1061), it is the first overt attack on his
opponent to appear in print. Erasmus had still not been able to see the bulk of
Lee's critical notes on his New Testament. The publication of the revised
edition in March 1519 (cf Ep 864) had added to his nervousness and for a
second time he had attacked Lee publicly, still, however, without mentioning
his name, in his *Apologia* against Jacobus Latomus (c April 1519; Epp 936:34n,
993 n6). English friends had attempted to mediate between the two opponents

and their efforts met with some success (cf Epp 993:40–1, 1026 n3) until the *Apologia* against Latomus appeared.

Convinced that Lee's intelligence was as mediocre as his scholarship, Erasmus was increasingly afraid that Lee, like Latomus, was but a willing tool in the hands of more formidable enemies secretly joined in a conspiracy against him (cf lines 50–6 and Epp 930:10–12, 993:32–9). Chief among these Louvain theologians of the old school was the venerable 'vice-chancellor' of the university, Jan Briart of Ath (cf Ep 1029 n2). Since Erasmus was officially on good terms with him (cf Ep 946) he could not reasonably object when Briart was proposed as an arbitrator in the controversy with Lee. By October 1518 (cf Ep 1053 n14) both progtagonists had submitted their texts to the 'vice-chancellor,' who had earlier examined the first edition of Erasmus' New Testament and had found nothing to criticize. But already by the end of October Erasmus withdrew the printer's copy of the text volume of the second editon from Briart as he had to send it to Froben's press (cf Ep 864 introduction). Subsequently Lee also reclaimed his notes after Erasmus had craftily tried to obtain copies (cf n3). Briart died in January 1520 without having pronounced an opinion, and both opponents were free to lay claim to some support from him; cf *Apologia invectivis Lei* (*Opuscula* 247–9).

Lee continued to withhold his notes from Erasmus, who retaliated with the threat that, in spite of his efforts to the contrary, his own admirers might join battle (cf lines 65–84 and Epp 993:49–51, 57–62, 999:344–51, 1053:152–76). He might not have used this threat, which was bound to backfire, had he been aware that Nesen's *Dialogus bilinguium ac trilinguium* (cf 329 below), a coarse attack on Lee, was to be published soon afterwards. Erasmus himself, however, showed hardly more restraint when attacking Lee in a new edition of his *Colloquia*, published about November 1519; see Epp 1041 introduction, 1061:374–430.

ERASMUS OF ROTTERDAM TO EDWARD LEE, GREETING

That you should differ from me on some points does not greatly distress me, for scholars have always had the right to disagree while remaining friends. But your method of proceeding in this matter will not commend itself, unless I am greatly mistaken, to any sensible person, since even Jan Briart Atensis   5
does not approve it, rightly devoted to you as he is. In all my thousands of notes, full of opinions and suggestions of every kind, it is neither new nor strange if you have detected some mistakes that had escaped me or if you disliked something that I had found acceptable. But the way in which you suddenly changed from friend to enemy and attacked me in writing while I   10
was away[1] will commend itself to nobody – and that too when I had done nothing to provoke you, and you had never confronted me while I was

present. Nor will the way you wrote against the old edition[2] when you knew I was preparing a new one. Nor this circulating of your piece in every convent, especially those in which you were aware there were people who do not wish me well. Nor this showing of your work solely to those whom you knew to be prejudiced against me, while you could never be induced, even by the influence of Atensis, to give me access to your book – no, not even to produce by word of mouth a single passage with which you had found fault. You have sprinkled poisonous abuse and actual falsehoods up and down your book (so people tell me who have seen it, and the pages I have intercepted[3] bear this out). You boast constantly of the hundreds of passages which you have refuted, and all the time you do not show me a single one. Is this, I ask you, a fair example either of responsibility or of Christian spirit?

If you wish to be useful to the public, why not publish? If you wish to put me right, why am I the one person not allowed to see it? If you wrote for your own benefit, why has your book such a wide circulation?[4] If you are diffident about your work, why advertise it everywhere? If confident, why so anxious that no one should read it who is not prejudiced against me? In this way, while you attack me before an audience which is committed on oath to your way of thinking and hostile to me, you make me no better and you make them worse. Have you considered meanwhile what effect this will have on the reputation which you pursue with so much clamour? If you had published your work immediately, we should all have admired the prodigious fertility of your brain, which in a few short months had devoured so much Hebrew and Greek,[5] that in your judgment Erasmus knew no Greek and Jerome no Hebrew – if indeed it is Jerome's version, as you always add out of respect, for fear you seem to underrate Jerome. Why, they tell me that three days after your first steps in Hebrew you had much fault to find with Reuchlin, and some even with Capito.[6] Yes, it might well have happened: the Holy Father, in admiration of your almost godlike brain, might have placed the wand of office in your hands and set you up as censor of the whole world, so that no book would be published or read without the approval of Edward Lee, the modern Aristarchus[7] of the whole realm of literature.

As it is, many people say that you are keeping close your famous annotations with intent to publish them after my death, hoping to win your case by default; and a barren victory it will be, if there is no opponent to give you a game. Others maintain that in the mean time you are on the look-out for complaints from all quarters, so that your book will be nothing but a patchwork of other people's malicious criticisms, of which only a very small portion will be your own work. There will then be the risk that instead of the

honour and glory for which you hoped you may get as little credit as
Latomus[8] did for his dreary dialogue, over which they say a whole battalion   55
of divines wore themselves out. No doubt you are very well pleased just now
with what you write; but do not suppose that it will please everyone when it
is exposed to the light of day. Young[9] as you are, I can forgive the desire to
shine that drives you on; but that you should choose this devious path to
glory, you who wish to be thought not only a theologian and an upright man   60
but something of a saint into the bargain – this all posterity will disapprove
of, though perhaps you win applause from some people now. You have been
acting this absurd part for nearly two years, and you enjoy it so much that it
seems you will act it to your dying day.

All the same, I do not resent what you have done to the extent of   65
wishing that anyone should be one hair's breadth[10] less well disposed
towards you on my account, let alone of hoping that some more serious
misfortune should befall you. But the trouble has now spread all over the
world; you would hardly believe how they come flying out from everywhere, the emissaries of those people who, in defiance of precedent, are   70
both beggars and bullies[11] at the same moment. Nor is there any country in
which my works have not earned me something in the way of friends; but in
Germany I have supporters in plenty, more enthusiastic than even I could
wish, and you know the restless energy of the Germans and their violence of
character. They have not yet entirely shaken off that native ferocity of theirs,   75
however much they may be ripening steadily under the influence of humane
studies. Look at the pamphlets[12] with which they cut to pieces anyone who
has done them an injury! I for my part have restrained[13] many of them from
writing, partly by word of mouth, partly by letter, and shall continue to urge
restraint as far as I can. But some of them, I hear, are threatening more violent   80
measures,[14] and if anything of the sort should happen (which God forbid),
not only should I be unable to remedy your trouble but, to judge by the way
people now put two and two together, some of the blame would fall on my
own head. And thus your trouble would mean a twofold inconvenience for
myself: I should be sorry to see ill befall for my sake a man to whom I wish   85
nothing of the kind, and men would not be wanting to suspect that I was
privy to the attack. As it is, I hope we shall see nothing of the sort, but at the
same time I fear that something may happen. If there is no danger, it was
friendly of me to be anxious; if there is, it was still more friendly to warn you,
and give you the chance, if you think fit, of taking such steps to meet it as you   90
in your wisdom may think best. Farewell.

Louvain, 15 July 1519

999 / To Ulrich von Hutten   Antwerp, 23 July 1519

This letter is a brilliant portrait of Erasmus' best friend, Thomas More. (It was supplemented later by two more fragmentary descriptions of More's character and personal environment in Epp 1233, 2750). One of More's reactions to another portrait – the painting by Quinten Metsys representing Erasmus himself – was Ep 684. That letter had been published in the *Auctarium* and thus could have inspired Hutten's request for a portrait of More (cf n1). The request fell on willing ears, to say the least. Erasmus had now abandoned earlier plans to immortalize More in another work (cf Ep 706:38n) and was eager to compose for the general public a description of More that could be published without delay in the *Farrago*. In giving it the form of a letter to Hutten, he also paid tribute to the latter – tying, as it were, one close friend to another, a move he later regretted (cf Allen I 27). See Germain Marc'hadour *Thomas More vu par Erasme: Lettre du 23 juillet à Ulrich von Hutten*, a private edition (Angers 1969) including the text, a French translation, and a commentary; M.M. Phillips 'Erasmus and Biography' *University of Toronto Quarterly* 42 (1972–3) 185–201; Bietenholz *History and Biography* 92–4.

    This letter was dated during the first of two consecutive visits Erasmus paid to Antwerp. Perhaps the main purpose of his first trip was to meet his old friend Richard Pace, then returning from a diplomatic mission in connection with the imperial election (cf Epp 996 n4, 1001:58–60. Pace reached Antwerp on 22 July (cf LP III 392), possibly later than expected. Perhaps he had been delayed by unsafe roads (cf Ep 1001:73–7), for he had been at Frankfurt on 3 July, at Mainz the next day, and at Cologne on 8 July (cf LP III 351, 353, 363). Erasmus may have reached Antwerp before Pace and composed or polished this letter while waiting. It was not merely feelings of friendship which prompted him to meet Pace at any cost; he was alarmed that Edward Lee, his bitter opponent, was also travelling to Antwerp to see the English ambassador (cf Ep 1074:74–7 and Pace's letter to Lee, Greenwich, 21 March [1520] in Froben's *Epistolae aliquot eruditorum virorum* 85–7; see Ep 1083 introduction). On 27 July Pace was at Mechelen expecting to depart for Calais and England on the following day (cf LP III 398); Erasmus had returned to Louvain by 31 July (cf Epp 1000, 1001:4–5).

    Erasmus' second absence from Louvain was primarily recreational (cf Ep 1013:27–31) and less rushed than the first. He visited several cities in Brabant and Flanders, dating again a series of letters from Antwerp between 7 and 15 August (Epp 1001–6, 1008–9). On the way there he had stopped at Mechelen to greet Bishop Philip of Burgundy who happened to be there (cf Ep 1001:9–11). From Antwerp he probably went on to Bruges where he met Cardinal

Campeggi on c 26 August (Ep 1025:6; cf Ep 1012). On the way back he may have stopped in Brussels (cf Ep 1040 n2) and on 10 September he was again in Louvain; cf Ep 1013.

ERASMUS OF ROTTERDAM TO THE HONOURABLE ULRICH VON
HUTTEN, KNIGHT, GREETING

The affection – one might almost say, the passion – that you feel for that gifted man Thomas More, fired as of course you are by reading his books, which you rightly call[1] as brilliant as they are scholarly – all this, believe me 5
my dear Hutten, you share with many of us, and between you and More it works both ways:[2] he in his turn is so delighted with the originality of your own work that I am almost jealous of you. Surely this is an example of that wisdom which Plato calls the most desirable of all things, which rouses far more passionate desire in mortal hearts than the most splendid physical 10
beauty. The eyes of the body cannot perceive it, but the mind has its own eyes, so that here too we find the truth of the old Greek saying[3] that the eye is the gateway to the heart. They are the means through which the most cordial affection sometimes unites men who have never exchanged a word or set bodily eyes on one another. It is a common experience that for some obscure 15
reason one man is captivated by this form of beauty and another by something different; and in the same way between one man's spirit and another's there seems to be a kind of unspoken kinship, which makes us take great delight in certain special people, and less in others.

Be that as it may, you ask me to draw a picture of More for you at full 20
length, and I wish I were as skilful as you are eager. For me too it would be nothing but a pleasure to spend a little time thinking about the friend I love best. But there are difficulties: it is not everyone[4] can appreciate all More's gifts, and I doubt if he would endure to be depicted by any and every artist. It is, I suspect, no easier to produce a portrait of More than one of Alexander 25
the Great or Achilles, nor did they deserve their immortality any more than he does. Such a sitter demands the skill of an Apelles, and I fear there is less of Apelles in me than of Fulvius or Rutuba.[5] I will try, however, to do you not so much a picture as an outline sketch of the whole man, based on long-standing and intimate acquaintance, as far as my observation or 30
memory will serve. Should any mission overseas eventually bring you together, you will realize what an incompetent artist you have selected for this task, and I am afraid that you will think me either envious or purblind – too blind to detect, or too envious to be willing to record more than a few of all his good qualities. 35

To begin with one aspect of More which is quite unknown to you, in

stature[6] and habit of body he is not tall, without being noticeably short, but
the general harmony of his proportions is such that nothing seems amiss. He
has a fair skin; his complexion tends to be warm rather than pale, though
with no tendency to a high colour, except for a very delicate flush which   40
suffuses it all. His hair blackish-brown, or brownish-black if you prefer;
beard[7] somewhat thin; eyes rather greyish-blue, with a kind of fleck in them,
the sort that usually indicates a gifted intelligence, and among the English is
thought attractive, while our own people prefer dark eyes. No kind of eye,
they say, is so immune from defects. His expression shows the sort of man he   45
is, always friendly and cheerful, with something of the air of one who smiles
easily, and (to speak frankly) disposed to be merry rather than serious or
solemn, but without a hint of the fool or the buffoon. His right shoulder
looks a little higher than his left, especially when walking, not by nature but
from force of habit, like so many human tricks. Otherwise there is nothing to   50
criticize in his physique. Only his hands are a trifle coarse, at least if one
compares them with his other bodily features. As for the care of his personal
appearance, he has taken absolutely no heed of it ever since boyhood, to the
extent of devoting very little care even to those niceties allotted to the
gentlemen by Ovid.[8] How good-looking he was as a young man, one can   55
guess even now by what remains[9] – though I knew him myself when he was
not more than three-and-twenty, for even now he is scarcely[10] past his
fortieth year.

He enjoys good, but not rude, health, adequate at any rate to support
all the duties of a good citizen, and is subject to no complaints or very few;   60
there is every hope that he will enjoy long life, for his father[11] is still alive at a
great age, but wonderfully active and vigorous for his years. I have never
seen a man less particular about his food. Until he reached manhood he was
content to drink nothing but water, a habit inherited from his father. Only,
for fear of causing any embarrassment in this regard, he used to drink his   65
beer out of a pewter tankard, so that the guests did not know – small beer
next door to water, and often just water. As for wine, the habit in those parts
being to invite your neighbour to drink in his turn from the same cup,[12] he
sometimes barely sipped it, so as not to seem entirely to dislike it, and at the
same time to learn to follow common usage. Beef, salt fish, and coarse bread   70
with much yeast in it he preferred to the dishes of which most people are
fond, though in other ways he was by no means averse from all the things
that bring harmless pleasure, be it only to the body. Dairy produce and all
the fruit which grows on trees have always had a great attraction for him,
and he is particularly devoted to eggs. His voice is not loud, yet not   75
particularly soft, but of a sort to strike clearly on the ear; no music in it, no

subtlety, a straightforward speaking voice, for he does not seem framed by nature to be a singer, though he is fond of music[13] of all kinds. His language is remarkably clear and precise, without a trace of hurry or hesitation.

Simple clothes please him best, and he never wears silk or scarlet or a gold chain, except when it is not open to him to lay it aside. He sets surprisingly little store by the ceremonies which ordinary men regard as a touchstone of good breeding; these he neither demands from other people nor tenders meticulously himself either in public assemblies or in private parties, although he is familiar with them should he wish to use them. But he thinks it effeminate and unworthy of a man to waste a good part of his time in such frivolities.

Court life and the friendship of princes were formerly not to his taste, for he has always had a special hatred of absolute rule and a corresponding love for equality. You will hardly find any court, however modest, that is not full of turmoil and self-seeking, of pretence and luxury, and is really free from any taint of despotic power. Even the court of Henry viii he could not be induced to enter except by great efforts,[14] although it would be difficult to wish for anything more cultured and more unassuming than the present king. By nature he has a great love of liberty and leisure; but dearly as he loves to enjoy leisure when he can, no one displays more energy or more endurance at the call of duty.

Friendship he seems born and designed for; no one is more open-hearted in making friends or more tenacious in keeping them, nor has he any fear of that plethora[15] of friendships against which Hesiod warns us. The road to a secure place in his affections is open to anyone. In the choice of friends he is never difficult to please, in keeping up with them the most compliant of men, and in retaining them the most unfailing. If by any chance he has picked on someone whose faults he cannot mend, he waits for an opportunity to be quit of him, loosening the knot of friendship and not breaking it off. When he finds open-hearted people naturally suited to him, he enjoys their company and conversation so much that one would think he reckoned such things the chief pleasure in life. For ball games, games of chance, and cards he hates, and all the other pastimes with which the common run of grandees normally beguile their tedious hours. Besides which, though somewhat negligent in his own affairs, no one could take more trouble in furthering the business of his friends. In a word, whoever desires a perfect example of true friendship, will seek it nowhere to better purpose than in More.

In society he shows such rare courtesy and sweetness of disposition that there is no man so melancholy by nature that More does not enliven him, no disaster so great that he does not dissipate its unpleasantness. From boyhood he has taken such pleasure in jesting that he might seem born for it, but in this he never goes as far as buffoonery, and he has never liked bitterness. In his youth he both wrote brief comedies[16] and acted in them.   120 Any remark with more wit in it than ordinary always gave him pleasure, even if directed against himself; such is his delight in witty sayings that betray a lively mind. Hence his trying his hand as a young man at epigrams,[17] and his special devotion to Lucian;[18] in fact it was he (yes, he can make the camel dance)[19] who persuaded me[20] to write my *Moriae encomium*.   125

In fact there is nothing in human life to which he cannot look for entertainment, even in most serious moments. If he has to do with educated and intelligent people, he enjoys their gifts; if they are ignorant and stupid, he is amused by their absurdity. He has no objection to professional buffoons, such is the skill with which he adapts himself to the mood of   130 anyone. With women as a rule, and even with his wife, he confines himself to humour and pleasantry. You would think him Democritus[21] reborn, or rather that Pythagorean[22] philosopher who strolled unthinking through the market-place watching the crowds of people buying and selling. Nobody is less swayed by public opinion, and yet nobody is closer to the feelings of   135 ordinary men.

He takes a particular pleasure in contemplating the shapes, character, and behaviour of different living creatures. Thus there is hardly any kind of bird of which he does not keep one in his household, and the same with any animal that as a rule is rarely seen, such as monkey, fox, ferret, weasel, and   140 the like.[23] Besides these, if he sees anything outlandish or otherwise remarkable, he buys it greedily, and has his house stocked with such things from all sources, so that everywhere you may see something to attract the eyes of the visitor; and when he sees other people pleased, his own pleasure begins anew. In his younger days he was not averse from affairs with young   145 women, but always without dishonour, enjoying such things when they came his way without going out to seek them, and attracted by the mingling of minds rather than bodies.

A liberal education he had imbibed from his very earliest years. As a young man he devoted himself to the study of Greek literature and   150 philosophy, with so little support from his father, a man in other respects of good sense and high character, that his efforts were deprived of all outside help and he was treated almost as if disinherited because he was thought to be deserting his father's profession; for his father is a specialist in English law. The law as a profession has little in common with literature truly so   155 called; but in England those who have made themselves authorities in that subject are in the first rank for eminence and distinction. Nor is it easy in that country to find any other career more likely to lead to wealth and reputation;

Lady Alice More
By Hans Holbein the Younger
Corsham Court, Lord Paul Methuen

and in fact most of the nobility[24] of the island owes its rank to studies of this kind. In the law, they say, no one can perfect himself without many years of 160 hard work. So it was not surprising that, when he was a young man, More's nature should swerve away from the law, being made for better things; but after a taste of the subjects studied at the university, he betook himself to it with such good effect that there was no one whose advice was more freely sought by litigants, nor was a larger income[25] made by any of those who gave 165 their whole time to the law. Such was the force and quickness of his intelligence.

Besides this he devoted himself actively to reading the works of the orthodox Fathers. On St Augustine's *De civitate Dei* he gave public lectures[26] before large audiences while still quite a young man; priests and old men 170 were not ashamed to seek instruction in holy things from a young man and a layman, or sorry they had done so. And all the time he applied his whole mind to the pursuit of piety, with vigils and fasts and prayer and similar exercises preparing himself for the priesthood. In this indeed he showed not a little more sense than those who plunge headlong into so exacting a 175 vocation without first making trial of themselves. Nor did anything stand in the way of his devoting himself to this kind of life, except that he could not shake off the desire to get married. And so he chose to be a god-fearing husband rather than an immoral priest.

However, he chose for his wife an unmarried girl[27] who was still very 180 young, of good family, and quite inexperienced as yet, having always lived in the country with her parents and her sisters, which gave him the more opportunity to mould her character to match his own. He arranged for her education and made her skilled in music of every kind, and had (it is clear) almost succeeded in making her a person with whom he would gladly have 185 shared his whole life, had not an early death removed her from the scene, after she had borne him several children. Of these there survive three daughters,[28] Margaret, Alice, and Cecily, and one son, John. Nor did he endure to remain a widower for very long, though the advice of his friends urged a different course. A few months after his wife's death, he married a 190 widow,[29] more to have someone to look after his household than for his own pleasure, for she was neither beautiful nor in her first youth,[30] as he used to remark in jest, but a capable and watchful housewife, though they lived on as close and affectionate terms as if she had been a girl of the most winning appearance. Few husbands secure as much obedience from their wives by 195 severity and giving them orders as he did by his kindness and his merry humour. He could make her do anything: did he not cause a woman already past the prime of life, of a far from elastic disposition, and devoted to her household affairs, to learn to play the zither, the lute, the monochord, and

the recorder, and in this department to produce a set piece of work every day   200
to please her exacting husband?

He shows the same geniality in the management of his household,[31] in
which there are no troubles and no disputes. If anything should go wrong,
he puts it right promptly or makes them agree; nor has he ever dismissed
anyone as a result of ill feeling on either side. In fact his household seems to   205
enjoy a kind of natural felicity, for no one has ever been a member of it
without bettering his fortune later, and no one has ever earned the least
shadow on his reputation. Indeed you would hardly find such close
relations anywhere between a man and his mother as exists between him and
his stepmother;[32] for his father had now remarried for the second time, and   210
he loved them both as if they had been his own mother. The father has lately
remarried a third time; and More solemnly swears that he has never seen a
better person. Such moreover is his affection for his kinsmen, his children,
and his sisters[33] that his relations with them are never oppressive, nor yet
does he ever fall short in his family duties.   215

From any love of filthy lucre he is absolutely free. To provide for his
children he has earmarked as much of his resources as he considers sufficient
for them; and the rest he spends liberally. In the days when he was still
dependent on the income from his clients, he gave everyone helpful and
reliable advice, thinking much more of their advantage than of his own; the   220
majority he used to persuade to settle their actions, on the ground that this
would save them expense. If that was not successful, he then tried to show
them how to carry on their litigation at the least cost to themselves; for some
men are so made that they actually enjoy going to law. In the city of London,
in which he was born, he has for some years acted as judge[34] in civil cases.   225
This office is by no means onerous, for the court sits only on Thursdays until
dinner-time, but it carries much prestige. No one ever determined more
cases, and no one showed more absolute integrity. Many people have had
the money returned to them which according to precedent must be paid by
litigants; for before the action comes into court, the plaintiff must deposit   230
three drachmas,[35] and the defendant the same, nor is it permissible to
demand any more. The result of this behaviour was that his native city held
him in deep affection.

He had made up his mind to be content[36] with this station in life, which
gave him quite sufficient standing and at the same time was not exposed to   235
serious risks. More than once he was forced to go on a diplomatic mission;[37]
and as he conducted these with great intelligence, his serene Majesty King
Henry viii would not rest until he had dragged[38] the man to his court. I use
the word 'dragged' advisedly, for no man was ever more consumed with
ambition to enter a court than he was to avoid it. But since that excellent king   240

had it in mind to fill his household[39] with learned, wise, intelligent, and upright men, he summoned a great many others, and especially More; whom he keeps so close to him that he never allows him leave to go. If serious business is afoot, no better counsellor than he; if the king wishes to relax his mind with more cheerful topics, no man's company more gay. Often difficult   245
issues demand an authoritative and able judge; and More can settle these in such a way that both parties are grateful. Yet no one has succeeded in persuading him to take a present from anybody. Happy indeed a commonwealth would be, if the prince would appoint to each post a magistrate like More. And all the time no pride has touched him.   250

Amidst such masses of business he does not forget his old and ordinary friends, and returns to his beloved literature from time to time. Whatever power his station gives him, whatever his influence can do with so powerful a king, is all devoted to the good of the commonwealth and of his friends. His disposition was always most ready to do good unto all men, and wonderfully   255
prone to show mercy; and he now gives it more play, because he has more power to do good. Some men he helps with money, to some he gives the protection of his authority, others he advances in life by his recommendation. Those whom he cannot help in any other way he aids with good advice. He has never sent anyone away with a long face. You might call More the   260
general resource of everyone who needs help. He thinks some great stroke of luck has come his way if he has been able to relieve the oppressed, to help the perplexed and entangled out of their troubles, or to reconcile the parties to a quarrel. No one more enjoys doing a kindness or less demands gratitude for doing one. And yet, though he is very fortunate on so many counts, and   265
though good fortune is often accompanied by self-conceit, it has never yet been my fortune to see a man more free from that fault than he.

But to return to tell of his literary pursuits, which have been the chief bond between More and myself in both directions. His earlier years were exercised principally in poetry; after that came a long struggle to acquire a   270
more supple style in prose by practising his pen in every sort of writing. What his style is like now, I need not set down, especially for your benefit, for you have his books always in your hands. He has taken delight especially in declamations,[40] and, in that department, in paradoxical themes, as offering more lively practice to one's ingenuity. As a youth he even worked   275
on a dialogue in which he supported Plato's doctrine of communalism, extending it even to wives.[41] He wrote an answer to Lucian's *Tyrannicida*,[42] on which topic it was his wish to have me as an opponent, to test more accurately what progress he had made in this sort of composition. *Utopia* he published with the purpose of showing the reasons for the shortcomings of a   280
commonwealth; but he represented the English commonwealth in particular,

because he had studied it and knew it best. The second book he had written earlier, when at leisure;[43] at a later opportunity he added the first in the heat of the moment. Hence there is a certain unevenness in the style.

It would be difficult to find a more felicitous extempore speaker, so fertile are both his mind and the tongue that does its bidding. His mind is always ready, ever passing nimbly to the next point; his memory always at his elbow, and as everything in it is held, so to say, in ready cash, it puts forward promptly and without hesitation whatever time or place demand. In disputations nothing more acute can be imagined, so that he has often taken on even the most eminent theologians in their own field and been almost too much for them. John Colet,[44] a sensitive and experienced critic, used to say sometimes in conversation that there was only one able man in the whole of England, though the island is blessed with so many men of outstanding ability.

True piety finds in him a practising follower, though far removed from all superstition. He has his fixed hours at which he says his prayers,[45] and they are not conventional but come from the heart. When he talks with friends about the life after death, you recognize that he is speaking from conviction, and not without good hope. And More is like this even at court. What becomes then of those people who think that Christians are not to be found except in monasteries?

Such are the men whom that most intelligent king admits to his household[46] and his privy chamber; admits, yes, and invites, and even forces them to come. These are the continual spectators and witnesses of the way he lives; these form his council; these are the companions of his journeys. He rejoices to have them round him rather than young men or women dissolute and vicious, or even rich men[47] in their splendid collars, or all the blandishments of insincerity, where one man would divert him to aimless pleasures, another would heat his blood with thoughts of tyranny, another put forward fresh tricks with which to fleece his people. Had you lived in this court, my dear Hutten, I have no doubt you would quite rewrite your *Aula*,[48] and cease to be a professed enemy of court life, though you too live with as honourable a prince[49] as you could wish, nor do you lack men who look for a better state of things, such as Stromer and Kopp.[50] But what are the few that you have in comparison with such a company of distinguished men:[51] Mountjoy, Linacre, Pace, Colet, Stokesley, Latimer, More, Tunstall, Clerk, and others like them? Whichever you choose to name, you will have mentioned in one word a world of all the virtues and all learning. I myself, however, have hopes of no common kind that Albert, the one ornament of our native Germany at this time, may gather more men like himself into his

285

290

295

300

305

310

315

320

household, and may set an important precedent for all the other princes, encouraging them too to wish to do the same, each in his own court.

There is the portrait, the best of sitters ill done by the worst of artists. You will like it less when you have the good fortune to know More better.   325 But I have done it to protect myself for the moment – to stop your complaining that I have not done what you asked, and your constant objections that my letters are too short. Though this has not seemed to me longer than usual in the writing, nor will you find it, I am sure, long-winded in the reading; my dear More's charm will see to that.   330

But I must not leave your last letter,[52] which I read first in print before it reached me, quite unanswered. The kindness of your distinguished Prince Albert I knew already from a letter[53] which he himself sent me. But how, pray, has it happened that the cup[54] should be familiar to everyone from your letter before it gets to me? I am sure you could not find a safer messenger than   335 Richard Pace, the English king's envoy, whether I were in Brabant or Britain. For what I can see, you are waging war valiantly with both pen and sword,[55] yet not with more courage than success. For I hear you have made a great impression on his Eminence Cardinal Cajetanus.[56] I rejoice that all is well with Reuchlin. The name of Franciscus Cinglius[57] shall not die; literature   340 must see to that, or risk a charge of gross ingratitude.

You shall have my news on another occasion; for the moment, only this. The favourite weapon here[58] is the most sordid insinuation, an art to which I must confess myself unequal. If there is anyone in your part of the world who wishes to learn the technique of innuendo, I will point out to him   345 a past master[59] of the system, whom you would say was clearly meant for it by nature. Cicero is less of an orator than this purveyor of scandal, and he finds many among us to believe him. The time is not yet ripe; but I shall soon be recommending the man to you as a candidate for immortality in the writings of the learned (which he deserves, and is pathetically anxious for) – but as a   350 monster rather than a man. Farewell.

Antwerp, 23 July 1519

1000 / To Lorenzo Pucci   Louvain, 31 July 1519

This is the preface to Erasmus' edition of Cyprian (Basel: J. Froben February 1520). St Cyprian became bishop of Carthage shortly after his conversion to Christianity and died a martyr in 258. He was one of the earliest Fathers of the western church, and although he was at times in open opposition to the see of Rome and perhaps excommunicated, the number of surviving manuscripts shows that his predominantly pastoral writings carried great influence.

An edition of Cyprian was probably discussed when Erasmus spent the summer of 1518 at Froben's press, preparing the second edition of his New Testament (cf Ep 864 introduction). Earlier he had taken charge of Froben's great edition of Jerome (cf Ep 396 introduction). The complete works of other church Fathers were perfectly suited to continue the co-operation between the scholar and the printer, and Cyprian was a logical choice for the first of these folio volumes, since the inadequacy of the preceding Cyprian editions underlined the need for critical scholarship. In 1521 Froben published an equally important edition of Tertullian, another early Father, prepared by Beatus Rhenanus. In 1522 the planning and production of subsequent volumes in this patristic series was no doubt an important consideration when Erasmus decided to settle in Basel (cf Ep 1242 introduction).

The search for manuscripts and early editions of Cyprian was conducted jointly from Louvain and Basel (cf Epp 925 introduction, 975, 984, Allen IV 23–4, V xx) and netted some texts not previously printed. On 3 October 1519 Bonifacius Amerbach wrote that Erasmus was still working on the Cyprian, lavishing nearly as much care on him as previously on Jerome; on 26 December he stated that the Cyprian kept Froben's staff busy day and night (AK II Epp 686, 711; cf Ep 715); finally, on 23 February 1520 Amerbach was thanked by Zasius for a gift copy (AK II Epp 719–20). This preface was reprinted with the Cyprian edition by the Froben press in 1521, 1525, and 1530, with new revisions each time. There is a modern critical edition of Cyprian in three volumes by Wilhelm von Hartel in CSEL 3 (1868–71).

This dedication to Cardinal Lorenzo Pucci (d 1531) links the Cyprian to the revised New Testament of 1518–19. When Erasmus was at Basel to see the New Testament through the press, he was visited by the cardinal's nephew, Antonio Pucci, papal legate to the Swiss cantons (cf Ep 860). A papal brief for the New Testament (Ep 864) was obtained in part through the good services of Antonio and especially of Cardinal Lorenzo, whose secretary, Paolo Bombace, was an old friend of Erasmus; cf Epp 865:24–9, 36, 905:5–7.

TO HIS MOST REVEREND FATHER AND LORD LORENZO PUCCI,
DESERVEDLY CARDINAL OF THE SANTI QUATTRO CORONATI,
FROM ERASMUS OF ROTTERDAM, GREETING
In that vast cataclysm of literature from which so many famous works of Antiquity have emerged corrupt or fragmentary, and by which countless 5 authors deserving of immortality have been completely swallowed up, it might seem foolish, most reverend Father, to lament the loss of one or two in particular, were not Cyprian rightly held to be a host in himself, whether one considers his eloquence, his learning, his eminence as a bishop, the apostolic energy that breathes in every word he wrote, or his glorious martyr's death. I 10

almost think we should find the loss easier to bear if he had perished utterly. As it is, while we infer from the fragments which some accident has permitted to survive what his lost works were like, those of us who are greedy for such treasures are tormented all the more. In fact, the reputation of his works became the reason why it is now so uncertain what and how much that great man wrote; for it led Jerome to think it a waste of time to make a list of his productions,[1] since in his own day they shone brighter than the sun and enjoyed a universal circulation – Jerome could not think it possible that such brilliance, such celebrity could by any accident be overtaken by the darkness of oblivion. The same misfortune has befallen us in Tertullian,[2] while some other mischance has robbed us of the catalogue of the works of Origen drawn up by Jerome,[3] as he tells us in a letter to Paula in which he compares the works of this Adamantius (as he calls him) with those of Varro,[4] who like him is well known as a most prolific author.

In any case, though we have the evidence of Lactantius[5] that Cyprian wrote a great deal, no one will form a correct idea how great was the calamity that deprived us of the rest until he has separated from such remains as we have those pieces that are spurious and wrongly ascribed. Cyprian shares with other authors the misfortune of having many works by other men mixed with his own, but he was more fortunate than Jerome in one respect: there are many pieces interspersed in Jerome's works which are simply not worth reading,[6] while nothing was ascribed to Cyprian that was not scholarly and the work of some great man. And so I have rejected nothing even of that class, and in fact have added a few things from early manuscripts, for one cannot reject something out of hand merely because it is not Cyprian's.

And let no one think that in applying these tests I have followed nothing but some will o' the wisp of my own imagining. The *Symbolum fidei*,[7] which in both printed and manuscript volumes still bears Cyprian in the title, is current among St Jerome's works under the name of Rufinus. The *De singularitate clericorum*[8] is to be found among the shorter essays of Augustine, though I am not certain it is not by Cyprian; Augustine's it cannot be, as is shown, apart from the language, by the scriptural quotations. As regards the rest, I shall add my own views in the appropriate places. The life is clearly an excerpt from the book written, as Jerome[9] tells us, by Pontius, Cyprian's chaplain, who was the inseparable companion of his exile until the final day of his martyrdom. For it seems to me unlikely that this is the distinguished work mentioned by Jerome in his life of Pontius, for the thing we possess does not deserve to be called so much as a sketch. Certainly the conclusion,[10] which deals with the translation of his body, is added by another hand, as is too clear to need pointing out, especially since it includes a mention of the emperor Charlemagne.

Then again, when St Jerome records that only eight letters from Cyprian to Cornelius, bishop of Rome, survive, while our manuscripts offer, if I am not mistaken, eleven,[11] it may be that they did not all come into Jerome's hands or, since it sometimes happens that different topics are dealt 55 with in one and the same letter, that some of them have been divided in two; this certainly happened to one of them, as I have detected and pointed out.[12] Besides which, many as were the Doctors once produced by Africa who were famous for their style and doctrine, among whom Tertullian and Augustine are the chief, yet scarcely any of them achieved a really pure Roman style 60 except Cyprian. (I refer to the ecclesiastical writers; otherwise Lactantius[13] would be an obvious exception.) For Tertullian, close-knit and forcible as his argument is, is difficult and obscure, and even slipshod in language, as Jerome[14] says in his letter to Paulinus, agreeing of course with the judgment of Lactantius. Even in Augustine the reader is pulled up from time to time by 65 a certain complexity and difficult involution of style, a complaint which Jerome brings[15] against him in his letters.

But both ascribe to Cyprian the highest gifts of style. Thus Jerome writes[16] in his letter to Paulinus: 'St Cyprian like a crystal spring runs on fresh and smooth,' and Lactantius[17] in the preface to book 5 of his *De* 70 *institutione religionis christianae* credits him not only with fluency, charm, lucidity, versatility, and polish, but in addition with force and energy in pressing his case. 'He was by nature,' he says, 'fluent, versatile, agreeable, and (the greatest of stylistic virtues) lucid, so that it would be hard to say whether anyone ever showed more eloquence in expressing and more 75 readiness in explaining himself, or more power of persuading his reader.' I only wish that St Augustine, like Cyprian an African and a bishop, had been as able to keep up with him in elegance of style as he was to surpass him in number of volumes. If only he successfully emulated the style which he so openly admires and praises! For it is from Cyprian's works in particular that 80 he chooses examples in the fourth book of his *De doctrina christiana*[18] to show that no department of eloquence is unrepresented among Christian authors, comparing Cyprian from time to time with Ambrose, as Quintilian[19] compares Cicero with Demosthenes. And again in his confrontations with the Pelagians and the Donatists he quotes Cyprian's opinions with great 85 respect.

For myself, I cannot deny that among orthodox writers I used to give first place to Jerome;[20] but when I looked more closely into Cyprian, whom previously I had read at random and without attention, doubt at once assailed me which I should prefer; so true is it that each with his own special 90 virtues makes an overwhelming impression. If Demosthenes is rightly put first on the ground that he comes nearest to the true and natural style of

speaking and is farthest from the unnatural atmosphere of declamation, then
in this way Cyprian far outstrips Jerome, being everywhere more serious and
less artificial; for Jerome, like Tertullian, is undisciplined in his humour and   95
sometimes flat in his digressions, and has a strong admixture of profane
allusions – all these being gifts (if we think them desirable) which Cyprian
not so much lacked as neglected or despised. You will find nothing in him
that might seem brought in to show off the writer's wit or that smacks at all of
artifice, as happens sometimes in Jerome. His manner of expression   100
everywhere is such that you feel you are listening to a true Christian, a
bishop, and a future martyr. His heart burns with the religion of the Gospel,
and his language answers to his heart. What he says is eloquent, but even
more than eloquence it shows vigour, and there is even more vigour in his
life than in his writings, as he himself somewhere puts it.   105

Such a personality was better matched by dignity than charm, although
some passages clearly show that he was not devoid of wit, when the subject
so required, as when he pours the cleverest mockery on a heretic[21] who
maintained that Cyprian could not be regarded as a bishop, or when he
refutes those who thought that anyone baptized in dangerous sickness by   110
sprinkling rather than immersion should be called a bedridden[22] rather than
a baptized Christian. For here, besides the unbroken grace that runs
through everything like blood through the body, he uses jokes and barbed
shafts as well. In one letter[23] at least, which begins 'Bene admones, Donate,'
he has made some satirical use of a grand and solemn style, and it is from that 115
that Augustine takes an example of neat, graceful, and brilliant language.
This great Doctor of the church, this champion of Christian piety, we owe to
the schools of the rhetoricians, so let no one think with stupid satisfaction of
his own lack of a rhetorical education. Let others exalt to their hearts' content
those whom we derive from the schools of philosophy, the logicians, and the   120
Peripatetics, nor would I wish to criticize them; Cyprian undoubtedly is
assigned first place among the orthodox Fathers by Pope Gelasius in the
Decretum,[24] distinction 15, section *Sancta Rhomana*.

At this point it will perhaps not come amiss to say something of those
tenets of his which are not accepted by the church of today, among which far   125
the best known is his view[25] that heretics who have been expelled from the
fellowship of the church and schismatics produce no effect by baptism. And
indeed this view was held not only by Cyprian, but by almost all the bishops
in Africa, Numidia, and Mauretania, as is abundantly clear from the acts of
the Synod[26] of Carthage, which I have appended to this edition. That even   130
Hilary[27] himself was at one time of this opinion, so that he would not admit
persons baptized by Arians unless they had been rebaptized by orthodox, is
clearly stated by Jerome. And yet Cyprian held the view subject to this

limitation, that while following what he himself believed to be best, he laid
down no law for others to prevent them from doing as they themselves   135
thought fit, nor did he suppose that anyone who disagreed with him must
for that reason be excommunicated. In fact, those who preferred to follow
the opposite view seem to me not so much to have been moved by arguments
as to have chosen the party that was farthest from the schism of the
Donatists, and at the same time to have seen clearly how dangerous it was to   140
open that window, if an irreligious priest were thought to produce no result;
yet this was a view apparently held by some in Antiquity. For the importance
of St Augustine's arguments on a sacrament and the effect of a sacrament, on
the character and different mode of action of him who baptizes and him who
remits sins, would be too long a topic to be suitably treated here. There is no   145
doubt that Christ gave the right to baptize to the same persons to whom he
entrusted the power of absolution; yet any priest who invokes for this
purpose the name of the Trinity does not *ipso facto* convey absolution. If the
question depended on human reasoning and if general agreement did not
deserve to be supported everywhere, the view followed by Cyprian might   150
well be preferred to the accepted view.[28] There are other points too, more or
less arising out of this, which we will touch on in their place.

Lactantius[29] has a story that a certain witty but irreligious person called
him Caprian instead of Cyprian; but we ought to find a good man all the more
acceptable if a bad man rejects him, and indeed he found nothing   155
unacceptable in Cyprian except the fact that he was a good Christian, for the
man shows pretty clearly what he thought of Christ by calling his teaching
an old wives' tale. And another point: if Jerome elsewhere[30] seems to deny
Cyprian a perfect knowledge of Holy Scripture, all he meant, I think, was
this, that he was too much handicapped by the storms of persecution which   160
then racked the church, and by martyrdom, to have fulfilled in the
explanation of the Bible the outstanding work he would have done had it
been permitted him. What he wrote is mostly concerned with familiar topics;
and Jerome often borrows from it when he treats of the same themes, just as
Cyprian (it seems likely) often borrowed from Tertullian. For we read[31] that   165
he was so delighted by Tertullian and so devoted to him that when he came
to ask his amanuensis for a volume he used to say simply 'Give me the
master,' paying no less tribute to his genius because he had separated
himself from the church, since of course he knew that gold can be picked up
even from a dunghill. He understood that what is good is good wherever it   170
may be, and he shunned the prophet's curse[32] on those who suffer their
judgment of things to vary according to the persons concerned or their own
feelings, calling what is good, bad, and making bitter what is sweet.

But I must delay your Eminence no longer. Most reverend Father, here
then is Cyprian, much more correct, for my efforts have removed many   175

blemishes, and somewhat purer (by the removal of pieces falsely ascribed to him) and at the same time more complete (by the addition from very ancient copies of some pieces hitherto lacking). Besides which, he appears, thanks to Froben's skill, in a form at once neater and more dignified than before. And his appearance will be successful, if your Eminence approves both my   180
industry and my design; for it is to you that I have chosen to dedicate this book, knowing how hard you work for the restoration of the Christian religion. Who could be a more appropriate patron for the restoration of the early Doctors of the church than you, who are among their principal modern representatives? Who could more fitly put forward the claims of a writer   185
close to the apostles than they who now take among us the apostles' place? And another thing too seemed to me very suitable, that Cyprian, to whom the judgment of the Holy See assigns the first place,[33] should appear under your auspices, who are deservedly preferred,[34] among so many leading lights of the order of cardinals, by Pope Leo, who owes his fame no less to his   190
intelligence than to his great place. Hannibal the Carthaginian, who fought with the inhabitants of Italy for control of the Roman world, enjoyed great fame among the Romans; Cyprian[35] ought to be still more famous, for he fought with Catholic Romans for the palm of Roman eloquence more successfully than Hannibal. Hannibal encountered Scipio in battle; Cyprian   195
seems to have challenged Pope Cornelius[36] to a contest of piety of a rare kind, in which both were equal in merits, both died the same glorious martyr's death on the same day, though not in the same year, and Cyprian won the palm of eloquence.

For my part, I have a further and special reason for dedicating this   200
book, such as it is, to your Eminence: in no other way could I put on record my heartfelt gratitude for the exceptional kindness so generously shown me, first by your nephew Antonio Pucci,[37] who was at that time papal nuncio among the Swiss, and later in Rome by your Eminence; whom I pray that Christ the Almighty may long preserve in health and wealth as a pillar of the   205
Roman See and the whole Christian polity.

Louvain, 31 July 1519

1000A/ From Maarten Lips   [Louvain, July–early August 1519]

Maarten Lips belonged to Erasmus' own order of canons regular and lived in the Augustinian house at Louvain. He kept two copy-books in which he recorded many letters exchanged between Erasmus and himself (cf Ep 750 introduction). This letter and Erasmus' reply, Ep 1000B, come from one of them, which is now in Rotterdam's Gemeente Bibliotheek (MS 15 C 4). In Allen's edition they are Epp 1035–6.

In editing this exchange, Allen hesitated between the tentative dates of July and October, noting that the end of July would be more plausible if N were to be identified with Maarten van Dorp. Henry de Vocht supported both this identification of N and the corresponding date (CTL I 394–5, 435). Neither can be proved, but in conjunction with the reference to Nesen's recent arrival (cf Ep 994 n1) they make good sense. At any rate the present exchange is less likely to have occurred after copies of Nesen's *Dialogus bilinguium ac trilinguium* (cf 329 below) had reached Louvain in early August, an event which presumably should have put an end to his friendly visits at the Augustinian house.

When Nesen arrived from Paris he had instructions to inform Erasmus of a recent letter to Dorp written by Nicolas Bérault on behalf of some friends of Erasmus (cf Ep 994:13–15) who apparently saw in Dorp a principal cause of Erasmus' difficulties in Louvain (cf Ep 930). Perhaps to save him embarrassment, Erasmus was not to be shown this letter, and due to his repeated absences from Louvain (cf Ep 999 introduction) learned only belatedly about its existence. When he did, he lost little time in writing to Bérault to clear Dorp's name (cf Ep 1002:38–44). Meanwhile Dorp had received Bérault's letter and, to make things worse, had been clumsily attacked in Nesen's dialogue. His answer was to rally himself uncompromisingly to the cause of Erasmus; see Ep 1044 introduction.

MAARTEN LIPS OF BRUSSELS TO ERASMUS OF ROTTERDAM,
GREETING

Soon after Nesen arrived here, the talk began to turn on N, and he told me many things I was sorry to hear. I wish you and I could talk it over. I could put it in a letter, but what I need is to hear your story too, what line he took 5 with you and how you answered. Would you perhaps be at leisure to come to my house now, this afternoon? About two o'clock this afternoon will suit me very well, but you can make it earlier or later as you please. Best wishes.

1000B / To Maarten Lips   [Louvain, July–early August 1519]

This letter answers Ep 1000A; in Allen's edition it is Ep 1036. For the source and the background see Ep 1000A introduction. It is clear that when Erasmus wrote these lines he had already succeeded in allaying Nesen's suspicions of N.

DESIDERIUS ERASMUS TO HIS DEAR MAARTEN, GREETING

I do beg you, my dear Maarten, not to sow discord between N and Nesen. Leave them to be friends on such footing as they can, and do not get yourself mixed up in anything of the kind. I will come and see you, if nothing happens meanwhile. In any case, if there is anything private which concerns 5 myself, tell no one, but send it by the bearer in writing. Best wishes from your sincere friend.

1001 / To Georgius Spalatinus   Antwerp, 7 August 1519

This letter acknowledging receipt at long last of Spalatinus' Ep 711 was written
at the time of Erasmus' second visit to Antwerp (cf Ep 999 introduction) and
subsequently published in the *Farrago*. Spalatinus was the secretary of the
elector Frederick of Saxony.

TO GEORGIUS SPALATINUS, INCOMPARABLE THEOLOGIAN,
FROM ERASMUS OF ROTTERDAM, GREETING

If you can spare a moment, busy as you are, and if it is quite proper for a
theologian, here is something that will make you laugh. About the first
August in this year of grace 1519, at Louvain, I had a visit from that rather   5
agreeable person, Petrus Alamirus.[1] He handed me a letter dispatched from
Aachen[2] and assured me that he had with him in Antwerp great bundles of
letters from my most distinguished friends on subjects of no ordinary
interest. Anticipation of this future feast kept me happy for several days. It
was about ten days later that I went to Mechelen[3] to greet my own bishop, I   10
mean his lordship of Utrecht,[4] who happened to be there at the time. As luck
would have it, I ran into Alamirus; I reminded him about the letters, and he
said he had them at hand. We arranged to meet in the cathedral, and even
fixed a time. In the cathedral, before a numerous company, he produced five
letters, some of them wrapped in a double blank sheet, and all enclosed in a   15
single common wrapper. Imagine my delight as I received them! For the
moment I had to be satisfied with learning who the writers were from the
addresses written on the back, for there were people there with whom I had
some business to transact; and so off I went to dinner. For I had promised to
dine with Jan Robbyns,[5] the dean of the cathedral, a man of unusual wisdom   20
and great integrity, but also very good company. He is the man on whose
shoulders rests the chief responsibility[6] for the College of the Three
Tongues.[7]

During dinner, observing that my fellow guests needed something in
the way of news to enliven the proceedings, I took out the letters I had just   25
received, and broke the seal. The first[8] was one from yourself, demanding
that I should answer a letter from you which you had, it seems, written to me
on behalf of the duke, and in fact in the name of the whole university. As I
had never received any such letter, and at the same time had answered[9] my
most recent letters from the duke and yourself a few days before, I could not   30
think what you meant. In the end, I looked at the signature and found that
the letter was dated from Altenburg on 13 November 1517. There was a roar
of laughter, as you might expect; I had found cinders[10] instead of gold, old
lamps for new. Disappointed there, I opened[11] a letter from Pirckheimer –

and found it written in 1518, on the first October. More laughter, and louder. 35
I broke the seal on one from Riccardo Sbruglio of Friuli, the court poet; that
too was dated 1518, on 13 November. I was now beginning to feel rather
foolish. I tried another, from Georg Behaim,[12] canon of Nürnberg; it was
dated 17 February 1519. One and the same man brought me all these, and
handed them over as though he had flown post-haste from the other end of 40
Germany; and they were all spotless, as if they had been written that very
day. There's efficiency for you! In future therefore you will entrust him with
any letter you want carefully preserved; but if you wish it to be delivered,
you will entrust it to someone else.

No doubt our excellent friend Jonas[13] and his colleague have given you 45
a letter from me, and an account of my feelings. I am distressed by the loss of
that medal[14] with the wonderful portrait of the duke, and the letter that came
with it. I knew that the prince-bishop of Liège[15] wanted very much to see
both; I happened not to have them in my pocket at the moment, and he was
delayed till a late hour by private discussion with the princess Margaret, 50
daughter of the emperor Maximilian, and was due to leave for Germany next
morning at daybreak. So I gave them to the page who had waited on us as
cupbearer when we were dining with the bishop, intending that he should
show them both to him and let me have them back. Some days later I learnt
from the physician[16] that the young gentleman had set off for Germany with 55
the others, nor has the bishop yet revisited the court here on his return from
Germany. But I regret the loss of the letter more than the medal.

Richard Pace,[17] who is an excellent scholar in both Latin and Greek and
was the English king's representative at the election of the emperor, gave me
on his return a most heartfelt and eloquent picture at full length of Frederick; 60
such force of character, such wisdom, such integrity, such a range of
knowledge! – in short, all the points of a distinguished prince. In my opinion
he won more credit by his refusal[18] of the imperial crown than certain others
by their pursuit of it. Yet no one makes a better ruler than the man who has
really considered how heavy is his task. So the burden of a famous title is laid 65
upon our shoulders. We can only pray Heaven that it may prove a blessing,
to ourselves in the first place and then to all Christendom.

When the rumour first reached us that the Empire was destined for
Charles,[19] there was a universal outburst of satisfaction and rejoicing in this
part of the world that went almost too far. Such however is the mingled yarn 70
of human life, that anxiety was soon there to keep company with joy. The
plague[20] never leaves us in peace, and in some places rages without mercy.
On top of that a large force,[21] I suppose some of the troops who were
engaged in the defeat of the duke of Württemberg, is planted on our
frontiers, and nobody knows who is in command, who controls them, or 75

what their intentions are; the one thing everyone can guess easily enough is
that they want money, and plenty of it. Many people are still terrified by the
example of Asperen,[22] which was annihilated two years ago; and we are
already repenting of the clemency which let those earlier armies go
scot-free.[23] Some even suspect that the present force is deliberately kept   80
going by the powers that be so as to have a weapon handy to oppress the
common people if they show any reluctance to do as they are told – and they
are told to do things almost past bearing. But in all this fate will find a way;
for my own part I am sorry for the poor common people, and cannot stomach
some persons' more than Turkish tyranny. Behind it all, I see how power is   85
being gathered into few men's hands, while the relics of our traditional
democracy[24] are gradually done away with. Why, in Spain even now you can
see obvious traces of the Saracen rulers under whose tyranny that country
languished long ago. If only princes could be persuaded of this one thing,
that the most glorious monarch is he whose subjects are free and happy!   90

His eminence Cardinal Albert, the prince-bishop of Mainz, has paid me
the compliment of a very friendly letter[25] and honoured me with a handsome
present, which I value all the more because it came from a very intelligent
prelate, and came unsought. The gift that is prompted by esteem is an
indication of confidence rather than a present.   95

I am publishing Cyprian,[26] corrected with considerable labour, as I
hope for Christ's mercy, and enlarged with several new treatises which I
have added out of very ancient manuscripts; I have also supplied some brief
notes, but not many, separated the genuine from the spurious pieces, and
am so far from cutting out things in this class that I have even added a kind of 100
appendix.

Please commend me and my work to your illustrious prince,[27] and be
sure to give my greetings to your society[28] of devotees of the humanities.
'Take pains and win the day.'[29] Farewell.

Antwerp, 7 August 1519   105

1002 / To Nicolas Bérault   Antwerp, 9 August [1519]

This letter answers Bérault's recent Ep 994 together with his preceding Epp
925, 989. It was published in the *Farrago*. Epp 1002–4 were probably all
composed during Erasmus' second visit to Antwerp (cf Ep 999 introduction)
and sent to Paris by the same messenger; see below n11.

ERASMUS OF ROTTERDAM TO NICOLAS BÉRAULT, THE
DISTINGUISHED TEACHER OF LATIN AND GREEK, GREETING
If I may send a single answer to your last three letters, and thus whitewash[1]

several walls out of one bucket, I am conscious of having written to you
frequently,[2] but with such laconic brevity that I may seem to you not to have   5
written at all; such is the pressure, my dear Bérault, of the mass of work by
which I am overwhelmed. If you calculate how much time has to be given to
religious duties, how much to sleep (of which I need a good deal, and drop
off again about dawn),[3] how much to nursing my health, and how much to
writing and revising my books, you will easily discover how little remains   10
which I can devote to answering all my correspondents. Though my efforts
do not aim[4] at expelling Thomas or Scotus from the universities in disgrace or
driving them out of their ancient inheritance. This is not within my powers;
and if it were, I am not sure that it would be desirable, unless we could see
some school of thought ready to hand which would be better than they.   15
Other people's endeavours are their own affair; I for my part shall never take
the responsibility for such confusion. Enough for me if theology gets more
sensible treatment than it has hitherto, and if we now and again fetch from its
fountain-head in the Gospels what most people hitherto have been content
to draw from pools that are not altogether clear. And I have not been wholly   20
unsuccessful: some men have been persuaded, some even compelled, to
become more serious theologians. As for the praises which you lavish on me,
all I can say is that your delusions about your Erasmus are a sign of great
affection.

So much in answer to your letter[5] from Paris of 23 March. Now for the   25
one that was brought by Nesen[6] – a sincere and faithful friend if ever there
was one. What you entrusted to Calvo, or what he passed on to me, I do not
rightly remember, but I am sure that he never came to see me in Basel, and I
never had anything from him. In Louvain he had extracted from me a long
letter to Grolier,[7] the governor of Milan, promising in return the proverbial[8]   30
mountains of gold. You can read the published letter; he talks proudly of
Grolier's reply,[9] though I myself have not heard for certain whether my letter
ever reached him. You say that a letter of great importance is on its way from
Etienne Poncher, the archbishop of Sens. A letter from such a great man, and
a man to whom I am particularly attached, would be important in my eyes in   35
any case; but that being said, I do not much fancy some great position if
coupled with burdens to match. My own spirit has always been a lover of
leisure and liberty; the turmoil of business I loathe. As for what you wrote to
Dorp,[10] Nesen was so far from telling me that I did not even learn from him
that you had written. Some few days ago I heard that he had received a letter   40
from you sent by way of Herman[11] of Friesland, in which you had some bone
to pick with him. If you were at all sharp with him, my dear Bérault, I should
be sorry: if Dorp makes a mistake, he does so more from over-readiness to
oblige than from malice aforethought. If the theologians are changing their

minds, some of them, and some of them becoming more moderate,[12] I am glad   45
of it, more for their sakes than my own.

   Now I must write some sort of answer to the letter[13] brought by Herman
of Friesland. That young man had been recommended to me in writing by
many people, warmly recommended; and I am grateful to them all for giving
me the chance to get to know an intelligent man, likeable in so many ways.   50
He had no ambitions except to talk and to see something of me, and I was as
generous with my time as the pressure of my work allowed. I now commend
him to you in reverse: pray add to your kindness to him, to please me. All
good wishes.

   Antwerp, 9 August [1518]   55

1003 / To Guillaume Hué   Antwerp, 9 August [1519]

This letter to the dean of the cathedral chapter of Paris was composed at the
suggestion of Nicolas Bérault (cf Ep 989:11–12) and evidently dispatched
together with Ep 1002. It was published in the *Farrago*, but Hué does not seem
to have answered; see Ep 1185.

ERASMUS OF ROTTERDAM TO GUILLAUME HUÉ, DEAN OF
THE CHURCH OF PARIS, GREETING
Nicolas Bérault, a man born for the Graces, devotes great effort in a recent
letter to arranging a match between you and me. If it were a contest of
learning or literary skill, he could not deter me more effectively than by his   5
words of encouragement. 'In these lists,' he says,[1] 'he would rather receive a
challenge from you than be the challenger; he has considerable experience
already in authorship of many kinds.' Even among equals the aggressor is
always in the wrong; who would think I had any modesty or common sense,
if I were to provoke you, as Thersites[2] provoked Achilles? As it is, however,   10
neither birth nor fortune is any obstacle to competition with men of the
greatest eminence in friendship and good will, and in this field he is thought
to be more modest who issues the first challenge; and so I have no hesitation
in complying with the wishes of yourself and Bérault. In this letter,
therefore, behold a challenge issued to one of our most learned men by a very   15
indifferent scholar, and to a pillar of integrity by a man of very moderate
rectitude – one who, all the same, will yield to none in the give-and-take of
friendship, and will not endure to take second place.

   I hear with the greatest satisfaction that the University of Paris[3] is
enthusiastically adding a knowledge of the three tongues to its original   20
subjects of study, in which hitherto it unquestionably always held, and still
holds, first place; and that it returns from time to time to the pure springs of

Holy Scripture, not sharing the opinion of those few (their own worst
enemies) who suppose that these studies conflict with true theology, while
in fact they do more than any others to promote all honourable disciplines.   25
This I attribute in part to the noble frankness of your Gallic turn of mind, in
part to the wisdom of that great bishop Etienne Poncher, a man designed by
heaven for the revival of humane studies and true religion; but above all to
your excellent king Francis. We are the only country[4] that cannot yet
congratulate itself on any movement of the kind. But yet we have good   30
hopes.

May it be the will of Christ the Almighty that, as princes everywhere
come to love and foster the humanities, so they may adopt a philosophy
worthy of those who are the vicegerents of Christ: in other words, may give
the widest possible berth to tyranny and barbarism, and do nothing through   35
ambition that will undermine the peace and liberty[5] of Christendom. As they
encourage by their favour the branches of literature in which the achieve-
ments of princes are normally handed down to posterity, may they
endeavour to achieve such triumphs as deserve to win the praise of all future
generations.   40

Farewell, honoured sir, whose name henceforth I shall enter in the list
of my important Williams.[6]

Antwerp, 9 August

1004 / To Guillaume Budé   [Antwerp, c 9 August 1519]

This letter was answered by Budé first with Ep 1011 and then again with Ep
1015. Thus it was probably sent together with Epp 1002–3 (cf Ep 1002 n11). It is
primarily an answer to Budé's Ep 915 but also acknowledges Epp 987, 992.
Erasmus published it in the *Farrago*.

Guillaume Budé was a most erudite Greek scholar and antiquarian who had
in recent months (cf Epp 744, 778 salutations, 924:20n) resumed a more active
role at the French court. His laboured correspondence with Erasmus,
oscillating between warm friendship and jealous suspicion (cf CWE 6 preface),
continues with this letter, which is written in Greek down to line 143. Erasmus
uses the Greek term 'amnesty' (lines 141–2) to suggest that the two friends
should let bygones be bygones and abandon their quibbling. While this term is
eagerly taken up in subsequent letters (cf 1011:41, 47, 74, 84, 136, 1015:129,
1066:12, 1073:15–18), no fundamental change is apparent in their relationship
as reflected in these letters.

ERASMUS OF ROTTERDAM TO GUILLAUME BUDÉ, GREETING
Many people[1] bring me word from you, and you yourself, my dear Budé,
have written I think three times,[2] to say you are not a little surprised that I

have been silent for so long, and do not answer the letter I had from you
beginning 'I have seen the comments etc.' Let me assure you there is no   5
reason except this: I value our friendship highly as a most precious
possession, or rather, I think it worth everything, and I could very much
wish that it might be seen by all men to be what I am quite convinced it really
is – inviolate and unalterable. I do not think that to maintain our unanimity and
hold it together we need Luis Vives[3] to act as a kind of cement between the   10
two of us; we need letters, gay and reasonably humorous letters, that others
too may see what great friends we are. Personally, I have never been in the
least put out by your humour and your jests, which are sometimes by no
means without their barbs, but are always playful. I am not hurt by your
abuse of me, but I fear for your reputation, which I count mine too, since   15
friendship makes all things common property. But Vives himself, when I
showed him your letter,[4] was still more surprised; for he never would have
believed, he said, that Budé could write such things to Erasmus, had he not
read the letter himself in your own handwriting.

Tell me now in the name of the Graces, my dear Budé, how should a   20
man reply to this sort of thing, which seems to have been written in an
ill-judged and slightly hostile spirit, and is also off the point and nothing to
do with Dionysus, as the saying[5] goes? To begin with, I had suggested[6] in my
answer that all your maxims and your epigrams had been foreseen and were,
as we say, at your fingertips, obviously because I envied your fertility and   25
that thrice-blessed memory of yours, to which you could add energy and
diligence to match. This well-meant and simple remark you twist[7] into
something critical and offensive, as though what I really meant in my
riddling fashion was that Budé owed his eloquence and his culture to
notebooks and reference books and nothing else.   30

On top of that you diverge somehow onto a sort of battle-ground,[8]
where you challenge[9] me on the score of jealousy and a desire to dominate,
as though I wished to prohibit and prevent everyone else from using flowers
culled from the classics – although they are already public and have become
common property – casting aspersions in passing on the excessive length of   35
my collection of proverbs. Once again I ask, how am I expected to answer
this? The facts speak for themselves, as the phrase is: what I set down to your
credit is distorted by you and made to sound offensive. How can I possibly
be jealous and obstructive, and make trouble[10] for those who wish to use
proverbial phrases in any way they please, as though I were forbidding men   40
to fish in the sea, when I have expended so much labour on this very
purpose, of making proverbs more available and accessible to everyone?
How am I an obstacle to the publication by others of their own collections,
when I have so often urged so many people to compete in that field? For I am

well disposed not only to average men but to the more distinguished people 45
who will put my reputation, if I have any, in the shade.[11] So I thought it much
better in face of all this to remain quite silent, and not to answer point by
point and so stir up strife maybe to no purpose and anger my friend, or by an
irrelevant reply to make myself a laughing-stock to those who enjoy poking
fun, who might well cast in my teeth Demonax' remark[12] about one man 50
milking a billy-goat and the other catching the milk in a sieve.

For I think it makes very little difference, so far as I am concerned,
whether I have worked for seven years[13] or seven thousand years on what I
now publish in what you call a constant series, even if it is perfectly clear to
those who are in contact with me and know my work intimately that I make 55
the opposite mistake, pouring out[14] almost all my things in careless
improvisation, rather than bringing them to birth, so that they are still
formless and unfinished like the whelps of a lioness or a she-bear. In this
department I have no claims to be thought better educated; it is you, I
maintain, who are both more fortunate and more sensible. I perhaps write 60
more than you, but I write worse; I produce more rapidly, but my
productions will soon be dead, while you take a long time to give birth, but
your offspring is immortal.

So much for that. As for Jerome and the Areopagites,[15] I gladly pardon
your slip of memory and willingly accept pardon when you offer tit for tat, as 65
the proverb[16] has it; though there was a kind of theft, on which a capital
charge would lie in Antiquity, as there does now; and you know well, I am
sure, that every judge can metaphorically be called an Areopagite.

As for what follows, surely it will be thought not only odd but rather
spiteful to say[17] 'If anything in my letter to Tunstall seems to you oddly 70
expressed and ill timed, you have my full authority as chief critic and arbiter
in all things to alter it and put it right,' clearly insinuating that any praise you
give me there is not seriously meant or from the heart; though I did not fail to
notice that even your praise of me was not free of criticism and double
meaning. But to speak quite openly, my excellent Budé, I enjoy praise from a 75
man who deserves praise himself; but were I somehow deprived of your
panegyrics, I should not be depressed or indignant. So if you were to have
second thoughts about this kindness or rather generosity, on your part, I
should return the whole gift at once.

Just see how unfairly, because I was too modest to accept your 80
encomium, you interpret this as pride and awkwardness, telling me to
descend if I will from the eminence on which you, if you please, have placed
me. Yet whoever takes it ill if a man begs to be excused on the ground that he
has been invidiously overpraised? Who does not rather welcome the
modesty of a man who refuses the offer? Then it will be the real Erasmus and 85

nothing else that comes to France,[18] if you strip me of the ornaments you have disguised me with.

Next you say,[19] I know not why, that there was something in your letter which I, being wholly made of lead, failed to understand. What this was I cannot guess, but I remember your saying clearly enough that you thought   90 of dropping the project for the sake of us both. That is something that even Davus[20] in the comedy I suppose could understand. Nor is that all: you accuse me of ingratitude, the worst offence of all, because, if you please, I gave no clear answer to such obscure offers, made to me as it were only in a dream, while all the time I owed you gratitude for bringing such good news.   95 It is permitted, I suppose, by your good leave, to be satisfied with my existing lot if I so wish, whatever it may be now or in the future, especially since, grateful as I am for your good intentions, I never asked you or invited you to open these negotiations. All the same, I remember urging you in a letter[21] not to take this project too seriously, indicating that I am not much concerned   100 about it. And why, after that, are you indignant with me?

Even more painful than this is what you say about the shrew,[22] and how I suffer from an excess of spleen which will soon prove fatal unless you administer the life-saving purge which will make me spew it up. In the same vein is that other sentence about practice in exchanging jokes with you, as   105 though it were something strange for me to return one of your pleasantries or as though I would not dare open my mouth in reply without gradual practice. How else, in the Muses' name, would some tyrant or oriental despot address a bought slave? Yet you write this as one friend to another, you being the person who first invited me to enter this arena; it is you who   110 write who are the merry man, the jester, who never resents any jests he may receive in reply; it is you who are the perfect gentleman who knows all the secrets of the Graces.

After joking at my expense and bombarding me like this, you change to threats, caressing my poor head with honeyed words. If that genius of   115 yours, you say,[23] is still tormenting you with mad fits of this kind, why not turn your pen, or rather the point of your weapon, against that one-syllable theologian who ponders mischief deep (as Homer[24] has it) at your expense? – and I in turn will sit out of range, as they say, and watch you struggle with him, hoping of course to enjoy the sight of a friend's misfortunes.   120

I forgive much that you say in haste, such as your remarks about Deloynes and Ruzé.[25] I do not see why you think me fond of adulation – me, who more than most men appreciate friends who speak their minds. Adulation has no place in friendship, and still less has this indulgence in abuse of one's friend. Since I am the only target for this kind of pleasantry,   125 either you have a peculiar idea of friendship, or it must be given another name. And on top of all this you accuse me of maliciously misrepresenting you,[26] because in comparing a passage from your letter I wrote 'you say' instead of 'you would say,' as though in Latin it made much difference to the argument whether one puts 'you say this' or 'you would say this.' What I was trying to convey was that the argument you put in my mouth does not fit me at all.

When I read this and much like it, it does not distress me, for I can take anything from a friend. But I fear that some tactless person, who is less familiar with the Graces' choir and takes up your French wit in a different sense, would form a less favourable idea than I could wish of my friend Budé. For I myself have no fears and am not put at risk. And so, most eloquent of men, I think it will be best if we entirely give up these pleasantries, which can cause ill feeling and engender bad blood, and in future confine our letters to one another to topics which are congenial to friendship and sound learning. On that understanding, let us make a clean sweep of everything we have said and done hitherto. Farewell.

I was not exactly pleased to gather from one of your letters[27] that you mean to desert the cause of sound learning, now that you have been co-opted into court circles. On the contrary, I feel myself that this is just the time to support those studies which you have not only loved passionately all your life but worked at with more diligence than almost anyone and championed with such courage. The prestige of the court will make it possible for you to do more now for the humanities, especially as you serve under a prince who seems to have it among his chief aims to give studies of this kind as high a standing as he can. Maybe you will even be allowed the leisure to finish that very scholarly work you started long ago. How can you suppose it is but little gain to our studies when More and Richard Pace[28] are recruited to the royal household? Thomas Linacre,[29] who lacked leisure at home to publish the work which you now see partly in print, has found it at court. It makes all the difference what the court is like to which you transfer yourself: at the moment some are, I perceive, of such a standard that compared with them our universities themselves are backwaters. You must just be careful to learn their ways gradually, and I do not doubt that you will soon agree that you have found court life to add spurs in your service of the Muses. Nor will you find it difficult to take your place; it is men of no resources and no reputation who have to fight their way up when admitted to court circles. You arrive at court with distinguished lineage, considerable property, and an outstanding reputation as a scholar, and you arrive with an invitation – almost under compulsion. If we had a court like that[30] in this country, I should join it without hesitation, despite my state of health, and even my age. Farewell once more, dearest Budé.

I beg you earnestly to make my excuses to Deloynes for not writing to him. I wrote an answer[31] to Ruzé when he was acting as envoy at Liège.

1005 / To Pieter Zuutpene   Antwerp, 10 August 1519

This letter was published in the *Farrago*. Pieter Zuutpene (also Zuetpene) of Cassel near Saint-Omer (d before 1552) was the legal advisor to Adolph of Burgundy, lord of Veere (cf below lines 43–4). He had studied together with Dorp and Adrianus Cornelii Barlandus and became a patron of the latter (cf Ep 1204 introduction). Erasmus had probably met him in March (cf Ep 952:14–15, 60–1); see Etienne Daxhelet *Adrien Baerlandus* (Louvain 1938; repr 1967) 19–20, 289–91; de Vocht CTL I 264.

ERASMUS OF ROTTERDAM TO PIETER ZUUTPENE OF CASSEL, GREETING

Such, I perceive, are the convictions of the majority of men, that they look for the sources of their happiness or unhappiness among the heavenly bodies.[1] For my part, I know no luminary whose propitious radiance surpasses a 5 sincere and congenial friend, and none on the contrary more fatal and sinister than the company of one who is counterfeit and insincere. Let others then watch the stars, if they will; in my view we should seek on earth what can make us happy or unhappy. Other men at the start of some enterprise consider anxiously under what aspect Venus, Jupiter, and Mercury confront 10 one another; I think it better to weigh carefully the men with whom one has to do, for some bring good fortune to themselves alone and bode harm to everyone else. And so words almost fail me, my dear Pieter, most open-hearted of men, to say how great a profit I consider to have come my way when you became my friend, for I could not wish to discover anyone more expressly 15 designed to suit my temperament and character.

In old days I thought myself abundantly blessed in one Pieter, Pieter Gillis,[2] a dear friend whom I would not exchange even for some legendary Pylades.[3] My felicity was doubled when I acquired you, a man so like him that I should hesitate which to put first. I say nothing of your distinguished 20 position, of your unusually wide reading, of your ability, which is so astonishingly adaptable to any kind of business; it is your frank and open mind, your straightforward character, the charm of your conversation, your modesty, your sense of honour, your active discharge of every obligation. What can they say to this, those people who condemn the spirit of the age as 25 past redemption, when such a character as yours is to be found even in the courts of princes?[4] In old days, I used to find it intolerable that gifted minds designed for literature and the Graces should be dragged off into some

kingly household; and now I see that virtue and liberal studies are held in
high honour by no one more than princes. It is therefore in the interest of all   30
who have such studies at heart, that a certain number of people like yourself
should live in courts, that men may never be wanting to fire our rulers by
their conversation with the love of literature and integrity, to add spurs to
their generosity, to guide them in the arts by which the imperishable glory of
an honourable reputation may be won. Think of the benefit that accrues to   35
learning of every kind from the presence at the English king's court of
Thomas More, of Thomas Linacre, of Richard Pace? in France, of Guillaume
Budé? One must count them fortunate that such princes have fallen to their
lot, and feel gratitude for their unselfish action if they make them such.

I know that nothing is so much to your liking as a life of learned ease,   40
and that the court has features, besides the distractions of business, which
must offend so pure a spirit as yours; but all this you ought to endure with
patience all the more because you serve under an excellent prince in
Adolph,[5] who from his earliest years acquired from Batt his tutor a
favourable attitude towards literature and men of high character and still   45
retains it, and who gives me his favour and support for no reason except that
he believes me to possess those qualities, which is very far from being so.
Knowing how important it is that the education of princes in their early years
should be entrusted to an upright man, he has placed his young son[6] with
Jan of Borsele,[7] a man (to sum up countless virtues in brief) very much like my   50
dear Batt. Someone of this sort should be attached to our prince Ferdinand,[8]
and in this respect I wonder very much that there is such delay, this being (I
suspect) the work of certain rich blockheads[9] I could name who find it to their
advantage that princes should be unable to think for themselves. I fear that
someone will put himself forward in the mean time who, under the guise of a   55
tutor, will play the part of a benefice-hunter, and the public weal will greatly
suffer. The theologians have ambitions in this department, and the man who
is to educate a prince should indeed be a theologian, but a real one, whom
greed and ambition cannot touch. Farewell.

Antwerp, 10 August 1519   60

1006 / To Jacob of Hoogstraten   Antwerp, 11 August 1519

Hoogstraten, prior of the Cologne Dominicans and inquisitor for the archbish-
oprics of Cologne, Mainz, and Trier, was a graduate of Louvain and a former
prior of the Antwerp house. Erasmus knew him (cf Ep 856:32n), but not very
well; moreover he had heard many things about him, some favourable, some
not (cf lines 7–8, 25–7, 42–8 and Epp 849:21–30, 877:19n). About May 1517
Hoogstraten had allegedly talked about prosecuting Erasmus because of his

New Testament (cf Hutten *Opera* I Ep 51.7). Erasmus, for his part, deplored Hoogstraten's attacks upon Reuchlin and his supporters. He had earlier considered writing to him (cf Ep 856:28–30) but had been held back by his desire not to get involved in the controversy (cf Ep 694 introduction). What made him change his mind now was, above all, the publication of Hoogstraten's *Destructio cabalae* (cf n13), in which he was explicitly attacked (cf n23). This letter was rushed to Basel for immediate publication in the *Farrago* (cf Ep 1009 introduction).

Hoogstraten did not, it seems, answer this letter. When the *Farrago* appeared he was visiting Louvain and causing Erasmus some anxiety (cf Ep 1030 n7). The inquisitor's prime preoccupation was, however, with Luther rather than Erasmus and the publicity gained by this restrained letter may have helped to achieve a partial reconciliation between Erasmus and Hoogstraten (cf Epp 1064, 1078 introduction). To readers of the *Farrago*, especially in Germany, this letter must have seemed significant: it showed Erasmus, for the first time since 1515, publicly siding with the Reuchlinists and actually defending the German scholar – notwithstanding his repeated protests that such was not his purpose. In reply to Hoogstraten's critique of his stand on divorce he also defended his conviction that church dogma, once established, was not beyond modification; cf lines 201–5, 285–8.

ERASMUS OF ROTTERDAM TO JACOB OF HOOGSTRATEN, THE
DISTINGUISHED THEOLOGIAN, GREETING
For some time now, as I read the pamphlets containing your disputes with Reuchlin, I have often been moved to write to you, by Christian charity in the first place, then by the common bond of our professional studies, by the special feeling that I have had ever since boyhood for your order,[1] and last but not least by an unusually strong predisposition in your favour, of whose courtesy and friendliness I hear so much. That you are greatly attracted by the liberal studies which are my own field is proclaimed aloud by what you write,[2] if nothing else; for since you aim everywhere at polish and elegance of style, it is clear enough what you must think of the humanities. Nor is it relevant how far you are successful; on the contrary, as it is clear that you industriously – I had almost said anxiously – pursue them, any lack of success shows how keen you were. Were it not so, it might seem that the graces of style flowed from your pen by nature against your will.

It was these things, as I say, which impelled me to bring to your notice what I felt to be important for your own reputation, for the advantage of your order, and for the tranquillity of the Christian commonwealth; but on the other side I was deterred by my experience of human nature, for I perceive that very few men make a success of imparting advice even in the most friendly spirit. To give counsel is a religious duty,[3] but fraught with peril too. There is an old saying[4] that 'counsel misjudged hurts him that gives it most.' But such nowadays is the breakdown of moral standards that even wise and true counsel often harms the man who gives it in good faith. This misgiving however was lifted from my mind by the suffragan bishop[5] of Cologne, a man   25 of incredible charm of character and winning manners. If the picture he painted of you was a faithful one, you will not take it amiss if I now give you some advice with the best and most affectionate intentions.

Long ago I had read Reuchlin's defence,[6] though only in snatches, with the most painful feelings, nor did I conceal my distress in writing to Reuchlin   30 at the way in which he had let fly at his opponents with abuse that was so obviously false and with so little self-control, whoever they might be – for at that time they were no better known to me than was Reuchlin himself. I expressed the same regret[7] among my private friends, among whom were supporters of Reuchlin who tried to pacify my feelings by saying that the ill   35 will should all be attributed to the people who should have been models of modesty and Christian gentleness and had in fact taken the offensive with such virulent and savage attacks; left to himself, they said, nothing could be milder by nature and more peaceful than Reuchlin. When I hesitated to believe them, they assailed me with what Pfefferkorn had written, and   40 Gratius and Arnold of Tongeren,[8] and other pieces which I need not mention now. About your own character there was a difference of opinion. Some maintained that you were easy enough by nature but were provoked into a passion by other people; on the other side a good number asserted that you consulted no one so much as your own ambition and greed, that you wished   45 to be thought important because you were despotic and ruthless by nature, and were thirsting for the wealth of the Jews because of your insatiable desire for money. My habit has always been, when I have to take something on trust, to lean for preference towards the better side rather than the worse; and at that time, as I could not refute all this, I did what I could none the less   50 to moderate the violence of what was being said.

Some time afterwards two things happened: I read the report[9] of the whole case, and your pamphlet[10] was published in which you refute Benigno's dialogue; that piece itself I had read only in snatches. May I tell you the effect it had on me? I speak with regret, but with perfect truth. I had   55 had a higher opinion of you before I read you in your own defence. How often I said to myself as I read, 'If only this man could see himself with my eyes!' I will not go into the other points which at that stage repelled me, nor do I touch at all on the merits of the case; that has nothing to do with me. But certainly in many places I found a complete lack of the gentleness and   60 self-restraint that one would expect of a Christian, a theologian, and a

member of the Order of Preachers. Many were the painful moments, and
often was I ashamed on your behalf, before I had read that preface[11] to the
end! My reflections then, my mental turmoil and my indignation, it would
give less offence to pour out to you in person, if we could have the   65
opportunity to talk things over.

Not so many days ago, I happened upon a small book[12] in someone
else's library containing several letters which attacked you furiously with
great freedom: the first, if I remember right, was by Reuchlin, the second by
the count of Neuenahr, the third by Hermannus Buschius, and the fourth by   70
Hutten. The bitterness of them all I should have found quite insufferable,
had I not previously read the things which seemed to have provoked them to
this intemperate rage. And so my feelings as I read were complex. At one
moment it was they whom I was sorry for, at another it was you, fearing from
time to time that fair-minded men of high standards might think that such   75
bitter invective could not be directed wholly against one who does not
deserve it; yet I thought them too good to write stuff like that, and hoped that
you would prove too good to be their target. For, a few days before, two
pamphlets[13] had appeared, in one of which you attack Reuchlin's *Cabalistica*,
and in the other you reply to Reuchlin's supporters, though the style of this   80
smacks more of Gratius.[14] Here again, I will not touch on the question whose
case appeals to me more; this field has not been entrusted to me, and if it
were, I can imagine I should gladly refuse. Nor do I claim sufficient learning
to think I could pronounce on such difficult questions, in the course of which
the word heresy is used from time to time. For at this moment I am not   85
concerned with Reuchlin's interests; it is your interests I am trying to serve,
and I am concerned with them up to this point: I want to see you in future
give more thought to your reputation, and remember decency. I doubt not
that you see this clearly yourself and bear it in mind; but I suspect that it
happens to you as it does to men in general: the violent rush and heat of   90
controversy distract your attention elsewhere. For I have no small confidence that you will take my advice, which proceeds from brotherly affection,
in a fair and friendly spirit.

First of all for the title,[15] which they attack bitterly as full of arrogance,
this does not move me much; for it might be thought to be the work of the   95
printer, were it not well known that you were in Cologne at the time. What
admits of less excuse is the way you repeat with emphasis in every chapter
'Reuchlin, the purveyor of cabalistic perfidy.' You will hardly persuade
anyone that this was done without your knowledge, when it occurs so
constantly all through the work. And whoever thinks you were responsible   100
will not have much doubt of your attitude towards Reuchlin. Yet it was of the
first importance, not only for your reputation but for your case, to proceed

solely by arguments and courteously, and not to give such a clear indication
of hostility. If it were part of Christian piety to let fly at anyone with a stream
of malignant abuse, Origen would have let fly at Celsus;[16] for Celsus   105
attacked the whole teaching and the life of Christ with insufferable
malignance, and in published volumes too. And yet Origen nowhere
inveighs against him as you do constantly against Reuchlin, who (to say
nothing else) has at any rate not been condemned yet[17] by those whose
function it is to pronounce on these things. Nor does Origen give himself   110
pains to distort or exaggerate Celsus' words towards the worst interpretation, as you seem to me to do constantly, with surprising heat, forcing
everything all the time towards a case of heresy.

But you will say 'I am doing my duty.' I like to see you do it, but I could
wish it done with sufficient moderation to make it clear to everyone that you   115
have nothing but the cause of Christ at heart, and to relieve you as far as can
be from the appearance of misusing the defence of the faith as a pretext either
to serve your ambition or your greed, or to satisfy some private hatred. What
could ever be written at all so cautiously that it could never be twisted by an
angry opponent into some sinister meaning? What is more, the man who   120
displays his personal animus immediately forfeits our confidence, however
just his cause, and I do not doubt that this has been the chief obstacle to your
achieving the results that they suppose you were pursuing. An inquiry was
entrusted to you, not the right of passing sentence – and how many times
you pass sentence on Reuchlin! – particularly when the case is still pending   125
before the judge,[18] and a judge moreover from whom they say there is no
appeal. Had you not already done all that could be expected of you, after
pursuing for so many years with so much clamour some pamphlet[19] so
obscure that maybe no one would have heard of it had you not made it
famous? when the pope, perceiving that the case was one of those that are   130
better forgotten than pursued at length, had already ordered you to be
quiet? If some error has arisen which is a source of danger to Christianity, it
ought first to be carefully investigated and discussed among the learned,
and then reported to the bishop. When you have done this, your duty as
inquisitor is finished. You have made your inquiries and put the right people   135
on notice; there is no need for you to confound heaven and earth and rouse
this tragic uproar.

How I wish you had spent that effort, that expense, those valuable
years in preaching the gospel of Christ! Unless my forecast is wholly at fault,
Jacob of Hoogstraten would be a greater figure than he is now, and his name   140
would be more popular, or at least would rouse less ill will, among men of
judgment. As it is, a good part of the unpopularity falls on your order; and

since it had often been grievously unpopular for many reasons in the past, it
was a pity to burden it with fresh resentment. Moreover, it behoved a man of
sense like you to consider whether that piece of Reuchlin's contained 145
anything that might do serious harm to the Christian religion. But the only
point at issue in it is that the Jews should not be unfairly treated. What was
the object of such a vigorous campaign to make the Jews unpopular? Which
of us does not sufficiently detest that sort of men? If it is Christian to detest
the Jews,[20] on this count we are all good Christians, and to spare. There are 150
people who view with grave suspicion, besides many other things, this in
particular, that with so many books being written everywhere, you have
chosen this one pamphlet for such prejudiced inquiries. You find nothing
amiss in the works of Agostino Giustiniani, of Silvester Prierias, of Tommaso
de Vio who is now cardinal of San Sisto; and yet there are many things in 155
them that shock the Paris theologians[21] not a little – for I myself have only
sampled them. This makes men say that you are blind to the errors of
Dominicans, and clear-sighted only when Reuchlin errs or one of his
supporters.

I say this, not to give my support to Reuchlin, but in the interests of you 160
and your party. My friendship for him is not such as to make me become
involved in his case, as you seem to suspect none the less; for they tell me this
is why you made such highly prejudiced references in your preface[22] to the
honourable count of Neuenahr, and that you had no other reason to criticize
me[23] also in the attacks you have published on the Cabala. For I am not 165
greatly elated by the courtesy with which you suppress the name Erasmus
after setting out the title of my work and a passage from it, in which you
repeat word for word what I wrote. What suprises me more than anything is
your dragging me into a business which you wish to appear as odious as
possible and to which I am a perfect stranger. May Christ be as merciful 170
towards me as I would be unmerciful[24] towards the Cabala! Nor did the
course of your argument give you much warrant to bring in this topic; you
dragged it in, I believe, by the short hairs and cobbled it on like a badly fitting
patch. And how you put venom in everything, how treacherously you
distort what I have written! What I said of myself and others like me you 175
continually interpret as an attack on the church, and you cite only one
passage, which you thought particularly suited for misrepresentation,
though I refer to the topic in several places. By comparing these you might
have discovered what I had in mind in writing what you object to. For in
another place[25] I record my pity for people who are loosely held together by 180
an unhappy marriage, and yet would have no hope of refraining from
fornication if they were released from it. Their salvation I wanted to secure

by some means, if it should prove possible, nor have I any wish for this to happen without the consent of the church. I am no innovator; I refer the whole question to the church's discretion.   185

But, you say, the church cannot do what you wish. In the first place, I do not lay down what the church can do; and if this proves to be quite impossible, I have merely expressed what every charitable man would wish for. I am no supporter of divorce; but I pity those who are set for perdition. Christian charity often wishes for something that is not possible, and it is   190 often a pious act to wish for something you cannot bring about. I point this out in brief and merely by way of comment, not as a matter of dogma; it is you who thereupon emphasize the word dogma in order to get me into trouble. You trembled all over, according to your account,[26] at what I said, so severely that you nearly collapsed in horror, and my brief comment, which I left to the   195 judgment of the church, you describe as an attack on the church as a whole.

After laying foundations such as these, which are so widely different from my true opinions, you prolong the discussion to great lengths, adducing every possible argument to prove that after a divorce remarriage is unlawful, as though I were unaware of the opinions of the early Fathers or   200 the decrees of the church on this subject. But it is possible that the spirit of Christ may not have revealed the whole truth to the church all at once. And while the church cannot make Christ's decrees of no effect, she can none the less interpret them as may best tend to the salvation of men, relaxing here and drawing tighter there, as time and circumstance may require. Christ   205 wished that all his people might be perfect, so that no question of divorce should arise among them; the church has endeavoured to secure the full rigour of the gospel dogma from everyone. How can you be sure that the same church, in her zeal to find a way for the salvation even of weaker brethren, may not think that this is the place for some relaxation? The Gospel   210 is not superseded; it is adapted by those to whom its application is entrusted so as to secure the salvation of all men. Nor is a thing superseded when it is better understood. But I have no mind now to enter into a maze of argument, especially as in my second edition I have put together almost everything pertaining to this problem, in a note[27] on the seventh chapter of 1   215 Corinthians.

Here too, my good sir, I am constrained to find you somewhat unreasonable. You thought proper to criticize this passage, when you knew quite well that I had prepared a new edition, which I had promised[28] in the earlier one. For it is unlikely that a fact had escaped you which was common   220 knowledge, even long before my recent journey to Basel,[29] which was of course for this very purpose. It will be thought therefore, either that you anticipated this in your passion for finding fault, or that you were unwilling to jettison

something you had already written. And so, as I say, I do not enter upon this
field of discussion, nor indeed does a letter admit of it; I merely protest that   225
your reference to me was less than fair. I spoke of interpreting for the best;[30]
pray observe how you interpret this for the worst, as though I were falsely
accusing the church of superseding Christ's decrees, while my opinion is
that we, by which I mean myself and others like me, are misusing the
interpretation of the gospel principles, with the result that the force of the   230
gospel teaching in our standards of behaviour is fading away.

Christ (to give an example)[31] so wished his people to abstain from
murder that he forbade all upbraiding and did not permit men to be angry.
We interpret this as meaning angry without just cause, and relying on this
interpretation many a man who is angry comforts himself with the thought,   235
'It is not without just cause that I am wroth with him.' Likewise Christ so
wished his people to abstain from perjury that he forbade an oath of any
kind. This we interpret as meaning that we must not swear without just
cause, and this interpretation is a pleasing delusion for those who use an
oath freely on the slightest occasion. In the same way, he so much wished   240
them to abstain from divorce as known to the Jews, who used to repudiate
their wives for the most frivolous reasons, that he forbade divorce
altogether. What interpretation the church can put upon this I do not decide;
I wish she could interpret it so as to promote many men's salvation. And yet
the church does admit divorce of a kind, and more reasons for it than Christ   245
allowed. And she has drawn a distinction between marriage consummated
and not consummated; the one she will not allow to be parted, the other she
will, provided there intervenes what for some unknown reason they call a
solemn vow.[32] None of this was part of Christ's teaching, nor was there
anything about the cases in which matrimony is or is not binding, on which   250
the orthodox were not of one mind in the early days and the church, or at any
rate the Roman pontiffs, have altered their own decisions.

When I saw how wonderfully the spirit of Christ measures out its
influence to suit the changing state of things and observed how great is the
authority wielded by the church, I suggested that, if it were possible, steps   255
should be taken towards the salvation of so many human beings on the way
to perdition. Nor do I make any final proposals on this point; I leave the right
of decision to the church and content myself with drawing attention to the
problem. What was there, pray, in all this that you must needs think fit to
exaggerate in such atrocious language? You sprinkle your discussion with   260
references to a certain doctor[33] who is grumbling and rumbling against the
church; worse, he 'puts holy mother church in the dock,' 'puts forward
dogmas other than those held by the holy Roman church,' and there is, you
say, some risk that 'a hotbed of sedition may dare to challenge ecclesiastical

authority,' that there may be a 'concerted growth of contempt for the   265
church,' and a danger that 'men will follow the vices of the flesh without
shame to their own destruction.' Doubtless you recognize your own words,
which will be widely thought not so much appropriate or well judged as
likely to cause a breach of the peace. Some people maybe will detect wit
when you remark that the doctor whom you have taken on gives a frigid   270
treatment of the words of Christ, while you yourself are more than a little,
shall we say, overheated; when you allow him nothing but tinselled verbiage
at one moment and a feeling for grammar (as you are pleased to call it) at
another; when you make him out to be a blinking owl or bat, while you feel
yourself, I suppose, to be an eagle. For my own part, when it comes to   275
theological matters, I think I am less clear-sighted than an owl, which can see
even in the dark; and yet, if I chose to go into this whole argument as
seriously as it deserves, you would find me perhaps not quite so near-
sighted as you wish me to appear.

But this would be a subject for more than one volume, and I have   280
already dealt with most of these questions in the later edition, as though I
foresaw there would be attempts to weaken my argument at that point.
Though even there I assert nothing absolutely; I give the judgment of the
church everywhere the reverence and authority which are its due; I am all for
discussion, I decide nothing. If you say that it is unlawful to take things   285
which are generally accepted and question them, what are we to make of the
saintly Doctors who are not afraid to submit for discussion whether the
Eucharist is a sacrament, whether simple fornication is a sin? I am not much
moved when you take me to task in passing, at the outset of your argument,
for saying on the basis of the nineteenth chapter of Matthew that a law was   290
introduced among Christians against the dissolution of marriage, and thus
making in your judgment two mistakes, one in holding that this prohibition
was introduced by the law of man and the other in thinking it derived from
that passage when it was clearly taken from the fifth chapter[34] of the same
Gospel. To answer the second point first, if both passages convey the same   295
meaning, how can it matter which we say it is derived from? – though it will
be more likely to come from the nineteenth, where the business of divorce is
specifically dealt with. Not but what I did not mean that passage as it stands
in the text; I used the word passage to mean the whole of this argument
wherever it is treated, otherwise it will seem to be taken neither from the fifth   300
nor from the nineteenth chapter but rather from the seventh chapter of
Paul's first Epistle to the Corinthians, for he there ordains[35] that a woman
who has departed from her husband and will not be reconciled should
remain unmarried. Again, in this place,[36] where an exception is made of

fornication, the right to divorce does not seem to be entirely done away, but   305
rather to be limited, because among the Jews it was unduly wide.

And then it cannot be denied that laws[37] exist made by the pope which
forbid divorced persons to contract another marriage, provided it is
established that the first marriage truly existed. If these were taken from the
words of the Gospel, I do not see why I should be rebuked for saying that a   310
law exists which forbids the dissolution of marriage. Of even less weight
than these is your complaint that I was inaccurate in saying that Moses
granted divorce to the Jews, finding a double error in those few words. He
did not grant it, you say,[38] he permitted it, as though there were any
difference between the two words, except that to permit is a general word for   315
conveying the right to do something, while to grant implies some sacrifice of
one's own rights, so that the latter verb is more appropriate to the sense we
want. Again, you say that Moses permitted it, but under authority from the
Lord; as though Moses could not properly be said to have commanded what
he instructed the people to do under command from God, or Matthew is   320
wrongly said to have taught what Christ taught him to say.

If you wish for some practice in writing, which seems, to me at least,
much better than to have other men write[39] in your name as some people do, I
could wish you would confine yourself to subjects which rouse less
animosity and do more good, or, if circumstances oblige you to treat   325
questions of this kind, that you could control your language and your
attitude all through, not only to win the approval of sundry brethren of your
own order, but so that all truly educated and intelligent readers, and even
posterity itself, may recognize that here is the mind of a true theologian. If
the subject calls for severity, let there be no bitterness anywhere; above all,   330
avoid any taint of ambition or greed, which are poisonous, and still more, of
hypocrisy. True religion sometimes has the right to be indignant; but its
indignation should be sweetly tempered with charity. There is no wisdom in
irritating those whom you can set right, nor should one alienate anyone who
can be won back by mildness. Heresy is a hateful word, and all the more for   335
that reason should one be as sparing of it as one can. Nowadays it is the
commonest word in some people's mouths. You in your wisdom, I agree,
rightly distinguish[40] 'heretic' from 'heresy,' and 'heresy' used of an impious
sect from 'heresy' in the sense of error which, if obstinately persisted in,
would make a man a heretic. But these most subtle distinctions are over the   340
heads of ordinary stupid mortals; when they hear of the heresies of someone
or other, all they understand is that the people mentioned must be heretics,
just as they cannot imagine how the French[41] can be said to be at war when
they themselves are not fighting. On the contrary, when they are speaking

in public and fear that someone is listening, they talk of Reuchlin's heresies;   345
by themselves and among men of their own way of thinking, they call
Reuchlin a heretic, losing sight no doubt of that scholarly distinction. Such
small value do those men set on other people's reputation who take such
loving care of their own.

For your part, I find you somewhat more reasonable in what you have   350
written lately, and I hope that hereafter you will surpass yourself more and
more in this praiseworthy course. You will find that you have done much,
not only for the Dominican order but for the whole order of theologians, if
you use your authority to suppress the brainless calumnies of some people I
could name who everywhere, in public or private discourses, in disputa-   355
tions, at the dinner-table or the council-table or in conversation and, what is
most serious of all, in the pulpit, which is a sacred and a public place, pour
out their poisonous attacks[42] on knowledge of the ancient languages and on
humane studies, the fair name of which they blacken by prating of Antichrist
and heresy and other such histrionic stuff, though it is clear enough what   360
the church owes to men skilled in those languages and in the art of writing.
These studies do not obscure the dignity of theology, they set her in a clearer
light; they are not her enemies but her servants. There is no immediate
connection between music and heresy, if a musician should happen to be
convicted of some lapse in that direction. The error of the individual must be   365
condemned, but liberal studies should be paid the honour that is theirs.

But it would take too long to recount what absurd stories[43] I hear about
some people every day who, while they try to bring the humanities into
disrepute with the ignorant multitude, let it appear to intelligent and
educated and honest men that their obtuseness is a match for their   370
effrontery. If theology joins in honouring these studies, they in turn will
prove a credit to her; but if she meets them with insult and calumny, I fear we
shall see, in Paul's words,[44] that while they bite and devour one another, it
will end in their mutual destruction.

I write this with sincere and honourable intentions, and do not doubt   375
that if you accept it in the same spirit, you will be grateful to me one day for
advice as sound as it is friendly. You will not, I suppose, take offence at
advice from a man like me, who is at least, if I mistake not, older than you, for
Moses did not reject the counsel of Jethro.[45] Farewell, honoured Father, and
let my name be entered in the list of those who genuinely wish you well. I beg   380
you most sincerely to commend me to Christ in your prayers; and may he ever
govern your mind with his most gentle spirit.

Antwerp, 11 August 1519

1007 / To Pope Leo x   Louvain, 13 August 1519

In the light of Epp 1006 and 1008 it would appear that Erasmus was still in
Antwerp (cf Ep 999 introduction) on 13 August, the date given as 'Ides' in the
Latin text of this letter. The more formal a letter is, the less certain its date. A
letter to the pope would be copied out with special care, probably by a
secretary who might well work from an undated draft in the absence of his
master and simply add the current date. Moreover, letters dated from the
Calends or Ides often suggest an approximate or anticipated date at the
beginning or middle of the month rather than a precise day (cf Epp 967A, 1010
introductions).

Erasmus was convinced that Leo's approval of his revised New Testament
(Ep 864) was more than an encouraging gesture (cf Ep 1010:31–2) and would go a
long way to prevent any future attacks like those prompted by the first edition,
such as Lee's critique, which was now Erasmus' greatest preoccupation (cf Ep
998 introduction). Lee's stand was typical of the attitudes of other Louvain
theologians who continued to oppose the Collegium Trilingue (cf the preface
and Ep 1001 n7) and the new learning in general. As Erasmus considered that
the latter had taken root in England and France thanks to royal protection
(lines 111–21), he now appealed to the pope for a general pronouncement of
universal validity to follow Ep 864, which applied only to his New Testament.
A similar appeal to Rome is contained in Ep 1062 to Cardinal Lorenzo Campeggi
and it is possible that Campeggi himself was asked to convey this letter to Leo x
when Erasmus met him toward the end of August (cf Ep 1025 n3); at the same
time the text was sent to Basel for speedy publication in the *Farrago* (cf Ep 1009
introduction).

TO POPE LEO X FROM ERASMUS OF ROTTERDAM, GREETING
Most holy Father, some time since there went forth into the hands of the
public a New Testament revised by me for the second time with incalculable
efforts, together with annotations enriched with not a little new matter. It
went forth, one would think, under happy auspices, recommended[1] by the   5
name[2] not merely of a pope but of Pope Leo, as popular a name as any in
Christendom. Already all men of true piety held it in deep respect,
dedicated[3] as it is to you as to a patron deity; but now they welcome it still
more eagerly as having received the solemn approval of the supreme pontiff.
He is a poor Christian who has no respect for something dedicated to the   10
head of Christendom; but anyone must be raving mad who sets out as an
ordinary man to reject what is approved by the vicar of Christ or has the
temerity to condemn as an individual what satisfies the supreme interpreter

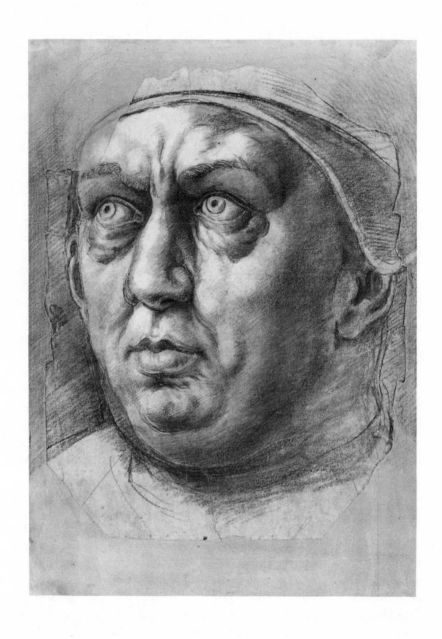

Pope Leo x
Drawing by Sebastiano del Piombo
Devonshire Collection, Chatsworth, Bakewell, Derbyshire
Reproduced by permission of the Trustees of the Chatsworth
Settlement

of the divine mind, to whose authority we owe even our belief in the
Gospel.[4] For in this I claim no credit for myself, except that of a spirit that will   15
refuse nothing in the way of nightly toil in hopes of helping others. It is your
doing that my work is welcomed with enthusiasm by every scholar, your
doing that it is so loved and so well thumbed, and that all men everywhere
are fired by it with the love of Holy Scripture. Those who took some offence
at the novelty of the earlier edition have now changed their minds[5] and admit   20
they were mistaken. Those who used hitherto to draw a cold and muddy
doctrine from stinking pools, now enjoy draughts from the crystal springs of
Christ and his apostles.

The earlier edition was warmly received by all open-minded, educated
men; and with their approval I might have been content, for anyone might be   25
satisfied when he has given pleasure to outstanding judges,[6] seeing that no
mortal man has yet been so fortunate as to please everybody. With
astonishing unanimity it won the approbation of all save very few, some of
whom were too stupid to be convinced by sound arguments, others too
proud to be willing to learn, others too obstinate not to feel shame if they   30
showed lack of firmness in pursuing the wrong course, not a few too old to
have any hopes that it might be worth their while, some too anxious for their
own reputation to let it be thought that there was anything they had not
known before – all of them men of such a kind that there was nothing gained
by wooing their good will. There is much force in that saying of Seneca's:[7]   35
some men are such that there is more credit in their disapproval than their
praise. And among these men hardly one is to be found who has read what I
wrote. They saw a threat to their dictatorship, some even to their finances, if
the world should come to its senses. What their own convictions may be, I do
not know; but at least they try to convince the ignorant and unlearned that   40
the study of the ancient languages and of what men call the humanities is
opposed to the pursuit of theology, while in truth theology can expect more
distinction and more progress from them than from any other subjects.

These men, cursed as they are from birth by all the Muses and the
Graces, make war without ceasing upon the subjects which are working   45
their way up in our own day to yield a still richer harvest, while their great
hope of victory lies in mere falsehood. If they use books as their weapon, all
they do is to betray their own folly and ignorance. If they match argument
with argument, the truth inevitably is manifest and prevails. So they confine
themselves to noisy protests before the illiterate public and foolish women,   50
who are easily imposed on, especially under the pretext of religion, which
they counterfeit with the greatest skill. They put up a screen of fearsome
words like 'heresy' and 'Antichrists'; 'The church is in danger,' they cry,
'and religion tottering,' theirs being of course the only shoulders that can

support it; and with this stuff, so loaded with prejudice, they slip in remarks   55
about languages and humane learning. These things, they say, that we
shudder to mention, take their rise from poetry; for poetry[8] is the misleading
name they give to all enlightened studies – to all, that is, that they have not
learnt themselves. This sort of rubbish they are not ashamed to vomit even in
their sermons, and expect to be regarded as the heralds of the teaching of the   60
Gospel. And they make free play with the names of the pope and the Holy
See, knowing how much all respect them, as is right and proper.

With this chicanery, these subterranean approaches, they prepare to
attack the new flowering of humane letters and the purified theology which
bears the impress of original sources. They stop at nothing, they invent   65
every form of calumny to use against those to whose efforts they can see this
progress to be due; among whom they reckon me also, though how much
influence I have contributed, I do not know. At least I have tried with might
and main to release men from those lifeless details which could bring no
result but premature old age and to fire them with zeal for a theology alike   70
more authentic and with higher standards. Nor have my efforts in this kind
been quite in vain, as is clear from this at least – the passionate attacks on me
by those who cannot abide to see anything valued that they themselves
cannot teach and are ashamed to learn. But I rely above all on Christ, who
knows me, and who is the prime object of my nightly vigils; after him, on the   75
judgment of your Holiness, on my clear conscience, and on the support of so
many eminent men; and of these barking curs I have never taken any notice.

What little powers I have, once and for all, are Christ's. His glory I will
serve, and his alone; I will serve the Catholic church and that church's head,
especially your Holiness, to whom I owe all I am and more. I might have   80
taken up other subjects and achieved wealth and position; I can produce
impressive witnesses to show that this is true. This seemed to me more what I
wanted: I would rather advance Christ's glory than my own. Ever since
boyhood I have been careful never to write a line that was irreligious or
indecent or subversive. If in the past I have published a few trifles with the   85
undue freedom[9] of the young, at least my present time of life is fit for nothing
that is not serious and sacred. No word from my pen has yet blackened one
hair[10] on any man's head, or made anyone a less good Christian; no discord
has ever arisen of which I was the cause, or ever shall. These are my
principles, and the malice of my enemies shall never shake them.   90

What others write is their own affair; I pass no judgment on another
man's servant – it is by his own master's opinion that he stands or falls. But it
grieves me sorely that some men's bitter squabbles should undermine the
tranquillity of our studies and of the Christian world. Nor is the affair

confined any longer to the clash of arguments; the battle grows more 95
barbarous, with monstrous abuse on either side, and poisoned pamphlets[11]
are the weapons; curse answers curse, and discord ripens into madness. No
man escapes an occasional slip, unless he is more than human. But human
errors, if they are such as must not be overlooked, should be corrected with
the mildness of a Christian. As it is, they distort even what contains no error, 100
and often too what they do not understand. Their bitter comments only
inflame sores that a little Christian gentleness might have healed, and their
severity estranges men whom courtesy might have retained. The word
heresy is on their lips at once whenever they disagree or wish to be thought
to do so; if there is anything they do not quite like, they appeal like 105
demagogues to the crass and ignorant multitude.

Such things sometimes arise from small beginnings, and often kindle a
vast conflagration; and thus it happens that the trouble, which was ignored
at first as negligible, slowly grows and bursts out in the end into a serious
threat to the peace of Christendom. In this field great praise is due to those 110
eminent monarchs[12] who have used their authority to quell this discord
when it began to grow, as Henry the Eighth in England and Francis, first of
that name in France. In Germany, that part of the world being parcelled out
among several lesser rulers, the same thing cannot happen; with us, since we
have lately begun to have a prince, and have one who is good and great alike 115
but very far away,[13] there are some who cause trouble and as yet go
unpunished.

Consequently, it seems to me that your Holiness would do for Christ by
far the most acceptable service you can render if you imposed silence upon
all contention of the kind, and secured in the whole Christian world what 120
Henry and Francis has done, each in his own dominions. Your Christian
policy has reconciled[14] great kings; it remains for it to restore their proper
peaceful atmosphere to things of the mind. This can be done, if on your
orders men who cannot speak would cease to cackle like geese at humane
studies, and those who have not yet learnt the language of blessing should 125
cease to curse the study of the ancient tongues, but each should actively
pursue his calling without denigrating those of other men. Then we shall see
what are called the senior faculties, theology, law, philosophy, and
medicine, receive no small advantage from the assistance of the humanities.
Add this great blessing to the debt already owed you by good literature (and 130
it owes your Holiness everything); and may Christ Almighty long preserve
you for the restoration and extension of his kingdom.

Louvain, 13 August 1519

1008 / To Christoph Hack   Antwerp, 13 August 1519

After Erasmus' severe illness in the autumn of 1518, rumours of his death
spread in central Europe (cf Epp 950:33n, 1021:13–15) and reached the circle of
his admirers at Erfurt. The one who composed the elegiac poem here
mentioned was no doubt Euricius Cordus, the recipient of Ep 941. In fact the
arrival of that letter reassured him that Erasmus was alive and caused him to
compose an ecstatic *Palinodia* in recognition of his error. Like the elegiac poem,
it was addressed to Hack. It was printed in an edition of Cordus' *Opera poetica
omnia* (n p n d). The preface indicates that on the suggestion of Johannes
Draconites (cf Ep 871) the elegiac poem had also been printed, but no copies
are known to exist. Two other epigrams by Cordus in praise of Erasmus are
reprinted in LB I (19) and the present letter is found in the *Farrago*.

Christoph Hack (or Hacke) matriculated at Erfurt in 1509 and was BA in 1512.
He became a priest and, after repeated visits to Wittenberg between 1517 and
1521, a Lutheran minister. He also met with Hutten and Reuchlin; see Carl
Krause *Helius Eobanus Hessus* (Gotha 1879) I 146, 236–7, 299, 336.

ERASMUS OF ROTTERDAM TO CHRISTOPH HACK, GREETING

An elegiac poem has reached me, of uncertain authorship, but the heading
clearly shows it is addressed to you. In it the author, whoever he is, laments
my death, and concludes by placing me among the saints. I would thank the
man for his courtesy, if I knew him; as it is, it must be your privilege to thank   5
him on my behalf. A man so devoted to Erasmus is all the more welcome,
since he paid me this tribute as to one dead and buried; for he who praises a
man during his lifetime does not entirely escape the suspicion of a wish to
please. But what penalty can I invoke upon these rascals who kill me off
twice a year[1] and, what is more heartless, bury me alive, forcing me over and   10
over again to outlive myself? What can I pray for these wretched creatures
except that they may be given more sense, so that they do not live for ever in
a state of death, as they have up to now? For seeing that God is love,[2] and he
is the life of the soul, how can we suppose these men to be still alive who hate
their neighbour so much (and he so far from doing them harm that he strives   15
to do good unto all men) that, since it hurts them to see him still alive, they
bury him from time to time with these baseless fabrications, enjoying his
death in fancy since they cannot in fact, and getting the most heartless
entertainment from the grief of those whose spirits they crush with their sad
stories. But we, whether we live or die, live or die unto the Lord.[3] Farewell,   20
my good friend.

Antwerp, 13 August 1519

1009 / To Albert of Brandenburg Antwerp, 15 August 1519

This letter answers Albert's Ep 988 (cf Ep 999 n53). It is the latest in date of the letters published in Erasmus' *Farrago nova epistolarum* (Basel: J. Froben October 1519) and Erasmus used it to state in public his reaction to the recent imperial election (cf the preface), carefully balancing his praise between the victor, Charles v, and the defeated Francis i of France. In the arrangement of the *Farrago* it follows directly after Ep 1007, Erasmus' appeal to the pope, but his work on the collection apparently did not end with these reverent tributes to the heads of Christendom. The last pages of the *Farrago* are taken up by Epp 1006 and 998, major defences against two prominent opponents which would be examined keenly by his critics. It seems, therefore, that these two letters were held back for careful revision and afterwards sent separately to Basel. When they reached Froben the *Farrago* was already being printed, and they had to be appended in haste (cf BRE Ep 133 of 12 November; Allen IV 9–10). The volume, a collection of Erasmus' recent correspondence and of many formerly unpublished letters of his early years, was produced under considerable pressure to meet the target of the Frankfurt autumn fair (cf Ep 1013A:10–12). As a result Erasmus immediately planned another, larger, and better collection. The *Epistolae ad diversos*, however, were not published until the spring of 1522 (cf Ep 1206 introduction). In the mean time the reading public was bound to accept the *Farrago* as expressing Erasmus' current positions on many controversial issues; in particular it seemed to lend considerable support to Luther (see P.G. Bietenholz in *The Sixteenth Century Journal* 8 supplement, 1977, 61–78). On 13 November Udalricus Zasius at Freiburg had received a copy, perhaps one still lacking the appended letters (cf AK II Epp 701, 703). By the beginning of 1520 Erasmus was distributing copies from Louvain (cf Epp 1056–7). Within weeks from this date Froben's stock of copies was already running low and he too considered a new edition (cf Ep 1066:93–7). Following a line of conduct adopted in preceding collections of his correspondence, Erasmus came close to suggesting that he had no part in the edition (cf Ep 1041:26–7, Allen Ep 1225:140–4), but in a private statement not designed for publication he spoke differently (cf Ep 1040:4–5). See also CWE 3 349–50; Allen I 595, 600.

TO THE MOST REVEREND FATHER IN CHRIST AND MOST
ILLUSTRIOUS PRINCE ALBERT, CARDINAL PRIEST OF THE
ROMAN CHURCH WITH THE TITLE ST CHRYSOGONUS,
ARCHBISHOP OF MAINZ AND MAGDEBURG, PRINCE-ELECTOR
OF THE HOLY ROMAN EMPIRE, PRIMATE, AND ADMINISTRATOR 5
OF HALBERSTADT, MARGRAVE OF BRANDENBURG, ETC,
FROM ERASMUS OF ROTTERDAM, GREETING

As I grow weary under the immense burden of my researches, I sometimes
derive not merely encouragement but fresh strength from the most generous
support of your Highness, who, while engaged in what is in itself the   10
greatest of all tasks (for what could be greater than to give the world an
emperor?) and was also severely complicated by the many difficulties that
assailed you in the course of it, could yet find time to read my ill-written
letter, and, having read it, to send a careful reply. I would express my
gratitude to your Highness for such singular courtesy towards a simple   15
person like myself, did I not choose rather to congratulate the Christian
world, which by the efforts of its wisest princes, and by your efforts
especially,[1] has been blessed with Charles as emperor,[2] the one man who
was rightly thought capable at this juncture both of supporting the great
responsibility of empire and of succeeding Maximilian. And perhaps a man   20
who could bear this mighty burden was less difficult to find than one who
could reproduce the virtues of the Caesar we have lost. But all men have high
hopes that we shall see our Charles restore and equal the glories of his
ancestors; I would not dare to say outdo them, but I dare form the unspoken
wish. Besides which, Charles is so successful that the imperial title, which   25
for several centuries past has carried more prestige than real authority, bids
fair to be matched by equal power. Many men have been entrusted with the
Empire, and it has made them great; Charles will add lustre to the Empire as it
is now. Others have ruled the world, and then claimed the imperial name;
Charles will claim for the Empire the leadership of the world. And he is of an 30
age to make us hope, under the favour of heaven, that the Christian world
will enjoy a very long spell of prosperity under his sway. Such too are the
kingdoms over which he rules that no man can strike more terror into the
barbarian enemies of the Christian religion.

　　For one thing we must all beseech the heavenly powers, that they may   35
preserve and continually encourage the virtuous disposition which Charles
now displays, so that the impious tumults of war may be driven out from the
whole Christian polity, and the people of Christ, rejoicing in perpetual
peace[3] and tranquil ease, may flourish exceedingly in the most honourable
arts and in the exercise of true religion; or at least, if need arise, that our 40
princes may turn their forces and their arms with one accord against the
enemies[4] of the name of Christian. If there is any other point on which
Charles is to be congratulated, we should do this, I think, on two counts:
one, that you voted for his election, and the other that, when he achieved
the imperial dignity, which he himself more deserved than sought to win, it   45
was with Francis king of France as his great competitor. As in old days
Hector's valour added lustre to Achilles' victory and Turnus' courage

increased Aeneas' glory,[5] so now it will be found that to have a great king as a rival for the same prize has made Charles' success more glorious. The Empire has been given in trust, not sold[6] – given to him who is able to hold it 50 most courageously and willing to rule it most religiously. Nothing remains except that the supreme Prince in whose hand alone are the hearts of all kings,[7] should bless the outcome of your choice, of Charles' efforts, and of all our prayers. To this end we must all strive, each in his place, for this concerns us all. 55

I had previously no reason to regret the small book[8] in which I tried to lay down as best I could the duties of a prince; a book which our dear Ferdinand, a young man born for virtue, has constantly in his hands. But now I am the more glad because I hope that such value as it has may reach the whole world. For as a man does the maximum amount of harm who fouls the 60 spring from which all drink, so that man's good action has the widest range who teaches the heart that is to rule over all men.

Richard Pace, the excellent envoy of an excellent king, was sure, I knew it, to win your approval in every way. On his return[9] to us, I can hardly say how delighted he was with his good fortune in having come to know, 65 and in turn to be known by, a prince such as your Highness, distinguished no less in character than in lineage or station. With what enthusiasm and in what glowing language did he, in answer to my eager questions, give me a full picture of you!

As for myself, what honour or assistance I can bring to Holy Scripture is 70 for others to decide; I am at least resolved to work at this till death. And my work is not displeasing to Christ, of this I am sure, for one reason at any rate, that I undertake it with a single purpose, to promote his glory. Why should he who preferred the poor widow's mite[10] to all the offerings of all the rich not approve my industry? Let others strive to please Christ by good deeds of 75 different kinds: this is all I can do, this is the sacrifice that shall win me his favour.

Consider too how much I owe to your Highness' generosity for Hutten's sake as well.[11] He will one day, as I foresee, be a great credit to our native Germany, on this condition, that God preserves him and grants him a 80 long life and that he does not lose the favour of your Highness; for this excessive levity in his nature (if I may say so) will be naturally corrected by increasing years. That you do not resent the man's[12] mistake in seeking to please someone else, with more zeal than discretion, by the dedication of a book, is to me evidence of a lofty spirit worthy of so great a prince. Your gift 85 has not yet arrived;[13] when it comes, I shall keep it always as something sacred, and shall display it too, as a pledge of your feelings for me and a

record of the opinion that you formed of me. My respectful best wishes to
your Highness, whose good will I should wish always to retain.

Antwerp, 15 August 1519 90

1010 / To the Reader [Louvain? c] 1 September 1519

This preface was published in a separate edition of Erasmus' Latin version of
the text of the New Testament, reprinted from the *Novum instrumentum* of 1516
(cf Epp 373, 384), without the Greek. This separate edition was printed by Dirk
Martens (Louvain [c September] 1519; NK 335). It proved a success, and similar
reprints followed one another at short intervals. Two of them, by Andreas
Cratander (Basel August 1520) and by Johann Froben (Basel July 1522), contain
new prefaces to the reader in the place of the present one. Finding them similar
in scope to this preface or to other well-known texts, Allen judged them
unsuitable for inclusion in the correspondence of Erasmus. For the same reason
they will not be translated in this edition. The one of 1520, however, attained a
certain notoriety in two German translations that were printed a dozen times
from 1522 to 1525, often under the misleading title *Von walfart*. For details on
subsequent editions see Allen's introduction to this letter and *Bibliotheca
Erasmiana: Répertoire des oeuvres d'Erasme, liste sommaire* ed F. Vander Haeghen
(Ghent 1893; repr 1961) II 57; H. Holeczek *Erasmus Deutsch* (Stuttgart-Bad
Cannstatt 1983–) I 73–80.

As on similar occasions the date of this letter, Calends of September in the
Latin text, could be putative and set to coincide approximately with the
anticipated date of publication (cf Epp 853, 1007 introductions). It is quite
possible that on 1 September Erasmus was away from Louvain (cf Ep 999
introduction), and he would not likely have waited for a vacation to supply
Martens with this short text.

ERASMUS OF ROTTERDAM TO ALL FAIR-MINDED READERS,
GREETING

In the face of all my protests, gentle reader, it has been decided to print the
New Testament in my version without the annotations, in other words, to
cast it naked and defenceless to the tender mercies of its detractors.[1] Other 5
men's wisdom, or their love of money, having won the day, the next best
thing, indeed all that remains, is to issue a formal warning. If you feel that
anything is in disagreement with the common and accepted version, you
must be in no hurry to interpret this as though my new version offered any
criticism or correction of the old. I have taken what I found in correct copies 10
of the Greek text, and have translated it in such a way that sometimes I give
our own text[2] the preference over the Greek, and from time to time put the

two together so as to leave it to the reader to decide which is the better reading. At least I have shown, nor can it be denied, that in our texts there are many corrupt passages, a certain number of passages translated in such a way as to be obscure or ambiguous or barbarous, and some which have hitherto been imperfectly understood.

In these places, if you feel that your studies have been assisted by my efforts, be grateful not to me but to Jesus Christ, under whose guidance we do all that is done aright. If on the other hand you find something which at first sight you do not like, be in no hurry to speak ill of me. Suspend judgment until you have consulted my annotations. Heaven forbid that you should wish to emulate the unheard-of impudence of some men, who privately and in public condemn what they confess they have not read, in which they show themselves more unfair than Zoilus[3] himself: he did read the Homeric poems diligently before criticizing some points in them, with good reason I dare say, and meanwhile clearly approved what he left untouched. These men shut their eyes and, like blindfold gladiators,[4] attack something they cannot see and condemn what they cannot understand and do not wish to. Such is their astonishing blend of ignorance and conceit that they take something which the supreme pontiff[5] after due inspection and examination has declared to deserve the attention of all who wish to learn, and this, without looking into it, they pursue with clamorous malevolence, especially among those who know no better. How came such unfairness, such perversity, I might almost say, among Christians? – worse still, among men who wish to achieve distinction by their profession of the religious life?

But a dispute with such people is not to my purpose. It is to you, dear reader, that I appeal, who bring to Christ's teaching a truly Christian spirit. If anything here is to your taste, enjoy it; and then be all the more fair-minded, if the man who has tried to be of service to you should fail of success in his pious undertaking.

1 September 1519

1011 / From Guillaume Budé   Marly, [early September 1519]

Budé replied twice to Erasmus' Ep 1004: first by this letter, which is rather reassuring, and a few days later by Ep 1015, which is somewhat more critical. This letter is entirely, the second is partially, in Greek. Both were first printed in *Epistolae Guilelmi Budaei* (Paris: J. Bade 20 August 1520) and afterwards also by Erasmus together with his answer, Ep 1066, in *Epistolae ad diversos*. Allen's collation indicated that the editors of the latter had followed faithfully a corrected reprint of Budé's own edition rather than any manuscript, perhaps on instruction from Erasmus himself, who was well aware of Budé's concern with accuracy (Epp 493: 47–55, 896 postscript).

All early editions of this letter give the date of 15 September, but it was actually written a few days earlier. Since Paris was infested by the plague Budé had gone to his country house at Marly. There he received Ep 1004, which had probably been carried to Paris by Haio Herman (cf Ep 1002 n11). Herman was expected to take this answer back with him to the Netherlands, but when it reached the capital he had left; so Budé finally sent it together with his second letter, on 15 September; see the postscript of Ep 1015.

BUDÉ TO ERASMUS, GREETING

It was a great pleasure to get your letter, which I had been looking forward to, as it happened, for some time. The letter was not so pleasant, however, when I opened it, at least on a first reading. It was the day on which Christophe de Longueil,[1] a man who at no distant date will be among those   5
renowned for their learning, had passed by my country house on his way to England with some pleasant companions, I thought, but intending to visit you and see the city of Louvain, as he told me, *en route*. Late that evening, when I was occupied with some learned work or other, one of my household reported that there was a young man[2] at the courtyard gate on horseback. I   10
came down at once, and the young man met me, after greetings, with the news that he brought letters from Erasmus and from another friend of mine. When I heard this, I can't tell you how I was filled with joy, and felt my heart all the time bounding in my breast.

So I took it and opened it, and when I saw at once that the beginning   15
was in Greek, it was a delightful surprise. Then, when I began to run through it eagerly in my excitement, as I read I was flushed and pale, smiling and showing my teeth, by turns indignant and grateful, relaxed and troubled, a prey to conflicting emotions, everything you can think of all at once – sometimes longing to be quit of this debate between us, and then   20
again warming to the fray. Thereafter, I thought the question over in my mind, and then for a short time, with my opinion swaying this way and that – for my judgment was pulled in opposite directions by conflicting sentiments – I was plunged in meditation, arguing with myself, until in the end I abandoned my vacillating state and came down on the side of what is   25
agreeable and reasonable, keeping tight hold, as you may well suppose, on the friendship that means so much to me. And that friendship reminded me that I ought not to consider your strictures on me nearly as much as I ought to give you credit for your kindly and affectionate heart.

At the same time it occurred to me, while I was then thinking this over,   30
that if I had committed any offence against the god of friendship – for such a

thing might perhaps happen during the playful imitation of a genuine contest which we reproduce in our letters – I ought to buy my pardon by some sacrifice, nothing ordinary or offered in any ordinary fashion. But it is a principle accepted by all of us who are keen students of heavenly things that   35
no sacrifice could appease the offended god more readily than confessing and repenting of our mistakes. And so, dearest of men, when you invite me[3] to adopt a more gracious and decorous form and content for the letters we exchange, I am so appreciative of your courtesy and of that spirit of yours that hates finding fault that I am perfectly delighted with your proposal that   40
we should let bygones be bygones, which I promise to abide by permanently. Be assured then that henceforward you will find your friend Budé as obedient to the principles of true friendship as any of your esteemed and tested friends.

All the same, I shall not hesitate, feeling as I do about friendship, to   45
make this one request of you, and I do not think you will object to granting it. What I ask is this. I will preserve the amnesty[4] and do nothing to break the peace between us, but to a limited extent I want to be allowed to remember what has passed, enough to bear witness to all men, be they friends or enemies of yours or mine, that whatever I may have, or may seem to have,   50
written or said about you or to you, while there may perhaps have been a touch of jealousy in it (which slips in somehow and sharpens one's temper, and perhaps ends by doing some damage, for emotions often increase in intensity for the worse), did not arise from any jealous spite or ill-natured wish to win; I swear it by Philosophy, whose divinity we must and do revere.   55
And indeed I should have no hesitation myself in calling as a witness to this the goddess of Truth-in-itself, who keeps true philosophers straight on their course, and sees into our hearts. And yet I for my part, who never take a solemn oath without some misgiving, and never on any casual occasion, felt no need, I think, at this time to prove our mutual good will, had it not been   60
for your friends, and the enemies of us both maybe, and still more those who cannot stomach our enthusiasm; for they seemed silently to put me to the proof and challenge me to swear this oath, suspecting no doubt that there is some hostility between us which they view with satisfaction, as a result of the skirmishes we have fought in the past by way of practice.   65

And you, my dear sir, if you are conscious of having done anything of the kind – in respect, I mean, of this contentious spirit of rivalry which goes further than it need – you would know if it is necessary for you too to purify your conscience in some such way as this. For no man of good will and friendly intent would think it necessary to recall now things that did, as a   70
matter of fact, surprise me in your letter, which were expounded cleverly and ingeniously but in a somewhat censorious spirit, and indeed were

discussed with needless accuracy, considering that the person concerned
was immediately going to propose an amnesty. Language which might
appease me and cast a spell over me would have been more in place, to   75
prepare me to be submissive and ready to accept your new rule; for had I
myself been in contentious mood, had I tried to make full use of this dispute
to gratify the more passionate part of my nature more emotionally, there
would never have been an end to this business, and from this excessive
competition between two friends a whole Iliad of unfortunate contention   80
would have arisen, as each of us, I suppose, claimed that he was always
right, whether justly or unjustly.

     Indeed it pleases me to think that I was the first to control myself, so
that I readily acquiesced in your admirable amnesty, though even that
would, I suppose, have been more reasonable, had you not introduced it   85
into that disputatious letter, which went so closely into various mistakes that
I seemed to have made by exceeding the limits of moderation in my dispute
with you. I do not deny the charges that can be brought against me, and in
the same way I should not be ashamed to retract my mistakes wherever this
might be practicable, and to ask forgiveness when I have done something in   90
haste when I should not have. Apart from anything else, I have derived this
benefit from your skill, that I shall now grow accustomed to endure in seemly
and orderly fashion the man who lays down the law to me and to give him a
careful hearing, even to the extent of overcoming my impatience, which
rebels above all against reasoned argument. For there is no state of mind less 95
amenable to reason, none that finds it more difficult to submit to self-control,
than this contentious spirit – and this although it strives so earnestly to seem
to have right on its side. It will be for you, dearest of friends, to consider
carefully how you may avoid giving the impression of disengaging from this
contest in a somewhat inconsiderate fashion; for when I saw you anxious, as   100
you said[5] you were, for my reputation, I thought it advisable in return, as a
matter of my own duty and my credit too, to take some thought for yours.

     What then, in heaven's name? Will some of our common friends put this
to your credit, if, when I have sent you three letters[6] in succession, you have
taken issue with only one of them, and that the worst, and one already   105
outdated, searching out every point in it that you do not like and so
misinterpreting it that I find what I sent you unrecognizable, while of the
two that were friendly and well-meaning you made simply no mention at all?
For the needless trouble with which you turn over and over the bitterness
and folly of my letter does not smack of a very sweet disposition; nor does   110
your silence regarding those good, friendly letters, which deserved to be
taken seriously, provide much guarantee, I think, of a permanent attachment[7] on your side. You say you are always the same where friendship is

concerned; do you not fear that no one will believe this, if you stand
self-convicted of such a long memory for the wrongs you have suffered? And   115
then, having set such an example, do you expect to persuade other men that
you take in good part everything that is said even if it is a little uncalled-for?
How can you, while you so much enjoy repeating all these charges in this
clever, captious way, and fasten so tight on every word I wrote, and yet have
tried to prove yourself beyond criticism on every point? 'Persuade me you   120
may, but I won't be persuaded,' as it says in the comic play.[8]

For my own part, dear friend, I freely confess my error, and ask pardon
if, under the weight of your harsh and pedantic criticism, which holds you
guiltless yourself of any fault, I have gone on at such length, however much I
am convinced that you are a true friend and wish me well. Both of us, it may   125
be, allow our judgments to be warped by feeling, our self-love being perhaps
a little bit too passionate, as the way of mankind is. And then again, I fear
that I may unconsciously be interfering with the repentance which I try so
hard to practise; for if a man has repented of his mistakes, and does not for
the future entirely avoid the points that were at issue, it will not be long   130
before he measures his length over the same obstacle once again. Henceforth
therefore I present myself in a state of irreversible repentance, ready and
willing to concur in whatever you wish, especially as I am not averse by
nature from those courteous and elegant exchanges – such being the field to
which I am summoned by you, the nursling of the Graces. So let our rule to   135
let bygones be bygones have the force of law from now onwards, and a
blessing on it. Whichever of us revives what has passed on either side shall
not merely stand arraigned for breaking the law, but shall incur a further
substantial penalty, to wit the enmity of our common friends. You see how I
play my part in your legislation, I vote for your policy, and join in ratifying   140
that element in your proposal which will strike out, I hope, and abolish all
causes of dispute. Remember then the proposal which you were the first to
introduce, and lead the way in finding a convincing and elegant method of
making sense of what has passed.

From my house at Marly, the fifteenth of Maimakterion[9]   145
Farewell, and may good fortune long attend you.

1012 / To Jan van Fevijn   Louvain, 9 September [1519?]

This letter was published in the *Epistolae ad diversos* dated August 1521, where
it stands on the same page as Ep 1013A. Both are given the year date of 1517,
which is unacceptable. In the case of this letter either 1519 or 1520 is possible as
Erasmus visited Bruges during the summer of each of these years. Allen leaned
toward 1519; Henry de Vocht (*Literae ad Craneveldium* 314; CTL I 402) preferred

1520, assuming that Gerard Geldenhouwer, the recipient of Ep 1141 (dated 9 September 1520), was then in Flanders and that this letter was sent along with his. In the absence of more precise evidence it makes sense to read this letter in conjunction with Epp 993:52–60, 994 n4, 998 introduction, 1004:165–7, 1006 introduction, 1007:107–17, 1016, 1022 introduction, 1025 n4 and 329–47 below, all of which reflect Erasmus' current troubles at Louvain and his desire for a more quiet abode. Some of his personal troubles were connected with the uncertain future of the Collegium Trilingue at Louvain. It appears that at times some consideration was given to moving the college to Bruges, where the new learning was generally welcomed and no conflicts threatened to arise from the presence of a conservative faculty of theology. From 27 October 1518 daily lectures on Greek grammar were held in the chapter hall of St Donatian's there (see de Vocht CTL I 514–20).

Jan van Fevijn (Fevinus) of Veurne, Flanders (1490–1555) had matriculated at Louvain in 1506 and subsequently obtained a doctorate in law in Italy. In 1510 he was appointed to a canonry at the chapter of St Donatian at Bruges and subsequently, as scholaster, took charge of the chapter's excellent grammar school. Fevijn and his cousin, Karel van Hedenbault (line 4), lived in the Prinsenhof, a palace of the former counts of Flanders which had been a favourite residence of the dukes of Burgundy, where Erasmus enjoyed repeatedly an elegant hospitality; see de Vocht *Literae ad Craneveldium* xci–xcix.

ERASMUS OF ROTTERDAM TO JAN VAN FEVIJN, CANON OF
ST DONATIAN'S AT BRUGES, GREETING

After the taste I had during those few days of the exceptional friendliness of many people, and especially of you and your cousin Karel,[1] I like Louvain less than I did, and should be happy to spend my life in Bruges, if I could find a convenient nest and a bill of fare to suit my philosophical appetite. I hear Karel has almost the same tastes that I have; he likes stylish rather than constant dinner-parties, and entertainment that is elegant and not prolonged. There can be no shortage of room in the prince's empty palace, and at the same time I noticed how your cousin took to me; about yourself I will say nothing for the moment. But there will be no shortage of company either, when among others there is my friend Marcus.[2] In short then, if you think fit, have a word about this with your cousin, for we can do this without being unfair to anyone. If there is no objection from any quarter, we shall easily agree about the rent; but if there is some reason why this is not convenient, write and tell me so. Until then, best wishes. My greetings to Karel, kindest of men, and to your kinsman Robert[3] and his wife.

Louvain, 9 September

Give my greetings to all your colleagues, but especially to the
precentor⁴ and to Nicolaus Fistula.⁵   20
   [1517]

1013 / To Jacob de Voecht   Louvain, 10 September 1519

This is the preface to a new edition of Cicero's dialogues *De officiis*, *Cato maior de
senectute*, *Laelius de amicitia*, and *Paradoxa Stoicorum* (Louvain: D. Martens [late
1519]; NK 2657; cf Ep 1053 introduction). It was reprinted at Basel by Johann
Froben (August 1520). A rough draft of this letter is in the famous manuscript of
writings by Erasmus at Copenhagen, Gl Kgl Samling 95 fol, f 194; see Allen III
630–4; C. Reedijk in *Studia bibliographica in honorem Herman de la Fontaine
Verwey* ed S. van der Woude (Amsterdam 1968) 327–49. When Erasmus first
edited and annotated *De officiis* at Paris in 1501 he composed a first dedication
to de Voecht (Ep 152) which remained unpublished, however, until it appeared
together with this new letter in Froben's edition of 1520. The Martens edition
may have been intended primarily for the use of students of the Collegium
Trilingue (cf de Voecht CTL II 11, 110–11).
   Jacob de Voecht (Voogd, Tutor c 1477–1541) had been pensionary (or legal
adviser) of the city of Antwerp since 1506.

ERASMUS OF ROTTERDAM TO THE HONOURABLE JACOB
DE VOECHT, PENSIONARY OF THE FAMOUS CITY OF ANTWERP,
GREETING
As those who have been stung by scorpions go to the same creatures for a
remedy,¹ so it seems right and proper to me, my dear Jacob, most scholarly of   5
men of law, that those of us who are devoted to literature, when we have
wearied our minds or weakened our bodies by more serious study, should
seek refreshment² equally from study, but of a more attractive kind. Your
truly devoted reader does nothing else all his life, as long he is allowed to
control his way of life to please himself, but read; he does not so much   10
abandon his passion for reading as relax it; he sometimes rests his mind, but
is never idle. Such men lay off now and again, but all the time they are doing
something; they take a holiday sometimes, but in such a way that they can
give a good account of their leisure hours. Sometimes, if you like, they are
idle; but their idleness does more for them than the unremitting addiction to   15
business does for some other men. A gallant and active soldier (to take a
fairly close parallel) in his summer or winter quarters, or in a time of peace,
when there is no call to take his place in the line or live out under canvas,
relaxes his mind none the less and rebuilds his strength in those sports

especially which have a military flavour. He attacks a dummy figure, he   20
shoots at a target, he whirls his sling and brandishes his spear, he fights in
the gymnasium, competes in the lists, swims across a torrent, leaps in full
armour onto his horse. In a word, his holiday from warlike duties is of a kind
to send him back to them with renewed vigour. There is a difference between
the pastimes of a gamester and of a distinguished prince, between the   25
scurrility of a buffoon and the humour of a man of worth and character.

In accordance with this principle, when my state of health lately
demanded that I should restore and repair my strength of mind and body,
which had been worn down with the continual and excessive labour of my
researches, I left Louvain and travelled[3] through several towns of Brabant   30
and Flanders in order at the same time to get away for a space from my books
and refresh myself with the company and conversation of my modest friends
in the learned way. Even so, I could not endure to be so wholly parted from
my beloved library as not to carry round with me two or three books as
companions on the journey, so that if at any moment I was not blessed with a   35
congenial old friend to share the carriage, at least I should not be short of
someone to talk to me and while away the time. Among these were Cicero's
Officia, Laelius, and *Cato,* together with his *Paradoxa Stoicorum;* the small size
of the volume had attracted me, for it would not add much weight to my
baggage. From reading this, my dear de Voecht, I gained a double benefit.   40
For one thing, I refreshed my memory of our early intimacy,[4] than which
nothing could have been more delightful, in a way that gave me extraordinary pleasure. And then I so fired my whole self with a zeal for honour and
virtue, that for a long time I had felt nothing of the kind while reading some
modern authors of our own country, who are Christians and teach the   45
mysteries of the Christian philosophy, and discuss these same topics with
what seems to us great subtlety, and yet leave us quite cold.

I know not the effect on others; the effect on me I frankly confess,
whether it is their fault or mine. I found myself thinking as I read: Is this a
pagan writing[5] for pagans and a layman for laymen? What justice, what   50
purity, what sincerity, what truth in his rules for living! – all is in harmony
with nature, nothing glossed over or half asleep. What a spirit he demands
from those at the head of public affairs! What a notable and lovable picture of
virtue he paints before our eyes! How many lessons he teaches, and how like
a saint – almost a deity! – on how we should do good to all men even without   55
reward, on the maintenance of friendship, on the immortality of souls, on
contempt for the things for whose sake the modern public, not merely
ordinary Christians but divines and monks as well, will do and suffer
anything. I was ashamed meanwhile at the thought of our own behaviour:
brought up on the Scriptures, encouraged by such examples and such   60

rewards, we profess the gospel teaching and do not practise it. Show our grandees a prince or magistrate as Cicero describes him: my life upon it, he will jeer at Cicero and his ideal as crazy. Who now takes up public life except in hopes of profit or to win high place? Who governs without seeming to have an eye for gain and to behave like the enemy of those whose interests 65 he ought to consider even at the cost of his own life? Where will you find among Christians a pair of friends to match the picture put forward by Cicero? Or old men who endure the troubles of age with such unbroken spirit? Or such noble conversations between old men and young?

Never before have I more clearly felt the truth of what Augustine[6] 70 writes: that the virtuous acts of pagans are a sharper spur towards goodness in ourselves than those of our own people, when we reflect what a disgrace it is that a heart illuminated by the light of the Gospel should not see what was seen clearly by them with only nature's candle to show them the way; that we, the soldiers of religion under Christ's banner, who look for 75 immortality from him as our reward, do not perform what they did, who suspected or fully believed that no part of a man survived the funeral pyre. And after all this, there is no lack of blockheads to deter students from reading books like this, because they are what's called poetical[7] and a serious danger to morals. But I consider them worthy to be read by teachers with the 80 young in every school, and read and reread to themselves by the old; and that is why long ago I emended them and dedicated[8] them to you, and now renew the dedication of a more accurate text, enriched with fresh material. For I have added first Cicero's book *De amicitia*, secondly the *De senectute*, and thirdly the *Paradoxa*, with brief notes on them all, which are indeed short 85 but will, if I mistake not, be found useful, in which my chief purpose is to discourage the faultfinding linguistic pedantry of certain people who at almost every word cry out, 'This is not Latin,' 'It is not found in the best authors.' Besides which, I have pointed out a certain number of mistakes which no one, so far as I know, had previously noticed. 90

It remains that, as de Voecht was always before my eyes as I worked on this book, so you, as you read it, should bear in mind your Erasmus, who loves you and cares for you as much as anyone. Farewell.

Louvain, 10 September 1519

1013A / To Gerardus Listrius Louvain, 11 September [1519]

This letter is Ep 660 in Allen's edition, but on second thoughts Allen himself assigned it to the year 1519 (Allen IV 67; cf below n2, n6, n8). It was first printed in the *Epistolae ad diversos* with the wrong date of 1517 (cf Ep 1012 introduction). Listrius, who was the rector of the grammar school at Zwolle, had written a commentary on the *Moria* which was published in 1515 along with Erasmus' text; cf Ep 495 introduction.

ERASMUS TO HIS FRIEND GERARDUS LISTRIUS, GREETING

On the contrary, it is for me to thank you for arranging for me that conversation with your brother;[1] so far was he from being unwelcome, I like the young man very much. So you have a wife[2] after your own heart: I wish you joy, and pray that Christ may make your felicity everlasting. If she also 5 thinks well of me, I have you to thank for that, not her; she likes me, but she has caught the affection from you. My *Moria* is translated into French,[3] but the translator has changed not only the language but the matter, and left out many things that he could not understand, while some of it was over his head. At this year's fair there will appear a new volume of my letters[4] of a 10 considerable size; next year I mean to revise what has been printed, and add some new letters to make a proper volume of it. I will write to Tilmannus[5] as you suggest, as soon as I have the chance of someone to take it, as I shall have shortly. What you propose about the *Enchiridion*[6] is not quite clear to me; if you will add explanatory notes, I shall be delighted, but if you want notes 15 from me, you must mark the passages that seem to you obscure. If the name Erasmus carries any weight[7] in your part of the world, I owe it chiefly to your readiness to think well of me.

Serious steps are being taken here to patch up a peace,[8] now that they have voided all their venom; the fact remains that a Christian spirit wins the 20 day everywhere. I am astonished at these men who profess the purity of gospel times, and let fly against a fellow creature's reputation in a manner so unlike the Gospel, rambling on about things they do not understand[9] to an audience that has no understanding either. They deserve not only to be mocked by the children but to be driven out publicly with a shower of stones. 25 But truth will prevail, never fear.

Give my greetings in return to Master Simon[10] and the prior of the Mont,[11] but specially to your precious little Justina, to whom I send my very best wishes. The prior of St Agnes I have not seen yet; I had no opportunity, being involved in so much petty business. Farewell, my learned Listrius. 30
Louvain, 11 September [1519]

1014 / To Beatus Rhenanus   [Louvain, early September 1519]

This letter is now missing, but Allen printed under this number an excerpt from a letter written by Beatus Rhenanus to Bruno Amerbach from Sélestat on 28 September 1519 (AK II Ep 684), which refers to Erasmus' missing letter. As had happened once before (cf Ep 594 introduction), a financial dispute with Johann

Froben and his associates had caused Beatus Rhenanus to leave Basel in the summer of 1519. He was living in his native Sélestat, from where he would not return to Basel until 15 September 1520, after a settlement had been reached (cf AK II Ep 749; Bietenholz *Basle and France* 28). Bruno Amerbach was preparing to leave Basel to settle his wife's estate with his father-in-law, Johann Schabler (cf AK II Ep 657). Beatus Rhenanus writes to him as follows:

Erasmus says in a letter to me that Froben ought to print the ancient *Panegyrici*, adding his own *Panegyricus* and the one Ausonius wrote for the emperor Gratian. Please therefore let Froben have your copy, which I have marked in the margins, before you leave, and please tell Froben this, for it did not enter my head when he was here three days ago.

The *Panegyrici veteres*, a collection of texts in praise of different Roman emperors, was first edited by Franciscus Puteolanus and printed by Antonio Zarotto (Milan: [c 1482]). Of this edition Bruno Amerbach owned a copy which is now missing but was no doubt used for Froben's reprint of December 1520. It included, as Erasmus had directed, his own panegyric on Philip the Handsome of Burgundy (cf Epp 179–80) and that of Ausonius, and also some others by Ermolao Barbaro, Pandolfo Collenuccio and Georg Sauermann, all addressed to members of the house of Hapsburg. A short preface to the reader, published over the name of Johann Froben, and a longer one by Beatus Rhenanus (BRE Ep 187) both attest to their recent reconciliation. For the delay between Erasmus' suggestion and the actual publication see BRE Ep 191.

1015 / From Guillaume Budé   Marly, 15 September [1519]

For the circumstances and the publication of this letter see Ep 1011 introduction. It is another reply to Ep 1004. Budé entrusted it for forwarding to the Paris printer Gilles de Gourmont or to a relative of his who visited him at Marly; see Budé *Opera Omnia* I 256.

BUDÉ TO ERASMUS

What is all this? In what I said in your praise in my letter to Tunstall[1] you did not fail to notice that there was criticism and double meaning? For my part, I am surprised at the way in which, artlessly no doubt, you stand self-convicted of the same sort of double talk in what you have written about me   5
(and you began it) in flattering vein. Your friend Vives[2] could give you evidence of this: I showed him a letter written to me by a man of very good judgment (though I put my finger over his name to conceal it), who drew my attention, as though I did not observe them, to the passages of criticism

scattered through what you have written. Though he himself did not see one   10
letter to the same effect from an Italian[3] who is greatly respected, who did not
address it to me but to one of his own acquaintances and friends, who lately
sent me the original. And though I thought it best to pass over that and much
like it in silence, and even to forget it altogether, you have now aroused my
resentment like an old wound, and almost turned suspicion into certainty;   15
unless you propose to deny that in the words I speak of you I set a precedent
against yourself – a precedent for taking the same view of you that you say it
came into your mind to take of me.

I should not like you to think this meant that I did not greatly enjoy that
letter you wrote me in Greek, to which I have already replied in Greek;[4] but   20
none the less you gave me a double reason to accuse you in some sort in
return, let alone to defend myself. How could it be otherwise? You repeated
over again everything I had written, outshooting all the rhetoric, all the care
and thought I had put into it – and it was you who said you let pass[5] and did
not mention many of my mistakes, while I in turn deliberately passed over   25
much in my reply. I know only too well that I let pass things in my defence in
the expression of which, and the working out of them on paper, I am
conscious that indignation has made its way into my mind or that I have been
swept off course by the strong feelings of controversy. I see clearly that I
have sometimes exaggerated and given way to passion. I have therefore   30
suffered myself with a good grace to be corrected by a friend, so far indeed as
concerns passages which cannot be modified by treatment. But you seem to
me to have failed so far to understand my mind – always granted that you
speak from your own opinion and not other people's.

First of all, when I said[6] that you have now, I hope, swallowed the pill   35
contained in my letter, I would urge you to consider whether I cannot give
this a more apt explanation than yours, like this: there was indeed bitterness
in my letter (for you sometimes accuse me of being spiteful and odd)[7] but all
the same I hoped you had digested it, or at least had swallowed[8] all that
indignation sufficiently to be quit by now of all memory of the wrong done   40
you (if one can speak of wrongs where there is no intention to hurt),
especially as you had unburdened yourself adequately of your indignation
against me, and seemed to me from the last page of your letter to bear my
bitterness (to give it that name, since you find it such) more calmly, and to
have no wish to recall it, for you kept saying that by now you know the kind   45
of man I am.

And then can you imagine the impatience and the discomfort with
which I read that passage where you rise to tragic heights, calling heaven
and earth to witness – where you adduce as offensive and reject as
tyrannical and domineering that remark of mine about getting 'practice'[9] in   50

exchanging jokes with me.' Have you forgotten your humanity, dearest of my friends, and that love of great things for which we have, I believe, the same enthusiasm? Do not think me so conceited as to suppose that I could associate with you except on equal terms and with a sense of what is due to both of us. Let me therefore give you my explanation of this remark, and then   55
complain if you dare that I do not treat you as an equal. You have often said that I am too much given to jests, drawn sometimes from an area of danger, so to say, and sailing close to impertinence, and they were just what you could not approve, for they seemed perhaps below the level of a modest and serious person like yourself. I on the other hand felt myself in that longer   60
letter[10] of yours so belaboured, so pelted with your jests, that you would have found it impossible, or at least unbearable, to say anything further, even had indignation and not humour been the moving force. Consequently I wrote, in my usual straightforward way, that you were now getting practice in exchanging jests with me. Something restrained me from saying   65
that you had now begun to be as unbridled and licentious in your sallies as you used to complain that I was. Do please reread the passage and think over what it means; and you will find, I hope, that the shafts of my wit are aimed more at myself than you. Or was it not really a reflection on myself when I said or hinted that you had departed from your true nature through the   70
malign influence of my letter and our exchange of humorous remarks? But you have almost made a high tragical crime out of it by your passionate protests.

Again, when you protest that I made you out to be too leaden-witted[11] to understand me, if I were not afraid to reopen wounds[12] that had already   75
healed over I would expound this passage; but to put you right in a word or two can do no harm, I imagine. Let me at least remind you then, when you put your finger, as it were, on one of your Williams,[13] of the business that I was then trying to put through for you and how important it was, and of the agreement we had come to. I would rather you had not mentioned him at all;   80
for apart from the fact that the confessor of our lord and master is sacrosanct, this man stands high in repute and in position, and as far as business goes has confidential connections, not to express my meaning more clearly. Besides which, he is one of those who are friendly disposed towards me and is a keen supporter of us both. But of course it was I and not you who stood   85
the risk, and so you did not give it so much thought. Though I do not yet touch the point on which I said in my humorous way that you were not sharp-sighted enough, in fact were unlike yourself. For that the words[14] 'in which I tried to bring to fruition for your benefit what we had decided on' were more than you could understand, I can hardly believe, especially as   90
your way is to receive what I say as meaning something more comprehensive

than I do myself, as is clear from what I have said. And if you think I wrap up
my ideas in riddles rather than express them, very well: whenever you
please, I will speak more clumsily and more clearly, though I can hardly
suppose that I need to do so.   95

As for what you say about gratitude for bringing good news,[15] as
though you were afraid I should expect you to be grateful for the efforts and
the interest I have put into this project, I acquit you already of that
obligation, if you are embarrassed by the responsibility; but I do not also
liberate you from the laws of friendship, which I should be pleased to think   100
will endure between us forever, as should you, so far as I can gather from the
evidence and from what other men tell me, as long as you will judge my
sentiments by your own and not from other men's opinion.

Very well then, think it out for yourself: is it friendly, is it like my friend
Erasmus, is it clever and elegant, confronted with the honey-sweet letters of   105
Deloynes[16] and my other fellow-countrymen, to arraign me on a charge of
libel as though I had said or hinted that you are fond of adulation, when in
fact you rejoice more than any man in the outspokenness of your friends? I
forbear at this moment to inquire whether it is true or no that you get the most
satisfaction and pleasure out of your most free-spoken friends. Was there   110
any other reason for the sort of collision that has come about between us,
who seemed previously to be such particular friends, except the liberties I
took at the beginning in my letters? But let it now be true and taken as
established; what follows? Did you suppose me to be so much my own worst
enemy, and to have such an evil genius at my elbow when I write, that I   115
would quarrel capriciously and recklessly with my circumstances, and even
let myself go in the abuse of the chief of my friends under the impulse of some
excess of feeling directed against you? What then? Was I already so unable to
control the critical and mocking element in my humour that I would apply the
insulting word flatterer to Deloynes, who is more kindly disposed to me than   120
anyone and enjoys, moreover, no ordinary reputation? For presumably I
could not say you were fond of flattery without myself calling him a flatterer
– so easy is it for you to cast at me whatever comes into your head! When the
moment comes that you have collected quantities of this sort of thing in great
detail in your Iliad[17] of my misdoings, you are at liberty, so far as I am   125
concerned, to add this to the list in rhetorical fashion in the gathering of your
friends, of those especially who take strong exception to my letters. Then if I
seem to them to deserve the names I am given for what I have said, it will
follow presumably from the amnesty[18] laid down by you that there should be
some audit on the other side of what I have suffered from you in return, and   130
that, when that takes place, if our exchanges should be found to be even and
equally balanced, we should be reconciled on equal terms in respect of all

charges and counter-charges. This will be the best way of ensuring that bygones will be bygones, and that in future you will not be able to use rhetorical pretexts like 'I forgive much that you say in haste, such as your remarks ...,'[19] though you cannot let even that same 'remarks' rest without distorting it to look like something scandalous. Is it really so, my good man (that is to say, my orator)? Will you maintain that you are conceding to me what you hang on to with clenched fists and teeth? And after exacting all your legal rights, every scrap of them, will you describe yourself as a fair-minded and kindly litigant?

Then as to what you write (whatever the ulterior motive) about maintaining our unanimity[20] and our not needing anyone to act as cement, I want you to bear in mind that I have never mentioned the topic to a soul, except to this extent: I have habitually asserted and upheld in every attitude of both body and mind that our minds are not shaken or moved by all this sort of verbal skirmishing to the extent of making possible any dislocation or separation in the established fabric of our friendship, but that none the less this appearance of disagreement has proved so lifelike that in the end it might be taken by zealous friends and ill-informed outsiders for disagreement in earnest. In this field I foresaw no need for me to take any special steps in advance, before I detected and saw clearly enough that you get more enjoyment from the sort of playful contest that is fought with foils on the weapons, which at least can do no harm. Not that you had any fears on your own behalf or on mine, not that you had anything to fear from me or I from you, but because you thought it better to give pleasure to the spectators than to keep them on tenterhooks in expectation of some lamentable outcome. And you easily persuaded me of the reasons for this policy, once I had begun to consider the question more carefully.

In fact, I consider that no estrangement and difference of opinion has arisen between us such as might ask for a reconciliation, let alone a mediator. By all means, as far as I am concerned, if I have ever spoken or written a word against you with uncharitable and hostile intent, to hurt your interests or diminish your reputation, immense as it is – designing I suppose with language carefully contrived to topple you from your pinnacle of fame – may the Lord strike me with equal misfortune. Bad temper has had its share; we have made mistakes, as is only human; we have been clumsy and perhaps unwise in the way we have treated our friendship, and given the impression that in this matter of reputation each of us is out for the other's blood, as sometimes happens in mock engagements, when the heat of battle overruns the rules of the game and the legitimate and agreed limits of give and take. In our own experience we see this happen sometimes in the lists at a tournament, and yet we see it rightly forgiven, when a man humbly offers

satisfaction and asks pardon for his error. What was done in the heat of the
moment is not inexcusable, nor does it ever stay rankling in the mind for a   175
whole day. Even then, I would assert that no resentment, no touch of
indignation was ever strong enough to develop into hatred. I assert this of
myself, and have no hesitation in supposing it true of you. And what if I
should find no cause for regret in any case in what we have written? Think
what strength it adds to our friendship when we part after a fairly sharp   180
dispute with no damage done, in such a way that each of us, having put the
other's disposition to the test, is confident that he has tried it out and fully
tested it, and is happy in that knowledge.

When you complain that I have become a courtier, and regret the loss to
literature as though I had deserted[21] or betrayed the cause I once espoused,   185
and therefore the humanities have lost one of their pillars, this will provide
me with material for making fun of you. But I will write in Greek, so that I can
entertain you with a more outspoken and candid account of the foray[22]
which fell to my lot this year as a member of the court – how far by the
kindness of providence I cannot say.   190

Farewell, from my house at Marly as aforesaid, 15 September.

Here's another confession for you, made in all good faith. Some days
after your letter arrived I sent mine, written in Greek, to your man Herman,[23]
but he had left the city already on account of the plague.[24] So it was sent back
to me from town, and I have amused myself by adding this one to it. It is   195
suprising how much I enjoy writing to you! But I shall not entrust both to the
same man, so that I can score two for them. Farewell once more.

1016 / To Etienne Poncher   Louvain, 2 October 1519

This letter was first published by Nicolas Bérault, Poncher's secretary, in his
edition of works by Marino Becichemo (*In C. Plinium praelectio* and notes on the
first book of Pliny's *Naturalis historia*, Paris: P. Vidoue for K. Resch, colophon
date of 23 July 1519). Obviously pleased with the commendation contained in
lines 34–9, Bérault had this letter added to the verso of the title-page or, in
view of the colophon date, perhaps had the title-page reprinted. As a result the
royal privilege, dated 29 July 1519, had to be squeezed onto the bottom half of
the page. This letter was later republished, with minor changes, in Erasmus'
Epistolae ad diversos. In Bérault's edition its date is given as 31 October, but the
date of 2 October which appears in the *Epistolae ad diversos* is more plausible, as
it agrees with the date of Ep 1017, which was given to the same carrier (see
below n1).

The letter was clearly not intended as a commendatory preface for Bérault as

it shows no marks of the sort of flattery usual on such occasions. Rather
Erasmus wished to remind Poncher with studied nonchalance that he expected
to hear from him in the near future; cf Ep 994 n4.

ERASMUS OF ROTTERDAM TO THE MOST REVEREND ÉTIENNE
PONCHER, ARCHBISHOP OF SENS, GREETING

Most reverend Father in God, although I have nothing of which I would
wish specially to inform your Lordship, the unexpected opportunity
provided by the kindness of the commendator,[1] the bearer of this, is my excuse   5
for a letter of greeting, if no more, to show that I have not forgotten a man to
whom I well know myself to be indebted on many counts. The weather[2] here
is so unseasonable that I can scarcely preserve my bodily health, such as it is.
But apart from the unseasonableness of the weather, I am buffeted by such
storms, raised against me by the enemies of liberal studies, that I never in my   10
life read or heard of or experienced anything more trying; there seems to be a
general conspiracy[3] against Erasmus, all against one. They have attacked me
with engines of every sort – have indeed to the best of their ability roused the
whole world against me. The trouble began with a few people, and gradually
spread, until in the end it took hold of almost everyone; for my own part,   15
with nothing but a clear conscience to support me, I have kept my balance in
this constant barrage of insinuations, believing it to be unchristian to repay
falsehood and abuse in kind. They have at last seen the error of their ways
and made overtures to me at their own request; how long it will last I know
not, but certainly, once peace[4] has been patched up, I shall not be the one to   20
break it.

I am sorry that Lefèvre is having trouble with the bishop of Rochester,[5]
a good Christian and a good scholar, but by nature not a man to let go easily
once he has grown warm in some dispute. I could wish that in those earlier
books he had refrained rather more from bitter words; and he has added   25
others, which means he has worked through the same topic a second time;
but these I have not yet read. What evil genius is it that confounds the
tranquillity of our studies with this kind of strife? How much better it would
be to agree together, and pass our time in the garden of the Muses! I have
now had two or three letters from Bérault[6] in which he warns me to expect a   30
letter from your Grace; and I assure you it will give me great pleasure,
whatever the subject. Whatever the country that houses him, your Grace
will find in Erasmus a devoted adherent; and I will prove the truth[7] of this, if I
am allowed to survive for one more year. The notes of Scodrensis[8] on the first
book of the world history, which have lately been printed in France under   35
Bérault's auspices, I have run through but not properly read. I for my part am

Etienne Poncher
Seventeenth-century engraving by an unknown artist
Bibliothèque Nationale, Paris

entirely glad to have anything in print anywhere in the world that helps to correct or explain so important an author. If only enough people would get to work on this subject to give us Pliny one day reborn complete![9] Farewell.

It would be impertinent in me to try and recommend the commendator   40
to your good graces, and be commender of a commendator, especially since with his help I hope to commend myself to you, for high in your good graces is where I wish to be.

Louvain, 2 October 1519

I hope Cop[10] the physician is well.   45

1017 / To Domenico Grimani   Louvain, 2 October 1519

This letter, which was published in the *Epistolae ad diversos*, is addressed to one of Erasmus' most influential patrons in Rome; see Ep 334.

ERASMUS OF ROTTERDAM TO CARDINAL GRIMANI, GREETING

Right reverend sir, some years ago I published a paraphrase of the Epistle to the Romans dedicated[1] to your Eminence, and it must, I think, have been a success, to judge by the frequent reprints. I was very anxious to know whether this attention on my part was agreeable to you, for I had no other   5
recompense in mind. The letter[2] which Andrea Ammonio told me you had written never reached me; and so I beg you to put yourself to the trouble of another letter, to tell me whether what I did met with your approval.

The most reverend archbishop of Canterbury is now urging me in a succession of letters to translate Origen's commentary[3] on the Psalms. If   10
there is a copy of this in your library, I would not presume to ask you to send it here; but I do beg you to let me have a transcript made at my own expense. I will see to it that in the finished work you are not deprived of any of the credit you have earned. This business I have entrusted to the commendator,[4] a man replete with every virtue, and as such held in the highest esteem   15
by his sovereign.

My respectful greetings to your Eminence, of whose good opinion I would gladly be assured.

Louvain, 2 October 1519

1018 / To Floris van Egmond   Louvain, 2 October 1519

This letter was published in the *Epistolae ad diversos*. Floris van Egmond was an old patron of Erasmus (cf Ep 178:48–54). At this time he must have sought Erasmus' assistance in finding a new teacher for his son Maximiliaan, who had been in Louvain for at least three years, studying with Adrianus Cornelii

Floris van Egmond
By Jan Gossaert van Mabuse
Rijksmuseum, Amsterdam

Barlandus. Floris van Egmond was perhaps involved in the unsuccessful attempt to secure Erasmus as a teacher for Prince Ferdinand (cf lines 17–18; Ep 917 introduction). If so, he can hardly have expected Erasmus himself to take a very active part in his son's education. But his gift (line 3) assured Erasmus' co-operation in suggesting a suitable teacher. As Maximiliaan was still at Louvain in 1521, studying Greek (cf Ep 1192), it may perhaps be assumed that Erasmus' recommendation was accepted (see de Vocht CTL I 485–6, II 124–6).

Maximiliaan van Egmond (d 1548) distinguished himself later as a military commander and was appointed governor of Friesland. His only daughter became the wife of William the Silent; see NNBW III 339–40.

ERASMUS OF ROTTERDAM TO THE RIGHT HONOURABLE
FLORIS, HEER VAN IJSSELSTEIN, GREETING
My honoured Lord, the gift that you have so generously given me was most welcome for more than one reason: it came from one of our great men, and it came unsought, to one who neither deserved nor expected it. I have pointed 5
out to your Highness' son, a boy of rare natural gifts, that he must assist me in returning thanks; for I shall not think I have thanked you properly unless I ensure that his progress in learning answers to your hopes. He has promised to do so; and young as he is, there is already such brilliant promise of learning to be seen in him as gives me very great hopes that your Maximiliaan 10
will turn out in time to be an ornament not only of his family but of humane studies as a whole. Arnold[1] is devoted to the boy, and is as attentive as he is affectionate.

There is a young man here by name Conradus Goclenius,[2] an excellent scholar in both Latin and Greek, with a happy gift of style whether in prose 15
or bound by the rules of verse, and a knowledge of philosophy above the average, of unblemished character and proven integrity; in short, worthy to have Ferdinand himself as a pupil. I can vouch for this on my own responsibility; and if you think he would be a satisfactory addition to your son's household, I can speak with him, and shall do so with as much 20
confidence as if my own son's business were concerned. But if you have other ideas, you may be sure that Erasmus is your devoted servant. Farewell.
Louvain, 2 October 1519

1019 / To Maarten Lips   [Louvain, c November 1518–October 1519]

This letter is known only from one of the two copy-books of Maarten Lips, which is now in Brussels, Bibliothèque Royale, MS 4850–7. In his usual fashion Lips gave a short argument of his own before copying Erasmus' letter to him. In his argument Lips recalled how Lee had been wavering whether or not to send

Lips his critical notes on Erasmus' New Testament, but then had decided not to, stating as a reason the advice of his fellow Englishmen. The last sentence of Lips' argument is unclear; Allen argued that it referred to a copy of the second edition of the New Testament that Erasmus had recently given to Lips (cf Ep 955), who had now lent it to Lee. Lips wrote: 'subsequently, in fear lest Lee should notice the numerous corrections made in that edition and use them for further attacks on Erasmus, [Lips] had enquired whether he should endeavour to conceal the fact of the corrections ... Erasmus assured him it would not matter.' Allen assigned this letter tentatively to early October 1519 in view of Epp 1026, 1029, both of which in fact repeat formulations contained in this letter (cf n2).

On the other hand, all that can be said with certainty about the last sentence of Lips' argument is that it refers to a gift copy of the New Testament with many corrections. If these were manuscript corrections, Lips would more likely be referring to a copy of the first edition that Erasmus had given him late in 1518 (cf Ep 898A). Just at that time the first edition was being rendered obsolete by the appearance of the second, a fact that could explain Erasmus' indifference to Lee's perusal of the book in question. The date of about November 1518 is also strongly suggested by the arrangement of Lips' copy-book. The letters seem to be recorded in chronological order and this one follows Ep 898A and precedes Ep 899.

Greeting. Take my word for it, Lee[1] is making a mock of you, and thinks himself on this account a very clever fellow. His mind is, not to suppress[2] his annotations, which he expects to make him immortal, but to get more material before he publishes. As for the book that was sent, there is nothing to fear on my side; nor do I see any risk to you, even if he does get to know. On the   5
contrary, if Lee knew everything, there would still be no risk to me from such a man; though I would rather have to do with a real lion[3] than with such a fox. Farewell.

1020 / From Bonifacius Amerbach   Basel, 7 October 1519

This laboured letter was composed by Bonifacius, the youngest of the Amerbach brothers. He had just turned twenty-four and was preparing to leave Basel to continue his studies in Avignon (lines 57–8). It was first published by Allen from Amerbach's rough draft in the Öffentliche Bibliothek of the University of Basel, MS C VI^a 73 f 186. Allen's hypothesis of a postscript added to the good copy is no longer relevant; see AK II Ep 694 introduction.

I do not think I shall be trespassing, dear Erasmus, the sole glory of our age, if after such a great display of misplaced modesty[1] (of which good men, moreover, disapprove) I address a letter to you, or rather a piece of foolishness – and, to be sure, it is very short. Longer I must not be, if only for the sake of all those liberal studies of which you are the prop and stay, taking 5 the weight of them on your shoulders like a second Hercules, when they were already near to falling, so that you have almost given them a new lease of life. On that account I should indeed deserve prosecution in the public interest, were I to interrupt your studies with my stammering stuff while you are taking thought for the salvation, the convenience, and the profit, in one 10 operation, of us all. What of the point that you should only be approached in reverence by the pure in heart? How few there are, even among the truly learned, who dare address a letter to you! You are, of course, as highly valued by all men as it is right and proper that true excellence should be valued; and rightly so, for your greatness is so accessible, your learning so 15 wide, your eloquence such a thunderbolt, that you would find it easy single-handed to put all other men of our generation in the shade or, to use a legal term, to obstruct their light. But if, though myself a mere cipher, I am not dismayed by all this glory, the reason is the kindliness that matches and is joined with your great learning, which has given me, little as I deserve it, 20 such a reception that beyond doubt I should be a monster of ingratitude, did I not give you an acknowledgment even in this foolish form.

You can see, greatest of men, what drives me on to write, or should I say with more truth, to waste your time: it is the wish to clear myself of any sinister suspicions arising from my silence, and then your singular kindli- 25 ness, to which I would attribute any lack of modesty that may be laid at my door. At any rate, I would rather be censured for lack of modesty than for ingratitude. For lawyers hold that injury inflicted on leading members of society incurs a heavier penalty; and in the same way I should like to think that no punishment can be adequate for the ungrateful, especially for those 30 who are ungrateful to the world's greatest men, in the list of whom I place you first. And so, that I may escape this stigma, here is a sample, a first taste, of my respect and gratitude. It testifies that to this Erasmus 'great and godlike,' whom men declare unanimously to be 'a mortal meant for immortality,'[2] – to him, I say, I am entirely devoted; to him I owe my self, 35 body and soul, and I know nothing holier and more venerable, nothing more truly the object of my admiration and respect and worship, than him and him alone. His supreme learning and supreme kindliness, his supremacy above our age in everything, I do not cease to extol wherever I am and wherever I may journey, though I am but an incompetent herald of your virtues; while 40 you should never be written of except by the high priests of the world of letters, just as Alexander would have his likeness taken by none but Apelles or Pyrgoteles.[3] If any men are your well-wishers, my life upon it, in the tribute of genuine affection I surpass them all.[4] But where my modest talents fall short in praising you, my love for you fills and rounds off the gap. 45

But less of this; for were I to open everything to the quick, not one day will be needed but a period of unbroken leisure. Let this then be accepted as a first sketch of my feelings towards you, which I hope may excuse my silence; and though I may still be silent in the future – as at least I ought to be, for you are so much greater than I – yet all the same you will know with the 50 certainty of an oracle that my regard for you will always be full of the purest affection. But you, who have once received me as a friend, must please retain me as one, and not hesitate to bless me in perpetuity with the favour which you have always shown me hitherto. And so I declare myself your obedient servant. 55

If you wish to hear our news, the plague[5] had hitherto treated us gently, but now grows worse every day. I shall be setting out shortly for Avignon,[6] where I hope to attend the lectures of Andrea Alciati of Milan, a greater man in jurisprudence than any I remember. From the works[7] he has lately published in Milan you can judge his quality. You will find a most 60 happy marriage of great legal knowledge with both Greek and Latin. He and our friend Zasius,[8] I would say, are the two pillars of the law; for they are at home not only in textual criticism, though that is theirs too, but in the active centre, in the very heart of the subject.

The theological disputation[9] held at Leipzig has now been finished. 65 The faculty in Paris will pronounce on it. 'Great Zeus, how subtle are the thoughts of men!'[10] Eck[11] is his usual self, everywhere trying to seem invincible and dreaming of triumphs. If he goes on in his accustomed fashion, 'I cannot pray he might be madder yet.'[12] He has challenged Philippus Melanchthon[13] with a pamphlet in his defence; but he will find, I 70 think, that the beast has horns.

But why tell you all this, when I meant to be laconic and not disturb you? Farewell, thrice-great Erasmus, luminary of the world of letters.

Basel, 7 October 1519

1021 / From Jan Šlechta   Kostelec, 10 October 1519

This letter, which was published in the *Epistolae ad diversos*, answers points raised by Erasmus in Ep 950. Jan Šlechta, a retired secretary to the king of Bohemia, was writing from his estate on the Elbe (north-east of Prague). Erasmus answered his letter with Ep 1039.

JAN ŠLECHTA OF KOSTELEC TO ERASMUS OF ROTTERDAM,
GREETING

Your letter reached me on 11 September, after I had given up all hope. Last
year I had sent you my letter[1] by an agent of a Leipzig bookseller who is in
business in Prague selling printed books, and he promised faithfully he   5
would send the original to you, wherever you might be, by a courier he could
trust, and bring back an answer. He gave me his promise, and I handed him
the letter; but after waiting this whole year for an answer from you and
getting none, I made up my mind that that letter never reached you, but had
been either lost or held up in someone's hands on the way or intercepted by   10
somebody. So your answer was all the more welcome and enjoyable because
it came so unexpectedly, and came from a friend who is the dearest of all my
dear and precious friends. I am delighted first of all at your unimpaired good
health, and hope that your critics, who spread the spurious news of your
death,[2] may long continue to be as far from the truth as they have been last 15
year and this, both here and in your part of the world, while you live on, and
not only equal but surpass the record of the aged Nestor.[3]

You say that certain churchmen, and some of the monks especially,
pursue you with undying hatred and from time to time get their teeth into
you like mad dogs on the sly; and this does not suprise me, for virtue and   20
vice, good and evil must ever be opposites. It is usual for good men and
criminals to be fond each of their own kind, and like makes friends with like;[4]
for resemblance, as you know, is the parent of good will, and difference
begets dislike. You have on occasion, with the brush of an Apelles,[5] painted
an exact picture of their way of life under its protective cloak of hypocrisy   25
and shown them up by irrefutable proofs as the Antisilenuses and Gnathos[6]
that they are; you have proved that they neglect their divine inheritance and
cling instead to the letter that killeth[7] instead of the spirit; otherwise you
would be their dearest friend and brother. Truth, to those who have a bad
conscience, has a most unpleasant and bitter sound and, as it says in the   30
comedy, 'breeds nought but hate';[8] hence all this hostility and strife, that
wells up from their jaundiced minds like water from a spring. But to spurn
and cast far from one the sham and worthless friendship of such men as they
are is better than to lose sight of truth and demean oneself to be their toady;
for it is certain that no man lives his life without incurring blame of some   35
kind. But that your pen is harmless and has no barb to it, we all know; for it is
faults alone that you point out and correct and reprobate – to people you are
always merciful. Who then can justly be indignant with you on their behalf
except the man whose bad conscience tells him that you mean himself? And
so it is all the more praiseworthy that you should combine an upright mind   40
and honourable way of life with learning and wisdom, by the light of which

you bring light to other people; and by dint of wide reading and writing and expounding and instructing you have brought forth fruit for all men hitherto.

But I prefer to write no more on this topic for fear it may seem my 45 intention to embrace and add lustre to your outstanding virtues and scholarship and saintly life in my underfed and barren style, which would be like trying to give the sun more light or add water to the sea. The New Testament,[9] which you have enriched so notably and copiously with the most important opinions of many standard authorities, reached me with 50 several smaller works of yours on 14 May. For I possess all your books, all those that you have written and entrusted for printing to Johann Froben in Basel, a good scholar and cunning as Daedalus[10] in the art of printing, and I greatly enjoy reading them. Thanks in great part to them, I have increased my library not only in size but in quality. 55

Although I know there is nothing you can do in Prague, I myself, and many others who have a great desire to see you, would gladly have seen you and talked with you here. But as this is rendered impossible, partly by your great press of business and partly by the unbroken and untiring toil of your researches, we must postpone this to a more appropriate and suitable time, 60 when if God please I may converse with you at some other time and elsewhere, since it cannot happen here. If this country cannot provide those who would travel into other parts of the world with reliable companions and the escorts needed to secure their safety, that, my dear friend, will no longer suprise you, if you remember that it is fenced in on all sides by steep and lofty 65 mountains and surrounded by a broad belt of impenetrable woodland and tall trees, such as you may have seen in great numbers in the Hercynian forest.[11] In the forest lurk numerous bandits, who beset the main roads and often inflict heavy losses on imprudent travellers, especially on merchants, some of whom they deprive not only of their possessions but of life itself. 70 And though nearly every month the people from neighbouring cities and towns capture an infinite number of robbers of this kind and make away with them by various forms of punishment and execution, yet this seed-bed of evil and poisonous weeds can never be completely rooted out and cleared; when one lot have been sentenced and executed, others immediately take their 75 places, just as used to happen with the hydra[12] destroyed by Hercules, whose heads grew again as they were cut off.

Towards the end of your letter you express some degree of surprise regarding the divisions in faith and religion which arose a fairly long time ago in this country and still continue and our failure during all that time to 80 find anyone, among either churchmen or secular princes, capable of reducing those divisions to some definite agreement; and you suggest that the reason for this is simply the love of money. This opinion of yours has my unquestioning support. How few men can you find nowadays, whether you survey the pope or the cardinals and bishops or other church dignitaries or   85 even individual monks, who do not pay more attention to self-advancement and monetary advantage than to the salvation of their neighbours' souls! If they would only listen to the life and teaching of our Saviour, who urges and adjures them to despise those worldly goods that are so fleeting, frail, and transitory, and to pursue religion and piety, charity, mercy, and the other   90 virtues; if only they would follow him! I am sure that no tribe, no country would be so cut off and distant, no journey so difficult and laborious, that they would not cheerfully and gladly shoulder the burden for the salvation of their fellow men, as was the practice of Paul and the other apostles, whose representatives and successors they so falsely and ineffectually boast   95 themselves to be.

But perhaps it will not be out of place if I develop this in passing, there being such divisions in faith and religion among my countrymen, to give you an idea how many and how varied these differences are, and the causes for it. To say nothing of Jews and Epicureans, who deny the immortality of the   100 soul, and similarly some Nicolaites[13] (for a certain number of all these are to be found among us), the whole population of this country and the margraviate of Moravia is divided into three sects.[14] The first consists of those who in all things follow and obey the Roman pontiff and recognize him as the true vicar of Christ, as the Germans do, and all other nations that   105 cleave to him as the shepherd of the Lord's flock. Among them are the majority of the upper classes, magnates and gentry, also several royal cities, and monasteries that were once rich and are now to a great extent ruined and despoiled, belonging to various orders.

Another sect[15] is formed by those who distribute the Eucharist to the   110 congregation in both kinds. To this belong a few of the nobility, many of the gentry, and nearly thirty royal cities. They hold to all the sacraments of the Holy Church and its rites and ceremonies, in the same way as the Romans themselves, differing solely in the practice at communion and in the fact that in the mass their priests sing the Epistle and Gospel in the mother tongue. To   115 these two practices they adhere with the greatest obstinacy, asserting that they have confirmation and approval of both in a letter from the Council of Basel which they call the Compacts.[16]

For on one occasion they sent to the council by command of the emperor Sigismund, who was then king of Bohemia, ten doctors of divinity   120 from the University of Prague, who argued with the theologians on the council in favour of the article about communion in both kinds and demonstrated that communion in this form[17] was instituted by Christ, delivered by the Apostle Paul to the Corinthians, and observed by all the early Doctors both Greek and Latin down to about the year 1200 without a break. All this the council investigated in detail, and after due examination granted them this same use and practice of communion as aforesaid, subject to these conditions: their priests both present and future were to administer the Eucharist to the lay people gathered for this purpose, either in one kind or both as each communicant should desire in accordance with his belief, having first given this solemn assurance to both parties: 'You who are about to communicate in one kind must not believe that you receive less than those who communicate in two,' and similarly that those about to communicate in two received no more than those who communicated in one; and in every other respect they promised to observe and follow the lawful ceremonies of the Roman church. In the same way they and all their successors were to accept and recognize the Roman pontiff and his successors as the true vicars of Christ and obey their instructions without the least reluctance. So they promised in good faith that they would perform these things all and singular and carry them out in practice, and on receipt of this promise approval was given to them for communion as aforesaid by a letter of the council, which they call the Compacts.

But all this was further to be confirmed and ratified by a letter (of the kind they call 'executory') from Pope Eugenius,[18] who at that time ruled the Roman church. He had originally given authority to the council; but later, when it came to his notice that certain decrees of the council had been concluded and determined to the prejudice of himself and future popes, he repealed and nullified all the decisions of the council, and so was unwilling to issue a letter approving of the concessions made to the Bohemians by the council, for fear of seeming to concede any authority to the conciliar decrees to which I referred. And so up to now they have been equally unable to secure this from succeeding Roman pontiffs; with the result that, recognizing how obstinate and unshakeable the policy of the popes is on this subject – for they refuse to confirm what was instituted by Christ, held by the early church and approved by the council – they are no longer prepared to obey them or hold them to be the true vicars of Christ and successors of St Peter.

And whereas their leaders had promised that the priests of their way of thinking, when about to give the people communion in one kind or in both, would address the congregation in the words I have already quoted, they rejected the whole thing as a falsehood, and are not willing to communicate any of the lay people except in both kinds, bitterly criticizing on this point their leaders who were sent to the council for having been so foolish and irresponsible as to be willing to agree to the false and one-sided terms offered by the council, since in the early Doctors both Greek and Latin it can be

found expressly stated[19] that those who receive Christ's body are given one 165
grace and those who drink his blood another. Since the grace conferred is
different in each case, how can it be true that those who receive the
sacrament in one kind are given no less grace than those who receive it in
both, and those who receive it in both are given no more than those who
receive it in one? To this they add that even if the ancient commentators on 170
Holy Scripture had not delivered the opinion I have quoted, yet one half of
the sacrament of salvation was on no account to be withheld from the lay
people contrary to Christ's institution, for this is nothing but pure sacrilege;
nor ought they to be wiser than the early and saintly church, which
maintained his institution inviolate for nearly twelve hundred years. And 175
when our party adduce certain arguments and various dangers which were
the reason for depriving the lay people of half the sacrament, they say the
drawback to this will be that such men are trying to be wiser than Christ
himself, who was quite unaware that that half of the sacrament would be
beset by the dangers which they have discovered and recognized, and that 180
this is claiming to surpass Christ in knowledge and understanding. All this
and far more is to be found in the treatises which they have written against
communion in one kind, which it would be long and tedious to dwell on.
Who then can be found suitable to arbitrate between us in a disagreement of
such great importance? 185

The third sect is of those they call the Pyghards.[20] They get their name
from a certain renegade of that nationality who came over here about
ninety-seven years ago, at the time when a sacrilegious criminal called Jan
Žyžka[21] had declared war here on church dignitaries and the clergy as a
whole and seized upon their property to tear it in pieces. Joining forces with 190
Žyžka, he infected with his poisonous doctrines first the ringleader in crime
and then the whole army he had put together out of brigands, murderers,
criminals in exile, and other dregs of rascality. This crop of weeds lasted
down to the time of King Vladislav,[22] who died a few years ago, and made
great progress during his reign; for once he had taken up the government of 195
the kingdom of Hungary and spent more time there than in Bohemia, he
cared little what happened here, provided all his subjects kept the peace.

These men regard the pope, the cardinals, the bishops, and all the rest
of the clergy as so many manifest Antichrists, calling the pope himself
sometimes a beast and sometimes the famous harlot[23] in the Apocalypse; and 200
since all the clergy do is contrary to the teaching and tradition of Christ, how
can they possibly possess any authority or virtue in the celebration of the
sacraments? The whole effect of their ministrations is neither liturgy nor
sacraments nor benediction, but pure blasphemy, abomination, malediction.
They choose their own bishops and priests, unlearned laymen of no 205

education with wives and children; they call themselves brothers and sisters and salute one another as such. They recognize no authority except that of the Old and New Testaments contained in the Scriptures; all Doctors ancient and modern and all their books they despise, nor do they attach any importance to their teaching. Their priests, when celebrating the office of the mass, do so without any priestly vestments, nor do they use for this purpose any intercessions or prayers save only the Lord's Prayer, with which they consecrate leavened bread. 210

Of the sacraments of the church they think and believe little or nothing. Those who adopt their heretical views are compelled to be rebaptized individually in plain water. They have no blessing of salt or holy water and have no belief in consecrated oil. In the sacrament of the Eucharist they believe there is no element of the divine, but only consecrated bread and wine which, they maintain, shows forth Christ's death by certain hidden signs; and therefore everyone who genuflects or bows to it or adores it falls into the sin of idolatry, since that sacrament was instituted by Christ to no other purpose except to keep alive the memory of his passion and not that it might be carried about hither and yon or held up by the priest to be exposed to view, since Christ himself, who is properly to be adored and worshipped, sits at the right hand of God the Father, as the Christian church confesses in the creed. Vows to the saints and prayers for the dead they consider vain and ridiculous, and the same goes for auricular confession and penance enjoined by priests for sins. Vigils and fasts they regard as the paint and whitewash of hypocrites, and the feasts of the Blessed Virgin Mary and the apostles and other saints as the inventions of idle men; but they keep Sundays and the festivals of Christmas, Easter, and Pentecost. 21

Many other poisonous doctrines held by this monstrous people could be added, had I not some respect for your more serious and valuable studies. If however the first two parties could be brought to agree, this nefarious sect as well (though it has lately made much progress, but especially on account of the dissolute life led by the priests) might with the king's help be exterminated or brought into a better kind of faith and religion.

But enough of this and more. I beg that you will take in good part my running on at such immoderate length, in which I have indulged with the sole object of giving you a true and reliable account of our manifold divisions. Whether this letter will reach you soon, I know not, since Apollo's shafts[24] are said to be flying thick and fast in Saxony. It was perhaps to avoid them that our friend Jodocus,[25] the rector of Erfurt University, retreated, it seems, to some distant place; for the letter which you gave him to be sent on to me was retained by him for four months, for no other reason except that he had no reliable courier coming in this direction. I hope, dear friend, that you may long remain in the best of health, and love me as you have learnt to do; when convenient, let me have something by way of reply, and I promise to do the same. Farewell.

From my castle of Kostelec, 10 October AD 1519   250

1022 / To Ortwinus Gratius   [Louvain, second half of
                                                  September – early October] 1519

The original of this letter, entirely in Erasmus' hand, is in the Österreichische Nationalbibliothek, Vienna, MS Pal. 9737 c f 2. The left-hand margin is torn away; with the exception of the date, however, Allen's readings and interpolations are accepted as a basis for this translation. This letter follows Ep 1006 to Jacob of Hoogstraten but is earlier than Ep 1030, which reports the presence of Hoogstraten at Louvain. Erasmus may have written to Gratius, who was a friend of Hoogstraten's at Cologne, hoping to receive some reaction to Ep 1006; and he may have written soon after 13 September to inform his opponents in Cologne of his reconciliation with the theologians at Louvain.

In the summer of 1519 Erasmus had suffered much animosity from a group of conservative-minded theologians at Louvain (cf the preface). This letter contains important details (to be supplemented by Allen Epp 1217:119–26, 1225:133–40) about an agreement to end all mutual recriminations reached on 13 September. It seems that on the initiative of Jan Briart of Ath (cf Ep 1029 n2), Erasmus was called to a meeting in the College of the Falcon attended by Nicolas Coppin and Jan de Neve, masters of the Falcon and of Erasmus' own College of the Lily. There the terms of peace were discussed and agreed upon. The following day was the Feast of the Exaltation of the Holy Cross, a feast day widely observed in Brabant. Since it fell upon a Wednesday Henry de Vocht connected it with a recollection in Ep 1162 and ingeniously suggested that it gave Coppin a pretext for inviting Erasmus and other theologians, including some of his bitter opponents, back to the Falcon for a banquet in honour of the accord (cf Ep 1033:21–9, Allen Ep 1162:107–11; de Vocht CTL I 402–6). From the beginning Erasmus doubted the solidity of the accord (cf Ep 1016:18–21), and in fact it soon suffered considerable strain. Ep 1053 apart, Erasmus did not publish his complaints about infractions until more than two years later in the *Epistolae ad diversos*, but his theological opponents had some reason to question his observance of the peace as well; see Epp 1029 n2, 1033:28–31, 1042, 1059.

Greeting. I have long had it in mind to urge you to turn your gifts from these spiteful disputes[1] to the course of study on which you had embarked. Your manner of writing shows that we may have great hopes of you, if only you would choose to be guided by moderation and good sense instead of this

devotion to controversies which are, I assure you, unworthy alike of a   5
scholar and a Christian. A different course would do much more for the
cause of truth. Enough of these controversies in which you have neither part
nor lot. What has become meanwhile of the simple pleasures of life and
learned work, if human beings are inflicting mortal wounds on one another?
To embroil yourself in the sort of battles you are fighting shows very little   10
sense, for the business has nothing to do with you. I have written a long
letter[2] on this subject to Master Jacob of Hoogstraten, and I have no doubt
that he took it in the spirit in which it was written, for I wrote as one writes to
a dear friend. Here too poisonous tongues have been at work, rending the
peace of this university. Several times the thing looked like breaking out in   15
uproar, had not the faculty of theology and other leading spirits in the
university taken steps about it. So they arranged a meeting to discuss it, the
discord was easily resolved, and peace patched up again, never I hope to be
further disturbed. This took place on 13 September last, and so Christ would
much rather have it. I wish therefore that in your part of the world and   20
everywhere else this sort of petty squabbling could be brought to an end and
all that has passed be forgotten.

I write in haste, for the courier is impatient. Another time I will write at
greater length and with a lighter heart, especially if I find you have taken my
advice, which is the best for you and for the cause of learning. Farewell, and   25
give my greetings to Hoogstraten.

Louvain ... 1519
Erasmus of Rotterdam
To the honourable Ortwinus Gratius, as to a dear brother

1023 / To Guillaume Budé   Louvain, 15 October 1519

This letter was published in the *Epistolae ad diversos*.

ERASMUS TO HIS DEAR BUDÉ, GREETING
Longueil,[1] a very good scholar whose company I enjoy for many reasons, has
brought, instead of a letter from you, only complaints that I have not yet
answered your last two letters.[2] From this I suppose that my last letter[3] has
never reached you, or at least had not reached you when he left. I received   5
your letter to Vives[4] from him today, but have not read it yet; Longueil has
made that impossible. John Colet, best of men and most reliable of my
friends, has died[5] in London of the dropsy. Mind you keep in the best of
health, dear Budé, and love me as I know you do.

Louvain, 15 October 1519   10

1024 / To Nicolas Bérault   Louvain, 15 October 1519

This letter was clearly sent with Ep 1023, and is printed together with it in the *Epistolae ad diversos*. The letter it answers is now missing.

ERASMUS TO NICOLAS BÉRAULT, GREETING

Longueil[1] has returned from England, and brought a letter from you. You need have no fears of a hornets' nest.[2] That letter of yours[3] worked wonders, and Dorp has reacted in a very friendly way. The theologians have made overtures to me of their own accord, and peace[4] is restored on the basis that   5
the past is forgotten. Dorp has even gone on record that he has changed his mind by publishing a speech.[5] Actually, I am quite sure that he can be relied on. With the others I am only so far in agreement that I shall wait and see how they behave. I will take pains to ensure that no one can accuse me of breaking the peace, but I shall keep an eye open so as not to be defeated in some   10
careless moment. I sent you a letter recently by Augustine,[6] that physician from Friesland, by whom I have also sent Dorp's speech. Give my greetings to Ruzé, Deloynes, and Du Ruel.[7] Farewell, my learned friend.
     Louvain, 15 October 1519

1025 / To Richard Pace   Louvain, 16 October 1519

Epp 1025–32 were all published in the *Epistolae ad diversos*. Addressed to patrons and friends in England, all but two served to introduce Antoon, the nineteen-year-old son of the powerful Jan van Bergen, who was then preparing to join the court of Henry VIII (cf Ep 760). He was accompanied by his tutor Adrianus Aelius Barlandus (cf Ep 1028:13–14) and also carried letters of introduction from Margaret of Austria dated 5 November 1519. On 20 November he was at Calais and during 1520 he held an appointment as one of Henry's cup-bearers (see LP III 496, 517, pages 1540–2). When Erasmus wrote these letters he was under the impact of the recent death of his good friend John Colet (cf Epp 1011 n1, 1023 n5). Several of them refer to his intention, which was fulfilled with Ep 1211, of setting up a literary monument for Colet.

ERASMUS OF ROTTERDAM TO RICHARD PACE, DEAN OF
ST. PAUL'S, LONDON, GREETING

I feel only half a man, with myself alive and Colet dead! What a leader his country has lost, and what a friend I have lost myself! I rejoice with you on your being appointed to succeed him.[1] I long to know whether you have any   5
news of your books.[2] I saw that eminent figure Campeggi[3] in Bruges; he had

sent for me, with unexpected warmth. I never saw anyone kinder or more
open-hearted. The king was threatening to reply,[4] and so was his Grace of
York; but I have heard nothing so far. Keep me posted, if there is anything it
would be useful for me to know.   10

There is someone on the way to your court, a most agreeable young
man called Antoon van Grimbergen, son of the lord of Bergen; he is a person
of some education and a sincere friend to literature and learned men. I
express no desire that you should make friends with him, I merely ask you to
make his acquaintance; and once you are acquainted, you will be friends in   15
spite of yourselves, he is such an excellent young man in both heart and
head. His father, as you know, is a man of great and well-deserved influence
here. It will do me no harm if he learns that his son and I have common
friends in your part of the world – the sort of friends whose acquaintance
will help him to turn out the sort of man his father passionately hopes for; for   20
he is an excellent and very intelligent old man.

I have kept my health so far with some difficulty in such an inclement
season.[5] In these coming winter months I aspire with Christ's help to finish
my remaining paraphrases.[6] It is a long time now that I have been sadly
waiting for a letter from you. Farewell.   25

Louvain, 16 October 1519

1026 / To Thomas Lupset   Louvain, 16 October 1519

Cf Ep 1025 introduction. Thomas Lupset, a protégé of Colet (cf lines 3–4) had
graduated BA at Paris earlier in the year and subsequently returned to England
where he was appointed to one of Wolsey's readerships at Oxford (cf Epp
967:40n, 1087:683–5). It was probably when returning to England that he
travelled from Paris to Louvain for a visit with Erasmus. Edward Lee, who had
not met him previously, seized the opportunity of presenting to him his case
against Erasmus. To no avail, however, as Lupset defended Erasmus loyally
and would continue to do so. See his letters in Froben's *Epistolae aliquot
eruditorum virorum* 75–9; cf Epp 1053, 1083 introductions and *Opuscula* 250,
256.

ERASMUS TO HIS FRIEND LUPSET, GREETING
It must be thirty years since I felt any man's death as I feel Colet's. I have a
great desire to enshrine his memory for the benefit of posterity. You were
very devoted to him: will you undertake the task of instructing me,
particularly if there is anything that you suppose I do not know? I have   5
devoted nearly three whole days to Longueil;[1] I like him in all respects, save

one, that he is too much the Frenchman, considering that he is my
fellow-countryman. A very distinguished young man is coming to settle in
your part of the world, Antoon van Grimbergen, son of that most intelligent
prince the lord of Bergen; he is a gifted person, of high character, sincerely   10
devoted to literature, and with a certain fondness for his Erasmus. Your
friends[2] here, Herman of Friesland and Nesen with Carinus and the others,
are all well.

Our puny friend[3] is busier than ever, but it is all underhand. My dear
Lupset, if you want to earn my everlasting gratitude by some kind action,   15
contrive somehow to get me a sight of that book. Three or four people in your
part of the world have a copy, and my friends are busy trying to get it
suppressed; yet all the time they make it worse for me, as he gets his attacks
better organized every day. The last thing to be expected is that he should
suppress it permanently. If you can do me this kindness, ask in return   20
whatever you please; I will deny you nothing. It would give me great
pleasure if you would write to me frequently. Farewell.

Louvain, 16 October 1519

1027 / To William Dancaster   Louvain, 16 October 1519

Cf Ep 1025 introduction. William Dancaster was a friend of Lupset (cf Epp 1026,
1229) and like him a protégé of Colet; he was left a sum of money in Colet's will
'to supporte hym in hys vertue' (S. Knight *The Life of Dr John Colet*, Oxford 1823,
401). In 1528 he was appointed rector of Ampthill, Bedfordshire and probably
died early in 1530; see Emden BRUO.

ERASMUS OF ROTTERDAM TO THE EXCELLENT WILLIAM
DANCASTER, GREETING

O the pity of it! What a teacher, what a patron we have lost, and what a
friend! 'Real tears lament the loss of coin'[1] – here we have a loss to be
lamented with tears of every kind. But what good does it do to weep and   5
wail? He cannot be called back, and we shall soon follow. In the mean while,
let us rejoice with him. He is now at peace, enjoying the vision of Christ his
Master,[2] who was ever on his lips and in his heart. I shall set down Colet's
life in writing, if you and others in your position will tell me what you know
and what I perhaps do not; and I do beg and urge you to do this. Give my   10
particular greetings to Master Gerard[3] his steward, to whom I am still obliged
to show myself ungrateful, so much am I beset on every side.

I have made peace[4] with the theologians, at their own particular
request, now that, having tried every means to my undoing, they see that all

their efforts are unsuccessful. If Christ[5] be for us, who can be against us?   15
Farewell, my dear William, and commend me to Christ the Lord in your
prayers.

Louvain, 16 October 1519

1028 / To William Blount, Lord Mountjoy   Louvain, 16 October 1519

For the source and contents of this letter see Ep 1025 introduction. Mountjoy
was a former pupil and reliable patron of Erasmus.

ERASMUS OF ROTTERDAM TO THE RIGHT HONOURABLE
WILLIAM, LORD MOUNTJOY, GREETING

Best of patrons, I can hardly refrain from jealousy when I think of your
court,[1] so full of learned men, while ours has nothing but rich ones, even
though circumstances force our nabobs to take some account of humane   5
studies. The lord of Bergen, who has heard from many sources of the
honourable tone at your court and the endowments of your king and queen,
has made it his first choice as a place to which to send his son Antoon, lord of
Grimbergen, a young man blessed with many gifts and with a character
worthy of his lineage, above all, a keen student of literature, and –   10
something he shares in common with yourself – one of my well-wishers. But
why need I recommend to you a person whom I know to be endowed with
qualities which you cannot fail to love? He brings with him his tutor
Adrianus Barlandus, a man of more than common learning.

You do not answer my letter,[2] but I suspect there is no reason except   15
that you are always slow to answer. I have felt Colet's death more acutely
than any in the last twenty years. But what use is it to weep and wail? He will
never return[3] to us, and we shall go to join him.

I have patched up peace[4] with the theological faculty, at their own
request, and have accepted it to this extent, that I shall never break it by any   20
fault of my own, nor will they ever enjoy my confidence. It is unheard-of,
such a conspiracy sprung from the bitterness of a single individual;[5] and the
peacemaking was his doing too, for he saw that the whole melodrama was
too much for him and that I, supported as I am by a clear conscience, would
not give an inch – was, in fact, at length beginning to show my teeth, and   25
meant to let fly if they had gone any further.

I am pretty well, except that age continually saps my bodily strength;
but I would not object to death if it found me busy on work that will promote
the glory of Christ. If your wonted feelings towards me have not changed,

mind you interrupt your old friend with a letter from time to time, for   30
wherever in the world I may be, I am all yours. Farewell.
     Louvain, 16 October 1519

1029 / To Cuthbert Tunstall   Louvain, 16 October 1519

> For the source and contents of this letter see Ep 1025 introduction. Tunstall, an
> English diplomat and future bishop of London, was a close friend and a patron
> of Erasmus.

ERASMUS OF ROTTERDAM TO CUTHBERT TUNSTALL, GREETING
I have made peace[1] with the backbiters; they had been anxious for it
themselves for a long time. Never did anyone hear or read of such a
conspiracy. They say Noxus,[2] and Noxus alone, was the man who originally
egged Dorp on and started the whole melodrama; I suspected as much long   5
ago and now know it for a fact. It was also he who set on foot the overtures
for peace, when he realized the action I was threatening if they did not call it
off, and how other people were girding themselves for the fray and his own
health was menaced by the agitation, while what he was getting ready for me
was likely to fall on his own head. I know that my defences are not to your   10
taste,[3] but I had to do what needed doing; in fact, you would applaud my
moderation if you knew how monstrous the business was. I know that you
encouraged Lee to suppress his book; but the only result meanwhile is that
he will publish it in more finished form, and when I maybe am dead or far
away. The last thing to be expected is that he should permanently suppress   15
what he is rewriting every day; he was never more fully committed to the
business than he is now. But I have no intention of disputing your opinion.
Dorp[4] has now gone on record by publishing a pamphlet that he has
changed his mind, and in other matters is behaving in a way that makes me
feel he can be trusted. With the others I have come to terms, and for my own   20
part I shall keep to them, and have laid my weapons aside; but my pickets
will remain[5] on the watch. This winter with Christ's help I shall finish my
paraphrases.[6] Colet's death would leave me inconsolable, did I not know
that tears will help neither him nor me.
     You are to have a new resident at your court, Antoon van Grimbergen,   25
son of an outstanding man, the lord of Bergen; he is a youth born to excel,
devoted to humane studies and those who pursue them, by nature civilized
and modest. You will, I know, be ready to show him how much you value a
man of honour. Longueil[7] has spent two whole days with me here. I saw
Cardinal Campeggi[8] at Bruges, and dined with him; his courtesy is quite   30

remarkable. I liked his character; all was open, with no trace of sham.

If it could be arranged, I should dearly like to have a copy of Lee's annotations, for they are preparing again for my third edition,[9] and from the man himself I can extract nothing. The feelings of the bishop of Rochester[10] cause me no misgivings, but this wretch is as crafty and unprincipled as can 35 be. If you have any instructions for me, you will find me most ready to obey. Farewell.

From Louvain, 16 October 1519

1030 / To John Fisher   Louvain, 17 October 1519

> For the source, the conveyance, and some of the contents of this letter see Ep
> 1025 introduction. John Fisher was a friend and patron of long standing.

ERASMUS OF ROTTERDAM TO THE RIGHT REVEREND JOHN,
BISHOP OF ROCHESTER, GREETING

My Lord Bishop, I had intended to send you in writing, at your Lordship's own request, all my notes on the three books[1] in which you refute Lefèvre's views. But it seemed too late to do this when your subsequent work[2] 5 appeared – which I have in fact not yet read, though I expect to read it shortly. I am sorry for Lefèvre; he is an excellent man, who bears a considerable load of unpopularity in Paris, principally among the Dominicans, for this reason in particular, that he is said to be a supporter of Reuchlin.[3] I hope your Lordship will be content with the victory which you 10 are said to have won already in the estimation of the learned world. The work is selling readily, so that in future whatever you are willing to send him will be gladly accepted for printing by the publisher. To start with, he proved surprisingly awkward,[4] so that I had great difficulty in getting him to budge. 15

Peace[5] has been patched up with the theologians, at their particular request, and I wish they had thought of it before and not preferred active ill will to reconciliation. But like the cauldrons of Dodona,[6] once set in motion they jangle on for ever, and especially some monks I could name, with their astonishing malice and shameless appetite for defamation, which is becom- 20 ing a disease. Jacob of Hoogstraten[7] is active at Louvain, taking refuge from the plague[8] in Cologne or, as others suspect, having been driven out by the monks to protect themselves for the unpopularity[9] he brings upon them. He has nothing in train at the moment, but I know nothing of his future plans.

As for Lee,[10] I am ashamed of complaining so much, and I pray that 25 Christ will give him a spirit more worthy of a priest and a divine. He is as busy now as he ever was, and all this time one can extract nothing from him.

Froben is threatening to reprint[11] the New Testament; and so I beseech you,
by your love of sacred study, by your charity so proper for a bishop, by our
mutual friendship, and by any value you may set upon my humble self, do at   30
least, if you are not willing to lend me the whole book (which I should much
prefer), do send me a note of the points which you think of some importance;
and I do assure you, I will not make heavy weather of it. If you are too busy to
be able to do me this kindness, let More at any rate be asked to undertake it, if
you think fit, even if you have to urge him. One thing is quite certain: Lee   35
will not keep his pitiful stuff a secret perpetually. His object is to produce
something as well documented as he can, and yet meanwhile he goes on
saying that he keeps it dark only to oblige his friends and to show his respect
for myself. If he waits to publish until I am dead, we shall both be in worse
case. He will be too late to enlighten or correct me, and any reply made then   40
will show him in a far worse light than if I were to reply myself. So on this
point I do beg you to let me put to the test that good will towards me which
you have always displayed.
    As I write this, I mourn the death of Colet, which afflicts me so much
that for thirty years I have never felt any man's death more. I know that it is   45
well with him: he is released from this wicked and miserable world, and
enjoys face to face the presence of his master, Christ,[12] whom in this life he so
much loved. But for the general good I am bound to lament such a rare
example of Christian piety and an outstanding preacher of Christian truth,
and for my own private sake such a faithful friend and incomparable patron.   50
One thing alone remains, one service I will pay him as a farewell tribute: if
what I write has any force,[13] I will not suffer his memory to fade from among
posterity.
    Duke Frederick of Saxony has written me two letters[14] in reply to one of
mine. It is he who is Luther's one protector. This he says[15] he does to serve   55
the cause and not the man, and adds that he will not suffer innocence to be
overwhelmed in his dominions by the ill will of men who seek their own
good and not that of Jesus Christ. By general agreement he was offered the
imperial crown and nobly refused[16] it, the day before Charles was elected;
nor would the imperial title have come to Charles had it not been declined by   60
Frederick, who won more honour by refusal than he could have by
acceptance. Thereupon, when asked whom he thought should be elected,
he said that no one seemed to him to be equal to the burden of that great
position except Charles alone. In return for this noble conduct, our people
offered him thirty thousand florins, which he steadfastly refused; and when   65
he was urged to allow ten thousand at any rate to be distributed among his
staff, he said 'They can take it, if they please; but no man will be still in my
service tomorrow morning who touches a penny.' And next day he mounted

Frederick III, Elector of Saxony
By Lucas Cranach the Elder
Hamburger Kunsthalle

his horse and rode away, so that they might not pester him any more. I had
this for absolute truth from the bishop of Liège,[17] who was present at the   70
election of the emperor.

The duke of Württemberg is resuming the war[18] after his recent defeat
and has got back a few small towns. We are expecting the return of Charles,[19]
our prince, from Spain next spring. Farewell, my Lord, and remember your
friend Erasmus all the more warmly now because now, bereft of Colet, he is   75
but half himself.

Louvain, St Luke's eve 1519

1031 / To Thomas Wolsey   Louvain, 17 October 1519

> This letter of recommendation for Antoon van Bergen (cf Ep 1025 introduction)
> was published in the *Epistolae ad diversos*.

TO THE MOST REVEREND THE CARDINAL OF YORK FROM ERASMUS,
GREETING

If your Eminence not only took my last letter[1] in good part, but read it
through with a smile on your face, as I was told at Bruges by my lord Cardinal
Campeggi,[2] I am full of gratitude, and the fact that you have not yet replied is   5
due, I know, to the flood of business. To me, however, a letter from your
Highness, should I be thought to deserve one, will be of as much value as the
most generous present. If I interrupt your Eminence once again, the
responsibility lies with the bearer of this, Antoon van Grimbergen, son of
that distinguished and most generous prince the lord of Bergen, who is   10
coming to stay in the English court, his father's purpose being that he should
turn out as befits his rank. He is a young man of good breeding and full of
modesty, not unlettered himself and a great lover of literature and learned
men; in short, of such natural gifts as to arouse very great hopes, if his native
promise can be enhanced by a proper education. His father is devoted to   15
him, not least because he is the youngest of his children and as it were the
sheet-anchor of his posterity. Being a very sensible man, he knows how
important is the choice of the society in which those years are to be spent,
when one stands at the parting of the ways between virtue and vice and can
by the lightest touch be impelled down one path or the other.   20

He is convinced that there is no court[3] where the tone is higher, for
besides a king whose standard of honour is the best of our time, with a mirror
of all the virtues for his queen, you have so many men of outstanding
accomplishments, renowned for their probity, justly respected for their high
principles, and eminent for wisdom and understanding. He well knows   25
what temptations beset our courts to entrap the slippery steps of youth. That

Henry Guildford
By Hans Holbein the Younger
Windsor Castle; reproduced by gracious permission of Her Majesty
the Queen

is why, being a very intelligent old man, he has chosen your court as the only academy (so to say) where a young man may receive not only the liberal education but the character that a good prince should have. For there is no doubt that this boy, born as he is in great place, will rise to still greater things 30 if he is spared. I am sure he has been commended to your kindness by letters from the most eminent princes, so that it is quite superfluous for me to add my commendation. But since he modestly suggested, rather than asked, that I should do so, I thought it right to give your Eminence this sketch of him. Not but what no one can recommend him more effectively than his own 35 character and his most attractive personality, to such as love the combination of a sense of honour and a liberal education, among whom your Eminence beyond dispute is first and foremost. May God in his forethought for the affairs of men long preserve you in prosperity.

Louvain, St Luke's eve 1519   40

1032 / To Henry Guildford   Louvain, 18 October 1519

This is the last of a group of letters given to Antoon van Bergen (cf Ep 1025 introduction) and published in the *Epistolae ad diversos*. Sir Henry Guildford was Master of the Horse and a prominent member of the royal household.

ERASMUS TO THE HONOURABLE HENRY GUILDFORD, MASTER
OF THE HORSE TO HIS MAJESTY

Nothing, as you know, my dear Sir Henry, is more attractive than excellence, which wins all men's hearts as effectually as any philtre ever could. So it is that the honourable reputation of the English court[1] spreads everywhere 5 like a sweet savour the news that besides a king notably gifted with all the endowments of an absolute prince, and a queen of equal merit, it is well supplied with so many upright, well-read, serious, intelligent men. And this has persuaded the lord of Bergen, a man of unusual judgment, which means he has eyes to both the past and the future, to choose this academy and no 10 other for the education of Antoon, his youngest child, whom nature seems to have designed for excellence; with the intent that on his return he should be not only untouched by the vices to which the courts of princes are so commonly exposed, but also equipped with the various forms of excellence which are suitable to his distinguished lineage and to the great mass of 15 business to which no doubt he will be called. To recommend the young man to you would be a waste of time. His character is such, his manners so charming, his sense of honour so exalted that he will at once engage the affections of all men of the better sort.

On this point too I feel that our lady of Rhamnus[2] is against me. Some 20

years ago, the generosity of his Majesty and the kindness of the cardinal of
York invited me[3] more than once to join that court, and I was encouraged by
William Mountjoy,[4] always a true and friendly counsellor. But my wits were
ill-starred, and they told their tale to deaf ears.[5] I knew that nowhere could a
court be found as free from corruption as yours; but who could have guessed   25
that a king's palace would prove such a home of the Muses? As it is, I must
follow the course recommended by my age and my state of health; but all the
same, I shall rejoice that things go so well with you, since there will be no
profit in lamenting that for me they have gone ill. Farewell, dear Sir Henry.
Louvain, St Luke's day 1519   30

1033 / To Albert of Brandenburg   Louvain, 19 October 1519

Before appearing in Erasmus' *Epistolae ad diversos* this letter was published in
eight or more editions, many of them without a printer's name and all
unauthorized, in Cologne, Wittenberg, Nürnberg, Augsburg, Basel, and
Sélestat (for details see Allen's headnote and Luther w *Briefwechsel* I 620). The
first perhaps were two Cologne editions which also reprinted from the *Farrago*
Erasmus' Ep 980 to Luther. The same combination occurs in an edition printed
by Michaël Hillen at Antwerp, without date (NK 2935), which was probably
arranged by Erasmus himself, perhaps as early as the end of October (cf Epp
1040 n4, 1042 n2).

In his *Spongia* against Hutten (1523; ASD IX-1 192–3) Erasmus claimed that this
letter had been sent to a member of Albert's household 'whom Hutten must
know best' to be given either to the cardinal or to the flames, as he saw fit.
Amazingly, Erasmus contended a year later that readers of the *Spongia* would
not realize that Hutten himself was meant (cf Allen I 28; Ep 1445). According to
Erasmus' account in the *Spongia* the letter was published rather than handed to
the cardinal and the result was trouble, Albert having to face the Roman curia
and Erasmus the Louvain theologians. The *Spongia* adds that when Albert
finally received the original letter, torn and soiled with printer's ink, he blamed
Erasmus and abruptly withdrew his support of him.

At the time he wrote this letter Erasmus' apprehensions were evidently
different from those expressed later in the *Spongia*. Hutten's close contacts with
Albert seemed to indicate that the young cardinal was indeed one of the
prelates who favoured Luther (cf lines 48–51 and Epp 938:12–13, 999 n56). As
late as 1525 Luther himself believed that Albert might perhaps join the Reformation as his relative, Albert of Brandenburg-Ansbach, Master of the
Teutonic Knights, had done (cf Luther w XVIII 408–11). Writing a few days after
Luther had been formally charged before the theological faculty of Louvain (cf
lines 63–6, 154–5, 249–50), Erasmus feared that Luther's case offered a pretext

for a renewed attack upon his own positions (cf lines 215–28). As a patron of humanists and the primate of the German bishops, Albert was well suited to receive a public plea for the freedom of learning and the right to expose ecclesiastical corruption.

This letter is a fundamental statement of Erasmus' views on the conflict; it contains many formulations that he was later to repeat on countless occasions. Luther's supporters were clearly pleased with it, although the reformer himself was not impressed. By 26 January 1520 he had seen it and expected that it would soon be in print. Presumably it was a printed copy that Hutten himself showed to Johannes Crotus Rubianus at Bamberg, who promptly forwarded it to Luther on 28 April (Luther w *Briefwechsel* I Ep 242, II Ep 281). On 27 April Melanchthon had sent a manuscript copy to a friend at Wrocław (*Melanchthons Briefwechsel* I Ep 84). The most remarkable echo of Erasmus' efforts, however, may well be a conciliatory letter to Luther of 26 February, written in the name of none other than Albert of Brandenburg (Luther w *Briefwechsel* II Ep 259); cf Ep 1101 introduction.

TO THE MOST REVEREND IN CHRIST ALBERT, CARDINAL
ARCHBISHOP, MARGRAVE ETC, FROM ERASMUS OF
ROTTERDAM, THEOLOGIAN, GREETING

Respectful greetings, most revered Prelate and likewise most illustrious Prince. I have received your Highness' present,[1] in material and workman- 5
ship alike remarkable and splendid, and a gift worthy of such a princely giver; but I can hardly think my humble self a suitable recipient, for it suits me better to drink from glass and earthenware[2] than from gold cups in high relief. Had the cup you sent me been only of glass, it would even so have been laid up among my chiefest treasures, for this reason if no other, that it 10
would have come from a man as good as he is great. But the gift that was in itself so welcome was made not a little more acceptable by my friend Hutten, who explained to me that it is called a loving-cup, as though sacred to the Graces, – for this reason, I suppose, that those who use it are joined, as it were, by a kiss of peace, and become one instead of two; and he told me 15
further that it possesses the power of cementing those who have drunk from it in a bond of the closest good will. Wishing to test this, I drank out of it to Guillaume, Cardinal de Croy,[3] when he visited me in my library a few days ago, and he drank in his turn to me. He is an exceptionally well endowed young man, and his nature seems not unworthy of his great endowments. 20

But I am sorry that it did not come before. The theologians of Louvain recently made up their differences with me, on the basis that they should silence the slanderous tongues they had aroused, while I should continue to restrain the pens of my friends as far as I could. At this party[4] – for there is no

binding agreement here unless is sealed with a drink – I would have   25
produced your cup, if I had had it; and if all and singular had drunk out of it,
perhaps our new regime of peace might have got off to a more promising
start. As it is, as a result of some letter[5] which was imperfectly understood,
and a still more false interpretation put upon it, our patched-up peace has
fallen apart, and after a brief period of tranquillity an even fiercer storm   30
seems to have arisen. I have no doubt that all this is contrived by the
machinations of Satan, who hates nothing worse than the sight of Christians
at peace among themselves; and so he uses every means to break up
somehow the tranquillity of life and learned work, and does this under the
pretext of religion, so as to work yet more mischief.   35

On this subject, if the stormy seas of business have left your Eminence
any leisure, there are several things which it is in my interest that you should
know, and perhaps also it is in your own; certainly it is in the interest of
humane letters, which should always receive the support of good men
against bad. The first point I must make is this, that I have never had any   40
connection either with Reuchlin's business[6] or with the case of Luther.
Cabbala and Talmud,[7] whatever they may be, have never appealed to me.
Those venomous conflicts between Reuchlin and the supporters of Jacob of
Hoogstraten I have always found extremely offensive. Of Luther I know as
little[8] as I do of anyone; his books I have not yet found time to read, except for   45
dipping into some of them here and there. If he has written well, none of the
credit is due to me; if the reverse, there is nothing that can be laid at my door.
One thing I do see: it is the best men who take least offence at what he writes,
not because they approve of everything, I imagine, but because they read
him in the spirit in which we read Cyprian and Jerome, or even Peter   50
Lombard,[9] turning a blind eye to many things.

That Luther's books were published, distressed me; and when some
short pieces, I forget which, began to be handed about, I did my best to
prevent their publication,[10] for this reason especially, that I was afraid they
would give rise to disorders. Luther had written[11] to me, in a very Christian   55
spirit in my opinion, and in my answer I urged him in passing to publish no
sedition, nothing derogatory to the Roman pontiff, nothing arrogant or
vindictive, but to preach the gospel teaching in sincerity with all mildness. I
did this courteously, in hopes it would have more effect. I added that there
were some here who supported him, in order to persuade him more readily   60
to adapt himself to their advice. These words have been read by some
blockheads to mean that I supported Luther, though none of them have yet
told him where he is wrong and I alone did tell him. I do not accuse Luther, I
do not defend him, nor am I answerable[12] for him. On the man's spirit I
would not dare pass judgment; for this is a most difficult task, especially if   65

the verdict is to be adverse. And yet, if I supported him as a man of high
character, which even his enemies admit; as a man on trial, and even jurors
on oath are allowed to pity without breaking the law; as a victim of
persecution, which common humanity dictates – and persecution too by
those who have found a trumped-up pretext to make a fanatical attack on the   70
humanities – where in all this would there be grounds for suspicion,
provided I did not meddle with the case? Last but not least, it is, I imagine,
my Christian duty to support Luther to this extent: if he is innocent, I should
be sorry to see him overwhelmed by some villainous faction; if he is wrong, I
would rather he were set right than destroyed; for this agrees better with the   75
example Christ has given us, who according to the prophet[13] quenched not
the smoking flax and did not break the bruised reed.

I should like to see that heart of his, which does appear to house some
glowing sparks of the gospel teaching, not overwhelmed but set right, and
then invited to preach the glory of Christ. As it is, certain divines well known   80
to me neither correct Luther nor instruct him; they merely traduce him with
their crazy clamour before popular audiences and tear him to shreds with the
most bitter and venomous denunciations, their mouths full of nothing but
the words 'heresy' and 'heretics.' It cannot be denied that the most invidious
attacks have been made on him here[14] in public by men who have not yet set   85
eyes on his books. It is a known fact that some have condemned specifically
what they still did not understand. Here is an instance. Luther had put in
writing[15] that we are not bound to confess all our mortal sins but only those
which are manifest, meaning by manifest those which were known to us
when we made our confession. A certain Carmelite divine,[16] understanding   90
this as though manifest meant openly committed, made a portentous uproar
over something he had not understood. It is a known fact that these men
have condemned as heretical in Luther's books things they read in the books
of Bernard and Augustine[17] as orthodox and even pious.

I told them at the beginning to refrain from this kind of public clamour   95
and to proceed by preference in writing or by disputation. First, I said, a
thing ought not to be condemned in public which has not been read or,
rather, not considered – for I will not say not understood; secondly, that it
was unseemly for theologians to use disorder as a weapon, for their
decisions ought to be a serious matter; lastly, that it was not easy to rant and   100
rail against a man whose life all know to be blameless. And then perhaps, I
said, it was not safe to touch on such topics before a mixed crowd containing
many people who much dislike confessing their secret sins. If they hear that
there are divines who say we are not bound to confess all our sins, they will
snatch eagerly at this excuse for a quite erroneous opinion.   105

Although this view of mine was shared by all the most intelligent people, yet my friendly warning gave rise to the suspicion that Luther's books were largely mine,[18] and born in Louvain; while there is not a letter in them that belongs to me or was published with my knowledge or consent. And yet, relying on this utterly base suspicion, and being beyond the reach of any protest, they roused the most tragical scenes here, which were the most frenzied things I have yet seen in my whole life. Besides which, although a theologian's proper duty is to teach, I now see many of them intent on nothing but compulsion or destruction and annihilation; though Augustine,[19] even when confronted with the Donatists, who were not only heretics but brutal ruffians as well, disapproves of coercion without instruction too. Men in whom gentleness was most to be expected seem to thirst for nothing but human blood, and are all agape for nothing so much as to seize Luther and destroy him. This is to play the butcher, not the theologian. If they wish to prove themselves eminent divines, let them convert the Jews, let them convert to Christ those who are now far from him, let them mend the standard of morality among Christians, which is as corrupt as anything even the Turks can show. How can it be right to hale off to punishment a man who, in the first place, put forward subjects for discussion which have always been discussed in all schools of theology, and have even given rise to doubts?[20] Why should a man be tormented who wishes for instruction, who submits himself to the judgment of the Apostolic See, who entrusts himself to the judgment of the universities?[21] If he does not put himself in the hands of certain people who would rather see him dead than right, we should not be surprised.

Above all, we must look clearly at the sources of this evil. The world is burdened with ordinances made by man. It is burdened with the opinions and the dogmas of the schools. It is burdened with the tyranny of the mendicant friars who, though they are servants of the Roman See, have risen to such influence and such numbers that the pope himself – yes, even kings themselves – find them formidable. To them, when the pope is on their side, he is more than God; in things which are not to their advantage, he has no more substance than a dream. I do not condemn them all; but there are very many of this description who, for gain and for despotic power, deliberately ensnare the consciences of men. With growing effrontery they now began to leave Christ out of it and preach nothing but their own new and increasingly impudent dogmas. Of indulgences they were speaking in such terms that even the unlettered could not stomach it. This and much like it little by little was sapping the vigour of the gospel teaching; and the result would have been, with things slipping always from bad to worse, that the spark of Christian piety, from which alone the spent fire of charity could be rekindled, would be finally put out. The centre of religion was tending to be a more than Jewish ceremonial.[22] Hence there is sorrow and sighing among men of good will. And all this is admitted in private conversation even by theologians if they are not monks, and by certain monks themselves.   150

It was these things, I think, that roused Luther's spirit to take the first bold step of opposing the intolerable impudence of some of them. What else am I to suppose of a man who does not seek high place and has no desire for money? Of the articles[23] on which they base their charges against Luther I enter into no discussion for the moment, I discuss merely the manner and   155 occasion. Luther made bold to doubt about indulgences; but this was a subject on which others previously had made brazen assertions. He made bold to speak, with some moderation, of the power of the Roman pontiff; but on this the other party had previously written with no moderation at all, the leaders of them being three Dominicans,[24] Alvarus, Silvester, and the   160 cardinal of San Sisto. He made bold to condemn the pronouncements of Thomas;[25] but these the Dominicans set almost above the Gospels. He made bold to discuss some doubtful points on the subject of confession;[26] but this is a subject on which the monks set endless traps for men's consciences. He made bold to neglect in part the pronouncements of the schools; but to these   165 they themselves give too much weight, and on them they differ none the less among themselves, and finally they change them from time to time, tearing up the old to bring in new.

This was torment to religious minds, when they heard scarcely a word in the schools about the gospel teaching, and those sainted authors who had   170 long ago been accepted by the church dismissed as out of date. Worse, in sermons they heard very little about Christ; almost everything concerned the powers of the papacy and the opinions of modern authorities, and all the preachers said now flaunted openly the money-grubber and the toady, the place-hunter and the charlatan. It is their fault, I think, even if Luther was   175 rather too intemperate. Whoever is a supporter of the gospel teaching is a supporter of the Roman pontiff, who is its principal mouthpiece, while the other bishops are his mouthpieces in their turn. All bishops are Christ's vicegerents, but among them the Roman pontiff is the chief. Of him we must suppose that he supports nothing more than the glory of Christ, whose   180 minister he boasts himself to be. Those men do him the greatest disservice who ascribe to him in adulation what he does not himself accept and what is not expedient for Christ's flock. And yet some of those who stir up these tragic commotions do it out of no zeal for the pope; they misuse his position to enhance their own interests and their own despotic power. We have, I   185 should suppose, a pious pope. But in such a stormy sea of business there is much of which he is unaware; some things too which he cannot restrain even if he would, but, as Virgil[27] says, 'The driver's steeds now carry him away, /

Nor will the chariot the reins obey.' And so the pope's pious duty can only
be assisted by a man who encourages truly Christian behaviour. It is no
secret that there are people who seek to arouse his holy fervour against
Luther, or rather against anyone who dares open his mouth in opposition to
their favourite ideas. But the greatest princes ought to consider the pope's
abiding wishes, and not his acquiescence secured by force or fraud.

Indeed I could show you with perfect truth what sort of men are at the
bottom of this tumult, did I not fear that while I try always to be truthful I may
be thought merely spiteful. Many of them I know well; many have
themselves displayed their true quality in the books they have published –
nor does any mirror give a clearer image of a man's mind and life. If only
those who assume for themselves the censorial staff, to purge the Christian
body of whom they please, as the ancient censors[28] purged the senate, had
thoroughly absorbed Christ's teaching and Christ's spirit! This happy state
is reserved for those hearts from which all the contamination of this world's
desires has been cleared away. Whether the men we treat of are in this class
will soon be discovered by anyone who does business with them on any
point that touches their pockets, their ambition, or their love of revenge. I
wish I could indicate to your Highness what I have both observed and been
told upon this subject; for I must not forget the self-restraint proper to a
Christian.

I say this all the more freely because I am in every way a stranger to both
Reuchlin's case and Luther's. I should not be willing to write anything in
that field myself, nor do I claim to possess sufficient learning to be ready to
keep an eye on what other men write; but I cannot refrain from letting you
into one secret – that those people have very different objects in view from
those that their words profess. They have long resented the new blossoming
of the humanities and the ancient tongues, and the revival of the authors of
Antiquity, who up to now were wormeaten and deep in dust, so that the
world is now recalled to the fountain-head. They are afraid for their own
shortcomings, they do not wish it to be thought that there is anything they
do not know, and they fear their own prestige may suffer. This is a sore place
that they have long kept under, but pain proves too much for pretence, and
it has lately burst. Before Luther's books appeared, they devoted great
efforts to this, especially the Dominicans and the Carmelites,[29] many of
whom, I regret to say, are even more criminal than they are ignorant. When
Luther's books had appeared, as though this gave them a handle they began
to tie up the ancient tongues and the humanities and Reuchlin and Luther
and even myself in the same parcel,[30] their distinctions being as much at sea
as their deductions. To begin with, what can liberal studies have in common
with a question of religious faith? And then what have I in common with

Reuchlin or with Luther? But they have cunningly confused all these things,   230
to lay on all who follow the humanities a load of ill will which all share.

Further, that this campaign is dishonest, this alone is enough to show:
they themselves admit that there is no author ancient or modern in whom
mistakes may not be found, and would even make a man who defended
those mistakes assiduously a heretic, and why, if so, do they probe so   235
invidiously into two or three and ignore the rest? They do not deny that
there are many errors in Alvarus, many in the cardinal of San Sisto, and many
in Silvester Prierias.[31] These are not mentioned, because they are Dominicans. Reuchlin alone is the object of their clamour, because of his skill in
languages, and Luther, whom they suppose to be equipped with the   240
subjects that I study, although in fact his acquaintance with them is but
slender. Luther has written much which is not so much irreligious as ill
advised; and of this what hurts their feelings worst of all is that he does not
attach much importance to Thomas,[32] that he reduces the profit to be made
from indulgences, that he does not think much of the orders of mendicants,   245
that he does not pay to the decisions of the schools the same respect as he
pays to the Gospels, and that he thinks the man-made subtleties of academic
disputation can be ignored. These, we can all see, are insufferable heresies.
Yet these they gloss over in the presence of the pope and produce charges
loaded with prejudice; only the chance of hurting someone calls out all their   250
unanimity and cunning.

In the old days a heretic was listened to almost with respect and was
absolved if he did penance; if he remained obdurate after conviction, he was
not admitted – that was the extreme penalty[33] – to communion with catholics
in the bosom of the church. Nowadays the accusation of heresy is a very   255
different thing; and yet on the slightest pretext at once they are all crying,
'Heresy, heresy.' In the old days a heretic was one who dissented from the
Gospels or the articles of the faith or things which carried equal authority
with them. Nowadays if anyone disagrees with Thomas, he is called a heretic
– indeed, if he disagrees with some newfangled reasoning thought up   260
yesterday by some sophister in the schools. Anything they do not like,
anything they do not understand is heresy. To know Greek is heresy; to
speak like an educated man is heresy. Anything they do not do themselves is
heresy. It is, I admit, a serious crime to violate the faith; but not everything
should be forced into a question of faith. And those who mind[34] the business   265
of the faith ought to steer very clear of every kind of ambition for personal
gain or hatred or revenge.

But anyone can see the goal they have set before them and the way they
are heading. And if their greed is once allowed free rein, they will begin to
show their resentment against all good men everywhere, and will end by   270

threatening the very bishops, even the pope himself. I should not protest if this were to be thought untrue, except that we have seen some of them doing this already. How far the Order of Preachers can go, to produce no other example, we can learn from Girolamo Savaronella[35] and that outrage at Bern.[36] I have no wish to refresh the memory of their disgrace; I issue a 27 warning of what we must expect if all their rash attempts succeed.

All that I have said hitherto lies outside Luther's case; I discuss only their methods and the danger of them. Reuchlin's case[37] has been reserved to himself by the pope. Luther's business has been delegated to the universities.[38] Whatever they may pronounce will be free of all risk for me. I have 28 always taken pains to write nothing indecent or seditious or at variance with the teaching of Christ. I shall never knowingly be either a teacher of error or a promoter of civil strife, for I will suffer anything rather than arouse sedition. But I had my reasons for wishing this to be known to your Eminence, not to give you good advice or show you the way, but so that, if 28 the adversaries of the humanities attempt to misuse your great position, you may know more surely what the best decision in this field is. And in my opinion, the more your Eminence can keep clear of this case, the more you will honourably preserve your own tranquillity. The *Methodus*[39] which I dedicated to your Highness, I have revised, and enriched with considerable 29 additions. May Christ the Almighty ever preserve your Eminence in health and wealth.

Louvain, 19 October 1519
Your Eminence's most obedient servant Erasmus of Rotterdam

1034 / To Ludovicus Carinus   [Louvain? autumn 1519?]

The following is an inscription in Erasmus' own hand in a gift copy of the Younger Pliny's *Epistulae* (Venice: A. Manuzio November 1508). Allen examined the volume when it was in the possession of Mr George Dunn. What became of it after Mr Dunn's death is not known. It may be noted that Erasmus was staying with Aldo Manuzio when the volume was being prepared. It was perhaps at this time that he gave it to Ludovicus Carinus, one of the students who had come to Louvain together with Wilhelm Nesen; cf Ep 994 n1. Above the inscription Erasmus writes: 'Maro: Adeo in teneris consuescere multum est' and Παροιμία: "Εργα νέων βουλαὶ δὲ μέσων εὐχαὶ δὲ γερόντων' ('Virgil: Such power has habit in the tender young; Proverbial: Youth acts, grown men take counsel, old men pray'). The Virgil quotation is from *Georgics* 2.272; for the Greek proverb, cf *Adagia* III v 2. Melanchthon has a story how Erasmus replied with this proverb when he urged him to support the reformers openly; see P. Melanchthon *Opera omnia* ed C.G. Bretschneider et al (Halle 1834–) x 304.

TO LUDOVICUS CARINUS FROM ERASMUS

Continue, my dear Ludovicus, as you have begun. Furnish yourself with such a provision for life as will not desert its owner even when life itself deserts him. Devote your youth to whatsoever things are good, remembering that what you have acquired in early years will cling most closely, nor is 5 any other age so quick to learn. With all good wishes.

1035 / From Maarten Lips

This letter has been assigned a new date and is Ep 1000A in this edition.

1036 / To Maarten Lips

This letter has been assigned a new date and is Ep 1000B in this edition.

1037 / From Edward Lee   [Louvain? winter 1519–20]

This letter is a preface published with Lee's *Annotationes ... in annotationes Novi Testamenti Desiderii Erasmi*, Paris: Gilles de Gourmont (cf Ep 1074:94–5) for Konrad Resch [February 1520]. (A volume in the British Library described in the *General Catalogue* as 'another edition,' 3226 b. 25, was destroyed in the second world war; see also Ep 1100 introduction). Gourmont's volume opens with an *Apologia* addressed to the students of Louvain and dated 29 December [1519], which is followed by an extensive index. Next come this preface and 243 notes based on the 1516 edition of Erasmus' New Testament, followed by addenda to these on the basis of the revised New Testament of 1518–19 and by a section of new notes; the last piece in the volume is Ep 1061. In view of the sheet signatures Allen suggested that the annotations together with this preface were probably printed ahead of the rest; but precisely when we do not know (cf n1). The date of publication can be determined with more precision, however. By 17 February 1520 Erasmus had heard at Louvain that Lee's volume was out or imminent (Epp 1066:99–100, 1068:18–20; cf 1072, 1073 introduction). By 27 February a very few copies had found their way to England (Rogers Ep 84), while others reached Cologne (Ep 1078:15) and Basel (Epp 1083:2–4, 1084: 71–4) not later than the first half of March.

Lee's critique of Erasmus' New Testament falls short of being a significant contribution to biblical scholarship, and on the whole Erasmus had little difficulty in answering his charges (cf Ep 1080 introduction). This short preface conveys both Lee's satisfaction and his resigned anticipation. He had succeeded in withholding his notes from Erasmus prior to their long-delayed publication and thus deprived him of a chance to answer in public before the charges had been divulged (cf Ep 998 introduction and n3); on the other hand, in view of the commotion Erasmus had made and his thinly veiled threats (cf Ep 998 n14), Lee had to brace himself for a devastating reaction; see Epp 1053, 1061, 1083.

EDWARD LEE TO DESIDERIUS ERASMUS, GREETING

Here at last, Desiderius Erasmus, is the volume of my annotations for which you have asked with so much urgency, and I trust the work will give you pleasure and satisfaction, not so much because I wrote it as because it bears your name in the title and is published after a whole year[1] of pressure from 5 you; still more perhaps because the whole world will thus become aware of my ignorance, which you take every opportunity to advertise, so that everyone will know that your picture of me is a good likeness. For my own part, whatever happens will not come amiss or be untoward. Let chance throw the dice as she pleases: I am ready. Farewell. 10

1038 / To Erard de la Marck   [Louvain? late October 1519]

This letter was first printed in the *Epistolae ad diversos* without a date. The year date of 1518 added in the *Opus epistolarum* has no value.

The prince-bishop of Liège had been in personal communication with Erasmus after his return from the imperial election (cf Ep 1001 n15) and before 17 October (cf Ep 1030:69–71). Allen and Henry de Vocht assumed very reasonably that on c 15 October Erard had stopped at Louvain on his way to Brussels and that it was on this occasion that he was met by three delegates of the Louvain theological faculty and invited to comment on Erasmus' remark (in Ep 980, brought to Louvain by Jacob of Hoogstraten; cf Ep 1030 n7) that he favoured Luther. Erard denied the allegation on his word as a priest. Erasmus could have met him on the same occasion, giving him reassuring explanations which were evidently accepted (cf Ep 1127A). Later in the day he would have failed to see the prince-bishop for a second time, as explained in this letter (cf de Vocht CTL I 427–31).

It is not quite clear, however, that Erasmus and Erard had met face to face and that they had done so in Louvain. What is certain is that Erasmus expected Erard to be at the court of Brussels when he wrote this letter and was counting on his support. It is possible that Erasmus himself did visit Brussels at about this time; see Ep 1040 n2.

ERASMUS OF ROTTERDAM TO THE RIGHT REVEREND ERARD, PRINCE-BISHOP OF LIÈGE, GREETING

For three days and more I have been wanting to come and see you, and have

been fast bound at home by an unbroken and most cursed fog.[1] I wanted to
make some amends for the way in which I failed to pay my respects to your 5
Lordship before you left here. Your physician[2] is responsible: he had
assured me that you would be with us for the whole day. That truly noble
prince Albert, cardinal of Mainz, whose more than human endowments you
lately admired at close quarters,[3] has sent me a cup,[4] as large and heavy as it
is notable for the workmanship. He adds that he gives me this present 10
although I avoid him, and that I shall find greater generosity awaiting me if I
give him the benefit of my company. This is indeed a gift worthy to be given
by such a prince, though an Erasmus drinks more appropriately from
common pottery.[5] He has moreover given it a name. He says it is called a
loving-cup, I suppose because when two well-matched parties drink out of 15
it, it is like a kiss – it makes them one, as often as they please; for those who
drink of it, he says, are forthwith cemented by mutual good will. If this is
true, what a pity the theologians of Louvain did not drain this cup with me
two years ago!

By their kind offices (so I am given to understand) my lords the princes 20
of Bergen[6] and the count of Hoogstraten[7] have to some extent turned against
me. Should opportunity arise, perhaps you would advise them to use their
normal good sense, and give more credence to men who have made it up[8]
than to those still in a passion. They were induced to attack me by suspicions
with no shadow of foundation, and the whole thing was a tribute to the 25
resentment of one individual.[9] When they made overtures of friendship, it
was because they had thought things over with more attention. One was the
outcome of passion, and the other of reason and sense. If you cannot get
them to do this, at least let them not pass judgment against me before they
have heard both sides. If they had known the whole story, they would have 30
an even higher opinion of their Erasmus than they had before. Farewell.

[1518]

1039 / To Jan Šlechta   Louvain, 1 November 1519

This impressive letter, which answers Ep 1021, was published in the *Epistolae
ad diversos*. At a time of fierce opposition at home (cf the preface) it was
designed to disseminate Erasmus' ideas in remote regions of central Europe
where Šlechta so far was his only correspondent. Answering this educated
Czech noble who could be expected to be as influential as he had shown
himself to be sympathetic, Erasmus chose to restate what he considered to be
essential (and non-essential) in the formation of a truly Christian mind.
Reviewing the troubles of Bohemia, he was also led to express himself on the
problems of authority in Christendom.

There are several indications that this letter served its purpose. In particular
the interest of the Czech Brethren (cf Ep 1021 n14, n20) should be noted.
Threatened with suppression in the reign of Vladislav II, the Brethren had
made repeated efforts to explain their position to a wider European public, and
from the time of the disputation of Leipzig (cf Ep 1020 n9), they were in
personal contact with Martin Luther. It seems quite possible that some of their
leaders saw this letter soon after it had reached its destination. If so, Erasmus
must have presented himself to their minds as an unprejudiced judge of
enormous prestige. Either in June or in August 1520 he was visited in Antwerp
by two emissaries of the Brethren, the physician Mikuláš Klaudyán and one
Laurentius Voticius, BA. Erasmus mentions this visit only in passing (Allen Ep
1183:7), but there is a fuller account of their meeting in Joachim Camerarius
(1500–74) *Historica narratio de Fratrum orthodoxorum ecclesiis in Bohemia, Moravia
et Polonia* (Heidelberg 1605; this account is reprinted in Allen's headnote to Ep
1117). It is perhaps based on information given by Jan Blahoslav in his summary
account of the Brethren (1556; printed in Jaroslav Goll *Quellen und Untersu-
chungen zur Geschichte der Böhmischen Brüder*, Prague 1878–82, I 124–5).

According to Camerarius the two Brethren presented Erasmus with a
statement of their faith, no doubt the *Apologia sacrae scripturae* edited by
Klaudyán (Nürnberg: H. Höltzel 16 December 1511; cf Ep 1154). He promised
to study it, and a few days later they returned to hear his reaction. They were
told that reading it in haste, he had not found a single error. At the same time,
however, he refused to give them any public endorsement, explaining that
otherwise his own writings might be suspected of heresy together with theirs.

Erasmus' continued occupation with the religious situation is evident in an
exchange of letters with Arkleb of Boscovice (Epp 1154, 1183), and in his
discussion on infant baptism and confirmation in a preface to the reader for the
paraphrase on Matthew, 14 January 1522 (LB VII preliminary pages); see
Konrad Bittner 'Erasmus, Luther und die Böhmischen Brüder' *Rastloses
Schaffen: Festschrift Friedrich Lammert* (Stuttgart 1954) 107–29; F.M. Bartos
'Erasmus und die Böhmische Reformation' *Communio viatorum* 1 (1958) 116–23,
246–57. This letter was translated into German by an otherwise unknown
Johann Froben of Andernach. It was edited with a title commending it as a
guide to end religious strife by Martin Bucer: *Ain Epistel ... an Johann Schlechten
von Costeletz* (Strasbourg: J. Schweintzer 1531); see Heinz Holeczek *Erasmus
Deutsch* (Stuttgart-Bad Cannstadt 1983–) I 252–9.

ERASMUS OF ROTTERDAM TO JAN ŠLECHTA OF BOHEMIA, GREETING
Your long letter, my excellent Šlechta, must receive a brief answer,[1] designed
only to show that I have received it and read it through; for I am too busy at the
moment to do more. To the voices of my critics, since they are made even

more ferocious by kindness, I long ago learnt to turn a deaf ear. In the old 5
days I used to think I had some moderate experience of human affairs,
having lived on familiar terms in different countries with various kinds of
men; but I have found such monsters among Christians as I would never
have believed had I not learnt the reality, to my great misfortune. All the
same, since they cannot be other than their true selves, I shall try to be my 10
true self, nor shall I cease to do good unto all men so far as my talent permits,
if only it lies with me. Perhaps it has pleased God that in this way I should
atone for my misdoings, by which I offend against him frequently. I will
forgive them, that he in turn may forgive me; for the holiness of life which
your words confer upon me, I would that Christ in his goodness, as the 15
author of all holiness, might some day confer upon me in reality.

You say that you beguile your spare time by reading my works.[2] This is
friendly of you, and might be profitable too, if only you will read what I write
in a critical spirit – for my books are not gospel – and also if you only take up
your Erasmus when you have no access to anything better. But you give me a 20
most vivid description of the country you live in, so that I seem to perceive
almost more in what you write than I should see if I had lived some years
there.

If your Germany is, as you say, a prey to widespread brigandage,[3] I
suppose this is due partly to the remnants of its former barbarism, partly to 25
the division of the country between so many lordships and petty princes,
none of whom is willing to yield to any other, partly to the habit, more
common there than in any other nation, of fighting for pay. Thus by
continuous brigandage they keep themselves fit for war, and when war is
over, they keep its embers alive by brigandage. And then, since however 30
unprofitable a thing may be, there is always profit in it for somebody, those
who make a living out of convoying strangers or merchants sometimes see to
it that a journey should not become quite safe, for fear there may be no
further use for their services. In my opinion, it would be wiser to deal with
evils of this kind by prudent measures to prevent their happening than by 35
punishing them when they have happened. To encourage the greatest
possible ease of communication, it might be possible to free a route from
forests that beset it, and to protect it with villages, towns, and castles.
Indeed, it seems to me little short of a disgrace that the cities and princes of
Germany do not take the same steps in their own territories as the Swiss,[4] 40
depending on the will of the people, do in theirs. But these ills will find a
remedy, perhaps in Charles[5] our prince, who is not only supreme in power
but foremost in his love of justice.

In any case, as far as concerns divisions in the faith,[6] it would be a more
tolerable calamity, in my view, if all shared the same error. As it is, not only 45

do a large part of you differ, they tell me, from the Catholic church, but you even differ in error and fight among yourselves. For an admixture of Jews is a thing you share, perhaps, with parts of Italy and the rest of Germany, but especially with Spain. But who would believe that men still exist who follow the foolish doctrines of Epicurus,[7] and deny that our souls survive after death? Here too you can frequently see people who live as though they did not believe that anything survives after death, but no one is mad enough to be either a leader of this doctrine or a follower: just as one can find plenty of Nicolaites, who hold their wives in common with many other men, but no one professes this as a belief, though no less an author than Plato[8] held something very like it. But I ask you, my dear Šlechta, are not such people ashamed to be called heretics? Nothing is more discreditable than such a name, yet even of that they seem unworthy. For what does a man believe who denies the immortality of the soul? What value does a man set on the Gospel who wishes to see promiscuity in wives?

It seems to me astonishing that nothing can be thought of so monstrous that it finds no followers. Pythagoras[9] forbade men to eat beans, and found men who would not touch them. Some taught that it showed proper feeling for sons to put an aged parent to death, and a nation[10] was found to do this as a matter of conviction. Some held that private property is impious, and persons arose, as St Augustine[11] records in his catalogue of heresiarchs, who spent their lives in idleness and lived on alms, rejecting other men from their society as impious who obtained by their own labours the wherewithal to maintain their wives and children. There were men who thought the redemption and salvation of the world were owed to Judas[12] the betrayer, and he even had disciples who worshipped him as the supreme god. Some chanted[13] innumerable psalms all day long and did nothing else, and this lunacy found its adherents. Some held that those who strictly observed the sanctity of marriage were irreligious, more wicked in fact than those who demanded that wives should be held in common, and they succeeded in forming a flock and giving it a name. Some preached that religion required parents to burn their children alive, and found people to accept such an irreligious principle. So great is the credulity of mortals, and such their infinite fertility of ideas. I believe myself that if anyone arose now and taught that religion required men and women to dance together naked in the market-place, he would not lack followers and patrons for his way of thinking. This makes it all the more important for those in authority to be careful not to teach anything or lay down any principles which do not square with the rule laid down by Christ.

But to ignore these monstrosities as they deserve, you tell me that the whole kingdom of Bohemia, and the margraviate of Moravia too, is divided into three sects.[14] How I wish, my dear Ślechta, that some cunning artificer[15] in religion would weld this trinity into a single whole! But as long as everyone is devoted to his own private advantage, neither public affairs nor private can go well, and scarcely a person can be found with any intellectual   90 gifts, except such as are spent on our current philosophy; and in this respect things are more reasonable among the Turks, they tell me, than in our world. I am thinking not of those tenets which we insist on regarding as matters of faith, but those which form as it were the springs from which the true religion of the Gospel flows: contempt of money and of worldly place,   95 control over the passions, of anger, hatred, and malice; for if a man be the slave of such desires as these, pray, what purpose is served by his profession of the faith? If avarice and ambition have too much power over us, if our lusts are too criminal, our hatreds too cruel, our envy too damaging, our malice too poisonous, to what end do we acknowledge Christ, who was made man in   100 order to wean us away from such things? If anyone wishes to be indignant with me for saying this, let him be indignant with the apostle James,[16] who says all this with emphasis and at greater length in his Epistle.

So, in your account of your sects, I am happy to see the one you mention first[17] in the first place, but I wish dearly that it were the only one.   105 What comes closer to the design of the hierarchy of heaven than a system of ordered ranks culminating in a single head? What could be more valuable as a defence against the divisions of the world? If some prince designs to seize despotic power, he will be kept in his place by the exhortations and prayers, the teaching and authority of the Holy See.[18] If some bishop behaves like a   110 tyrant, the common people will have somewhere to apply for help. Should someone arise who brings in the devil's doctrine, the Roman shepherd will be there to bring forth from the pure sources of gospel philosophy things worthy of Christ's steward and vicegerent. If on any point the supreme pontiff will not answer,[19] first of all it is impossible that he who is set over all   115 men should give all men satisfaction; and secondly it is our duty, so far as we can, to put a favourable interpretation on all things. Besides which, for a good part of what happens we must thank not the pope himself but those in whom he trusts, as he must do. We should also remember that while he presides over mankind, he is but man himself, and that if mutual concord is   120 to last long, two things are needful: he must be mild and give us our head in many ways, but we in turn must obey him as the times demand, especially since the apostle[20] teaches us that we must obey even wicked and wayward princes as far as we can without doing violence to our religion.

In this department, as it seems to me, the second faction make a worse   125 mistake in rejecting with contumely the jurisdiction and traditions of the Roman church than in thinking it religious to receive the Eucharist in both kinds. I only wish that on this point Eugenius[21] had thought fit to consider the public peace rather than what touched him personally, if what you say in your letter is true. Though here, if the Bohemians had asked my advice, I should have told them, although their opinion on this question may well be true, to comply rather than stand out, especially as the greatest part of Christendom follows this custom. And yet, to say frankly what I think, I wonder very much why it was thought right to alter what was instituted by Christ himself, since the reasons they produce do not seem of much weight.

As for the sect of the Pyghards,[22] that it should stand further from the rule of concord in the Gospel is less surprising, since as you say it takes its rise from a criminal founder. For if the Roman pontiff is Antichrist because there has now and then been an impious pope, or if the church of Rome is the great harlot because it has sometimes wicked cardinals or bishops or ministers of another kind, then by the same token we should never obey any bishops, any pastors, any kings; not to add, for the moment, that once this window is opened anyone is free to label as irreligious whomever he happens to dislike. How much more satisfactory is Augustine's opinion[23] that the character of the minister cannot vitiate the gift of God conferred upon us through the sacraments, even if the severest penalties await those priests whose impious behaviour causes the unlearned and the weak to speak ill of the name of our Lord Jesus Christ, which they should adore. Suppose that, breaking all the bounds of decency, they go on to be openly criminal, they must of course be somehow restrained, but it is not for the first comer to attack them; nor do I approve the use of weapons, for fear that if the precedent of violence be once admitted, it will run wild among the innocent as well.

That they should choose priests and bishops for themselves does not disagree with the tradition of the Ancients. That was how St Nicholas[24] was elected, and Ambrose[25] but the formula for canonical election was not yet widespread – in the same way that kings in old days were chosen by the people. After a time, the constant tumults among the mob caused the thing to be entrusted to the decision of a small number. Apart from that, the choice of unlettered men of no education would be more tolerable, if their lack of learning were made up for by holiness of life. As it is, the people suffer twice over, if they are as impious as they are ignorant.

If they call themselves indiscriminately brothers and sisters, I do not see why one should take exception. I only wish the same affectionate address survived among Christians everywhere, provided only that their words were borne out by their behaviour. In giving less weight to Doctors of the church than to the Scriptures – paying more attention, in other words, to God than men – they are quite right; but to reject their authority entirely is as

wrong as to accept it everywhere. Again, though it is not untrue that Christ
and the apostles celebrated in everyday clothes, yet it is impious to despise a   170
custom instituted later by the Fathers with some salutary purpose in mind.
They are only ceremonies, but these ceremonies make the holy mysteries
more acceptable to the people. And if nothing else, what is the object of
disagreement on a point which could be observed without any trouble,
unless the Roman pontiff were to allow them to use their own rites to   175
preserve an ancient tradition, in the way he has authorized rites for the
Greeks and the Milanese[26] which are very different from ours? As for their
special preference for the Lord's Prayer, that is part of our office also. It is
folly to connect your sacraments with one single prayer; but they do not do
much better who introduce whatever vain wording they please from any   180
source.

On festivals their opinion is not far from Jerome's generation.[27] But in   190

   As for their views on the sacraments, they are more fantastic than a
religious hearer can easily tolerate, except that out of that mass of evil we can
extract one good thing: a warning not to put our own admirable system to the
wrong uses – personal profit, vainglory, tyranny even. I wonder they have   185
the face to despise vigils and moderate fasts, seeing they are so often
commended to us in the language of the apostles; though I would rather
men were drawn towards them by exhortation than driven into them by
orders.

   On festivals their opinion is not far from Jerome's generation.[27] But in   190
our day the crowd of feasts has grown beyond all reason, though there are
no days on which more misdemeanours are committed by the mob; and the
most cruel thing about it is that men are obliged to be idle whole days at a time
who have no other resources on which to keep their wives and children, and
maybe their parents, except their daily wages. To force them to keep holiday   195
and give them nothing – what is this but to force them to starve? Let there be
plenty of feasts, but in the churches, which can be attended by the rich, and
yet the poor can be allowed to live. At least they might be permitted when
service is over to return to work that has God's blessing on it; for what can be
more blessed than to work with the labour of your hands to support your   200
children and your household? In our day every superstitious movement
means the institution of some new festival; indeed we often see it to be a
favourite project with certain bishops for each of them to add a new feast-day
to the calendar, as though this at least would be an enduring monument to
the credit of his tenure of the see. As however it is the duty of the obedient   205
multitude to perform what is laid down for them by the leaders of the church,
one might have expected them in their wisdom not to burden the people
unadvisedly or strike a blow at public morals with new foundations of this
kind.

Thus far I have been learning from your letter what the evil is; and now   2
I wish someone would discover a trustworthy and efficient cure. And I think
this could be done, if men of good will and authority could devote
themselves wholly to it, especially as we have an emperor in Charles who is
whole-heartedly devoted to the interests of the Christian religion, and so
mild and merciful a pope as Leo. Union can be successfully achieved, if each   2
side will make some concessions to the other. It may well be that many in
your part of the world reject the rule of the pope of Rome with horror
because they have heard the laments of neighbouring regions,[28] where men
complain that they are pitilessly pillaged and oppressed by the cruelty of
those who manage the pope's business affairs. But, unless I am quite wrong,   2
it will be easy to secure from the pious and merciful nature of Pope Leo that
the confused reckoning of earlier years should be written off and his
demands for the future reduced to a minimum, especially if they trust
themselves to him as to a father in sincerity of heart. He will think it sufficient
profit if he can banish discord and re-establish peace and unity. The emperor   2
will put his authority behind this – and he is recognized as their monarch, I
believe, even by the Bohemians. For the rest, in what concerns orders and
sacraments, there must be no kind of dissent from the orthodoxy practised
everwhere; and it may be possible to allow some dispensation from the
legislation of more recent popes. On the liturgy it will be easy to make them   2
some allowances, although I would prefer all Christians everywhere to use
the same rites and the same prayers. As it is, there is excessive variation, for
every man invents things to express his own feelings, and another adds
something to what he finds in use.

Another thing, it seems to me, which would reconcile many nations to   2
the Roman church, to which all gravitate now as though to some common
head, would be a readiness not to define everything over a wide field in the
way we should willingly think appropriate for the subject-matter of the faith,
but only such things as are clearly laid down in Holy Writ or without which
the system of our salvation cannot stand. For this a few truths are enough,   2
and the multitude are more easily persuaded of their truth if they are few. As
things are, we make six hundred articles out of one, some of them of such a
kind that one can be ignorant of them, or unconvinced, without peril to one's
religion. And such is the nature of mortal men that we cling tooth and nail to
what has once been laid down. Besides which the whole of the Christian   2
philosophy lies in this, our understanding that all our hope is placed in God,
who freely gives us all things through Jesus his son, that we were redeemed
by his death and engrafted through baptism with his body, that we might be
dead to the desires of this world and live by his teaching and example, not

merely harbouring no evil but deserving well of all men; so that, if adversity   250
befall, we may bear it bravely in hope of the future reward which beyond
question awaits all good men at Christ's coming, and that we may ever
advance from one virtue to another, yet in such a way that we claim nothing
for ourselves, but ascribe any good we do to God.

   These above all are the things that must be implanted in the hearts of   255
men until they become second nature. If any man wishes to pursue more
abstruse questions touching the divine nature or the substance of Christ or
the sacraments, so that he may raise his mind on high and withdraw it from
lowly things, he is welcome to do so with this restriction, that to believe what
commends itself to this man or that should not at once become compulsory   260
for everybody. A long-winded legal document soon gives rise to controversy, and many definitions are a hotbed of dissent. Nor need we be ashamed if
our reply is sometimes 'God knows how it happens; enough for me that I
believe it does happen.' I know that the body and blood of Christ must be
received pure and in purity by the pure in heart, for Christ wished this to be   265
a most holy sign and pledge both of his love towards us and of the concord of
Christians among themselves. I will therefore examine myself to see if there is
anything in me which is not in harmony with Christ, or any point of
difference between me and my neighbour. But how the ten categories[29] are to
be found therein, and how the bread is made to change its substance by the   270
mystic words, and how the same body can exist in so small a form and in
different places – all this, in my opinion, has not much to contribute towards
progress in religion. I know that I shall rise again, for Christ, who was
himself the very first to rise from the dead, has promised this to all men. But
what my body will be like, and how it can be the same body when it has so   275
often been reduced to quite different shapes, are questions the reasonable
study of which at the proper time I would not disapprove of; but to spend
much time on them contributes very little to true religion. As things are,
these problems and countless others like them, on which some men pride
themselves, divert men's minds from the only things that really matter.   280
Finally, it will be a very great contribution towards the establishment of
world-wide agreement, if lay monarchs, but above all the Roman pontiff,
abstain from tyranny[30] and greed of every kind. Men start back easily when
they see servitude awaiting them, when they realize that they are not so
much being invited to join in a religious exercise as cozened that they may be   285
fleeced. If they feel that we mean no harm and may do good, they will easily
give credence to our faith.

   I will forgive the length of your letter, as you ask me to, but on
condition that you often send me letters like it; for we bear more easily what

we are accustomed to. Jodocus Jonas[31] was with me at the very time of his   2
election as rector of the university; I seldom saw a better man. Farewell, my
excellent friend.

Louvain, 1 November 1519

1040 / To Maarten Lips   [Louvain, October–November 1519]

> This letter was preserved in Lips' copy-book now at Rotterdam (cf Ep 1000A
> introduction). An approximate date can be assigned from the presence of
> Hoogstraten in Louvain and from a comparison with Ep 1038:20–2; cf n2, n3.

ERASMUS OF ROTTERDAM TO MAARTEN LIPS OF BRUSSELS

His suggestion[1] is pure fiddlesticks; I got wind of it in Brussels.[2] Hoogstrat-
en[3] is now at Louvain. He has secured a copy of my letter to Luther, and
thinks it will serve nicely to show me up as being in favour of Luther, I
having published[4] it expressly to prove that Luther and I have nothing in   5
common. And suppose I did favour him, would there be anything monstrous
in that? He[5] has been working on the people at court, especially my lord of
Bergen;[6] but there were some who understood the question too well for that.
I suspect however that certain of them have been putting their heads
together[7] – Briselot, Hoogstraten, the suffragan of Cambrai, and Egmon-   10
danus with them – not so much against me as against Luther. I am suffering
severely from the rheum. Thank you for your present. My dear Maarten,
there is no call to throw doubts on our friendship. I wish I could come and
see you. My new *Colloquia*[8] is in the press. Best wishes.

1041 / To the Reader   [Louvain, October–November 1519]

> Dirk Marten's authorized edition of Erasmus' *Familiarum colloquiorum formulae*
> (cf Ep 909) had been reprinted several times in quick succession, for instance by
> Michaël Hillen at Antwerp in April–May and again in September 1519 (NK
> 2867–8). Another reprint by Martens, Louvain (n d; NK 2869) was partly
> revised, slightly enlarged, and had this letter appended (cf ASD I–3 18, 113–20;
> Ep 1061 n38). It is clearly contemporary with Epp 1033, 1040 and was intended,
> above all, as a protest against recent unauthorized publications of private
> letters. The truth of some of its statements is open to question, but Erasmus
> apparently trusted that those with access to his original letters would not
> challenge him (cf n3, n7, n8); see P.G. Bietenholz 'Erasmus and the German
> Public, 1518–1520: The Authorized and Unauthorized Circulation of His
> Correspondence' *The Sixteenth Century Journal* 8 Supplement (1977) 61–78.

ERASMUS OF ROTTERDAM TO THE FRIENDLY READER, GREETING

I am sorry to say, dear reader, that another point[1] has arisen on which I have thought it better to issue a warning, even out of season, than that anyone should be misled. It was downright unfriendly that lately, when letters[2] addressed to Reuchlin had already been some time before the public, the printers should without stopping to think have added some letters of mine which were by no means written with a mind to publication; but it is much worse that they should have made some offensive alterations. I will pay what penalty you please if in the original which I wrote to Reuchlin you can find the words 'not ... a Christian but a Christian ape,'[3] to say nothing of the other passages. I know Reuchlin is too sensible a man to let this happen, and have no doubt it was done without his knowledge by those who wish Reuchlin well with more zeal than discretion; and it was they who added those offensive headings[4] 'The Reuchlinists' and 'Erasmus in his masterly works prepared to defend Reuchlin at all points.' I am no 'Reuchlinist.' I belong to no man's party, and detest these factious labels. I am a Christian, and I know what 'Christian' means; I will not tolerate 'Erasmists,' and 'Reuchlinists' is not a word I know. Between me and Reuchlin nothing has passed but the civilities of ordinary friendship,[5] and to become his champion is a thing I have never undertaken, nor does he feel the need of it. His case is a matter for the supreme judge[6] on earth, who has taken upon himself the responsibility of passing final sentence.

I find some lack of wisdom in these people too, who take a private letter written to a friend and publish it, especially when they have altered it as they think best. In the letter in which I replied to Luther, a mention of the bishop of Liège[7] was added; in the same letter as published by I know not who[8] in Basel this is not to be found. In the same way, in a letter[9] from Eck to Jacob of Hoogstraten which was being handed round among a group of people in Brussels[10] some rather ill-tempered reflections upon a certain most illustrious duke had been suppressed; though this seems to me a fault in the right direction. I feel no embarrassment at having answered Luther; if he challenged me, I would answer the Grand Turk. I wish well to the good things in him, not the bad; more accurately, I wish well to Christ, not Luther. If I do answer him, it is to correct him on many points at the same time. I corrected him politely, because I know that to be more effective. On these terms, I imagine, a great many people wish him well, in the sense in which Cyprian wished well to Tertullian,[11] many to Lactantius, even more to Origen.[12] In saying this, I should not wish to do Luther any harm. I am neither prosecuting him nor counsel for the defence nor judge. This is a matter for those to whom the duty has been specially assigned[13] by the supreme pontiff. Not but what I fail to see any cause of scandal in wishing

him well quite apart from that inquiry. He is, as even his enemies allow, a
man of high character; and he has a warmth of heart which although when
exasperated, not without just cause, flared up too far, might yet, if diverted
to other ends, prove a capital instrument in the cause of Christ, who did not   4.
quench the smoking flax[14] but revived it. How unlike those who prefer
destruction to instruction and would rather kill than cure! The laws with all
their severity allow judges even on their oath to do their best for the accused.
Humanity ordains that we wish well to the oppressed.

In saying this, I am very far indeed from being on Luther's side, and as   5(
much averse as any living man from every sort of controversy. As for the
letter[15] which, being imperfectly understood, and a worse interpretation put
upon it, gave rise to these suspicions, Luther himself regrets its publication,
as he declares quite clearly in his last letter[16] to me. I wish therefore that those
who bring books into the world would refrain from taking these liberties,   5!
which lead to strife, and not misuse their skill, which was invented for the
benefit of learning and public morals and not to disturb the peace of our
Christian polity. If it is impossible to restrain their rashness, at least for your
benefit, dear reader, I wished by the evidence of this document to put my
view on record. Farewell.   6(
    From Louvain

1042 / To [Jan van Winckele?]   Louvain, [October–November 1519]

When this letter was first published in the *Epistolae ad diversos*, neither the name
of the person addressed nor the date were given. A wrong date added in 1529
is easily corrected (cf n1, n2). As for the addressee, Henry de Vocht (CTL I
441–3) proposed to identify him with Jan van Winckele (d 1555) who became a
doctor of medicine in 1515 and lived in the family mansion at Louvain which
after his death became a college for law students. In 1549 he set up rules for the
college to be founded, one of which debarred its inmates from any involvement
in the humanities that might be detrimental to their legal studies. In 1517–18
Winckele had entertained Erasmus and Maarten van Dorp for dinner (de Vocht
Literae ad Craneveldium Ep 85) but by the end of 1519 his true priorities may be
gathered from the *Dialogus bilinguium ac trilinguium* (see below 345) and the
Epistola de magistris nostris Lovaniensibus (de Vocht CTL I 585–6; cf Ep 1033
n16, n24). The *Epistola* ridicules Winckele as a prominent opponent of the new
learning, uncultured, conceited, and incompetently attending Jan Briart of
Ath (cf Ep 1029 n2) in his illness.

ERASMUS TO A CERTAIN OPPONENT, GREETING

The way in which you misused your powers of speech before peace[1] was

restored did not escape my notice; but now, since there has been a general
agreement to let the past be forgotten, I hear that every entertainment at
which you assist is regaled by you with the most poisonous attacks on my   5
position, my way of life, and my reputation. Even were I a person who
deserved to have such things said of him, you know very well how
disgraceful it is to seek your revenge in abusive remarks, and that too at the
dinner-table; while you do this, you set a pernicious example to your
company, and especially on a subject of which you know nothing. You   10
would have done better, instead of rattling on like this, to thumb the *Canons*
of Hippocrates, and thus equip yourself with some answers to give to the
patients who consult you. I know the course of your suspicions: they arise
from a failure to understand two letters,[2] and I can easily explain this to
anyone whose brain is sound. But what can you do with those who are   15
raving mad?

But it would take too long to explain this. To be brief, if you refrain from
this poisonous language, you will do a greater service to your reputation. I
have endured a great deal rather than be the cause of any tumult, and now
that peace is restored I mean to cling to it tooth and nail. As for Luther, I 20
neither attack nor defend him. The facts will teach you that this is so. I am
therefore unwilling to become involved in these men's activities, and this I
will prove with true and solid arguments. If then you continue to attack my
reputation with that wanton insolence of yours, beware lest my patience in
its turn may be exhausted, and you may find yourself a thousand years   25
hence a byword in the great catalogue of poisonous toadies, boastful
ruffians, and bad doctors. I hope it may not come to that. Christian principles
suit me better, and I invite you to adopt them. Farewell.

Louvain [1518]

1043 / To Philip of Burgundy   [Louvain, c November 1519]

This dedicatory preface appeared in Erasmus' paraphrase of the shorter
Pauline Epistles, *Paraphrasis in epistolas Pauli ad Timotheum duas, ad Titum unam
et ad Philemonem unam,* first published by Michaël Hillen in Antwerp, late in
1519 (NK *0442), then by Johann Froben in Basel in March 1520, and repeatedly
thereafter.

The paraphrases on the Pauline Epistles began to appear in 1517 and proved
singularly successful (cf Epp 710, 916, 956). The completion of this undertaking, which Erasmus saw as his main project for the winter months of 1519 (cf
line 3 and Epp 1025:23–4, 1053:570–2), was accomplished with this volume
and the paraphrases prefaced with Ep 1062. It can be assumed that this letter
was written between the completion of Erasmus' manuscript and the appear-

ance of the book. Late in 1519 Edward Lee tried unsuccessfully to have Hillen publish his *Apologia* (cf Ep 1037). In Ep 1061:130–4, 716–41 Lee charged that Erasmus prevented the publication by hastily thrusting this paraphrase upon Hillen. Only one incomplete copy of Hillen's edition is known today. In the *Apologia invectivis Lei* (*Opuscula* 286) Erasmus claimed that the paraphrase was only given to Hillen because Dirk Martens, the Louvain printer who had published the earlier paraphrases, was short of journeymen, and that the printing took no more than twelve days. Zwingli (*Werke* vii Ep 113) seems to confirm that a copy had reached Basel before 4 January 1520.

The recipient of this dedication, Philip of Burgundy, prince-bishop of Utrecht, was hardly a model of episcopal virtues after Erasmus' own heart (cf Ep 603:5n). Although he felt a special loyalty to the shepherd of his native diocese (cf line 7 and Ep 1001:10–11), much of this letter may be taken as an admonition that the spiritual side of the episcopal office should not be neglected because of pressing temporal concerns.

ERASMUS OF ROTTERDAM TO THE EXCELLENT PRELATE AND DIS-
TINGUISHED PRINCE OF UTRECHT, PHILIP OF BURGUNDY, GREETING
In these wintry months, my Lord Bishop, though the fields lie bare and barren everywhere, the good corn-land of literature never ceases to bear some kind of crop, nor is midwinter ever so bleak that the harvest-carts of   5
learning cannot come home full. To me it seemed right that some share of this harvest should be set aside for the bishop, as the leader in this sort of husbandry. For when we do our best to aid the business of the Gospel, we in our turn are taking a part of your pastoral burden upon our shoulders. I have done this the more readily because the subject itself invited me to do so; for I   1
have made a paraphrase to explain St Paul's two Epistles to Timothy and one to Titus, to which I have added by way of epilogue the letter he wrote to Philemon, in order not to leave it out in the cold, last as it is in order, albeit on such a different topic. Not but what in St Paul there is nothing that is not proper to a bishop. In the first three he gives a wonderfully vivid picture of a   1
true and really Christian prelate, the gifts that a man should possess who is to be called to such a high and difficult office, and the service he must render to fulfil the task entrusted to him. How difficult it is to be a bishop beyond reproach, how disastrous the effect on society of a shepherd of the Lord's flock who is not genuine appears, to say no more, from this: on no other   2
subject did Paul ever set down his principles with greater emphasis or more anxious thought. How often he repeats the same precept and underlines it, beseeching, urging, appealing to all that is holy, sometimes with winning words and promises, sometimes with threats, sometimes inspiring by his own example or that of Christ.   2

Here is Paul then, so anxious for those whom he had shaped by his own teaching and ordained by the laying-on of his own hands, whose faith and honour he had many ways of knowing intimately: far greater the danger today of entrusting so difficult an office unadvisedly to any man! In olden time each individual city was presided over by its own bishop, and in those 30 same cities only a small fraction professed the religion of Christ. I need not add that in those days Christ's blood, so lately shed, was still fervent in men's hearts and the fire from heaven conferred in baptism still glowed; and now both of these seem, I know not how, to have grown cold in our modern way of life. Thus it was that the bishop ruled a flock that was not only smaller 35 than today, but did his bidding of its own accord. And so it seems to me much harder today to be a faithful bishop and uncorrupted, not only because one man has the care of so many towns, but much more because most bishops, besides spreading the teaching of the Gospel, which is the chief and proper function of a bishop, are further burdened by the administration of their 40 secular authority.

Yet it is wonderful to see how ill Christ and the world agree together, how hard it is for heavenly and earthly cares to meet. It is the hardest thing there is to fill either part, that of a good bishop or of a prince who seeks his people's welfare: what a task it must be for a man torn in both directions so to 45 manage his business as to satisfy the demands of both religion and earthly state, to please your mortal prince without offending that Prince who is immortal, to stand well at court and yet not stand ill in heaven! In olden time the man who took upon himself a bishop's task had forthwith to prepare his spirit to face all the tempests of persecution. I almost think that the 50 tranquillity of our own time, if such it can be called, is more full of dangers than the storms of old.

Yes, things have changed, nor is it possible for the principles which should guide a bishop to be in all ways the same; and we should not condemn out of hand what differs from the pattern of ages past. The 55 cross-currents of human affairs do not always allow a prelate to achieve what he may judge the best result, just as a mariner, however skilled and vigilant, sometimes grasps the wheel in vain when he is carried away in the power of winds and waves. And yet that man will wander less from the true and perfect image of a good bishop, who has Paul's pattern as a target always 60 before his eyes, like an experienced navigator who, though he may be forced to deviate somewhat from his true course, will never take his eyes from the pole-star, so that it may not be his misfortune, as the saying[1] goes, to be the whole wide sky off course. If one cannot keep level with Paul, it is something all the same to follow him as best one can. He who strives for the best will not 65 lack Christ's help; your Highness is his vicegerent, and all mortal endeavour is vain without his help. Farewell.

1519

1044 / From Maarten van Dorp   The Hague, 28 November 1519

Allen based his text of this letter on an early sixteenth-century manuscript copy (Öffentliche Bibliothek of the University of Basel, MS G II 13a ff 46–7) and on the printed text appended to Dorp's *Oratio in praelectionem epistolarum divi Pauli* (Basel: J. Froben March 1520).

Dorp had been annoyed and alarmed by the agitation against him in both Paris and Louvain (cf Ep 1000A introduction and page 331 below). Immediately after Erasmus' reconciliation with the Louvain theologians (cf Ep 1022) he published for the first time his *Oratio* (Antwerp: M. Hillen 27 September 1519; NK 739), which supports a programme of humanistic education. In October, while the peace appeared to be holding, he had left Louvain to visit his aged father at The Hague. In a recent letter to him Erasmus must have written of renewed hostility against himself in Louvain (cf lines 3–6), thus raising in Dorp's mind the spectre that he too might soon be attacked again, and worse than before, as the unsparing German Erasmians prepared to defend their master against Lee and perhaps Hoogstraten (cf lines 67–8; Ep 1083 introduction). He reacted with this candid and warm expression of loyalty to Erasmus, who was evidently glad to follow Dorp's suggestions (cf lines 57–61, 64–7) and arrange for another edition of Dorp's *Oratio* with Johann Froben's press, where it was being printed as early as January (cf BRE Ep 147, Zwingli *Werke* VII Ep 118), and published in time for the spring book fair, this letter having been added. It appears that it soon became known to Luther (cf n16), and in spite of a discreet omission (line 47) in the printed text, it aroused predictable animosity against Dorp at Louvain. Yet, though he regretted its publication (cf BRE Ep 166) Dorp never again faltered in his support of Erasmus; see de Vocht MHL 215–27 and CTL I 444–5.

MAARTEN VAN DORP TO THE EXCELLENT DOCTOR ERASMUS OF
ROTTERDAM, GREETING

I cannot imagine, my most scholarly friend, what has happened to these people[1] to make them turn everything upside down so badly that they cause trouble to several excellent men who have rendered such service both to   5
learning and to Christendom. I promise you, I promise the Lord God, they will never have me as a partner in making such confusion. How much more worthy of a Christian is a sane and straightforward understanding of

everything that sees it all in the most favourable light! Those who do
otherwise are surely guilty of damaging the work of scholars everywhere. I   10
beg you, my dear Erasmus, as leader of the learned world, by the glory of
Christ do not lose heart at the misbehaviour – feeble and misguided as it is –
of certain people who are both few and powerless. Take courage, rather,
from the highly favourable opinions of you and of your learning expressed
by so many distinguished princes and prelates and so many learned men all   15
the world over – opinions that are quite true and quite unfailing.

Here at any rate they are sincerely on your side, they admire the
distinction of your work so much and speak so highly of it, that I doubt
whether any mortal in history has been in the same position, not even Jerome
himself. As God is my witness, dear Erasmus, I am not making this up. Every   20
scholar of standing expresses pleasure at the appearance of my oration,[2] to
see me frankly setting forth what I feel and think without any disguise. That
eminent and at the same time most scholarly of lawyers, Master Nicolaas,[3]
president of Holland and the other provinces, is so much pleased with it that
nothing makes him more cheerful at dinner than prolonged conversation   25
about you, and especially to hear your praises sung; and for this reason he
shows me much attention. Some of the lords of the council do all they can to
earn my gratitude, because they have been told, and have read in my
oration, that I am your sincere supporter. All our lecture rooms,[4] all our
gatherings of learned men and every group of important people – all ring   30
with the praises of Erasmus; among the latter the chief is that eminent,
distinguished, and learned man the heer van Assendelft,[5] who takes a very
special pleasure in what you write and has your books in his hands almost
the whole time, when he has any leisure.

As for me, they are keen here to put gold in my pocket. There is no lack   35
everywhere of excellent men in the religious life who praise you to the skies,
as is right and proper; among whom two in particular have urged me most
keenly to attach myself to you, though there was no need of urging. One is
the warden[6] of Mechelen, a most intelligent man with a great knowledge of
affairs and a capital scholar; next to him, Amandus[7] the Greek and Hebrew   40
scholar, whom I think you know. They are so keen on your pious labours
that they could not be more so if they were their own. In Germany, in
England, in France, think of the thousands of men who support you with
such sincerity that they could not be more devoted to hearth and home. How
mad of me not to have struggled tooth and nail against the growth of any   45
horrible suspicion that I might be the sort of person to stand against a man
like yourself, and take the side of – never mind who etc.[8]

Why did I not make this clear from the beginning? Why did I put it off so

long? My dear Erasmus, I was carried away by some freak of fate; but 'better turn back than hold a course ill-judged.'[9] How thankful I am to have   50
published that oration, and thus made clear to everyone how repugnant I found everything that happened! – for I never approved of what they were trying to do. But this was the point on which I freely confess that I went wrong, dear Erasmus, for I know your kind heart: I ought to have expressed my opinion openly. If this happens again, may it be the death of me, for what   55
little I am worth.

    May I beg you, when you have a suitable opportunity, to mention me[10] somewhere in a friendly way, so that everyone may see that we are in complete agreement; you can do nothing that would give me greater pleasure. Several letters[11] are in existence from you to me, and mine to you; if   60
any of these are fit to be printed, they would serve my purpose. The abbot[12] of Egmond, a holy man whose native goodness makes him hate these disputes, has friendly feelings for you. With him and with everyone I shall not hold back, nor shall I keep the matter to myself. My oration, incompetent and ignorant as it is, I should dearly like to see printed in Basel at the Froben   65
press. If you favour this, it is as good as done, for Rhenanus or Froben can deny you nothing. When you write to More or Pace or Rhenanus or Hutten or Budé, please make kindly mention of your friend van Dorp.

    My father,[13] who is an old man now and nearly eighty, told me to send you his warmest greetings. Perhaps you may not remember how he knows   70
you. He had a delightful conversation with you a little over two years ago in Arras[14] College. Master Jacob Mauritszoon[15] the councillor, who was formerly pensionary of Gouda, and is wholly devoted to you, asks me to send his best wishes. I am in great demand here among the best people, both scholars and men of position. I rarely dine at home, not that I love   75
dinner-parties, but for the sake of the conversation.

    Luther,[16] as I lately wrote and told you, is in high favour here. There is a man[17] well known as a scholar, a gifted mind and a tireless worker and still in the prime of life, who once lived at Louvain with a great reputation for learning, who has written in support of him, expounding and defending   80
everything on a solid basis of Holy Scripture. I have read the book myself, and will bring it with me; that is his own wish. He is a man of high spirit, and rich.

    Please greet Dr de Neve,[18] and ask him to forget troubles of long ago. I am sure that if he knew the whole story he would bear me no resentment.   85
Give my cordial greetings to Berselius and Rescius[19] and the others. Father Jan Koolman,[20] the parson of St Agatha's, a saintly and learned man with an enormous appetite for your books, whom you met at dinner with me in

Louvain, sends you his respects. Farewell, and let me have an answer if you
conveniently can, for I may not yet leave here.   90
    From The Hague, the Monday after St Katharine's 1519

1045 / From Germain de Brie   Paris, [c December] 1519

Germain de Brie first met Erasmus in Italy (cf Ep 212) and remained his friend
when he embarked upon a comfortable ecclesiastical career at the French court.
He wrote Latin verse, and the patriotic stance of one of his poems (cf Ep 1087
n4) was mocked by Thomas More in his epigrams, published in 1518 (cf Ep 620
introduction). Erasmus attempted to forestall a public controversy with Ep 620,
and here now is Brie's long-delayed reaction.

    Together with Ep 620 this letter was printed as an appendix to Brie's
Antimorus (Paris: P. Vidoue for K. Resch 1519; ed and tr in More Y III-2 469–547),
an attack on More in verse followed by copious notes in prose and other topical
material. The date of 1519 in the colophon of the printed edition would seem to
correspond with the date assigned to this letter (cf n1). The copy of the
Antimorus that Brie sent Erasmus together with this letter (cf line 32) may have
been in manuscript or in print. The publication of Brie's entire collection may
have occurred somewhat later as it begins to be noted by the middle of March
1520 (cf Luther w *Briefwechsel* II Ep 265; Zwingli *Werke* VII Ep 124; BRE Ep 159; AK
II Epp 728, 735). For More's reaction see Ep 1087; cf M.-M. de la Garanderie in
Colloquia Erasmiana Turonensia ed J.-C. Margolin (Paris-Toronto 1972) I 359–79.

GERMAIN DE BRIE TO DESIDERIUS ERASMUS, GREETING
Yesterday I happened to visit my friend Budé, as I often do, and he showed
me a volume[1] of your letters recently printed in your part of the world, and in
it a letter from you to me which he said he had just read. Very likely you gave
it to some courier for delivery to me before you handed it to the printer; but at   5
any rate it never reached me, and to Budé at that moment I owe my first sight
of it. I would say that it gave me pleasure, did I not think it unnecessary to
say that separately of any individual thing you write, for your works as a
whole are all popular with your friend Germain, and well live up to your
name.[2]   10
    As concerns Thomas More[3] (for I have a mind to begin now by
answering the argument which you put last in your letter) you say you hear
that I am preparing an attack on him with some sort of pamphlet with teeth in
it, to use your own expression, though it is not unbiased; and since, as you
say, you are equally devoted to both of us, you urge me not to do so. It is   15
expedient, you say, also for the cause of humane studies in general that their
disciples should agree among themselves, now that the enemies of literature

are banding together so unpleasantly. I acknowledge, my dear Erasmus,
your quite exceptional fairness of mind. I acknowledge that your loyalty and
affection for me are something out of the common. I acknowledge the   20
outstanding good will and charity and zeal that you show towards humane
studies and those who pursue them. These things in their own right have
each such force, they carry such weight with me at least, that there can be
absolutely nothing I would not readily do for my Erasmus on the lightest
hint. But may the Muses themselves abandon me when I most need them, if   25
my *Antimorus* (for so I call my little collection aimed at More) was not already
in the printer's hands and a great part of it already struck off; and as
witnesses to this I can cite both Budé and Bérault, to whom I had given a hint
of the publication of the *Antimorus* a few days before. You know them both, I
think, as men of such tried and tested honesty, that I suppose the evidence 30
of either one of them would be enough to prove my point with you.

As for the *Antimorus* itself, of which I am sending you a copy, when you
read it (and I beg you to find time to read it, although I know you devote your
time solely to the reading and writing of things of the very highest class), you
will agree that it is by no means the pamphlet with teeth in it that you expect. 35
It is in fact quite toothless, for though I snap in it, I have no fangs; I am
humorous but not malicious, I poke fun but stop short of personalities, I let
myself go but in moderate language, I rebuke without severity, and play the
teacher without wielding the rod. More has wantonly attacked me with
insults and with imprecations although, as you say, I am unknown to him   40
and, as I maintain, I have done him no wrong; he has aped, no doubt, that
barbarous Cyclops in Homer[4] who, when he saw that Ulysses had already
embarked and could be reached in no other way, expressed his rage by
praying for the destruction of the hero and his companions. By the common
right of reprisal I could arm myself with the same kind of weapons and go   45
down to meet my adversary in the arena. But no: I thought I should gain
much more general approval and indeed show greater modesty if I took
More's abuse as meant for humour, his malice as jesting, his accusations as a
joke, his imprecations as irony, and his curses as common abuse. And I have
done so; whether with success or no, I leave to the judgment of yourself and   50
other readers of my collection. One thing I really do believe, unless my
forecast is quite misleading: that among those who weigh the arguments on
the two sides, favouring neither except on their merits, I shall certainly not
be criticized for replying to More – who challenged me first, although I had
never attacked him in writing or in speech and had no such intention in   55
mind – and for replying in such a way as to point out a thousand thoroughly
discreditable mistakes (which could not be allowed to circulate any longer
without grave damage to their author's reputation and an indelible stigma of

ignorance) in a spirit of friendliness, goodwill, and loyalty, which is what I
am doing.   60

Under this head I do not see how one man could owe another a greater
debt. As far as your judgment goes, my most learned friend, although you
urged me, when the position was no longer open, to suppress my book (thus
making an open declaration how much you desire to see unanimity among
your friends), yet now that it is published you will hardly, I take it, condemn   65
the man responsible for publication, unless you wish to lay down one set of
rules for yourself after publishing your *Apologia*[5] against Lefèvre and
another set for me and my *Antimorus*. I have done in my book exactly what
you did in yours: only when attacked did I defend myself against the enemy,
though I did not fight with the same ferocity as you, not being equipped with   70
the same sort of weapons; for you in your *Apologia* are fully armed and hotly
engaged at close quarters, while in my *Antimorus* I am unarmed and at long
range, and not wholly serious. All the same, your attitude was not
unbecoming for one who played the part of a champion of Christian piety,
and mine in turn might be thought suitable for one who wears what is only a   75
poet's mask. Why, More's position would indeed be privileged, for pity's
sake – it would amount to a dictatorship, if he were allowed to attack others
freely and without a second thought, while they were debarred from
answering back; for after all, especially among us who live in France and not
in his Isle of Never-never,[6] he has authority to sign a letter, but not a   80
death-warrant.

And so, notwithstanding that it was More who struck the first blow
when he deliberately attacked me, a stranger who had done no wrong, and
that it was his abuse of me and no black streak in myself that drove me to take
my part in this tragedy, all the same, now that we have both donned our   85
tragic masks and come on stage and shown that we can both sustain our roles
with might and main, he as challenger and I as defender – he being in any
case, as you say in your letter, a man I ought to know and like – let me not
stand in the way if he thinks it right that all this tragedy, at your instigation
and with you (shall we say?) as producer, should end in comedy; let us clasp   90
hands, and with Erasmus as our *pater patratus*[7] sign a treaty and be joined in
good will on both sides. If he prefers to watch the outcome of the tragedy as it
now is, I equally have no objections to its running through to its last act.
More's acting is not brilliant enough to frighten me off the stage, nor is he
such a doughty fighter that if he prefers to join battle I must refuse to meet   95
him, provided he descends into the arena to do battle in his own armour, not
like Patroclus[8] in the arms of Achilles, and gives me fair warning with a blast
of the trumpet.

As for the second topic in your letter, I can hardly put into words how

delighted I should be if you could be induced to come and live in my native
France, either by the invitation[9] of this king of ours and his most lavish
promises, or by the prospect of the most agreeable society of the many
friends whom you have here – friends of no common and ordinary sort but
distinguished men in high position. They have all been hearing rumours for
some time now that Erasmus is coming to join us, and the summit of their
wishes is that he should at length come in the flesh and be with us in person.
Where you are concerned, most learned Erasmus, I must by all means speak
the truth as one faithful friend to another (in so describing you I do not think
I can be wrong). There is no living man anywhere whose name is better
known, whose reputation is more widely spread among all our devotees of
humane studies, than yours. I myself think that you will do a great wrong
not only to yourself but to all of us, who so eagerly long to behold our
Erasmus and to make him welcome and to talk with him, unless you really
come to us, if not to settle and to live here permanently, at least as a visitor
and an honoured guest (though that you should settle here would be my
choice). As for your host, everyone wishes to be of service to you, and
everyone (as far as I can see) is competing to receive you on your arrival in his
own house; but this one thing I do beg urgently of you with all the emphasis I
can command, that you should stay with me and choose a lodging in my
house, where you will find me so appreciative and so open-handed as a host
that you will be able to count on all that is mine as yours. My fortune may not
be very ample, but it will provide enough for us both: food, clothing,
servants, a horse to ride, and a modest purse besides with money always in
it – to say nothing here of the garden attached to my house, which is so
pretty, I assure you, so delightful, so lovely and pleasant to look upon (a
thing which, as you know, is very highly valued in Paris) that the Muses
themselves, I think, need never tire of haunting it.

In fact it is our long-standing friendship, begun in Venice and
cemented after that in Padua,[10] that makes me invite you in such a familiar,
not to say audacious, fashion formally to become a guest under this humble
roof of mine; especially since I suspect that not a few people are getting ready
gardens worthy of Maecenas and positively Lucullan palaces,[11] in which
you can perform that formality on a much grander and more splendid scale.
But I perceive that Apollo prefers the company of the Muses, unassuming as
it is, to the lavish banquets of Jove, which (if we may believe Homer[12]) he
does not much frequent unless Jove specially invites him, when he wishes to
consult him about some matter touching either Greeks or Trojans, for the
assembled gods are anxious and Juno is already lodging a complaint.

It remains to lodge a mild complaint with you at this point about your
printer who, thinking to make my name more illustrious, printed my other

letter[13] to you and thereby covered me with shame. For to append something written by my humble self to Erasmus' work is to mix roses and wind-flowers[14] or to tag lead onto gold. Not that I accuse him of any malice prepense; but I wonder he could take so little thought for another man's reputation. For though I do not entirely regret that letter, yet, had I thought   145
it would be published, I would have seen to it, I do assure you, that a more elegant and polished piece should have left my hands to go before the public. As it is, since it was your letter to me that gave me my reason for writing this, I thought it best, as yours is already published in your part of the world, to put it in print here too and prefix it to mine, so that, if anyone is   150
brave enough to open what I write, he may read your letter and find mine easier to understand. Farewell, and cherish your affection for me, as I know you do.

Paris, 1519

1046 / To Jan Robbyns   Louvain, 1 December 1519

This letter was published in the *Epistolae ad diversos*. The recent agitation in Louvain against Erasmus and Luther (cf Epp 1033, 1040, 1042) was bound to aggravate the difficulties encountered in the establishment of the Collegium Trilingue, which was made possible by the generous bequest of Jérôme de Busleyden (cf Ep 691 introduction). Jan Robbyns (or Robijns), an intimate friend of the late Busleyden, now acted as a prominent and generally respected patron of the new foundation (cf Epp 805, 1001:20–3). He was now being approached by Erasmus at a moment when its survival seemed to be in jeopardy (cf Ep 1066:70–86).

The trouble had started when Wilhelm Nesen (cf Ep 994 n1) defiantly announced a private lecture course on Pomponius Mela within the framework of the Collegium Trilingue, not having bothered to matriculate in the university or apply for the requisite permission to lecture (*venia legendi*). Official opposition could be taken for granted, and to forestall it Nesen's private pupils seem to have staged a prank during the night of 29 November which could be interpreted as a threat of violence and intimidation against the rector, Jan Calaber. When the senate met at 9 AM on 1 December, it was decided not to tolerate Nesen's irregular lectures, but at the same meeting the *venia legendi* was granted to the Trilingue's new professor of Greek, Rutgerus Rescius. Within hours, however, Rescius was arrested under suspicion of involvement in the prank against the rector. At this moment Erasmus stepped in to save the college its only teacher at the time. Although it took some time for Rescius to receive full restitution for the unjustified arrest (cf Ep 1240), the raise suggested by Erasmus was granted at once by the trustees of the Trilingue, while Nesen

continued his efforts to arrange a lecture course; see Ep 1057; de Vocht CTL I
453–78.

ERASMUS OF ROTTERDAM TO JAN ROBBYNS, DEAN OF MECHELEN,
GREETING

You see before you, Mr Dean, the tragicomedy of human life. What would
you? The play must go on, and cannot go otherwise. Paul[1] rejoices that he is
the prisoner of Jesus Christ. Rutgerus[2] can rejoice that he is the prisoner of   5
the College of the Three Tongues. Conceal it how they please, this college is
treating those men disgracefully. True, these portents promise it, to my
thinking, a glorious future. Such was the birth of the Roman empire; so
began the glorious progress of the Hebrews; such was the birth, the
spreading, the final establishment of the Christian religion. Nothing ever   10
grew great without hard times in the early stages. You will hear the whole
story from Bartholomeus,[3] who was not only an eyewitness of the danger but
close to it. Human affairs being, as they are, rarely black and white, it would
have been like your kindly self to lend at least some support to your
professor even if someone had done wrong. As things are, he being what he   15
is, the most harmless of men, it is still more your duty to stand by him.
Whether a better scholar could be found, I do not know; you could hardly
find a more devoted teacher or one of higher character. He and I dine at the
same table, we talk freely on all subjects over our wine. He has been
provoked in countless ways; they make a dead set at him, for fear of trouble   20
with more masterful men than he is; and yet I never heard him utter an
ill-tempered word.

There's a true Christian spirit for you! A moment ago I compared
Rutgerus to St Paul; he goes one better in this respect, that Paul's
persecutors went wrong because they were estranged from the gospel way   25
of life, while it is the standard-bearers of our Christian doctrine who with
their eyes open and of set purpose plan these things. They have inhibited
Nesen too, who was starting a course on the *Geography* of Pomponius Mela;
had he set up a brothel of some sort in his private house, they would let him
alone. 'Tis a noble university indeed, if you compare it with others, but it   30
deserves a different class of men to be its rulers. In many ways, it seems to
me, Rutgerus deserves to have his salary,[4] which has already been raised by
a certain fraction, put up to eighteen livres. Steps have been taken to find a
Latin professor,[5] which will meet I think with your approval. On the Hebrew
chair[6] I can form no opinion, but I will consult those who no doubt can. May   35
the Lord Jesus preserve your Excellency in good health.

Louvain, 1 December 1519

1047 / From Johannes Thurzo   Wrocław, 1 December 1519

This letter from the bishop of Wrocław was published in the *Epistolae ad diversos*; it answers Ep 943 and is answered in turn by Erasmus with Ep 1137. A manuscript copy, probably taken from Thurzo's rough draft, is preserved at Munich in the collection which is the source of Ep 850. This letter was accompanied by gifts (lines 37–44) which reflect the Thurzo family's involvement in mining and related industrial developments, predominantly in Bohemia and Silesia. The bishop's father, Johannes Thurzo of Bethelenfalva (1437–1508) started a smelting operation in 1469 near Cracow, where the writer of this letter was born. The older Johannes is singled out for praise at the end of the first book of Georgius Agricola's *De re metallica* (Basel: H. Froben 1556) 18. Reinforced by a similar gift from Agricola's friend Matthias Meyner (cf Ep 1122), this connection would finally lead to Erasmus' commendatory letter for Agricola's *Bermannus*, published in 1530; see Ep 2274 and G. Agricola *Ausgewählte Werke* ed Hans Prescher (Berlin 1955–) VIII 76, 827–8.

TO ERASMUS OF ROTTERDAM, GREETING

I cannot set forth, most learned Erasmus, the pleasure your letter gave me, although it took nearly seven months[1] on the way; there was nothing I had more looked forward to, and in the event nothing more welcome could have happened. And so I welcomed it, as the phrase[2] goes, with open arms; I 5
welcomed it and read it, and can never even now have enough of the reading of it. I had often, I confess, been filled with the greatest admiration and delight by the most scholarly writings of Erasmus, that great scholar, addressed to others, when I saw them reproduced in printed letters and in some other man's hand; but now there is no further room for elation and joy, 10
for I have set eyes on the handwriting of the most learned and most highly gifted of men. And so this letter from you will be treasured as a most select and precious present, and will be a perpetual record of your memory which oblivion will never do away.

There is however no reason, most honoured Erasmus, why you should 15
give my letter (my litter, rather) such high praise; I know my own worth, and very gladly keep myself within my own skin.[3] But I might rightly be thought discourteous did I not thank you even for this, and no less rightly should I be thought conceited if I accepted the things you say about me. But you surely must be reckoned most unfair to yourself, when almost the whole world 20
quite rightly loads you with praise, and you indulge in excessive modesty, if I mistake not, in this regard, and are so far from accepting it that you reject it entirely and turn away. Our debt to you is certainly far greater, especially

since it is your championship alone which has restored the splendour of all
the truly liberal disciplines, freed from the darkness of barbarian neglect and   25
squalor, and at the same time the old genuine theology also in its pure form;
and those sacred studies which had been reduced almost to extinction
flourish anew in the whole world as though reborn, with you their parent
and their leader.

As far as I am concerned, your letter and all your works, so full of   30
industry and piety alike, place me under a deep obligation and bring your
memory before me every moment, however true it may be that there is
absolutely nothing of mine in your possession which could call to memory in
return a humble mortal like myself. And so, in order that the zeal of my
singular love and respect for you may be steadily better known, and that the   35
memory of your devoted Thurzo may pass from time to time before your eyes,
I send you a present – not indeed of great value: four timepieces,[4] small glass
vessels which measure the hours as sand gradually runs through them, the
working of which is, I suppose, the modern equivalent of the ancient
water-clock. As you handle these and reverse them, they will be able to   40
remind you of me every hour. I have added four little pieces or shavings of
pure native gold, lately dug up just as you see them, in underground caves
and in the very bowels of the earth within the jurisdiction[5] of my diocese, in
order that the bright living gold may declare you most worthy of immortality;
and with them a cap for your reverend head made of the pelts of Pontic mice   45
which my people, still using the borrowed word, call sables. These skins, as
they nestle soft and comfortable on your head, and protect it with their
soothing warmth, shall serve as evidence or symbols of my affection for you.

I send these to you not because I suppose that you, who are honoured
every day with gifts from kings and powerful princes, are in need of such   50
things and much finer ones, but that the strength of my affection and of the
very deep respect of which I told you before[6] may be made clear to you. I beg
you most sincerely to accept readily and with pleasure the things I have sent,
such as they are. And this I am sure you will do, if you measure my modest
present not by its value but by the warmth of my feelings and the sincerity of   55
my devotion to you. Had you to be given the presents you deserve, scarcely
would the wealth and resources of the whole world, much less the treasures
of any single potentate, be found adequate to what you are worth. For the
rest, dear Erasmus, the sum of my wishes is that you continue, as you have
begun, to give me your affection, and that you abide in health and wealth.   60

From Wrocław, 1 December 1519

Johannes Thurzo, bishop of Wrocław, with my own hand

1048 / To Maarten Lips [Louvain], 1519

Epp 1048–9 and 1052 form a sequence; the first two were evidently written by
Erasmus at Louvain shortly before a planned visit to Antwerp; the third
appears to be a follow-up from Antwerp. All three were copied by Lips onto the
same leaf of his copy-book now at Brussels (cf Ep 1019 introduction); the first
two were published by Erasmus in the *Epistolae ad diversos*. The date of 1519 was
added to both letters in the *Opus epistolarum* of 1529. This date is confirmed by
the arrangement of Lips' copy-book; thus the trip to Antwerp may be either the
one of December (cf Ep 1051), as Allen assumed, or perhaps an earlier one in
August (cf 999 introduction) and closer in time to Ep 955 (cf below n2).

Lips prefaces his copy of this letter with a brief argument, recalling that it had
been delivered to him by Erasmus' secretary Johannes Hovius (cf Ep 867:189n)
and dealt with 'a calamity caused primarily by the theologians, which Erasmus
finally overcame by means of wonderful patience and various skillful devices.'
The last statement may well refer to the 'peace' concluded with the Louvain
theologians in September 1519 (cf Ep 1022), but Lips' argument no doubt was
written at the time he copied Erasmus' letter and he may not have done so until
some weeks after he had received it.

ERASMUS OF ROTTERDAM TO MAARTEN OF BRUSSELS, GREETING
Your letter, dearest brother, duly arrived, but I did not answer it immediately. I had decided to pay you a visit, but I have been prevented by a constant
succession of business. I beg you not to let yourself be tormented by this
melodrama, which is quite dreadful; your resentment can do me no good and 5
can certainly do you harm. Do not give this nonsense a second thought; take
comfort in your studies in theology, and in the theology of Christ, which
delights in good men and makes the best of bad ones.

I think I can get a Hebrew Old Testament[1] in Antwerp. If you have not
changed your mind, I will arrange to buy it; if you have different views, let 10
me know what you would like done.[2] Farewell in the Lord, dearest Maarten.

1049 / To Maarten Lips [Louvain], 1519

Cf Ep 1048 introduction. In his argument to this letter Lips mentions a letter full
of poison sent to the Louvain Dominicans and 'said to have come from the
priory of St Maartensdal' where Lips was a canon. 'Many people suspected
Johannes Fagius, an old man, because he spread around lies about Erasmus in
the manner of ignorant folk.'

ERASMUS OF ROTTERDAM TO MAARTEN OF BRUSSELS, GREETING

Greeting. I am overwhelmed by so much laborious research that, however much I might wish to, I have no leisure to visit you. Johannes Hagius[1] swears he is not the author of that scandalous pamphlet. I suspect that Lee wrote it, or at least provoked its writing, unless my powers of divination are at fault. The question seems to me of no importance, for my conscience is clear; but if I could know for certain who it is, he will find himself made an awful warning to the rest, whoever he is, that tool of Satan. As for you, take comfort in the study of the Scriptures and steer clear of strife, which upsets your peace of mind and cannot make much difference in my own affairs.

I go to Antwerp tomorrow and will buy the Hebrew book, unless you have changed your mind. Farewell, dearest Maarten, my son in years,[2] my brother in our holy calling; be of a good courage, think nothing of the uproar raised by these wretched creatures, and look for strength to Christ in Heaven.

1519
Your devoted friend Erasmus

1050 / To Adrianus Cornelii Barlandus   [Louvain, c December 1519]

This letter was published in the *Epistolae ad diversos*; the year date added in the *Opus epistolarum* is evidently wrong. When Barlandus resigned from the Latin chair of the Collegium Trilingue (cf Ep 1046 n5), Conradus Goclenius was chosen to succeed him, apparently in preference to another candidate (cf Ep 1051) who had had Barlandus' support. Hence the latter's disappointment and Erasmus' admonition to accept Goclenius in good grace. Erasmus too had at first, it seems, supported another candidate, but he thought highly of Goclenius (cf Ep 1018), who was to become a close personal friend and a pillar of the Trilingue. The letter appears to have been written soon after the appointment had been made.

ERASMUS TO ADRIANUS BARLANDUS, GREETING

I am not willing to believe what some people tell me, that you are for some reason indignant with Goclenius and even speak ill of him; this would be most unlike your fairness of mind, nor does he deserve it. He is a very learned man and as honourable as he is learned, who is jealous of no man's reputation. What is more, it is right at this time for all who love humane studies to close their ranks,[1] while the hosts of the Philistines are gathering all around. I am well aware that there are people in this university who from some congenital defect speak ill of others, even of men who have done them no harm, and from whom indeed they have received kindness. They perhaps are incurable; but you, my dear Barlandus, must continue to be what you have always been, and not let yourself be affected by their society. Farewell, and when it suits you, we will talk at greater length.

[1518]

1051 / [To an Unsuccessful Candidate for the Latin Chair]

Antwerp, 7 December [1519]

This letter was published in the *Epistolae ad diversos*; the year date added in the *Opus epistolarum* is wrong. It is clearly addressed to an unsuccessful applicant for the Latin chair at the Collegium Trilingue in succession to Barlandus (cf Epp 1046 n5, 1050 introduction), and evidently not the one supported by Erasmus. Henry de Vocht (in CTL I 488–93) proposed to identify him with Alaard of Amsterdam, who had earlier in the year proposed to lecture on Erasmus' *Ratio verae theologiae* under the auspices of the Trilingue, but had been refused the authority to do so. Alaard was at Louvain at the time and could well have applied for the position, solicited Erasmus' support, and vented his irritation against him on being passed over in favour of Goclenius. Henry de Vocht offers no evidence to show that Alaard was in fact a candidate, but it is true that henceforward Erasmus mentions him with angry contempt. In 1524 he reminded Goclenius of the 'tragoedia Alardica et Paschasiana' of which his correspondent was fully informed (Ep 1437). This was, according to de Vocht, a reference to Alaard's anger, described in this letter, which was shared by Paschasius Berselius, who would have supported Alaard's candidature; cf Ep 1065 n1; see also A.J. Kölker *Alardus Aemstelredamus en Cornelius Crocus* (Nijmegen-Utrecht 1963) 39–45.

ERASMUS TO A CERTAIN LOOSE TALKER, GREETING
I should never have had so a low opinion of you, had you not declared yourself so openly. I told you many times, and it was quite true, that the thing was not in my power and that when you spoke to me about the chair things had already gone some way. Suppose (what is quite false) that the 5
executors[1] had entrusted the choice entirely to my discretion, and that I had passed you over and chosen Goclenius as the better man: what reason was there to rave against me like this, exactly as though I had cut your grandfather's throat? Personally I am not upset by this; it is you I am sorry for. If you had had a chance, I would have done what I ought. I knew that the 10
executors were simply not disposed to take you, even if you had put up another twelve livres[2] of your own money. I did not like to tell you this; what was the point? Believe me, by carrying on like this you are putting many people against you; men like persuasion and not compulsion. No doubt it is behaviour like this which makes the Abbot[3] so niggardly in his dealings with 15
you. I have, I think, never done anything against you before, though I may have done nothing for you. So now I recommend you to have more sense in

future, and for your own good; for there is very little indeed that you can do
to my hurt. Farewell.

Antwerp, eve of the Conception of the BVM [1518]   20

1052 / To Maarten Lips   [Antwerp, 1519]

Cf Ep 1048 introduction. The following argument is given by Lips in his
copy-book: 'He sent me this letter from Antwerp with the complete works of
Chrysostom, inscribing them not, as was his wont, to Brother Maarten but to
the whole college, for I had told him that our subprior needed them passionately. The author to whom he again refers was never discovered.'

Greetings, dearest brother. I have bought the Chrysostom.[1] About the
Hebrew book I will take steps as soon as I can. That Hagius[2] did not put his
name to it is not surprising; for if he had put his name and had been a layman,
his life would be at stake. For the pamphlet is not merely slanderous[3] but
inciting to rebellion. Consider for your part whether there are any   5
arguments with which it can be refuted. Best wishes to you and all yours.

1053 / To Thomas Lupset   Louvain, 13 December 1519

Edward Lee maintained that the publication of his *Annotationes* against
Erasmus (cf Ep 1037) had been cunningly stalled by the latter until after he had
had the time to compose this elaborate letter. Although Erasmus ridiculed Lee's
suggestion by saying that he could write letters such as this in half a day and
that this one was not published until after Lee had sent his book to Paris for
printing (cf *Apologia invectivis Lei: Opuscula* 256, 259), it is clear that Erasmus
was determined not to lose the initiative in his controversy with Lee (cf Ep 998
introduction) and that this letter was printed as soon as it had been written.
According to Lee it was offered for sale at Louvain on c 14 December (cf Ep
1061:739–41). At first it appeared as an appendix to some copies of Dirk
Martens' recent reprint of Erasmus' edition of Cicero's *De officiis* (cf Ep 1013).
Only one copy with that appendix has been found so far; it is in the library of
Eton College (see Robert Birley *The History of Eton College Library*, Eton 1970, 44,
77). Subsequently this letter was reprinted in Froben's *Epistolae aliquot
eruditorum virorum* 29–46 (cf Ep 1083 introduction) and in Erasmus' *Epistolae ad
diversos*.

Although given the form of a personal letter, this text was clearly conceived
as a public defence. Lupset may have been chosen as its addressee in view of
his recent visit to Louvain and because he had close ties to Paris as well as to
Lee's and Erasmus' common friends in England (cf Ep 1026 introduction, n3).
Lee was soon to reply in great detail in Ep 1061.

ERASMUS OF ROTTERDAM TO THOMAS LUPSET, GREETING

A letter from a certain eminent friend[1] of mine, who at the same time is no enemy to Lee, informs me of a widespread rumour in your part of the world – and not only widespread but very widely believed – that I and my friends are responsible for Edward Lee's inability to bring to birth here the attack on me 5 which he has been in labour with for so long now, and to be delivered of his bantling with some printer for a midwife; in fact, that we are frightening the man with threats[2] until he dare not publish what he has written. These reports, part of the proverbial[3] uncertainties of war, ought no longer to surprise me, for one hears them almost daily and should long ago have 10 grown used to them; what I do very much wonder is who the authors of this most shameless of all inventions can be. I cannot be induced to believe that Lee, whatever his qualities as a man, has such effrontery that he can find it in him to maintain this story, for he himself is perfectly well aware that the facts are quite different. I am not so obtusely credulous as to have been convinced 15 by anyone, nor shall I ever be convinced, that Lee intends to suppress in perpetuity those distinguished fruits of his nightly toil over which he has laboured now for several years and which are his hope of immortality and the base he himself chose on which to build his reputation. I knew well enough that he is too good an economist in such things to allow so much 20 labour and lamp-oil to go for nothing. Nor is my sense of smell so defective,[4] far from suspicious as I am and entirely straightforward by nature, that I could not pick up the scent of what he had in mind. Had I been too stupid to detect this, there was no shortage of people to tell me what Lee's first object was, namely that should anything befall me (for we are all mortal) or should 25 some chance remove me to a distant part of the world, that would be the moment when he could safely and (what is more) successfully publish his annotations. 'Sweet is the fruit when the guard's back is turned.'[5]

He knows the truth of the old saying[6] that dead dogs do not bite back. Perhaps too he has read in his Quintilian[7] (for he seems at some stage to have 30 dipped into good literature) that the man who wants to tell lies will find it safest to tell them about the dead. And then he is well aware, urged on though he is by the thirst for glory and reputation, how greatly he stands to profit by this delay. All this time he is collecting from all sources every malicious criticism voiced in discussion-group or drinking-party, all the 35 suggestions of Dominicans or Carmelites,[8] the comments of candidates for the bachelor's degree in divinity (for they were put on to this business[9] by men who afterwards shall not be deprived of their due credit), the nibbling away by licentiates[10] and worthy master doctors, if they find any disposed to be prejudiced against me. And all the time he is on the scent to detect what 40 reply is to come from me or from someone else on my behalf; all the time as he reads he has second thoughts on some things which their author had thought too well of in the first heat of composition; all the time inspiration, or it may be spite, suggests some new topic of malignant invention, for resentment makes men not only eloquent but even resourceful, and, as the satirist[11] has it, indignation sometimes 'rounds off the verse that nature had denied'; while finally even his daily reading contributes something in the way of addenda. Thus it results, of course, that in the end his work, when it comes out, is not only fuller and better documented, but contains fewer errors. He confessed to me himself the last time we met[12] that he had reworked almost the whole thing from top to tail, as they say: he had cut out much which the second edition of my New Testament had rendered superfluous and made many alterations, changing his mind in some places as a result of more careful thought.

Actually, that he should do this, now that he has resolved to go to war, does not greatly surprise nor much annoy me. He is out for his own interest, and maybe the laws of war permit the use of all devices against the man you wish to overwhelm. In one point however I find his wisdom not a little defective: that in the conversation I mentioned, after admitting to me seriously that his whole work was being rewritten, he yet urged me to believe his assurances that he would never publish the book. So his purpose in spending so much effort on rewriting it was, once it was rewritten, to suppress it! The language of truth is not only simple but consistent, and none suffer more often from a slip of memory than those who do not mean what they say. Or maybe this was not a slip of memory, but my own stupidity gave him confidence to suppose that I should believe on the spot something not only so incredible but coming from such a source as himself.

And so there was I, convinced that he would by all means publish what he had written, so strongly convinced that I could not ever be induced to change my mind, even by people whom I normally believe implicitly, and found myself on this one point in disagreement with those with whom I am usually most happy to agree; I knew well how much he would gain and I should lose by delay, and indeed what risks for me and what hopes for him lay in the postponement of his work. Who then would not think my sanity in danger if I took all possible steps to prevent his book from coming into the hands of the public, as they say I did? I always thought and always said the same thing:[13] I wished his work, whatever it might amount to, to be published as soon as possible. If they can produce a single letter in which I take a different view or anyone who has heard me say anything different, I surrender.

But of this I cannot produce a more suitable witness than Lee himself. At our first meeting,[14] soon after I had left Basel, we entered into a discussion, and it was in St Peter's church, in the way that leaders in a war, when peace is not fully established, commonly meet in some neutral place that is safe for both sides. He there boasted that he had marked more than three hundred passages which no one could get round; and so I, to prevent a furious dispute which would be a disgrace to any Christians and particularly to professional theologians, proposed that he should choose one of three alternatives. The first, which was, I said, most akin to the spirit of a Christian and appropriate to our long-standing friendship – for he had declared that, though a new friend, his conduct would be such as to yield to none of my old friends in loyalty and readiness to be of service – the first was to let me see his annotations. For the part of the volume which contained my own annotations was, I told him, printed off but not yet published,[15] and would not be published until the whole work was finished; it was therefore possible to alter a certain number of sheets – not, at this stage, without some pecuniary loss; but my reputation and the convenience of the reading public meant more to me, I told him, than money. And so, if he had pointed out anything of importance, I would mend it, but taking good care at the same time not to purloin another man's credit; I would, I assured him, frankly record, with honourable mention of the name of Lee, the source to which the reader owed this benefit.

This offer, which was so fair that it met with approval even from those whom I then suspected and later discovered to be by no means impartial towards me, he entirely rejected; and I then passed on to my next and inferior alternative. Let us come to a confrontation face to face, compare our two volumes, and settle the question by word of mouth, for thus he need have no misgivings which might make him fear for the safety of his manuscript. When even this did not satisfy him, I proceeded to suggest that he should issue his book at the risk of us both, for no other course remained. As far as he was concerned the book was virtually published already – but not from my point of view; a number of copies had been made, but it was being read solely[16] by the sworn members of his faction, and the rumours spread by him and his supporters were doing me far more harm than the book itself would have done if published, for rumour always exaggerates what it puts about, especially if there is anything bad in it. If he himself was deterred by either the cost or the labour of publication, I told him that I would see the book was printed at my own expense[17] and on my own responsibility. Besides which, if he did not trust me, he could keep a transcript for himself, by which I could be immediately refuted, if I had added, omitted, or altered anything.

That this is what happened, Lee himself, I think, will not attempt to deny. If not, this if nothing else will show that I am not inventing, that Lee once complained to common friends in a letter, when they had already seen a sample of the work and were strongly dissuading him from publication, that he was being challenged to produce it by myself. I always told Dirk of Aalst[18] that if Lee were to hand the manuscript over to him, he should publish it, and would have my approval in doing so. When I discovered that he had approached two printers in Antwerp[19] with a view to publication but without success, it is common knowledge how indignant I was that his resolution should have come to nothing. Shortly afterwards I sent for a printer and urged him with all the force I could to open negotiations; but Lee had changed his mind and had already slipped away. Rumour had it that he had sent the book to Cologne[20] to get it published there. I wrote to two of my friends, telling them to let it be published; only would they please see to it that I got a copy of the printed volume promptly, for Lee's supporters were putting it about that the printing of the book would be so contrived that it should pass from hand to hand among those who disapproved of me, and I should only secure a copy a year later. And I am led by many indications, which I will perhaps adduce on another occasion, to believe that this was true. I can produce witnesses now who heard me undertake to see that Dirk should print the book, so that Lee himself might supervise the proof-correction. Those who wish may ask Lee's brother Wilfred,[21] through whom as a kind of Hermes he sometimes communicated with me, how often I urged him through the medium of his brother to publish. Finally, he was said to have made overtures already to Michaël[22] the printer in Antwerp, and that nothing stood in the way except that he was uncertain how I should take it. I told him in reply to get on with it; I was strongly in favour. This I am able to prove from a letter written in my own hand. And after all this, what brazen effrontery to circulate a perfectly baseless story that I did all I could to prevent the book's publication!

I will now say a few words also on the question of threats,[23] concerning which I marvel not only at their impudence but at their astonishing ingratitude. I had observed that certain people who give me even more enthusiastic support than I could wish had some scheme on foot to attack Lee with outrageous pamphlets and even, if he continued, to go to work with the cudgel[24] as well as the pen. I besought them for all I was worth to do neither, declaring undying hostility to anyone who might for my sake have attempted anything so barbarous and so unworthy of the cause of literature; but I trusted their promises and the sort of men they were so little that I thought I ought also to warn Lee[25] about it, for fear that anything might happen to him, if he were taken off his guard, which might do him harm and at the same time rouse public feeling against devotees of the humanities. For as far as I am concerned, the man does not exist, I think, who after reading what I write or

forming any acquaintance with me is not perfectly convinced that I detest   165
nothing so much as examples of defamatory libel[26] or the use of violence.
And so I looked at it like this: if there was any danger it was friendly to warn
him, and even if there is none it was friendly to be concerned. Nor had I any
doubt that he would take my warning in good part. If he misunderstands my
friendly action, I would rather waste this small exertion of good will than   170
that he should know how great is his debt to me, in this affair at least. Let him
produce the letter[27] I recently wrote him; it will show the straightforward
and friendly spirit in which I warned him, and will show also that I
challenged him to publish his work and did not deter him. In fact, the sole
reason my friends were so angry with him was that he boasted everywhere   175
so insolently about his book and never published it.

Nor have I failed to see the trick Lee has played here. When he was not
yet ready for publication, he tried meanwhile to gain a little reputation by
pretending that he withheld the book to please me. Later, when he was
passionately anxious to publish and thought that he was more or less   180
prepared, he began to protest publicly that he was being challenged to
publish by me, so as not to offend his friends[28] who urged him so hard not to
publish. And so, if you hear of any people after this repeating the same
nonsense, tell them with my compliments that they are either entirely
deluded or shameless liars. In the end, if anyone is still unconvinced by what   185
I say, a test is quite easy. Even now, let Lee hand over his book, and unless I
arrange for it to be printed in Basel or somewhere else, and that with no
expense on his part, let everyone believe that hitherto I have stood in the
way of its publication.

If I firmly reject a manifest falsehood, I will no less frankly confess what   190
is true. It was easy to suspect that offensive attacks of various kinds would
be scattered throughout this work. For one thing, I knew that Lee, whatever
his attitude may be now, undertook this business in an entirely hostile spirit,
as I will prove by the clearest arguments when the case requires. For
another, I pressed him frequently and urged him to tell me why he took such   195
precautions not to let me of all people see the book he had written against
me, although he gave so many people access to it; and at length his reply was
that there were some things in it that would anger me – as though it was not
more offensive if he wrote things about me to other people which he did not
dare show to me in person. And again, the two or three notes which I had   200
succeeded by chance in intercepting[29] showed clearly enough what the rest
of the work would be like. Consequently I told him to make his points with
argument and not scurrility, and with reasons rather than insults, which
would, I said, mean a straightforward task for him in writing and for me in
replying. I should never take offence, I said, if he were to disagree with me in   205

a thousand places; in fact, I should be grateful to have my hard work reinforced by his. If however he mixed insults in with it, it would double both the work and the disadvantages for us both: he would risk acquiring the reputation of a man without decency or ballast, and I should be faced by an unpleasant dilemma. If I answered his insults, I should be thought to resemble him; and if I did not, the majority perhaps would think that I admitted the accusations he had heaped upon me.

I think this policy struck every man of good will as both wise and friendly. And yet my attitude always was that I wanted to see the book, whatever it was like, appear as soon as possible, and would rather suffer anything than the petty triumphs of certain tedious idiots. For I am not as unsympathetic to Lee as some people make out. I know how strong is the urge to win a reputation, how sharp the spur of the desire for fame, how hot is youthful fire,[30] especially in one who has now entered the arena of public opinion for the first time. To what lengths are we not driven by the thirst for an immortal name? – for the story of Erostratus[31] that we read is no fable. He has a nature as eager for glory as naphtha is for flame, and there was no lack of precedents to pour oil, in Horace's phrase,[32] on the live coals.

To say nothing of earlier examples, he saw how much fame at least, if not glory, had lately been secured by Ortwinus Gratius[33] from two or three minor confrontations. He knew the truth of Pindar's saying[34] that it is war wins men renown, and those whom tranquillity keeps dark are brought into the light by discord; nor had he overlooked, I dare say, that Greek proverb:[35] 'In stress of war even Androcleides passes for a general.' He saw clearly that to gain a public reputation as an author is a long and difficult road to glory, not very unlike that road of which Hesiod[36] tells. He detected a different route, shorter even than that recommended by Lucian's fluteplayer[37] to one of his pupils, when he told him to exhibit a sample of his skill to those who were universally regarded as the best fluteplayers of the day, for if he were approved by those whose judgment was most respected by the public, he would soon find himself famous throughout Greece. The way pointed out by that fluteplayer was honourable enough, to be sure; but some people still do not find it short enough. Men prefer a hollow reputation to one that is more solid but must be waited for. He who criticizes another man's writings gets, to begin with, as much of a name in one year as his author has acquired by the labours of many years. And then the critic is commonly thought cleverer than his victim. Last but not least, there are plenty of people to spur him on, to urge the flying steed,[38] to cheer him, to repeat that honey-sweet phrase 'Well done,' to applaud, to rouse him to fresh efforts in mid course, and 'with swelling breath the bulging bottle fill.'[39]

One result of all this is that, even if Lee has written some silly schoolboy things, I shall not give them a hostile reception, provided he does not torment us for too long with his birth pangs, his promises, his boasting, his threats, his constant criticisms, and his subversive attitude to everything. If he has followed my advice and never lost sight of Christian modesty,   250 considering how he himself ought to behave rather than the desires of certain persons who misuse the gifts of others to damage the new growth of liberal studies, he will win quite a warm welcome not only among serious students but even from me as well. For why should I feel it as a disgrace, if in so many thousand passages which I have either emended or explained he   255 detects something which my own eyes had failed to notice as they hurried on to other things, or finds some passages where he thinks he must disagree with me? I did not write my annotations on the footing that all other men must be deprived of their right either to add, if someone is able to find fresh material, or to correct, if I have been under a delusion; for I am not only   260 human but a man of most limited gifts and learning scarcely up to the average. Even had I not stated this myself,[40] nobody ought to think me so arrogant that, while not hesitating in a number of places to disagree with the most approved Fathers, Ambrose for instance and Augustine and Jerome and Cyprian, I lay down the law for everyone else, forbidding them to   265 disagree with me. I now therefore put it on record in a clear and audible voice, first that I wish my own rights in this matter to remain intact, and secondly that, so far from deterring others from this activity, I challenge them and invite them to do likewise.

And it may well be that Lee had read nothing of this. For I remember   270 how in conversation once he urged me seriously to put it on record somewhere in a preface that my principle in editing the New Testament was not to avoid at all costs a departure from the Greek; and when I shortly afterwards replied that I had stated this long ago more than once in my prologues, he said that he skipped the prefaces and hurried on to the   275 business. 'Well,' said I, 'if everyone else did as you do, what purpose would it serve to go on record?'

One claim I think I can make with justice, that no one before me has ever annotated more fully or with more care. To say nothing for the moment of the fact that in this work I do not profess to write a note on everything worth   280 knowing, but only on points affecting the integrity of the text. If anyone takes it into his head to include notes of different kinds, he will not immediately put me in the shade unless he provides a fuller treatment where our subject-matter is the same. And yet such is my zeal for sacred study that I desire to be put in the shade, not merely by Lee but by everyone. The glory of   285 Christ and the general good of those who love sacred literature – these are the objects to which my labours, such as they are, have been devoted; why should I suddenly change, and be grudging to those for whose sake I have endured so many nights of toil? Why indeed should I grudge myself the benefit, if someone is willing at his own expense to enlarge or correct my knowledge? What is there, pray, in this to make Lee angry with me or to prove me unjust to him? If he does not approve my choice of subject-matter, why choose to work in the same field himself? And since the subject is almost entirely dependent on a good knowledge of Greek and Latin, why does he not allow me, who am, I think, a somewhat better scholar in both tongues than he is, the same freedom that he allows himself, when he has newly started[41] Greek and not made, I think, so much progress as yet in Latin that he can disdain to be on the same footing as myself? And then why not allow me freedom in the New Testament, when he takes every licence in the Old,[42] although he has dipped into Hebrew quite lately – the more so as I have at my back the agreement of so many approved copies and the authority of so many orthodox Fathers, while he, apart from copies of the Hebrew text in circulation nowadays and a few dictionaries, has almost nothing to fall back on? Last but not least, why should it not be lawful for me to do with the encouragement and approval of Pope Leo[43] what he takes upon himself on his own authority?

I do not say this because I disapprove of Lee's industry, but to make it clear that neither of us has any reason to be jealous or resentful of the other. Those who contend that it is unlawful to make any change at all in our Vulgate texts are plainly mad, as I have abundantly shown in the *Apologia*[44] prefixed to my New Testament. If there are some things in my work that he does not like, what was the need for this warlike attitude, for all these noisy attacks, these whispered scandals, trumped-up charges, and abusive letters? Did I not personally invite Lee[45] to do me this service before he had touched Greek, or I could suspect that he would do so? I have not the effrontery to disapprove of a man for doing what I urged him to do; but his manner and method of doing it will be approved, I think, by no intelligent man and no man of good will, for in this department Lee was thought to have been unfair even by the man[46] who thinks everything fair that goes against the humanities and against myself.

Had he preferred to take right reason for his guide rather than anger or spite or jealousy or ambition or some other such emotion, he would not have become the leader and the tool of the masters of innuendo who under some malignant star[47] now lord it here; he would have done me no harm and won for himself a reputation at once greater and more truly earned.

In the first place, though it is most difficult to help others and very easy to do them harm, he ought to have laid the foundations of the reputation he seeks in well-doing rather than the reverse. As it is, when they hear the

name of Lee, which was hitherto obscure, strangers will ask, 'What manner
of man is this Lee?' and the reply will be, 'The man who first led a vendetta   330
against Erasmus.' It needs more genius and wins more praise to produce new
work than to try to prove one has genius and a dash of learning at the
expense of other men's books; it is a more distinguished thing to be the
author of some new work than to play the critic Momus-like on the works of
others – though Momus[48] only found fault, he did not indulge in calumny;   335
he was outspoken, but not slanderous. Surely the guest would be
insufferable who, as he sat at a table furnished with much thought and great
expense, deliberately ignored the good things, took merely a taste of every
dish, and if he found something he did not happen to like, roundly damned
it and protested to his host. How much more civilized to invite the host to   340
your own house and give him a rather better dinner!

And so, had he acted openly and with Christian mildness, every
right-thinking man would have approved his efforts. I should have thanked
him myself and joined in the chorus of praise. Had the force of his genius and
the fire of youth swept him into war, the next best thing was to wage war in   345
an honourable fashion: by valour, not trickery; by force, not fraud; in open
field, not by stealth. Those who prepare fire and slaughter and destruction
for their enemies send envoys first to protest, to demand redress, to lay
down the conditions on which, if they are met, they do not refuse to lay
down their arms. But Lee first professes himself to your face a friend second   350
to none and then suddenly becomes an enemy, having suffered no injury
and made no protest. Worse still, to wreak his spite on me, what made him so
friendly with men[49] of whom he previously both spoke and thought in most
unflattering terms? If he denies this, I have evidence at hand to refute him.
Why did he keep silence in front of me and become all boldness and threats   355
once I was far away?[50] Why did he wait for the most suitable moment to do me
harm, knowing that things here were inflamed by a conspiracy of certain
people, and then become the nail that scratched that sore,[51] the noxious
humours that gathered round that boil? And since he saw that evil-speaking
was an endemic disease in our country, why was it this incomparable friend   360
who first set the cauldrons of Dodona[52] sounding, who thought up and
started the noise that by perpetual passage from one to another will make its
way all over the world? Why bring these false charges against my first
edition when he was well aware that I was publishing a new one?

I was absent for that purpose in Basel. The news spread, and it was true   365
enough, that I was ill. Perhaps rumour, as so often happens, exaggerated
and said I was dead.[53] This gave Lee sudden courage, and he filled the whole
of this country and his native England with those famous six hundred
passages. If he did this with no ulterior motive, why did he not let me see on

my return what he boasts of ceaselessly in front of everyone? If he wished to show me the picture of myself (those are his words), why am I the one person not given a chance to read it? If he wrote for himself alone, how comes it that his book is multiplied in so many copies and flits through province after province in the hands of his sworn allies? – and it surprises me to see them so loyal in a campaign of slander, for nowadays one can hardly find loyalty even in an honourable cause. If he wrote it for all to read, why does he not publish it? If he decided to suppress it, why boast of it, as he does, everywhere? Why share it with so many people? And why does he so often take it to pieces and remake it? If what he used to say is true, that there is nothing in it which could call for an answer, why does he not dare to take the risk in even a few passages? How can he now disagree with himself in so many passages? If he has confidence in his book, why devote all his efforts to prevent it falling into my hands? If he does not believe in it, why all this mystification? If he longs to publish it, why does he so anxiously conceal it? Why not make use of the offers so often made him? Why complain to his friends that I challenge him to publish? What means this puzzled inconsistency: 'I will, I won't, I won't, I will'? If he is acting in simplicity and good faith, why does he show his book above all to the men he knows to be no friends of mine – to men, moreover, whose friendship he seeks for no other reason than that they are no friends of mine? Why does he refuse a sight of it only to those he knows to be my true friends? He told me himself, when I asked why he did not give Thomas More access[54] to his book, that More was a true friend of mine. And yet More is a friend to us both, though a fellow-countryman of Lee's as well, which might give him, one would think, an extra claim. He thought it a strong enough reason to refuse him the book, that he was my intimate friend.

But all the time he is enriching and correcting his work. I am not against this; but let him at the same time frankly confess the truth. He ought not to pretend to suppress something to please me, when he postpones it for his own convenience. He ought not to suggest that he is being forced to publish by pressure from me, when he himself longs to do so. And yet all the time he fails to see that while he makes his book bigger he is making the credit it will bring him smaller. If he had published forthwith this book of which everyone had heard quite enough, everyone would have believed that it was all his own work. There is now some danger of a popular outcry that we are confronted with Aesop's crow,[55] decking herself out with other birds' feathers, so that even if his work does prove worth having, only the smallest share of the credit will be paid to him.

And now pray consider, I beg you, how on this point too he does not see where his own interest lies. He is waiting for some chance to remove me from the scene. Can this be right? Does a brave man choose that moment to appear on the field of battle? Will he win an award for bravery? Will men applaud his return in triumph? Has he instead no fear of being thought – and it is a most dishonourable charge – to do battle with the dead? Did any man ever earn credit who won a case by default? But let that be: he has chosen a 415 victory that is safe rather than glorious. But I am afraid that here too he may have got it wrong. I do not doubt that in place of my single self many men[56] will arise who will answer Lee with less mercy than I should have shown him; for though attacked on all sides with so many calumnies, I have not yet let myself be driven from my ancient principle, my determination not to let 420 any man's name be blackened[57] by anything I write, although there has been no lack of books published in which I am criticized with great impertinence.

Other men have invented a new sort of defamatory libel.[58] There are gangs of conspirators who have consigned themselves on oath to the infernal powers if they do not utterly destroy the humanities and classical 425 theology; and they have sworn to hold forth against Erasmus everywhere: at drinking-parties, in markets, in committees, in druggists' shops, in carriages, at the barber's, in the brothels, in public and private classrooms, in university lectures and in sermons, in confidential conversations, in the privacy of the confessional, in bookshops, in the taverns of the poor, in the 430 courts of the rich and in kings' palaces, among superstitious old men and blockheads rich as Midas,[59] to the ignorant public, and to foolish women – through whom like the serpent[60] of old they find a way to deceive their husbands. There is no place they cannot penetrate, no lie they will not tell, to make me, a general benefactor, into an object of general hatred. 435

For this holy purpose they train up their emissaries, who are no less carefully taught how to poison the minds of simple and uneducated people and to establish the kingdom of Satan than Christ's own disciples were taught to preach the kingdom of God. For this truly evangelical purpose they make use for the most part of those evangelical characters[61] to whom the 440 world gives alms as beggars and whom it tolerates as bullies. This I should be very sorry to see distorted into a general criticism of any of the orders; let it fall on those alone who, by their claims to a kind of despotic rule, oppress their good colleagues who are possessed of Christian gentleness. They bring in too as auxiliary forces those who can be hired by a crust of bread to commit 445 any outrage. Whom have they not suborned to act his part in this play? Whose peculiar nature, whose foibles have they not taken advantage of? And the authors of this play are those who dispute with such meticulous care about making good pecuniary loss, nor do they deny that loss of good name is more serious than loss of money. If anyone dares murmur a syllable 450 against sophistical theologians or utter a word about the superstitions of

Carmelites or Dominicans, at once all hell breaks loose. 'Christ's church is in danger,' they cry, and appeal to all the powers, above and below. They themselves, while showing such great malice, such obstinacy, and such a genius for conspiracy in spreading their lies against a man whose object is to do good to all men and to hurt no man fancy themselves religious characters and pocket saints.

Defamatory libel[62] is a capital charge. These men, knowing they have behaved as I describe, have no hesitation in proceeding forthwith with unwashed minds to Christ's most holy table. They think it suffices if they somehow give their faults a respectable name, as though assassins and murderers had any difficulty in somehow justifying their crimes in their own eyes. Let us consider, if you please, how much difference there is between their behaviour and defamatory libel, or homicide for that matter. To begin with, the man who utters a defamatory libel infects with his crime no one but himself; these men make everyone whose tongue they can fill with poison and then use as their tool responsible for other men's disgrace. One writes at his own peril; they shelter behind a screen of sanctity and actually expect to be praised for their misdemeanours. The one man openly avows his hostility to his victim and usually abandons all claim to be believed; these men, earning respect from their costume, sprinkle their poisonous language on an undeserving victim in sacred places, disguised as the teaching of Christ. Besides which, a defamatory libel, even if the author is uncertain, makes definite accusations and can be replied to; which was done, we are told, even by several emperors.[63] When these men spread their calumnies, there are many of them and they are scattered and often concealed; you cannot tell whom to reply to – you feel the wound and cannot locate the man who shot you. If they are ever detected, they have the method of denial[64] at their fingertips, even if they have never learnt rhetoric: I said nothing, that is not what I said, what I said has been wrongly reported.

Indeed, supposing you could detect everything, who could have the law on so many people? Scarcely any libel can be so widely circulated as these men's calumnies, which travel over the world as not even the apostles travelled. No chamber is so private that they do not find the way in; they are present everywhere in the whole world as blood and lymph are omnipresent in the body. One ought to add that a libellous attack can sometimes be excused by necessity,[65] for instance when a despotic ruler must be influenced by fear because it is not safe for any man to rebuke him. These people aim their clamour against someone who is obvious and accessible to all and prepared to give anyone an answer. Nothing is dearer to any man than his own life. And yet to good men honour is dearer even than life, for they can bear to lose their lives but will let no one deprive them of their honour. He therefore who deprives them of it out of deliberate villainy is surely more criminal than an assassin or even a poisoner. The most criminal form of homicide is to carry poison round with you, not in a phial but on your tongue. 495

These attacks have never hitherto been able to make me forget the modesty proper to a Christian, any more than to make me cease to do what I can for learning; and Lee therefore had nothing to fear, even if some of his remarks were impudent or childish. I am not without experience of such things, and think it nobler and even more courageous to bear another man's impertinence than to return it. Not that there is any lack all the time of people who try to taint me with the disease of impudence because I sometimes touch on the common habits of mankind, because I sometimes differ from approved and generally accepted authorities, because I sometimes reject a thing with indignation. If disagreement is an insult, who ever wrote that did not here and there disagree with all the others? If it is insulting to criticize the faults of men in general, why do they describe and advertise in public sermons the mysteries of secret vice? – a thing I have never done. And if I sometimes seem needlessly indignant, it would be right to consider the source of that indignation. Aeneas[66] treated Turnus cruelly, but his cruelty is reckoned to the credit of his tender heart, for it was the belt of the dead Pallas that overcame the mercy that was natural to Aeneas. I saw the saintly Doctors of the church regarded, some of them, as obsolete and out of date, and all in a corrupt, confused, and filthy state. I saw the teaching of the gospel almost overlaid with the petty comments of men, and the gospel texts buried in mistakes as though in brambles and in tares. Of course at this point it was piety, and not a choleric nature, that made me emphatic. No gentle, peaceful voice could rouse the world from such deep lethargy. If I showed indignation here, I do not much regret it. But where do I appear unduly heated when defending myself from an injury affecting me alone? I would rather have a spirit like this than resemble those who are gentle and mild when Christ suffers wrong and are almost beside themselves if you subtract the merest ounce from their income or their reputation. 500 505 510 515 520

I have written all this to you at such length so that by using this letter as a kind of shield you can easily ward off the perfectly shameless nonsense of the people concerned. But will there ever be a limit to these trumped-up charges, will they ever stop them and be ashamed of themselves? When will the hydra-heads of this far too fertile monster cease to renew? What pestilent demon, what fury, what evil genius first inflicted this pest on our studies as Christians? For there simply must, it seems to me, be an element of fate in so widespread an evil. One might think that Alecto,[67] who not long ago was confounding princes and peoples in the impious tumults of war, had now 525 530

turned her attention to the ending of all learning. The war between scholars
now carried on with tongue and pen is almost more disastrous than those
waged hitherto between princes with the sword. And all this time, immortal
god, where is the sisterhood of the Muses? Where are their comrades, the
Graces, in all their simplicity? Nor was it enough, had this pestilence seized
only upon profane learning. It has invaded precisely that literature which
alone could teach us Christian concord and give our minds freedom and
peace from all the tumults of desire. This was the one harbour left us in which
we could take refuge from these waves and storms of human life.

Everyone knows what various ills the whole of human life is heir to.
That we might be able sometimes to recover from them, there lay open before
us the paradise of Holy Scripture. There we could pace slowly at our leisure
through delightful groves. There we could cool our hot and weary breasts
from crystal springs. There we could breathe a freer air; there we could
pluck, from where we pleased, the sweetest fruits of the mind; there we
could gather delightful blossoms with the fingers of the spirit. But how did
that deadly serpent creep in even here, and poison this peaceful happiness
with the venom of discord? Who mixed the deadly aconite with those
health-bringing herbs, fouled those clear springs with poisonous filth, and
spoilt those trees that grew for our salvation with an admixture of Dead Sea
fruit? In place of charity, of modesty, of Christian readiness to think the best
of others, jealousy, spite, anger, strife, and ambition control our studies.
And where meanwhile is that clear eye of which the Gospel speaks,[68] when
jealousy passes judgment? What has become of charity, which strives to do
good even to the wicked, when spite enjoys absolute sway and those who
do good to others receive ill-treatment for the good they have done? What
place is left for sound judgment when anger passes sentence, madness
executes it, rashness urges it on, and all ends in blindness? How can there be
an end of evils while contention links one quarrel to another and out of every
evil breeds fresh evil? How can truth win the day when ambition turns the
sum of things topsy-turvy? Can anything seem right to him who is already
resentful, jealous, or prejudiced when he opens a book, and opens it only to
look for things that he can criticize – indeed, who often forestalls his own
judgment, and damned the book before he read it? I see the whole thing run
by a group of minds banded together, ready for the worst, who have no more
hope of better things than gladiators.

And so I have almost made up my mind, when I have finished my
paraphrases[69] on St Paul, which with Christ's help I hope to do during these
winter months, to make music thereafter for myself and the Muses,[70] or
rather – much more – for Christ. Let anyone else who will descend into the
arena; I think I have fought long enough with this kind of monster. It is

sometimes a good plan to give way before wickedness that has no remedy,   575
for anything one does for wicked men is fruitless and they do still more
damage when roused.

But it is time for me to finish my complaints, although there is no
finishing their madness. One very just complaint I share with you – that
death has removed John Colet,[71] a most sincere friend to me, and to you an   580
exceptional patron, a teacher, almost a father. A true theologian, a
wonderful herald of the gospel teaching – how that man had drunk in the
philosophy of Christ! How greedily he had absorbed the true heart and spirit
of St Paul! And how the purity of his whole life echoed that heavenly
doctrine! How many years he taught the public without fee,[72] another way in   585
which he recalls his beloved St Paul! I never had a conversation with him that
was so trivial or so far from serious that I did not leave him a better man, or at
least a less bad one. All the more, my dear Lupset, is it for you, who spent so
many years in his familiar society, to emulate both his scholarship and his
piety. Farewell.   590

Louvain, St Lucy's day 1519

1054 / To Nicolaus Praepositus Edanus   Louvain, 19 December 1519

This letter was printed in the *Epistolae ad diversos* (dated 31 August 1521 on the
title-page). The addressee has not been identified convincingly: Praepositus
may either be a title or a common surname; Edanus could point to several
locations in the Netherlands and elsewhere. Nor is it really clear that letter and
postscript belong together. Assuming that they do, the postscript would
support an identification proposed by Allen. Jacob Proost (Praepositus) of
Ieper (cf Ep 980: 61–5) was by 1521 openly committed to the cause of Luther's
reformation; deliberately or otherwise, his name in the address may have been
altered. Nicolaas van Broeckhoven (line 12) had been since 1517 the master of
the Latin school at Antwerp. Jacob Proost had been since 1518 prior of the
Augustinian house in the same city. In 1521–2 both were investigated on
account of their religious views and obliged to recant their errors in public.
Little is known about Proost's early life, and no connections with Mainz have
come to light so far.

ERASMUS OF ROTTERDAM TO THE EXCELLENT NICOLAUS
PRAEPOSITUS EDANUS

Honoured sir, I hear from a bookseller in Mainz that a work[1] on the
antiquities of Mainz and its neighbourhood is being printed for him, in
which it is said that there is a mass of masonry worth seeing known as the   5

Emperor Ferdinand I
By Hans Maler
Kunsthistorisches Museum, Vienna

Drusiana. If you have any record of this either in your notes or in your
memory, I beg you earnestly to let me have it. Farewell.

Louvain, 19 December 1519

Erasmus

I hear there is a house empty near the school, and that it lies more or less   10
in your discretion whom it should be let to. With your knowledge of affairs
you are aware how badly housed Nicolaas[2] of 's Hertogenbosch is, and what
a contribution to one's happiness is made by a good house; nor need I
recommend to you a man you all know well. So I beg you, if you can let that
admirable man have it without any inconvenience to yourself, to follow your   15
natural bent, and this kindness will earn my gratitude as well as his. Farewell
once more.

1519

1055 / To Ulrich von Hutten   [Louvain? late 1519]

To show the continuation of friendly relations between Erasmus and Hutten
Allen inserted here an excerpt from Hutten's letter to Philippus Melanchthon,
dated from Mainz, 20 January 1520 (Hutten *Opera* I Ep 150; *Melanchthons
Briefwechsel* I Ep 72). Referring to his forthcoming return to Franz von
Sickingen's castle of Landstuhl, Hutten wrote:

When I am there, I will do what I can for Erasmus as well, who writes me a great
rigmarole on the subject of his rivals. First we must get Ferdinand on our side;
Franz is most anxious to do him some service. After that it will be easy to drive
out the rascals.

Reasonably, Allen assumed that Hutten referred to a missing letter from
Erasmus, contemporary with Ep 1053 and like it concerned with Lee's
activities. Erasmus had promised Hutten another letter at the end of Ep 999,
which had been published in the *Farrago*, and it is unlikely that Hutten's
reaction here was prompted by Erasmus' brief reference to his enemies in that
final paragraph of Ep 999. Allen inclined to connect Hutten's remarks with a
passage in Lee's *Annotationes* (f cc verso; reprinted in *Opuscula* 269–70; cf Ep
1037) where Lee mentioned threatening letters received from Germans who
told him that he would risk his life if he were to go to Paris or Germany (in order
to publish his book). Lee noted Erasmus' alleged explanation that a thrashing
was intended by his cryptic remark in Ep 998:80–1 and further added that some of
the threatening letters had also mentioned a noble and learned young man who
planned to come to Louvain and punish him (cf Ep 999:337, 348–51, 1053:155–7).

Hutten did in fact later take up his pen both to attack Lee (cf Ep 1083 n8) and to reassure Dorp, who was also afraid of Erasmus' German friends (cf Ep 1044 n10). In June 1520 Hutten visited Erasmus in Louvain on his way to Prince Ferdinand in Brussels (cf Ep 986:34–6) and Erasmus' recollection of their conversations are confirmed by Hutten's own remarks here (cf Ep 1114 introduction). In preparation for his trip Hutten dedicated to Ferdinand his *De unitate ecclesiae conservanda* (Mainz: J. Schöffer March 1519), an attack on the papacy (cf Hutten *Opera* 1 Ep 155 and page 47*). Sickingen had served the Hapsburgs during the imperial election and been named to Charles' council in October 1519.

1056 / To Maarten Lips [Louvain, c January 1520?]

This letter is found in Lips' Rotterdam copy-book (cf Ep 1000A introduction); it was also published by Erasmus in the *Epistolae ad diversos* and reprinted in the *Opus epistolarum* of 1529, with the date of 1518 added. Allen assumed that the books accompanying this letter and Ep 1057 were copies of the *Farrago* (cf Ep 1009 introduction), and that Lips might have received his around 1 January 1520 as a New Year's present (cf CWE 5 xi). Since a copy of the preceding edition of Erasmus' correspondence, the *Auctarium*, had been sent to Lips with Ep 897, and no other volume of letters comes to mind whose date of publication would fit the other data given in this letter, Allen's arrangement may tentatively be accepted.

ERASMUS OF ROTTERDAM TO MAARTEN LIPS OF BRUSSELS

If I may send a single letter in answer to two of yours,[1] I am surprised that you alone hear no news of Erasmus, whose name now goes the rounds even in the taverns.[2] I send you a volume of letters as a present. To have a go at Lee would do no good, my dear Maarten, either to you or to myself. Do you think that Christian charity, which embraces all things, must be confined within such narrow bounds that you cannot be friendly with Lee[3] unless you cease to be friends with Erasmus? These rows, which almost seem predestined, are nothing to do with you, for which I count you more fortunate. No, you read the Fathers,[4] to your heart's content.

Do not trouble yourself about my revised proverbs;[5] I have corrected a few places only, and you can easily write them into your copy. The book will appear in perhaps a year's time. Farewell.

[1518]

1057 / To Joost van der Noot   Louvain, 7 January [1520]

This letter was published in the *Epistolae ad diversos*. It is addressed to a young
and well-connected (cf n1) member of the Council of Brabant, Joost van der
Noot (d c 1525). Son of Jan van der Noot, who was between 1500 and 1537
repeatedly alderman and burgomaster of Brussels, Joost had matriculated at
the universities of Louvain in 1510 and Bologna in 1516.

This letter apparently summarized the appeal which Wilhelm Nesen
presented the same day to the Council of Brabant in response to the
university's decision not to allow his lectures (cf Ep 1046 introduction). The
university's case was presented by Erasmus' old adversary, the Carmelite
Nicolaas Baechem (cf Ep 1040 n7) and assisted by a notary. The council
deferred its decision, but after more hearings it upheld the university's case,
thus clearing the way for the university to reaffirm its decision as a general rule
on 23 January; see de Vocht CTL I 460–4; and for Nesen's further moves Epp
1083 introduction, 1088 n4.

ERASMUS OF ROTTERDAM TO THE LEARNED DOCTOR JOOST
VAN DER NOOT, COUNCILLOR OF BRABANT, GREETING
My excellent Joost, if my lord the chancellor,[1] who is as wise as he is eminent,
gives his support in the case before him to academic freedom, he will most
fully carry out the wishes of our sovereign, who beyond doubt wishes his   5
university to be a most flourishing home of liberal studies. Their objection
about a request for permission to lecture is a pure invention, of which many
of them are already ashamed, brazen as they may be in other respects. We
owe the whole business to a small cabal of men satisfied with their own
attainments and more intent on filthy lucre than good letters; they care little   10
how much progress the young men may make, provided they can lord it over
Louvain as they please. Nowhere is there a university whose young men are
better behaved and less disorderly than Louvain at this moment. These
people have long been trading on the students' good nature and treating
these young men of gentle birth almost like bought slaves. But, as the man   15
said to the consul, 'You're no consul to me, if you will not treat me as a
senator.'[2] If there is any sedition or disorder, the responsibility lies with
them, not with the young men. In this business I have neither part nor lot. I
give no lectures and attend none; I take nothing from anybody, and give to
quite a few. But I am deeply concerned all the same by the common cause of   20
university studies. Nesen is a stranger, and not familiar with our language;
all the more reason for supporting a man who is, in any case, learned,
honourable, and modest.

I send you as a present a volume of letters,[3] with which you can while away a few hours when you have the leisure. Farewell, and commend me to my right honourable lord the chancellor.

Louvain, the morrow of Epiphany [1519]

Your sincere friend Erasmus

1058 / To Nicolas Bérault [Louvain, mid December 1519–mid February 1520]

This letter is now missing. Allen inserted the number on the strength of the following passage in Erasmus' *Apologia invectivis Lei* (*Opuscula* 258; cf Ep 1080 introduction):

At length a letter arrives from Paris, from which I learn that the book is being printed there. Immediately I send off someone there too with a letter to Nicolas Bérault, telling him that they must do nothing on that account that might make trouble for any Englishman. My business is with Lee, and Lee only; apart from that I am devoted to the whole nation. Besides which, no one is to sharpen his pen against Lee and attack him with abuse, although I have no doubt that his own book is highly abusive. All they are to do is to see that I get a copy of the book as soon as possible.

The book mentioned is Lee's *Annotationes* (cf Ep 1037). At the earliest the message to Bérault could have been roughly contemporary with Ep 1053, which according to Erasmus was not written and printed until after Lee had sent his *Annotationes* to Paris. At the latest the messenger sent to Paris could have been the carrier of Ep 1066. Erasmus' approach was prompted by Bérault's eagerness to defend Erasmus against his detractors (cf Ep 1000A introduction) and by the potential implications of the controversy between Germain de Brie and Thomas More; cf Epp 1026 n3, 1045.

1059 / To a Member of the Louvain Faculty of Theology [Louvain, c January 1520]

This letter was published in the *Epistolae ad diversos*. It was probably written not long after Briart's death (cf n3) and perhaps addressed to Nicolas Coppin, who had presided at Erasmus' reconciliation with the Louvain theologians of 13 September 1519 (cf Ep 1022; de Vocht CTL I 529) or to Jacobus Latomus, whom Erasmus was coming to consider as a principal opponent (cf Epp 1113:13–15, 1123), or perhaps to another theologian.

ERASMUS OF ROTTERDAM TO A CERTAIN THEOLOGIAN, GREETING

Honoured sir, Homer[1] expresses surprise that mortal men can never have

enough of war, although of all other things they soon have more than they
want; but I think it is still more astonishing that we never have enough of this
civil strife. I hear that renewed efforts are being made against me with great   5
enthusiasm by certain persons I could name, and an enquiry is on foot
against my books;[2] a thing which could never have occurred to them except
in a moment of resentment and desire for revenge. I was hoping that, now
Atensis[3] is dead, the course of our studies would run smooth, and did not
expect that in this department our great Elijah would leave behind him his   10
Elishas.[4] It is time for you to show yourself the man you promised you would
be. In my letters,[5] though they were published before peace was made, there
is nothing to hurt[6] any man's reputation, unless he chooses to identify
himself. Farewell, and have a care for the tranquillity of our studies, by
which you stand to gain more than I do.   15
    Your sincere friend, Erasmus

1060 / To Thomas Wolsey   Louvain, 1 February [1520]

> This letter was published in the *Epistolae ad diversos*. In conjunction with Ep
> 1062 it continues Erasmus' efforts to have Pope Leo x restrain the Louvain
> theologians (lines 48–51). It also contains a first reaction to some recent
> criticism of Erasmus in England (lines 27–35) and, in view of his embattled
> position in Louvain, may be interpreted as an attempt to revive the negotia-
> tions for his permanent settlement there; see lines 3–6.

TO THE MOST REVEREND THOMAS, CARDINAL OF YORK,
FROM ERASMUS OF ROTTERDAM, GREETING
I am now paying a well-deserved penalty for my own unwisdom. If only I
had accepted[1] the generous offers freely made to me by the king's majesty
and by your Eminence, I might now be living a pleasant and gracious life in   5
your country, with scholarly friends around me; and as it is, I am compelled
to struggle with a quarrelsome crew who have no gratitude and no sense of
decency. Some distempers of the body are the work of destiny, and I
perceive that in the same way there are predestined epidemics of the mind,
whatever their source; whether it be the stars,[2] or the effect of different   10
influences on our bodies or, as I tend to think, the Enemy of mankind, who
rejoices in nothing more than in our discords. Who else could have infused
such venom into our studies – even in theology, on which depends the
sound health and honourable estate of the Christian religion? Such are the
spite and bitterness with which nowadays even the theologians everywhere   15
dispute among themselves, so venomous the pamphlets[3] in which they
excoriate one another and the sermons before public audiences in which

they tear one another to shreds, that in my view it might be better to exchange the study-table for the cabbage-patch.[4]

And in this regard none behave more disgracefully than those who profess poverty[5] and yet plan to set themselves up as tyrants. Many leading scholars all over the world[6] express their thanks to me for my New Testament, which has now appeared in two editions, among them several bishops and even the Holy Father himself, Leo, tenth of that name. Yet these men shamelessly blacken my name in front of the public with their seditious clamour before they have even read my book, though I have done them service. Here too some men of that kidney have raised their heads, and in your country I hear tell of a man[7] who protested noisily before a crowded congregation that I wished to correct the Gospel of St John, because in my rendering I had used *sermo* instead of *verbum* – as though St John had written in Latin, and as though the Son of God had not been called *Sermo* rather than *Verbum* before me by Cyprian, Hilary, Jerome,[8] and countless others, or as though *sermo* were not a better equivalent than *verbum* for the Greek word *logos*. Before a learned audience could anything be more foolish? And before the unlettered multitude could anything be more inflammatory? And meanwhile where is the sweet reasonableness of scholarship, of which Jerome[9] speaks? Where is that cheerful exercise in the field of Scripture without risk of hurt? And all this time both parties lose a great part of the good they might be doing. By importing personal prejudice into their preaching, which ought to tell of Christ and nothing else, they lessen their power to rouse the public to religion; and my books are read either by fewer people or with less profit because these men have spoilt the public image of them, which counts always for so much, to such an extent that if one were to read a book by Augustine under the conviction that it was by the heretic Pelagius,[10] one would get the least possible benefit from it.

Your Eminence is the support of liberal studies[11] in your own country, while among us they must still do battle with the defenders of traditional ignorance. How I wish you might find it possible to defend the peace of sacred study not only in Britain but all over the world! And this will easily come about, if your Eminence will write to the pope[12] and urge him to use his authority to suppress this passion for attacking other people: let every man do credit to his own convictions without vilifying those of others, just as St Paul[13] glorifies his own gospel without casting aspersions on the gospel of Peter. If on some points clever men disagree, let there be Christian humility in the discussion, not devilish spite; let argument be the weapon used, and not seditious clamour, so that the winner may leave the field with more credit and the loser with more understanding. Your Highness will do great things and deserve well of our Christian polity if you can find it possible to defend the peace of our studies by your authority, as you are doing now. I have written[14] on this subject at some length to our Holy Father Leo. But how little   60 is there that we weak men can do!

I have completed paraphrases[15] of all the genuine Epistles of St Paul, a work which is destined to live, if I mistake not, and is so fortunate as to have won the approval even of men who can like nothing by Erasmus. I wish it were open to me to set your name[16] like a beacon at the head of my work. But   65 it was finished at long intervals and in more than one campaign, and so I have dedicated different parts to different persons. But I shall try to find something no less destined to endure, which I will dedicate to your Highness; for I am resolved to continue at this work till death, although I feel myself getting slower every day, not so much from age as from the unbroken   70 toil of my researches, or rather, from the weariness of controversy, for in itself the work is enjoyable. My respectful greetings to your Eminence.

Louvain, 1 February [1519]

1061 / From Edward Lee   Louvain, 1 February 1520

This letter was published as the last piece of Lee's volume containing his *Annotationes* and *Apologia* against Erasmus (cf Ep 1037 introduction); its date may well be the anticipated date of publication, since parts of it, at any rate, appear to be written prior to the death of Jan Briart on 8 January 1520 (cf lines 15–21). Basically defensive in its stance, it supplies many details about the tortuous progress of Lee's feud with Erasmus. Lee's recollection of facts and dates appears to be accurate, while in the analysis of these events bias stands against bias. The letter opens with a point-for-point reply to Erasmus' Ep 998, quoting the text of that letter almost completely and verbatim (lines 2–369). Before the examination of Ep 998 is completed (lines 527–85), other texts begin to occupy Lee's attention: Ep 1053, first quoted in lines 370–4 and more consistently from line 611 to the end, and also recent additions to Erasmus' *Colloquia* (lines 374–430). Some further attacks on Lee both by Erasmus and others are mentioned in lines 585–9.

By the time Lee wrote this letter emotions were running high on both sides as each protagonist had some reason for accusing the other of conducting a smear campaign. One can sympathize with Lee, who sensed hypocrisy behind Erasmus' self-righteous assertion of superiority, but one must also note that Lee charged Erasmus repeatedly with defiance of the church and orthodox dogma (lines 267–9, 459–61, 608–9, 848–60, 939–41). Erasmus' sensitivity in this respect was well known (cf Epp 597:37n, 659) and may go some way toward explaining his fierce reactions both before and after this date. For his reply to Lee see Ep 1080 introduction.

EDWARD LEE TO DESIDERIUS ERASMUS, GREETING

I think, Desiderius Erasmus, that the most convenient way to answer the letter[1] from you which was recently printed in Basel and which was on sale in the bookshops before the whole of it had yet reached me will be to take its paragraphs and discuss them sentence by sentence and phrase by phrase, 5 prefixing first your own actual words and then at once adding my answer. In this way I shall preserve the order of your letter, and shall omit very little which has much bearing on the issue. This then is how you begin.

Erasmus That you should differ from me on some points does not greatly distress me, for scholars have always had the right to disagree while 10 remaining friends. But your method of proceeding in this matter will not commend itself, unless I am greatly mistaken, to any sensible person, since even Jan Briart Atensis does not approve it, rightly devoted to you as he is.

Edward If one has the right to disagree while remaining friends, why make all this fuss for no reason whatever except that I disagree with you? As for my 15 method of proceeding not being approved by Atensis either, I do not know what you mean, any more, I think, than he does; for what you pile up against me later in the letter I will deal with when we come to it. When you call Atensis 'rightly devoted to me,' I at least have not put him hitherto sufficiently in my debt by doing him any service to earn even common 20 affection; whereas I owe him a debt, and so do you, for the impartial kindness with which, at the request of us both, he undertook the task of comparing my annotations with your second edition,[2] which he would have completed if you had let him.

Erasmus In all my thousands of notes, full of opinions or suggestions of 25 every kind, it is neither new nor strange if you have detected some mistakes that had escaped me or if you disliked something that I had found acceptable.

Edward Exactly, as you say, neither new nor strange; and I am the more surprised that you, who have not been attacked in any way whatever, pursue 30 me so spitefully.

Erasmus But the way in which you suddenly changed from friend to enemy and attacked me in writing while I was away will commend itself to nobody – and that too when I had done nothing to provoke you, and you had never confronted me while I was present. 35

Edward I am no enemy to Erasmus even now, after so much provocation. For your enemies I have such a hatred that I would exterminate them if I possibly could – by which I mean your mistakes. I never attacked you in writing while you were away. Before you left for Basel to publish the new edition of your work, I had brought my annotations to an end, as nobody 40 knows better than yourself, for you saw them all[3] before you left here. Whether you had done anything to provoke me I leave to the judgment of any fair-minded man who may hereafter read my *Apologia*.[4] And yet my intention was not to give tit for tat, nor is it now. I should have confronted you while you were present, had I had the leisure for such a waste of words; for everyone knows that Erasmus can turn black into white.   45

Erasmus Nor will the way you wrote against the old edition when you knew I was preparing a new one. Nor this circulating of your piece in every convent, especially in those in which you were aware there were people who do not wish me well. Nor this showing of your work solely to those   50 whom you knew to be prejudiced against me, while you could never be induced, even by the influence of Atensis, to give me access to your book – no, not even to produce by word of mouth a single passage with which you had found fault. You have sprinkled poisonous abuse and actual falsehoods up and down your book (so people tell me who have seen it, and the pages I   55 have intercepted bear this out). You boast constantly of the hundreds of passages which you have refuted, and all the time you do not show me a single one. Is this, I ask you, a fair example either of responsibility or of Christian spirit?

Edward I did write against the old edition, that is, I noted down in the old   60 edition what seemed to me to be its faults, which I should not have done unless you yourself had bewitched me with some extraordinary incantation, and more than once, to do so. I had never intended to publish, did you not press for it so much. No monastery in the world, so far as I know, has a copy, with two exceptions.[5] One of these has one on the understanding that it is   65 made available either to no one or to very few people; the other is to keep it for me only, as it does all my possessions, which are there for safe keeping. We are all human, and love our own trifling productions and do not let them perish. I have given access to the book to no one whom I knew to be prejudiced against you or to bear you ill will, indeed, with the sole exception   70 of Atensis and a few copyists, only to those who either are friends of yours or do not know you even by sight. For More and Latimer are your friends, and the bishop of Rochester[6] had the volume with your consent. Nor was there any reason why I ought to be induced by the influence of Atensis or anyone else to hand my book over to you, who had nothing in mind except to lay   75 snares for me. As I have said, my intention was not to publish. Even had I wished to publish, the thing at that stage did not look like a book; there was nothing smoothed or squared up,[7] nothing polished or perfected in the whole work. Had you got the volume into your power, it would not have been open to me afterwards to alter anything; it would in fact have been   80 already in your power to publish my unformed and shapeless work whenever you pleased. You would thus have achieved the object of all your arts: you would have made me a monkey and a byword.

That I shared many of my annotations with you both by word of mouth and in writing[8] is a thing I am greatly astonished that you can have the face to deny, since I have answers in my possession written in your hand. Why should I not have shown them, except for your dislike of well-meant advice? And to that several of your answers[9] will bear witness. To the remainder, which I did not send myself, you were given access by a man[10] who betrayed me; and this will be most clearly proved by a letter from the traitor himself sent to you, but which is now in my hands. But I know why you deny that you ever saw anything. You are particularly anxious not to be thought to have had one jot of help from me. And yet in this regard some passages in your second edition[11] will cry out against you. For at this point I put off my natural modesty, in order both to recognize and reclaim my own material, which you, ungrateful man, do not admit to be mine.

Poisonous abuse I do not use anywhere. If in some places I write with rather more freedom than you would wish, I did this not without precedent, and because the subject-matter demanded it. I do not consider that Christ used abuse, but the language of rebuke, when he calls the Pharisees[12] hypocrites and whited sepulchres, or Paul, when he said to Ananias,[13] '[God] shall smite thee, thou whited wall,' or Polycarp,[14] a disciple of the apostle John, who replied, when asked by Marcion whether he recognized him, 'I recognize the first-born of Satan.' Paul[15] tells us that he who sins in the sight of all men should be rebuked in the sight of all men. And yet I never presume to rebuke you; I tell you openly what I do not like, and in some places I have tried to make you see yourself, because you seemed to me to have forgotten yourself.

As for your accusation of falsehood, it would be mad to tell lies in a book which the world will read. And though you do this yourself, I do not take a precedent from that. What I thought I had arrived at by guesswork only I put forward as a guess and not as certain knowledge. If you find that I have set down a falsehood even in a single passage (for that I have never told a lie I know for certain; but I am not always in such complete control of myself that I might not have let something slip), tell me, and I will withdraw it. At any rate it is a most disgraceful thing to tell lies in public; and I am surprised that you should do it a number of times, being both a theologian and a monk. I have never boasted that I have refuted hundreds of passages.[16] This is your invention, like the rest. I take a precedent for what I have done from Holy Scripture. If thy brother hath sinned against thee, correct him between thyself and him. If he will not hear thee, bring two or three witnesses. If he will not hear them, tell it to the church.[17] This order I have strictly observed, so that now, having vainly tried the first two methods, I am obliged to adopt the third, and shall tell the church.

Erasmus If you wish to be useful to the public, why not publish?   125

Edward Would that I might have the good fortune to be able to be useful! That at least is what I would wish. But though I wished it and attempted it, I have twice been prevented[18] by you, who now urge me to publish. First, you interrupted the business when the type was already set for the first press; and then you put such a spell on the second printer, with whom I later came   130 to an agreement, that although in our first conversation on the subject he had seemed to want the book, later, when you gave him your paraphrase on Timothy,[19] he would not accept any reasonable proposals, not even those which he previously offered of his own accord. If you so greatly desired the publication of my annotations, why, when you knew that I had begun to   135 treat with this printer and had indeed already agreed on certain points, did you butt in with your paraphrase – and that too though he was a printer with whom you previously had no familiar dealings, to whom indeed they say you were previously somewhat hostile because he had printed and published the dialogue of Dr Jacobus Latomus?[20] If you took such a lively   140 interest in my book, why did you twice close the printing-houses against me? I had definitely decided to spare no expense to get it published; and I fancy you must have spared none to get it rejected, for I cannot think the printers are so careless of their own advantage that they would be willing to forgo so much profit without any recompense.   145

Erasmus If you wish to put me right, why am I the one person not allowed to see it?

Edward I put you right? – you who put everyone right in your masterful way, and are quite capable, as they say, of pecking the crows' eyes[21] out.

Erasmus If you wrote for your own benefit, why has your book such a wide   150 circulation?

Edward Not at all: I wrote for your benefit rather than my own. I get no advantage out of it, except that for the daily labour of more than six months I am most spitefully traduced by you. How much advantage you have got, your second edition will indicate; how much more it might have been, the   155 reader will decide. My book does not have a wide circulation: those who saw it before publication are not twenty in the whole world, and those who had copies outside my own hands are not so much as four.

Erasmus If you are diffident about your work, why advertise it everywhere? If confident, why so anxious that no one should read it who is not prejudiced   160 against me?

Edward I leave the book to the reader's judgment. I am not entirely diffident about it, yet I have not sufficient self-confidence, nor do I value the work highly enough, to advertise it everywhere. Hitherto I have never been too pleased with myself to be willing to undergo other men's criticism; and if you had done the same, we should not now be going through this sorry business.

Erasmus In this way, while you attack me before an audience which is committed on oath to your way of thinking and hostile to me, you make me no better and you make them worse.

Edward I do not traduce you before an audience who are committed to me on oath to be hostile to you. Atensis, though he had my book, was a friend of yours; but when I found you resistant to criticism, I recalled the book from him. The bishop of Rochester[22] is neither committed on oath to me nor hostile to you. The abbot of Winchcombe[23] wishes all men well. I think he has never seen you; and he at least is an admirer of great minds and of humane letters. My friend the prior of St Mary Overey[24] lets no one see it. Whether you have been made better by my labours, that is, have profited by them, the reader must decide. At least I have made no one worse; no one, that is, thinks less well of you than you deserve. If when I differ from you I am right, why should not scholars agree with me? If when I differ I am wrong, I am not such a Suffenus[25] that I would have anyone agree with me against you. I shall always think it a gain to be taught something.

Erasmus Have you considered meanwhile what effect this will have on the reputation which you pursue with so much clamour? If you had published your work immediately, we should all have admired the prodigious fertility of your brain, which in a few short months had devoured so much Hebrew and Greek that in your judgment Erasmus knew no Greek and Jerome no Hebrew – if indeed it is Jerome's version, as you always add out of respect, for fear you seem to underrate Jerome. Why, they tell me that three days after your first steps in Hebrew you had much fault to find with Reuchlin, and some even with Capito.

Edward Had I thirsted for glory, the shortest road to it would have been not to disagree with you but to agree with you, as in the play:[26] 'He says yes; I say yes. He says no; I say no.' This is what you, as a dispenser of immortality, promised me in our first conversation and again afterwards more than once: that you would make my name immortal if I helped you in this work. I thought this meant 'if I frankly disagreed when the facts warranted it'; you on the other hand meant 'if I cringed, if I admired whatever you said and never tried to do anything.' I stupidly got this wrong; otherwise I should now have been on your list for immortality.

It would indeed be prodigious, if I have been able after a few months to make such progress that I have been able to judge that these words are or are

not in the Greek, which is all I presume to do. But that little seems a great deal
too much to you, because I point out so often that your note belies the   205
meaning of your text; whether from carelessness or on purpose is for others
to judge.

I never thought Erasmus knew little Greek; he knows as much Greek as
I would willingly purchase with all I possess. But there is no reason to take it
amiss if there are those who put certain people ahead of you or at least on the   210
same level. Nor do I claim for myself the right to judge; but that is what some
persons think. Nor shall I fight to the death about this.

Nor did I ever say that Jerome knew no Hebrew. I should be plainly
mad to say anything of the sort. At any rate I will not deny that I said to you
long ago, when we were talking about various things in St Peter's[27] church at   215
Louvain, that the psalter sung in church seemed to me in places to be a whole
world away from the Hebrew original, and I could not sufficiently wonder
whether it could be Jerome's. If I said anything wrong, let me be put right by
a Hebrew scholar, and I surrender. And what a Christian spirit this shows,
to take a remark which was neither foolish nor arrogant and mix it in with   220
your calumnies! If I wanted to get tit for tat, do you suppose you never said
anything thoughtless in my private ear that you would be sorry to have
spread abroad?

When you say on the authority of some persons unknown ('they tell
me' are your words) that three days after I began to learn Hebrew I had much   225
fault to find with Reuchlin and much with Capito, I wonder how anyone
could be so utterly shameless as to tell you that, a thing which almost
everyone who sees me every day knows to be a lie. I to find fault with
Reuchlin and Capito? Could anything in the world be further from my
judgment than to find fault with my Hebrew teachers, for whom I cannot   230
show sufficient respect? – one of them[28] being the father of the Hebrew
language among Christians, the other[29] the most successful compiler of a
Hebrew grammar, who so generously passed on the rudiments and so
skilfully reduced them to order, that I need nothing further. One of them, if I
were looking for a perfectly accomplished scholar, I should perhaps place a   235
little higher than anyone else; in the other I often admire that fertile genius
which has enabled him to combine with the most exalted (I mean, sacred)
studies an uncommon skill in the three tongues.

But you find it easy to do what you do always. This is a theme on which
you dwell continually, to make me unpopular with all learned men. Twice[30]   240
now you have depicted me as an enemy of the three tongues, though I am
anything but that; now you accuse me of attacks on great scholars, though
nothing could be further from the truth. I appeal to the evidence of those I
live with. Is this the way by which you wish to be thought to teach me the

duty of a Christian, indulging even in trumped-up charges to make my name   24
offensive to the learned? Where is this pattern of a responsible man or a good
Christian, my excellent Erasmus? If I intend to bring definite charges against
you, I shall bring unquestionable evidence for what I say, or else I give in. I
shall produce the letters and notes in which you have answered me, and
some other evidence perhaps which cannot be gainsaid. I do not wish hints   25
and guesses, if I produce any, to be given more weight than the names
themselves deserve. My case against you will not be based on false
accusations or stories that cannot be checked.

Erasmus Yes, it might well have happened: the Holy Father, in admiration
of your almost godlike brain, might have placed the wand of office in your   25
hands and set you up as censor of the whole world, so that no book would be
published or read without the approval of Edward Lee, the modern
Aristarchus of the whole realm of literature.

Edward Thus you are pleased to make fun of me, as you habitually do. I,
being well aware that I am a nobody, do not think myself worthy of the   26
honour of being among the pope's advisers. I know 'how scant the gear I
have at home.'[31] But everyone knows that you assumed for yourself long
ago, of your own accord, this office of being the Aristarchus of the whole
realm of literature, sparing neither ancients nor moderns: you pass judgment
on all men with a kind of absolute *ex cathedra* authority; you damn even   26
things you have hardly dipped into; you tear up by the roots the opinions of
our forefathers and do not allow even the decrees of the church to remain
inviolate; you appear to others besides myself to give superficial support to
the ravings of heretics; you claim a special jurisdiction over theology; you
despise everyone beside yourself, as I have experienced in respect of certain   27
persons who are, if I mistake not, more learned in theology than you are
yourself. Am I mad enough to aim at that position, when you fill it like this
already? I have always had a respect for scholars. I have never despised the
most trifling work, whoever the author. Your work at least I do not despise,
even if I sometimes disagree with it. Your zeal in this field I have never   27
disapproved of. The only thing I feel the need of in you is a little more
diligence and modesty, and maybe in some passages rather better judgment.
It would have been better to do nothing than to do it confusedly and in a
hurry[32] and half asleep. You were writing a work for the world at large, and a
work full of peril unless you could prove equal to it, so that it was almost   28
wicked not to have all eyes on the watch, not only your own but other
people's.

Erasmus As it is, many people say you are keeping close your famous
annotations with intent to publish them after my death, hoping to win your

case by default; and a barren victory it will be, if there is no opponent to give   285
you a game.

Edward I have no quarrel with your shade; as far as I am concerned, when
God wills and when the fit moment comes for your salvation, may it rest in
peace. At any rate I could never wish for your death; rather do I pray to God
and the heavenly powers that you may live many years to serve liberal   290
studies, provided you are willing to be the sort of man demanded by our
generation and by your Christian duty and your double status.[33]

Erasmus Others maintain that in the mean time you are on the look-out for
complaints from all quarters, so that your book will be nothing but a
patchwork of other people's malicious criticisms, of which only a very small   295
portion will be your own work.

Edward If anyone can recognize his stolen plumage in my annotations, he is
welcome to claim it back. I have not picked up one single passage from any of
the theologians. If this is not so, let them know me for a liar. Nor do I think
my annotations so brilliant that there will be much competition for them.   300

Erasmus There will then be the risk that instead of the honour and glory for
which you hoped you may get as little credit as Latomus did for his dreary
dialogue, over which they say a whole battalion of divines wore themselves
out.

Edward As I hope for the unbiased judgment of scholars, credit is not what I   305
hope to get from this, except perhaps in so far as I have tried to be of use. You
are now pressing me to try my luck. I know that some men will approve my
side of the case, and others yours. It may be that neither of us will win much
honour and glory out of this contest. My lot will be less unhappy than yours,
because I do not expect great good luck; though my arguments ought to gain   310
something in the eyes of unbiased judges from the fact that I am dragged
unwillingly into the arena.

Erasmus No doubt you are very well pleased just now with what you write;
but do not suppose that it will please everyone when it is exposed to the light
of day.   315

Edward It will be a happy day for me if it does please me later; and it will do
so if it pleases the learned world. Thus far at least it gives me no pleasure. It
would be foolish to forecast the verdict, when one writes for the whole
world.

Erasmus Young as you are, I can forgive the desire to shine that drives you   320
on; but that you should choose this devious path to glory, you who wish to
be thought not only a theologian and an upright man but something of a
saint into the bargain – this all posterity will disapprove of, though perhaps
you win applause from some people now.

Edward I am not moved by the thirst for glory, and of this Erasmus is a   32°
proper witness, who offered me immortal glory[34] unasked, and I did not
accept it or even thank him for it. I only wish I were an upright man! Why you
should call me something of a saint I do not know, unless it irritates you that I
say what they call hours of the divine office every day; the rest of the day as a
rule I spend at home on my own business and in reading. I offer none of the   33°
external signs of sanctity, nor have I ever had the ambition to be called a
saint. Surely it will be enough for me as long as I live if I am a Christian. O
how I wish I were! For the name of true Christian covers many things I do not
find in myself. And yet I shall try to be one day what I ought to be always.
Erasmus You have been acting this absurd part for nearly two years, and   33
you enjoy it so much that it seems you will still act it tc your dying day.
Edward Not at all; it was Erasmus acted it, for Lee has done nothing at all
unless provoked to it by Erasmus. How I wish your eyes could have seen
into my heart! – that you might see with what reluctance, each time that you
struck, I abandoned the studies I had planned, in order to answer to your   34°
wishes. When I was plunged in quiet, counting myself happy that I could
enjoy the ease that meant so much to me and, as I thought, was likely to
remain unbroken, a sudden arrow from your quiver struck me, expecting
nothing and full of the thoughts of peace, and this happened four times[35] –
an arrow designed to rouse not me alone but my friends, and to breed   34°
universal confusion, so that for a long time now, with Erasmus to give the
lead, there has been no subject of conversation in Louvain and hardly any
among my native English, except Lee. If only you did not enjoy the action of
this play so much more than I do! Things would never have reached this
pitch of tumult. Nor do I mean to act my part in it to my dying day. Now that   35°
your ambition is fulfilled to publish my ignorance to the world, you may find
after this that you are telling your tale in a deaf man's ear. Had you allowed
me, I should perhaps by now have got somewhere in Greek and Hebrew
studies. Unhappy indeed am I, that I am dogged by such a reason for being
so often torn away from the leisure that I love to enter this odious arena – I   35°
who have never before learnt to fight, and now have to fight against you,
who are the most bellicose and most skilful warrior of them all.
Erasmus All the same, I do not resent you to the extent of wishing that
anyone should be one hair's breadth less well disposed towards you on my
account, let alone of hoping that some serious misfortune should befall you.   36°
But the trouble has now spread all over the world.
Edward It is marvellous how you dare say this, who have done all you can to
rouse the whole learned world against me and have even poisoned the
minds of several friends in England.[36] In fact you are now sowing tares

between me and certain men of the highest character and learning; but I trust 365
that with their usual wisdom they will turn a deaf ear to these incantations of
yours. And what more serious misfortune could you hope to happen to
anyone than that you should blacken his name everywhere? – which you are
now trying to do to me by every means in your power. What you say here is
not unlike what you say somewhere[37] so sanctimoniously about yourself, 370
that you do not think the man exists who after reading what you write or
forming any acquaintance with you is not perfectly convinced that you
detest nothing so much as examples of defamatory libel or the use of
violence. This is admirably borne out by those two most virulent and
baseless accusations which you vomit in my direction in your *Colloquia*,[38] 375
which you published as a young man, but not long ago in your old age, with
all a young man's indiscretion, you crowned with this crazy supplement and
almost nothing else. I will copy here the actual conversations:

AUGUSTINE Suppose I bring two or three shadows, I mean unwanted 380
guests?
CHRISTIAN By all means, only don't bring dark shadows.
AUGUSTINE Suppose I bring N?
CHRISTIAN What, the famous Scotist?[39]
AUGUSTINE Scotus himself, if you like. 385
CHRISTIAN Right: he shall be admitted. But he must leave behind at home his
sophistical riddling, his trumpery talk, his innuendoes, his arrogance, his
bitterness, his sardonic laugh,[40] his thrasonical[41] bragging, and his self-
satisfaction.
AUGUSTINE He'll find it easier to leave his tail[42] behind. 390

Let the world recognize in these words, if it can, its great theologian, its
moral critic, its monk, its paragon of humility, that famous modesty so
simple-hearted and at the same time so typical of Erasmus, that typical
seriousness and decency and sense of honour. If this book is not defamatory, 395
what is?

But where in all this, you say, do we hear your name? There is plenty
here from which it is easy to guess who your target is. 'But, my good man,
what have you to do with tails?' Are you not ashamed of such a childish and
ridiculous libel on the English people, who have treated you by no means 400
badly? – and when you are well aware that the facts are actually quite
different? If this is your famous humility, show it towards other people;
humility like this is no use to me. I should slightly prefer being the target of
other men's selfishness to being buttered up by humility like this. Impu-

dence itself could have said nothing more impudent. Did I wish to compete   40
with you in this kind of humility, I have no lack of opportunity, and even less
lack of material.

But I will not follow your example. I will not stray outside my brief, for
the subject of my contention with you is not vulgar abuse but holy things.
Not, however, that I am short of resources with which to overcome your   41
bitter attacks and those of your friends. I shall simply despise them; why
should it make a scrap of difference[43] to me if Erasmus' humility towards a
noisy ruffian who attacks someone with a torrent of raving words is by now
almost proverbial? Besides which, your false accusations lack all probability,
for everyone knows by experience that the language of hatred falls far short   41
of the truth. And yet some people have found a more honourable excuse for
you, that you are carried away by your own words.

I should by now be ashamed to produce another of your trumped-up
charges – it is so foul and disgusting, stinking as it does of the privy – were it
not that it provides a second specimen of Erasmus' famous modesty. It runs   420
like this:[44]

AUGUSTINE What useful purpose do these vacuous studies serve?
CHRISTIAN They can be used for wiping the buttocks, and are fit for
wrapping mackerel and the like.   42
AUGUSTINE For my part, I know a man whose tongue I would rather divert to
such a task.
CHRISTIAN I on the other hand know someone by whose tongue it would be as
risky to be wiped as by aconite leaves.
AUGUSTINE He really deserves then to eat aconite, the rapscalleon.[45]   430

I ask you, Erasmus, are these words worthy of you? Are they worthy of a
man who wishes, like you, to be thought a theologian and the world's great
critic? Could one say anything filthier, more revolting, more poisonous? Is
there a noisy ruffian, a buffoon, a low comedian, the keeper of a privy who   43
could have voided anything so foul on anyone? Not to mention other things
which you ought not to have held in such contempt, at least you should have
remembered the priesthood we both share, and it should have prevented
you as the Lord's anointed from so disgustingly befouling one who is the
Lord's anointed no less than you.   440

But I pity you too much to take any pleasure in a more serious
counter-attack, for on your own showing you betray yourself and give a
lively picture of yourself in your own true colours. Far be it from me to
behave in a way that has always been foreign to my character and to libel a
man in public. For when you accuse me so often of poisonous malice, this at   445

least comes from giving your suspicions too much play, with no sure
evidence or proof. On the contrary, you cannot produce a single witness
who ever heard me utter a single careless word in criticism of you except on
the topic of this dispute over your New Testament and in defending myself
against your calumnies. Christ,[46] rejecting a calumny, answered that he had   450
not a devil, and Paul opposed Peter to his face because he did not walk in the
right path.[47] Why may I not use these as precedents, at one point for
rejecting calumny, at another for frankly correcting a brother who has gone
astray? If I have offended you in so doing, the fault is not mine but yours,
who do not allow fair treatment to be meted out to you, while never ceasing   455
to behave most unfairly yourself. Suppose that in the course of establishing
my innocence the heat of the moment drove me a little further than was just:
this was not so serious that it could be set right only by the widespread
publication of the most impudent and mendacious accusations. There is one
thing at which I remember you protested, my accusing you in a letter to a   460
friend of malignant attacks on Holy Scripture; and this I do not wholly deny
nor am I quite certain that I wrote as you say I did. It may be that I blurted out
something rather too unguarded to somone I know[48] who was no true friend
but disguised as one – your friend not mine – who even betrayed me to you.
This man, being over-anxious to please both sides, told me some things he   465
had heard partly from you and partly from your friends which I did not much
like, and as I had not much leisure in which to reply and yet he was very keen
that I should answer, I may well have let fall some hasty remarks in a fit of
indignation.

But be it so; never mind. Even if I wrote something of the sort to other   470
friends as well, after the way you had already maligned me in a number of
passages this is still not of such capital importance, for my business now is to
prove this.[49] Unless I succeed in proving it, I have lost my case. Nor do I stray
outside my brief if I did say this. But tell me: do you find me such a
mountebank, such a man of straw, changing every moment to something   475
fresh, so much attracted to every novelty and roaming the world like a
second Ulysses, that you have to call me a rapscalleon,[50] changing the last
vowel but one to make a closer allusion to my own name? Your generosity at
least made me smile when I first read this – the way you adorn me with all
your own distinguished qualities until you leave hardly anything for   480
yourself. I could turn this against you more aptly if I so wished, but I shall not
do so, nor is there any great need for it. Erasmus is a well-known figure. And
what a taste it gives one of your modesty when in letters[51] to friends you call
me in one place a venomous little serpent, in another a monster rather than a
man, in another a past master of innuendo! And how entirely irrelevant,   485
except that you must find a target everywhere for your poisonous spittle, is

the passage where you call me a little creature, pale and skinny! And all this without a qualm! If I were to let myself briefly play the fool like you, I am a match for you in stature, and it is truer to say that I look down upon you, while you are somewhat more stoutly built[52] than I. But as for being pale and skinny, our lot is very much the same, except for what you have added by more obstinate studies and also by being not a little older than I am myself.

But now it occurs to me why you are so pleased with yourself. Some people call you the great Erasmus. I wish you joy of the title. Some even Erasmus the supreme. I go along with them too to this extent, that if I am only a contemptible little creature in your eyes, in mine you can be an Atlas, who is supposed to carry the sky on his shoulders though in fact he does nothing of the kind. But how redolent of your Christian spirit and of that charity for which Erasmus is so famous, that in a passage in your *Farrago* of letters lately published in Basel you should write to the bishop of Rochester[53] first of all that I seem to you to have a natural gift for the purveying of slander, and then 'If I had on my conscience even the least part of all his malignant slanders, I would not dare approach Christ's table'! Slanders, slanders, slanders – it is your favourite word,[54] which you use more often than any other. Why have you forgotten the boast you make in another context,[55] that your writings have made no one blacker by a single hair? Do I emerge no blacker from all this, at least if you had your way, after these strenuous efforts to blacken my reputation? Could you accuse me of anything more godless than of daring to approach Christ's table while I am still unclean and have so many slanders on my conscience, thereby making myself guilty of the body and blood of the Lord? At any rate, if I am not blackened, this will have been due to no restraint on your part but to the common sense of your readers, who take nothing on trust from an authority like you. But who art thou, O man, that judgest another man's servant, who stands or falls[56] to his own master? Judge not,[57] that thou mayest not be judged.

At this point I could if I wished get my teeth into you in my turn, but I restrain myself. I simply should not have said what I have said already, except with the object of drawing a kind of sketch of that restraint of which you are so greatly proud, to stop you from winning a reputation on the basis of bare words to which your acts by no means correspond. But when you say[58] that the trouble has now spread all over the world, it is your letters and your friends' letters and not mine that are responsible. I have written about this commotion to no one except to some friends in England[59] whom we both share, nor are there many of them. You, who have friends wherever you please, have spread this rumour wherever you please, and with no proper regard for the truth.

Erasmus[60] And you are aware of the uncontrollable energy of the Germans and their violence of character. But among them I have supporters in plenty more keen than I could wish. Letters from me have restrained some of them from writing, and I shall continue to urge restraint as far as I can. But some of them, I hear, are threatening more violent measures, and if anything of the sort should happen (which God forbid), not only should I be unable to remedy your trouble but, to judge by the way people now put two and two together, some of the blame would fall on my own head. I hope we shall see nothing of the sort, but I fear that something may happen. If nothing results, it was friendly of me to be anxious; and if something does result, it was friendly to warn you, so that, if you think fit, you may take such steps to counter the trouble as you in your wisdom may think best.

Edward I cannot readily be induced to believe that the German soldiery take all this to heart; they have nothing to do with a bath.[61] But the scholars of Germany are honourable men, as I can gauge from the leading position they now hold in the world of learning, and nothing is harder to imagine than that they should rush into some base and criminal behaviour. I would not readily ascribe such infamy to the learned men of my native England as you do to the Germans. On the contrary, whatever you may say, I am convinced that German scholars are men who never allow their emotions to decide and in any question affecting the world of learning do not seek an answer with drawn swords. If things reach the stage of an appeal to force of arms, Erasmus is welcome, as far as I am concerned, to sit as sole judge on his professorial throne and give us what rules he pleases with impunity. I have not learnt to do battle with the sword. And yet I only wish I might be accounted worthy to fall by the sword in so godly a cause! If they threaten to publish more violent attacks, who stirred them up to attack me except you, who will say anything that can damage me? Is any man such a brute that he flies into a rage of his own accord with no reason to provoke him? Or rather, what is there so serious that it can have aroused them? In fact, even supposing all your assaults on me in this letter, which are as false as they are virulent, were true, surely there is nothing here so criminal that it can be avenged by nothing but the sword? Evidently, if there is truth in the threats you utter obliquely as though under cover of someone else, you have said worse things of me in idle talk than what you write. For your written charges are too slight to move any man of sense to take up the cudgels.[62]

And where now is that Christian bosom of yours that breathes nothing but endless charity and reticence and all that is friendly and straightforward? Do these words give you so much self-satisfaction? When you lay down the principles of Christianity, is this on the basis that if you are able to sketch them in words you are free to attempt any criminal deeds, and that the man who plans a crime is in no danger if he can make others responsible who are maybe quite innocent? No no, this will not do: either show yourself the man you so often give yourself out to be or take off the mask and let the world 570 see your true self. This is a serious discussion about Holy Scripture, and you, who wish to be thought on other occasions a patron of peace, how can you mix it up with swords and staves? I myself am a man of no account and may be no loss; but you should consider in advance what the church of God must suffer if through your influence a precedent finds its way in, whenever a 575 difference of opinion arises about Scripture, of appealing to assassins to decide it. And I certainly believe that posterity will regard the name of Erasmus as a plague and as a pestilence in time to come and an object of execration; for you will do more harm to posterity than, even were I to die, you will to me.   580

     And do not have such faith in your powers of deception as to think that if anything happens to me on this account you will be able to wriggle out of the infamy of the deed, even though you swear by all things sacred and profane. If a clandestine attack is made on me, Erasmus is undoubtedly the person responsible. How well you have restrained your pen is shown by 585 your *Apologia*[63] addressed to Jacobus Latomus, by the dialogue of the trilinguals,[64] by the libellous posters[65] fixed to the church doors in Louvain, and not least by the volume of your letters lately published by the house of Froben[66] and your letter to Lupset.[67] I am not such a fool as not to be well aware of these deceptive tricks of yours. You are active in everything and do 590 not wish to seem so. You are an enemy and you wear the mask of a friend. You act your part as though your audience were stocks and stones, and think yourself the only man who can put across conjuring tricks of which no one apart from you will be aware. If only you really were the man you wish to be thought! In that case there would be no difference of views between you 595 and me. The church would be a happier and more peaceful scene. If you go on as you have begun, stirring up all these disorders in the literary field if anyone is not on your side, or giving others a precedent to do the same, what then? I only hope I may be wrong in my foreboding that the time will come when Holy Church must suffer grievously from this party strife. I am many 600 years younger than you, and if I wished to preach you a sermon you would perhaps think nothing of it. Let Paul[68] be your teacher; learn from him to endure anything rather than that the church of God should be made to stumble because of you, and if you follow Paul as your master, you will choose what is best not only for yourself but for the church. And I, whom I 605 dare say you take to be your sworn enemy, shall pray God constantly to inspire you with a spirit of sound judgment and of peace, in which you may learn to know yourself and to discipline your intelligence for Christ's service

to the building up of the church and not its destruction, so that in this way
you may earn true and solid glory from both God and men.   610
    But now, since it gives no one pleasure to waste such precious time on
such a worthless kind of controversy, which will be no credit to either of us
and tedious for any god-fearing reader, I will take certain paragraphs in the
letter to Lupset,[69] which was intended to prejudice the public mind before
my book appeared, and refute them, but without citing your actual words as   615
I did for your earlier letter.[70] And as you go to great efforts to persuade your
reader that you put no obstacles in the way of the publication of my book,
you force me to repeat from the egg, as the phrase goes, what I have often
said before, and set it out openly and at greater length.
    In the first place then I assert with confidence that you did interfere   620
with the publication of my book. The relevant facts are these. When the
printer[71] already had the type of the first forme ready for the press, he told
me that he did not dare proceed, because the work contained an attack on
you; and on the day before, in the evening, your servant[72] was seen by one of
mine going into the printing-house. Then, when I asked his partners in the   625
morning what Erasmus' servant was doing there the evening before, one of
the two replied that he had gathered from the master printer that the man
had been there and had spoken to him, but he himself did not know what
had been said. I went straight off to the printer and asked him, for I
suspected at any rate that something was afoot, and my business had gone   630
very slowly. The printer, not content merely to deny that your servant had
been with him, swore to it as well. I had already had my doubts whether the
man could be trusted. However, I said nothing and turned it over in my
mind, and foresaw what in fact happened. Another hour had hardly passed
when he roundly refused to go on with the job. Later, he proved willing to   635
renew our agreement, but on pretty unfair terms; for having promised, when
he wanted the work, to give me thirty free copies, he now tried to stipulate
that I must take two hundred from him at my own expense. Even so, I should
have accepted this condition had I not already been in doubt whether I could
trust the man. For you may well believe that I had not failed to detect what   640
you yourself were aiming at, namely that the quires should be shown you
treacherously by the printer as they came off the press, so that you would be
free, if the matter were very urgent, to stop him in mid-career from going any
further; or if by any chance you were to let the work go forward, you might
have secured a delay sufficient to have allowed you to write an answer in the   645
interval, so that your reply too might be published simultaneously with my
own work.
    You confessed to me yourself, with a half smile, that even had the

printer gone straight ahead the business would have had to be prolonged all
the same into a third month, while he had agreed with me that the book   6
should be on sale in three weeks. Hence it is clear enough that you had laid a
plot against me. Nor is there any lack of people who think that the first sheet
was printed secretly and taken for you to see. And two things make me
believe this was so. One is that after the printer had withdrawn from his
agreement, when I told him to unlock the type and distribute it into the cases 6
without more ado with a member of my household as a witness (for this was
another trick which at that time I had myself foreseen), he was unwilling to
do so, though otherwise there was no adequate reason why he should
refuse, unless the object was to print the quire secretly and show it
treacherously to you. Another was that one particular member of your   6
household repeated one particular comment on that first quire in the hearing
of one of my own people. Moreover the printer himself pleaded this excuse,
that one of his partners wanted to show you the sheets secretly the moment
they came off the press, and that was why he had withdrawn from the
contract, that he might not be tainted with the discredit of this when another 6
man was guilty. And yet, whatever lies he may tell now, it is certain that he
planned this treachery himself; only it was you who put him up to it.

    There is another point. Later on, in a certain conversation between us
in St Peter's[73] church in Louvain, when I had said that I should not have
given the book to a printer unless you had told me yourself that you would   6
be very glad to see this, you flatly denied that you had ever said so. But
unless the rumour could be suppressed, you said you would rather the book
were not suppressed but published. But I can now produce a fact more
reliable than any evidence. I could give you the name of a man[74] to whom you
said that you were now sorry that you had hindered the publication of the   6
book. Yet I could believe anything sooner than that the man concerned
should invent anything to your discredit; for he is one of the people who
revere you.

    Once this man had refused the business, I next tried Hillen; and he
seemed almost eager for the job and said that Wednesday[75] would be a good   6
day to start work. Scarcely an hour elapsed and he changed his mind,
undoubtedly because you and your supporters had either bribed him or
frightened him with threats. And yet you make a great parade of having been
sorry that the business should come to nothing, and of having sent for the
printer soon afterwards and arranged with him to make a new agreement;   6
but it was I, you say, who now changed my mind and withdrew. How can
you tell such shameless lies without flinching! After the rejection of my work
at ten o'clock on the Saturday morning, I stayed in Antwerp the whole of
Saturday and the whole of Sunday until seven on Monday morning, and all

that time no one came near me. In fact, to make sure that I did not return   690
without your knowing you kept a careful eye on my movements, and
followed my coach in the next one from Mechelen as far as Louvain; and even
so you were not satisfied, but to make sure I was in the coach you got down
from yours and peered into mine, which my servants saw you do and told me
afterwards, for at that moment I was busy with something else. This is well   695
known to that one-eyed Pieter[76] of yours, who is always singing your
praises, and who was in your company at the time. I change my mind and
withdraw! Far from it: I was bitterly disappointed that I had returned home
having done nothing; for the rumour had already got around that I was
planning to publish my book, so that the rejection put me to shame. Had not   700
More's letter[77] forewarned me when I was already making new plans I
should not have given way like this. Did you not admit to me yourself that
when you heard that Hillen also had changed his mind, you said: 'That
settles it. There are no printers here besides those two who have Greek
type'?   705

   Again, on the second occasion, who was responsible for the failure of
my approach to Hillen? You arranged things in such a way that every day a
new sheet was shown you secretly, and you could have had the book
thrown out of the press at your own sweet will whenever you pleased, so
that in this way I was at your mercy and likely to lose my labour and lamp-oil   710
at a hint from you. As for your saying that when Hillen was doubtful in what
spirit you would take it if he printed my book, you told him in reply to get on
with it because you strongly approved his doing so, I know people who
were assured by you that in reply you said you had no wish to stop his doing
so nor did you encourage him to do so. This reply showed that you had not   715
made up your mind but were more inclined to think that he should not. But
to show more clearly that this was what you felt, you promptly sent him your
paraphrase[78] on the Epistles to Timothy and Titus, though in any case you
knew that I had already made an agreement with him, as at this point you
freely admit. And so you are not very consistent, or rather, you openly give   720
yourself away. If you had been so keen to see my book published, you ought
not to have intervened with anything else that would stop the business
going forward.

   But who is such a blockhead as not to see clearly how cunningly you
dealt with this problem? Once you had arrived in Antwerp, immediately   725
after my agreement,[79] the printer, who had previously been ready to start on
my book from one hour to the next, put the thing off until twelve days before
Christmas, which was about six weeks after the appointed day. Who can fail
to see, especially if he looks at the outcome, that this long delay was
arranged for your benefit, to give you time both to finish your paraphrases   730

and to put together and publish this letter[80] of yours as a means of filling
everyone's mind with prejudice by your trickery and falsehoods? You knew
of course that this would be greatly to your advantage, because the man who
makes the first protest generally gets a more respectful hearing than he
deserves. And yet I did not fail to send my brother[81] to Antwerp on the day   7:
agreed on. As soon as Hillen saw him, he said he had your paraphrases on
his hands. Afterwards however, after consulting your supporters, as is
generally agreed (for you were already in Louvain, probably putting
together this letter), he named for the start of the work the precise day[82] on
which this letter to Lupset first issued from Dirk's[83] press in Louvain and was   74
put on sale. And so it is clear even to a blind man that this delay had no other
object except to enable you, before my book was in the press, to dazzle
everybody with this new story – which you meant to force on the reader like
an oracle while he still knew no facts – and to seem at the same time to be
urging me to publish my work, as though you hoped by this to convince your   74
readers that you did not hinder the publication of a work which you are so
intensely anxious to see published.

Relying on these magic arts and your famous skill with the pen you
have promised yourself that you can convince anybody; but maybe it is only
stupid people and those who do not look far enough beneath the surface.   75
Me you will never convince, though you may think me stupid. For you make
a great parade, as though you could force me to adopt your opinion on any
subject, being yourself of course well aware that the facts are quite different,
while I am not aware of this. In fact, you are well aware that things are quite
different from what you say; and even those who are in your counsels are   75
well aware in their hearts, though they say nothing, and condemn you, you
may be quite certain, as a liar. And there is no lack of those who think the fact
that last summer some of your supporters barred me[84] from Germany and
Paris, if I wished to have a thought for my own safety, points in the same
direction: it was to stop my book being printed there, for in this country, as   76
you knew well, you had closed all the printing-houses against me.

This is the chief point, the main head of that letter; and I think I have cut
its head off. Now for the rest of it. You never said a single word to me about
Dirk,[85] although apart from that there was no hope that he, who was always
your sworn vassal, could be properly trusted in any business of mine. I never   76
said I had marked three hundred[86] passages which no one could get round. I
may have said there were some things to which a good answer would not be
easy. When you recount the offers you made[87] to me, you include some
points of which I never heard. The fairest proposal of all you do not mention,
which was that we should both agree to submit the problem to Dr Johannes   77
Atensis as arbitrator, nor the further point that you had evaded his decision

by a subterfuge.[88] Nor do you say a word about the enforced idleness to which you had reduced me. Why not? Because all these things tell against you, as can be seen at greater length in my *Apologia*. To put it in a nutshell, that this happened as you say[89] it did, Lee does very much deny. 775

That I was challenged by you to publish, I do not dispute. And yet, slippery customer that you are, your efforts all seemed aimed in another direction. Had you permitted, the world would long since have had my book. For when you say[90] my supporters were putting it about that the printing of the book would be contrived so that it should pass from hand to 780 hand among those who disapproved of you and you should only secure a copy a year later, is anyone crazy enough to believe you when you say that? Was there ever a printer who does not make the books he publishes available to everyone and with all eagerness? And I had fully made up my mind (there are people who can vouch for this) to send you the book as soon as it was 785 printed and copies should have reached me. But the idea of sending the book to Cologne had never entered my head. I did not enter on this business with any hostile intent. I have never acted more straightforwardly in anything, and that remains true down to this day. That I am estranged from you is your fault, not mine. All the same, I never was your enemy, nor am I as yet. 790

One thing I never remember saying to you is that when I first had your New Testament in my hands I skipped the prefaces[91] and hurried on to the business. And another thing too that I flatly deny having said is that I had cut out much[92] which the second edition of your New Testament had already rendered superfluous, a book which at that time, the time of that last 795 conversation between us, I had not even seen, or, if I had seen it, I had not yet compared it with my annotations. Nor is there any reason why you should accuse me of a slip of memory[93] because I said that I had rewritten my work and also that the time would never come for me to publish the book. One of these statements I made in March, when with your agreement I was to 800 send the book to the bishop of Rochester;[94] and at that date your second edition was not yet on sale. The other I made after that, in July, after getting letters from many friends urging us to agree. This was a concession I was willing to make to the wishes of my friends. And at that time I clearly bore in mind what I said, provided my lord of Rochester was willing to act as 805 arbitrator and you gave me no further provocation to publish.

Nothing here has been prompted by any but the most honourable motives, and God knows this is true; he also knows how much I have loathed this dispute and how greatly I enjoyed my old freedom to spend my time on Greek and Hebrew. You have interrupted this so many times with no 810 provocation on my side but, I can only suppose, in hopes that great credit for yourself or some major disaster for me will result from this conflict, or even, it

may be, because you say one thing and mean another. For I also had had to
cope with the rumours which were afoot, the blame for which is yours and
not mine. I on my side have merely defended my own cause against false   8₁
accusations; you on yours have never relaxed, in front of children, laymen,
coachmen – for I understand you uttered a lot of nonsense in a hired carriage
among other places; so that in all this it is you, not I, who are the bronze
cauldron from Dodona,[95] for the noise you make is everywhere and never
stops, and you have not been silent for a moment since the day when at your   8₂
instigation I first started on this line of work. The last thing, of course, that
you can tolerate is advice from a friend, especially if he is a simple soul whose
advice comes from the heart, as it should from those whose friendship is
sincere.

When however you make me out to have such a thirst for glory[96] that I   8₃
am willing to earn it either by crime or impudence – for you equate me with
Herostratus and with someone called Ortwinus Gratius – you seem to me to
contradict yourself by making me at the same moment both eager for glory
and perfectly mad. Obviously I should be worse than mad if, when I had a
reputation waiting for me, as you promised me I would have, and could   8₃
secure it so easily just by shutting my eyes to your errors and playing the
toady, I tried to acquire one by another route which is not only toilsome and
full of pitfalls but in many respects highly perilous. The reputation you offer
was mine for the asking, if I wished; I was to be universally acclaimed as 'Lee,
the friend of Erasmus and the Muses and of all polite literature.' Anything to   8₃
be hoped for from the uncertainties of this dispute will come belatedly in any
case, bringing little satisfaction because so much risk and trouble is
associated with it, and little permanence because it will always be exposed to
the yapping of so many Erasmian curs. But your modesty is such that you
always give me credit for something peculiar to yourself. It is you who, in   84
order to earn a reputation, arm yourself with a kind of censor's rod[97] and
pass judgment on everyone, not yielding before Antiquity; you who wish to
be thought to see further in your sole person than all those great and wise
champions of Holy Church could ever see. While if I sometimes protest
against you in your sole person and the various pressures you bring to bear   84
on me, though I may use more freedom than you would wish, it is never more
than is your due.

You pay what I have done the compliment of comparing me with an
incendiary. An impartial judge might well consider which of us two more
resembles an incendiary, I who attempt with pious zeal to liberate the   8₅
Scriptures and the doctrines of the church from foul aspersions (and would
that I could prove as equal to the task as I could wish!) or you who cast so
many aspersions on them, who take pains to have texts befouled by

heretics[98] spread through the world, with the risk that the true and genuine
reading too may sometimes be corrupted, who even seem more than once to   855
take up the cause of heretics, so that you in particular, if anyone, appear to
set fire, not like Herostratus to the temple of a goddess made with hands, but
to the church of Jesus Christ which he redeemed with his own blood,
following the example maybe of Arius[99] and other plagues. And this is fire of
a sort that can hardly be extinguished, if you go on as you have begun.   860

The subject you took up I have never disapproved of. Nor have I ever
claimed that in Greek and Latin I could, as the phrase goes, unloose the
latchet[100] of your shoes. Nor would I wish in any case to be your equal,
unless I possessed other qualities besides which are denied you. What skill I
may have with the pen I am now trying to discover for the first time, and I feel   865
I have none. And yet for better or worse I must stammer away when thus
spurred on by you. You allow yourself more liberties in the New Testament
than I would myself in the Old; for in the New you point out what you do not
like in order to instruct your reader, while I merely put together a volume of
notes[101] to aid my failing memory, like one who still crawls rather than walks.   870
For it will not be found easy to make progress in the Hebrew Bible without
stumbling unless you have first collected the roots of Hebrew words. This is
all my work amounts to – to help the memory, not to impart instruction. I can
at least say that had these troubles permitted I should somehow by now have
brought the business to a conclusion.   875

And how straightforward, how modest, how Christian is the spirit in
which you attempt to sow tares among the brethren by saying[102] that to
wreak my spite on you I have become so friendly with men of whom
previously I both spoke and thought in most unflattering terms! I have no
doubt that those you allude to have too much sense to believe such an   880
authority as you. I have always respected this order;[103] but of any close
friendship between us there has been no evidence hitherto. Apart from two
or three, maybe, I can hardly greet any of them up to now by name, nor have I
ever had much to do with them. I never provoked one of them to attack you –
let them brand me as a liar if I ever did so – nor have I ever spoken or thought   885
of them with less respect than they deserve.

You tell a libellous story[104] that when a rumour spread that you had
died in Basel, I at last had a favourable opportunity, as I supposed, and filled
the whole of this country and my native England with those famous six
hundred passages. That rumour never reached me. After your return from   890
Basel, when you were lying sick with some illness, I know not what, in the
house of Dirk[105] of Aalst, I remember once hearing from that Jew, Matthaeus
Adrianus, that your life was almost despaired of. May I never enjoy good
health myself if my immediate reaction was not that I should be extremely

sorry if that were true, for your death would be a great loss to humane &
learning.

It would be monstrous of me if I had boasted of collecting six hundred
passages,[106] when the book had already been with Atensis for something
like two or three months, so that he could give you access to my annotations
if you wished. And so, apart from the bad impression I should have made on $
Atensis of being a man who could not be relied on, you would have detected
with your own eyes how unreliable I was. If the whole of this country and
my native England was filled with copies, one of two things must follow:
either you had no friends either here or in England while I was well supplied
with friends as loyal as Achates,[107] or your desire to have the book was a $
mere figment and you had no wish to see it, while I provided a way for you to
have it by spreading it so widely. How could they possibly have escaped you
and your friends for so long if they had been so widely put about? On this
point no one with a spark of intelligence could believe you; and from this we
can measure how reliable you are elsewhere. $

Another tale of the same kidney is your saying[108] that I refused a sight
of them only to those I knew to be your true friends, and that when you
asked why I did not give a certain person access to my book, I replied that he
was a true friend of yours. In Louvain, none of the theologians apart from
Atensis saw it; and he was then your friend, nor do I think he has yet become $
an enemy. As for the scribes who had made copies, I am not sure whose side
they are on, except that I know one of them secretly let you see[109] my
annotations. In England three friends of yours saw them, the bishop of
Rochester, More, and Latimer; among your enemies, as far as I know, they
were seen by absolutely no one. Apart from these I am not aware that four $
people in England of any description saw them. And when you say I replied
that I did not show a certain person the book because he was your friend, I
flatly deny that I said any such thing. It is strange that you do not name the
person concerned. But this, like everything else, is a device to secure your
reader's confidence; and I hope that, now you have been shown up so often, $
you will not deceive him again.

Such is the answer I have been forced to make to two letters of yours
beyond what I had ever expected. I had supposed that my *Apologia* embraced
a full and proper response to your calumnies, sufficient to dissolve them all
completely, and now these two letters bring a number of new charges $
against me which appear more concrete because they are set out with your
many rhetorical tricks; and so it seemed prudent not to pass over them, for
fear I might seem to admit them. If I have answered some of them at
unnecessary length, making too much of my opportunity, I was provoked to
do so by the repetition of the same matter in these two letters; and the context $

encouraged me, because I was reminded of things I had previously forgotten
but which I thought relevant. Furthermore, if after such numerous and even
bitter attacks I seem to have returned your fire somewhat too fiercely, I
deserve to be excused for having done so under provocation, and not so
much for my own sake as in defence of the church, my zeal for which   940
sometimes drove me to excess. God knows that I have not given much scope
to my feelings, even if I have not been able at all points to demand of myself
the degree of moderation that you might wish. I have said straightforwardly
and openly what I felt. I have used no deceit and given hatred no place,
deliberately. And yet, while it seemed simple and honest to refute charges   945
which I do not accept, it was a serious and very unpleasant step to enter on a
contest with you, a man of such widespread repute whom I had once
thought a friend of mine and who is indeed a more than common friend of the
many friends we share. But I am not obliged to be responsible for what I
cannot avoid. I had absolutely made up my mind to keep silence and enjoy   950
my freedom, had you let me do so; for nothing has ever happened to me so
unpleasant as this dispute.

Farewell, from Louvain, 1 February 1520.

1062 / To Lorenzo Campeggi   Louvain, 5 February [1520]

This preface introduces a volume containing Erasmus' paraphrases on Ephesians, Philippians, Colossians, and Thessalonians. This sequence completed his
rendering of all the canonical Epistles that he considered to be the work of Paul
(cf n15). Like the paraphrases that preceded it, it was probably printed at first
by Dirk Martens at Louvain, or possibly elsewhere in the Netherlands (NK
*0439), but no copy of such a first edition seems to have survived. By 1 March
1520 the new texts had reached Basel (cf AK II Ep 722), where Johann Froben
issued them with the date of March in the colophon. For Froben's second
edition of March 1521 Erasmus revised this preface, enlarging it substantially.
Allen and this translation follow the revised text, which must have been
written at the time that Erasmus addressed Campeggi again in Ep 1167, a letter
that shows considerable resemblance to some of the revised passages here.

The dedication gave Erasmus a welcome opportunity to repeat his request
for a papal pronouncement that would silence the Louvain theologians
opposing the Collegium Trilingue (cf Ep 1046 introduction) and Erasmus
himself (cf the preface; Ep 1053 n62). An appeal to this effect had been directed
to Leo x with Ep 1007, and Campeggi, when he met with Erasmus in August
1519 (line 200) had no doubt been asked to support it in Rome. A similar appeal
had been launched with Ep 1060, addressed to Cardinal Wolsey. It appears
that in Erasmus' mind Wolsey and Campeggi continued to be closely associated

(cf Ep 1060 n16). There is no trace of a response from Rome to these *démarches*, but Erasmus was soon to be gratified on another, more limited, request (cf Ep 1079 n1). As previously in the case of Epp 1001 and 1006, the nature and subject of this letter offered Erasmus an opportunity to comment on the patterns of change he perceived in the course of both political and ecclesiastical history.

TO THE MOST REVEREND FATHER IN CHRIST LORENZO
CAMPEGGI, CARDINAL OF SAN TOMMASO IN PARIONE, FROM
ERASMUS OF ROTTERDAM, GREETING

Whenever I survey the mutability of human affairs, my lord Lorenzo, brightest ornament of the college of cardinals, I seem to see precisely some 5 Euripus[1] or whatever may be more inconstant than that, so incessant are the changes as they surge this way and that, up and down, and cannot long continue in one stay. They reach a climax and swing back to what was left behind, until once more they come to such a point that we are obliged to turn our course from some excess that has now become intolerable; and what is 1 more, were one to try to stand against the sea or bend its course a different way, one could never do this without putting all things in serious jeopardy and immense upheaval. It was thus that in old days the kings of Rome gave place to a democracy or at least an oligarchy, which in its turn reached such a pitch of licence that there was need of tribunes of the people and dictators 1 and after that even of emperors, whose power then rose to enormous heights and provoked once more a desire for earlier forms of commonwealth. But it would be an infinite task to collect in this way the many different shapes that things have taken as they rise and fall in turn, and flourish and decay, and bloom once more and shoot again from time to time in a new shape. What is 2 more surprising is that even sacred studies, which ought to be the most consistent thing there is, have their own ebb and flow.

In olden days the Christian philosophy was a matter of faith, not of disputation; men's simple piety was satisfied with the oracles of Holy Scripture, and charity, a natural growth, had no need of complicated rules, 2 believing all things and never coming to a stop. Later, the management of theology was taken in hand by men nurtured in humane learning, but mainly in those fields of learning which today we commonly call rhetoric. Gradually philosophy came to be applied more and more, Platonic first and then Aristotelian, and questions began to be asked about many points which 3 were thought to pertain either to morals or to the field of speculation about heavenly things. At first this seemed almost fundamental; but it developed by stages until many men, neglecting the study of the ancient tongues and of polite literature and even of Holy Writ, grew old over questions meticulous, needless, and unreasonably minute, as if drawn to the rocks on which some 3

siren sang. By now theology began to be a form of skill, not wisdom; a
show-piece, not a means toward true religion; and besides ambition and
avarice it was spoilt by other pests, by flattery and strife and superstition.

Thus at length it came about that the pure image of Christ was almost
overlaid by human disputations; the crystal springs of the old gospel   40
teaching were choked with sawdust by the Philistines;[2] and the undeviating
rule of Holy Scripture, bent this way and that, became the slave of our
appetites rather than of the glory of Christ. At that point some men, whose
intentions certainly were religious, tried to recall the world to the simpler
studies of an earlier day and lead it from pools most of which are now sullied   45
to those pure rills of living water. To achieve this object, they thought a
knowledge of the tongues and liberal studies (as they call them) were of the
first importance, for it was neglect of them, it seemed, that brought us down
to where we are.

And here at once there is a great uproar at the very outset, one party   50
cleaving with clenched teeth to things as they are, the other breaking in with
undue violence, more like an enemy than a guest. Both sides are wrong; both
suffer. So it was in the old days, when the Jews rejected the new wine of the
gospel teaching, accustomed as they were to the old wine of the Mosaic law,
and saw as a disgrace to their earlier code what really filled out and   55
beautified it; they thought it novelty and hated it, when they were really
recalled to the original truth. In this way a kindness can turn into an injury, if
the physician applies his remedy without sympathy and tact, and the patient
sees the man whose concern is about his health as though he were an enemy.
How much more fitting that those who profess the learning that is commonly   60
called new and is therefore unpopular, though it is very ancient, should
effect their entrance courteously and not break in like enemies;[3] not instantly
throwing any man over sixty off the bridge,[4] as the old custom was, but
gradually taking root, the new guests and the ancient tenants side by side.
The humanities are not brought in to do away with subjects which are   65
taught, to the great benefit of the human race, in all our universities, but to
purify them and make them more reasonable than they have been hitherto in
some men's hands. Let theology by all means be the queen of sciences: no
queen is so effective that she can dispense with the services of her
handmaidens. Some she allows to counsel and some to adorn her, and she   70
believes it part of her glory that those who serve her should be honourable
women.

If only those who are keen to enliven traditional learning with all that
the humanities can offer would contribute their services courteously and
peaceably, and those who have grown grey in the ancient subjects would   75
not be so grudging towards themselves and their juniors but would welcome

the new arrivals to share the rights of citizens in a generous spirit, we should
see each group bring ornament and profit to the other, for both will share
their advantages and the benefit will be doubled. As it is, while we bespatter
each other with mud or, it would be truer to say, throw stones at one
another, both parties lose the advantage that was theirs and both leave the
field having suffered great loss. In the pamphlets[5] in which each side tears
the other to pieces there is more abuse than argument. In their academic
discourses there is more spite than scholarship, more bad language than
good judgment, more prejudice than liberty. In their sermons the gospel
teaching, which ought to appear in its purest form, is infected with human
emotions. It is a sin to declaim in offensive language against the studies
which have been accepted hitherto, inarticulate though they may be; but
those men's sin is more grievous who climb into the pulpit, from which one
ought to hear the gospel trumpet-call that heralds the glory of Christ, and
there cry, in words designed to stir up strife, 'Keep your children away from
Greek! Greek is the mother of heresies. Touch not the books of' this man or
that man (for they do not refrain from mentioning names) 'who corrects the
Lord's Prayer, criticizes the Magnificat, and emends the Gospel of St John.[6]
Do your duty, ye magistrates! Back them up, citizens! Keep this great plague
far from the world of men!'

If words like these are used before the inexperienced public, what can
be imagined more subversive? If before people of education and intelligence,
what could be more crazy? And yet the men who do this in public wish to
pass for pillars of the Christian religion. They do not stop to reflect that,
while they profess Christ's teaching, as they do, their attacks on the
reputation of those who do them good service, or who at least strive to do so,
are diametrically opposed to their professions. Besides which, they forget
that all the time a great part of their efforts is wasted, both for them and for
the common people, as long as this behaviour loses them all their credit with
their audience. Who would put his trust in a man whose spite and hostility
are plain for all to see? And on the other side, the works of those who are
keen that their laborious nights should advance both learning and true
religion to the best of their power are less profitable when such men read
them – unless we suppose it makes little difference whether you take up a
book with an open mind or a mind already occupied by hostile convictions
or, at best, suppositions. Last but not least, what is sown is not the Gospel
but the pestilent tares[7] of strife and hatred; and when these have once seized
upon the minds of men, they are not easily weeded out.

Nor is it easy to credit what small sparks, as they gradually spread, can
often start an immense conflagration. Nothing in human affairs is so
flourishing that discord cannot turn it into disaster. And nowhere should

discord be more strictly avoided than in scholarship, and in sacred studies above all, the authority of which ought to be specially effective in quelling the tumults of men's appetites. What does he teach if not peace, who teaches   120
Christ? If the salt[8] has lost its savour, what is there left with which to season this tasteless mess? If the light of Christian philosophy is darkened by the appetites of men, what will be left to lighten the darkness of our minds? Everyone knows that a great part of our religion depends upon our system of study. And now here too the Eden of our life has been ruined with his venom   125
by that cunning old serpent, so that it seems to me far preferable to cultivate any garden[9] rather than scholarship; for chives and cabbages will bring more profit to the man who grows them than nights of toil spent by the lamp.

But for some time now your thoughts have been silently protesting, 'What can be the object of all this?' Why, in hopes that on the advice of you   130
and others like you our beloved pope Leo will complete the circle of immortal glory which he has so prosperously begun to form. Long ago he rendered a more than human service to the Christian world; for when kings and peoples were in confusion, warring wickedly on one another, he brought them into agreement,[10] and perhaps he will confer a no less eminent benefit on us, if in   135
the same way he restores to our studies the tranquillity that should be theirs. For in them so bitter is the hostility, so venomous the language, so bloody the fighting, that it is not yet clear to me which is the greater evil for the human race, the armed conflicts of which I spoke or these feuds among the learned. His most serene majesty the king of England, Henry, eighth of that name,   140
with the support of his *fidus Achates*[11] the cardinal of York, and no doubt with advice from you, has done this for his native country; and Leo ought to do the same for the world at large, of which he is head, acting as vicegerent of Christ, who loved nothing more than concord. I doubt whether any monarch or emperor of Antiquity was ever honoured with a more splendid tribute   145
than the inscription[12] lately set up, they say, in honour of our Leo: 'To Leo x, who gave peace back to Christendom.'

And further, it is not only in theory and in general that this duty belongs to him, to whom belongs all that belongs to the advancement of religion and piety; it is particularly his affair not to leave the ancient   150
languages and humane letters exposed to assault from any quarter, seeing that he himself, whose judgment carries supreme weight, sets so high a value on them that he engages men[13] from every land at great personal expense to teach them in Rome, in the conviction that the Eternal City with all its famous monuments will gain no small further distinction thereby. That   155
most intelligent mind of his perceives, of course, that a knowledge of these tongues is necessary, not only for the teaching of academic disciplines but, beyond that, to extend or fortify the boundaries of Christendom. What

kingdom ever became united or long endured without the cement of languages which all men shared? Consider now for yourself how greatly it concerns him if the New Testament,[14] which I undertook with his encouragement, revised with further encouragement from him, and dedicated to Christ and to him, is to be misrepresented by any ignorant and worthless fellow before men no less ignorant. For my own part, the loss of my reputation moves me little, provided (as is right) the gain is Christ's, the glory Leo's.

And if the question is asked how concord can be re-established, I think it can be done very easily if he proclaims with all the authority of an oracle that every man should promote and promulgate his own convictions without offensive criticism of those of others, so that on both sides this frenzy of tongue and pen is restrained, by those especially of whom this moderation is most to be expected. If there is a difference – and often enough, just as tastes differ, so do attitudes of mind – let all dispute be confined to courteous confrontation, and never issue in frenzy. Furthermore, if anything seriously concerns the integrity of the faith – for that must not be dragged into everything by the scruff of the neck – let the question be discussed above all by those who know the mysteries of the faith; secondly by such as will not under cover of the faith pursue their own personal ends; last but not least, let it be done with judgment and moderation and not with subversive clamour. It is not perhaps to all men's liking that some persons, no matter who, should decide whether they are Christians or not.

I had no doubts of my ability to convince you of this, for I well know how your marriage of learning and fairness of mind abhors all virulence. Nor will it be hard for your Eminence to persuade our Holy Father Leo, whether because he rightly values you so highly for your distinguished gifts or because of his very own nature he is so wonderfully disposed towards peace and concord. The aid I ask is not great; but in case it should seem an inadequate reward to have the name of Lorenzo Campeggi exalted by the whole company of educated people for all time to come, here is a small addition offered on my own account: a paraphrase on the five Pauline Epistles which remain out of all his genuine letters,[15] completed in one recent spell of work. For I did not finish this task in the right order or all at the same time or with one burst of energy; and thus it has come about that the various parts are dedicated to different names. I have good hopes that this work at least will live, seeing that it wins approval even from those who criticize everything of mine as though by avowed intent. At the same time I thought to pay off, at any rate in part, the debt I owe to your Eminence; for I have forgotten neither what I owe to your unheard-of generosity[16] nor what I have promised you in writing.[17] Pray accept therefore this payment on account, until I can scrape together the means to pay in full.

When I dined with your Eminence at Bruges,[18] your last words to me at   200
parting, I remember, were that in whatever court Lorenzo Campeggi might
be found, I could be sure to find a friend who sincerely wished me well. May
I say in my turn that in whatever country Erasmus may be found, you may
believe you have there a most devoted servant. My respectful best wishes to
your Eminence.   205
    Louvain, 5 February [1519]

1063 / To Beatus Rhenanus   Louvain, 5 February 1520

> The only source for this letter is a copy in the Öffentliche Bibliothek of the
> University of Basel, MS Ki. Ar. 18ᵃ f 176, preserved among letters addressed to
> Bonifacius Amerbach. The copy is in Beatus' hand and was presumably made
> to relay Erasmus' request for his friends to reassure Dorp (cf Ep 1044
> introduction and n10) from Sélestat to Basel (cf Ep 1014). The request was
> repeated by Beatus in a short letter to Bonifacius Amerbach of 5 March 1520
> (BRE Ep 156; AK II Ep 726). Amerbach affected to be, or perhaps was, reluctant
> and only complied with Erasmus' wish when his teacher, Udalricus Zasius,
> also urged him to do so (cf Ep 1084:27–9).
>   This letter was probably part of a packet dispatched to the Upper Rhine
> region (cf Ep 1064). An earlier packet had apparently been sent from Louvain at
> the turn of the year when Jan Briart was dying (cf n3) but had been lost,
> according to Hieronymus Froben, through the carelessness of the young and
> scholarly messenger; see Zwingli Werke VII Ep 118.

ERASMUS OF ROTTERDAM TO BEATUS RHENANUS, GREETING
The intrigues[1] here are still so intense that nothing could be more
unpleasant. All the same, Dorp is sticking to his guns, and I feel sure that he
will be consistently his true self in future. Please therefore spur on Zasius
and Bonifacius and other people, if you can, to write to him in a friendly and   5
complimentary spirit. Give my greetings to Sapidus and Volz and Wimpfeling.[2] You know, I expect, that Atensis[3] has departed this life. Farewell, my
dear Beatus.
    Louvain, 5 February 1520

1064 / To Johannes Oecolampadius   [Louvain, c 5 February 1520]

> This letter is now missing, but Allen printed under this number an excerpt from
> a letter written by Bernhard Adelmann to Willibald Pirckheimer, Augsburg 4
> March 1520 (J. Heumann ed Documenta literaria varii argumenti, Altorf 1758,
> part 2, 189). Adelmann wrote:

Johannes Oecolampadius
Collection of Mrs Carl J. Burckhardt-de Reynold, Switzerland

Erasmus wrote recently to our preacher that he had finished a paraphrase on all the genuine Epistles of Paul, that Atensis and Colet have died, Dorp is sincerely reconciled to him, and Hoogstraten has visited him twice at Louvain and put the blame for his opposition to Erasmus on Atensis. Unless the great men at court had supported him, Erasmus says he would long ago have been stoned by that gang of monks and professional pedants. He complains bitterly about one of the Carmelites, and about a man called Edward who, he says, has also attacked six of Luther's Theses.

The preacher referred to is Oecolampadius, frequently designated in this way in other letters of Adelmann to Pirckheimer. After just a few months Oecolampadius had left his position at Basel (cf Ep 797:3n) late in 1518 to become cathedral preacher at Augsburg, but this new appointment too was of short duration (see Ep 1095 postscript). The letter he had received from Erasmus clearly belongs to the early months of 1520 and in view of its similarity with Ep 1063, which had reached Beatus Rhenanus shortly before 5 March, may have been dispatched by the same messenger. Jan Briart died on 8 January 1520 and John Colet on 16 September 1519. For Jacob of Hoogstraten's visits to Louvain and for his agitation see Epp 1006 introduction, 1030 n7; for the Carmelite, perhaps Nicolaas Baechem, cf Epp 1040 n7, 1072 introduction. Which of Luther's theses were attacked by Edward Lee is not clear.

1065 / To Antoine de la Marck   Louvain, 16 February [1520?]

This letter was first published in the *Epistolae ad diversos* dated 31 August 1521 on the title-page. The date of 1519 added in the *Opus epistolarum* of 1529 has little authority and may be discarded in favour of 1520. 1521, the only other year date possible, is effectively ruled out by internal evidence.

   With Ep 956 Erasmus had dedicated to the young abbot of Beaulieu his paraphrase on Galatians (lines 4–5). The powerful house of de la Marck had long wavered in its allegiance between Hapsburg and France. In 1518 it was united in the Hapsburg camp (cf Ep 748:29n), but while Erard de la Marck, prince-bishop of Liège, remained loyal to Hapsburg, his brother Robert and his sons, among them Antoine, reverted to the French alliance under the terms of an agreement reached at Romorantin on 4 February 1521. In the same month attempts were made, with French assistance, to promote Antoine to the see of Liège in place of his uncle Erard (see Harsin *Erard de la Marck* 365–7) and the Franco-Hapsburg War was gaining momentum (cf Ep 1228).

   The king mentioned in line 20 must be either Francis I or Charles V, who still is so referred to by Erasmus in Ep 1070:15, but is regularly styled emperor ('Caesar') a year later. Antoine could not conceivably have recommended

Erasmus to Francis I before 1521, but there is no other evidence that Erasmus was then seeking special favours from the French king or indeed had much reason to praise him for favours already received. If Francis I were intended this letter could be embarrassing for Erasmus and would not likely be selected by him for publication soon after the events of February 1521. If on the other hand the king is Charles v, the year could be either 1520 or 1521, but the title of king suggests 1520 for the composition, while the events of February 1521 sufficiently account for Erasmus' decision to publish the letter.

ERASMUS OF ROTTERDAM TO THE NOBLE YOUTH ANTOINE DE LA MARCK, ABBOT OF BEAULIEU, GREETING

The man[1] you know of had persuaded me that I should establish some considerable claim on your Highness if I took the initiative in dedicating[2] to you some part of my researches. As I now see, this had the opposite result: I seem to have displeased you precisely by my attempt to earn your good will. That you are, as always, open-minded, sincere, and consistent, there is no room for any doubt. I do not know whether the man who had encouraged me to pay you this attention is equally responsible for its failure, or whether my work itself fails to commend itself to your judgment.

As for your promise, I would not have it lie heavy on your conscience. You made me an offer unasked and of your own free will, which I neither invited nor expected; and of my own free will in turn and unasked I release you from it. I will not hold it against you that what you attempted did not succeed as you proposed, provided you do for me what is in your power to do – I mean, to return the affection which I feel for you. I am now learning from experience that a large part of human happiness consists in not setting a high value on anything. Had I depended anxiously upon your promises, I should be undergoing torments of disappointment; as it is, my hopes were not deeply committed, and I suffer very little by the loss of them. The king[3] himself has done far more for me than you had dared to promise. So far am I from any resentment at your failure to fulfil your undertaking, that I am the more grateful to you for wishing to do something and making the attempt. Farewell, my honoured Lord.

Louvain, 16 February [1519]

1066 / To Guillaume Budé   Louvain, 17 February [1520]

This letter answers Budé's Epp 1011 and 1015; it was published in the *Epistolae ad diversos*. For its conveyance and for Budé's answer and further reaction see Ep 1073 introduction.

ERASMUS OF ROTTERDAM TO THE HONOURABLE GUILLAUME BUDÉ,
HIS GOOD FRIEND, GREETING

I have many reasons for not liking that doubly ill-tempered letter,[1] either for
its bad Greek or for what you too think its impertinence; but I approve it for
this reason at any rate, that it provoked two letters from my friend Budé   5
which are as full of good things as they are lengthy. To answer them was out
of the question, even had you not forbidden me to answer,[2] for I am at
present not so much busy as overwhelmed[3] by my researches. Your first
letter, which speaks such good Attic throughout that it can be taken for a
native of Athens rather than Paris, ordains, as though my offences against   10
you were now duly paid for in full, that in future the rule between us shall be
to let bygones be bygones;[4] and then you add a second letter half in Greek
and half in Latin, which is not a little more quarrelsome than its predecessor;
but so far am I from resenting this that I am delighted with the bargain I have
made. I therefore authorize you, if anything occurs to you, even in the   15
future, on which you think a protest is called for, to pour out your feelings at
your own discretion, without prejudice to the rule which we have ratified
between us.

    But why need I still confess my own shortcomings, when you have
done this for both of us, and especially for me? I accept your confession, and 20
grant you absolution as you have absolved me, that the words of St James[5]
may be true of us: 'Confess your transgressions to one another, and pray one
for another, that you may be healed.' It is a divine attribute, not meant for
mortal men, never to make a mistake. In natural gifts, in learning, and in
command of both the tongues, of course I gladly yield the palm to you. It is   25
not my custom to enter into competition in these things with anyone, much
less with Budé, a sort of Milo[6] of our age if I may so put it, the champion of
our literary arena. The credit for an open mind and a warm heart, in which at
least I hope to go equal shares with you, I do not give up quite so readily. But
this too you wrest from me by force, so invincible are you on every point,   30
noble creature that you are.

    On every other point then, either I own up or I grant that what you say
is fair and reasonable. One exception I do make – what you say[7] in your
second letter about Deloynes, when you somehow reach the conclusion that
you could not call me a lover of adulation without yourself calling him a   35
flatterer. What a suggestion, my dear Budé! Friendship is a sacred thing, and
it is unlawful to touch what must be kept inviolate. I am not mad enough to
write or think like that about such a man. I have reread that Greek letter[8] of
mine, and find nothing in it from which it would be possible to infer what
you say; and in any case no thought was further from my mind. What was to   40

prevent my being a lover of adulation, and yet having no one to flatter me? So I wonder, dear Budé, how such an idea entered your head. And indeed, if I had anyone to flatter me, it would not immediately follow that he must be the man, on whom no suspicion of the sort could ever possibly fall.

As for your letter to Tunstall,[9] when you do not deny that there was an element of double-talk in it, and turn the same accusation back on me, what you yourself are willing to admit is for you to say; I shall not confess that it is true of me until some mortal is discovered who has heard me saying a word about you different from what I have put into my letters, whether in that perfectly unfettered conversation we have with our cronies, uttering whatever comes into our head, or over the wine when things often come tumbling out fit or unfit to be uttered, or if I have ever allowed any of my friends, I will not say to criticize your reputation, but to set me on a level with you or above you, without a sharp and serious protest.

Now I do not know how highly you value that too sharp-sighted Italian[10] commentator, who pointed out to you (as if you could not see clearly for yourself!) some things written by me that had a double meaning. I at any rate shall never be grateful for such a service. The outcome of what you call your foray[11] as a member of the court I learnt partly from your letter to Luis Vives,[12] which was so elegant, so scholarly, such an all-round success that I, who am rarely jealous even of my enemies, was jealous of one of my dearest friends. He is now engaged in rhetoric[13] and, I must say, with astonishing success. You would never think his subject-matter arose in this part of the world or in this age of ours; when he fights a case, it is not imaginary or academic, but true and serious. His gifts I always found adequate, but in his diction I used to feel a wish for greater flexibility. He is now so good at all points that I see no one in these days (and I hope I hurt nobody's feelings) who can challenge his supremacy in this field. That Greek letter which you promise[14] me I shall not cease to plague you for until I get it out of you.

The performance[15] which is staged here endlessly by a body of conspirators opposed to the College of the Three Tongues and to humane studies as a whole is something so disgraceful and so tedious that I cannot describe it to you, my dear Budé. Had any such project been put forward in the city of Rome, which is already richer than anywhere in such distinctions, the cardinals even so, and the pope himself, would encourage it with every kind of support and privilege and would think that their city, already so rich, had gained no mean distinction. But these men, faced with a scheme so generous, designed to be of such great and universal utility and to bring such immense credit to the prince and all his dominions, are so disgusted and so terrified that the Romans of old were not more frightened of the Gauls when they had captured the city and were now laying siege to the Capitol.[16]

You would be still more indignant if you knew that in this discreditable play there are three or four chief actors, who are such stupid blockheads that you would think them unfit to be given charge of your cabbages.[17] And yet they get their own way, by having no shame and no principles and by a new 85 system of closing their ranks.[18] If these men talk sense, your king[19] is mad when he engages people with characteristic generosity to adorn the kingdom of France with public lectures on the ancient tongues, and Leo[20] the Tenth is mad when he spends so much on bringing men to his city who can teach the tongues and humane studies; and countless others are mad too, 90 among them the king of England,[21] whose munificence attracts teachers of these subjects to both the universities of his dominion.

You have seen, I expect, my *Farrago*[22] of letters, but the editing is very careless. They are asking a second time for a copy with revisions, for the copies went very quickly; it often happens that the worst books are the most 95 saleable. If you think anything should be left out or altered, let me know; for to this task I am now obliged to devote myself.

I was already hoping to make harbour, tired of wrestling with this sort of slanderous attack. But a book[23] has been published in Paris, I hear, which drives me back into the arena. My chief wish was to be allowed to resign and 100 retire in peace; and next to that, that my opponent might be a man of honour. As it is, I am faced with a man of whose nature I cannot bring myself to speak.

I beg you particularly to give my warmest greetings to Deloynes and Ruzé, and if I have done something to annoy them, make my peace; though I cannot think this is really necessary. Best wishes to you and all yours, my 105 great supporter and incomparable friend.

Louvain, 17 February [1519]

1067 / From Jakob Wimpfeling   Sélestat, 19 February 1520

The original letter in Wimpfeling's own hand was preserved in MS 0331[m] of the University Library of Leipzig, a collection lost in the second world war. It is the earliest of a number of letters addressed to Erasmus at one time in the possession of Bonifacius Amerbach. By way of Netherlands, England, and a Württemberg diplomat these finally entered the collection of Professor J.F. Burscher at Leipzig, who first published most of them in his *Spicilegia*, 1784–1802; see *Briefe an Erasmus von Rotterdam*, ed. J. Förstemann and O. Günther (Leipzig 1904) viii–ix.

Wimpfeling, the patriarch of Alsatian humanists, returned to his native Sélestat at the end of 1515 and lived there until his death in 1528 at the age of seventy-eight. This is his last surviving letter to Erasmus.

Greeting. I wish my friend Erasmus length of days, that you may bring forth new creations every day and enlarge the old ones, as your custom is; for these are my consolation under the harsh treatment I have suffered[1] from men to whom I have always wished well. But such are the rewards of this world, and I am heartily tired of it, hoping that with Jesus as my guide I shall 5 soon be through these storms and reach the haven of peace. Every good wish for your prosperity; you are my one consolation, for your *Enchiridion*[2] and *Compendium*[3] are a constant source of pleasure.

Sélestat, Quinquagesima[4] 1520

Your devoted friend Jakob Wimfeling of Sélestat 10

To Doctor Desiderius Erasmus of Rotterdam, supreme among theologians and most beloved of teachers

1068 / To John Fisher Louvain, 21 February [1520]

In this letter, which was published in the *Epistolae ad diversos*, Erasmus acknowledges (line 5) three letters from Fisher which are now missing but may all have reached him after he had written Ep 1030. In his *Apologia invectivis Lei* (cf Ep 1080 introduction) Erasmus frequently refers to Fisher's interventions in his dispute with Edward Lee (cf Ep 1026 n3). In particular he mentions a letter from Fisher which, he says, had been long in reaching him and finally arrived shortly after the publication of Ep 1053 (c 14 December 1519). According to Erasmus, Fisher had by then recognized that Lee's notes could not be supressed permanently and therefore recommended a procedural agreement by which Lee should give Erasmus his manuscript notes and then be free to publish them as soon as they had been purged of any personal slights. Thereafter Erasmus would show similar restraint when publishing his rejoinder (*Opuscula* 258–9). While Fisher's proposal failed at first to quell the worst outbursts of mutual denigration (cf Epp 1053, 1061, 1083), it provided a basis for the eventual truce (cf Ep 1100).

In the *Apologia invectivis Lei* (*Opuscula* 267; cf 247, 250, 256, 264, 271) Erasmus also mentions a promise on the part of Fisher to communicate to him Lee's notes as soon as they were in his hands (cf Ep 1030:28–35), and generally seems to confirm the assurances given in this letter that Fisher's efforts at mediation were welcome. Some traces of impatience notwithstanding, Erasmus seems in turn genuinely eager to be of service to Fisher by persuading him to end his controversy with Lefèvre d'Etaples.

ERASMUS OF ROTTERDAM TO THE RIGHT REVEREND JOHN, BISHOP OF ROCHESTER, GREETING

If your Lordship suspects[1] me of having taken offence, either because you

have replied to Lefèvre or because you have not sent Lee's book, you do not
yet know your Erasmus. And here are three letters already in which you   5
suggest something of the sort. Believe me, there is nothing in it. I have no
more doubt of your feelings towards me than I have of my own. In the first
issue of your pamphlet[2] you made fun in a number of places, and (so many
people thought) rather sharply, of Lefèvre's loyalty to the church. In the
second,[3] not only is the style more polished, but there is less ill humour.   10
Only I was surprised that you took such great pains to drag the question of
orthodoxy into this business. Lefèvre takes this very hard; and I should like
him to be comforted, all the more since he both admires and respects you.

     As for the New Testament, I can tell you to take courage. If some
rumour has been spread among monks and the unlearned, this is not   15
surprising, seeing how Lee does nothing else, as though that were his
purpose in life. And he works through the monks; he knows who can help in
a thing like this. But when it once comes out, this book we have heard about
for so long, it will be a case of 'The mountain laboured, and forth crept the
mouse.'[4] The world is not so crazy that a pronouncement from Lee will set it   20
by the ears. Just let the book appear; and I think this must soon happen.[5] You
will find there is peace[6] between Lee and me, once he has published his
book, which he has been brooding over for so long. For he will never be
unlike himself. Whether he is disastisfied with you, I do not know; to me at
least you have at all points given the greatest satisfaction. You seem to me to   25
be entirely ignorant of Lee, if either his resentment or his friendship moves
you in the slightest. My feelings you will never hurt, even if you do disagree
with me in print. I do beg you therefore, if you ever nursed such a suspicion
hitherto, dismiss it utterly, and convince yourself that my feelings towards
you will always be what a humble dependant with a long memory ought to   30
feel towards a patron who has done so much for him.

     With best wishes, from Louvain, 21 February [1519]

1069 / To Maarten Lips   [Louvain, last week of February 1520]

This letter, which comes from Lips' copy-book now at Rotterdam (cf Ep 1000A
introduction), and Ep 1070 belong together, in that Lips' answer to this letter
(now missing) induced Erasmus to redefine his complaint in Ep 1070. He seems
to have written this letter when he had just seen Lee's *Annotationes* (cf Ep 1037
introduction), shortly after 21 February (cf Ep 1068:18–21) and before he had
made up his mind to reply to Lee, which he did before the month was out; cf Ep
1080 introduction.

ERASMUS OF ROTTERDAM TO MAARTEN LIPS OF BRUSSELS,
GREETING

As far as I am concerned my dear Maarten, you need not fear that Lee can do
me any harm, or N[1] either. You do me less than justice if you think there is
more profit in my work than in Lee's; he does not write for the public or for   5
the general good, but to advertise himself. I doubt if you will see a contest
between him and your Erasmus; there will be no lack of others[2] who can take
him on. Best wishes.

1070 / To Maarten Lips   [Louvain, last week of February 1520]

This letter is a sequel to Ep 1069 and like it was copied by Lips into the
Rotterdam manuscript, but it was also published by Erasmus in the *Epistolae ad
diversos*. The planned excursion (line 14) may be Erasmus' forthcoming visit to
Antwerp; cf Ep 1079 introduction.

ERASMUS TO MAARTEN LIPS OF BRUSSELS, CANON OF
ST MAARTENSDAL AT LOUVAIN, GREETING

I am not complaining that you do me less than justice, but at the form this
takes – that you think my notes preferable to Lee's, as though Lee had
written anything of the sort. As for Luther,[1] this witch-hunt they are starting   5
is both foolish and dangerous; they will realize later that what I am
supporting is not Luther but the peace of Christendom. No matter what
Luther has written, no intelligent person can be happy with the present
uproar. You would be right to be dissatisfied with your present lot,[2] were it
not true that all mortals everywhere have plenty to put up with. The easiest   10
way to lighten a necessity that cannot be avoided is to bear it as best you can;
to change your servitude, perhaps for something worse, makes no sense.

I am not abandoning you, but I am weary with overwork[3] and propose to
make an excursion; not far, however, from Louvain, for fear I am overwhelmed by Lent.[4] I hope the king's arrival[5] will put a stop to these shameful   15
disorders. Ask our friend Luxembourg[6] to come and dine here quietly
tomorrow, and come yourself also, if you can. If you can, I know you will.
Best wishes, dearest Maarten.

From my study, [1519]

1071 / To Nicholas of Luxembourg   [Louvain, February 1520?]

The only source for this letter is Lips' copy-book now at Rotterdam (cf Ep 1000A
introduction), where it follows Epp 1069–70. The arrangement of this

copy-book, however, is not always chronological. This letter may follow Ep 1070 simply because the latter contains Erasmus' only other reference to Nicholas of Luxembourg, who is not otherwise known.

DESIDERIUS ERASMUS OF ROTTERDAM TO NICHOLAS OF
LUXEMBOURG, MOST WATCHFUL HEADMASTER OF THE SCHOLARS OF
ST MAARTENSDAL

Dear Nicholas, you are the kindest of men; but was it necessary to make sure of your reception with a present of wine? A sight of you would have been 5 much more welcome; I have all the wine I need. I would ask you to dine tomorrow, but I have today given my promise to the cardinal.[1] If you will come to supper, you will be a welcome guest. If you would prefer conversation only, come and see me today. Best wishes.

1072 / To the Reader   [Louvain, end of February 1520]

This letter was published as a preface to Erasmus' *Apologia de 'In principio erat sermo'* (Louvain: D. Martens February 1520; NK 780). This short *Apologia* does not relate to Edward Lee so much as to two other critics who had attacked Erasmus' rendering of the beginning of the Gospel of John (cf Ep 384:48n). Their names are not mentioned in the *Apologia*, but one of them, the Franciscan Henry Standish (cf Ep 1060:27–30) was eventually identified in Ep 1126; the other is described in the *Apologia* as a Carmelite and bachelor of theology, who was egged on by his mentor and attacked Erasmus in a sermon at Brussels, no doubt as part of a concerted action (cf Ep 1040 n7). The mentor presumably was Nicolaas Baechem; the bachelor conceivably Jan Robyns (cf Ep 946:4n).

This short *Apologia* must have been ready for printing by the time Erasmus finally received Lee's *Annotationes* (cf Epp 1037, 1068:18–21) in printed form. Since the *Apologia* did not require an introduction, he seized this opportunity to announce to the public his forthcoming reply to Lee (cf Ep 1080 introduction) who had also chosen the rendering of John 1:1 for a target in his early attacks on Erasmus (cf Ep 886:60–6) and who was a protégé of Standish (cf Ep 1113:6–9). Logically enough this preface and the following text were joined together with the *Apologia invectivis Lei* in an edition of Eucharius Cervicornus (Cologne, March 1520; cf Ep 1080 introduction). For other reprints see Allen's headnote and NK 781.

This preface was dropped when Erasmus published an enlarged version of the *Apologia de 'In principio erat sermo'* with Froben's edition of *Epistolae aliquot eruditorum virorum* (cf Ep 1083 introduction). The enlarged text, which appeared without a preface, is reprinted in LB IX 111–22.

ERASMUS OF ROTTERDAM TO THE READER, GREETING

Edward Lee's book has suddenly appeared. Of its quality, since it is an
attack on myself, I express no opinion; the wise reader will decide on the
facts. In the mean time I would make one request of everyone: to suspend
judgment until the appearance of my reply. I have written an answer[1] to his   5
defences in these last three days, attempting the extremely difficult task of
replying to abuse without being abusive myself. I now address myself to his
notes, to which ten days at most will be allotted, although he took more than
two years; and yet in the old days defending counsel was allowed more time
on the clock[2] than the prosecutor.   10

Reader, farewell, and keep the other ear free and open for my reply.

1073 / From Guillaume Budé   Marly, 26 February [1520]

Like Epp 1011 and 1015, this letter was first published by Budé in his *Epistolae*
of August 1520 and reprinted from there in Erasmus' *Epistolae ad diversos*. This
letter answers Ep 1066, which had been delivered to Budé's country house
near Paris by two unidentified Germans the night before he wrote this answer.
Erasmus had sent Ep 1066 to Paris by a servant (see below) whose main task
may have been to bring back a copy of Lee's *Annotationes* (cf Epp 1037, 1072
introductions). This would explain the need for Budé to reply at once if the
same messenger was to take his answer back to Louvain (lines 2–11). However
that may be, it appears that this letter did not reach Erasmus at Louvain before
he left for Antwerp (cf Ep 1079 introduction). On 7 March Vives wrote to Budé
from Louvain (cf Ep 1004 n3) and transmitted greetings from Erasmus, who had
not received a letter to which he could reply.

The second paragraph and some shorter passages of this letter are written in
Greek. Its main interest perhaps lies in Budé's studiously indifferent reference
(lines 64–72) to Erasmus' desire to escape, at least temporarily, from Louvain.
One of his purposes in writing Ep 1066 was to inform Budé unobtrusively of the
continuing conflicts at Louvain and of his longing for a quiet haven. And he
may have been more explicit in contemporary exchanges with Bérault and,
conceivably, Germain de Brie, which he did not publish (n4). There are some
clear indications that the royal invitation to Paris (cf Ep 994 n4) was now more
attractive to Erasmus (cf Epp 1045:99–127, 1080:5–6) since alternative plans for
a move to other destinations had failed to progress (cf Epp 1012, 1025 n4, 1065,
1078 n15, 1092 n1). On 2 May [1520] Budé wrote to Vives (still from Marly):
'Please give my greetings to Erasmus, as I have not heard from him since his
servant departed from here with a letter from me, but his arrival is daily
expected at Paris' (Budé *Opera omnia* I 301). Budé was more likely referring to

Erasmus' arrival than to the return of his servant. Late in June Erasmus was at
pains to explain to Brie his failure to come; see Ep 1117:5–6, 30–5.

GUILLAUME BUDÉ TO ERASMUS, GREETING

About the third watch of the night two Germans arrived here, and
brought me your letter when I was on the very point of going to bed. I had sat
up working until nine o'clock, which as a rule I only do on fast days;[1] for I
read nothing after a meal unless absolutely obliged to. Yet I have no fixed   5
hour for going to sleep, and so I often drop off during the morning; for this
last fourteen years I have not had three nights, I suppose, free from
headache,[2] so far am I from enjoying the *summum bonum* of the Epicurean
philosophers, which was freedom from pain. So I am writing this to you this
morning in order not to delay the courier;[3] for Bérault[4] asked me not to,   10
having provided him with a companion who carries a letter.

First of all then, dearest of men, I pray to all the gods and goddesses
that you may have the same affection for me that I always have for you; and
then that God may grant us whatever is best for us and make us good men
and men of good repute. By this I mean not only mutual exchange of   15
affection, but also the maintenance of the amnesty[5] between us as we
formally agreed. We must use the proper language, if only for the good
omen. And the said act of amnesty shall have universal force and effect,
having been read a third time and passed. This rule at any rate I am resolved
to abide by, as surely as if it had been posted up three market-days running.   20

And so I shall not reply to your charges, for you and I are pretty well
agreed that this is the only way to escape this monster that has come between
us; but I must contest what you say[6] about my admitting to deception. Pray
make well and truly sure that you have really understood that passage in my
letter. And then, when you give evidence that you never spoke against me,   25
as far as I am concerned this may well be the truth, nor do I consider it
necessary to cross-examine you in my turn; we have disposed of this quite
sufficiently in previous letters, if indeed it can ever be disposed of.
Supposing some of your friends did so speak, as I believed on the evidence
of witnesses who could read and write, I am not so inconsiderate as to   30
suppose that even if they set out to do it for your benefit, you should be held
responsible for their foolishness or their imprudent zeal. And though I did
perhaps purge my stomach before that with too strong a tincture of aloes, yet
since then I have decided to wash out my ears with vinegar,[7] to make sure
they do not admit any messages containing criticism or complaint without   35
examining them first, for I have often been misled by my excessive credulity. I
think this must have happened to you in the matter of those letters of yours

which you call ill-tempered[8] and I call uncommon witty; but afterwards, when you put a drop of vinegar into them even at that time, they lost much of their brine and saltiness.[9]

When you yield[10] to me both the palm and the glory of ability and learning, I do not accept your offer. That was not the point of that dispute between us; which I wish to regard as settled on the understanding that I should be seen to have got nothing out of it, for fear that it might not be disinterested. And in any case may I never take it into my head to conduct a dispute with anyone on a subject which cannot be decided without bitterness and prejudice to the detriment of my tranquillity. For judgment, impartial judgment at any rate, one usually has to wait till after death; though I know on sufficient authority that this suspicion once found a lodging in your bosom. For heaven's sake, did you not once write[11] without misgiving, 'What does Budé expect? I have already got out of his way, and now I yield him first place as the more cultivated man. Does he expect me to act as his lackey?' What? Have I reached such a pitch of insolence that such an idea could enter my head? Even if I had had the good fortune to be your guide and the architect of your fortunes? This was mere gossip, and you carelessly believed it. It is my view that the time has come to clear our minds of these petty suspicions on both sides.

What you tell me[12] about those enemies of liberal learning is quite extraordinary. I at once begin to be sorry for you already, if you now have to descend into that arena or, alternatively, to abandon all you have done for an admirable foundation and for the last wishes of the prelate[13] who left that memorable and most generous legacy to promote the studies of gifted men. Our champions of philosophy here are in general less narrow-minded people. So if you were to leave where you are for a short time, as rumour has it you have decided to do, the loss to your own affairs and to the interests of your province would be made up for, I believe, by an immense saving of labour and tedium. In this city,[14] as a rule, one can live, if not handsomely, at least honourably and conveniently, in the society of men of the highest standing and of first-class repute in the profession of polite literature. You know the balance-sheet of your affairs better than I do, and get help, I dare say, in drawing it up from friends who are good men and true; I was short of something to write about, and added this to my letter.

The story of my expedition as a member of the court you cannot expect from me in the near future; at the moment you are busy and have no time for trifles of the kind, and I am out of spirits and have no leisure. For in these last few days I have had letters[15] from Rome, from Venice, from the court, and elsewhere; and when I had begun to answer them, yours arrived. I also have another project,[16] which will claim most of Lent, if I can once get it started. I

transferred myself down here, as a place where freedom from care is always
to be found; but anxiety and business cling closer than my shadow and   80
follow me, whatever peoples or places I may visit. This was all I could write
you before the morning office, for it is a feast-day.[17] Farewell.

From my house at Marly, 26 February

Please give Vives my greetings; I had no time to write to him, and in any
case I had nothing to say except to wish all success to the distinguished mind   85
and the hard work to which you bear witness. I wrote to him on the first
February or the following day.[18] Farewell, restorer and standard-bearer of
the humanities, and may you long so continue in prosperity.

1074 / To Wolfgang Faber Capito   [Louvain, end of February 1520]

The original letter in Erasmus' hand is in the Öffentliche Bibliothek of the
University of Basel; MS Ki. Ar. 25ᵃ no 99, but the text breaks off after two
sheets, leaving the letter incomplete. First published by Salomon Hess in 1790,
it must have been written soon after Erasmus had finally seen Lee's
Annotationes (cf Ep 1037 introduction) and reached Capito before the middle of
March (cf Ep 1083:31).

This letter, with its almost neurotic pitch, marks a climax in Erasmus'
ceaseless preoccupation with Lee's critique. Erasmus' charges against Lee are
clearly unreasonable, but this may well have been intentional. In the Latin text
Erasmus consistently refers to himself in the third person (as he had done in
the *Compendium vitae*; cf CWE 4 403–10). Presumably he wishes to provide his
supporters in Germany, by whose zeal and temper he had often professed
himself troubled (cf Epp 967:107–23, 149–61, 998 introduction and 65–91), with
inspiration and ammunition. This letter and Ep 1075 are clearly part of a
campaign to mobilize his friends against Lee (cf Ep 1083 introduction).

Capito was bound to take an interest in this controversy, as his name figured
in it (cf Ep 998 n6). On 10 December 1519 Caspar Hedio noted that Capito had
written an attack upon Erasmus' critics at Louvain, but was suppressing it at
Erasmus' request, awaiting his signal for concerted action (Zwingli *Werke* VII
Ep 107n; Allen IV 92). In the missing part of this letter Erasmus seems to have
modified his earlier request (cf Ep 1083:31–7). As a result Capito announced in
Ep 1083 (17 March 1520) that he intended to attack Lee in print. While Erasmus
released Ep 1083 for immediate publication, he may have continued to dampen
Capito's zeal with ambiguous advice. Capito also wrote to Luther on 17 March
1520 (Luther w *Briefwechsel* II Ep 267) that he did not see how he could remain
silent in view of Lee's attack on Erasmus and the condemnation of Luther by
the Universities of Cologne and Louvain (cf Ep 1070 n1). But his only known
attack on Lee is a letter written after his transfer from Basel to Mainz and dated

from Mainz, 13 August ('Ides') 1520. It is addressed to Martin Gerthofer or Gertophius (cf Ep 1083 introduction), a priest in his native Dietenheim in Württemberg, and was published as a preface to a reprint of Erasmus' own *Apologia invectivis Lei* (Mainz: J. Schöffer, colophon date of June 1520).

The English viper has burst out at last! Before us stands Edward Lee, an eternal blot on that isle so highly thought of. For eighteen months now he has been boasting of his 'pious annotations.' The whole world awaited a work of scholarship; and here before us is a book running over, raving mad I would say, with brawling and fishwives' abuse. Strip this from the book, 5 and heavens! how worthless, how tedious is what remains! I would describe the monster for you, but I fear posterity will not believe that such a beast was ever born in human shape. No harlot was ever so brazen, no pimp a more abandoned liar. His own and other people's respect for the truth are of no account. Lying is the one thing for which you might say he has a gift; and yet 10 he is not gifted enough to make his lies hang together. He is a mass of inconsistencies, with an insane thirst for petty scores, which he pursues in the most pitiful fashion. He wishes to be thought a theologian, an expert in the three ancient tongues, a bit of a saint; and with this in view he haunts the Carthusians, the Minorites,[1] and other monks of approved religious life. He 15 makes them some present from time to time, actually buying what ought to have been refused if freely offered.

This creature had taken a dislike to the name Erasmus before he had ever set eyes on me, being jealous even then of my reputation among his own people; for before he had seen my New Testament or knew any Greek, he 20 said to someone I could name that he had no doubt he could cut up Erasmus' New Testament in many places. Then he moved to Louvain.[2] When his Erasmus arrived there too, he wormed his way into acquaintance with the new arrival. I, in my easy-going way, overlooked the attack he had made some time before and admitted the man to my ordinary circle of friends. He 25 had begun at that time to learn the elements of Greek,[3] to equip himself already for his chosen profession as a mischief-maker, and in this I gave him some help, suspecting no evil even then. Some time later he was allowed as far as my private study, and saw me preparing a second edition of my New Testament. For the work was almost finished before I showed it to Lee. 30

Fearing that he might not achieve the modest reputation which he meant to secure like a drone from another man's labour, he began to read the New Testament himself in the earlier edition; for by now he had nearly learnt to read Greek. Some time later, relying on my good nature, he admitted that he too had made a few notes. I asked if I might see them. He sent one 35 wretched half page, and would send no more until that was safely returned.

He also sent them in no proper order, Matthew first,[4] then Mark, then
something from the Pauline Epistles, being perhaps afraid I might copy
them. When he saw that I did not set much store by them – for I myself had
already revised the whole work two or three times, and had altered almost all   40
the things detected by Lee, for out of all his notes scarcely two or three were
of any use, and only so far of use that they made me reread and compare the
passage more carefully – then the ambitious little man resented the fact that I
did not always agree with him and began by degrees to scatter his poisoned
darts. When I had scribbled on his papers 'Remember that the man you   45
correct is only human; and so are you,'[5] the foolish fellow took offence and
sent no more. I thought no more of it, indeed I was almost glad to be quit of
him, having detected that the idle drone had designs on my reputation and
that what I was writing would not be my own, but I must let that rascal claim
half the book; so I went back to Basel[6] and finished my work. Scarcely had I   50
been away a couple of days, when Lee spread the news through England,[7]
through Louvain, and everywhere that he had marked three hundred places
where I was wrong. Some Englishmen whom I could name were delighted.
On my return,[8] when I heard of it, I protested to him. His reply was the
purest nonsense, as you can guess from his letter.[9]   55
   At length Lee appealed to the judgment of Atensis.[10] Atensis, when he
realized the nature of the man and saw that the business would end in
trouble, refused to arbitrate. Meanwhile Lee was threatening to publish his
work, and would not give me access to it – refused in fact to produce a single
brief note verbally, though I often challenged him to do so. All the time he   60
never ceased to boast of his 'book' and his 'sacred annotations,' as he said
they had been described by a certain abbot.[11] He wrote hundreds of letters
packed full of lies, which he has as much ready to hand as a spider has silk.
At every opportunity he spread venom directed at me, for his tongue is the
most poisonous thing there is. He got copies made, and hawked them round   65
the monasteries and the lodging-houses, displaying them to everyone he
supposed to be no good friend of mine. He sent it to England; but took
marvellous care all the time that it could not fall into my hands. He thought of
nothing else.
   At long last some of my scholarly friends saw the book in England.   70
They disliked it[12] to a man, either for its venomous tone or for its ignorance
and folly. They wrote to him most severely and terrified him with threats, to
make him suppress a worthless book that would be a discredit to the whole
of Britain. They told him to make his peace with me. Richard Pace[13] came to
see me here, being at that time envoy from the king of England to the imperial   75
electors. He made the same proposals when he was here that he had
previously made by letter. Proposals for peace were put forward, the

condition being that Lee should suppress his book, when I wanted above all that it should be published. At length, as there was no end to the boasting and the backbiting, I challenged him to publish his work. He pretended that he wished to do so, although this was not his intention. He knew what he was doing: he wanted to enjoy this borrowed reputation by seeming to suppress the work in order to oblige me and our common friends, while he kept the whole world in suspense, waiting to see these labouring mountains bring forth the proverbial mouse.[14]

Soon a more bitter attack[15] from one quarter made him lose all control, and he was given further confidence in particular by certain Englishmen and friars, who spurred the man on in a way that was by no means good for him. In Antwerp he did not dare publish it, fearing that an answer would be ready before his own work was finished. So just see what a trick the man plays! He deliberately spreads a rumour that the work is being printed at Bonn,[16] the other side of Cologne. I send to Bonn, and discover at the price of six florins wasted that this is a mirage. He had invented it to put my suspicions off the scent; and all the time the work was being printed by Gourmont,[17] to whom he had dispatched his own brother.[18] Now at last the work has appeared, and the true nature of the monster is made plain; and even so the wretched man, whose talent is for libel and slander, has hired two or three hack scribblers, in his new annotations[19] and in the more recent *Apologia*, while none the less claiming for himself a certain neatness and elegance of style which he is pleased to call Erasmian. Such is the petty ambition of a worthless wretch!

Now just see the tricks with which he tries to secure a little credit for himself! He strings his lies together like bits of flimsy thread. Although he himself and many others know it to be false, he has a story that I should not have attempted a revision of my New Testament unless this will-o'-the-wisp had put me on to it; while in fact I had promised to do[20] so already in my first edition, and as soon as I returned from Basel after first publishing the work devoted myself to that entirely, first at Antwerp, then at Brussels, and afterwards at Bruges,[21] as many witnesses can testify, before I had ever seen Lee. Nor has this wretched little man, who is more vain than any woman, any misgivings in lying so shamelessly in hopes of his scrap of credit. He has the face to say that I had the whole of his work before I went to Basel to make the second edition; whereas I never knew that the work had been transcribed by the person who according to Lee's story made a copy for me, until quite lately I learnt this from Lee himself, when Lee's work was already in the printer's hands. He has no fear of contradiction from the man who made the very first transcript of this work – whom he calls a traitor[22] because he showed me two or three short notes he had had from Lee. Lee has the

effrontery to say that I showed his book to certain Englishmen in my own
study. Could any street-walker be more brazen, more utterly shameless? He   120
became aware that I was trying by every means to get hold of the book, while
he on the other side put all his efforts into keeping it from me; and yet his
story is that I had a copy of it. And now any corrections that I made were
made, he claims, at his instigation. The man cannot even lie consistently! At
one moment he writes that he did not want to let me have his book for fear   125
that I should publish it uncorrected; at another he says that I always had a
copy. At one moment he wishes me a long life[23] that I may be spared to do
service to the church; at another he says that to the church my books are a
menace.[24] He denies spreading any rumours about the book; and yet he
admits that it was copied in Louvain six times[25] and that in England many   130
people had read it. He pretends to have said what he did not say, and denies
saying what he said.

He does the same about Erasmus. Never was anything so glib, so
irresponsible! He had promised three hundred notes, and produces twice
that quantity[26] of slanders. On facts he is frigid and foolish, in scurrilities he   135
is hot enough – raving mad, indeed – and yet his petty, mad-dog spirit is
never satisfied. And even so, this same book of his is not entirely his own
work. In his last invective[27] he employed a hireling hack, and the same in his
new annotations; the parts which are really his give themselves away by an
elegance and tedium peculiar to their author. The poison is there, but he   140
cannot bring it out except by another man's pen. After which this
three-halfpenny booby is as pleased with himself as if the world were likely
to believe this to be a human being speaking. Such is the authority of his
advice, the heavy frown of his censure, the lofty severity of his castigation.
He is such a crow set off with other birds' feathers,[28] such a worthless mimic   145
pretending to be what he will! He never stops to think how learned and
judicious Englishmen will laugh as they read this stuff, men who know what
the wretch is really like and who know their Erasmus, how far he is from
deception and unaccustomed to dress himself in other people's plumage –
more likely, in fact, to dress others in his own. Orestes[29] himself could not   150
write more like a madman; and yet the poor wretch is very happy, because
somehow or other he has secured himself a reputation. He might be forgiven
for the outpourings of some ungovernable passion ...

1075 / To Paul Volz   [Louvain, beginning of March 1520]

From the reference to Wimpfeling (line 13) it can be assumed that this letter was
written shortly after Erasmus had received Ep 1067, which cannot have been
before c 1 March. His state of agitation over Lee suggests that this letter is

roughly contemporary with Ep 1074. It was first published in the *Epistolae ad diversos*.

Volz seems to have been in doubt whether he should continue as abbot of Honcourt (Hugshofen) near Sélestat, a position he had held since 1512. A man of contemplative temper, he was not well suited for his administrative duties and had not been successful in his assigned task of introducing the Bursfeld reform among his lax flock. He resolved his dilemma in 1525 by leaving the abbey and subsequently the Roman church; for a similar case of doubts about the monastic vocation, cf Ep 1070 introduction.

Erasmus' strident remarks about Lee did not fail to impress Volz, who criticized the Englishman in his letter to Maarten van Dorp of 20 June 1520, which was published in Froben's *Epistolae aliquot eruditorum virorum* (cf Ep 1083 introduction) and edited by de Vocht in MHL 381–4.

ERASMUS OF ROTTERDAM TO THE MOST WORTHY ABBOT PAUL VOLZ, GREETING

It is hard for me to give you advice on a question when I am not sure whereabouts on your foot the shoe rubs. If you know any manner of life which can provide the tranquillity your spirit longs for, in your weariness (as 5 I suppose) of our mortal tumults, show me the way, and I will join you. I have now long had enough of everything, for I can see that it is borne along by some kind of fate. But I fear that troubles follow us into every walk of life; and so, if you can bear to continue in the life you live now, I would rather you sought the tranquillity you aim at in your own spirit and not somewhere 10 outside. If you cannot, I pray that Christ may be willing to grant to whatever you do a happy issue. Oecolampadius[1] too is planning a retreat, and Wimpfeling[2] also, he tells me, has his eye on the harbour. I alone am left in this stormy sea, and Colet[3] has gone before.

Christ has added to my lot a dark particular Satan,[4] who has 15 abandoned all else and devotes himself to rousing the world against me; for he has a natural genius for intrigue – and even so I have to work hard sometimes to save him[5] from catching it hot. My dear Volz, I could never have believed there is so much venom in the human heart. Yet he says mass[6] frequently. He threatens destruction to anyone who dares to speak well of 20 Erasmus, although they speak no ill of himself. Farewell, reverend Father, and beloved friend in Christ.

[1519]

1076 / To Heinrich Gruntgen   Louvain, 7 March 1520 [?]

This letter first appeared, without a date, in the *Epistolae ad diversos* (dated 31

August 1521 on the title-page) among the letters newly added in that edition (cf
Ep 1206 introduction) so that the year date is likely to be either 1520 or 1521.
The year date of 1520 was actually added in the *Opus epistolarum* of 1529 and
may be accepted for want of proper clues, but it has little authority. On 7 March
1520 Erasmus was probably not in Louvain (cf Ep 1079 introduction), but his
movements in March 1521 are equally uncertain and, as always, the place date
could either refer to his permanent residence or could have been added by a
secretary who copied the letter in his absence.

   Heinrich Gruntgen (Gruingius) came from a good family of Kalkar. Elbert
Groenken was burgomaster there in 1489 and town councillor in 1495–6; Gerit
Groentkens was burgomaster in 1532; see *Annalen des historischen Vereins für den
Niederrhein* 51 (1891) 142; 64 (1897) 135–6, 141. Heinrich was dean of the
chapter of Emmerich for about thirty-two years until his death on 20 November
1547; see H.F. van Heussen *Historia episcopatuum foederati Belgii* (Leiden 1719) I
286.

ERASMUS TO HEINRICH GRUNTGEN, DEAN OF EMMERICH, GREETING
Your brief letter told me many things in few words. First, that you are a man
uncommonly well versed in humane learning; next, that you are endowed
with exceptional modesty and kindliness; and lastly, that you are well
disposed towards my humble self, correcting me as you do in such friendly   5
fashion,[1] and have a pretty good idea of me, in that you correct me so
forthrightly, understanding no doubt how far I am by nature from the
common run of men, who tend to take offence when offered one of the
kindest offices one man can perform for another. Henceforward therefore
your name will be found written among my special friends.   10
   On the passage which you have altered I fully subscribe to your
opinion, and it shall be mended at the earliest opportunity, not without some
honourable mention of yourself. The thing was done in a hurry, and I had no
time in such a vast sea of historical material[2] to check everything. I owe you a
debt, my excellent friend, and shall owe you still more if you will often repeat 15
the performance. Farewell.
   Louvain, 7 March 1520

1077 / From Paschasius Berselius   Louvain, 8 March [1520]

   The autograph of this letter in the University Library of Wrocław, MS Rehdiger
   254, Ep 26, has no year date, but 1520 is clearly indicated by the reference to
   Erasmus' expected reply to Lee's book. This letter was sent to Erasmus when he
   was visiting Antwerp (cf Ep 1079 introduction). For Berselius' recent relations
   with Erasmus see Epp 1051 introduction, 1065 n1.

TO ERASMUS FROM HIS FRIEND BERSELIUS, GREETING

A letter[1] attacking Lee has appeared here, addressed from Ghent to all
devotees of learning. I have arranged to have it printed with care by Dirk.[2]
Many people read it, and greatly enjoy it. I have posted it up in more than ten
places[3] to bring discredit on Lee. Everyone finds it sweet as honey; only Lee   5
and his long-tailed[4] followers think it virulent poison.[5] You will shortly hear
the whole story,[6] which has its funny side. Work away meanwhile at what
you are doing.[7] We are all waiting for your reply. Dirk's presses are taking
things easy. You would do him a real service if you would order them to
strain away at your defences. Give them to the boy who brings this letter, if   10
you think it a good idea, and in a few days they will be finished. There is
nothing Dirk desires and longs to do more than to print something that will
make Lee wither away, – burst, rather, with spleen and fury. Farewell, dear
Erasmus, and if you want me to do anything, let me know. I will do it with all
diligence. Forgive me if I write so carelessly to a master for whom I care so   15
much, and my most respected patron. Farewell again and again.

Louvain, 8 March

If it is not inconvenient, give my particular greetings to Pieter Gillis.

To Master Erasmus of Rotterdam, most learned of men. In Antwerp

1078 / From Hermann von Neuenahr   Cologne, 14 March 1520

This letter was published as the first piece in Froben's *Epistolae aliquot
eruditorum virorum* (cf Ep 1083 introduction). It followed an earlier exchange of
letters, now missing, which must have taken place at the time of Hoogstraten's
visit to Louvain late in 1519 (cf Ep 1030 n7) and is mentioned in Erasmus'
Spongia against Hutten (ASD IX-1 138; cf Ep 1053 n20). According to Erasmus
Neuenahr had written to ask whether he should continue his feud with
Hoogstraten (seeing that Erasmus had earlier deplored another contribution of
his to the Reuchlin controversy; see below n9). Hoogstraten (who had already
been given a taste of Neuenahr's influence; cf Ep 877:18–35) offered to issue a
formal apology to his opponent and Erasmus advised Neuenahr to remit the
offence in the spirit of Christ. As late as 1529 Erasmus had still in his possession
a copy of Hoogstraten's apology to Neuenahr (cf Allen Epp 1196:294–300,
1892:56–8, 2045:200–6, 2126:116–28). This letter shows Neuenahr attempting
to render Erasmus a similar service; but while counselling moderation to
Erasmus, he shows none in his own references to Lee, a combination of
circumstances which made his letter particularly suitable for the opening of the
Epistolae aliquot eruditorum virorum.

TO THE RIGHT LEARNED THEOLOGIAN ERASMUS OF ROTTERDAM
FROM HERMANN, COUNT OF NEUENAHR, GREETING

So he has appeared in print at last, this scarecrow of a Lee, no leonine figure
but a proper donkey – the ass of Cumae[1] – whose braying threatened dire
peril to the learned world for two whole years! In the end however his   5
ferocious appearance has frightened us much less than the noise that was
current about him. This Lee,[2] whom we feared as a wild and savage beast,
proves to have no claws and no strength, nothing but an unlimited supply of
verbiage, and he has rushed into the fray in unwarlike and most ridiculous
fashion. Are these, for pity's sake, the famous annotations, which were to   10
throw heaven and earth into confusion? Is this the triumph of which certain
men in black[3] gave us here such a horrifying picture in advance? If this is how
Lee and his lackeys triumph, we need wish them nothing but an unbroken
series of triumphs for the future.

When copies of Lee's *Annotationes*[4] first arrived here, my friend   15
Gerhard[5] and I sat down to compare one passage with another, being afraid
at that stage that Lee might be what he was said to be. But we soon saw there
was nothing to worry about: this mischief-making document contains
nothing but pure malevolence and the seeds of fraternal discord. Blind with
anger and spite, he does not understand what he is saying, but pours out   20
sound and fury without sense.[6] I could not bring myself to read his defence
all through; it seemed to me that a Christian's ears could hardly tolerate such
a spiteful attack, which contains little enough learning, far less profit, and no
Christian charity whatever. Never have I taken such a dislike to these
logic-chopping natures, though I have never liked them, for they seem born   25
to arouse turmoil in the Christian religion and disturb the public peace. If
this is what it means to be a professor of Holy Scripture, who would not be
ashamed to be called a Christian? If these are the arts which adorn the study
of theology, what would I not be rather than a theologian? There is a kind of
standard of self-control which even the common sort of men do not easily   30
transgress; but this has so little place among certain persons, who deck
themselves with the name of theologians, that it seems better to fall into the
hands of robbers[7] than into theirs. Our friend Reuchlin[8] has felt the truth of
this, and is hardly free to breathe again even now. I have felt the evil myself,
and the same fate, Erasmus, is waiting for you. I am heartily ashamed that I   35
did not keep my mouth shut. I now wonder what had happened to my
self-restraint;[9] but who would not occasionally exceed the limits of self-
control, especially under such provocation? You however will show the
genuine spirit of a true theologian; if you are injured, you will not overlook
it, but when you detect it, you will not carry vengeance to excessive lengths,   40
so that your reputation for the serious mind and modest heart proper to a

theologian will be quite untouched. Nor need you take into account what he has done, but what will be right for you and good for humane studies and a credit to us all.

These were just your own sentiments when you were lately[10] giving advice to me, and the opinion you expressed with the intention of restoring my self-control was indeed what one would expect of you. Now you in your turn will not take it amiss to receive advice from me, and that in your own words, though you are old and I am young. Your confidence and your hopes will be increased by the support of Pope Leo the Tenth, under whom humane studies have so greatly flourished that no one is such a fool as not to see it. Furthermore, in place of the emperor Maximilian the star of Charles has now risen upon us, in which the splendour of his father and grandfather shines again, or rather, if one may say so, the radiance of his forbears pales in comparison with his glorious sun. Of our fellow Germans I can promise you great things; this nation can show more princes, nobles, and ordinary citizens versed in the liberal arts and open in outlook than any other. There remain a few beggarly jackdaws and black-beetles;[11] 'no plough can tame that fern.'[12] Some think it was they who suborned Lee, so that they could use him most unfairly as a stalking-horse in order to put this business through, while they themselves sit safely in their kitchens. How far this race of men gives us a good example of the patience of Christ, I think you know well enough by experience, for you have painted them in their true colours. Lee is now playing the part of the ass among the monkeys in the fable.[13] He had better look out, for fear he has to play it out to a finish, for in the first part he has not been very successful. I await your *Apologia*[14] with impatience; please see that it comes out soon, and crush these chattering frogs. In all this, if there is anything I can do for you, I will not fail; you will find me always your faithful henchman. I think myself happy enough, if I endure persecution from men of this kidney, for I long to be a follower of those in whom there is no guile.

I look forward to your arrival[15] next spring. There is no plague[16] abroad here to frighten you away; do but come with all speed, and among the woods of Bedburg[17] we will converse together at length of our affairs; for much remains to be said. Or if you wish to visit our prince,[18] you will approach him in my company, and will give him very great pleasure, I have no doubt. The leading men at his court are on your side, and the prince himself has the most distinguished opinion of you, and so do his brothers. In a word, the nobles of Germany are returning to their senses; they now begin to hate barbarism and to welcome openness of mind. My brother[19] and all his household and kindred wish you well. Best wishes.

Cologne, 14 March 1520

1079 / To Silvestro Gigli   Antwerp, 15 March 1520

Epp 1079–81, published together in the *Epistolae ad diversos*, were addressed to
members of the papal court of Rome. They show that in his desire to escape
from his troubles in Louvain Erasmus included Rome – together with Paris (cf
Ep 1073 introduction), Holland (cf Ep 1092:2–5), Basel (cf Ep 1078 n15), and
England (cf Ep 1098 introduction) – among the places he considered visiting in
the near future (cf the preface).

For the time being he had gone to Antwerp. Already in February he seems to
have planned this visit as a holiday, much as in years preceding (cf Ep 1070 and
CWE 5 preface). In view of his desire to be exempted from the dietary rigours of
Lent (n1), the private home of his Antwerp friend Pieter Gillis (cf Ep 1077
postscript) was perhaps preferable to room and board at the College of the Lily.
But then Lee's book (cf Ep 1037) appeared and consequently the visit to
Antwerp also gave Erasmus an opportunity of preparing his rejoinders away
from his adversaries and in the proximity of the printer he had chosen to
publish them (see Ep 1080 introduction). He must have left Louvain a few days
before 8 March (cf Ep 1077), and he was apparently back there on 19 March (cf
Ep 1085), only to return to Antwerp in April (see Ep 1091 introduction).

Gigli, who had resided in England until 1512, now acted at Rome on behalf of
Henry VIII and Cardinal Wolsey. He had earlier assisted Erasmus in the matter
of another papal dispensation; cf lines 11–12 and Epp 447 introduction, 521, 567.

ERASMUS OF ROTTERDAM TO SILVESTRO, BISHOP OF
WORCESTER, GREETING

Right reverend Bishop, I was expecting your Lordship to call me ungrateful,
having returned no thanks for your long-standing kindness to me. And
now, with unparalleled generosity, you add new treasures to the great pile   5
of good things you have done for me all this time. I have received a copy of
the diploma[1] and am much pleased with it. Nothing could be imagined more
considerate or more in accordance with my wishes. But on this subject I
would rather nothing more were sent until I can write and say where I
should like it sent; for I hope to be in Rome myself and kiss your reverend   10
hands – and that shortly, unless the return of Charles[2] my master brings me a
change of plan. I know what I owe to your Highness, and am in no danger of
forgetting it. If however you knew the storms of business that overwhelm
me, you would not only forgive but even pity me. If I live one more year, I
shall bear witness[3] that I know how much I am beholden to you. My best   15
wishes to your Lordship, to whom I am wholly devoted, as is right and
proper.

Antwerp, 15 March 1520

1080 / To Francesco Chierigati   Antwerp, 15 March 1520

Cf Ep 1079 introduction, and for Chierigati's former contacts with Erasmus see
Ep 639. He had been papal nuncio to England (1515–17), but little seems to be
known about his obligations towards Bishop Gigli; see line 12.

This letter contains the first clear indication that Erasmus was preparing a
reply to Lee, whose *Annotationes* (cf Ep 1037) had reached him by the end of
February. Perhaps he meant at first to leave the task of answering Lee entirely
to his friends (cf Epp 1068–9), but as his irritation grew (cf Epp 1074–5) he
himself took up his pen, answering in the first place Lee's introductory analysis
of their conflict (Ep 1061). This, Erasmus claimed, was done in three days,
apparently while he was still at Louvain (cf Ep 1072); the resulting composition
was the *Apologia invectivis Lei* (*Opuscula* 225–303). Completed or not, Erasmus
took the manuscript with him to Antwerp and had it published by Michaël
Hillen, probably at the beginning of March (NK 782). It was reprinted with
Erasmus' *Apologia de 'In principio erat sermo'* (cf Ep 1072) by Eucharius
Cervicornus at Cologne with the colophon date of March 1520, and in June at
Mainz by Johann Schöffer (cf Ep 1074 introduction). The *Apologia invectivis Lei*
resembles Lee's Ep 1061 in offering a highly subjective account of the conflict.
The validity of Erasmus' statement (lines 10–11) that unlike Lee he was refraining from abuse perhaps depends on one's assessment of Lee's charges of
heterodoxy. It is clear, however, that both in Ep 1053 and in the *Apologia
invectivis Lei* Erasmus surpasses his opponent in the art of innuendo. Besides,
intentionally or not, Erasmus encouraged others to insult Lee (cf Epp 1074
introduction, 1077 n3).

The refutation of Lee's critical *Annotationes* to the New Testament was a more
extensive but also more scholarly task. Two sets of *Responsiones* (LB IX 123–284)
were printed consecutively, again by Hillen, in April (NK 864–5; cf Ep 1092) and
subsequently reissued by Johann Froben at Basel together with Lee's *Annotationes* (cf Ep 1100 introduction). Erasmus later estimated that it had taken him
thirty to fifty days to write the three answers and to see them through the press;
cf Epp 1098:31–2, 1102:20–1; Allen I 22, Epp 1134:25–6, 1139:40–2.

ERASMUS OF ROTTERDAM TO THE HONOURABLE DOCTOR
FRANCESCO CHIERIGATI, APOSTOLIC CHIEF SECRETARY, GREETING
Dear Chierigati, kindest of men, if you were my own brother, what could
you do that would be more considerate? I like the diploma[1] very much
indeed. But at the moment it is uncertain whether I am to stay here any   5
longer, for I am summoned to France. So do not let anything be sent here
unless I write and say so. And perhaps within a few months I shall be in
Rome; meanwhile, pray take steps to ensure that I find you in lively spirits.

Edward Lee has published a book attacking me, full of abuse, at some
damage to my reputation, but more to his. I am now composing a reply, but   10
without the abuse. That is why I write to you so briefly. Farewell.

I know how much I owe to your revered patron, Silvestro. I shall not be
wanting in gratitude, when opportunity offers. Farewell once more.

Antwerp, 15 March 1520

1081 / To Lorenzo Campeggi   Antwerp, 15 March 1520

Cf Ep 1079 introduction and n1.

ERASMUS OF ROTTERDAM TO CARDINAL LORENZO CAMPEGGI,
GREETING

My most reverend Lord, I send a book[1] dedicated to your Eminence as a
token, however inadequate, of my grateful feelings towards you. What was I
to do? No more suitable opportunity presented itself. There will be one, I   5
hope, in the future. As it is, I am engaged with numerous monsters, though I
am no Hercules and barely half a man. I hope it will be possible in a few
months time for me to revisit Rome, which I once learnt to love, unless the
return[2] from Spain of Charles my master causes a change of plan. God grant I
may find in good health those whose well-being is very near my heart. My   10
respectful best wishes to your Eminence.

Antwerp, 15 March 1520

1082 / To Hermann von Neuenahr   Antwerp, [c 15 March] 1520

This letter was published as an introduction to Juan Luis Vives' *Declamationes
Syllanae quinque* (Antwerp: M. Hillen April 1520; NK 4062). In his own preface
addressed to Prince Ferdinand Vives mentioned Erasmus, and in revising it for
a later edition credited him with having urged the publication of his work (see
Vives *Opera* II 317–21). Hillen probably took advantage of Erasmus' presence at
Antwerp (cf Ep 1079 introduction) to solicit this letter of recommendation from
him. In writing it, Erasmus allowed himself to be guided by the praise of Vives
he had formulated in Ep 917. Beyond this, he seems to be noting a shift in Vives'
interests towards rhetoric and literary invention and away from dialectic and
Stoic theorems (cf Ep 957 introduction) a shift which he warmly welcomed; cf
Epp 1066:62–8, 1107:14–15.

ERASMUS OF ROTTERDAM TO THE HONOURABLE HERMANN,
COUNT OF NEUENAHR, CANON OF COLOGNE, GREETING
Surely the heavenly powers must love your Lordship, most gifted of men, for

they have added to your lineage and wealth such a noble spirit that it is your first care to adorn your family and fortune with the genuine and lasting distinctions of integrity and scholarship. And how fortunate you are that your exceptional exertions should thus be seconded in every way by favouring wind and tide![1] Truly your castle[2] is Apollo's dwelling-place and your woods are dedicated to the Muses! – and following the example of the Younger Pliny,[3] you hunt in them continually, but never without books, so that if huntress Delia[4] does not favour you, at least the goddess Philology is on your side, and you do not return home empty-handed. Why, I should be jealous of you for living the life of the gods, were you not too dear to me for anything good to happen to you which I do not feel I share.

You in your turn want to know what is happening here. The *Ptochotyrannophilomousomachia*[5] still rages. That's a long word, you will say. Not so long, I assure you, if you compare it with the reality, for those curs bark quite endlessly against humane studies. And how fare you meanwhile? you ask. I, the familiar champion and preacher of peace and tranquillity, have entered the ring; I deal out black eyes and receive them in turn. O you poor wretch! I hear you exclaim already; but you would say so all the more if you knew the monster[6] against which fate has matched me. But this you will learn from his book, the most ignorant and most malevolent that has appeared for many centuries. Maarten van Dorp,[7] one of your keenest well-wishers, acts like a true theologian, for he has extricated himself from the tumult and the faction, and lives a pleasant life devoted to higher studies.

Luis Vives, while others rant,[8] combines vigour and eloquence, reviving in himself the precedents of Antiquity;[9] for as you know, in this department of learning even the Italians have hitherto been wanting. This distinction our friend Vives confers upon his native Spain. Spain once could show in this field, as in others, outstanding men, her Senecas and her Quintilians, but they were to be found in Rome. And now he claims this eminence for his own Valencia, so that it could appear to contend with Rome in something more than mere identity of name.[10] Ranting is easy enough, but eloquence I regard as a most difficult thing, and especially eloquence like his, if my judgment has any value. For he manages it with such skill[11] that if you took away the author's name you would think you were reading, not a production of our own country or generation but a survivor from the great creative days of Cicero or Seneca. The theme which he develops is invented, but he does it so that you feel some serious matter is afoot. He treats both sides of the question, but so plausibly that he seems already a convinced supporter of the side for which he argues. He strictly observes the rules of the art,[12] but conceals his own artfulness so well (which is, as you know, a

large part of the art itself), that you would think his work spontaneous. He   45
never sinks into commonplaces, never wanders away from his theme. You
might think he was pleading against the clock[13] for a friend on trial for his
life. His keen eye in the discovery and presentation of argument I admire
less, because I know he has had long and successful experience in almost all
branches of philosophy; such a source of strength to him is his wonderfully   50
versatile intellect, whichever way he turns it.

While he was engaged on those subtle but inarticulate subjects which
are now so popular, no man showed more acumen in disputation or proved
himself a better sophist. Now he is engaged wholly on more humane studies,
and engaged to such good purpose that in this generation[14] I know scarcely   55
anyone whom I would dare set against him; for even if we grant that others
may equal Vives in powers of eloquence, I see no one in whom you might
find so much eloquence combined with such great knowledge of philosophy. His mind is fertile, sane, and vigorous; his memory exceptionally well
stored, his energy inexhaustible, his years green even now. Out of all this   60
we can promise ourselves some great and far from ordinary results. I hope
there will be many hereafter who follow this splendid example; whether they
will equal it, I know not. If you wish well to his Eminence Cardinal de Croy[15]
(as I am sure you do, if you wish well to those who sincerely pursue the
humanities), you will think him fortunate to have this man to direct his   65
studies.

Give my greetings to your Gerardus Episcopus;[16] they call him bishop
every day, I hope he will some day become one.

Antwerp, 1520

1083 / From Wolfgang Faber Capito   Basel, 17 March 1520

Subtle direction on the part of Erasmus, and the momentum gained by the
campaign once it was under way in Germany, produced a whole series of
polemical publications directed against Edward Lee's attack upon Erasmus (cf
Ep 1037).

*Epistolae aliquot eruditorum, nunquam antehac excusae, multis nominibus dignae
quae legantur a bonis omnibus, quo magis liqueat quanta sit insignis cuiusdam
syconphantae virulentia* ([Antwerp: M. Hillen April–May 1520]; NK 765) was
arranged by Wilhelm Nesen, as is evident from two of the letters it contains,
which were addressed to Nesen by Thomas Lupset. Among the remaining six
pieces are More's long letter to Lee (Rogers Ep 75), and also Epp 1083–4, which
can hardly have been available to Nesen for publication without Erasmus'
consent. In fact Erasmus himself worked closely with Hillen during his visits to
Antwerp (cf Epp 1079, 1080, 1091 introductions).

Hillen later reissued the *Epistolae aliquot eruditorum*, supplemented by an *Appendix epistolarum quibus eruditi viri detestantur Edouardi Lei virulentiam* (NK 128). As the appendix contained, among other pieces, Epp 1095 and 1109, Hillen's second volume likely dated from June–July 1520.

A much larger collection of twenty-eight pieces, *Epistolae aliquot eruditorum virorum, ex quibus perspicuum quanta sit Eduardi Lei virulentia*, was printed following Erasmus' *Apologia de 'In principio erat sermo'* (cf Ep 1072) by Johann Froben in Basel, in a volume to be dated from July–August 1520. In addition to all the letters previously published by Hillen it contained fourteen new pieces, including Epp 1053, 1078, 1089, 1105. The last letters of the collection suggest that the editor was Hermannus Buschius and that he was then staying with Froben. Buschius also contributed some verses to Gerthofer's pamphlet (see below). Again Erasmus had given considerable encouragement to this venture, acting partly through Nesen (cf Epp 998, 1074, 1085, 1088 introductions), although by the time of publication, his concern may have cooled (cf Ep 1100 introduction).

Another contribution to the controversy was *Recriminatio Ioannis Gertophii, adulescentis Germani, adversus furiosissimum sycophantam Eduardum Leum* (Basel: A. Cratander June 1520). The author, Johann Gerthofer of Dietenheim (cf Ep 1074 introduction), dates his preface from Ulm, 9 April 1520. On 30 March 1522 he matriculated at the University of Wittenberg. For his knowledge of events at Basel see Ep 860 introduction.

For the background of *In Eduardum Leum quorundam e sodalitate literaria Erphurdiensi Erasmici nominis studiosorum epigrammata* (Erfurt: J. Knapp 3 June [?] 1520; Mainz: [J. Schöffer] 1520) see Ep 1088.

For the authors and promoters of *Duae epistolae, Henrici Stromeri Auerbachii et Gregorii Coppi Calvi medicorum, quae statum reipublicae christianae hoc saeculo degenerantis attingent; adiecta est Andreae Franci Camicziani epistola ad Pirckheimerum; subiunctis etiam in fine libelli in Leum epigrammatis* (Leipzig: M. Lotter 1520) see Epp 999:314–15, 1085, 1123, 1125.

In the well-known tract *Hochstratus ovans* Lee is lampooned along with Jacob of Hoogstraten. Several anonymous editions appeared in 1520; see NK 1111; Hutten *Operum supplementum* 1 461–88; de Vocht CTL 1 437. In the *Spongia* against Hutten (ASD IX-1 142) Erasmus denied any connection with the author and the publication.

This letter was published in the collections both of Hillen and Froben. It appears to have been written soon after Capito had first seen Lee's book and upon receipt of Ep 1074. For his further reactions see Ep 1074 introduction.

WOLFGANG CAPITO TO ERASMUS OF ROTTERDAM, GREETING
I wrote in my last letter – three days ago, I think – about Edward Lee's book, which Konrad[1] the Paris bookseller, who is Froben's kinsman, printed there

at his own expense and brought with him. If you will permit a Capito to give
advice to an Erasmus – which is asking Minerva[2] to take lessons from a sow –   5
it is best to forget the whole episode as a flash in the pan,[3] and laugh it off
with a light heart. There is no reason whatever to fear that a book so dull, not
to say raving, can do any harm to your reputation with serious and learned
men. What this cockscomb is after is the repute of having once challenged
you. If you truly understand your own position, you will not think him   10
worthy of this honour. Everyone can see that Lee was provoked to these
flights of impudence by the desire for fame and reputation. When he could
not secure an immortal niche for his name in your *Annotationes*,[4] he tried to
make himself known as best he could at his own expense. His poor ambitious
little heart is grieved because you do not acknowledge that such learning as   15
you may have is derived from him. The poor fellow thirsted for fame, and he
will get what he thirsted for – and more of it than he wanted, for we shall
make him more famous than Erostratus,[5] if the pens of Germany have any
power. He makes up to me with some insincere words of praise,[6] thinking me
too stupid to detect such tricks. Let him keep his kind words to himself; no   20
one in Germany would endure to be praised by a man from whom praise
carries more discredit than his hostility. He also makes up, the donkey that
he is, to Hutten and Reuchlin. He must think us blockheads, not men; but he
will find we are men, not the toadstools he thinks us. The crow will get the
treatment he deserves, nor shall we rest content when we have stripped him   25
of his borrowed plumes.[7] Hutten's pen,[8] I hear, is hard at work. Oecolampadius,[9] though by nature the mildest of men, waxed surprisingly angry at
these outrageous attacks, and he is a man of truly Christian spirit. Zasius,[10]
the distinguished professor of Roman law, cannot sufficiently marvel at so
much arrogance in so ignorant a man, and such devilish venom in a priest.   30
    What you urge upon me twice already,[11] I will carry out as far as I can;
for when you tell me to publish absolutely no reply, that is more than I can
bring myself to. The course that you allow as second best, that if I answer at
all, it should be in moderate terms, I will follow as far as his own lack of
moderation permits; though he needs medical treatment rather than refuta-   35
tion, if I rightly infer his state of mind from what he writes. Certainly I will
spare his countrymen,[12] as you tell me to, and fairly enough; they have had
no part in it, no more than a piece of garden ground in which aconite springs
up, though the rest of it is full of wholesome greenstuff. I should by now
have sent you a foretaste of my work,[13] if a safe messenger had offered   40
himself. I will however publish nothing until it has been revised or approved
by Rhenanus,[14] for fear I am carried away by the heat of composition. I have
not yet read the whole of Lee's book; one thing is clear already, that if you
take away the heat of controversy and innuendo, the rest is very frigid stuff.
    I would have written more, but the last boat is just leaving for   45

Frankfurt;[15] I had to hurry. I will act the part of a most faithful friend, as events will soon prove. Farewell.

Basel, 17 March 1520

1084 / From Bonifacius Amerbach   Basel, 19 March 1520

An autograph rough draft of this letter is in the Öffentliche Bibliothek of the University of Basel, MS C VI[a] 73 f 329. The good copy was evidently sent with Ep 1083 and like the latter was printed in the collections of both Hillen and Froben; see Ep 1083 introduction.

TO THE GREAT ERASMUS OF ROTTERDAM FROM BONIFACIUS AMERBACH, GREETING

What think you, dear Erasmus, sole glory of our age, of the truth of the old Greek saying[1] that ignorance breeds rashness and reflection makes men slow to act? How long can I continue to abuse your kindness? I know how deeply 5 involved you are with most important work on authentic theology; I know how the subject appeals to you continually as to some saviour Hercules, and how tirelessly you watch over it; yet this makes me none the less ready to trouble you with my nonsense. Yet if I do get a bad name for rashness thereby, you must please blame nobody for this – only my very great 10 affection for you; and as this is always filled with anxious fears,[2] the more I write the less self-confident I am. You see, it drags me in my reluctance or drives me against my will to express my heart's attachment to you willy-nilly in a new letter from time to time. And so, if you find me more tiresome than I should be and than your great researches will allow, please be ready to put a 15 kind interpretation on it. Granted that I do not deserve your indulgence, and that you have other friends who are distinguished scholars, such neverthe-less is your kind heart that you will not turn away from a man who is wholly devoted to you. I may be the worst scholar of them all, but in the warmth of my affection, at least, I shall never yield to anyone, whoever he may be. And 20 so, that you may not always find my long rigmarole unduly tiresome, here is another brief note in which my heart goes on record that it will always be what it is right and proper for you to find in one devoted to you.

May all be for the best! I hear that Maarten van Dorp[3] has had a change of heart and is now a supporter of your doctrines, or rather of the lessons of 25 authentic theology. This news was most welcome to everyone here, and to no one more so than to Dr Ulrich Zasius, the great jurist. I wrote[4] to congratulate him, though against my will, to please other people, for Zasius drove me to it and bound me by oath. As I may not refuse him anything, in this matter I was particularly glad to do as he wished, especially since you 30 and Dorp are now friends again, which is the best thing for us that could happen. Blessed indeed you are, and show true greatness! – for not content with restoring the full extent of liberal studies, you do battle with the barbarian hordes, and in the process turn sophists into human beings and 'vain babblers' into theologians.   35

Of our own news there is not much worth telling. You know, I think, what a wretched time we have had this past year. We lost my brother Bruno,[5] cut off by the plague, which plunged us in mourning. His death will have been a blow to you, I do not doubt; for close as he was to us by birth, he was even closer to you in the great devotion he felt for you, which made him   40 worship your books and feel a religious enthusiasm for yourself. But he is dead, much as we would wish him still alive; he passed on, just when he was first in a position to do something for good letters, and his death was a very great loss to us. I have remained up to now in Basel on account of my brother's death; but in early spring I set off for Avignon,[6] to continue the   45 studies I have begun and to enrol in the faculty of law, if that seems a good plan, though I do not know if there is anything I should be worse at than acting as a hired mouthpiece. Still, it will be a new way of life. Dr Ulrich Zasius is much involved in business for certain princes[7] and has no time to write at the moment. By the next courier he will write to you and to Dorp,   50 and has told me meanwhile to send you his warmest greetings.

But, I say, who is this Lee, this queer fellow in both name and nature,[8] who is continually criticizing your notes on the New Testament in a manner not so much queer as quibbling? He must be crazed beyond hope, he has made himself such an outstanding exhibition of crass stupidity. Don't think I   55 say this to please you; I mean what I say. What cursed impudence, to attack with such frivolous rubbish things which are true and beyond cavil! Where did the man find such audacity, not to say madness? How valiantly he lays about him with abuse, and what a child or a ninny he is when it comes to arguments! Is it so true that nothing anywhere is safe from the tooth of   60 malignity? Apollonius[9] was quite right: a wise man is in more danger from ill will than a sailor from tempest or a soldier from the enemy. Yet what can a gnat do against an elephant?[10]

But why write all this to you when you are busy with more important things? May the Almighty bless you and keep you through a long life for the   65 benefit of us all and of sound learning. Greetings and best wishes, dear Erasmus, light of the literary world; remember that Bonifacius loves you dearly, reveres, and respects you, and do not fail to think kindly of him, yes, and to love him in return.

From Basilea Rauracorum (alias Basel), 19 March 1520   70

A few days ago, when I had to write to Zasius[11] about something,

1503·

Willibald Pirckheimer
Charcoal drawing by Albrecht Dürer, 1503
Kupferstichkabinett, Staatliche Museen zu Berlin

among other things I made some mention of Lee's latest notes. As I was writing this, he sent me a full reply,[12] at no point more true and well expressed than where he touches on the latest criminal attempt by Lee. As this concerns you, I thought it imperative to add it to my letter, so that you might get an even clearer idea of that great man's opinion of Lee, inasmuch as this was written to someone else and not to you. Here it is. 75

'What is all this about that sophist Edward Lee? How right our ancestors were when they used to say that fate seems sometimes to make men race to their destruction as though they were running for a prize! Otherwise, would the giants ever have tried to scale heaven? What else is that sophister trying to do, if not to assail heaven, by which I mean the citadel of all divine and human learning? Such are the labours which that incomparable hero undergoes, and is ever fresh to face new ones: following masters such as Jerome and Cyprian he opens the majesty of theology before us, winning the applause of gods and men – such men at least as possess any learning or sound judgment. And out of his native darkness crawls this worm, to gnaw at the splendid harvest which is ours without having won respect himself in any field of study. If one expects grammar, he blunders every now and then; if power of expression, he stumbles and stammers away; if skill in argument, he pounds like a pestle, or any blunter thing there is. No sample of philosophy breaks surface at any point. His theological apparatus he handles in such a way that it is abundantly clear that what he cites was suggested to him by other people. Numbskulls of this type dare write books in this learned age of ours, and dare to write them against Erasmus! Henceforward who would not dare to do so, if this Lee has? Woe upon thee, O hapless sophister! Woe to the mother who bore thee, and to the womb – say rather, to the planet that presided at thy birth! When the Germans in this land of scholars see your nonsense, what do you suppose will happen then? How they will trounce you! How your reputation will be torn to shreds! A thousand ways of rending you and your writings will not be enough, unless the scraps of you are reduced to annihilation.' 80 85 90 95 100

That is what Zasius thinks! Farewell once more, and best wishes, prince and sole ruler of the world of learning.

1085 / To Willibald Pirckheimer   Louvain, 19 March [1520]

This letter was first published in Willibald Pirckheimer *Opera* (Frankfurt 1610, repr 1969) 277. Pirckheimer's answer, Ep 1095, shows that he too responded eagerly to Erasmus' appeal for a concerted attack upon Edward Lee; cf Epp 1074, 1083 introductions.

Greeting, dearest Willibald. I was approached in Antwerp by a gifted young man,[1] your sister's husband, who brought me greetings from you and at the same time offered me his services.

Edward Lee's book[2] is out at last – the most poisonous and false and mischievous thing that ever was, and the most foolish and ignorant besides. And yet the man is so pleased with himself; and he has invented something blockheads can enjoy. I wrote an answer to his calumnies on the spur of the moment; compared with them, what Hoogstraten and Pfefferkorn[3] write is pure honey. As for the question at issue, I laid about me to some purpose in refuting him. But in any case, how you ought to deal with this monster,[4] born to be the plague of humane studies, you will learn from the letters of several friends to whom I have entrusted this task.

Unless frightened off by the plague, I may perhaps move bag and baggage to Germany[5] this spring. Meanwhile, mind you look after yourself, dear friend, and benefactor without equal.

Sincerely, and in haste, Erasmus
Louvain, 19 March
To the worthy Doctor Willibald Pirckheimer, my incomparable friend

1086 / To Maarten Lips   [Louvain? late in March? 1520]

The text of this letter comes from Lips' copy-book now at Rotterdam (cf Ep 1000A introduction). When Erasmus wrote it he was able to send Lips a copy of his completed *Apologia invectivis Lei* (lines 3–4), presumably in print (cf Ep 1080 introduction). At the same time he was preparing the first of his two *Responsiones* to Lee's critical notes, where the reference to Gregory of Nazianzus (n2) occurs. Erasmus was probably writing from Louvain as he was preparing to set out on one of his repeated visits to Antwerp (cf Epp 1079, 1091 introductions). On the other hand, he may have been writing from Antwerp, preparing to return to Louvain, perhaps in April, although in that case he might perhaps have mentioned the messenger who was to take charge of Lips' answer.

DESIDERIUS ERASMUS OF ROTTERDAM TO MAARTEN LIPS
The Carmelite,[1] whoever he was, was more richly supplied with humourless wit than any lickspittle in the comedy. I enclose a copy of my *Apologia* in reply to Lee. You will soon have my answers to his *Annotationes*, in which it will be clear how far Lee falls short of what we expected of him. If the Nazianzen[2] is still with you, please turn up the genealogical poem and see if he says anywhere that Joseph had two fathers, Jacob his natural parent and Eli by

adoption, and make a note of the place and send it to me. For I must be off on Tuesday morning. Farewell.

1087 / From Thomas More   [Greenwich? March–April 1520]

This letter – quick and perceptive in many places, but also long-winded and repetitive – was never revised for public circulation and first appeared in print in *Thomae Mori ... lucubrationes* (Basel: N. Episcopius, 1563). After the Anglo-French war of 1512 Germain de Brie composed a poem (below n4) in praise of the valorous deeds of a French captain. This poem provoked More to comment on Brie's labours in a series of critical epigrams which were eventually published without More's knowledge (cf below n2 and Ep 1093 n16). Brie, in turn, answered passionately if belatedly, with the *Antimorus* (cf Ep 1045). This letter resembles in many points More's public reaction to the *Antimorus*, an *Epistola ad Germanum Brixium* (London: R. Pynson [April] 1520; Rogers Ep 86; More Y III-2 551–694). Both appear to be written under the impact of More's first acquaintance with the *Antimorus* (lines 588–90). Erasmus too must have seen Brie's printed collection headed by the *Antimorus* at about this time. He reacted with Ep 1093, putting forward peace proposals which induced More to suppress his *Epistola ad Germanum Brixium* (cf Ep 1096). Although More's reactions may seem excessive to modern readers, he showed more self-control than did Erasmus in his controversy with Edward Lee, even allowing for the difference that Erasmus had suffered a challenge to his orthodoxy, More only to his national sentiment (cf Ep 1061 introduction).

More's presence at the royal court in Greenwich is documented for 29 February and c 8 April; see Rogers Epp 85, 89 and cf Ep 1089.

THOMAS MORE TO THAT EXCELLENT AND MOST LEARNED MAN
ERASMUS OF ROTTERDAM, GREETING
Did you ever, my dear Erasmus, best of men and scholars – did you ever see a more charming character than our friend Brie? As soon as he takes a fancy to conceal something, he supposes it is hidden from all other mortals too. For   5
the greatest blockhead could not fail to realize how absurd and offensive and discreditable it was to make quarrelsome and scurrilous attacks on anyone unprovoked, and again and again he asserts and repeats and emphasizes that he was provoked by my epigrams and was purely on the defensive throughout, so that though he found himself the target of curses and   10
execrations he hits back at his assailant with nothing but pleasantries and wit and humour. But of the impudence, the falsehoods, and the insults with which he had previously challenged all England, never a word; not a word

either of the fact that the difference between us was a live issue long ago in all
the confusions of wartime, and had long been dead, until he revives it now   15
after all this time, when peace is fully restored. Our modern Phormio[1] is
inspired with such self-confidence that, though he could easily discover that
his case is rejected by everyone with a real knowledge of the facts, he
behaves all the same as though he had fully and clearly established it before
the appropriate tribunal; and now, being I suppose sure of his position, he   20
lets fly at will against me, and bales out (wit and charmer that he is!) all the
bilge-water in his bosom. Having decided that two or three epigrams[2]
written for fun are to be regarded as invective, as though he only has to say
something to carry universal conviction, he convinced himself at the same
time that everyone would approve his action, if he were to take a few lines   25
humorously directed long ago against a very bad-tempered pamphlet of his,
and in wartime too, and reply after all these years, when peace is ratified and
established in such a spirit of concord[3] as no two peoples have ever shown
before, in a book that is simply poisonous. He hopes no doubt that no one
will be either sharp-sighted enough to be able to see something he himself is   30
content to wink at or such an unseasonably severe critic that he will ask for
evidence other than Brie's own story, especially as he boasts of the justice of
his cause with such self-confidence.

I at least should have found him somewhat less impertinent, if he had
dangled all this tinsel only before the eyes of the ordinary public, among   35
whom he might have found some who still knew nothing of the subject,
many to whom both of us were strangers, and some who enjoy a quarrel
however unjustly, and if this ox were not flaunting his pack-saddles thus in
front of you, who are not only familiar with the contest from stem to stern
(unless you have failed to read *Chordigera*,[4] for all the rest I know you have   40
read) but also know the contestants themselves under the trappings and
through to the skin, as the saying[5] goes. Besides which he knows that
quarrels of this kind, even when they arise from just causes, are unpleasant
and hateful to a man with your open-hearted and kindly nature. All the more
so the very silly, very unjust, and very uncivilized quarrel he is pursuing   45
now, which you have already condemned in a kind of preliminary inquiry,
as he could have seen from the letter[6] you sent him, in which you add
reasons for your opinion, one of which pays too much respect to us both and
was thought up in the interests of courtesy rather than truth, as though he
and I were the sort of people whose friendly relations were of any   50
importance to the cause of literature, while the other at least was perfectly
justified – that humorous pieces I threw off long ago in the heat of a war
ought to be wiped off the slate now that peace is restored. Of your two
reasons, the one that was more courteous than true he allows, as concerns

me with a touch of scorn, but in his own case he is frank and modest and   55
accepts it;[7] the other, the truth of which could not be denied, he has passed
over in silence, and once more tries to throw dust in our eyes with this talk of
provocation, claiming[8] that I attacked him first and in a hostile spirit.

And indeed if Brie, devoted as he is to metaphors from comedy, ordains
that the action of this play shall start with the second act, that is to say with   60
my epigram, I cannot deny that I did give him provocation. If he follows
normal practice and allows the first act to take its proper place, there will, I
think, be no doubt that the confused working-out of the plot has nothing
comic about it. To begin with, who would not be astonished at the egregious
impudence of a man who protests so often that he is the injured party, when   65
he knows all the time that his *Chordigera* is on sale everywhere? Nor should I
have pursued it with an epigram, had he not attacked my countrymen as a
whole with such abusive falsehoods. In this regard I do not see what he can
invent to excuse his calumnies. Can he say that my epigrams preceded his
book, when their satire is entirely directed at that book's ignorance,   70
plagiarisms, and falsehoods? Can he maintain, like the sharp little attorney
that he is, that his *Chordigera* contains nothing offensive? Let him be as
impudent as you like, he will not deny that at the outset of the *Chordigera* he
accuses us of breaking treaties and shamelessly calls us perjured.[9] And yet
he dares to open with the remark that he carries an olive-branch in the midst   75
of arms, having presumably such an affection for falsehood that he regards
perjurer and treaty-breaker as terms of endearment. Does he suppose it no
concern of mine if my countrymen are attacked by him with falsehood and
calumny, merely because I myself am not mentioned by name? For so he
seems to suggest; as though the same reasoning, and indeed the same   80
eloquent assertions, would not justify the footpad in taking the traveller to
court who had withstood him perhaps rather uncivilly, on the grounds that
he did not attack the man but merely had designs on his purse.

It may be said perhaps that though I did not attack him first, I did at
least write with more bitterness; for there are limits even in self-defence. But   85
I, with the barbarity of a Polyphemus,[10] in furious anger pursued Brie (our
modern Ulysses, of course) with curses and execrations. So he maintains,
not stopping to think how grossly he lies. He consoles himself with the hope
that there must be many people who have not learnt the whole story and can
easily be persuaded to believe him, and that thus he will be victorious   90
without a battle; while with you and those who know he is satisfied if he can
secure the modified approval of 'I should have thought he was speaking the
truth if I did not know the facts.' But I shall either defend myself with the
truth; or alternatively, I would rather lose the day than owe my victory to the
ignorance of my judge. And so in this field at any rate, I shall not follow   95

Brie's example, who right at the end of his crazy collection printed my lines on Abingdon[11] (which I threw off as a joke to tickle the ass's ears of a certain person whom nothing would satisy unless it rhymed), omitting two epigrams of mine on the same subject which explained the humorous purpose of the lines. He could hardly do anything more maliciously   10
misleading. I at least will do the opposite. I will get his *Chordigera* reprinted, and add my epigrams at the end. I will also append his collection,[12] so that he cannot complain that anything has been left out; and in this way I hope I shall make it downhill work for all educated men to judge whether Brie has as good a case as he so pompously maintains.   10

He calls us perjurers and treaty-breakers; he distorts the whole sequence of events to the credit of his own people and to our discredit by what he himself calls fictions but are really brazen lies; he recounts the lot of it in such absurd terms that nothing so absurd was ever seen before; he dresses it all up in other men's verses, so that you might think you were   11
reading the cento of Valeria Proba,[13] except that she put her material together neatly, and Brie cobbled his up so ineptly that every seam projects into a kind of knot like a great scar on a wound, or gapes as the ground does in a drought. With all this, I did nothing in those epigrams, by which he claims he was so grievously injured, except to poke fun at the faults I have   11
mentioned, and at any rate there was, I think, no bitterness in it; so that I wonder very much where in my epigrams he can have found the curses and execrations[14] which this witty man, as he prides himself on being, turns into humour. Does he mean by execrations and curses what I say in one of my epigrams,[15] where I produce a humorous excuse for his having to invent, as if   12
no one had returned safe home from the *Chordigera* who could tell him the story of what actually happened? – for I added that Brie ought to have been in the ship himself, that he might see with his own eyes the events he was to describe, for so he would not be obliged to lie like this so disgracefully and hand falsehood down to posterity as though it were true. Apart from this   12
one point, I am certain that Brie will never find anything against which he can direct a trumped-up charge of either curses or execrations.

Although on this same point either his charges are egregious inventions, or at any rate he shows himself egregiously ignorant of the meaning of the words execration and curse. There may be someone who also thinks I   13
was rather cutting, though if he were to take a small sample of Brie's *Chordigera* I trust he would excuse me without difficulty; but there will be no one to call this execrations or curses, if he knows any Latin at all. That level is not reached even by Martial's remark,[16] which was far more cutting than mine, about the poet Theodorus, who was perhaps as a poet not unlike Brie;   13
for when Theodorus' house was burnt down, Martial exclaims that it was an

outrage, and the gods ought to be ashamed of themselves, that the same fire did not also consume its owner. Whereas I, though I did think Brie deserved to be well and truly present in the *Chordigera*, so that he could escape the need for such shameless lies, did not wish that that had happened to him; I did not call down upon his head the fire which after all many people escaped who were in the vessel. If one thinks and declares a man worthy of something, one does not in the same breath call that fate down upon his head. For Brie too, I suppose, thinks thieves deserve to be hanged, and the same of adulterers, and no doubt of perjurers too, though they are not so very many parasangs distant[17] from liars; and yet I cannot think him so heartless as to call down that fate simultaneously on all these classes, who form a large part of the human race. A wish of this kind would be most merciless; it would also perhaps be none too safe for Brie himself.

But besides that epigram there are nine others,[18] in the first of which – and what I say is perfectly true – I point out in simple language that all writers will lose their credibility if by his example they get the habit of following their emotions rather than the facts. In two I make fun of the way in which he describes Hervé[19] fighting like a prodigy. One is a humorous comment on Brie's combination of boasting and lack of sense, for besides many other utter absurdities he imagines Hervé prophesying about himself as if he were a nursling of Apollo, and to make this possible he has him deliver a long speech in the midst of the flames, as though he were perfectly at his ease. Furthermore, though there were many survivors from both ships, since several of our smaller vessels came to the rescue, he chose to burn everybody up rather than leave a survivor from whom he might have been thought to have heard a story which he could write up. In one epigram I referred to the lines invented by Brie for Hervé's cenotaph.[20] Two of them make play with the fact that Brie had decorated his *Chordigera* with lines stolen from the poets of Antiquity. In two I showed that I felt a need for more thought and more ingenuity in the *Chordigera* in both invention and arrangement of the subject-matter.

When I wrote these pieces, I was the injured party, public affairs were in turmoil, and I spoke the truth. Even so, I never published[21] them or showed them to anyone by themselves – always joined with other things, so that the reader's attention was either diverted from them as much as possible or at any rate was not monopolized by them; while his *Antimorus* on the other hand offers nothing but abuse of me by name, as crazy as it is offensive. Last but not least, when I heard that moves were on foot to print my epigrams in Basel, you know yourself what steps I took[22] to get what I had written against Brie, and a few other things, omitted; some of them seemed to me not serious enough, although they are far removed from the indecency which is for some people, I perceive, about the only merit some men's epigrams have to recommend them. And at the same time I had no wish to criticize anyone by name even slightly, however much he might deserve it.

If in this respect my efforts, as far as Brie is concerned, came to nothing, I am delighted; he makes it very clear that he deserves to have quite different things said about him. Take the places where he asserts, so frequently and so falsely, that I began it, and that I gave mortal offence with a string of insults, calumnies, abuse, curses, and execrations. If he has discovered all the things he lists, although – seeing how things then were, and what he had deserved – I could have defended what I had done on principles which every nation recognizes, yet I will admit forthwith that I am as great a barbarian as the Cyclops Polyphemus, which Brie maintains. If on the other hand he has not discovered in my work the things that he objects to, I think it only fair that Brie should acknowledge that he has wholly invented the passage where he complains of my curses and execrations in order to provide a place where he can drag in Polyphemus, a giant who to be sure needs plenty of room; for he was so much in love with that elegant fiction that, rather than be obliged to leave it out, he preferred to invent a target at which he could discharge some shafts of humour. If Brie were not more blind than Polyphemus himself, he would easily discern that there is not much credit in this for him, if he passes over criticisms made of him as though they did not exist and raises up other charges against himself which he can easily shoot down.

I had written an epigram on one of my countrymen[23] who made himself ridiculous by going over entirely to French fashions when we were at war with France. In another passage,[24] Brie having called us treaty-breakers and perjurers, I had touched in passing on the fact that in the war with France we had a religious cause and did our duty towards the church of Christ, whose vicegerent we were aiding, while the French were the other way round, for they encouraged schism and opposed the pope. This precise point I have no wish now to reopen, nor was it at my wish that it was published long ago. And yet, had Brie pretended (for he is a great hand at fiction) that he was moved to anger by these passages it might perhaps have been easier to forgive him, as a man who seemed to have been imposed on by a false idea of honour, in fact by an inordinate love of his country, which seemed to make him intolerant even of valid criticisms of it, or at least ready to maintain points which have been abandoned in the treaties. And now, like the blockhead that he is, he has chosen to make a case in which he has the same obstacles to surmount as in the other: that it was he who wrote first, he who provided the occasion for it, that his charges are false, that the point at issue has been decided, or rather, has been rendered void and extinguished by international treaties.

There is another most dishonourable thing which I pass over. In public he first gave cause for offence, and in private he poses like this as the injured party. How this can be, he cannot explain; but the curses and execrations piled on him by me he himself clearly shows to be his own invention. And so, since he began it by attacking me in print, and falsely too, while my reaction was confined to epigrams (the subject of which was such that, if he denies their truth, he will achieve nothing except to make everyone understand that he has lied twice over), an honourable retreat was not only possible for him, it was his duty. And he would have done so, I am sure, had he not preferred to make his distinguished impudence universally known. His former errors might have been forgiven to his youth, if nothing else, or blamed on the state of things. And now, all these years later, in all this peace and concord, when our two princes are very nearly bound by ties of hospitality[25] (for this is now in preparation), he must needs begin again at the beginning and repay the handful of epigrams I threw off against his book with a poisonous pamphlet in which, as he could think of no answer to make on his own behalf, he has turned entirely against me, pouring out nothing but unmixed calumny and abuse that would disgrace a madman.

In the first place, if at any point Froben's workmen, or even the man, whoever he was, who made the copy for the printer, were perhaps not quite up to the mark, he ascribes it all to me, although he sees that no book ever had such a happy passage through the press that it contains no errors at all, and although he finds in it no list of corrigenda. And yet in their very errors they have generally shown more felicity than Brie in his corrections. Look at the mischief-making and the falsehood of his charge that I attack the prince's father![26] – though I myself speak only of evils which the prince set right with such incomparable success at the outset of his reign, evils which afflicted the body politic for some years before that, thanks to the perfidy of some men on whom the king's father had relied too heavily at a time when ill health prevented him from managing things himself, though he was in other ways a supremely experienced ruler. And yet Brie, for all that in his spiteful way he diverts on to the king these evils which came about through other men's villainy, uses this to declaim with astonishing virulence against myself, all whirling fists and buffettings and threats of exile! And as though he felt imprisoned in the constraints of verse and could not range as freely as he wished, he added venomous notes in the margins to direct the reader's attention to these points, in case perhaps he took too little notice of the verses.

And in this fashion, while making it signally clear that he has all he needs for making mischief except power to match his malice, yet the pretty fellow is proud of his witty performance, though his laughter is the laughter

220

225

230

235

240

245

250

255

of Ajax.[27] Ajax, when the armour was assigned to another man, lost his   260
reason and hung up cattle and belaboured them, roaring with laughter all
the time and highly delighted with the groans they uttered, madness having
convinced him that they were Agamemnon and Ulysses, on whom he longed
to wreak vengeance. Brie is like that: he pursues a vile obstinate invention of
his own, hounding it on to destruction, beaming with self-satisfaction   265
because, mindless as he is, he fails to observe that every man – and I mean
every single man with any spark either of decency or of common feeling –
when he hears this wild Brie laughter, does not merely scoff at him as a
madman but is revolted by this gladiators' spirit of fighting to the death.

And in spite of all this, it is just as though he were writing this stuff for   270
some blockhead Coroebus or Margites[28] and not for Erasmus; as though,
with Erasmus ready to overlook the impudence with which he attacked me
first, he had so successfully blinded everyone without exception that what
he himself did not choose to see became at once invisible to everyone; as
though he had now proved his case that I began it, although the facts prove   275
that what I wrote came later; as though wartime conditions were still in force,
so that it was proper for him to seek revenge with his venomous inventions
for a few heedless words uttered long ago and quite harmless too, at this late
date when on both sides princes and peoples alike have so far grown into
amity that soldiers actually forget the wounds of which their bodies still bear   280
the scars; as though I myself had assailed him bitterly and rained all sorts of
imprecations on him, while he in return had merely sprinkled me with
unmixed pleasantries, unmixed humour, unmixed wit, and had not in fact
voided over me a flood of crazy invective and ravings for which poisonous
would be too mild a word. In the light of all this it is remarkable to see the   285
confidence and certainty with which he promises himself not merely
forgiveness, as though his reply was unavoidable, but actually praise for his
moderation; for when attacked (as we are asked to believe) with curses and
execrations (which are non-existent), though he had the right to bear
equivalent weapons when he entered the lists, he shows his amazingly   290
generous nature and admirably versatile talents by snapping with no fangs
(such is his boast),[29] by being humorous without calumny and funny without
giving offence and sarcastic but stopping short of personal abuse, by
rebukes without severity and instruction that needs no rod; to crown all, in
fact, by turning my abuse into joking, my offensive remarks into humour, my   295
insults into witticisms, by making irony out of my execrations and mere
scoffing out of my curses.

Would not any casual reader think that Brie had delivered a pretty
peroration, provided he knew nothing at all of the case? For should any
reader happen on it who has looked into his *Chordigera* and my epigrams and   300

his idiot *Antimorus*[30] (should anyone have such abundant leisure that he is able to make such a worthless use of his precious time), he will find in those epigrams of mine neither abuse nor insults nor offensive remarks nor curses nor execrations; while in Brie on the other hand he will find nothing but undiluted scandals and bad language and poisonous picking of quarrels; he 305 will see teeth, but they are broken on the grindstone, and a teacher's rod, but no learning; he will see that the man's criticism consists in foolish attacks on what he does not understand and his teaching in shameless innuendo against anything he does understand; – and then how he will laugh at that laughter of Brie's that makes Brie a laughing-stock! How he will mock at the 310 mockery which recoils so severely on its author! How humorous he will find Brie's humour, which reminds one of a camel dancing![31] What a subject for mirth he will find in the mirth of our Germain, in whom he will recognize a true cousin german of Aesop's donkey;[32] for the way the donkey imitated the frisking of that pet dog as he put his muddy feet and claws on his master's 315 shoulders and was chased with sticks back into the kennel was not much less absurd than Brie's imitations of the poets. With what elegant irony he will outflank Brie's irony, which is, to be sure, so inelegant that it reminds the reader of that painter who was as much a painter as Brie is a poet, and having painted a hound and a hare so much alike that no one could tell the 320 difference was careful in the end to make it clear by labelling them which was the hound and which the hare.

Brie's use of sarcasm is usually such as to fill him with pitiful forebodings that most of the praise he wishes to be taken as ironical will be accepted by many of his readers as serious; and from this danger he saw no 325 escape except to declare that he was being ironical in a marginal note.[33] Being a cautious man, he naturally took precautions to avoid being bound by his own act and deed, as though his praise of me had been seriously meant. There was only one place[34] where he saw no need to warn us in a marginal note that he was being sarcastic, because the elegance of that passage gave 330 him such confidence, although he lists it in the index (as he hopes it will be thought) of my mistakes and (as the facts show) of his own slanderous malice and ignorance. He makes fun[35] of a dialogue in my *Utopia* in which a friar is having a discussion with a jester: 'In reporting and developing this dialogue,' says Brie, 'More displays with ease the sharp edge of his wit, the 335 vigour of his language, and his incorruptible judgment.' For my part, dear Erasmus, my learned friend, I do not think so poorly of Brie, nor have I such a good opinion of myself, that I would not readily admit I could never have expressed the elegant diction of friars or the keen logic of a jester so prettily as the living truth with which Brie could have expressed them. It makes such 340 a difference to be familiar with these niceties of style and to approach the jester yourself, not in name alone[36] (as Brie so courteously and so often concedes that I do) but in nature (for which a wholly justified claim is presented by his *Antimorus*).

And then, when he talks about critical judgment, by which I take it he   34!
means that it is absurd to introduce the barbarous diction of friars into a book which you wish to be in Latin (to say nothing for the moment of the fact that the Greeks are thought barbarians by Latin speakers and Latin speakers by Greeks, though all authors so often interlard their Latin with Greek and get praised for it too), I do not foresee, I will not say my own style, in which Brie   35(
detects everywhere such blatant blunders and barbarisms (thanks to his own blatant facility in false accusation and his own blatant ignorance), but Brie's (which Brie himself thinks steeped in all the charm of all the Graces) ever reaching the standard of Latinity one finds in Plautus; and yet Plautus thought he was doing nothing absurd and committing no affront on the   35!
Latin language when in a Latin comedy he introduced a Carthaginian character from time to time speaking Punic.[37] This precedent, in my opinion, pretty well covers the man who, in a type of composition closely akin to comedy, brings on the stage a friar of this type speaking his own language, which is a sort of pidgin Latin. And yet you yourself know, dear Erasmus,   36(
how much I was dissatisfied with that dialogue and how gladly I should have omitted it, had it not given more pleasure than I can say to those persons whom no one with any education and judgment of his own could fail to rate for education and judgment as far above Brie 'as soars man's eye hence to the ethereal heaven.'[38]   36!

I would mention some of these people by name here too, but it would be a waste of time, for you know them already, nor have I any wish to expose honourable men, men who indeed deserve honour, to the malignity of this yapping cur, who goes into such a decline when he hears another man well spoken of that I really think it would have finished him off had he not   37(
vomited some of his mad rage on Beatus Rhenanus,[39] modelling himself for resentment on Aeschines;[40] though he falls as far short of Aeschines in literary gifts as I do of Demosthenes, of whose reputation Aeschines was so jealous that he brought a public prosecution against Ctesiphon too because he had spoken well of Demosthenes, and was plotting to have him sent into   37!
exile, a plot which soon recoiled, and rightly, on his own head. Finding therefore that Beatus Rhenanus has commended my epigrams to Willibald,[41] which was one good scholar and good man commending them to another, Brie flies into an incredible rage, and with passionate virulence and puny muscles draws his leaden sword with its blunt edge to attack Rhenanus. A   38(
toady he calls him, or, if he won't accept that, he is ignorant, uneducated, and stone-blind for not detecting that my verses are what they seemed to Brie

to be as he examined them through the spectacles that envy provided. But the gnat that attacks the elephant[42] is wasting his time; and what sort of creature Brie is, he makes clear of his own accord.   385

To sing Rhenanus' praises I have no desire as things are now, for fear they tell me it is one mule scratching another mule's back,[43] and if I had a mind to it I could not do it properly; everyone knows and they all freely admit that fertile as Germany is in men of creative gifts she has no more elegant stylist if it's style you want, no better scholar if you wish for learning, and if   390 you ask for character, no better man. Indeed I do very much wonder why Brie chose Rhenanus as the sole target of his fury. Is he the only man who differs from Brie in his estimate of what I write? – as though I had not been highly praised in print,[44] I will not say by you and Pieter Gillis, for you might be thought somewhat misled by your affection for me, but by Busleyden,   395 Hutten, Desmarez, Nijmegen, Vives, Grapheus, Zasius, and Budé, with whom I was at that time so far from being linked in friendship that we had not yet exchanged a single line; and the same is true of Rhenanus himself, to say nothing of many other people not unknown as scholars. If Brie were to imagine that they are all flattering me, I'm sure I am much obliged to him for   400 making me such a great man. If he declares them all blind, ignorant, and uneducated because they disagree with him and credit a man whom he so often calls a fool and labels crazy (not to take the list any further) with somewhat more sense at least than anyone, by what I hear, has yet ascribed to Brie, himself excepted – even so, no one has invested him with such   405 absolute and dictatorial powers that his personal opinion must be universally accepted without at least some remaining right of appeal to public opinion.

Brie takes it hard,[45] it seems, that Rhenanus should have preferred my epigrams to those of Marullus and Pontano;[46] but he ought to have looked rather more closely in assessing the value of Rhenanus' praise. It is true that   410 he pays me a much more generous tribute than modesty allows me to accept, but in the area where Brie particularly takes offence he does not praise me so effusively that Brie was bound to be jealous. Rhenanus does not prefer me to Pontano or Marullus in all respects or think me a match for them. He compares us only in respect of natural gifts, not in knowledge of Greek, so   415 there is no call for Brie to be so indignant at the sight of an Englishman matched against a Greek. Is there any reason in nature why a man actually as good as any Greek should not see the light 'in mist and fog, the home of muttonheads?'[47] Though I myself have neither so much pride nor so little self-knowledge that I can accept the tributes paid me by Beatus Rhenanus,   420 who, as I say, matches me in natural gifts against such men as they, but in usefulness puts me above them, at least to the extent of thinking that anything I contribute in the way of sound principles does my readers more good than all the filth and wickedness with which they defile their pages; and he supposes the benefit they get from my simple and straightforward verses greater than the charm of Marullus' riddling lines. Surely all Rhenanus does in this is to prefer any good there may be in me to the bad there is in them.

Praise of this kind does not preclude that their virtues should exceed mine, as they certainly do, and it ought not therefore to appear so partial as to arouse envy. For that matter take Budé (to say nothing of the others), a man whose experience of public affairs is as great as it is in literature, where he holds some kind of primacy: the things he has written about me are such that though I now know them to be due to the courtesy of a man who loves to think well of others – which is equally true of the preface contributed to Brie's *Chordigera* by that excellent scholar Aleandro[48] – all the same I would far rather they should prove to be true than that I should be a better poet than Pontano or Marullus, or better at Latin and Greek than the two of them together. And yet it is surprising how suddenly Brie turns about and devotes himself (of all people) to the care of my reputation; for it is, he says,[49] only from a devoted concern for it that he has called my attention in such friendly and kindly and loyal fashion to all those errors, so many thousand of them and so disgraceful; the idea being no doubt that with his assistance things should be quietly removed which could not circulate any longer without making me a perfect byword and earning me some sort of indelible black mark for ignorance. And on this score he thinks I owe as great a debt to his well-meaning labours as one man can owe another.

This elegant and graceful attitude so forcibly appealed to Brie that he now repeats as a serious proposition what moved everyone to mockery who read it in the *Antimorus*, forgetting for the moment those verses[50] in which with astonishing ingenuity he puts forward a scheme by which he now thinks it probable that I could put all this disgrace to rights. And the scheme is that I should arrange to have returned to me from every quarter all the copies of my book which have now been printed anywhere, and having purged them in this way should then reissue them. And yet Brie is so much frightened of my doing just this, of my despatching more than five hundred emissaries to every country under the sun and recalling all the copies, that he threatens to take steps to see that uncorrected copies continue to be available in his possession and that of a number of other persons (a result I think he would find difficult to achieve without sending out emissaries for the purpose in his turn), which can demonstrate my errors to the world, those errors which he now urges me to eliminate privately so that no one can hold them against me in future, in such a way that not all the waves of Ocean could wash my record clean.

Here is another example of his long memory or his self-consistency. In 465
that letter to you he says[51] his *Antimorus* has no teeth in it, because he snaps
in it without fangs; and yet in his eleven-syllable lines[52] (which he turns off
so neatly that he can sometimes squeeze thirteen syllables into one line) he
says that his elegiacs steep themselves in my blood. The fact is that when he
imitates poets he is as absurd as a monkey imitating a man, and his attempts 470
at concealment are as futile as those of any grey mullet or cony that thinks, as
soon as it puts its head into the sand, its whole body is sufficiently
concealed; so true is it that no wolf[53] ever had a shorter memory than his and
no feather, no puff of wind was ever more consistently inconsistent.

Look now at that place[54] where he says he would have taken your 475
advice had not his book been already in the printer's hands. I am greatly
surprised that a man to whom Erasmus' lightest nod is of such importance
should give so little weight to your letter[55] of warning that he would rather
persist in wrecking his own reputation with such a crazy pamphlet (and
particularly with his thirst for glory) than write off a small sum of money. He 480
is after all a man, to use his own words,[56] who is well off in respect not only of
food and clothing but of servants and a horse to ride and a purse with money
always in it; who has a house and garden to which Apollo and all the Muses
would like to move in a body and abandon Parnassus, if Brie does not bolt
the door. And yet I'm surprised if he would have done as you told him, 485
considering that after so much good advice, before the trouble started, he
was not willing[57] to listen to Budé or Bérault or Lascaris or Deloynes or to his
Eminence the cardinal[58] who died in France lately. Be that as it may, if he
thinks it was your goodness of heart[59] that made you dissuade him from
publishing the *Antimorus*, he now thinks all the same that if you do not 490
approve of it now it is published, you are being quite unfair, because you lay
down a different set of rules for him in his treatment of me from those you
adopted for yourself in dealing with Lefèvre.[60] Nor do I doubt that Brie
regards himself as very sharp and an expert in legal procedure, tying you
down as he does with such a weighty precedent that, if you wish to escape 495
the appearance of injustice, you cannot possibly give judgment against him.

For my own part, dear Erasmus – and this I say openly to all comers, but
to none more readily than yourself, for I have observed that from this aspect
at least your mind is entirely one with mine – I have such respect, such
admiration, and veneration for Jacques Lefèvre as I ought to have for a man 500
who by his attainments and character has done more to deserve this than
anyone for several centuries; and I doubt whether anyone has worked
harder, apart from his devotion to the Scriptures, to the exposition of which
he has made a useful contribution, to bring over our universities at long last
from their foolish waste of words and pointless logic-chopping to a sober 505

and strict devotion to philosophy and to the branches of learning they had so long neglected. This fact is so generally admitted that as a rule he receives the most laudatory tributes even from those who differ from him sometimes very widely indeed on individual statements; and yet nothing arouses them more than Lefèvre's habit (as it seems to many people) of asserting somewhat too absolutely things which would have caused no offence had they been laid down and defended with more moderation, and of making definite statements in an unduly contentious spirit – so easily does a sort of pious enthusiasm often carry a good man too far.

But how little resemblance there is between your defence[61] and that perfectly absurd complaint of Brie's is beyond all doubt for anybody unless he is quite ignorant of the facts. I do not propose therefore to develop this aspect of it and compare one case with the other and match pamphlet against pamphlet, as though this were the only way to make it clear that at no point, either when it began or as it has gone on ever since, did Brie's crazy reactions correspond to what you did; so let me not be thought to rouse controversy over a case which is quite clear, or seem to have stirred up sleeping and buried fires from their ashes to no good purpose, or be obliged in any way to give offence to Lefèvre, for whom I have the greatest respect, or be credited with attempting to suborn the judge before whom I now plead my case and procure your support by flattery. One thing at least he does say[62] (except that he described himself as light-hearted when he should have said light-headed) which in other ways is not wholly untrue: that you fought at close quarters while he operated at a distance. You went to the heart of the matter, not with a sword as Brie says (he seems to imagine you as a gladiator) but with the point of a needle, while Brie is only skirmishing at long range in a lunatic fit, discharging abuse such as any drunken old woman might have poured out at the first comer and most of which was well suited to the man himself, without succeeding in getting anywhere near the target; or if he was sometimes lucky and got close to it, then as often happens on hard ground to a weapon dispatched with insufficient force, it either simply overshot the mark or glanced off it. So his long-range equipment achieved at least this result: it provided evidence that he was a by no means inadequate marksman, granted only that in the kindness of one's heart one was always willing to move the target to the spot where his arrow fell, and a very pretty controversialist, if he could find someone to whom the abuse was applicable which he himself could draw from an unfailing well of scurrilities. And when there is no one on whom this filth will stick, what can he do for the time being except drench himself in it?

But the moment comes when, as though really moved by a letter from you, he begins to take a more pacific line and, if I think fit, now that each of

us has come on stage (as he puts it),[63] having donned our tragic masks (as worn by warriors in the olden time when they advanced to do battle) and shown that we can sustain our roles with might and main (I, that is, with a handful of epigrams and Brie with whole volumes), I as challenger and Brie   550
as defender (for he is careful to repeat these words lest otherwise someone might not believe them), at long last he does not refuse to clasp hands and, with Erasmus as our *pater patratus* (a practice in ancient times confined of course to the stage), to sign a treaty, especially as you think me a man whom he ought to know and like. At the same time, for fear that peace so easily   555
achieved might be somewhat too lightly valued, or that it might give me too good a conceit of myself, he qualifies his offer, mindful as ever of his own prestige, to the effect that if I prefer to watch the outcome of the tragedy as it now is, he equally has no objections to its running through to the last act. My acting is not brilliant enough to frighten him off the stage, nor am I such a   560
doughty fighter that if I prefer to join battle he must refuse to meet me, provided I descend into the arena to fight in my own armour, not like Patroclus in the arms of Achilles, and give him fair warning with a blast of the trumpet. Look at the astonishing tricks with which Brie adorns and glorifies this minuscule dispute, in which it is almost true that he is simply sparring   565
with himself! He matches himself and me together as actors both comic and tragic and gymnasts and warriors, and it is wonderful to see what a skilful mixture he makes of these very different things; how neatly he equips fighting men with masks and comic actors with armour, and brings in a *pater patratus* to sign a treaty between actors disguised as army commanders. How   570
he brings fighting men onto the stage and warriors onto the playing-field! And so, with a skilled use of the figure they call *epimonê*,[64] he maintains his simile so elegantly that in about three lines he completes for us a tragical-comical battlepiece.

As for this treaty, dearest Erasmus, you must not put yourself out.   575
Suppose there is a contest between More, that tiny creature, on the one side and on the other Brie, that noble victor crowned with many a palm[65] and not much more than a palm high himself; this does not threaten the world of letters with such enormous peril that we need Erasmus as our *pater patratus* to achieve a peace, unless anxiety over the outcome of this heroic duel has   580
the same effect on the princes of the literary world as that famous battle of the frogs and the mice had on the anxious gods in Homer,[66] who found it more formidable than their own conflict with the giants. For when you say[67] in your letter that I am exactly the sort of man who ought to be friends with him, I admire your goodness, for you are campaigning for peace at every   585
opportunity. But, dear Erasmus, 'of such an honour all unworthy I,'[68] the honour I mean of being counted among the friends of such a mighty nabob,

to whose *Antimorus* I have now written an answer[69] for better or worse, which shows perhaps too little reverence for such a great man but in the light of the facts at any rate is perhaps unduly modest, as others judge. And you, dear Erasmus, what do you think? I long to know. It is true that I had what I wrote printed very promptly, and it might perhaps have been safer to take time to polish it, especially as it has to come before a rival with such keen sight that he can descry a fault where no fault is. But I thought it better to leave him many bones on which to try his teeth and weary them or break them in the end than to fill my head for long with all this nonsense. And I should have thought such a crazy pamphlet simply unworthy of any reply, had I not felt it right to follow the advice of some of my friends, who advised me to protect myself against the man's perfectly ludicrous calumnies. This was my sole object; not to exchange abuse and give him as good as I got. Otherwise, had I not decided to consider what was fitting for me to say rather than what he deserved to hear, however lordly Brie's contempt for my style as unwarlike, effeminate, and limp, I would at least have made him feel the truth of Ovid's line[70] 'An easy case makes all men eloquent.'

As it is, though he has not merely let fly at my talents and my character but has taken secret steps to secure my undoing so far as it was in his power, and in the literary way has left nothing of mine alone without getting his teeth into it, I on the other hand have touched on nothing of his except just those volumes in which his target is either myself or my native country. On what he is capable of, taking the question as a whole, I pass no judgment and I make no examination. I know how little weight my opinion of him would carry, though even now I take a kinder view of him than many men whom he has done less to offend. All the same, I have never down to this day heard anyone give a truly favourable verdict on Brie without feeling at the same time that so far he has produced nothing grand enough to correspond to the airs which that boastful little man gives himself; for at one moment he boasts that poetry is his natural field, what the open plain is to a horse,[71] at another he prides himself on competing with Antiquity or robbing Hercules[72] himself of his club by force, or threatens with some lack of modesty that he will breathe forth the thunderbolt. Such are his boasts, and other people who compare them with his poems give as their considered opinion that he is not only insane but incurable.

As for me, although Brie shows himself in my case a ferocious prophet as well as judge, such that he not only damns everything I have written up to now but asserts that I shall never write[73] anything worth reading hereafter, yet I take a somewhat kinder view of him, basing my judgment mainly on both the *Chordigera* and the *Antimorus*, in which he attacked me in a fit of bad temper – for this very fact still gives me some hopes that that sour talent may

one day ripen. Though what he writes is so foolish at the age he is now, he is
not, I perceive, one of those men whose talents mature so early that he   630
cannot still continue and ripen in another way. Of course, if I thought he had
already reached his full development and vigour, his *acme* (to use the Greek
word), I could expect nothing except to see a man whose spring was spent in
a coma and his summer in uncontrollable rage enjoy an autumn of unbroken
frenzy.   635

When he says[74] my acting is not brilliant enough to frighten him off the
stage, I can at least admit that I neither have nor claim to have anything about
me that could frighten anybody. Nor can I deny that Brie's acting is such a
terrifying performance that it might drive from the theatre not only a
poor-spirited little creature like myself who am easily frightened by a pale   640
image in its mask[75] but the whole body of spectators, by spectral forms
affrighted, if those lines[76] of Brie's are to be trusted which the silly fool, a
second Morychus,[77] inserted in his *Antimorus*:

> As this I wrote, from their infernal marsh;   645
> The Furies rose; there stood Alecto, there
> Megaera terrible with visage harsh,
> Tisiphone with her snake-knotted hair.

If only Brie would take off those needlessly tragical masks, the rest of   650
his performance at any rate has nothing about it sufficiently remarkable to
make any man stiffen to attention as if he'd seen Medusa's head; nor does my
experience suggest that his strength is formidable enough to make Patroclus,
or Thersites[78] anyhow, run to Achilles to ask help from his armour against a
Hector such as this. But if he has made up his mind to bring on stage with him   655
not those pasteboard Furies but his own fury and rage; if he is resolved to let
all his thunders roll, and has decided to brandish that portentous thunderbolt which falls (so he boasts) from his lips whenever, in a private and
particular fit of resentment I suppose, he conceives 'wrath not of Jove
unworthy'[79] – why, then, as far as I am concerned, he can play to empty   660
houses, and the amulet to protect me against such threatening apparitions
shall be silence. However, there shall arise perhaps some Hercules, helper of
those in need, who has had some practice in subduing monsters like this and
will take from Brie's hands in his turn the club which Brie forcibly took from
him, using as his weapon I fancy a cane or a birch. Brie's brand of thunder is   665
such that Strepsiades[80] himself would not hesitate to fart in its face. And for
this conjuror's trick, this thunderbolt, very figure to suppress it is Cacus,[81]
himself no mean exponent of the art of terrifying; or, if his skill is insufficient,
the name of Cacus by itself would remind us of the weapons which he had

had to use himself against that kind of thunder. Are hapless mortals to perish   6·
by that thunderbolt's hot breath? No, no! Into that open mouth, agape with
three-cleft bolt, 'to piss, or worse, we have the right.'[82]

I hope, my dear Erasmus, that we shall see you when the kings meet at
Calais,[83] and if you come, both kings, you need not doubt, will make you
welcome. Otherwise it would be impertinent for humble friends of yours like   6·
me to demand or expect that for our sake you should endure the fatigues of
such a journey, when it is more properly our duty to come and see you, as I
shall certainly do if the wish to pay your respects to the kings does not bring
you there, having asked my prince to allow me a few days leave. Meanwhile,
dear Erasmus, farewell; and without any reduction in your usual friendship   68
for Brie, keep a warm corner as you usually do for More, for you are as dear
to me as I could possibly be to myself. Our friend Lupset[84] is lecturing at
Oxford to large audiences on the humanities, both Greek and Latin, with
great credit to himself and no less profit to his pupils. He has succeeded my
friend John Clement,[85] who has devoted himself entirely to medicine, in   68
which one day he will be second to none, unless (which God forbid) the
Fates deprive his fellow men of his society.

Farewell once more, and give most cordial greetings in my name to
those capital scholars Dorp, Nesen, and Vives.

1088 / To Justus Jonas   Louvain, 9 April 1520

This letter is known from a copy preserved in the manuscript that is also the
source of Epp 872, 983 (Forschungsbibliothek Gotha, MS chart. A 399 f 231). The
three texts were not published until 1880. This letter resembles Ep 872 in its
very private nature, and in this case too various circumstances mentioned
elsewhere would seem to prove sufficiently that the manuscript copy is an
accurate rendering of what Erasmus actually wrote. The letter illustrates
Erasmus' efforts (cf Ep 1083 introduction) at mobilizing his German supporters
for a concerted attack upon Edward Lee. These efforts netted, among other
things, the Erfurt collection of epigrams against Lee, for which Jonas was no
doubt in part responsible (cf Ep 1083 introduction), and also two incensed
letters by Conradus Mutianus Rufus, addressed to Johann Lang (24 May 1520)
and Jonas (29 June 1520), the first of which was perhaps written for
publication, but is not included in Froben's Epistolae aliquot eruditorum virorum
(cf Der Briefwechsel des Conradus Mutianus ed K. Gillert, Halle 1890, Epp 590–1).

Reinhold Weijenborg argued in Antonianum 58 (1983) 445 that this letter and
also Epp 872, 983 are spurious and actually invented by Jonas in order to give
the impression that Erasmus had solicited the epigrams published by the Erfurt
circle a few days earlier. Weijenborg interpreted the date of Knapp's edition of

the epigrams (cf Ep 1083 introduction) in a very unusual fashion. 'Feriae divini ternionis' is more likely to refer to Trinity Sunday (3 June 1520) than to the last three days of Holy Week (5–7 April 1520), as Weijenborg claims. Moreover if Jonas had intended to connect Erasmus with the collection of epigrams, why would he date his faked letter after its appearance and not before? And why would he have Erasmus solicit the writing of letters rather than epigrams? There can be no doubt that Erasmus wished to receive a bundle of letters attacking Lee, just as he states here (cf Ep 1074 introduction), and that he received some (cf Ep 1083 n9) but eventually decided to suppress them; see Ep 1157.

TO THE WORTHY JODOCUS JONAS FROM ERASMUS OF ROTTERDAM
Thank you for your last very kind letter.[1] I have replied[2] to Lee in such terms that in future he will not be able to utter a sound unless he is content to pile up abuse, of which any prostitute is capable. The second act remains: my friends are to write letters highly critical of Lee, but taking care to praise[3] 5 English scholars and the great men in England who support them, and bearing down on Lee and no one else; and him they are to laugh at as a foolish, boastful, deceitful little man, rather than attack him seriously. I should like to see many letters of this kind put together, so that he may be overwhelmed all the deeper. I should like them to be collected from the 10 learned writers and sent me by safe hand, and I will revise them myself and see to their publication. Great variety in them is desirable. I have written to Wilhelm Nesen,[4] so that he can show you what to do.

I would as soon the Dominicans did not know what a friend I have been[5] to Luther! The university here has developed incurable insanity. 15 Atensis[6] has died, but Baechem[7] and Latomus[8] are behaving insufferably, one blear-eyed, the other club-footed. Give greetings to all my friends, and if they love their old acquaintance, let them treat Lee as he deserves. Farewell.

Louvain, Easter Monday 1520

1089 / From Richard Pace   Greenwich, April [1520]

The only source for this letter is Froben's *Epistolae aliquot eruditorum virorum* (cf Ep 1083 introduction). For Lee's connections with Pace and other English friends of Erasmus see Epp 999 introduction; 1026 n3, and for the concern this caused Erasmus see Ep 1083 n12.

PACE TO HIS FRIEND ERASMUS
You told me in your note that you had answered Lee's defences.[1] I read the piece myself, or rather I drank it at one draught from cover to cover, struck

with astonishment at the moderation you show everywhere, which I should
never have thought it possible for you to maintain on such a subject had I not   5
seen it with my own eyes. This will warm the heart of any educated reader.
Others will be more careful in future, I dare say, not to make these abusive
attacks, when they see the gentle and religious spirit in which you know
how to use your teeth. If they are angry with Lee in Germany, I am not
surprised, but I greatly regret it. Not surprised, because Lee is trying to   10
besmirch the most precious jewel in the crown of Germany; regretful,
because they have been given an opening to rage against a fellow-
countryman and friend of mine. Farewell.

From Greenwich, April

1090 / From Thomas More   [Greenwich? end of February–April 1520]

In this letter More states his reaction to Edward Lee's printed *Annotationes*. It is
to Erasmus' credit that he published it in the *Epistolae ad diversos*, for despite the
loving consideration More always shows for Erasmus' touchiness, he does not
conceal his suspicion that his friend must share with Lee the blame for their
unfortunate controversy. Thus the letter was clearly not suited for inclusion in
Hillen's or Froben's collections of *Epistolae* against Lee (cf Ep 1083
introduction).

Allen and Rogers assigned to this letter the date of April 1520, assuming that
Erasmus answered promptly with Ep 1097, dated 2 May. It may be noted,
however, that More had twice written to Lee as soon as his printed
Annotationes reached him at the English court (Greenwich, 27 and 29 February
[1520]; Rogers Epp 84–5, both published in Froben's *Epistolae aliquot eruditorum
virorum*). The first letter advised Lee to return to England without delay; the
second expresses a loving regard for Lee, as does this letter for Erasmus. It
would seem to be in line with More's feelings if he had written to both
protagonists at roughly the same time, while Erasmus could have delayed his
answer to More until his reply to Lee was printed.

THOMAS MORE TO HIS FRIEND ERASMUS, GREETING
Though it was never concealed from me, Erasmus dearest of all my friends,
how much better your judgment is than mine, nothing has cast such a bright
light on this as the advice[1] we gave you and Lee that that pamphlet of his
should be permanently suppressed, while your view on the other hand was   5
that its publication should be allowed[2] at the particular moment when it was
so actively expected, so that the whole sad story might one day reach a
conclusion, rather than wait till the public interest should have died down
and then publish it all the same, stirring up fresh troubles. And so we forced

you rather than persuaded you to agree to this truce; but though you say you   10
never broke the agreement, and Lee solemnly swears that he observed it, it
was continually broken all the time. Which of you broke it I cannot say for
certain, for I was a long way away when it all happened, and you and he
were bandying accusations back and forth all the time; I am only bound to
regret that my advice carried sufficient weight with the two of you to bring   15
about a truce but would not carry enough to secure that the truce was
observed. For I would rather have had the book[3] published then, at a time
when feelings were not running so high and its publication would be a
milder affair, than that it should come out now after all this time, when
resentment has increased and its effect must be exacerbated. For it has come   20
out, and is rather more bitter than I might have hoped or than might have
been salutary to experts in this field; among whom one looks in vain for the
humility which even ignorant men should be ashamed not to display
towards one another. But for you surely, my dear Erasmus, it cannot be right
– assuming that the complaints he adduces are genuine – to be surprised if   25
he shows a certain bitterness in pouring out his feelings after being so badly
hurt; if, on the other hand, he has been misled by some phantom of the truth,
you ought to make allowances even so. For what we believe to be true moves
us with just as much force as what is proved to be so.

It is, I suppose, hardly necessary to advise or exhort you to display true   30
Christian humility, which in all it undertakes toils solely for Christ's sake,
who ought to be the only object before your eyes. The world may be
ungrateful and not take the trouble to reward you, it may be grateful but not
have the power; so much the more solid the reward you will receive from
him. If you have made such sacrifices to secure great advantage for the   35
world, if you have worn out your health by so much toil for the advancement
of humane studies, and yet have been repaid evil for good by the jealousy of
men who owe you (and you almost alone) what little tincture of a liberal
education they may possess, in all this you are made more like unto Christ;
and in no way can you more faithfully imitate him than by returning good   40
words for evil, just as it was your good deeds that called them forth.
Farewell, Erasmus my heart's dearest friend.

Yours, if he is his own, T. More

1091 / To Lieven Algoet   Antwerp, 13 April 1520

This letter was published in the *Epistolae ad diversos* with the date above, which
may be accepted in the absence of other evidence. The following letters show
that Erasmus spent much of April 1520 in Antwerp before returning to
Louvain, apparently between 3 and 5 June (cf Epp 1098–9). He had visited

Antwerp earlier in that same spring, possibly more than once (cf Epp 1079, 1086 introductions) and an important reason for his visits was no doubt the completion and printing of his answers to Lee (cf Ep 1080 introduction).

Lieven Algoet of Ghent (d 1547) was studying at he Collegium Trilingue when he entered Erasmus' service, apparently in the early summer of 1519, perhaps upon the recommendation of Marcus Laurinus (lines 29–31). He may have continued his studies under Conradus Goclenius (cf Epp 1046 n5, 1437) but was increasingly employed by Erasmus to carry his letters. For possible references to such errands at about this time see Epp 1058, 1063 introductions, 1073 n3. Algoet stayed with Erasmus for six years. Later on he received with Erasmus' aid employment at the court of Mary of Hungary; see Franz Bierlaire *La familia d'Erasme: Contribution à l'histoire de l'humanisme* (Paris 1968) 55–9; de Vocht CTL II 136–9.

ERASMUS TO HIS FRIEND LIEVEN ALGOET, GREETING

Several things have happened unexpectedly which delay my return for some time. I therefore think it advisable to repeat in writing the same instructions that I gave you before setting out. You must not let my absence tend to make you less keen on your studies, when it ought to have the opposite effect. The 5
more time you have free from the things you do for me when I am at home, the more you should concentrate on your reading. That was certainly what I hoped when I left you at Louvain, with your good in mind more than my own. So you must make sure that this plan of mine does not disappoint me, and do all you can to secure that I find nothing when I get back to lessen the 10
happiness of my return. You know what Terence[1] says: ' 'Tis always so, when master's back is turned,' and 'Who does his task from fear of punishment / Is good while he's afraid he'll be found out; / If he can hope to hide, shows his true self.' That other remark is more meant for you: 'He whom by kindness you have made your own / Will do his duty with a willing 15
heart; /Here or not here, he'll be the self-same man.' Personally I have always found this principle of Micio's congenial; it will be for you to see that I have no reason to regret this attitude.

Avoid, as you would the plague, the society of some people whom Menander's tag[2] really fits: 'Evil communications corrupt good manners.' 20
Keep in close touch with Carinus,[3] not a finger's breadth between you. It is true he is not much older than you in years, but he has such a high character and such a thirst for learning that there is scarcely anyone from whose society you will emerge a better man or a better scholar. Nature has given you qualities full of promise; we can all be glad of this for your sake, but you 25
deserve no credit for it unless you improve nature's generosity, like some fertile soil, by your own labours, and great disgrace will be your reward if

you prove not to have made the best of yourself. It is no secret from you that your excellent parents have high hopes of you, and you know what you owe to Marcus Laurinus,[4] who recommended you to me with real fatherly   30 affection. I will not mention at this stage what you owe to me, for I have always treated you not as a servant but as a son; but that you have lived in intimacy with Erasmus undoubtedly makes many people expect more of you. All this you cannot live up to except by very hard work; and you are now at an age when it is easy not only to learn but to work hard. Others are retarded   35 in their studies by lack of money or of books or teachers; you are well supplied with all these by the kindness of your friends, and unless you make yourself the sort of person it is right you should, there will be no excuse; the whole blame will fall on you.

Here then are reasons quite enough, I should suppose, to fire you with   40 the desire to be a good man and a good scholar; and there is yet another which should add a spur to any noble mind, that you can see in Louvain so many boys and young men pursuing distinction in the two tongues not only with zeal but with success. Finally, it is right and proper that you should fulfil the promise of your family name, so that men never arise (which God   45 forbid) to turn you humorously from *pankalos* (as Greek would have it) into *pankakos*, making you by the change of a single letter not Allgood, the true meaning of your surname, but Allbad. No, you must strive with all your powers to prove that this name fell to your lot not by pure chance but through the purpose of some deity.[5] I give you this serious warning, not   50 because I mistrust the goodness of your nature, but because when we passionately wish someone well, we begin to fear where no fear is.

If any letters have arrived at home which you can see are of no great importance, keep them till my return. If there is anything that had better not be postponed and you have no reliable person by whom to send it, run over   55 here yourself. Farewell.

Antwerp, 13 April 1520

1092 / To Nicolaas Everaerts   Antwerp, 17 April [1520]

This letter comes from a collection of autograph letters once belonging to Antoon Vivien of Dordrecht (cf Allen's headnote). It was still accessible to Jean Leclerc, the editor of LB, but has since vanished.

Nicolaas Everaerts of Grijpskerke near Middelburg (d 1532) studied and taught law at Louvain, receiving his doctorate in 1493 and serving as the university's rector in 1504. From 1496 to 1502 he was the official at Brussels of Erasmus' former patron, Bishop Hendrik van Bergen. Thus he was perhaps an early acquaintance of Erasmus, who may have met him again at Louvain in

Medal of Erasmus, with the figure of Terminus on the reverse
Made by Quinten Metsys in 1519
Historisches Museum, Basel

1502–3. In 1505 he was appointed to the Great Council at Mechelen. In 1509 he moved to The Hague as president of the Council of Holland. One of his sons was the famous neo-Latin poet and medallist Johannes Secundus; see NNBW; de Vocht CTL II 430–53.

TO THE HONOURABLE DOCTOR NICOLAAS, DOCTOR OF CIVIL
AND CANON LAW, RIGHT WORTHY PRESIDENT OF HOLLAND, FROM
ERASMUS OF ROTTERDAM, GREETING

My right honoured Lord President, I hope to visit Holland[1] this summer, if nothing new befalls. Meantime, I send your Excellency Erasmus in lead,[2] modelled by no mean artist and at some considerable expense. I send also two little books[3] in which I reply to Lee the Englishman, a wretched fellow, the most arrogant and ignorant and malignant thing this world has yet produced. England herself abhors her own offspring. I hear that in your part of the world also there are Dominicans[4] who rant away to the ignorant multitude and call on the crowd to start throwing stones; and unless governments take a stand against these rascals, the thing will issue in civil strife. Why cannot they preach the Scriptures, and keep quiet about these things which they do not understand?

A third book is now in the press, which will soon find its way to you, unless you should happen to revisit Louvain first; for so I have heard from your son,[5] who dined with me lately in Antwerp. His mind seemed to me as spotless as his habit. Please greet my other friends to whom I have no leisure to write just now, Sasbout,[6] Carolus,[7] Mauritszoon,[8] Bernard[9] the dean, and, if they are with you, two great men to whom I am much indebted, my lords of Nassau[10] and of Veere.[11] Farewell.

Antwerp, 17 April
Your sincere friend Erasmus

1093 / To Thomas More   Antwerp, 26 April 1520

This letter was published in the *Epistolae ad diversos*. Although Erasmus only refers to having read Brie's *Antimorus* and does not acknowledge receipt of More's Ep 1087, this letter covers so many points raised in Ep 1087 that it is safe to assume it presents Erasmus' reaction to it (cf n13). More probably thought so too, although in his reply he exercised polite restraint and merely expressed regret at the lateness with which this letter followed the publication of the *Antimorus*, see Ep 1096:3–9.

ERASMUS OF ROTTERDAM TO THOMAS MORE, GREETING

I was hoping that my letter[1] might have carried some weight with Brie. But

no: his *Antimorus* has come out, and is on sale here. For the author's own
sake, to whom I am attached because of his friendly attitude towards both
the humanities and myself, as expressed in what he has written, I wish either 5
that the book might have been kept dark for ever, or at least that Brie might
have copied the modest and courteous tone of your epigrams.[2] Yet I could
have wished even those had never been published, rather than that this
passionate dispute should have arisen between you, from which the cause of
the humanities must suffer; for I do not see how they can hold their ground 10
unless they are defended against these obstinate and well-organized
barbarians by a band of armed scholars standing shoulder to shoulder.[3] But
since what's done can't be undone, my fervent wish, now that this rogue
plant has sprung up in an evil hour, is that we may take steps to deal with it,
so that if it cannot be pulled out by the roots, at least it may not spread. And 15
this I wish, my dear More, not only for Brie's sake, to whom I am much
attached, but for yours, to whom my attachment is much deeper. Not that I
think there is any risk that his *Antimorus* will do any harm to your reputation
– I wish it might not have done more harm to his own – but because I am
seriously afraid that if you answer and give him tit for tat, the result will be 20
that what they all now think of him they will think in future of you both.

I know how hard it is, when one is answering a book like this which is
all prickles, not to be offensive oneself; and yet if you of all people[4] err in that
direction, no one who knows you will think it as easy to excuse you as Brie.
To say nothing for the moment of you both as scholars, the position you hold 25
and your standing and your knowledge of the world mean that you must rise
above squabbles of this kind, which are as petty as they are spiteful, and not
take pains to recompense one insult with another. I hear every day what
educated men are saying of Brie since he published his book; I do not enjoy
hearing these things said of him, and much less would I wish to hear them 30
said of you. And so, though I feel the difficulty,[5] when one has been attacked
in such a venomous pamphlet, of moderating one's reply so as to give one's
passions no play, yet I think the best course would certainly be to neglect and
despise the whole affair as it deserves.

Nor would I give you this advice, my excellent More, if there were 35
anything in the *Antimorus* which could have cast any aspersion on you such
that it might be worth while trying to wipe it off. It is all the kind of thing to
which the reader can see the answer for himself as he goes along. Everyone
can see that what Brie objects to is your having so rashly and hastily
published your epigrams, though most of them were written over twenty 40
years ago and almost all of them over ten, and even now it was not you[6] who
published them. They can see that he is carping at you for mistakes some of
which are the copyist's and some the printer's,[7] and most of them such that

they cannot be complained of without condemning the greatest writers. They see that your epigram on the *Chordigera*[8] was written long ago in the   45
middle of the war, and that Brie had no reason to revive a wartime dispute now after so many years when peace has been signed and sealed. They see Brie poking fun at your epitaph on Abingdon,[9] and with unmistakeable ill will concealing what cannot be concealed, that the absurdity of that poem was intentional. Apart from that, the passage where he attacks your poem   50
congratulating the prince[10] on his accession leaves every educated man so aware of Brie's lack of moderation in both feeling and expression that I, who am, as you know, not too bad as a defender of my friends, can find no way of excusing him except that he wrote in complete ignorance of English affairs; had he understood them, he would not have written that, and would have   55
admitted, angry as he was, that you had paid a splendid tribute to the king in really kingly language.

     Everybody thinks this, my dear More, and says so: what reason can remain for you to torment yourself into writing a reply, which is only, as they say,[11] to tell a twice-told tale, and nothing to be got from it except that while   60
no one at the moment is suffering from loss of reputation in the eyes of educated men except Brie, you run the risk of getting some share of that for yourself, if it should happen (and it is not easy to avoid, if one loses one's temper pen in hand, as sometimes happens) that you write without mercy and repay abuse in the same coin. Not the least part of your enviable   65
reputation is your equable temperament and the unruffled charm[12] of your character, and I should be sorry to see any sacrifice of this. But if you have made up your mind to take a different course (and I hear you have a book[13] against him already in preparation), do be content to defend yourself. Reject the charge that you were offensive and began it all by your spite without   70
casting it back at your opponent; fight with reasons and not abuse, and your moderation will magnify his ill will. All the same, even granted that you took that line, I would certainly much prefer you to keep silent and let the whole thing be buried in oblivion. This may be difficult just now, but it will gradually become possible if, as I hope, it is what you wish.   75

     I had written to Brie telling him to suppress[14] the *Antimorus*, which I kept hearing at the time that he was planning, and had the courier shown any diligence, I might have succeeded, if Brie's letter[15] speaks the truth. But, as you can see from his answer, the book was already in the press before he saw my letter. But of you, my dear More, I have far higher hopes than of Brie;   80
for when I see that I should have persuaded him if my letter had reached him in time, I ought to have no doubt that I shall easily win you over to control your emotions for my sake to the extent of not assailing yet further with fresh pamphlets a man who likes me and whom I like in return. One or other of you

must make the first move to end this controversy, unless you want the 85
contest to go on for ever turn and turn about. Your standing and your
character demand that the initiative should come from you. Believe me, my
dear More, though Brie has behaved in all this in such a way that even he
perhaps is sorry for it by now, and if he could start again he would not do it
(no one is so fortunate as to be wise all the time), yet he is a man, if you knew 90
him better, whose character and whose wide reading would delight you, nor
would you easily find anyone whom you would be more ready to make
friends with. Nor ought you to demand that everyone should keep his
emotions under such strict control as we have learnt in view of your record
and our long experience of your wisdom to expect without hesitation from 95
you. Brie had written some things in his *Chordigera* which gave you, as the
injured party, the right to reply even more bitterly, especially as things then
were; yet once your epigrams, the charm of which made them universally
popular, had made him a public laughing-stock, you ought not to be
surprised if, as a spirited young man with a thirst for fame, he was diverted 100
by some degree of resentment from thinking over what he had done and
concentrated on your verses, thinking himself the injured party and not
realizing that he had neither the right nor the ideal opportunity to seek
revenge.

I know you do not set such a high value on the few epigrams you threw 105
off against him that you could not bear for my sake to suppress them; for
unless your instructions had come too late,[16] you were arranging to do this of
your own accord some time ago, when you heard to your regret that the book
was going to be published entire. I shall therefore secure that with your good
will they are omitted in future[17] when the book is reprinted, and in return 110
that the *Antimorus* is given no circulation. Thus it will come about that for
want of fuel this fire will gradually die down. If however you have so
obstinately resolved to pursue this quarrel, yet in the name of our
friendship, which is neither recent nor of any common kind, I beg you again
and again to consider very carefully how you propose to treat the business. 115
For my part, if I had the choice, I should prefer, I repeat, for you to say
nothing and to despise a topic that really deserves to be despised. If this
cannot be, I should hope for the next best thing, that you should do as you
have managed to do up to now and continue to show yourself the victor by
your scholarship and the goodness of your case, and not by abuse as well. In 120
that way, as I see that one of my two friends has been wounded in this
ill-judged engagement, I shall at least be able to preserve the other
permanently intact, who is so dear to me that I prefer him alone to all my
other friends; though I should be more blest if I might preserve both. For as

man can have nothing more precious than a good and faithful friend, it is   125
reasonable to reckon no loss so heavy as the loss of friendship.

I have written this in the midst of the confusion[18] in which you know I
live just now. Farewell, most warm-hearted friend.

Antwerp, 26 April 1520

1094 / From Jan de Hondt   Courtrai, 28 April 1520

The original letter, autograph throughout, was in the Burscher collection at
Leipzig (see Ep 1067 introduction).

Jan de Hondt was canon of Courtrai in the place of Erasmus and responsible
for the payment of Erasmus' annuity; cf below n3, n6, and Ep 751 introduction.

Right worshipful and dear sir, with my humble duty: I received some days
ago and on my return from attending a synod[1] in Tournai the letter which
your Worship kindly wrote me dated on the Wednesday[2] in Easter week last
past. Enclosed in it was a blank form[3] of receipt intended to have the
quittance for St John Baptist's day next following entered in it; and you   5
asked me among other things, if I have the means available and do not find it
inconvenient, to send your Reverence the money due that same quarter-day
following by the hand of Michael[4] your messenger; and I am to know that in
this I shall be doing your Reverence a service, since I understand that you
expect shortly to be away and perhaps to move to a distance. In order   10
therefore to comply as is proper with your request and thereby to stand more
highly in your Reverence's regard, I send you as requested the entire sum
due on the said quarter-day next ensuing, that is to say sixty-five common
Rhenish florins, the greater part of this sum in good and current coin, that is
to say in stuivers,[5] and the balance in gold of good and proper weight. The 15
blank receipt I have now filled in, inserting nothing therein that might prove
an unfortunate precedent or burden to your Reverence for the future, but
faithfully complying with the trust reposed in me.

At the same time, worshipful sir, I must not conceal from you what a
hidden risk there was while I was still at Tournai and the rural deans present 20
on that occasion were submitting their accounts in the usual manner, for this
reason: that my friend Barbier[6] had failed to send his letters of *significamus* (as
they are called), otherwise known as letters certificatory, of his residence
and regular attendance at the court of his Catholic Majesty. This lapse of
memory, had I not repeatedly and urgently appealed to the officials of his   25
lordship the bishop of Tournai,[7] very nearly had this result, that the fruits of
the parish church of St Gillis-Waas[8] and of two chaplaincies, at St

Niklaas-Waas and Ghent, had by now been confiscated and made over to my lord of Tournai aforesaid. I secured however by my entreaties, as I say, that none of this money should be lost, provided that between now and St John   30 Baptist's day next I exhibit and prove to the said officials the appropriate letters of *significamus*. I wrote some time ago that it would be expedient to send such a letter every year on the approach of Easter, and what the reason was why this same letter has not arrived by now I do not know. For the rest, your Worship writes that as regards relinquishing the benefices which   35 Barbier holds from me direct and the assigning of an annuity by the second chaplain of the Lord of Chièvres,[9] you have entrusted the whole matter to Barbier's discretion, provided I approve. If Barbier comes here with the king on the visit we have so long hoped for,[10] I will make such arrangements with him as seem honourable, nor will I be a party to any transaction in which   40 anything is proposed that may be unacceptable or prejudicial to your Reverence; rather, I will protect your interests just as though they were my own. Your Reverence shall assuredly not find me any different from the man described to him by others.

My honoured master Jacob van Thielt,[11] precentor and canon of   45 Courtrai and secretary of the bishop of Tournai, has a worthy young man whose name is Johannes Soti,[12] a native of Aardenburg, of poor family but gifted, whom he has educated for several years on account of his gifts, and who is by now well grounded in literature and music. He is sending this man to Louvain to the College of the Lily to be instructed in the liberal arts, and   50 hopes thereafter to promote him to something higher, if the course of his studies continues as it has begun. Canon van Thielt, with cordial greetings to your Reverence, begs you to be so good as to recommend the young man to the regent[13] of his college. In the mean time, dear sir, my very best wishes, and believe me anxious to serve you day and night with all my powers.   55

From Courtrai, 28 April 1520

Your Reverence's humble servant Jan de Hondt, canon and rural dean of Courtrai

To the right worshipful and learned Doctor Erasmus of Rotterdam, doctor of divinity, dwelling in Louvain in the College of the Lily   60

In Louvain

1095 / From Willibald Pirckheimer   Nürnberg, 30 April [1520]

Pirckheimer's rough draft of this letter is preserved in the Stadtbibliothek Nürnberg, MS PP 33. It lacks the date and the postscript and differs in many details from the text actually sent, in which a number of vigorous expressions are toned down. In a marginal note added to the heading of the rough draft

Pirckheimer refers to a copy of Lee's book sent by Wilhelm Nesen. In fact, the
Bodleian Library in Oxford possesses a volume (Mar. 869) containing Lee's
Annotationes (cf Ep 1037) with a dedication from Konrad Resch to Nesen and
another from Nesen to Pirckheimer. The same volume also contains Erasmus'
first *Responsio* and the *Apologia invectivis Lei* (cf Ep 1080 introduction), the three
pieces probably having been bound together on Pirckheimer's order.

   This letter was published both in Hillen's *Epistolae aliquot eruditorum* and in
Froben's enlarged collection (cf Ep 1083 introduction) and subsequently also in
Erasmus' *Epistolae ad diversos*. These printed versions, which evidently follow
the letter actually sent, are the basis of Allen's text and of this translation.
Pirckheimer is answering Ep 1085, obviously anxious to contribute his share to
the campaign against Lee; Erasmus in turn replied with Ep 1139.

A LETTER FROM THE HONOURABLE WILLIBALD PIRCKHEIMER,
COUNCILLOR OF NÜRNBERG

That kinsman[1] of mine, my dear friend, does his duty in showing you respect
and bringing you my greetings therewith, for he well knows the warmth of
my feelings for you. We shall be able to invoke his help in sending letters,   5
which seem fated either to be delivered very slowly or even to be completely .
lost. For a long time I have had nothing from you, although I have written
several times, and unless I had discovered from your *Farrago*[2] of letters that
you had sent me an answer, I should not know even now. How faithfully my
letters too have been delivered to you is clear enough from the reliability of   10
my friend Alamirus,[3] if nothing else. Be that as it may, I have read this most
tedious attack[4] by Edward Lee, or rather, I have run my eye over it; for who
could endure to read a book so devoid of mind, of modesty, of literary skill,
of every human quality? I have also read your *Apologia*[5] which promises at
the same time an answer to his *Annotationes*.   15

   Would you like to know what I think? I wish you had either kept
silence or answered the man as he deserved. But (you will say) there was a
risk that your silence might be thought to mean acceptance of his criticisms.
As though everyone of any character and education was not likely to
understand at once that everything spewed out by that lunatic who has lost   20
all control of himself is pure calumny and the most impudent falsehood! We
know truth when we see it. And that poor madman is so far beside himself
that he frequently gives himself away. Ruffians and ragamuffins ought not to
cost you a moment's peace. Though even in that class those who are not
quite so stupid as the rest see and condemn the man's prodigious arrogance   25
and ignorance and venom; and these are abominated even by those who do
not wish you well, and are furious with the champion who has left them on a
lee shore, defending their cause so clumsily that he would have done better

to have kept his mouth shut. So I could wish that, once you had decided that
you ought not to keep silence, you had replied to his false and spurious   30
restraint with no restraint at all and loosed off the whole armoury of your
eloquence against the poisonous and hellish invective of such a cursed
fellow.

But you preferred not to forego restraint, not to return evil for evil – a
sound decision to be sure, and one that all good men will commend. But if   35
you do this always, think what you must expect from the envious, once they
see that any brazen blockhead can revile his Erasmus with impunity and
mock you as he pleases. I beg you therefore for the sake of your reputation
and in the name of our mutual friendship, not to think in future that every
noisy rascal deserves a reply; or, if you think a reply absolutely necessary, 40
put up some cook or stable-boy to do it for you. Remember who you are – too
big a man to descend into such an arena with men like him, from which even
as the victor you can win nothing but disgrace. Unless you do this, a mob of
malignant scribblers must inevitably overwhelm you in the end. For these
men never rest; they rave all the time against merit and scholarship and truth 45
itself. And can you wonder? How could they bless who have learnt nothing
except how to curse? Their minds, their gifts, their characters are such that it
is far better to be maligned by them than praised, and to be criticized than
commended.

In any case, being themselves too inarticulate to find words for their   50
virulence, too lazy to forego their pleasures for the moment, and above all in
fear that they will collect fewer cheeses[6] as the world's dislike of them daily
grows, is it surprising if they look for a comedian such as Lee to don the mask
and costume and act another man's play,[7] getting an unenviable reputation
as his reward? Such a man must have neither shame nor brains, only a   55
tongue that knows no restraints and the confidence of a prostitute. In this
line our Lee surpasses everyone hitherto seen on the stage, although we
have witnessed some signal examples of effrontery. Anyone can see who
stitched this buskin, but it is Lee who puts it on, in order to act a farce on
behalf of many others, which means to show the world a frightful monster   60
made up of ignorance, arrogance, vanity, impudence, and venom – in a
word, just such a creature as you depicted in your pamphlet[8] answering
Latomus' dialogues, with marvellous brevity but absolutely to the life.
Whoever you had in mind when you wrote that, at any rate your description
fits exactly the picture of what Lee has done. And this is the one place where 65
he seems to me to show some human intelligence: that he recognized his
picture.[9] I know you have some skill as a painter; but no one could give so
lifelike a portrait of Lee as he gives himself. He was satisfied with his whole
self, and his whole self he has set down. Suppose you had described a man

conceited to the verge of lunacy, so pleased with himself that he wonders not   70
to find all turn to roses[10] where'er he walks, admiring nothing but himself,
his handsome, scholarly, and saintly self, although he has no good qualities
at all and nothing in his bosom but vinegar – however true your words, it
may be that not everyone would have believed you. And now we have the
whole thing in Lee's self-portrait.   75

For my part, dear Erasmus, I have complete trust in your single-minded
integrity. But I would hardly have believed that so much folly and arrogance
and deception and stupidity and malice could exist in any human heart – if
we are to call Lee human, and not for preference a most savage beast. Had
there been any person more wicked or more crazy, Lee would have been   80
their choice as viceroy of this province, which has been their sphere of action
for so long. Nor is their programme new. They have a long-standing passion
for the defamation of distinguished men and for resistance to everyone with
high aspirations. To say nothing of earlier examples, is there any part of the
world that does not know the perverse, calumnious, and monstrous   85
intrigues with which they have harrassed that celebrated figure who has
done so much for Germany and for the humanities, Reuchlin? To say nothing
in the mean time of the disgusting abuse they have spewed out at that
excellent, that truly noble character, the count of Neuenahr, or at the valiant
Hutten, or for that matter at me and all Reuchlin's friends. What have they   90
not set on foot against the admirable Jacques Lefèvre?[11] For of their
long-continued machinations against Luther[12] it is perhaps better to say
nothing, for fear that I too – for this is an old objective of theirs – may be
haled off to court as a friend of his and compelled to defend a charge of
heresy.[13] One thing everyone knows: they have reached such a pitch of   95
confidence that they have taken this business out of the hands of the pope
himself, to whom the jurisdiction in this case particularly belongs, although
they knew he already had it in hand, and have condemned the author of
heresy before the pope could have passed judgment.

In any case, as I hope for the Graces' favour, what else have they   100
achieved by all this false testimony and slander and abuse except to advertise
their own stupidity as a match for their malignance, and to make themselves
hateful alike to God and man? For it is their own fault if things have come to
such a pass that all men of judgment now find nothing more acceptable than
what they utterly reject, and value most highly the man of whom they have   105
the lowest opinion. Well done then! – you who have been accounted worthy
by those foul and slanderous characters to be the target for their venomous
invective through their accursed mouthpiece, that mountebank Lee. No
higher praise could be given you than to be honoured with their vitupera-
tion, nor would you ever gain the approval of men of judgment and good   110

scholars unless you were disliked by Lee and ignorant hypocrites like him. You therefore, dear Erasmus, should remain quite unmoved if jealous and truly pitiful persons torment themselves and give their nature full play, with the result that always follows. You have laid such solid foundations of true excellence and achieved such a reputation for integrity and erudition that jealousy, however sharp its tooth, cannot undo it. What is more, you have made friends everywhere of such high standing and high quality that, even if you remain silent, they have the power and the courage to defend you against the invective and the lies of these accursed noisy rascals.

But I must cease to praise you, or Lee will burst with envy, and I pray he may enjoy the long and lingering death which he deserves. But first I must record a charge on which I have lately defended you. A good number of us were together the other day, and the talk turned among other things to you. After several people had spoken most highly of you and of your work, a most saintly man who happened to be present, a theologian[14] of the mendicant persuasion, was listening to your praises with evident distaste, and kept shaking his head, croaking[15] something from time to time beneath his breath. I noticed this, and asked him if there was anything in you that he disapproved of. He assumed a look of great gravity, and replied that many things about you were rightly criticized. He could not be driven into producing one; but at last when I pressed him he said, 'Although I had decided to remain silent, yet since you press me, and I should not like anyone to think I was moved by jealousy to say what I did, that Erasmus of yours of whom you speak so highly, is very fond of chicken dinners; and this I know not from hearsay, but when I made the acquaintance of the man at Basel, I saw it with these two eyes.' 'Did he steal them,' said I, 'or pay for them?' 'Oh, he paid for them' was his reply. 'Well,' I said, 'that confounded fox is far worse, that takes fowls every day out of my hen-yard, and never pays anything.' I asked him whether he reckoned eating chicken to be a misdemeanour. 'Very much so,' he said; 'It is the sin of gluttony, and all the worse when committed regularly and by persons who have taken vows.' I added, 'Perhaps on days when it is not allowed.' 'No,' he said, 'but we men in holy orders ought to refrain from all kinds of delicate fare.' 'But, worthy Father,' I said, 'if I mistake not, it was not porridge and barley groats on which you built up a belly like that,' for he was rather stout, 'and if all the chickens with which you lined your stomach could still cheep, armies and blaring trumpets would not drown the noise.' You see with what energy I have defended your impious and nefarious eating of chickens or *ornithophagy*.

You think perhaps I am telling stories, but I am ready to take my oath by St Hypocrisy in person that I tell you the truth. But let me not seem to praise

everything about you: there are some points on which even I might properly take you to task. Why did you prevent Lee, that divinely gifted character, from sleeping, or perhaps, like the shepherd in the story,[16] from drinking, until he had learnt the whole of Greek and Hebrew in six weeks? Happy   155
indeed might the church have been, had you left him to enjoy his delightful slumbers! Now, I think, he has something to occupy him into extreme old age. But we must not be hard on the man, for he has scattered a little credit[17] on us in places, and if we do not recognize this, I fear he may call us the most ungrateful of all mortals. It will be our duty therefore to honour the name of   160
Lee with some annual celebration, until he agrees that his kindness has been adequately repaid.

You say you mean to come to Upper Germany, and for many reasons I think this an excellent plan. Apart from the fact that here you will be far less exposed to the attacks of wasps like Lee, it will give you very great   165
satisfaction to find what friends, and how many of them, you have made everywhere. I would invite you to come to us first, if the plague[18] were not breaking out again and I were not looking for some place of refuge. But I hope it will soon stop, for most energetic steps are being taken to deal with it. About the time of King Charles' arrival[19] we shall expect you; the plague will   170
cease to spread meanwhile, and in accordance with ancient custom the new king's first council is usually held here. I have shown Alamirus some of our rooms here, in which I shall put you up, and they are not unattractive; he himself called them palatial. Moreover, I promise to set before you in plenty not only chickens but cocks and their sons and daughters withal. In the   175
mean while, farewell, dearest friend. Never forget that you are far more blessed in the abuse of those who bear you ill will than in the praises of your friends. Those men would never find your praises so unpalatable were they not perfectly certain that learning and integrity have earned you immortality while still alive.   180

Farewell once more, from Nürnberg, 30 April.

Your sincere friend Willibald Pirckheimer

Having written this, I was informed that our friend Oecolampadius[20] became a monk on the twenty-third of April, in the monastery[21] of the Saviour near Augsburg, which is of the Brigittine order, in which women   185
usually hold the highest posts. I wish he had known better what was good for him.

1096 / From Thomas More   [Greenwich? early May] 1520

This letter was first published in Erasmus' *Epistolae ad diversos*. The place and month date added to a reprint in More's *Lucubrationes* (Basel 1563) appear to be

correct. This letter gives More's reactions to Erasmus' admonitions in Ep 1093
concerning his further conduct in the controversy with Germain de Brie (cf Ep
1087 introduction). While his public reply to Brie's *Antimorus* was already in
print, it seems that he now did his best to suppress it (n17); but he was less
accommodating with regard to his epigrams against Brie; see Ep 1087 n2.

THOMAS MORE TO ERASMUS, THAT EXCELLENT AND LEARNED MAN,
GREETING

Brie's *Antimorus*, dear Erasmus, had been in London for a long time before
your letter reached me. I was wondering a little[1] what you had so much at
heart that made you so slow in writing about it, unless either the *Antimorus*   5
reached your part of the world rather later, maybe, or you were somewhat
slow because, until you heard that I was preparing a pamphlet in answer,
you supposed I should despise the book of my own accord, as likely to
damage its author more than me and clearly unworthy of a reply. And so I
should certainly have done, dear Erasmus, had not certain friends, very   10
good scholars and very wise men too, persuaded me otherwise. They
thought Brie an object for mockery rather than resentment, but they had
nothing like the affection for him that I see you have.

It is nearly two years[2] ago now that I heard he was getting something of
this kind under way and had the idea of writing to him myself, in the most   15
friendly possible terms, and at the same time of giving him some advice
which would have been somewhat more in his own interests than his
present intemperate behaviour. In the mean time, however, I understood
from most reliable news from Paris that the man was so much carried away by
his feelings that no persuasion from his friends[3] could restrain him, and even   20
advice from Bérault and Lascaris and Budé – men of the highest standing! –
could not make him change his mind, while the authority of a great man like
Deloynes or of his Eminence the cardinal,[4] who has lately died over there,
had no effect at all, so fast was he wasting away with a passion for revenge
and pitifully consumed like Narcissus with some sort of love of his own   25
verses; though fresh ones were born every day, and he used to carry them
round like a new-born babe out of its cradle and dandle them at dinner with
Deloynes or the cardinal. Nor was he always quite so happy when he took
them home again, hearing sometimes from good scholars and men of
judgment criticisms which, had he had any sense, he would have made   30
himself. Much of this I have been told in letters from those parts, but in
particular a certain John,[5] a Greek by birth but as learned in Latin as he is in
his native tongue, a man of high character and reliable beyond any doubt,
told me much by word of mouth; and when I realized from this that Brie was

too much carried away to admit of any overtures, I changed my mind and   35
abandoned my wish to write.

At the same time, 'He is letting himself go,' I thought, 'to the extent of
being reluctant to keep quite silent, but he is spending so much effort and so
much time on this that it is not unlikely, with the distance and the delay, that
the first resentment and a sort of quick reaction that affects us when things   40
happen suddenly are calming down, and he will enjoy himself in wit and
humour.' Wrangling and abuse and calumny I thought he would entirely
refrain from, for fear that his attacks would rightly be considered ill timed, if
he assaulted a man more savagely in peacetime than he had himself been
assaulted in time of war. And then I had read his *Chordigera*[6] seven years   45
before; though it abounded in faults of invention and arrangement and
language yet it did offer a sample of his natural gifts, which I thought would
ripen someday with the years (and I saw that the years had passed), and
therefore I was in hopes that he would publish something scholarly and well
finished, which would give pleasure even to me, at whom the publication   50
was aimed. For I am not as a rule much offended if humour is allowed a
certain licence.

But when Brie's famous bantling, the *Antimorus*, appeared, madder
than Morychus,[7] more venomous than any poison, and more illiterate even
than the *Chordigera*, I could do nothing but laugh, which was reasonable   55
enough, murmuring to myself the old saw,[8] 'Seeking gold I found live coals.'
And indeed, just as the glowing coals of Etna burnt up Empedocles,[9] so did
those coals singe Brie in a similar search for glory, and made him as black as
any cinder. And so I had decided to issue no reply at all; but other people
whose opinion on my affairs I trusted more than my own took a different   60
view. They admitted that no educated man existed who would not feel sick at
the sight of such dull, poisonous, mad stuff; but they gave it as their opinion
that his calumnies, absurd and foolish as they were, and besides that, by no
means obscure if one attends to the fore and aft of the whole business, would
yet not be lucid enough for many people, who might perhaps read his   65
Antimorus when they might have no access to the *Chordigera* or to my
epigrams. They persuaded me therefore to put all this together into a single
book[10] and set it all before the reader, and then to write something to throw
some light on the story, that the reader might need nothing more but his own
critical faculty.   70

You can see, dearest Erasmus, what drove me to a reply. And so I do
not feel it necessary to answer your arguments; for unless other people had
pushed me in a different direction I should have agreed with you myself all
the time. But I see Brie has persuaded you that it was only through the

courier's negligence that you did not succeed in getting him to suppress his   75
Antimorus entirely. It greatly surprises me, dear Erasmus, that you should
accept this as though you found it proven. 'Why should I not believe it,' say
you, 'when he puts Bérault and Budé in the box,'[11] both witnesses of the
highest probity?' I agree, Erasmus, he produces men of such integrity that
either by himself might convince one of anything. 'Then why,' you ask,   80
'should what Brie says not win the day?' For this one reason, my dear friend:
he produces two witnesses, but both give hearsay evidence and neither is an
eyewitness; and 'one witness with eyes in his head is worth ten who have
but ears.'[12] What other evidence can Bérault or Budé possibly give except
that on such and such a day they heard from Brie himself that the *Antimorus*   85
was in the press? That is what Brie means when he says that he told them of
the publication of the *Antimorus* some days before he had read your letter. So
you will believe Bérault and Budé; but whom will they believe meanwhile?
Surely Brie himself?

Do you see now, dear Erasmus, how that specious bit of evidence,   90
'Whom saw I brought you yesterday at nightfall?'[13] issued eventually in
bundling up Canthara? Not to mention in the mean time that he can never
produce any witnesses to prove that he had not read your letter before he
saw it in print, when he might have received it and concealed the fact, so that
he could use this argument to you afterwards without let or hindrance.   95
Besides which, his *Antimorus* consists of not more than eight[14] quires, which
normally take as many days to print, and we cannot infer from Brie's words
that it was half finished when he read your letter; so he compresses into very
narrow limits the 'some days' in which he says he told Bérault and Budé that
the book was being published. 'But why,' you ask, 'should Brie invent such   100
a thing?' Does it seem to you so suprising if a man of poetic turn invents
something to please himself? Though there was also a reason why he should
invent. Each of them had often told him not to publish such a foolish book, as
full of abuse as any fishwife, and he wanted perhaps to test whether they
would receive it, once he had done it, in the same spirit in which they had so   105
often told him not to do it. It sometimes happens that we object strongly to
the doing of something as long as the question is open; but when it reaches
the point of being too late to put it right, we acquiesce, and gloss over with
words what had gone wrong as far as we can.

But I, my dear Erasmus, want you to see in truth how much more truly   110
your friend More is ready to do as you tell him than Brie is; and so although,
when your letter arrived, my book was not actually at press but was entirely
printed off (and this I could establish not by a couple of hearsay witnesses
who have learnt of it from me, but more than ten with eyes in their heads who
have really seen it – in fact on the evidence, I suppose, of your own eyes, for   115

I do not doubt that the book has reached you before this letter), and although the advice of so many friends urged me to publish it, yet when I had had this letter from you, the one man whose opinion weighs more with me than all the votes of everyone else, I did not follow Brie's example. Though his purse (so he writes)[15] is always heavy with coin, Brie sets such a high value on your   120 instructions, whose lightest word he obeys (or so he tells us), that he could not face the trifling expense of buying up all those books of his and throwing them on the fire once and for all, so as to conceal from every eye that great nonsense of his by which the great name of Brie, which the poor dear man so much thirsts to immortalize, will be discredited. Not so I, dear Erasmus: apart   125 from these two, one of which I had already sent to you and the other to Pieter Gillis, and five more which the printer[16] had sold (for it was just when they were put on sale and had begun to be in great demand that your letter intervened), I bought up the whole lot and keep them shut up,[17] so that before any fresh steps are taken on my side, we may be able – or rather you   130 may be able after taking counsel with yourself – to decide what you wish me to do.

     And so, dear Erasmus, it is now your turn: let me urge you to look closely at your decision, for this is the case of a friend who is determined, whatever you decide, to do as he is told. You recommend that any attack of   135 mine on Brie should be omitted when my *Epigrammata* are fortunate enough to be reprinted,[18] and that on the other side Brie's *Antimorus* should be given no further circulation; but for my part, dear Erasmus, I think I have many reasons, so far as Brie is concerned, for concluding that he is too tender-hearted towards his own verses to endure to be weaned away from a   140 pursuit by which he expects, so far as it can be in his power, to endow his beloved offspring with immortality. My own *Epigrammata* never gave me much satisfaction, as you yourself, Erasmus, can testify; and unless that book had had an appeal for you[19] and certain other people greater than the charm it had for me, perhaps it would not exist anywhere today. As it is, see   145 how things are turned inside out! Suppose you and I had made a compact that you should be authorized to condemn such of my epigrams as you might please, provided you had no power over some few that I might choose to exempt: why, the only lines against which you unsheath your knife under our agreement would be the only ones I should protect by exemption. Such is   150 the charm they begin to have for me, now that I see many men moved to like them by Brie's bitter and foolish poetizing. Not that I mean by this to stop you from doing what you please with my verses, who can do what you please even with me.

     Now when you say that Brie is a person whom I should find on closer   155 acquaintance to be the sort of man who more than anyone deserves to be my friend, for my part, dear Erasmus, I do not give myself such airs as to think anyone's position too humble to make friends with him, provided he is not the sort of rascal for whom no one ought to feel any affection; and so I readily agree that Brie is not unworthy to deserve the friendship of greater men than I. He does certainly seem to have rather more – I will not call it pride, but a sort of nobility of spirit and grandeur of attitude – than could ever make him in any way suited to a person of humble and modest gifts like myself, unless I were willing to be as unsuitably coupled in friendship as ill-matched oxen drawing the plough awry.[20] And yet, my dear Erasmus, if this is what you advise, I would not reject his friendship, for I can easily adapt myself even to doing as I am told by better men than myself. At least, so far as his scholarship is concerned, I believe him to be keen to learn and not wholly stupid, and also a man who will one day be made different by experience. All the same, in what he has published hitherto, to tell the truth – and this I could demonstrate – he is not free from bad mistakes and has not kept the rules of metre, and in invention he often sinks further than would be acceptable in a child. And yet, with all his faults, I do not think so well of myself as to suppose that I am comparable to him in erudition, though you, my dear Erasmus, either blinded by affection or (which I think nearer the truth) with a sort of courtesy towards me, set me above him. To speak frankly, so far am I from hating him that, my judgment having now been purged, I can even love him in the cause of literature.

But in the case before us, pray consider rather carefully what you wish to be done before you issue your orders. It comes to this: if I do not reply, many people will think that I provided the reason for this most tedious dispute, and without provocation of any kind attacked him with insults, curses, imprecations; and this would have been no less brutal than I have now shown it to be false, if you will let my book come out. As regards the book, your second precept is that if I am absolutely determined to publish it I must take care that (as you say I have done hitherto) I may be seen to defeat Brie solely by being a better scholar with a better case, and not by abusing him as well. But, my dear Erasmus, while as far as scholarship goes I am content to be level with Brie, I have no doubt that my case is far stronger than his, however much Brie may assert that his is valid and demonstrable and sure to win; that is the opening gambit prescribed by the rules in the defence of a guilty party. In abuse I shall gladly let myself be beaten, for I am determined never to fight with that sort of weapon. Yet it can easily happen that something which seems to me, as the victim, to have no bitterness in it, might be judged by a man who sees things rather differently to be somewhat offensive. Should this by some chance ever happen, I shall not be so afraid of my readers' sense of justice as to think they will not, even in my case, dear

Erasmus, however serious the character your affection disguises me with, making out everything in me to be larger than life, the fact remains that while I still converse with mortal men and am not yet entirely deified, if I may be flippant on this not wholly serious subject, I am not afraid, I repeat, that my humane and human reader will not make some allowances in me too for those human feelings which no human being has entirely thrown off. Farewell, dearest Erasmus.

When we reach Calais,[21] for which the king is preparing to leave shortly, I hope we shall be able to discuss these things more fully face to face. For I fully expect to see you at this meeting of the kings, and Brie too; for the queen[22] of France will be there, and Brie being her secretary cannot fail, I suppose, to attend. So, as far as I am concerned, you will easily settle things as you think best. For though without any reason he has behaved towards me in such a way as shows that he would have ruined me had he had the power, none the less, since I value you, my dear Erasmus, as more than half of myself, I shall be more influenced as regards Brie by his being your friend than my enemy. Farewell once more.

1520

1097 / To Thomas More   Antwerp, 2 May 1520

This letter is Erasmus' answer to Ep 1090; it was published in the *Epistolae ad diversos*. Epp 1097–9 present part of Erasmus' efforts to justify his stance against Lee before the latter's countrymen (cf Ep 1083 n12). This letter was probably dispatched together with Ep 1098 and with copies of Erasmus' now published answer to Lee's book; see n6.

ERASMUS OF ROTTERDAM TO HIS FRIEND THOMAS MORE, GREETING
I knew very well, my excellent More, that the advice to which you refer, however unwelcome to me, sprang from a most affectionate heart, and therefore I could not fail to take it in good part, though from time to time I did seriously protest that you were promoting[1] Lee's interests rather than mine. I had acquired a thorough knowledge of the man's nature, which was made for troubles of this kind. He was already well alight of his own accord, and even so he had others to pour oil daily on the fire. I have often wondered in my own mind that you did not have the same understanding of Lee's nature, seeing that you had lived so long in his society.[2] Nor did I ever accept that truce; in fact when Pace the peacemaker on returning[3] from his mission in Germany, with the best intentions but following a policy that was very unfortunate from my point of view, tried to bring us together, I resisted most obstinately, protesting that this truce offered no results except what I most

wished to avoid; for nothing Lee had done, I said, had damaged me more 15
than the rumour that he had attacked me in a book which he endlessly
boasted of but never published, only showing it to a few people under the
oath of secrecy, thus securing for me that maximum of ill will in a manner
designed to teach me nothing and protect him from any possibility of being
refuted. 20

I took the same line with Lee himself that I did with Pace. But when I
perceived that you had agreed on this as the right course, I thought it better
to abandon my own interests than to oppose your minds when they were
made up. For since, now the book is out, it is such as to win the
whole-hearted disapproval even of those who were his supporters up to 25
now, in hopes to use it as a weapon to undo me, what a game we should have
had with that cursed book which circulated exclusively among a few friends
on oath and twopenny blockhead abbots[4] and was displayed only to the
initiated, seeing that this book in which he has had a number of helpers[5] is so
stuffed with nonsense? If you have a mind to test this, compare what he has 30
published to the world with what he wrote for his chosen friends. But all this
is now ancient history.

For the rest, when you exhort me to remember true Christian humility, I
do assure you I have not forgotten it; though I do not doubt there will be
people to interpret this humility of mine as cowardice or fear or what they 35
please. I set to some time ago to answer him. Part of the work[6] has appeared,
and will, if I mistake not, make it clear that I surpass Lee as much in
moderation as I do in scholarship. That I should receive some recompense
from this world, I do not urgently demand or particularly expect. But I do
marvel at the madness of some people, who abandon everything else and 40
make it the sole object of their devoted labours that scholars should derive as
little advantage as possible from all my work, and think it the finest
achievement of their whole lives, if they can stand in the way of public
benefit. Farewell, you and all your household, most worthy candidate for
immortality. 45

Antwerp, 2 May 1520

1098 / To Henry VIII   Antwerp, [3 May] 1520

This letter, published in the *Epistolae ad diversos*, was probably sent together
with Ep 1097. The last paragraph may suggest that Erasmus had not entirely
abandoned his hopes for a move to England (cf Epp 1025 n4, 1073 introduction). In view of Henry's reputed interest in theological matters it was
appropriate to present him with Erasmus' replies to Lee (cf Ep 1080 introduction), especially as the latter was well connected in English court circles.

ERASMUS OF ROTTERDAM TO HIS MOST SERENE MAJESTY
HENRY VIII, KING OF ENGLAND, GREETING

May it please your Majesty. No small part of human life and felicity is rooted
in humane studies; and the more they are attacked in this generation by some
very stupid persons I could name, the more, Sire, they should be supported   5
by the favour and protection of princes, towards whom they will show
themselves not ungrateful. Those studies in particular deserve support
which tend towards true religion and the glory of Christ our Prince; and in
this respect I could but wish that all other kings and heads of state might
follow your Majesty's example. Not but what there are some who do so now,   10
and many who will soon show themselves your rivals in this pious work. It is
little enough, I know, that I can do in the field of letters; but as I hope for
Christ's mercy, all that I have written hitherto, or ever shall write, has been
and shall be devoted to his glory. Thus far at least my labours have won the
approval of all men of good will, among them the pope himself.[1] Yet a few   15
have conspired[2] against me who are so far soaked in the old vinegar that they
cannot take my new wine. Few in number and stupid as they are, they are
loyal members of their faction, and would gladly see humane studies
extinguished, even at the peril of their own salvation, so much do they
resent their breaking everywhere into new bloom.   20

It was they, I suspect, who put up Edward Lee to rant and rave against
me. Not daring to take the boards themselves, they found a young man eager
for reputation and full of self-confidence, and suborned him to play the part
on their behalf. How I wish he had either written in a different style, or were
not an Englishman![3] I owe him nothing; but in the spirit of a Christian I wish   25
him a better fate than he wishes for himself; to England I owe more than to
any other nation. I send your Majesty with this a book[4] in which I reply to
him, but refrain from personalities; if your Majesty has the leisure to glance
at it, you will see how far the outcome is from fulfilling his promises. He will
not resume his abusive tactics, if he has any regard for his own reputation; to   30
my arguments I do not think he will ever find an answer. In this business I
have wasted about forty days.[5] I only wish I could have spent that time on
some piece of work that might have either helped prosperity to appreciate
your great distinction or promoted the glory of Christ to the best of my
ability.   35

I pray that Almighty God in Christ may by his blessing ever forward
and enlarge the noble and religious projects of your Majesty, and may permit
me to live long enough to tell one day how much I am conscious I owe to your
truly royal generosity, knowing that you will always deign to visit with your
accustomed favour myself the least of all your dependants.   40

Antwerp, feast of the Exaltation[6] of the Holy Cross, 1520

1099 / To Richard Foxe   Louvain, 5 May 1520

This letter was published in the *Epistolae ad diversos*. Although it appears to be dated after Erasmus' return from Antwerp to Louvain (cf Ep 1091 introduction), it is conceivable that it left for England together with Epp 1097–8, which were serving much the same purpose. For Foxe's connection with, and earlier support of, Edward Lee see Epp 898A introduction, 973.

ERASMUS OF ROTTERDAM TO THE RIGHT REVEREND RICHARD,
BISHOP OF WINCHESTER, GREETING
My Lord Bishop, Edward Lee's frenzied attack on my reputation with such open slanders give indescribable offence to all right-minded men; for he has done harm not so much to myself as to everyone who has the cause of the 5 humanities at heart, for whose benefit I have toiled hitherto with all my powers. Countless letters from my friends, countless warnings from me could not deter him from branding a dark stain on his own reputation no less than on mine. His book has come out – an ill-omened thing – and with some loss to my repute but far more to his own. His abuse[1] I have answered more 10 temperately than some men would wish. His arguments[2] I have answered to such effect that he can never reply, I know well enough; and yet all through I refrain from abuse.

Not content with this, they say, Lee has got ready another book[3] of far greater venom, which he has sent to Paris to be printed. He does not listen to 15 sensible advice from his friends, nor will he ever make a stop unless restrained by your authority. Oh, how I wish that had been done before this volcano erupted! He has suborned in London a Carthusian called, I think, John Batmanson,[4] a young man completely ignorant, as appears from what he writes, but conceited to the point of mania. If your authority can hold Lee 20 back from these raging fits, you will benefit not my studies only but Edward's too, who is now wasting his own time as well as mine. Farewell.

Louvain, 5 May 1520

1100 / To the Reader   [Louvain? beginning of May 1520]

This preface was printed with a new edition of Edward Lee's *Annotationes* (cf Ep 1037 introduction), published at Erasmus' request by Johann Froben at Basel, with the colophon date of May 1520. As is clear from the last sentence Erasmus had asked Froben to include in the edition his own *Responsiones* to Lee (cf Ep 1080 introduction). His letter to Froben, accompanied by the material to be printed, including probably this letter, had arrived shortly before 18 May and printing was under way by 25 May (Zwingli *Werke* VII Ep 140; BRE Ep 166). In time for the Frankfurt autumn fair Froben published altogether four texts with a collective title-page (although there were individual title-pages too which permitted the sale of each text independently). In addition to Lee's *Annotationes* and Erasmus' *Responsiones* (with a colophon date of 21 July 1520) the volume contained a reworking of Erasmus' *Apologia de 'In principio erat sermo'* (cf Ep 1072 introduction) and Froben's *Epistolae aliquot eruditorum virorum* (cf Ep 1083 introduction). This last addition ensured that the element of personal invective which Erasmus had removed from Lee's pieces and his own (cf n1), was amply restored by the efforts of his friends.

Erasmus' intention, in so far as he was responsible for the Froben volume, was perhaps to make a conciliatory gesture in response to the proposals of Fisher (cf Ep 1068 introduction) recently endorsed by More (cf Ep 1090). Such a gesture seemed advisable in view of a recent rumour (Ep 1099:14–15) that Lee considered a further attack. Lee, however, does not seem to have renewed his attacks on Erasmus, at any rate not directly and in print, while the latter was somewhat less generous. His *Epistolae ad diversos* (dated 31 August 1521 on the title-page) included the highly offensive Epp 1053, 1103, 1109, and 1139, but offered at the same time expressions of regret in view of the immoderate language his German friends had used against Lee (cf Epp 1123, 1129, 1134) and offered an assurance of peace and good will (Ep 1132). Erasmus also used restraint on other occasions (cf Epp 1061 n38, 1105, 1121 introductions). In 1523 he recalled that he had met Lee in Calais at the meeting between the English and Hapsburg courts (July 1520; cf Ep 1106 introduction) and that they shook hands to show that their war was over (cf ASD IX-1 160). Lee was then probably on his way back to England (cf Ep 1140 introduction), and Erasmus sought and received assurances that the conflict had not damaged his reputation with Henry VIII and his queen; cf Allen Ep 1127A:2–7.

ERASMUS TO THE FAIR-MINDED READER, GREETING
Many people were anxious to obtain what Edward Lee had written against my annotations, and copies were very scarce. I have therefore arranged for the work to be reprinted as it was published by the author, adding and subtracting nothing except the personal attacks[1] in which he had framed the   5
body of the work, since I supposed that he must by now regret such a display of ill temper and was certain that in English circles[2] as well as others it roused the extreme disapproval of every right-thinking and educated man. I did this all the more readily because, though some good is to be derived from his annotations and my answer, squabbling of this kind brings the reader no   10
profit at all. Dear reader, farewell.

1101 / To Albert of Brandenburg Louvain, 15 May 1520

This letter was published in the *Epistolae ad diversos*. On the basis of the correspondence, such as we have it, it does not appear that Albert had responded, directly or through others, to Erasmus' ill-fated Ep 1033. By now Erasmus had reason to fear the cardinal's displeasure, and his desire to appease Albert in the course of a personal visit, rather than a renewed invitation on the part of the cardinal (following the one conveyed with Epp 986:37–9), may account for this letter and likewise for Ep 1152. As far as is known, Erasmus received no indication that his visit would be welcome, and it never took place.

ERASMUS OF ROTTERDAM TO HIS EMINENCE ALBERT,
CARDINAL ARCHBISHOP OF MAINZ

I am continually opening my wings with the desire of flying in your direction, my most reverend Lord and most excellent Prince, but always something arises to tie me here. Charles[1] my master is expected daily. 5 Arrangements are in train for a meeting about the first of June of the two kings of France and England, of course in the greatest splendour; and I am under notice to be present. In the mean while I send you a reflection[2] of my humble self; for the picture of your Eminence is already in my possession. So you will not be far from owning the whole of Erasmus: the better part of me, if 10 there is good in me anywhere, you possess as it is set forth in my books,[3] and my physical appearance has been set forth by a famous artist in molten bronze. If there is any Erasmus left over, your Eminence will be able to claim it all as of right, for I am and ever shall be devoted to you, whatever country may contain my body. May Christ the Almighty long preserve you in health 15 and wealth.

Louvain, 15 May 1520

1102 / To Johannes Oecolampadius Louvain, 15 May 1520

This letter, which was published in the *Epistolae ad diversos*, was in reply to one now missing, in which Oecolampadius had announced in general terms his intention of entering a monastery (cf Allen Ep 1139:112–13). Ep 1103:32–4 shows that by the time Erasmus wrote the following he did not yet know that his younger friend was actually in the abbey of Altomünster (cf Ep 1095 n20, n21). It seems that he inclined to treat Oecolampadius' intention as the temporary consequence of a breakdown.

ERASMUS OF ROTTERDAM TO HIS FRIEND JOHANNES
OECOLAMPADIUS, GREETING

I wish you may find what you desire, my excellent Oecolampadius. If I were
certain of this, you would have me as a companion; but I fear that this
weariness will go with you still. Such is the life of man; it is in the spirit that   5
we must seek for peace. The index[1] to Jerome, so long awaited, is now
become a torment. Your health can still be mended, for your age is not past its
prime; but I must expect to die in the midst of my labours. Had I but had a
little good fortune[2] joined with this spirit of mine, the world would not thus
be put upon with impunity by these – what am I to call them? Controversy I   10
cannot like; in all else I will serve to the utmost of my power.

I should by now be in Germany,[3] but the conference of kings[4] detains
me. Charles is expected daily. The English and French kings are preparing a
meeting on the coast at Calais about the first of June. The archbishop of
Canterbury[5] says I must be there. Luther's books had nearly been burnt in   15
England, nor was there any way out; but a way out was found by a friend of
yours,[6] a man of no importance, but he kept his eyes open. I am not the man
to pass judgment on what Luther writes, but I cannot swallow this dictatorial
procedure. Farewell, dearest Oecolampadius.

I have replied to Lee in three pamphlets[7] written within roughly one   20
month. Other steps have been taken in a more roundabout way. Now I shall
attempt, or rather, have already attempted a paraphrase[8] on the two Epistles
of Peter; I prefer this to wrangling with these ranting nobodies. I am tired of
this sort of Christians, Pharisees rather; I would rather be a publican[9] and
ashamed of myself.   25

Louvain, 15 May 1520

1103 / To Johann von Botzheim   Louvain, 16 May [1520]

Johann von Botzheim (c 1480–1535) was descended from a family of Alsatian
nobles. He studied at Heidelberg under Jakob Wimpfeling and afterwards in
Bologna, where he obtained a doctorate in civil and canon law. Since 1510 a
canon at Constance, he was to become a faithful friend of Erasmus. He died at
Überlingen, where the chapter had moved when Constance joined the
Reformation; see NDB.

Originally published in the *Epistolae ad diversos*, this is Erasmus' first letter to
Botzheim, evidently in response to an approach that had been encouraged by
Urbanus Rhegius (lines 5–6). When writing to Erasmus, Botzheim had also
written to Maarten van Dorp; both letters were on their way by 6 March 1520 (cf
AK II Ep 727) but are now missing. The letter to Dorp was encouraged by Udalricus

Zasius in response to Erasmus' initiative (cf Ep 1044 introduction and n10; de Vocht MHL 232–3). The date of 1518 added to this letter in the *Opus epistolarum* of 1529 must be corrected in view of the references to Dorp and to Richard Pace as dean of St Paul's.

ERASMUS OF ROTTERDAM TO THE EMINENT JOHANN VON
BOTZHEIM, DOCTOR OF CIVIL AND CANON LAW, CANON OF
CONSTANCE, GREETING

Your letter, honoured sir, was all the more welcome, in that it united the gaining of a new friend with the remembrance of an old one. Urbanus[1] has been dear to me for a long time; Abstemius[2] I accept with pleasure. I give you as much joy of your good fortune as if it were my own. The rest gave me pleasure all through.

Only, when you say that a defence – against Pace,[3] I presume – is circulating in your part of the world, this pains me deeply. However it was that he let fall that remark about Constance, I know that he meant no harm. In the same work he makes many sallies at my expense[4] too, which I wish he had left unwritten; for some people will distort anything in order to make mischief. I know Pace intimately. He is by nature the most fair-minded, upright, friendly person in the world. This is simplicity, not malice. He is a good scholar; but this book, as is clear on the surface, was an extempore effusion. And I have taken steps to see that it is not reprinted without revision by the author. For my own part, in this most unpleasant uproar aroused not only by the Dominicans and the theologians but by Edward Lee, the most arrogant, venomous, and foolish object this earth has ever spawned, I have found Pace as faithful a friend[5] as any man could be to his own brother. He is much liked by all the grandees, and more than anyone by their excellent king. He has lately succeeded[6] John Colet in the distinguished office of dean of St Paul's, and will doubtless be promoted to the very highest positions. And so, if you are at all indignant with him, I should like to see you put it quite out of your mind, for my sake if nothing else. There is no greater service you could do me. Henceforward you will find the name of Botzheim among the leaders in the record of my friends.

What you said of Zasius made me jump for joy. Would that we might have that wonderful old man among us for many years! Your letter made my friend Dorp[7] a very happy man. He means to answer his friends, but for the moment has no time to spare. Before long he will answer them all. Give my warmest greetings to my excellent benefactor Urbanus the urbane, and to Oecolampadius[8] if he is in your part of the world, and to the worthy Johannes Fabri.[9]

I am excessively busy as I write this; I will write with more care another time. Farewell, from Louvain, 16 May [1518].

1104 / To Juan Luis Vives   Louvain, [April–June 1520]

While the precise date of this letter is a matter of speculation it should clearly be read in the context of Epp 1108 and 1111, which reflect on Vives' visit to Paris in May 1520 (cf Ep 1108 introduction). This letter could be Erasmus' reply to a first letter sent by Vives after his arrival in Paris, which dealt briefly with some of the topics treated more elaborately in Ep 1108. Or it could have been written in anticipation of Vives' departure for Paris. It is true that Vives did not have to be told about Nesen's difficulties (n7), as he was in Louvain at the time, but this letter may have been intended for him to show in Paris. Finally, it could also have been written as a first reaction to Ep 1108, covering familiar ground but failing to pay much attention to the section of Ep 1108 that deals with Budé; on second thoughts Erasmus would then have written another, more adequate reply to Ep 1108 in the form of Ep 1111. This subsequent exchange was published together in the *Epistolae ad diversos*, whereas Ep 1104, suppressed at first, only appeared in the *Opus epistolarum* of 1529, when it was no longer realized that it had been superseded by Ep 1111.

ERASMUS OF ROTTERDAM TO LUIS VIVES, GREETING
Really, my learned Vives, you are the most fortunate of men: you secure a welcome from people by speaking ill[1] of them, while I speak kindly and get nothing but hatred and ill will. I have tried to open the fountain-head of true piety and religion, I have done my best to restore theology, sunk far too deep   5
in wrangling with more sophistry than sense, to its ancestral dignity; and certain monks[2] I could name rave against me as if I had committed sacrilege, while you find these sophisters, an irritable race of men in popular esteem, all sweetness and light. Very well, since things have gone so happily for you, keep it up; work night and day to recall studies in the university to   10
better things.[3] Long ago I learnt to admire the University of Paris for its sincerity and its cultivated atmosphere; could it not, all those years, bear with a man like Fausto,[4] and not bear with him merely but support him and promote him? When I mention Fausto, much will occur to you which I would rather not entrust to a letter. With what spite he used to rave against   15
theology! How far from pure were his own principles! No one was unaware of the life he led. The French forgave all that wickedness in consideration of his learning, though that had not advanced much beyond mediocrity.
    The leading figures in this university cannot endure the College of the

Three Tongues,[5] although, while it costs them nothing, it renders great   2(
assistance to the studies of us all and is an ornament not only of this
university but of all the prince's dominions. They cannot endure professors
of most unblemished character, pure principles, and learning far superior to
Fausto's. The University of Paris[6] has certainly always held the first place in
the kind of studies which it has made its aim, and yet it is happy to receive an   2)
increase in polite learning from any source. They find a place for men who
wish to lecture on any subject for any fee they may choose, whereas here
they showed just as much venom in preventing Wilhelm Nesen[7] from
attempting to lecture without fee on the *Geography* of Pomponius Mela as if
he had taken steps to set fire to the whole town. Not so many years ago this   3(
university was in the doldrums; now that it has acquired some repute from its
support of the humanities, it is astonishing how it carries its head high and
gives itself airs and proposes to rule the world. But all this trouble, such as it
is, we owe to two or three people;[8] and they, even if they cannot learn sense,
will eventually be overwhelmed by the tide of humane studies that rises day   3!
after day, especially if in this struggle you play the part of a Camillus.[9]

What you say of Budé[10] is nothing new, but I always take special
pleasure in listening to the well-earned praises of a man I love so much. Nor
will he ever estrange me from him, though he were to pursue me with bitter
invective; so unlikely is it that a little skirmishing in pen and ink can separate   4(
two minds fast bound in concord by the Graces.

I send you a brief laconic letter; when Lucullus asks me to dinner, he
sups with Diogenes[11] in return. But you will ascribe this to press of business
and not policy. Farewell.

From Louvain   45

1105 / From Philipp Engelbrecht   Freiburg, 24 May [?] 1520

This letter is known only from Froben's *Epistolae aliquot eruditorum virorum*
against Lee (cf Ep 1083 introduction). The writer was a poet and professor at
Freiburg who had met Erasmus at Basel in the summer of 1515 (cf Ep 344:58).
There is no evidence that his desire for an answer by Erasmus (lines 16–18) was
ever met. The date is puzzling. If it is accepted, lines 4–5 are hard to reconcile
with the fact that Bonifacius Amerbach had left Basel for Avignon on c 1 May
(AK II Ep 739). In fact this letter appears to be primarily written in response to
Epp 998, published in the *Farrago* of October 1519, and the writer does not
show any awareness of the publication of Lee's *Annotationes* (cf Ep 1037
introduction) which occurred in February 1520. See also n1.

TO ERASMUS OF ROTTERDAM THE THEOLOGIAN FROM
PHILIPP ENGELBRECHT, GREETING

I cannot refrain from writing to you, dearest Erasmus, especially as I now
have a man available to carry my letter most conveniently. I understand that
my friend Zasius[1] and Bonifacius Amerbach will do the same; and I should 5
think it criminal if I, who have taken the same oath of allegiance in the service
of literature, although perhaps without much success, now tried to get out of
doing my duty. Not that I am unaware how fully occupied you are in
promoting the cause of the humanities, so that you have scarcely time to read
even the shortest letters from your correspondents; yet to refresh the 10
memory of our old companionship and at the same time to assure you of my
devotion to your interests, I was unwilling to allow a courier who offered
himself so opportunely to set off in your direction without a letter from me.
And you certainly should not object to this; for you will be able to steal a few
moments from your studies, enough to spare something for me without 15
disgust by way of light relief. Nor would it be unlike your kindness of heart
to give a mark of approval to my friendly feelings towards you; and if you do
this, you will seem to relieve the endless tedium of my exile,[2] which has
broken my spirit almost to the point that ever since returning to our common
studies I can hardly make steady progress. For I have been ten months in 20
exile on account of the pestilential atmosphere which has carried off many
hundreds and indeed thousands of people. But my absence was in one way
more agreeable, in that I had permission to be absent without loss of credit by
a public decision of our literary society.[3]

Meanwhile, I have heard from sundry sources that there is a man, 'of 25
rarest spirit he,'[4] who (of all absurdities) has compiled a whole Iliad against
your annotations on the New Testament. There were people who seemed to
look forward with the keenest anticipation to a criticism of this kind, in
hopes that such a mere listing of names might at least deprive this man
Erasmus of the authority conferred by supreme erudition. Those on the 30
other hand who looked up to you as beyond the reach of any competition in
genius, maintained that they were impatient for his nonsense solely in order
to see what kind of novelty this Bactrian camel[5] might produce. But here we
heard the same old story, only with the addition of an author who makes
such arrogant plans against you: a man whom you depicted brilliantly in the 35
last letter[6] of your *Farrago*, giving him a friendly warning not to descend into
this arena. I foresaw at once what his bantling would be like, not because he
differed from you here and there, for difference of opinion between scholars
is always legitimate, and in any case we can forgive an unknown man his
ambition to show off his learning like that; but my forecast was inspired by 40

the great promise shown by this late-learner, which has enabled him within the space of a few months to devour so much Greek and Hebrew[7] that every question in those literatures should be referred to him alone, a leaden straight-edge like the one they use in Lesbos.[8] This is the true reason why we so keenly expect this happy event, that the little newcomer may delight us   45 with its wonderful charms; and perhaps he will be delivered of what he has by now been in difficult labour with for nearly two years, unless it is an elephant[9] he has in his belly.

Your defence against this man I now picture to myself, for you cannot leave yourself undefended; and you will make such short work of your   50 opponent that I think he will be the most pitiful object possible – he will find you playing Apollo to his Marsyas.[10] It is true that among those half-educated characters none ever deserves a reply from you; yet this will be required by the filthy nature of some people, who were hoping for a signal triumph if you remain silent. For you know what this class of men[11] are like,   55 who under a perfectly religious exterior practise the most shameless despotism, which might somehow be tolerable, if they did not loose their fury against liberal studies too. A certain monster of this kind I lately heard braying like a donkey in front of the common people, and comic it was, for he generally thinks up 'some massy theme that panting lungs scarce match';[12]   60 and when you look into it, you find it has nothing in common with the gospel teaching.

More power to your genius, our great leader in theology! Pursue your allotted task without interruption, as you always do; for all the learned world is quite convinced that to put an end to these disastrous monsters you   65 are our heaven-sent Hercules.[13] From this proud position none shall displace you, for all that you write breathes to good purpose the spirit of Christ the Almighty God. Greetings from my brother Anton,[14] who is devoted to you; he is now bishop-suffragan to the see of Speyer. Farewell, dear Erasmus.

Freiburg im Breisgau, 24 May 1520   70

1106 / From Thomas More   Canterbury, 26 May [1520]

This letter and Erasmus' answer, Ep 1107, are among the six letters published for the first time by Adrianus Cornelii Barlandus in his *Epistolae aliquot selectae ex Erasmicis*, 1520 (cf Ep 646 introduction). Both were reprinted in Erasmus' *Epistolae ad diversos* and subsequently (with a wrong year added to the date) in the *Opus epistolarum*. This letter serves primarily to express More's admiration for the writings of Juan Luis Vives, whom he knew to be close to Erasmus. The whole letter, especially the postscript, suggests that More did not at this time know Vives personally. On the possibility of earlier contacts, perhaps in

Flanders, 1515, see Ep 545:16n (but cf Ep 911:63n for another case where an identification in the margin of the *Farrago* is plainly mistaken).

On the day this letter was written Charles v arrived in England for the first phase of the long-envisaged 'meeting of the monarchs' (line 98). In the wake of the treaty of London (cf Ep 964:39n) plans had been drawn up for meetings of Henry VIII with Francis I on one hand, and with Charles v on the other. After the imperial election (cf the preface), Franco-Hapsburg relations were approaching a breaking point – war would actually break out in the spring of 1521 (cf CWE 8 preface). The Hapsburg diplomats were eager to arrange for talks prior to Henry's meeting with the king of France, and Cardinal Wolsey wished to learn what they had to offer. An embassy of distinguished Burgundian nobles went to the English court to arrange the visit of Charles v, who was preparing to leave Spain for the Netherlands and subsequently Aachen, where he was to be crowned (cf Ep 1155 introduction). On 26 May the new emperor landed at Dover. For the next three days the two monarchs remained together at Canterbury, where Charles met his aunt Catherine, Henry's queen, for the first time. The Hapsburg diplomats had not come empty-handed. They promised to meet the English request for further trade agreements with the Netherlands and Wolsey was offered the principal revenues of two Spanish bishoprics. An agreement of uncertain nature was reached on 29 May. Charles then set sail for the Netherlands and reached Brussels on 1 June, to the great satisfaction of his subjects, who had been longing for his return (cf Ep 1007 n13). Meanwhile, on 31 May Henry VIII crossed over to Calais for the exhaustively prepared reunion of the courts of England and France at the 'Field of Cloth of Gold' on the border near Calais (7–24 June). The giant display of pageantry and chivalry produced some greatly needed cordiality but failed to prevent a close liaison between England and Hapsburg. Before he returned to England Henry VIII met again with Charles v at Gravelingen and Calais (10–14 July). Here talk was about a match between Charles and Henry's daughter, Mary Tudor, notwithstanding her engagement to the French dauphin. See Brandi *Kaiser Karl v.* I 96–8, II 109–10; J.J. Scarisbrick *Henry VIII* (Penguin 1971) 109–19; LP III lxvi–lxxxvi, 449; J.G. Russell *The Field of Cloth of Gold* (London 1969).

Erasmus' moves at the time of these gatherings are far from clear. Thomas More, who accompanied Henry VIII, here expresses once again (cf Epp 1087:674–6; 1096:205–7) his hopes for a rendezvous. Archbishop William Warham had also encouraged Erasmus to attend the Field of Cloth of Gold (cf Epp 1101:5–8, 1102:12–15; BRE Ep 166). Some of his letters were dated from Louvain on 16 May, 21 June, 6 and 30 July (Epp 1103, 1115, 1119, 1122). In June he was much troubled by illness (cf Ep 1112 introduction) although he apparently managed to visit Antwerp by 25 June (cf Ep 1117). But he did go to

Calais and had a formal audience with Henry VIII who raised in conversation the touchy subjects of Martin Luther and Edward Lee (cf Epp 1113 n10, Allen Epp 1127A:2–7, 1342:842–9). With Wolsey he apparently exchanged little more than a handshake (cf Ep 1132). He also wrote two epigrams in honour of the encounter between Charles V and Henry VIII which were perhaps intended to appear amid the festive decorations (Reedijk poems 109–10). After his visit to Calais Charles V went to Bruges where his court was between 25 and 29 July, and possibly longer. Erasmus too was at Bruges in the company of Thomas More (cf Epp 1129, 1141, 1145), who belonged to an English mission sent there for trade negotiations with the Hanse merchants. Henry VIII's instructions for his envoys were dated from Calais, 10 June, and they reported to the king from Bruges on 15 September (Rogers Epp 94, 98), long after Erasmus had left. Perhaps we may assume that Erasmus accompanied Charles V's court to Gravelingen and Calais (10–14 July) and thereafter from Calais to Bruges.

THOMAS MORE TO ERASMUS, GREETING

The young man[1] whose case you recommended to me I had already discussed with his father before you wrote. The boy himself had asked me in a letter some time ago, being convinced that my opinion would have some weight and influence with him. I did all I could; whether I did any good, I am   5
not sure. His father gave me a not entirely inflexible reply; and yet (for I know the man has an eye to the main chance) I think his reply was as forthcoming as it was more from a certain reluctance to oppose me than because he said what he really thought. What it came to was that he would, follow my advice about his son; but at the same time he made it clear that he   1(
would rather see him rich in coin than in culture. But the boy himself, I can see, is resolved to abandon not only his paternal inheritance but his father too, rather than let himself be torn away from liberal studies; clearly, with a mind like that, he deserves the support of everyone and all the help they can give him.   1

The schoolmaster[2] from Louvain I have found a place for, such that I do not doubt he will be permanently grateful to you. His master is much pleased with his scholarship; and when he heard that it was you who had recommended him, it was his idea to ask me to let him have the young man, and I complied without hesitation, as that was just what on other grounds I   2(
had decided to propose. For in my own household there was no place for any more servants.

In those first days, while he was staying with me, he showed me some things by Luis Vives which were as stylish and as scholarly as anything I have seen for a long time. How few people one can find (indeed one can   2
hardly find one anywhere) who at such a tender age (for you tell me[3] in a

letter that he is still quite young) have absorbed such encyclopaedic learning! I am positively ashamed, my dear Erasmus, of myself and others like me, who make the best of ourselves with two or three slim volumes and those generally not much good, when I see Vives so young and the author of so much that is penetrating and very well written and shows such abstruse reading. It is a great thing to be good in either of the ancient tongues; but he shows himself a past master of both. It is still greater and more fruitful to be well versed in important subjects; but who can show himself to be equipped in more fields and more important fields than Vives single-handed? But much the greatest thing of all is to have imbibed the humanities so well as a learner that you can in turn pass them on to others as a teacher; and who teaches more lucidly, more attractively, more effectively than he? I cannot sufficiently admire the qualities in his *Declamationes*[4] which you detected with such insight and expressed so eloquently; but most important of all (for in oratory it is the most important thing), he can not only hold the history of those times in a memory more ready than the memory anyone has of his own experience, but he can invest the stories of men who died so many centuries ago with such lively feeling that he seems not to have got what he is presenting out of books, but to have seen it and felt it and been engaged in events as they happened for better or worse; and he can judge their policies not tepidly, on the basis of an account by someone else, but with fire in the light of his own fears and hopes, his perils and successes. If he were as good as this on one side only, he would still deserve our admiration; but as it is, he shows himself such a master on both that you might think him a chameleon, which changes colour as its background changes.

How I wish, my dear Erasmus, that certain people who are now too ambitious and hope to be thought good writers would wake up and reorient themselves by the example of your friend Vives! – and I hope it more because they despise everything else than because they either pursue eloquence or properly attain it; for even in their dreams they never conceive any idea of what style is. These men neglect the other arts, and from what subject do they expect to derive their title to distinction? Orator or advocate are not names anyone will rightly confer on a man who neither pleads causes in real life nor declaims on imaginary themes. He will be a very thin and bloodless poet, whose verses are shaped by no philosophical principles, no precepts of the art of rhetoric, no practice in the conduct of discourse. Vives, after distinguishing himself in rhetoric beyond almost all the men who profess nothing else, goes on to leave untouched none of all the other arts which are worth knowing; there is none in which he is not so well versed that you would think he had spent his life on nothing else.

And so, though there is nothing of his that is not universally popular, I

The Field of Cloth of Gold
Windsor Castle; reproduced by gracious permission of Her Majesty
the Queen

take a special kind of pleasure in his *In pseudodialecticos*,[5] not only (though this is certainly one reason) because he makes such elegant fun of their absurd quibbling arguments, opposes them with powerful reasoning, digs   70 them up by the roots, and overturns them with inescapable logic, but also since I see him treat some themes in that book on almost the same lines as I had thought of for myself when I had not yet read anything by Vives. I approve of them now in Vives' book not because as my own arguments they had appealed to me before (for we often approve something that we see put   75 forward by other people, if we had already thought of it for ourselves); but it is good for my self-esteem, when I had previously suspected that some point was not receiving the expression it deserves and am now confirmed in my belief that it is by no means foolish, by seeing that Vives too accepts it. And then it attracts me and gives me satisfaction, when I see that the same   80 argument has taken possession of the minds and thoughts of both of us and has been treated by us in such a way that, though he is fuller and writes better, yet in some things we produce not only the same matter but almost the same words.[6] And so I readily flatter myself that something in the way of a kindred star joins our minds with some sort of secret power and sympathy.   85

I am glad to think that he has such a good position with his eminent master the cardinal.[7] I hope the favour of that deity may set right the injustice of Fortune, who always gives the worst treatment to those who deserve the best and, as though she had a grudge against learning and virtue, oten lavishes her favours on the exaltation of ignorant and vicious men. But the   90 cardinal, for whom it is almost as easy to make any man prosperous as it is for Fortune herself, is sure to show special generosity to such a man, whom he has made a member of his inner circle, and to whom he owes so much of the distinguished learning for which he is now not a little more illustrious than even for his exalted station; such is his well-known goodness, such the   95 credit he will gain with posterity by so doing.

Farewell, dearest Erasmus; I hope we shall soon greet each other face to face in Calais at this meeting of the monarchs. The emperor lands today. Tomorrow morning early the king will go to meet him, perhaps even this same night which now approaches. You would hardly believe the joy with   10 which not only the king and the nobles but the people too received the news which made it clear that the emperor is due here. Farewell once more, from Canterbury on Whitsun eve.

There is one point, my dear Erasmus, which I would mention to Vives if I knew him personally. As it is, since I am not certain how he would take such   10 uncalled-for kindness from a stranger, you can tell him at a suitable opportunity. There are in his *Aedes legum*[8] and also in his *Somnium* (which in other respects far surpasses what many other people have spent sleepless

nights on) some things which are too abstruse to be clear to any except
specialists, though it would be for the good of the literary world that   110
everything of his should be as widely understood as possible. It would be
easy enough to remedy this, either by adding an explanation or by putting
very brief notes in the margin. It will also throw much light on his
Declamationes,[9] if he will briefly summarize the story even on a single page at
the beginning.   115
    Farewell once more.
    [1519]

1107 / To Thomas More   [Louvain, June 1520]

This answer to Ep 1106 was evidently written between the arrival of More's
letter and Erasmus' departure for Calais; cf Ep 1106 introduction.

ERASMUS OF ROTTERDAM TO HIS FRIEND THOMAS MORE, GREETING
Dear me, what an example of the hopelessly perverted judgment of the
common run of parents! They take anxious thought for their children's
bodies and their mental endowments are neglected, though it is useless, and
indeed it may be disastrous, to own riches and not know how to use them.   5
As for the youth, I tender you no thanks, nor have you done anything new;
you have just been like yourself, as always.
    You speak of Luis Vives' gifts, and I am delighted to find my estimate
confirmed by yours. He is one of that band of people who will put the name
of Erasmus in the shade.[1] But in none of the others do I take such an interest,   10
and I love you all the more for your open-hearted concern for him. He has a
wonderfully philosophic mind. The mistress to whom all do sacrifice, but
very few with success, he roundly despises; and yet with gifts like his and
such learning he cannot fail of Fortune. No one is better fitted to break the
serried ranks of the sophists,[2] in whose army he has served so long. I shall be   15
in Calais, if my health[3] permits, to embrace all my friends for the last time and
bid them goodbye. Farewell, friend beyond compare.
    [1519]

1108 / From Juan Luis Vives   Bruges, 4 June [1520]

Vives reached Paris and met with Budé during the first half of May 1520 (ie
between the letters in Budé *Opera omnia* I 299–303 and 307). He left on 30 May
(lines 231–2). This letter is an account of his visit, carefully composed to
document his newly won appreciation of the University of Paris and of Budé. It
deals at some length with Erasmus' fame among the Paris humanists, the

Juan Luis Vives
Collection Duque del Infantado
Photo: MAS

excellence of Budé, and the cordial friendship between him and Erasmus, notwithstanding some 'light-hearted' criticisms. This letter was answered by Ep 1111, and conceivably at first by Ep 1104. It was published in the *Epistolae ad diversos*.

JEAN LUIS VIVES TO DESIDERIUS ERASMUS OF ROTTERDAM, HIS TEACHER, GREETING

Having proceeded with Cardinal de Croy[1] to the border of our prince's dominions, dear Erasmus, most learned and best of men, I took a fancy to enter France, both to visit those who are still there of my old acquaintances[2] and friends, and to acquire new friends whose conversation and society I should enjoy while I was there and whose letters would be a delight when I had left. It had happened, I thought, most unfortunately that at that time I had published an attack on pseudologicians[3] and especially those in Paris; so that I did not doubt that I should find many men of the variety they now call sophisters unlikely to be pleased to see me. But in actual fact my experience was very different from what in my excessive anxiety and suspicion I had imagined.

I reached Paris with no fatigue from my journey, for I had enjoyed it, and sent my servant to tell my friends I had arrived. They came round at once in crowds, greeted me warmly, and said how glad they were to see me. They also brought other people to visit me next day and the remaining days – sophisters of high renown. In the course of conversation, as often happens, we soon got on to the subject of what they were studying, and I too. I was most careful to gloss over and conceal my letter to Fortis[4] (who was there in person), thinking that I had published it at a most unfortunate moment. At that point Fortis could not keep silence any longer about my letter to him. They all laughed, and admitted not only that they had taken it in good part, but that they were actually most grateful to me for having devoted my efforts to showing up their wild absurdities. The state of mind of the Parisians, they assured me, is quite different now from the days when I studied there myself, although some still adapt themselves to the play and the audience, and lack either the enterprise or the perseverance entirely to abandon the old characters that were so popular and the plot that won so much applause. There are several of the Spaniards, they said, whose example is a great stimulus to better things: Juan Población[5] is an expert in the whole of mathematics and also a successful student of the humanities, Francisco de Melo[6] and Gabriel Aquilinus[7] have done the same. Juan de Enzinas[8] promises likewise; a young man who is the most lively disputant of them all, at least on their fictitious topics, and has a thousand arts, if tackled with the same weapons, of pique and repique and equally of side-stepping, of

ducking, and avoiding. They told me of many qualities, and I saw many more
for myself, in Dom Martinho[9] of Portugal, a kinsman of his king,[10] who
would need a whole letter to describe him as he deserves; when he tasted the
bitterness of the traditional sophistries, he was so disgusted that he devoted   40
himself entirely to this genuine and truly humane learning – or should I say,
plunged into it? The latter, I think, so that its sweetness might wash the old
bitterness off his tongue. He has made great progress in these disciplines;
and because he thought I was some good at them, he gave me the most kind
and friendly reception.   45

It would be a long story to recount who the men were and what
honours they paid me, being of that same opinion that there was something
in me – not only persons of high standing and noble birth, who respect and
cultivate the fields of learning proper to their rank and way of life and leave
meaner things to meaner men, but even leading theologians in the   50
university. You would hardly believe how ready they were to think well of
one, and how much more kindly their interpretation of everything than that
of many whom you know. If they are ignorant of something, this distresses
them; they bear no grudge against those who do know it, and encourage
those who wish to find out.   55

I dined with them – often in fact, and enjoyed it. At table we had barely
exchanged two words when your name came up at once in various contexts,
and there was much talk of you after dinner. My dear Erasmus, I would
recount it all, if you would endure to be praised in a letter to yourself. What a
pity I am not writing to someone else! So reluctantly I must not repeat what   60
they said about Jerome[11] restored by your efforts to his true self and about
the New Testament recovering its original purity – a labour which has done
more for Christian piety than a thousand years of declamation in the
lecture-room; how much they admire your paraphrases, which give us Paul
expounding his celestial doctrines in a form they can understand; all the   65
pleasure and profit they derive from your *Adagia* and your *Copia* and the rest
of your secular works; and how your *Moria* is a general favourite and offends
no one, no doubt because the self-confidence of these theologians is tougher
and more courageous than that of other men. How boorish and uncivilized I
am if I keep silence on all this, and how cruel you are to tell me to be silent!   70
But the time will come when I shall not do as you tell me.

One thing you will now have to suffer willy-nilly, that there is no
aspect from which they do not find you paramount, admirable, faultless. I
could give you the names of a dozen men of that order who promise you and
offer you all they can do, their diligent and enthusiastic support; they will do   75
anything for you, their houses are open to you if you go there, their
resources and households and wealth and friends are at your disposal. They

beg you, they urge you to press on, undeterred by the yelping of the ignorant, to serve the Christian religion and the cause of learning in general; they make it their business that in theological disputations the contestants 80 shall not waste their time on trifles. And this really is so. If anyone produces a theorem at the Sorbonne woven out of old Suisset's[12] cobwebs, the audience with frowning brows protest at once, reject him with hand-clapping, and drive him out of the lecture-room. Moreover in their philosophical encounters, if any paradox-monger appears, armed with some 85 oracular utterance weighed down with many a syncategorema,[13] and sorely in need of an Etruscan soothsayer[14] to unravel it – a thing which elsewhere is highly to the taste of the crowd of students in their fusty gowns – he meets now with shouts and catcalls and clapping of hands, and is thrown out of the classroom with great uproar. I do not doubt that you rejoice at this with your 90 love for humane studies, and I must say I found it a very pleasing sight, though that community has not yet succeeded in driving that kind of riddling sphinx out of its number.

And all that I have said so far relates to the satisfaction and pleasure which I enjoyed in Paris to no small degree. One thing at least makes an 95 immense contribution not only to the pleasure but to the profit of my travels; and that is, that I had the good fortune to meet and talk with your old friend Budé, now mine too[15] or, may I say, our mutual friend. In Christ's name, what a man! Whether one looks at his gifts, his learning, his character or – what counts for least in such a man – the position he holds (for most highly 100 honourable as it is, it yet pales into insignificance compared with the wealth and distinction of his other endowments): born in a station of particular eminence, and of the highest standing in his class of society, which has come to him as the head of his family, and endowed with means of which a man of his birth need not be ashamed. But this is not the side from which one would 105 form an opinion of him: beside his other qualities his birth and position pale like stars before the sun.

How I enjoy writing to you, and writing about Budé! His praises are sung with a loud and clear voice by the books he has published, and you yourself never cease to admire and extol his virtues; I would much rather 110 hear of them from you than tell you of them. He has read so much, and read it to so much purpose! All that he has written down to this day demonstrates that there is nothing he has not read, and that he has read it all with the closest attention. His memory is truly admirable. Really, you might call the man's head a whole library rather than a head: he has it all so much at his 115 finger-tips – history, mythology, antiquity, the entire range of subjects and vocabulary. Latin he writes and speaks so well that there is no reason why he should not have enjoyed a great reputation in the age of Cicero, had he

lived then; Greek so well that Greeks themselves[16] confess that he can teach
them their own language. His great experience of philosophy is proclaimed   120
by his five books *De asse*[17] and the amount he knows will hardly be credited
by anyone who has not observed him at close quarters and learnt to know
what they call his inner life. His familiarity with the classics I should not wish
anyone to learn from my report; let the *Annotationes in Pandectas*[18] and the
books *De asse* be his teachers. This last book of his has put to shame all your   125
Ermolaos and Picos, Polizianos and Gazas and Vallas[19] and the whole of
Italy; so that Tunstall,[20] that capital scholar, was as shrewd as he was
accurate when he wrote that Budé would have made himself ridiculous if
before he published his work *De asse* he had given out that he proposed to
write one. Nor was that man far wrong who put on its title-page 'To cavil at   130
this is easier than to copy it.'[21] Need I mention his character? Everything
provokes admiration and respect – so easily approached, so civilized, and so
fair-minded too; such a sense of duty towards God and man. The way to the
highest positions lay wide open before him, had he been willing to deviate a
finger's breadth from that precise and fully-rounded virtue that is his. This   135
he preferred to all the promises, all the blandishments of Fortune. Never has
he been dazzled by the glitter of riches and turned his eyes from what is just
and right.

  You know how true all this is, and your eloquence does not make his
qualities greater than they really are. I doubt if you could, they have already   140
reached such a high level; but at least you exhibit the facts and make them
credible. You have a great affection, and indeed love, for Budé. There are
very few Italians to whom you would not prefer him, and he is the only man
in these countries north of the Alps of whom that can be said, such is your
feeling for him, such your admiration and respect for his gifts and his   145
attainments. He in his turn, not to repay you but because this is truly his
opinion, maintains that you are the greatest literary figure of our age and
places you on a pinnacle of learning. For your gifts, your scholarship, and
your writings he has a religious veneration, and he is the most zealous
supporter of your name and fame. Long may this mutual affection and   150
respect and admiration last! You are two bodies, but a single soul. Could
anything be more agreeable than this sight to all lovers of learning, or give
them greater joy? It is true that in some light-hearted letters[22] he has criticized
you a little sharply, as those perhaps will think who do not know the two of
you, and in a way that did not befit your friendship; but for this there were   155
many reasons, as I know from both of you and from the facts. First, because
each of you was always seeking for some reason to write a long letter to the
other, yet not to be always praising him. Praise cannot go on forever; or if it
can, there is moderation[23] in all things. And then inspiration itself flags

without some antagonist, as it were, to stimulate it; and so at first it amused 160
you both to provoke each other with some harmless pricks. What becomes of
an orator, if he is the only speaker in a case or is not stimulated and urged on
by an opponent? He cannot fail to become sluggish and pedestrian. Gaius
Erucius, says Cicero,[24] spent very little trouble on his prosecution of Roscius
Amerinus, because it never crossed his mind that there would be anyone to 165
reply.

And so first of all we came to speak of the works you have both written,
a field of discourse by no means limited; for you have written so many things
and so learned, which are constantly in the hands of all who wish to learn.
And so, while each asks the other to explain the reason for something he has 170
done and each of you expounds the purpose behind his writing, lightly
turning aside or even throwing back upon his friend something which at
least surprised the other if he did not actually disapprove of it, this was the
original source of your disagreements. Each of you was put out at not
receiving the other's approval in every respect. Then, while you are 175
expounding at greater length what you are trying to do and why, out comes
your *Apologia*[25] against Lefèvre, and the skirmishing warms up: Budé thinks
you have gone too far, or at least you are represented as having done so, to
discourage you from writing any further attack on Lefèvre, while you seem
to yourself to be extremely moderate and restrained. 180

The next stage was those remarks which some people find already
excessive and severe and hard to bear, though in your own eyes (and this
one fact is quite enough for Budé) they never seem to pass beyond the limits
of friendship; nor do I think they have, when I consider the whole question
with some care, for both of you have been outspoken, relying on the 185
sincerity one friend uses to another. And those jests which to an outsider
appear double-edged and barbed are harmless between friends; they do not
wound or bite, they scarcely even pierce the skin, but merely tickle. For the
intention with which they were uttered was not at all to give pain, and in the
words themselves if there was no honey there was at least no gall, only salt, 190
and the sort of humour that is another direct product of friendship – and
friendship of no common kind, but the special and real sort, such as existed
once between Cicero and Atticus and Brutus,[26] who often assailed one
another with letters like this.

At any rate, as regards Budé's feelings towards you, though I know 195
well that you have gone into them thoroughly and fully understand them,
there is no limit to what I could vouch for. He showed me letters he had had
from certain furies (a better name for them than men), who were trying to
come between you and make you two separate people instead of one, citing
suspicions maliciously distorted and sowing seeds of discord that might 200

have come from Alecto's[27] private store. I said what seemed to me best at the moment to pacify and settle Budé's feelings in case all that poison had left anything bitter behind; but my remarks were quite unnecessary. For while as regards all other people he keeps a very firm grasp on any friendship once formed, and does not easily abandon even a friend who has done him wrong, you are so rooted in his heart with affection and respect that violence could not displace you. I can vouch to you on his behalf, as I did to him on yours, that your friendship will last forever, and with your common ground in literature and study in general it can never fail to bring both pleasure and profit. Nor would I dare answer for this, unless I knew you both to be endowed with sufficient sense always to believe the facts rather than rumours and backbiters and friends who offer advice distorted by some interest of their own. But enough on this subject, I hope that you two have laid the foundations of your friendship so well and truly that it will stand forever in its own strength, secure against all attempts to sever or weaken it. 205

210

215

I return to the story of my wanderings. My friends thought it would be a great shame if I took a fortnight's holiday from lecturing, and they proposed to me that my noisy nonsense should be heard in Paris too. I agreed, and to avoid too serious a topic, chose a dream,[28] so that if I should have fallen asleep, it would not have seemed out of keeping. So lying at my ease and dropping off from time to time, I told them some dreams I had had about the *Somnium Scipionis*; and on waking up, prepared at once to take my leave. I had many reasons for going, but was retained for some time by friends both old and new whose kindness was an embarrassment; they had already upset my digestion with all their suppers and their drinking-parties. And things would have gone on longer, had I not most opportunely had a letter from the cardinal in which I was immediately recalled. When I read that, I bade them an affectionate farewell, with all their breakfasts, dinners, luncheons, and suppers, with all their pint-cups and their pasties great and small; and on the fifth day after leaving them, which was Trinity Sunday,[29] travelling in a light carriage, I reached Bruges, and here I am writing to you next day. 220

225

230

Farewell, and every good wish, my beloved master.

1109 / From Hermannus Buschius   Mainz, 5 June [1520]

This letter was first published in the appendix to Hillen's second edition of *Epistolae aliquot eruditorum* and subsequently in Froben's *Epistolae aliquot eruditorum virorum*, a production with which Buschius was personally involved (cf Ep 1083 introduction). The letter also appeared in Erasmus' *Epistolae ad diversos.* After Erasmus had been unable to secure an appointment for him at Louvain (cf Epp 884, 1046 n5), Buschius continued to live an unsettled life. Erasmus showed his appreciation for his support with a lengthy reply to this letter, Ep 1126.

TO ERASMUS OF ROTTERDAM FROM HERMANNUS BUSCHIUS

I was met at Mainz by your servant, on his way back from Basel[1] and expecting to leave immediately. From him I learnt that in my absence your defence[2] and a letter had been delivered to me in Speyer[3] – your defence against Edward Lee, a man as light-weight as his name[4] suggests, which 5 means a pretty rascal. By this extraordinary publication of his all he has achieved is to appear ridiculous to every man who has a particle of human brains, and make himself a byword, just like that famous beetle[5] who went in search of the eagle and suffered for it. I am grateful to you over and over again, my most learned friend, for having thought to send me this most 10 elegant present. I wish my power to take vengeance on the worthless ruffian who has attacked you were equal to my affection for you, dear Erasmus. Unquestionably you would see, even from what he writes, the uncommon hatred which your friend Buschius feels for this fury, for no one's sake except your own. But thank heaven you do not need the resources of 15 Buschius or anyone else to defend you, for you will be more than enough by yourself with your domestic resources for the whole barbarian faction and not only for Lee. May Christ preserve you to us, great man that you are, for you were born to be a public blessing to every lover of learning. And so I promise myself he will, as surely as he will be the scourge of all slanderous 20 tongues, and specially of such as under the name and guise of religion devote themselves to one object above all, the overthrow of all religion worthy of the name.

Your two previous books[6] I had already read, having found them by chance in Worms, and I noticed from them that you were to add a third. I 25 shall therefore read it most eagerly when I get home, and therefore too I shall make for home sooner than I intended. I have written this on the spur of the moment, and in any case even after much thought I am not a very skilful writer. Pray therefore lay criticism on one side. Farewell then, and keep up your strength to put Lee, the most worthless of all two-legged animals,[7] to 30 shame, if he has enough decency left in him to know what shame is.

I write from Mainz, in the house of that honourable man Marquard von Hattstein,[8] who is a great lover of serious subjects and all who pursue them, and specially of you and Capito. He has asked me to send you his most particular greetings, and commends himself to you as he might to some 35 supreme pontiff. Give my greetings also in your part of the world to Nesen and to Maarten van Dorp, whom I love with my whole self now I know[9] that he is wholly fond of you. But enough of this nonsense! Farewell once more.

5 June, before sunrise

1110 / To Johannes Sapidus   Louvain, [c May–July 1520]

This is the preface to Erasmus' *Antibarbarorum liber unus* (Basel: J. Froben, colophon date of May 1520). Reprinted at least ten times during Erasmus' life, the work is now edited in ASD I-1 1–138, and translated, with an introduction and notes, in CWE 23 1–122. This dedicatory letter to Sapidus, master of the famous Latin school at Sélestat, may be seen as another tribute (cf Ep 353:9n) to the literary society of Sélestat, with the *Antibarbari* presenting a model for its concerns and activities. It came at the time when Sapidus joined the fray against Edward Lee by addressing a letter to Lee which was published in Froben's *Epistolae aliquot eruditorum virorum* (cf Ep 1083 introduction and n9). Other letters in that volume were either written or addressed to Beatus Rhenanus, who was also living at Sélestat at the time (cf Ep 1014).

Since 1517 Erasmus had been determined to publish this most significant of all his early writings, an indication that he believed its message to be valid and, indeed, timely (cf the preface). This letter provides some precious information about the history of the work (cf Ep 30:17n). Begun in the late 1480s (lines 24–6) it was subsequently cast in the form of a dialogue and divided into four books. During his stay at Bologna in 1506–7, Erasmus revised the first two books, but that manuscript along with others left in the care of Richard Pace (lines 41–6) was never recovered, although Erasmus continued to hope for the eventual return of the second book, in particular (cf Ep 1210). It was this hope which had prompted early plans for a publication in the spring of 1517, but in the months following, after his settlement in Louvain, this hope was fading, while other early works began to appear in unauthorized editions (cf Epp 909, 967:173–96, 1041:4–7, and below n6). Eventually he accepted the need of rewriting at least the first book on the basis of the pre-Italian version (lines 51–5). The result was the *Antibarbari* now to be published.

The manuscript reached Basel by April 1520 and production of the book began (cf Zwingli *Werke* VII Ep 131; BRE Ep 165), although this dedicatory preface was still missing on 25 May (cf BRE Ep 166 and above Ep 1109 n1); hence the delay in publication until after 22 July (cf Zwingli *Werke* VII Ep 148). Typographical evidence shows that this preface was set in type after the rest of the book. Distribution had finally begun in early August, when it was sent out together with the *Epistolae aliquot* against Lee, and Sapidus and Beatus Rhenanus received gift copies; cf BRE Ep 174.

ERASMUS OF ROTTERDAM TO HIS FRIEND JOHANNES SAPIDUS,
GREETING

There is a strange power and active force, as it were, in nature, my dear
Sapidus, which I infer from this fact among others that, though in my
boyhood the humanities were banished from our schools and there was no   5
supply of books and teachers, and they had no prestige to spur on a gifted
student – quite the reverse: discouragement of them was universal, and
drove one into other subjects – in spite of this, a sort of inspiration fired me
with devotion to the Muses, sprung not from judgment (for I was then too
young to judge) but from a kind of natural feeling. I developed a hatred for   10
anyone I knew to be an enemy of humane studies and a love for those who
delighted in them; and those who had acquired any reputation in that field I
looked up to and admired as more than human. For this spirit even now, as
an old man, I have no regrets. It is not that I condemn the interests of other
men, for which I felt no such sympathy; but I see clearly how cold, how   15
maimed and blind a thing is learning when deprived of the patronage of the
Muses. In any case it is a shameful story, the stupidity with which some men
reject what is far the most excellent province of knowledge, dismissing as
'poetry'[1] all that belongs to an ancient and more civilized culture. These were
the men who, when I was a boy, spitefully enough put obstacles in my path   20
and kept me away from my first love; and I had planned to take my revenge
with pen and ink, with this one proviso, that I would attack no man by
name.[2]

I had not yet reached my twentieth year when I set to work. Then, a few
years later, I had the idea of refashioning the same matter as a dialogue to   25
make it easier reading. I had arranged the whole work in four books. The
first was to refute the objections habitually raised against us by the
superstitious or by those who have the form of religion rather than its
substance. In the second a fictitious character like Glaucon[3] in Plato railed
against eloquence with all the force eloquence can wield, and robbed the   30
inmost arsenal of rhetoric of all its panoply in order to deploy it against
rhetoric itself – with such success that John Colet of blessed memory, when
he read the book, said to me seriously in familiar conversation, 'Your book
has quite persuaded me to abandon eloquence.' And when I advised him to
suspend judgment until he had heard the character who championed   35
eloquence, he asssured me that my attacks could not be weakened. Book 3
was a refutation of the arguments in the second book; but I had not yet
finished it. The fourth was a separate apology for poetry, the poetry I had
loved so tenderly as a boy. This I had not yet set in order, and had only a
great pile of material for future use.   40

The first book I had supplemented in Bologna, with publication already

in mind; the second I had revised. When I was about to leave Italy, I
deposited them with Richard Pace,[4] a man endowed with virtues and
accomplishments of every kind, and while they were in his keeping both
were lost, by the fault of others whose honesty that most honourable man   45
assumed to be equal to his own. The loss of the first book hurt me little, to be
sure, for there was too much immaturity about it, and I had piled up in it all
my crudest arguments. As for the others, I could wish they had survived; but
those drones thought otherwise who, while attempting nothing of any note
themselves, undermine the work of others.   50

After my removal to Louvain I learnt that book 1, in the form I had set
down long since, enjoyed too wide a circulation for me to suppress it; it had
in fact already come near to being published by certain supporters of my
humble self whose zeal outruns their discretion. To prevent that happening I
myself revised the book and sent it to the printers, though in other respects I   55
would rather it had been suppressed entirely; especially since a book on this
subject has now been published by Hermannus Buschius called *Vallum
humanitatis*,[5] which is scholarly and trenchant and well written. But I
thought it had better face the world with such revision as I could give it than
in the form taken by the manuscript copies, which were badly corrupted.   60
Book 2 shall join it if I can secure a text. The rest of the work shall be added
out of my own head, unless the persons who are keeping my own drafts
secret prefer to behave like honourable men, and not like petty thieves of
other men's midnight oil.

Those who do not wholly reject this portion, the worst of the whole   65
work, must please keep their eyes open in hopes of tracing the remainder.
This will make me the readier to publish other things too which I now have in
my desk, roughed out, such as a work on letter-writing.[6] In the meantime
this fragment shall be dedicated to you, my dear scholarly Sapidus, who in
educating the young of your town show such devotion to high character no   70
less than to sound learning. Keep it up! Continue as you have begun, and do
not rest until, so far as one man can, you have driven all barbarism out of our
native Germany.[7] It is time we learnt to know ourselves, after so long being
treated almost as animals by men who credit themselves with every virtue.
Farewell.   75

From Louvain

1111 / To Juan Luis Vives   Louvain, [c June 1520]

This answer to Ep 1108 was published in the *Epistolae ad diversos*; cf Ep 1104
introduction.

ERASMUS OF ROTTERDAM TO JUAN LUIS VIVES, THE ACCOMPLISHED
PHILOSOPHER, GREETING

Your letter, my learned Luis, found me depressed and rather weary[1] and in a
state of some dissatisfaction with myself, and cheered me wonderfully, for it
gave such a picture of that most prosperous journey of yours and brought it   5
so clearly before my eyes that I felt like your fellow traveller. Really you must
have been born under some lucky star! – for a renegade like yourself to have
launched a skirmish against your old companions-in-arms the sophisters,
and in Paris particularly, where, as it seemed to be the reigning queen and as
it were the citadel of the subject, there was some danger that you might be   10
pelted with stones or stung to death by hornets. I am simply delighted with
this public progress in their studies; and as a private person too I rejoice to
think of the University of Paris, with which I long ago became familiar
through several years spent there not unpleasantly. And what may we not
hope for hereafter, if the Sorbonne[2] has thrown over its logic-chopping and   15
welcomes a solid and true theology? What joy to see the Muses invited back,
who before this were perfect strangers to our public seats of learning! –
though I should wish to see their reception confined to the driving out of
barbarism and frivolous quibbles. They must not be allowed to overwhelm
subjects of which the acquisition is essential; and so far are they from   20
obstructing these that they will make it easier to acquire them properly. For
we must not spend our time on polite literature and nothing else, as some
people do in Italy, behaving too much like gentiles: once they have packed
Jove, Bacchus, Neptune, Cinthius, and Cyllenius[3] into a set of verses, they
fancy themselves finished scholars. The humanities do not receive the   25
honour that is their due until they are mingled like a seasoning with other
and more serious subjects.

Be that as it may, I often wonder how it is that while almost every
university in the world enjoys a kind of change of heart and settles down as
it were to steady progress the good people of Louvain alone put up such an   30
obstinate resistance to the humanities, especially as they are not greatly
distinguished even in this sophistical department of learning. Three years
ago I was told by John, bishop of Rochester,[4] who is a true bishop and a true
theologian if ever there was one, that in Cambridge University, of which he
is perpetual chancellor – for so they call the highest officer of the university, 35
who has perpetual tenure – sophistical disputation has now been replaced
by sound and sober discussion between theologians, from which they come
away not only better scholars but better men. Oxford University put up some
resistance at first, the work of certain monks; but they were coerced by the
authority of the cardinal and the king, who were sorry to see that most   40

distinguished and ancient institution deprived of such a blessing.[5] Of Italy
why need I speak? – these subjects have always been supreme there, and
these almost alone, if you except medicine and jurisprudence. The University of Alcalá[6] derived its original reputation entirely from the welcome it
offered to the ancient tongues and the humanities; its chief ornament is that   45
distinguished old man, who deserves to outlive many Nestors, Antonio de
Nebrija.[7] In Germany there are almost as many universities as there are
towns, and of these there is hardly one that does not provide large salaries to
attract public teachers of the tongues. In Cologne, by some freak of fortune,
the more humane subjects have never been highly valued, since power there   50
belongs, they tell me, to swarms of Dominicans and Franciscans. But at least
it has always been open to anyone[8] who so wished to teach, and even to be
paid for it.

But in Louvain the trouble has been that the leading men prevent
anyone from giving instruction in any humane subject, even without a fee! I   55
cannot tell you how they conspired against something which would be a
great benefit and a great credit, not only to the university but to the whole
region. An ancient regulation[9] was produced that no one had ever heard of.
The authority of the whole university was brought to bear; the protection of
the king's court was invoked; lay magistrates were summoned to give aid;   60
finally the police were called in. No stone was left unturned, no expedient
untried. You yourself were not merely a witness of this commotion, you
played some part in it. All these efforts had no other object than to prevent
anyone from offering a contribution from the humanities to the studies of the
university, particularly at a time when the subjects taught were highly   65
respectable and the teachers of such high character, and lecturing with such
integrity that you might sometimes hear things in sermons which contributed less to a high moral standard. In Paris, Fausto[10] was permitted to lecture
on any poet of his choice, even on that rubbish the *Priapeia*,[11] and to do this –
to say no more – in his own peculiar style. In Louvain, Nesen was not   70
permitted to expound the *Geography* of Pomponius Mela. Rome itself,
Milan,[12] to say nothing of our universities, woos those who can teach the
tongues, and attracts them with large rewards. Here, a College of the Three
Tongues, which will be no less useful to every subject of study than
creditable to the whole of the emperor's domains, has been founded by the   75
munificence of the Busleyden family, and we have used every device to
oppose it with a zeal that could hardly be surpassed. And yet I doubt
whether anywhere in the world polite literature is stronger than it is here; I
seem to see Horace's[13] 'Like as the oak with cruel axe' (you know the poem)
all over again.   80
When you write, moreover, that in that part of the world most people

have a very high opinion of what I write, I recognize of course the generous attitude of the French towards me, but I fear that you have added in something of your own feeling for me. And I fear that I may one day regret having rejected France, which has so often invited me to come with   85
munificent proposals.[14] But here are fetters of some sort which tie me here, and I am held here by the very people whose hostility might well drive me elsewhere. I am not allowed to leave the arena, and to the contests there is no end. Nothing invited me to move to Louvain except a more healthy climate and a more pleasant place; and I seem to have come to insoluble disputes.   90

As for Budé, you are absolutely right to praise him so highly; I have a habit of sometimes exalting him to my German friends until they are jealous. Then, as they cannot deny that he is supreme in every department of literature, they tend to defend themselves by saying that he is of course very good, but there is no one else. 'And yet on this count,' my answer is, 'France   95
leaps our native Germany; for Germany has no one equal to Budé, though she has many average scholars, and some above the average.' That skirmish between us I have long since forgotten, so far am I from any feelings on the subject. And towards Lefèvre my feelings are such that I should listen impatiently to anyone who spoke of him otherwise than one would of a most   100
upright and most learned man.

Cardinal de Croy is dear to me for many reasons, and I now have a new one, that he has restored you to us, and rescued you from the perils of chronic indigestion.[15] Farewell, Luis my scholarly friend, and pray let us see you here well and cheerful, as soon as possible.   105

Louvain, [1521]

1112 / To Thomas Wolsey   Louvain, [c June 1520]

This is the dedicatory preface to Erasmus' *Paraphrasis in duas epistolas Petri et unam Iudae* (Louvain: D. Martens n d; NK 842). It was reprinted by Valentin Schumann (Leipzig 1520) and Johann Froben (Basel, dated January 1521 in the colophon), and thereafter jointly with the paraphrases of other epistles.

By 15 May work on the paraphrase had just begun (Ep 1102:21–3). At that time Erasmus expected to visit the English court at Calais (Epp 1101–2, 1106 introduction). Since he owed Wolsey a dedication (Ep 1060:67–9), he probably endeavoured to have the book ready to present personally at the gathering of the monarchs. He was hindered by ill health (cf Epp 1107:16, 1111:3, 1113:35, 1114:18–21, 1115:50–1), 1116, but the book was in print towards the end of June (Epp 1116, 1117:134–5). Allen suggests that both book and preface may intentionally have remained undated as time was so short that Erasmus could not be sure whether Martens could have the book ready for a presentation to

take place in July at Calais. As it turned out, Wolsey was too busy to grant
Erasmus the private audience he had hoped for and on 7 August he still
awaited an indication that Wolsey had welcomed the gift; see Ep 1132.

TO THE MOST REVEREND FATHER IN CHRIST THOMAS, CARDINAL
PRIEST OF ST CECILIA, LORD ARCHBISHOP OF YORK, PRIMATE OF
ENGLAND, AND LORD HIGH CHANCELLOR OF THE WHOLE REALM,
FROM ERASMUS OF ROTTERDAM, GREETING

Often had I looked about me for some offspring of my labours which might   5
answer to your eminent position, that eminence which hitherto has
discouraged me from daring to dedicate to you any of my works;[1] and after
all, I find I have been foolish on two counts. In the first place, how could
there be anything in me, whether in expression or invention, which, even if I
courted a breakdown, could achieve the standard of your greatness,   10
whether one considers your exalted station, your intellectual gifts which are
so worthy of that station, or the kindness with which your generosity daily
lays under obligation not so much me as our whole programme of studies in
humane letters and in true theology? Secondly, are you the man to judge the
worth of a book by the size of the volume rather than its utility? And so   15
although, before I had finished the labour of my paraphrases designed to
expound the Pauline Epistles (those at least which are certainly genuine),[2] I
soon had with my already depleted strength to take up arms[3] against my
detractors, yet none the less with levies hastily raised I drove them off, and at
once with the same forces attacked the two Epistles of the apostle Peter and   20
one of Jude. For at the same time I thought to myself that what is offered to
divine beings or to very great men needs to be not so much adequate as apt,
just as in ancient times it would have seemed absurd for a man to offer a
hundred oxen to the Muses or a chaplet of ivy to the god of war. And so it
seemed to me appropriate first of all that Peter should go to such an   25
outstanding religious leader, being himself the incomparable head of the
Christian religion, so that the true and genuine philosophy of the Gospel,
which was born and first promoted under his leadership, should under your
pious care, which makes itself felt more day by day, be restored[4] after its
partial collapse. So true is it that human affairs tend always towards the   30
worse[5] unless we make great efforts in the opposite direction.

  And if the difficulty of the work is allowed in some sort to recommend
it, this was a much harder task than the size of the volume suggests. This is
due partly to Peter's style, which is much more complex than Paul's, and
partly to the absence here of ancient commentaries which might help us. For   35
the notes supplied nowadays by what they call the *Glossa ordinaria*[6] are taken

word for word from the commentary of your countryman Bede, a man who
lacked neither learning nor industry by the standards of his time; and this
was done with remarkable skill. Part of the notes were banished to spacious
margins, part were cut down to fit the narrow space between the lines of the   40
Epistle. The title was almost entirely removed, I know not why.

Everywhere there are a number of places which need a careful and
attentive reader: in the first Epistle,[7] for instance, the passage about Christ
and how he preached in the spirit to the spirits in prison, who had once been
unbelievers, and again on the preaching of the Gospel even to the dead; in   45
the second,[8] on the demons being reserved unto judgment, on the railing
accusation which the angels do not bring against themselves (though I have
explained this passage, which was obscured by Bede, differently), on the
earth consisting of water and through water, on the heavens and the
elements being reserved for destruction by fire[9] – all passages in which some   50
men have found an occasion of error; in the Epistle of Jude,[10] the passage
about the condemnation of blasphemy, thought to be taken from the
apocryphal book of Enoch, from which a prophecy is quoted a little further
on, although we are not told that Enoch wrote anything. This Epistle I have
added for this reason, that it shows surprising agreement[11] with the second   55
Epistle of Peter not only in style and ideas but even in wording, as though it
were explaining some passages in that Epistle, as for instance that about the
judgment of blasphemy.

On the first Epistle of Peter no doubts have ever been raised; but there
are doubts about the second, although it mentions the Lord's transfigura-   60
tion,[12] at which not more than three disciples were present as witnesses.
Hence, if it is not Peter's, it must be by someone who wished to be taken for
Peter. The Epistle of Jude was slower in reaching authority, since it adduces
evidence from what is called the Book of Enoch, in which there are said to be
things out of step with Catholic doctrine. But nothing forbids the use of   65
evidence from apocryphal writings in a suitable place, just as Paul[13] cites a
parallel from Epimenides. In any case, since in the first of the two Peter
records that he has written by the hand of Sylvanus,[14] and in the second
openly records that it is the second, saying,[15] 'This second epistle, beloved, I
now write unto you,' I do not see how the facts can be explained unless   70
either the second epistle is not Peter's or Sylvanus wrote it on Peter's
instructions. If it was written by Peter himself, he would seem to have
written three, of which the first has perished. Of the time and place of
writing nothing is certainly known, though they suppose[16] that the first was
written in Rome, which in the conclusion he called Babylon, in the reign of   75
the emperor Claudius.

But my preface must not be longer than the book itself. It is my great desire that this labour of mine, if it in any way deserves it, may be commended by the free and open approval[17] of your Eminence to all who wish to learn. The reason is not that I myself have any designs upon your Highness – I have never had the right spirit, nor am I now of a suitable age, for ambition – but because the support and approval of those in high estate wonderfully fires and encourages those who are learning. Apart from many accomplished scholars, there are now growing up in your native England, under your generous auspices,[18] many young men of the highest promise, who will one day do greater things and with happier results, if their zeal is fanned by the breeze of your encouragement. Would that henceforward our studies might make this their goal – to attract the minds of men to the best subjects by the charms of a moderate expenditure of time and effort, instead of pretending that all is difficult and lengthy, and thus striving to make ourselves look wonderfully learned, while our noblest minds are discouraged from pursuing the noblest subjects. Many others will achieve this more successfully, I do not doubt, but with more devotion than I have shown there will not be very many. And if your Eminence will continue, as you have begun, to support these most religious endeavours, you will both win God's full approval and leave a most honourable record to posterity. May Christ the Almighty long, long preserve you in health and wealth.

1113 / To Philippus Melanchthon   Louvain, [shortly before 21 June 1520]

The only known source of this letter is a manuscript copy in a contemporary hand preserved in a volume of letters and documents which were perhaps collected at Wrocław and are for the most part concerned with Luther. The volume is now in the Forschungsbibliothek Gotha, MS Chart. B 20 f 25 verso.

As in the case of Ep 872 the authenticity of Erasmus' text, copied and preserved in circles evidently sympathetic to Luther, seems adequately documented by analogies to some other letters which Erasmus actually published. This present one was clearly not intended for wide circulation and the Wittenberg circle respected the author's intention. On 5 May 1520 Luther mentioned that he and Melanchthon had recently written to Erasmus (Luther W *Briefwechsel* II Ep 284). This present letter is Erasmus' answer to both (line 32 and Ep 1119: 31–2). Its date can be derived from the presence of Hutten in Louvain (line 42). Hutten also wrote to Melanchthon and the two letters were evidently sent together; on 14 July Melanchthon sent them, original or copy, for Georgius Spalatinus to read (*Melanchthons Briefwechsel* I Epp 98, 100). By 1 August, when another messenger became available, Erasmus found the time for a long letter addressed to Luther directly, Ep 1127A.

ERASMUS TO PHILIPPUS MELANCHTHON

I am delighted to hear, my dear Philippus, that you still make such progress in divinity. One thing I would urge again and again: you must be careful of your health.[1] With us here, the criminal conspiracy[2] against truly Christian scholarship and humane studies knows no rest. New monstrosities arise 5 every day, the latest being Lee, who is as spiteful as he is ignorant, and was born to do evil and speak evil unto all men. He has in England two numbskull abbots[3] and a Minorite called Standish,[4] now a bishop, who gets a mention in my proverbs. These men have put up a Carthusian,[5] a young man with no pretensions to learning, but a diabolical hypocrite, just Lee all over 10 again. He writes like a fishwife against me, against Lefèvre – raving mad, like Orestes[6] in the play. Briart[7] has departed this life, for no reason except that this melodrama was too much for him. A big share in all this wickedness belonged to Jacobus Latomus,[8] and still does, for he has made up his mind to be king of this place. 15

Of Luther I hear differing accounts. I am in favour of the man, as far as one can be, although everywhere people connect[9] what he stands for with what I stand for. It was clearly likely to happen that his books would be burnt in England.[10] This at least I stopped by writing a letter to the cardinal of York, and he also, on my advice, made a public statement imposing silence 20 on all this foolish clamour before popular audiences, with special reference to Standish, who was present. The cardinal is a supporter of liberal studies. He had found nothing to take offence at in Luther, except his denial[11] that the primacy of the supreme pontiff is part of the divine law. Luther's supporters – and they include almost all men of good will – would wish that 25 some of what he has written were more courteously and moderately expressed. But it is too late to tell him so now. I can see that things are heading towards civil strife.[12] I pray that it may serve Christ's glory. Perhaps it must needs be that offences come,[13] but I should prefer not to be responsible for the offence. As for that lot, I can see their machinations 30 clearly, and they are diabolical, with no object except to put down Christ and set themselves up as tyrants in his name. Remember me to Dr Luther, and to all your friends.

I write in a hurry, with the unexpected chance of someone to carry a letter, and in indifferent health.[14] 35

Louvain

Your friend Erasmus

I have greatly enjoyed this answer of Luther's[15] to the condemnation by his enemies in Cologne and Louvain. At last they begin to be ashamed of having passed judgment in such a hurry. I would rather my name had not 40 been brought in; for that puts an onus on me and does not help Luther at all.

Philippus Melanchthon
Lucas Cranach the Younger
Kurpfälzisches Museum, Heidelberg

Hutten[16] is here, and will leave shortly for Charles' court; but there is no court where these beggar-bullies[17] are not installed already. Farewell again, dearest Philippus.

1114 / To Luigi Marliano   [Louvain, around 21 June 1520]

This letter, published in the *Epistolae ad diversos*, is addressed to the Italian humanist and physician Luigi Marliano. He had accompanied Charles v to Spain in 1517 and there was appointed bishop of Tuy, among other indications of his growing influence with the young monarch.

This letter serves as an introduction for Ulrich von Hutten, who visited Erasmus at Louvain on his way to the court of Brussels. Equipped with another introduction by Franz von Sickingen (cf Ep 1055), Hutten hoped to enter the service of Prince Ferdinand as a means of stepping up his promotion of church reform and humanistic studies. His hopes, though often unsound, were always lively. If we are to trust Erasmus' partisan remarks in the *Spongia* (1523), Hutten told him in deep secret of his plans for armed struggle against the church and in a lighter mood they joked about how Hoogstraten was to be hanged (cf ASD IX-1 138, 202). Perhaps Erasmus was in fact as alarmed about Hutten's plans as he thought he had been when he wrote the *Spongia* (but cf Ep 1119:38–9). Hutten, however, left him reassured that their friendship was as firm as ever. See W. Kaegi 'Hutten and Erasmus' *Historische Vierteljahrsschrift* 22 (1924–5) 225–7.

The date of this letter cannot be determined precisely. On 4 June Hutten described his departure from Mainz for the Netherlands as imminent (Hutten *Opera* I Ep 171; Luther w *Briefwechsel* II Ep 295). He was still on excellent terms with Cardinal Albert of Brandenburg, but within weeks Albert complied with requests for Hutten's dismissal sent to him from Rome (Hutten *Opera* I Epp 174, 176, 179–80). On 21 June Erasmus apparently expected Hutten to be at Brussels and also hoped himself to go there in two or three days time (Ep 1115:47–50). In Ep 1113 he had stated that Hutten was visiting him on his way to the court. In this letter he did not as yet expect – or perhaps no longer expected – that he would himself be able to travel to Brussels. Thus the letter may have been given to Hutten during his visit at Louvain, or it may have been sent to Brussels for him shortly after Ep 1115.

ERASMUS OF ROTTERDAM TO THE RIGHT REVEREND LUIGI MARLIANO, BISHOP OF TUY, GREETING
It is a great joy to me, my Lord Bishop, to know that your Lordship has been restored to us, for I am no longer left with no patron at court, now that Le Sauvage[1] is dead and Barbier[2] not yet returned. For you will, I have no   5

doubt, maintain the same feelings towards my humble self as you have
always shown hitherto; and this you will do, not so much for my benefit as
for liberal studies in general, which I support with passion, and consequently find many people who do not support me. I send you the *Apologia*³ I have
written in answer to those who were traducing me before popular audiences   10
for my rendering 'In the beginning was the Utterance.' This will suffice to
show you their stupidity and spite.

The bearer of this letter is Hutten, whose name you will know as a
warrior with a sense of style and the most warlike of stylists; but he is a very
open-hearted young man and worthy of your affection, unless I am quite   15
wrong. For your advice,⁴ which I learnt in a letter from Barbier and which
was both kindly and wise, I am grateful, and I intend to follow it. I would
have come to see your Lordship in person, but my health⁵ is still poor; this
very hot weather, which must have been brought upon us by some modern
Phaethon turned loose in the chariot of the sun, has been nearly the death of   20
me. My best wishes to your Lordship, to whom I present my most humble
duty.

[1519]

1115 / To Joris van Halewijn   Louvain, 21 June 1520

This letter was published in the *Epistolae ad diversos*; for the circumstances in
which it was written cf Ep 1114 introduction. Halewijn had accompanied
Charles v to Spain (cf Ep 794:92), but was now attending the court at Brussels
and would be present at the meetings with Henry viii at Gravelingen and
Calais (cf Ep 1106 introduction; LP iii 907).

Halewijn had earlier translated Erasmus' *Moria* into French, and copies of his
translation had circulated for some time (cf Ep 641), presumably in manuscript.
Although it is not normally thought to be identical with an anonymous French
version published in Paris by Pierre Vidoue on 2 August 1520 (cf Ep 641:6n),
Halewijn's renewed interest, as reflected in this letter, preceded the printing of
Vidoue's volume by just a few weeks, which might seem to be a strange
coincidence. In February 1536 when Pierre Vitré considered doing another
French translation he only knew of one earlier version and apparently thought
that the translator was still alive (Ep 3101). Halewijn died in 1536–7.

TO THE HONOURABLE JORIS, LORD OF HALEWIJN AND COMINES,
FROM ERASMUS OF ROTTERDAM, GREETING
It gave me very great pleasure to find that you have not yet forgotten your
humble friend Erasmus and that, great man as you are, you think him worthy
of a letter. The passage which troubles you in the *Moria*¹ – in what sense do I   5

say that some things really exist – will be clear to you if you remember the
Platonic myth about the cave and the men born in it, who wondered at the
shadows of things as though they were the reality. What we apprehend with
our senses does not really exist, for it is not perpetual, nor does it always take
the same form. Those things alone really exist which are apprehended by the   10
contemplation of the mind. Plato teaches this in many passages, and
Aristotle supports him in the *Metaphysics*.[2] Paul[3] too in the fourth chapter of 2
Corinthians says 'We behold not the things which are seen, but the things
which are not seen. For the things which are seen are temporal; but the
things which are not seen are eternal.' As however God exists most perfectly   15
of all things, because he simply exists and is removed as far as possible from
the coarseness of sensible things, so those things which approach him most
nearly are said most truly to exist. Thus the soul exists more truly than the
body. Now although the philosopher, withdrawing from sensible things,
practises the contemplation of things intelligible, yet he does not perfectly   20
enjoy them except when the spirit, liberated from the material organs
through which it operates now, exercises all its force. Further, although
there are some powers which the spirit exercises by means of organs which
are less under the sway of matter, as when it understands or remembers,[4] yet
it is a point at issue among philosophers whether the mind, which the   25
Greeks call νοῦς, can do anything at all in the body, for want of a bodily organ.

You say that so far you have had no satisfaction either from writers on
the method of learning Latin[5] or from the many people who have published
books lately to show how much Latin they have learnt. It may be that Cicero
himself will not satisfy you, just as there have been men who thought that   30
Virgil knew no grammar and Livy was provincial. Personally I approve
neither those who entirely neglect the rules and hope to acquire a method of
speaking Latin from the texts nor those who are devoted to the rules and
spend no time in reading the authors. I like few rules, but good ones; and the
rest I think one can gather from reading the best authors or from the   35
conversation of anyone who can speak as they wrote. If anybody does not
like this method, I do not see what remains except to take refuge in ludicrous
incantations and the absurdities of polygraphy,[6] from which I have never
seen anyone get any profit. Moreover, if the style of those who write today
appears impure, the reason may well lie in the taste of those for whom we   40
write: maybe we have to immerse ourselves from time to time in those
barbarous authors who are ubiquitous; and another cause may be that even
among the Romans no respect is paid to a classical Roman style, and there is
no incentive to do anything about it. There is no other snake in the grass,[7] as
far as I can see. I would adopt your view more readily, if someone would   45
appear who could write pure Latin without any rules.

There is in your part of the world a young man of good family, Ulrich von Hutten by name,[8] a master of Latin, a good scholar, and a civilized person; and you will do better to discuss the point with him. I shall be there in two or three days' time, if my strength permits; for I have barely recovered   50
yet from illness.[9] That is why I have dictated this letter instead of writing it. Farewell, honourable sir.

Louvain, 21 June 1520

1116 / To Gerard of Kloster   [Louvain, c 21 June 1520]

This letter is known only from Maarten Lips' copy-book now at Rotterdam (cf Ep 1000A introduction). It would appear that the Austin prior of St Agnieten-berg was present at Louvain on one of his repeated visits (cf Ep 1013A n11) and was staying at the Austin house of St Maartensdal where Lips lived (cf Ep 1140). For the date cf Epp 1112 and 1115:50–1.

DESIDERIUS ERASMUS OF ROTTERDAM TO CANON[1] GERARDUS,
THE VENERABLE PRIOR OF ST AGNES, GREETING

Most excellent Father Prior, I live under the tyranny of the doctors and exist on drugs, not food. So I can neither come to see you nor ask you to dinner. If it should be convenient to visit me, I should greatly enjoy a talk, and you will   5
perform two duties at a stroke by visiting both a friend and an invalid. I send you a book[2] written while I was ill; near the end I was taken so bad without warning that I could scarcely dictate the Epistle of Jude and the preface. The fever has now gone, but I am physically very weak.

Farewell, reverend Father.   10

1117 / To Germain de Brie   Antwerp, 25 June 1520

With this letter, which was published in the *Epistolae ad diversos*, Erasmus continues his efforts at ending the controversy between Brie and More (cf Epp 1045, 1087, 1093, 1096). Provoked by a fresh rejoinder on Brie's part (cf n21), Erasmus indicates tactfully but firmly that he judges Brie's position to be weak; he also repeats many of the arguments More had put forward in Epp 1087, 1096.

Erasmus' visit to Antwerp followed weeks of ill health (cf Ep 1112 introduction). As on other occasions (cf Epp 963:6n, 1205), he may have been seeking the vicinity of the sea for relief from the heat of summer (line 18; cf Ep 1114:18–19) and may have been staying, as he normally did, with his good friend Pieter Gillis (cf Ep 1079 introduction). For a meeting with two Czech

Brethren which may have occurred during this visit to Antwerp see Epp 1039 introduction; Allen 1129:23–5.

ERASMUS OF ROTTERDAM TO HIS FRIEND GERMAIN DE BRIE, GREETING

While I was on my way to Antwerp in a carriage, I happened to meet an Englishman[1] on horseback who gave me a letter from you which you say is the third.[2] You protest that I have not answered, but still more that I have not 5 been to pay you a visit;[3] and unless I can clear my name with powerful arguments, you wish me to run the risk of seeming to dislike all my Paris friends. Finally, you do not refuse to make it up with More, to please me, contenting yourself with my judgment that you are a better scholar than he is; for so you understand something, I know not what, that I had written to 10 Bérault.[4]

I must send you a short answer, for time is short. If you could have seen, my good scholarly Brie, the trouble I had to take in refuting the false accusations of other people and especially Lee, if you could see the bundles of letters which I sometimes have scarcely the time to read, and the amount of 15 work I devote continually to writing, correcting, and revising books, a kindly man like yourself would easily forgive my silence. On top of all this is ill health contracted from the hot weather, from which I have suffered severely, and it still keeps me very weak and to some extent dictates to me. And then no one has appeared who said he was on his way to your part of 20 the world.

Even supposing laziness were the reason I have not written more, it does not immediately follow that I thoroughly dislike the people to whom I send no answer. I can return the affection[5] of them all, write back to them all I cannot. There is hardly anyone to whom I am more sincerely devoted than 25 Budé,[6] and yet he has sent me two or three letters which I have not yet answered. Besides, I am no less desirous of enjoying the delightful society of Budé, yourself, Bérault, Deloynes, Ruzé, Du Ruel, Lascaris, Paolo Emilio,[7] and Cyprianus[8] than you are of setting eyes on this frail body of mine, as you say in your letter. But this whole miserable business of Lee[9] suddenly 30 knocked me sideways, and I had to give it nearly a month and a half. On top of that the return of our prince Charles,[10] and also some business connected with Spain,[11] have compelled me to change my course, though not my purpose. If I did promise to come,[12] it was barring accidents like this; it is always an understood thing that they form an exception. And I am no less 35 cheerfully in your debt and no less thankful for all the kindness you had planned to show me than if I had been able to enjoy it.

The disagreement that to my great regret has arisen between you and More[13] is something about which I had intended to write to you in some detail; for I had already written to More about it with unusual care. But so far this has not been possible. I wrote a short letter to Bérault,[14] to stop the trouble, however it arose, from going any further. But this was not done to please More. I perceived that he had so little fear of your *Antimorus* that it was he himself (so they write and tell me) who arranged to have it printed,[15] and that on the advice of some of his wisest and most honourable friends, among whom I know there were several men who were on your side until you published your book. Now they have changed over, finding you deficient in the common courtesy that ought to go with liberal studies. I wanted to see your quarrel made up, not because I thought More's reputation was in any danger from a pamphlet like this (which almost nobody here reads; certainly I have yet to meet anyone who thought well of it), or because I distrusted his powers if it should come to open conflict, but in the conviction that it contributed both to the public standing and to the progress of our studies if the devotees of good literature agreed among themselves and the Graces kept company with the Muses, especially since there is such a rancorous conspiracy everywhere against men of our way of thinking. I had the waste of More's time in mind more than his reputation, for all scholars would reckon him too great a man to suffer from such petty criticisms. But for your reputation I was very much concerned; I have it specially at heart, and wished to see it grow greater and better day by day. I thought it also contributed to the reputation of France, which by common consent has never yet produced anything with so much rancour in it as your pamphlet against More.

More provoked you, but you provoked him first; and he did so with much more courtesy than you show in your reply, as even your French friends[16] agree. And he wrote in the war, you after all those years of unbroken peace; nor did he publish what he had written, but allowed his friends to extract it from him, provided they revised it. It is no surprise in a man with poetic gifts if he embroiders the truth a little to exalt his subject, nor is there any serious disgrace in being misled by love of one's country. This is all that More charges you with; and you make a wicked attempt[17] to get him into trouble with the king as a critic of his royal father's reputation. His remarks on the mistakes in your poem did not deserve so much fuss. I do not now consider whether there is anything in the criticisms you bring against him in your turn, for I have no intention of disputing with my friend Brie, nor does More need me to defend him; it is I, rather, who need help from him. Nor have I any desire to act as judge between two friends, for fear I must lose one or the other.

And so I wonder very much, my dear Brie, what came into your head, that you should understand some words or other in my letter to Bérault[18] as   80
meaning that I had settled the question and given you the first prize for learning. I desired to have you both as lifelong friends, and had no idea of estranging one of you by passing judgment, especially while there was still a hot dispute between you. I do not clearly remember what I wrote to Bérault, but am prepared to swear that nothing was further from my thoughts than   85
the interpretation you put upon it. What I meant was this: that in any competition in the field of scholarship there is only one prize that one should aim at in such a contest, and that is somehow to show oneself the better scholar, if one can. I pointed out what you should have aimed at, not what you had achieved. However much I might have set your learning above   90
More's, I think you too modest and sensible a man to be willing to agree. I made no pronouncement which of you is the better scholar, nor is it necessary that I should, and I very much doubt whether it is my place to sit in judgment on the scholarship of yourself and More; I know what other people think.   95

I have not seen many things of yours, nor have I tested your learning at close quarters. Of More's things I have read a number, and he and I are intimate friends. My feelings towards him are those of any man who knows him well. He has incomparable gifts, a most fertile memory, and the greatest readiness in self-expression. He learnt Latin with great success as a child,   100
and Greek[19] as a young man, and that under the most learned teachers, Thomas Linacre and William Grocyn. In the Scriptures he has gone so far that the greatest theologians cannot overlook him. The liberal disciplines he has studied not without success. In philosophy he has advanced beyond the average, to say nothing of his professional knowledge of the law, especially   105
English law, in which he scarcely yields to anybody. His wisdom is something exceptional. This is why the king, who is very intelligent, was not satisfied until he had brought More into his most intimate councils.

And so, my dear Brie, the word-play[20] you are so fond of between More's name and the Greek for 'fool,' falls very flat indeed. Even his bitterest   110
rivals give his wisdom generous praise. The attitude you wish to adopt of looking down on him and treating him as a kind of joke is not likely to commend itself to men of learning and judgment. For while I reckon you among our outstanding men, I fail to see from what aspect you can despise More, whether you consider his fortune or his natural gifts, his mind, his   115
character, or his learning in any field. And the more I admire More's gifts (and I am not the only one to do so), the more did I want to see peace between you, for your sake more than his, and for my own sake too, that there might be no shadow on our friendship. What has been done cannot be undone; all

the same I should like to see this disturbance, such as it is, evaporate. You   12
think it hardly possible that your *Antimorus* should get out of date; but
unless I am much mistaken, no one will reprint it, if you are content to have it
so. Many people take it ill that you should have attacked More, again in a
preface,[21] when he had not yet made any reply to your pamphlet.

But I must stop. My dear Brie, if you wish me to use my influence with   12
More that both of you may forgive and forget, I will go on as I have already
begun. But if you expect More to come to you cap in hand, you are sadly
mistaken. So far as I understand his feelings, I shall do pretty well if I can
secure that he should refrain from a more unpleasant attack on you; and that
he should do so is, I think, important both for the public standing of our   13
studies and for your reputation.

You say you are turning your mind to questions of theology, and have
my paraphrases[22] continually in your hands. I am bound to approve your
design. I have edited for immediate publication a paraphrase on the two
Epistles of Peter and one of Jude. While I was engaged on this, I fell ill, but   13
am gradually recovering. Farewell, Brie, my learned friend. Greet all my
friends particularly.

Antwerp, 25 June 1520

1118 / To Richard Pace   Antwerp, [c 25 June?] 1520

This letter was published first in the *Epistolae ad diversos*, but the place and year
were added only in the *Opus epistolarum* of 1529 and cannot be accepted with
much confidence. The references to Lee and the Collegium Trilingue support a
date of either 1519 or 1520. The letter might thus be placed either at the time of
Pace's mission to the German electors (May or July 1519; cf Epp 968, 999
introductions) or at the time of the meetings of the monarchs in and near Calais
(June–July 1520; cf Ep 1106 introduction). Pace accompanied Henry VIII across
the Channel, as did Thomas More, and Erasmus probably expected them to be
in easy reach of one another by the time this letter would reach Pace, a factor
which may rule out May 1519. As Pace seems to be moving from a point near
Erasmus to the place where More is to be found, he was perhaps returning to
Calais from Mechelen or Brussels. Allen ingeniously proposed to connect this
letter with the Englishman on horseback who met Erasmus on his way from
Louvain to Antwerp (cf Ep 1117:3–4) and thus could have been Pace's
messenger. Erasmus' remarks, however, can be explained in different ways
according to the date chosen.

ERASMUS OF ROTTERDAM TO RICHARD PACE, GREETING

Your note reached me very late, when you were already set for boot and saddle. I wanted a word with you, and perhaps there may yet be an opportunity. I congratulate you sincerely on your promotion,[1] though Fortune can never reward your merits as they deserve.

In case we have no chance to meet, I commend to you a piece of business[2] which means more to humane studies than it does to myself. What Lee, that son of perdition, has on foot does not concern me personally; it does concern your native Britain, which has some interest, I imagine, in the veracity of a man who sings her praises. I know the credit that England has gained from my work is very small; yet Lee seems to begrudge her even that little.

The theology faculty have brought up a fresh ruse[3] against the College of the Three Tongues; More's letter[4] will show you the sort of thing. Farewell, best of patrons.

Antwerp, 1520

1119 / To Georgius Spalatinus   Louvain, 6 July 1520

This letter was published in the *Epistolae ad diversos*.

ERASMUS OF ROTTERDAM TO THAT MOST UPRIGHT OF THEOLOGIANS
GEORGIUS SPALATINUS, COUNCILLOR TO THE MOST ILLUSTRIOUS
DUKE OF SAXONY, GREETING

Alexander,[1] as promising a young man as one could find, has given me your most welcome letter,[2] together with two medals which bring back to me a lively image of your excellent prince. Such a present has raised my spirits more than if he had sent me an Attic talent[3] of gold. He has sent me himself in silver and gold, and I reply with my own image in bronze.[4] Each of us is done in the material he deserves. What is there in that prince of yours that is not golden? – who with a strength of mind surpassing the heroes of old despised the Empire[5] freely offered; who with characteristic sense of honour and integrity could not be persuaded by any inducements to confer the imperial crown on anyone except the one man whom he thought among all the princes of our time to be most fitted to carry the burden; who persistently rejected a large sum of gold offered him by our side; who with admirable wisdom and unparalleled skill adorns and enriches his dominions, and that without injury to his neighbours but rather to the general advantage of them all; who has blessed Christendom with a new university,[6] which he has turned in a few years from an empty and sluggish place into a flourishing centre for all languages and literatures, encouraging humane studies with such tact that supporters of the old learning have no cause to complain of him. The world of letters would show gross ingratitude, did it not enshrine this great man's merits in work that will never die. I owe him a great debt on my own account, but much more in respect of what he has done for the humanities. I only wish that before I die I might enjoy the privilege of seeing 25 your famous prince and his flourishing university. If I mistake not, I shall be in Germany[7] this autumn; I shall try hard to visit you, provided it can be done in safety. Meanwhile, I shall place the likeness of your excellent duke among my greatest treasures, and shall carry it about with me always as a favourite possession. 30

I wrote[8] recently to Philippus Melanchthon, but with the feeling that I was at the same moment writing to Luther. I pray that Christ Almighty may moderate Luther's pen and his mind in such a way that he may be the greatest benefit to the religion of the Gospel, and bring into a better frame of mind those people who seek their own glory at the price of Christ's shame, 35 and their own profit at his loss. In the ranks of Luther's opponents I see many who smack of this world rather than Christ. Yet there are mistakes on both sides. If only Hutten[9] had kept his pen under control! I admire his gifts particularly. How I wish Luther would take a rest for some time from these controversies, and treat simply the facts of the Gospel, with no personal 40 feeling mixed in! Perhaps we might see better results. As it is, he burdens the humanities as well as himself with unpopularity, which is disastrous for us and does him no good. And there is a risk that the corruption of public morals, which everyone agrees needed public action to remedy it, like the plague once stirred up will take root more and more. The truth[10] need not 45 always be put forward, and it makes a great difference how it is put forward. Farewell, my honoured friend, and commend me to the prince your master.

Louvain, 6 July 1520
Your sincere friend Erasmus

1120 / From Konrad Frick and Lorenz Effinger   Freiburg, 12 July [1520]

This letter is known only from a rough draft in the Öffentliche Bibliothek of the University of Basel (MS C VI[b] 3 f 246). It is in the hand of Udalricus Zasius and follows two other rough drafts by Zasius (f 245), addressed to Jan Hannaert (d 1539), styled chancellor of Charles V, and to Johann Salzmann (cf line 13). All three are dated from the same day (in this letter the year is partly torn away) and were evidently composed by Zasius at the request of the two abbots. Erasmus' answer is Ep 1148.

Konrad Frick was abbot of Schuttern from 1518 until his death in 1535. Lorenz Effinger of Villingen in the Black Forest was elected abbot of Ettenheimmünster in 1500 and ruled the abbey until his death in 1544. He is described as learned, a good administrator, and a patron of art. The two

Benedictine abbeys were located in the region of Lahr between Freiburg and
Strasbourg. Both joined the Bursfeld congregation in 1463, and both were
sacked by the rebelling peasants in 1525 and finally suppressed between 1803
and 1806. In the fourteenth century the lords of nearby Geroldseck took over
the protective 'Vogtei' over both abbeys. They used their position for endless
acts of encroachment and oppression while the abbeys replied with protests
and litigation. After the death of Maximilian I, who had greatly esteemed
Gangolf I von Geroldseck, the two abbots attempted to have the 'Vogtei'
transferred to the Hapsburg government of Ensisheim. Gangolf reacted with
the occupation of Schuttern, carrying off its supplies of grain and wine. In 1521
the Hapsburgs took Schuttern under their own protection and threatened
Gangolf with persecution. Agreements followed but brought only temporary
relief. In 1530 the two abbots went to the diet of Augsburg to give evidence of
their plight again. See G. Mezler and J.G. Mayer in *Freiburger Diözesan-Archiv*
14 (1881) 147–8, 162–3; *Germania Benedictina v: Baden-Württemberg*, ed F.
Quarthal et al (Augsburg 1975) 215–24, 562–72.

TO THE VENERABLE AND HONOURABLE DR ERASMUS OF ROTTERDAM,
THE EMINENT DOCTOR OF DIVINITY AND LEADER IN ALL LIBERAL
DISCIPLINES, OUR MASTER AND MOST HONOURED FRIEND[1]
Greeting. We have been encouraged, great Erasmus, prince of scholars, by
the bearer of this,[2] a man of solid industry and reputation, to write at least   5
these few lines to your Excellency. We were spurred on by Zasius, whom
you know, who sings your praises untiringly and assures us that you are fire
caught from heaven, and deserve no less reverence than any of the ancient
pillars of the church. We were encouraged further by your exceptional and
admirable courtesy and kindness, which stand out (so we are told) even   10
above your countless other gifts. At the risk of discourtesy, therefore, we
summon up our courage to address you, and to lay before you frankly the
state of our affairs, which Dr Johann Salzmann's[3] explanations will make
clear to you.

   To this day we have been attacked by the baron of Geroldseck[4] by no   15
process of law, and – to put our grievance mildly – he has from time to time
used violence against our dependants and threatened to use it against
ourselves; while he refuses to bring our differences to court, he proceeds to
insult us, to vilify us, and to sully our good name. His insolence is such that
unless our illustrious king gives us protection at the seat of judgment, and   20
that too with some force, as he has already begun to do, we fear we may be
unable to withstand any longer the party of nobles that has attached itself to
him and their violent attacks. In this matter, most honoured Lord, pray lend
us your support, if no other way is open to you, by word at least: speak for

us, plead our case, write for us; and born as you are to promote all good and   25
heavenly causes and the well-being of mankind, do what you can for the
calamities which we endure in innocence by lending us your kind and
valuable help to secure at least the chance to claim the rights for which we are
ready to stand up in court.

Given any opportunity of returning your kindness, we shall ever be   30
most ready to do all we can to further your desires. Farewell.

Freiburg, 12 July

Konrad, abbot of Schuttern and Lorenz abbot of Ettenheim, in the
province of Breisgau

1121 / From Udalricus Zasius   Freiburg, 13 July [1520]

This letter is found in Zasius' *Opera omnia* (Lyon: S. Gryphius 1549–50). One
would assume that it was taken to Louvain by Johann Salzmann (cf Ep 1020 n3),
although its text – at least as published in Zasius' *Opera* – does not refer to the
business of Ep 1020. Rather this letter is for the most part a sequel to Zasius'
earlier attacks on Edward Lee (cf Epp 1084:78–102, 1105 n1), which were to
appear in print before long. The reason that Erasmus made no use of this letter
and actually never seems to mention it was probably that meanwhile he had
decided that the campaign of his German friends against Lee had gone far
enough; cf Ep 1100 introduction.

ZASIUS TO ERASMUS, GREETING

What think you, great Erasmus? Does not Edward Lee look as though he had
virtually committed suicide as a member of society, now that he has cut the
throat of his own reputation with these foolish attacks on you? – and it is the
opinion of Paul the jurist[1] that loss of reputation is worse than loss of life. For   5
heaven's sake, how men's condition differs! There are you, constantly
promoting the salvation of mortals by your life-giving teaching, and Edward
on the other hand interfering as though he wanted no one to be saved. Caius
Caligula[2] once wished that the Roman people had only one neck, so that he
could cut the throat of the whole population at one stroke. Lee's objective is   10
not unlike that. A man like Lee constantly attacking an Erasmus: what is this
but to put his knife to the throat of the Christian faith and of Christ's faithful
people, and to aim at the jugular vein of all that scholarly society that
depends upon you? True and genuine theology is a young plant which you
have set out and nurtured with a new and greater skill, and it is not yet   15
established on its own roots; and does Edward Lee now try to cut down your
sapling as it grows?

God forbid! The whole of educated society rises against this enemy of

the general good; it is public action that must overwhelm a public enemy. I
believe that among cultured people, if they are men of good will, if they wish   20
to promote the public weal, there is no one who does not heartily disapprove
of Lee's unwholesome design and who would not join in any campaign
against him in defence of the common figure-head, leader, and father of the
humanities. There are not a few of us in Germany who, like the Roman
nobles who conspired with Mucius Scaevola[3] against Porsena, have sworn   25
to make common cause for the commonwealth, which means for Erasmus,
against Lee. Go on therefore, great hero, as you have begun, and care
nothing for an absurd man, a man of no account. The eagle does not chase
flies,[4] and great men pay no attention to such offscourings. After all, the
Lord[5] also will be at your side, and he will keep your feet that you may not   30
fall into a snare.

    But enough of this. I want to know how you are, for you are my patron
deity. What about Dorp[6] – a man almost beyond compare, if only his life
would correspond – is he still with us? Is he still a defender of the true
theology? Budé[7] has written to me very strictly and not very kindly about   35
some small points which I had put together for the benefit of novices in the
second book of my *De origine iuris*, and I was not slow in replying. I send you
a copy of both, but do not propose to publish them; if I must compete with
good men, let it be in courtesy, not controversy.

    The kindness of our king,[8] which I am now privileged to enjoy,   40
requires an answer to the best of my ability. For all my years, I maintain very
difficult courses in civil law with some reputation and in a new and polished
style. My physical powers may be failing, but my brains do not desert me. I
should like however to be relieved of my membership in the regency,[9] that I
may have more leisure to devote to study for the benefit of my audience. If   45
you can help me in this, I shall gladly confess that I owe you a blessing.
Farewell, and live long in good health for the benefit of all mankind.

    From Freiburg, 13 July 1520

THE DIALOGUE OF THE TWO-TONGUED

AND THE TRILINGUALS

Dialogus bilinguium ac trilinguium

translated by
PAUL PASCAL

annotated by
PETER G. BIETENHOLZ and PAUL PASCAL

The letters in this volume contain some echoes of the wide attention that the *Dialogus bilinguium ac trilinguium* gained around 1520; surprisingly, it has not so far been available in an English translation. Probably in July 1519 the Paris publisher Konrad Resch issued a short piece attributed to one Konrad Nesen: *Eruditi adulescentis Chonradi Nastadiensis Germani dialogus sanequam festivus bilinguium ac trilinguium, sive de funere Calliopes*. The title-page also indicated the address of Resch's firm, the *Ecu de Bâle: Sub scuto Basiliensi venale comperies*. This dialogue was quickly reprinted in Basel without an indication of place, printer, or date and, again without a printer's name or place, and with many additions, by Lazarus Schürer in Sélestat, who added at the end the date of 1520.

The dialogue was the kind of lively and learned lampoon that could not fail to be noted in humanist circles as soon as it became available. Edward Lee recalled that it was in circulation at Louvain after his return from Antwerp, where he had met Richard Pace, late in July 1519. Pace subsequently felt obliged to deny that he had brought the pamphlet from Germany, declaring that he had not seen it until after his return from Antwerp to London.[1] On 3 August Maarten van Dorp in Louvain had heard about a satire against the Louvain professors, but evidently not seen it as yet.[2] In September a copy was sent from Basel to Beatus Rhenanus at Sélestat and another to Udalricus Zasius in Freiburg.[3] On 6 October Konrad Grebel sent one from Melun, near Paris, to Joachim Vadianus.[4] While all of these may have been copies of the Paris edition, the above evidence points to the likelihood of a speedy reprint at Basel, and Bernhard Adelmann, canon of Augsburg, may have owned a copy of the second edition as early as October 1519.[5]

All three editions attribute the dialogue as well as the short epistle to the reader to Konrad Nesen of Nastätten in Hesse, who matriculated in 1525 at the University of Wittenberg and was later syndic and burgomaster of Zittau in Lusatia. He is not known to have visited either Paris or Louvain and may have given little but his name to the book. Beatus Rhenanus expressed – ironically, I think – admiration for Konrad's accomplishment, seeing that not long ago he had struggled with elementary Latin grammar.[6] Konrad may, however, have presented a copy of the Paris edition to Johann Reuchlin.[7] On the other hand, many circumstances suggest the involvement of Konrad's elder brother, Wilhelm Nesen. He had met Erasmus in 1515–16 in Basel, where he had worked for the printers, and won his esteem and affection.[8] Subsequently he had gone to Paris and from there had visited Erasmus at Louvain in March 1519.[9] One result of that visit was Nesen's decision to move from Paris to Louvain, where he arrived in July or August and was lodged, like Erasmus himself, in the College of the Lily.[10] The fact that he admired Erasmus greatly and clearly enjoyed his confidence would explain the affinity of views and the similarity of some expressions found in the dialogue and also in some of Erasmus' works and contemporary letters. His visit to Louvain in March had acquainted Nesen with the local scene and the personal features of Erasmus' adversaries at the precise time when the master felt himself to be the victim of a far-flung conspiracy and was seeking the support of his friends in Paris.[11] During his last months in the French capital (April to July 1519) Nesen would appear to have composed the dialogue, possibly with some help from more experienced scholars, and arranged its publication with Konrad Resch, an associate of Johann Froben at Basel. The first printed copies must have reached Louvain at the time of Nesen's arrival in July or August, or shortly thereafter. The date of 25 February at the end of Konrad's epistle to the reader probably is, like Konrad's name, a ploy, chosen to fit the epistle's excuse that the dialogue was a carnival amusement.

These assumptions are strongly supported by the role assigned in the dialogue to Maarten van Dorp.[12] The relations between Erasmus and Dorp, while much improved, still had their difficult moments as late as April 1518,[13] but in the ill-starred spring of 1519 the former critic was solidly on Erasmus' side. Erasmus' friends in Paris, however, among them Nicolas Bérault[14] and evidently Nesen, continued to see in him a traitor, and so did many others.[15] When Nesen arrived at Louvain in July or August, Erasmus had to act swiftly in order to clear up this misunderstanding, but despite his best efforts[16] he could not forestall all private and public statements bound to distress Dorp. On 3 August Dorp knew that a satirical attack against him was afoot[17] and began to do all he could to assure the literary world of his loyalty to Erasmus.[18]

There is good reason, then, to assume that Erasmus was unaware of the publication of the dialogue and in fact highly embarrassed when copies appeared in Louvain. As a threat of more attacks to come, the dialogue may in a way have helped to bring about the solemn reconciliation between Erasmus and his theological opponents, which occurred on 13 September.[19] That reconciliation, however, could hardly have come to pass, had the theologians considered him to be the author or instigator of this malicious lampoon. Erasmus' highly publicized crusade against libel and slander[20] is compatible with the assumption that Nesen was generally held responsible for the dialogue, but would be incongruous if he himself were. None of these arguments precludes the possibility that back in March Erasmus had learned about, and indeed encouraged, Nesen's project, although the dialogue contains neither specific formulations nor characteristic thoughts that are exclusively attributable to Erasmus. In another instance, though less important than the discrepancy of judgments with regard to Dorp, the dialogue differs from the views expressed by Erasmus at the time.[21]

Erasmus repeatedly complained that some works were attributed to him merely because they were in 'rather better Latin,'[22] and this satirical dialogue may be a case in point. In November 1519 Bernhard Adelmann agreed with Willibald Pirckheimer in attributing it to Erasmus,[23] but Pirckheimer may later have changed his mind. Bonifacius Amerbach's first reaction seems to have been that Erasmus was the author.[24] Perhaps already referring to the additions of the Sélestat edition, Zwingli wrote on 4 January 1520 that the dialogue had been 'merrily enlarged,' or 'enriched' (*auxit*) by Erasmus.[25] On the other hand, Richard Pace thought that the tract was too puerile to have been composed by Erasmus and instead pointed to Erasmus' supporters in Germany.[26] Beatus Rhenanus praised the dialogue highly in a letter to Wilhelm Nesen.[27] If his reference to Konrad Nesen's sudden accomplishments is, as I think, ironical, the passage may be read as a compliment for Wilhelm as the true author. In the lampoon *Eccius deodolatus* of 1520, often attributed to Pirckheimer, it is pointed out that the Louvain professors continued to persecute Nesen because of the dialogue, although its author rather was a 'creature' of his.[28] Edward Lee, finally, held Erasmus responsible for the dialogue, but his remarks can be taken to mean either that Erasmus had written it or caused it to be written.[29] Matching this ambiguity, Erasmus replied in the *Apologia invectivis Lei* that Lee had no basis for 'pressing' the dialogue upon him. He glibly added that he could not know who the author was. To Lee's charges in Ep 1061 he replied with a general remark about the tendency of fathering upon him certain libels penned by other people.[30] Much later, in 1532, he replied rather cryptically to an imputation made by Martin Bucer concerning the dialogue.[31] He appears to concede Bucer's point, but what that point was we do not know. We do not have any statement by Erasmus to deny explicitly his authorship or involvement, but neither do we know of any specific charges addressed to him that would have called for such a denial. He may well have been embarrassed by the publication of the dialogue, but there is on the other hand no evidence to suggest that he was unduly upset. Wilhelm Nesen continued to enjoy his support and to render him services of a highly confidential nature.[32] Nesen also continued his campaign against the theologians of Louvain with another satire in response to the Louvain condemnation of Luther.[33] This anonymous *Epistola de magistris nostris Lovaniensibus*[34] shows a much closer affinity to the *Dialogus bilinguium ac trilinguium* than any of Erasmus' writings.

Schürer's text was photomechanically reproduced (with an introduction and notes) in de Vocht CTL I 544–74. W.K. Ferguson included a critical edition based on all three early editions in his *Opuscula*, 191–224. The English translation here presented normally follows Ferguson's text, but in keeping with CWE practice the additions in Schürer's reprint are usually not identified as such.

PGB

By the learned youth, Konrad of Nastätten in Germany
The Merry Dialogue of the Two-tongued[1]
and the Trilinguals
or
The Funeral of Calliope.[2]

KONRAD OF NASTÄTTEN IN GERMANY TO HIS FRIENDLY READER, GREETING

As I observe that serious studies should be tempered with playfulness, and that in Paris it is the accepted custom, on the days that warn us of the approach of Lent,[3] for the youth to occupy themselves without any constraint in literary amusements,[4] I too have chosen to disport myself in the popular fashion, and I have playfully produced *The Dialogue of the Two-tongued and the Trilinguals*, making fun of the conditions of this age, but so frivolously that I would myself be unable to render any accounting of my project. Whoever you are who read this, smooth your brow and put on a face worthy of the subject, and of the season. Farewell.

Paris, 25 February[5]

BY KONRAD OF NASTÄTTEN IN GERMANY
The Dialogue of the Two-tongued and the Trilinguals.

Speakers:[1] Mercury, Baramia, Titus, Pomponius

Mercury Hail, trilinguals!
Baramia Hail, all hail!
Titus Hail to thee too, omnilingual![2]
Pomponius Hail, Mercury, of gods the most linguacious!
Mercury What if I take three languages and make nine out of them?
Baramia That's easy enough for you to do, with your mastery of magic and conjuring.
Titus Go ahead and do it, then.
Mercury There are three of you?
Pomponius Unless I'm mistaken.
Mercury And each of you has three languages?
Pomponius Granted.
Mercury So you have nine languages, unless you would deny that from a threesome triplicated there results an ennead.
Titus Well, aren't you the proper sophist! I suppose you could just as well produce five eggs from two, if you wanted to.
Mercury Yes, and in fact from a half-black, half-white[3] monk a pitch-black beast.
Baramia If only you could do the same with money as you do with languages! However, in this matter you show more favor and skill to the Midases than to us. We trilinguals hardly ever have a single gold piece.
Mercury It is not my role to impart all things to all,[4] while I strive to please all.
Pomponius Well, you might just give us a backward glance sometimes.
Mercury To put it bluntly, languages and money never go together. Easier were it for a Crassus[5] to produce a sesterce, or even a talent,[6] than a word. Their tinkling is in the strongbox, yours in the mouth. But how are you getting along with the Muse-chasers?
Titus Like lambs with wolves.
Mercury Ha, ha, he! What are you saying?
Titus No armistice, no truce in the war. It's more like pigs in marjoram,[7] I would say.
Mercury Why not show yourselves heroes?
Pomponius Indeed we are better than heroes, but we are thwarted by regiments and platoons of good-for-nothings. More than that, they are all absolute snakes.[8] Sometimes each of us does battle single-handed with

thousands of them, and when any one of the beasts is finished off, ten spring up in its place.

Mercury How marvelously prolific the most evil things have always been!

Baramia But where are you hurrying off to now, Mercury?

Mercury To Frankfurt.[9]

Baramia Frankfurt? Why there?

Mercury How can you ask? To bring good fortune to the affairs of thieves, impostors, perjurers, usurers, and peddlers.

Baramia I believe it.

Pomponius Immortal gods! What is this procession that I see from afar? Woe, woe!

Titus Woe, woe.

Baramia Woe, woe.

Mercury That's them! That's a story I was going to tell you about. But first I will surround us all with a thick cloud, so we can observe at ease and in safety; thereby we will perceive as through a glass sharply.

Baramia What? Can they see far enough to recognize us from such a distance?

Mercury Abroad they see everything, at home they are blinder than moles and Tiresiases.[10]

Pomponius But why are you so afraid of these fellows, Mercury, when you are a god?

Mercury Why shouldn't I, alone and unarmed, be afraid of so many who are armed?

Baramia Armed? I surely don't see any arms.

Mercury They're better armed with poison than the Mars of Homer[11] himself ever was with his full armor.

Titus To the devil with them![12] What manner of monster are they?

Mercury Watch your language! They're all gods and goddesses.[13]

Pomponius Does heaven contain such monsters?

Mercury Surely you didn't think that there are no gods anywhere except in heaven? There are, even on earth; and their majesty is so sensitive that they would have no qualms about farting on Jupiter himself, if anyone attacks them.

Pomponius You don't say! They must be Fevers and Pallors, or such monsters as Veiovis.[14]

Mercury Not that; a bit more dangerous than that. At doing harm, they are artists and heroes; at doing good, mere phantoms. In fact, they consider it their greatest benevolence to rest content with injuring only mildly. But I will point them out one by one when they come closer. After all, you know that I am the god for everybody, or, as the Greek proverb[15] has it, Mercury to share. I would not want to come right out and offend them.

Baramia What have you to do with monsters like that, you who are the friend of the Muses?

Mercury I am honored by them; by none more substantially.

Baramia In which of your capacities?

Mercury In the name of profit; for there is no class of gods or men more avaricious than these.

Baramia What's this I hear? Are they in business?

Mercury They don't grow rich by dealing in merchandise, but by trapping, buying, retailing priesthoods, preying on inheritances – that source of profit is now the richest. In fact, there is nothing that these fellows do not convert into gold; in that they surpass the very alchemists. Why, they even have holiness for sale; they convert their pretended contempt for gold into the very essence of gold.

Baramia That's a theologian's disease you're describing!

Mercury They are indeed theologians, but they have embarked on rivalry with certain monks, with whom they compete in every evil thing, and they often come out ahead.

Baramia By Jove, predatory gods!

Mercury Fornicators, in fact; profiteers, supreme impostors – they are, as I have said, worldly. But quiet now, they are all coming within sight.

Pomponius What are they carrying?

Mercury A coffin.

Pomponius Whose?

Mercury Calliope's.

Titus Don't say it! Is Calliope dead?

Mercury Not at all; in fact they are carrying her off alive.

Baramia Please, what horror is this, Mercury – they are carrying her off alive?

Mercury To be sure; so that they can hurl her down somewhere. They will not even accord her burial.

Baramia What has she done to deserve that?

Mercury Her crime is an atrocious one.

Pomponius What crime is it please? Not incest?

Mercury Don't be silly. Nothing like that. That's an honor among them.

Pomponius Embezzlement?

Mercury That's a malady of others.

Titus So what are we to imagine about Calliope?

Mercury She has been condemned for heresy.

Titus What kind of crime is that?

Mercury That was a pretext,[16] not her crime.

Pomponius Who was the judge who condemned her?

Mercury They themselves acted all the parts, judge, prosecutor, and defendant.[17]

Pomponius If heresy was the pretext, what then was her real crime?

Mercury Lese majesty. Calliope had conspired against their sovereignty with her followers, striving to eliminate their tyranny.

Pomponius Do such monsters reign anywhere?

Mercury There's nowhere that they don't reign, in the palaces, in the senates, in the law courts, in the schools, in the markets, in the ecclesiastical courts, in homes, in the very bedrooms. They infiltrate everywhere; although at the same time they claim that they are not concerned with this world but have their place in the clouds and the mists. It's a fact that they are outside of this world, but in the same sense that bilious phlegm is outside the body of a diseased person.

Titus Plague take them! But where are her other sisters? In Homer brother stands by brother;[18] why then in this case haven't sisters rallied to their sister?

Mercury What could unarmed maidens do against so many? In the course of the upheaval, they scattered.

Baramia Does Apollo then no longer have his bow?

Mercury Well, at that moment he happened to have his lyre in his hands; and, although his bow was close by, most of his arrows had no points. He has left them with Vulcan to be mended. As soon as that is done, he will easily disrupt their triumph.

Baramia But who is that god, or goddess, who is leading the motley column?

Mercury Gods avert such a plague from the earth! It is the bane of both immortals and mortals!

Pomponius What is it, Mercury?

Mercury Ate![19]

Pomponius Gods forbid. Why such a plague from me?

Mercury Ate, I say.

Pomponius No, rather from anyone else than from us!

Mercury How often must I say, Ate, Ate? I tell you, it is Ate. Or, if you prefer it in Latin, Noxa personified.

Titus You mean that Ate[20] who ruins all, whom Jupiter once cast headlong from the sky?

Mercury The very one.

Titus What you say seems very unlikely, Mercury.

Mercury How so?

Titus She doesn't match her description in Homer.[21] He represents her as having feet that are soft but nimble, and as stepping on the heads of men and women and disrupting everything everywhere. This one can hardly creep. She seems to me more like the goddess Podagra as your Lucian[22] portrays her.

Mercury She was that way once, when she had the vigor of youth; but now you see her as an old woman.

Titus But Homer represents her also with piercing eyes. This one is completely blear-eyed;[23] in fact she seems almost to be missing an eye.

Mercury Because of the way she blinks with one of them?

Titus Right.

Mercury Her vision is no less keen on that account, if she takes aim like an archer or a carpenter.

Titus 'Like sighting along a rule with one eye.'[24]

Baramia But that Ate, I thought, was an enormous beast who single-handed could throw into confusion all who dwell in heaven or earth. This one is hardly two feet tall. She seems to be some sort of pygmy.[25]

Mercury Have you never seen a seps?[26] A little creature almost shorter than its own name. And yet there is nothing more instantaneously lethal. Have you never seen the Spanish fly? It, too, has a fatal poison. But Ate alone, miniature evil that she is, surpasses hundreds of Spanish flies in venom.

Baramia So much venom in such a little body?

Mercury Indeed, the whole of her is nothing but venom, ever since Tisiphone[27] immersed the whole of her in the Stygian swamp when she was new-born. What the juice of ambrosia is to us, what blood and gastric juices are to you, that's what pure poison is to her. It is distributed through her whole body, as with a viper; but its power is particularly in her tongue.

Baramia I wish I had that tongue.

Mercury What would you do with it?

Baramia Wipe my arse.

Mercury To my mind you would be better off wiping it with a nettle than with such poison as that. I wouldn't care to let even a rotten chamber pot touch such a tongue. Wolfsbane kills on contact, but even from a distance this one breathes out incurable poison.

Baramia Why are her jowls swelling and hanging down so? Does she have a mouthful of pap?

Mercury Not at all. I think she has a mouthful of tumor.

Baramia It would suit me better if she had a mouthful of *merde*.[28] But why does she keep contorting her face that way, to the left and then to the right?

Mercury That's her threatening gesture, when she demands to be appeased.

Baramia I would gladly appease that goddess by planting a trident in her head.

Mercury But why are you putting on spectacles?[29]

Baramia To study this strange monster more carefully; and in fact I do see something that I hadn't noticed before. She is tied up and is being pulled at the same time from front and rear. I ask you, Mercury, who is that who has pierced Ate's nostrils with an iron ring as if she were an ox, and is pulling her about at will? Is it Megaera?[30]

Mercury No.

Baramia Alecto, then?

Mercury Not her either.

Baramia Tisiphone then?

Mercury Not at all.

Baramia And yet she certainly looks like one of the Furies. But the poets tell of no more than three.

Mercury There were no more than that as long as the Furies remained virgins. But recently Cacus[31] raped Tisiphone; the result was the birth of this controller and mistress of Ate, far more baneful than her mother and her aunts.

Baramia So what's her name?

Mercury Chole.[32]

Baramia But how does she suffer such an insolent mistress when she has such a fierce spirit?

Mercury Indeed the fool thinks that she is being especially regal when she is driven headlong by her mistress. That's the way Ate is.

Baramia Who is that who has her bound by the ankles and is hounding her from behind?

Mercury That is Ate's rather unpleasant attendant. She keeps changing her name. Sometimes she's Podagra, sometimes Chiragra, sometimes Cephalagra.

Baramia I hope she also turns into Glossagra.[33] But either my eyes deceive me or Ate is growing a beard.

Mercury Does that surprise you? When she used to be associated with the nymphs of the court[34] she was considered to be powerfully well-testicled.

Baramia What then? Did she touch the waters of Salmacis?[35]

Mercury No. Jupiter decided that she would be neither an outright man nor a woman. Her voice sounds somewhat female; her facial fuzz is ambiguous;

her mind is female and then some. But what is around her groin is so unfemale that you would call her a Priapus[36] or a satyr.

Titus May all the gods and goddesses damn her!

Pomponius Throw the bastard out![37]

Baramia Verily, verily. But what is Ate doing with the epomis?[38]

Mercury Didn't you know that the investigation of heresy was the responsibility of the wearers of the epomis?

Baramia So Ate is Magister Noster?[39]

Mercury I don't know about that; but you see the garment.

Titus Few men can plough, though many ply the goad.[40]

Mercury It is as you say.

Pomponius So, since age has deprived her of strength, she doesn't do as much damage as she used to.

Mercury On the contrary, never before has evil so increased with age.

Pomponius How is it possible, for an old woman with the gout? She is hardly even alive.[41] Even if the will to do harm were amply present, the faculties would be lacking.

Mercury You aren't looking at it right. How is it then that doddering tyrants rule? Isn't it through others? And that way they rage even more cruelly. By the eyes of others, by the feet of others she accomplishes everything. This whole procession is the limbs of Ate. But do you see that one squinting and clinging close to her?

Pomponius I do. What is the name of that god?

Mercury His name is Phenacus,[42] and he is properly so called. Compared to him an octopus is not an octopus.[43] He is an evil plague everywhere, utterly hated by both the Graces and the Muses, although he smiles blandly. He once wheedled his way into the company of the Muses, so that when he deserted them he could do them worse harm.

Pomponius Is he Ate's husband then?

Mercury No, he's her mind, as he goes by turns from one body into another.

Pomponius You are describing a monster, all right! But where are the Litae[44] that once accompanied Ate?

Mercury With Jupiter. For Ate was bent on ruining them by any means. Nothing could be mended once she had disrupted it; and she hated whatever was good for humans.

Titus If only Jupiter would inflict on that utterly wicked one an Ate more wicked than Ate!

Baramia Not just one Ate, but hundreds of Ates!

Mercury But you couldn't find hundreds of Ates who would add up to this one Ate.

Baramia So we must pray that she may be to herself what she is to others.

Mercury No one can do that better than you.

Baramia I'll do it: Arami Barach, chelam, diuara![45]

Mercury She has Podagra against her. If anyone sacrifices a monkey to her (that is a victim she likes), she will easily finish off this plague.

Baramia I wish she had arthritis and linguitis, or anything she could have that would be more appropriate. But who is that headless Philip?[46]

Mercury You mean the one who is somewhat blear-eyed?

Baramia That's right, the one wearing a patchwork cloak,[47] white outside and black inside.

Mercury That's the garment, they say, that was once worn by the divine Elijah.[48] But if you could examine this god more deeply, you would swear that compared to his foul mind, his gray garment was whiter than snow.

Baramia What's the point of his hiding his dark garment with a white one?

Mercury Obviously, the better to impose on fools.

Baramia Who is he?

Mercury Momides,[49] great-grandson of Momus; but he is a pale reflection of his great-grandfather. That one would blame, to be sure, if something was done not quite rightly. But this one is a mere sycophant, who chooses to rage against all good things with his impure tongue.

Baramia How could such a fool be born of Momus? As far as his face and his bearing indicate, he seems stupider than Corebus.[50] I would sooner believe he was born of a sow or a donkey. For Momus, whatever else he may have been, was very clever.

Mercury You're not far off the mark. This is the way it went: Jupiter, holding a grudge against Momus because of his outspokenness, when he saw that he was prolific, placed the heart of a donkey in the chest of his firstborn, and gave him the brain of a pig in his skull.

Baramia I wish he had added donkeys' ears.

Mercury He has those, and indeed splendid ones, my good fellow. But he hides them under a venerable patchwork, being a little smarter than Midas[51] himself. Then Momus, as he was not unaware of his descendant's stupidity, and as he could not undo Jupiter's decree, advised him to disguise his foolishness with a philosopher's garment, to inspire reverence, so that at least among fools (of whom there is a great multitude everywhere) he might appear to be something.

Baramia But what is that entourage of women he is bringing with him? Are they vestals?

Mercury On them he exercises his sexual parts. For none of the gods is more lascivious than he. Instead of a belt he has a white vest, full of incantations.

Baramia But who is that woman clinging to his arm? Is that his wife?

Mercury Not at all; this kind of god prefers promiscuous celibacy to chaste marriage. But it's true she takes the place of a wife, or whatever there may be that is sweeter than a wife: she is Philautia,[52] the sister of Moria. From her he daily begets children more foolish than both parents; a popular pun calls them, because of their outstanding stupidity, Camelites.[53]

Baramia A stock to be uprooted!

Pomponius An abominable monstrosity, may the Muses love me! But who is that peering sideways and moving his head back and forth like a madman?

Mercury That is the cousin of Philautia.[54]

Pomponius What is he wearing on his head? He has some sort of a helmet.

Titus It looks like a pot to me.

Pomponius You're looking at it wrong. That's a screech-owl that you see.

Mercury You're both looking at it wrong. It's a falcon, a bird held in favor by princes.

Titus He seems like Vertumnus[55] to me, the way he keeps changing the whole bearing of his body.

Mercury If you could see the spirit shifting within, then you would say that.

Pomponius Who is that godlet, strolling all over, whispering things into the ear of this one and that one, pale, skinny,[56] with eyes cast down, wearing a sardonic smile,[57] all covered with thorns and burrs?

Titus Smooth-lee as a hedgehog.[58]

Mercury That is Phthonides;[59] but he is much more baneful than his father.

Pomponius Immortal gods! What do I see? He is dragging a long tail.[60]

Mercury There he has venom more harmful than a scorpion. Why, he himself feeds on venom. And so it happens that the land which gave us this demon has been almost free[61] of poisonous creatures since he left it, as he had used up whatever venom there was there.

Baramia What land produced this monstrosity? Tartarus, perhaps?

Mercury Hibernia, they say, or the ends of Scotland.[62]

Baramia I wonder why he is so scrawny and pale.

Mercury Well, you would wonder even more if you knew how satisfied with himself this little manure god is. He considers Jupiter nothing[63] compared to himself.

Baramia What does the pen behind his ear signify?

Mercury He is always itching to write something, and he has a tongue more damaging than a viper's.

Pomponius My, they certainly are giving Calliope a nice funeral! We still haven't seen everything. Here comes a huge herd of pigs[64] squealing and grunting something or other.

Titus The leader of the disgusting troop is a huge pig. Oh, what a monster!

Mercury He is descended from Gryllus.[65]

Pomponius The one who disputed with Ulysses in Plutarch?

Mercury The very one.

Pomponius But that one spoke Greek and had some sense, and in fact he wasn't all that bad as a sophist.

Mercury Circe long ago has taken away the human mind of this one. Instead of Greek he speaks French,[66] or rather he grunts it. And he hasn't completely given up sophistry, except that what he retains is a crude type, worthy of a pig. All the rest of him is nothing but pig.

Titus Why is he limping?[67]

Mercury Recently when he was caught committing adultery – for he is no less lascivious than satyrs – as he dashed away in fear, he dislocated his ankles.

Titus Those smaller ones following, are they his sons?

Mercury No.

Titus What then?

Mercury They used to be men, but the descendant of Gryllus has the same power that Circe once had. Any youth that eats from the same trough straightway turns into a pig.

Titus A new type of god! But tell me, Mercury, what are they grunting, or humming, as it were?

Mercury Let's listen.

Chorus of pigs

> Thee, god, we adore
> As we cart off this whore
> Who scorned all our teachers
> As ignorant creatures,
> Said the wine they swill is coarse,
> But their Latin's even worse,
> Was indifferent as can be
> To viz and QED
> Now we'll hurl her from the rocks
> And tell the people she was unorthodox.
> So no one will dare with gnawing beak
> Against any Magister Noster to speak.[68]

Pomponius Immortal god! What kind of poem is this? Worse than piggish, by Hercules. And yet how sweetly self-satisfied they are! But as I look more closely, I see that they are all two-tongued.

Mercury That's the way with this kind of god.

Pomponius One tongue isn't enough?

Mercury No.

Pomponius How so?

Mercury They need one to flatter you to your face, another to slander you behind your back; one to bark at you publicly, another to deny stoutly what they said; one to persuade someone to undertake this or that, another to persuade someone else in turn not to let it be done.

Titus You're describing sycophants, not gods.

Mercury Compared to these, sycophants are not sycophants.

Titus But I see two laymen running up. How out of breath they are from rushing, and how gladly these others receive them, as if they know them!

Mercury Ah, yes, those fellows are campaigning to be added to the roster of the gods.

Titus One of them[69] is brandishing a helmet woven of thistles, like a sacred object.

Mercury That is a Carian through and through, newly arrived from afar; or, if you like, straight from Paphlagonia,[70] the traditional home of fools.

Titus But what is his descent?[71]

Mercury He is of the stock of that Bacchus[72] who sat outside, but overlooked the things within.

Titus The other[73] is draped with chamber pots and commodes. Are those his weapons, do you think?

Mercury He used to want to be thought of as a doctor, and he falsely claimed to be the son of Aesculapius. Now, draped as he is with chamber pots, he has come to help these.

Titus But who are the ones I see running up from all sides in shining white columns? You could call them magpies in reverse.[74]

Mercury They are the ulcers of the earth, and the auxiliaries of these gods. But they will all receive a rather poor welcome, if they don't watch out.

Titus A new garb! While they're carrying imperial crowns on their heads, they're wearing beggars' pouches.

Mercury With those they have long imposed on gods and men. But before long their mysteries will be revealed, and those who are now fatted by the foolishness of the people will be reduced to starvation. You see they are all wearing masks, but the Silenus within[75] will be revealed, and the world will recover its senses.

Titus May the gods bring it about! Why does Jupiter not use his thunderbolt against them, or Saturn his sickle, or Neptune his trident, or Pallas her spear, or Apollo his bow, or even Cloacina[76] not throw something at them?

Mercury The truth is that these fellows terrify the very gods with their sycophancies. However, you haven't yet seen the end of this drama. Apollo will not desert his sisters or let them be mocked with impunity, if I know him.

And, in fact, unless my eyes deceive me, I see him coming now. By Jove, how he is hurrying, although he is weighted down with a heavy quiver and arrows! I foresee a bloody triumph over them.

Pomponius How I would like that!

Mercury I see Pallas in her armor.

Pomponius Is she that tall warrior-maiden, conspicuous with a crested helmet?

Mercury The very one.

Pomponius But what is that column of armed maidens that I see following her? Are they Amazons?

Mercury No, they are Calliope's sisters.

Titus What have the Muses to do with weapons?

Mercury The situation demands it. It's weapons, not lyres, against these monstrosities, more brutish[77] than any beasts; of all creatures, they alone are driven wild by harmonious song. But look, now Apollo is drawing, he is taking aim at someone.

Pomponius Ate, it would seem; and in fact it is, for she is falling and biting the earth with her mouth. Woe, woe! How the others are fleeing in panic, and keep looking back! But I wonder that in flight the son of Gryllus is not lame,[78] but rather winged.

Mercury Indeed he was never lame where doing harm was concerned. He is running, but he won't get away; already I see an arrow sticking in him.

Titus The girls are taking Phthonides prisoner. What will they do with him?

Mercury What else but what Apollo did to Marsyas?[79] But do you see Momides[80] scrambling frantically to escape and falling into the deep muck, so that instead of being half black and half white, he is now all black?

Titus I do see him, by Jove, a jolly sight; and I wish it was a privy he had fallen into.

Pomponius In fact, into the abyss.

Mercury Phenacus[81] is showing his true nature; again he has deserted and is supplicating the Muses. But they won't trust him, although the Muses are simple-hearted, no less than the Graces.

Pomponius How the one in the helmet[82] is trembling! In fact his helmet has now fallen off. But Pallas herself has thrown a noose on him too, considering him unworthy of her spear, I suppose.

Titus Who would not burst with laughter, seeing those pigs running off in all directions; grunting, to be sure, but not as they were a while ago?

Mercury They're doing as pigs generally do. But do you see Calliope alive and even smiling, and hurrying to her brother's embrace?

Pomponius I see her.

Titus I never saw a funeral with a happier ending.

Baramia Nor I.

Mercury But now I will dissolve the cloud, as it is safe for you to address them openly.

Pomponius So we shall.

Mercury Farewell then; and you will see to it that these matters are celebrated in all languages.

Titus It will be taken care of.

Mercury And I hurry off to continue on my mission.

KONRAD OF NASTÄTTEN IN GERMANY, THE END OF *THE DIALOGUE OF THE TWO-TONGUED AND THE TRILINGUALS*, OR *THE FUNERAL OF CALLIOPE*

Notes

Preface

xi

1 Cf Allen Epp 1206:46, 1225:124, 151–2; Bietenholz *History* and Biography 26–7, 32–3, 73–7.
2 Cf Epp 603, 745.
3 Cf Epp 1041, 1110, 1193–4.
4 Cf Ep 1262.
5 Cf cwe 6 preface and Ep 864.
6 Cf Ep 1000.
7 Cf Ep 1208 introduction.
8 See Epp 1174 n6, 1334, and perhaps also Ep 1304; cf the following note.
9 Cf Epp 1043 introduction, 1062, 1112, 1171, 1179, 1181, 1248, 1255, 1333, 1381, 1400, 1414.

xii

10 Cf Epp 851, 943–4, 950, 1021, 1039, 1137, 1154, 1183, 1242–3.
11 Cf cwe 6 preface; Epp 1025 n4, 1073 introduction, 1078 n15, 1155 introduction. Erasmus refers to 'our native Germany' in Epp 1110:72–3 and 1111:96.
12 Cf Epp 1001:58–90, 1009, 1030:54–71.
13 Cf Ep 691 introduction and cwe 5 index.
14 Cf Epp 930:12n, 934, 1046, 1057 introductions.
15 Cf de Vocht ctl i 530, ii 62–3.
16 Cf Epp 950:20–2, 1002 n4, 1003 n3, 1007:127–9, 1125.
17 Cf Ep 904:20n.
18 Cf Epp 936:43–6.
19 Cf Epp 968:21n, 993:90–1. The first efforts to bring about such an examination were no doubt touched off by the appearance of Erasmus' New Testament in 1516; see Ep 505:9–16.
20 Cf Ep 972:10–13.

xiii

21 Allen Ep 1225:107–11
22 Allen Ep 1581:484–90

23 Cf Ep 1053:35–40; cf Ep 946 introduction.
24 Cf Zwingli *Werke* VII Ep 107.
25 Cf Epp 1040, 1042, 1046, 1050, 1057.
26 Cf Epp 934, 993 n5, 998 introduction.
27 Cf Ep 1029 n2.
28 Cf Allen Ep 1225:118; it may be noted that even when Briart was still alive, the *Dialogus bilinguium ac trilinguium* suggested that he was 'pulled about at will' by another man; see above 340.
29 Cf Ep 1022.
30 Cf Epp 1030 n7, 1040.
31 Cf Ep 1059.
32 Cf Ep 1037.
33 Cf Ep 1080 introduction.

xiv
34 Cf Ep 1100 introduction.
35 Cf Ep 1083 introduction.
36 Cf Ep 1061:92–6.
37 Rogers Ep 75:222–46
38 Cf Epp 1045, 1087, 1093, 1096.
39 Ep 1233, cf Epp 999:20–35, 2750.
40 Cf Epp 1211.
41 Cf Ep 1009 introduction.

Notes to Letters

993
1 hellish language] Cf Ep 1053 n62.
2 'Scotish'] A pun on the Englishman Edward Lee (cf Ep 998 introduction), whose systematic and pedestrian criticisms qualify him for a comparison with the followers of John Duns Scotus (d 1308) and other representatives of the despised scholastic theology; cf Epp 843:86–9, 1061 n30.
3 youngster] Erasmus continued to see in Lee an over-ambitious youth, even though his age was now about thirty-seven; but cf also Allen Ep 1139:60.
4 Greek proverb] Aristotle *Rhetoric* 1373a3
5 Latomus' dialogue] Jacobus Latomus (Jacques Masson), a theologian in the University of Louvain, was the author of a recent attack upon humanistic education. Erasmus believed that he was personally implicated and answered with a discreet apology; cf Ep 934.
6 statement] See LB IX 106A. Lee was not named, but the attack was more transparent than Erasmus was prepared to admit; cf Ep 936:34n.
7 plenty of people] Cf Ep 998 n12.
8 Luther's ideas] For Erasmus' limited support of Luther and for his efforts to make the limits understood see Epp 938–9, 980. Ep 1022 reflects the measure of his success.
9 one man] The context here suggests that Jan Briart of Ath, the chief administrator of the University of Louvain, was intended (cf Ep 1029 n2), although

Erasmus uttered similar threats against Edward Lee; cf above lines 50–1; Ep
998 introduction.

10 'famed ... o'er'] Ovid *Amores* 1.3.25
11 plague] As far as the physical disease is concerned there are many indications
   of its ravages at this time and in the following months (see also Luther w
   Briefwechsel I Epp 205–6; AK II Ep 714; BRE Ep 128). In the beginning of August
   Bonifacius Amerbach referred to a letter (now lost) from Erasmus, according to which astrologers had predicted that the plague would last for four
   years and would afflict the whole globe; see AK II Ep 670.
12 Truth] Cf *Adagia* II iv 17.
13 Balaam] Following the emended text in Erasmus' *Opera* III (Basel 1538); cf Num
   22:21–35, Pet 2:15–16, Epp 909:65–7, 1510. The *Farrago* of 1519 had Baal,
   but despite 1 Kings 18:26–9 Erasmus would hardly have likened himself to
   Baal.
14 old saw] One of Publius Syrius' maxims (*Sententiae* F 13 and B 10), quoted in
   Adagia I v 67
15 Black Friars] For Erasmus' misgivings about many members of the Dominican
   order, individually and collectively, cf the indexes of CWE 5–8.
16 official resolution] See preface and Ep 972:10–13.

994
1 Nesen] This young German had spent some time in Paris and from there had
   visited Louvain in March 1519, carrying Ep 925. Soon after taking charge of
   the present letter he must have followed up his earlier trip by actually moving
   to Louvain, and arrived some time before Erasmus wrote Ep 1002. Nesen
   was accompanied by Ludovicus Carinus, only slightly younger than himself,
   and by Crato and Nikolaus Stalburg, sons of a Frankfurt patrician, whom
   he had tutored at Paris. In Paris this group had probably been joined by
   another young man, Haio Herman of Friesland, who had made the move to
   Louvain somewhat ahead of the others (cf Ep 1002 n11). Herman, Nesen, and
   no doubt the Stalburg brothers too found lodgings in the College of the
   Lily, where Erasmus himself lived (cf Ep 1026:11–13; de Vocht CTL I 390–4).
   Nesen, who was evidently close to Erasmus, lost no time in causing him
   serious embarrassment; see 330–33 below.
2 two of them] Cf Ep 925:3n.
3 the most recent] Ep 925. In Ep 1002:25–6 Erasmus does not seem to recall that
   it too had been delivered by Nesen, the carrier of the present Ep 994.
4 important proposition] Erasmus still expected Poncher's letter in October (cf
   Ep 1016:30–32) and no doubt assumed that it would deal with the royal
   invitation to settle in Paris, which had first been relayed to Erasmus by Poncher, among others. Poncher had met Erasmus early in 1517 at Brussels and
   made him a generous offer of his own (Epp 522, 531, 1434). The royal invitation had recently been renewed (cf Ep 926:37n) and in view of his current
   troubles at Louvain (cf Epp 998, 1022 introductions), leaving seems to have
   been a serious option for Erasmus (cf Ep 1012) and a further, and specific,
   reaffirmation of the French offer was accordingly desirable; cf Epp 1002:34–7,
   1003, 1004:165–7, 1045:99–127 and see further Ep 1073 introduction.
5 written to Dorp] See Ep 1000A introduction.

6 New Testament] The second edition, August 1518–March 1519; cf Ep 864
introduction.

7 defenses] No doubt the preliminary pieces placed at the head of the New
Testament text volume, the *Paraclesis*, an *Apologia* repeated from the 1516
edition, and the greatly amplified *Ratio verae theologiae*; cf Epp 745 introduction, 809:111–14.

8 Deloynes ... Ruzé] The first an old friend of Erasmus, the second one of recent
date; both were intimate with Guillaume Budé and like Bérault himself
associated with the region of Orléans.

995

1 wandering life] Prior to his mission to England Campeggi had accompanied
the emperor Maximilian I on some of his travels, representing Pope Julius II
and subsequently Pope Leo X. He had also been envoy to the ducal court of
Milan.

2 image] A figure of speech which Erasmus too used frequently (see Epp 981:22–
8, 1033:197–9, 1101:10–11; cf Ep 953:9–13). For the books referred to see
Epp 396, 597:37n, 710, 916, 956.

3 Psalms] Ps 8:6 (Vulgate)

4 My own studies] They did not lead to any publications.

5 by the whole gamut] A proverbial expression, cf *Adagia* I ii 63.

6 first and second] Presumably Campeggi had received the two volumes of the
revised edition of the New Testament (cf Ep 864 introduction). One volume, apparently still unbound as it had only just arrived from the press,
accompanied Ep 961. This was probably the text volume which Froben had
published in March 1519. The same letter announced that the other volume
would follow shortly. As the volume containing the annotations had been
in print for some time when Erasmus wrote, Campeggi's copy was then perhaps at the binders. In spite of the singular used in line 85 below it appears
from this passage and from Ep 996:33 that both volumes had been sent by the
same messenger.

7 dialogue] The *Julius exclusus*; cf Epp 502 introduction, 961:40–55; cf also CWE
27 156–67.

8 much longer] See Ep 1025 n3.

9 diamond ring] It was listed among Erasmus' possessions in 1534 and also in
the inventory made after his death. In his last will of 12 February 1536
Erasmus left it to Justina Froben, whose husband, Nicolaus Episcopius, was
one of Erasmus' executors; see Allen XI 364; E. Major *Erasmus von Rotterdam*
(Basel [1936]) 38, 54.

10 the man] See Ep 996 n5.

996

1 temple of Apollo] On the Palatine hill at Rome. The temple and the famous
library attached to it were founded by Augustus; see Suetonius *Augustus*
29; Ovid *Tristia* 3.1.60–4.

2 solemn pronouncement] Ep 864

3 cedar-oil] Cf *Adagia* IV i 54.

4 Pace] Erasmus had met Pace in May 1519; see Ep 968 introduction.

5 devotee of Bacchus] Most likely the one-eyed Pieter Meghen, who had
   travelled to England for Erasmus on several previous occasions and was
   evidently fond of drink (cf Epp 412:47n, 653 introduction). In the spring of
   1519 he had been with Erasmus (cf Ep 1061:624, 696; *Opuscula* 255) who attempted in vain to place him in the service of Henry VIII; cf Ep 937:2n.
6 your own words] Ep 995 salutation
7 Attalus] King Attalus III of Pergamum (c 170–133 BC), famous for his riches
   and for a will bequeathing his kingdom to the Roman people
8 Dutch dumpling] Cf *Adagia* IV vi 35 and III i 1 (ASD II-5 34); III ii 48.
9 Gospel] Eph 1:18
10 some work] The promise was soon honoured; see Ep 1062.

997
1 Gospel precept] Cf Matt 25:14–30.
2 Greek proverbs] Cf *Adagia* I x 13.

998
1 away] In Basel in the summer of 1518; cf Ep 843 introduction.
2 against the old edition] Cf the preface to Erasmus' *Responsio ad annotationes Lei*,
   LB IX 123–4.
3 intercepted] See Epp 898A, 899 introduction. Moreover in the *Apologia invectivis Lei* (*Opuscula* 250) Erasmus himself reported how he had obtained a
   few notes by bribing a secretary with access to Briart's copy.
4 wide circulation] Cf Epp 993:27–32, 1061:150–8, 902–8.
5 Hebrew and Greek] Lee dealt with this frequently repeated charge in Ep
   1061:202–7, 861–75.
6 Reuchlin ... Capito] Both had published a Hebrew grammar (cf Epp 324:14n,
   600:26n). Erasmus had himself once rated Capito above Reuchlin (cf Ep
   413:15–16). In his reply to this passage (Ep 1061:224–38; cf *Opuscula* 278–9,
   286–7) Lee paid tribute to the two Hebrew scholars, but did not succeed in
   appeasing Capito; see Ep 1074 introduction.
7 Aristarchus] Aristarchus of Samothrace (d 145 BC) was considered the father of
   grammar and critical scholarship; thus his name was used to connote the
   mastery of that discipline; cf Ep 1061:256–64.
8 Latomus] Cf Ep 993:37–47.
9 Young] Cf Ep 993 n3.
10 one hair's breadth] Cf Ep 1007 n10.
11 beggars and bullies] The Dominicans; cf Ep 993 n15.
12 pamphlets] Such as the *Epistolae obscurorum virorum* and other attacks upon
   the opponents of Reuchlin; also the vitriolic pamphlets of Hutten (cf Epp
   622, 967:115–72). A collective attack upon Lee was in due course organized by
   some German friends, not without Erasmus' participation; see Epp 1074,
   1083 introductions.
13 restrained] See for instance Epp 636:29–31, 904:20n, 967:107–10, 180–5.
14 more violent measures] Perhaps a reference to the intentions of Wilhelm
   Nesen, of which Erasmus cannot have been entirely unaware; see 330–2 above.
   However, Allen noted a passage in Lee's *Annotationes* (cf 1037 introduction) in
   which Lee claims that he asked Erasmus about the meaning of these words

and received the reply 'a thrashing'; see Epp 1053:156–7, 1055, and Lee's reaction in Ep 1061:559–85.

999

1 you rightly call] Apparently in a letter now lost (cf lines 20–21) and presumably written before Hutten's Ep 986, which Erasmus answers at the end of this letter. It is also conceivable, however, that the alleged request is no more than a literary fiction on the part of Erasmus; for an analogous case see Ep 1211.

2 works both ways] Four years later Erasmus publicly withdrew this statement of Hutten's compatibility with More; see Allen I 27:29–32.

3 Greek saying] Cf *Adagia* I ii 79.

4 it is not everyone] Cf *Adagia* I iv 1.

5 Fulvius or Rutuba] Two Roman gladiators (mentioned in Horace *Satires* 2.7.96–7) who were evidently not suited to match the accomplishments of the celebrated painter Apelles. Erasmus uses the same comparison elsewhere; see for instance *Adagia* IV v 1.

6 in stature] Some details of the following description of More were borrowed verbatim by Beatus Rhenanus when he wished to portray Erasmus (cf Allen I 70:529–39, 545–6). More recently H.W. Garrod used this description for his portrait of P.S. Allen (cf Allen VIII xx). One is reminded of Erasmus' fondness of a Homeric verse pointing out that the god will always lead like to like; see *Odyssey* 17.218 and *Adagia* I ii 22.

7 beard] More never grew a beard, but the version of Holbein's portrait of him now in the Frick collection in New York makes it evident that he did not shave every day; see Stanley Morison *The Likeness of Thomas More* (London 1963).

8 Ovid] *Ars amatoria* 1.509–24

9 by what remains] Cf *Adagia* IV ii 3.

10 scarcely] So in the *Farrago*. In the *Epistolae ad diversos* 'scarcely' was replaced by 'not much.' This change supports the modern view that More was probably born on 6 or 7 February 1477 or 1478. He first met Erasmus in the summer of 1499; see G. Marc'hadour *L'univers de Thomas More* (Paris 1963) 34–41, 103.

11 his father] John More (c 1451–1530) was knighted and at the height of his legal career in London (c 1520) was promoted to the King's Bench; see Reynolds *More* 7–9.

12 same cup] For Erasmus' dislike of this habit cf *Adagia* I vi 53 and the colloquy about the syphilitic bridegroom, Ἄγαμος γάμος, ASD I-3 599.

13 fond of music] Cf below lines 197–201 and Ep 1087 n11; N.C. Carpenter 'A Song for All Seasons: Sir Thomas More and Music' *Comparative Literature* 33 (1981) 113–36.

14 by great efforts] Cf Epp 829:6–8, 832:38–42, and below lines 237–8, 303–5.

15 plethora] Cf *Adagia* III vi 37; Hesiod *Works and Days* 713.

16 comedies] More's additions to a comedy entitled 'Solomon' are mentioned in his earliest preserved letter (Rogers Ep 2). For his impromptu acting when he was a page in the household of Cardinal John Morton see the beginning of William Roper's *Life* (cf below n25); for later interest in drama among

More's family circle see A.W. Reed *Early Tudor Drama* (London 1926; repr 1969).

17 epigrams] Many were published with the assistance of Erasmus; cf Epp 550 introduction, 635, 1093 n16.

18 Lucian] In 1506–7 More and Erasmus translated a collection of Lucian's dialogues and declamations, including the *Tyrannicida* (cf below lines 277–9), to which each composed a reply (cf Ep 187 introduction, ASD I-1 360–627, More y III-1). These translations were primarily intended as an exercise, but the choice of texts also confirms an anti-Stoic tendency, which is reflected in the following lines and likewise in Erasmus' *Moria*.

19 make the camel dance] Cf *Adagia* II vii 66.

20 persuaded me] A very generous tribute; cf Epp 222, 337:134–46.

21 Democritus] The 'laughing' and skeptical philosopher of the fifth century BC, inventor of the atomic theory which was later taken up by Epicurus, who believed that pleasure was the goal of human action; cf Ep 222:16–20.

22 Pythagorean philosopher] See Diogenes Laertius 8.1.6.

23 monkey ... and the like] Cf the colloquy *Amicitia*, ASD I-3 706–7.

24 nobility] Another case in point was in Erasmus' view the brother of his opponent Edward Lee; see Allen Ep 2780:29–33.

25 larger income] According to Harpsfield, More earned about four hundred pounds sterling annually as an under-sheriff. This sum should be compared to his relative poverty after he resigned the chancellorship and to the hundred pounds a year Erasmus hoped to obtain if he were to settle in England; see Ep 694:11n; William Roper and Nicholas Harpsfield *Lives of Saint Thomas More* Everyman's Library (London 1963) 27, 64.

26 public lectures] Given in the church of St Lawrence in the old Jury, of which William Grocyn was the rector

27 unmarried girl] Jane, daughter of John Colt of Netherhall, Essex (cf Ep 221:35–6). She is probably the young woman recalled by Erasmus in the colloquy Uxor μεμψίγαμος and in *Moria*; see ASD I-3 301–13, IV-3 132–3.

28 three daughters] The number was given as four in the *Farrago*, but changed to three in the *Epistolae ad diversos*, no doubt because one daughter, Margaret Giggs, was adopted. At the same time the three names were added, the second being mistaken. More's three daughters were Margaret (1505–44) who married William Roper on 2 July 1521 (cf Ep 1233), Elizabeth (b 1506?) who married William Daunce on 29 September 1525, and Cecily (b 1507? d before 1540) who was married, the same day as her sister Elizabeth, to Giles Heron. More's youngest child was his son John (1508/9–47); see Reynolds *More* 4–6, 151, 342; Rogers Ep 43.

29 widow] Alice (1471–after 1543), widow of John Middleton, who died in October 1509. More married her in the summer of 1511; cf Ep 232:4n. She had a daughter, Alice Middleton, whose name may have caused Erasmus' confusion in line 188 above.

30 neither beautiful ... first youth] Cf for example Martial 1.64.4.

31 household] Some of those mentioned below, and later on More's sons-in-law, were at times part of the household; cf Holbein's sketches for his lost family portrait.

32 stepmother] After the death of Agnes Graunger, the mother of his children,

Sir John married three more times. Alice Clerke, who survived him, became his last wife apparently between the summer of 1519 and that of 1521, as the following sentence referring to her was added only in the *Epistolae ad diversos*.

33 sisters] Known to us are Jane (1475–1542), wife of Richard Staverton; Agatha (b 1478/9) and Elizabeth (1482–1538), wife of John Rastell of Coventry; see Reynolds More 342 and passim; J.B. Trapp and H. Schulte Herbrüggen '*The King's Good Servant' Sir Thomas More* (London 1977) 8–9 and passim.

34 judge] More was under-sheriff, that is judge in the court of the sheriffs, from 1510 to 1518; cf above n25.

35 three drachmas] The text printed in the *Farrago* read 'six' drachmas; this was subsequently corrected to 'three' in the *Opus epistolarum*. This change and other revisions appearing in the reprints may be the result of more accurate information received from England. The fees in question were part of the judge's remuneration; Erasmus expresses them in terms of an ancient silver coin.

36 content] Cf Ep 388:137–45.

37 diplomatic mission] See Epp 388:102n, 623:23n.

38 dragged] Cf above n14.

39 household] See below lines 303–6.

40 declamations] To the examples mentioned by Erasmus it may be added that Juan Luis Vives recalled in the preface of his own *Declamatio pro noverca* (1521) how More studied with his children the first declamation of Quintilian and, in the process, asked Vives repeatedly to compose a rejoinder to Quintilian's address to the judges; see Vives *Opera* II 484–5.

41 even to wives] This is one form of communal life in Plato's *Republic* (5.449–61) that was in the end banished from *Utopia*.

42 *Tyrannicida*] See above n18.

43 when at leisure] During a diplomatic mission to the Netherlands in 1515. For the sequence of composition see J.H. Hexter in More Y IV xv–xxxiii.

44 Colet] Dean of St Paul's in London; for his death see Ep 1023 n5.

45 prayers] Cf Ep 786:58–61.

46 to his household] For the following cf Ep 834 introduction.

47 rich men] Here as in Epp 1005:53, 1028:4–5 the Latin text alludes to the riches of Midas, *Adagia* I vi 24.

48 your *Aula*] A dialogue critical of court life; see Ep 863:36.

49 a prince] Albert of Brandenburg, cardinal and archbishop of Mainz; cf below lines 320–1, 332–3 and Ep 1009.

50 Stromer and Kopp] Heinrich Stromer and Gregor Kopp were physicians and humanists attached to the court of Mainz.

51 distinguished men] Cf Ep 855:36–51 where much the same list is given, with two exceptions. William Latimer, an Oxford scholar, is not normally associated with the royal court, although he was the tutor of Reginald Pole and a close friend of More and Pace. John Clerk (d 1541) is not otherwise mentioned in Erasmus' correspondence. He was chaplain to Thomas Wolsey and in 1519 was appointed judge in the star chamber and dean of St George's, Windsor. In 1523 he was created bishop of Bath and Wells; see Emden BRUC.

52 last letter] Ep 986

53 from a letter] Ep 988, which had apparently reached Erasmus before the original of Hutten's Ep 986, brought by Richard Pace
54 cup] A gift from Albert of Brandenburg, announced in Ep 986:40–8. By the middle of August it had still not arrived; cf Ep 1009:85–6.
55 pen and sword] Cf Ep 951:31–3.
56 Cajetanus] Perhaps Erasmus recalled merely that Cajetanus, like Hutten, had attended the Diet of Augsburg in July 1518 where both had spoken out in the matter of the papal crusade and where Cajetanus had conferred upon Albert of Brandenburg the dignity of cardinal (cf Ep 891:26n, 27n). Hutten and Cajetanus, however, were bitterly opposed to one another, especially with regard to Luther (cf Ep 923:23n; for a recent attack on Cajetanus see Hutten *Opera* I Ep 117 end). Moreover no love was lost between Cajetanus and Albert, and Cajetanus' diplomatic agitation against the election of Charles v had rendered him notorious in the eyes of many Germans (cf Hutten *Opera* IV 157–9; Luther w *Briefwechsel* I Ep 167). Therefore Hutten and other German contemporaries presumably thought that Erasmus' statement here was ironical, and it may well have been intended that way. For another critical reference to Cajetanus written for quick publication, see Ep 1033:161.
57 Cinglius] Franz von Sickingen's name is spelt by Erasmus in the same way in Ep 1166; for other strange forms of it cf LP II and III.
58 here] In Louvain
59 a past master] Evidently Edward Lee, thought by Erasmus to be craving for fame. For the following threat cf Epp 998 introduction and lines 71–84, 1055.

1000
1 list of his productions] Jerome *De viris illustribus* 67 (PL 23:714)
2 Tertullian] Tertullian was probably born in Carthage c 160 and died after 230; his works were published by the Froben press in 1521; cf the introduction.
3 Jerome] Ep 33 (CSEL 54:255–9 and PL 22:447; the latter is much closer to the faulty text Erasmus was reading)
4 Varro] Marcus Terentius Varro (d 27 BC), Roman antiquarian
5 Lactantius] *Divinae institutiones* 5.1.24 (CSEL 19:402)
6 not worth reading] Cf Ep 902A:2–3.
7 *Symbolum fidei*] This commentary offering the earliest Latin version of the apostolic creed was retained by Erasmus in his edition of Cyprian, but it is actually by Rufinus; see CC 20:127–82.
8 *De singularitate clericorum*] A work indebted to Cyprian's ideas, but probably by a follower; see CSEL 3-3:173–220.
9 Jerome] *De viris illustribus* 68 (PL 23:714). The life of Cyprian by Pontius (CSEL 3-3:xc–cx) is a text whose value as a primary source is now subject to controversy, but it is a great deal more authentic and sophisticated than the short text with that title available to Erasmus and printed by him among the preliminary pieces of his edition (1520; ff b⁴–b⁶). A reader of this passage later wrote to Erasmus to offer a better text of Pontius' life; see Allen Ep 1260:23–5.
10 conclusion] On f b⁶ verso of the 1520 edition; Erasmus' critical note is on f b⁵ verso.
11 eleven] The exchange is now considered to include nine letters by Cyprian

and two by Pope Cornelius (251–3), some of them printed by Erasmus for the first time.

12 pointed out] In a preliminary critical note (1520; f a⁵ recto). Although printing them separately, Erasmus recognized that two letters addressed to Magnus belonged together. They are united as Ep 69 in CSEL 3-2:749–66.

13 Lactantius] Apparently Erasmus here considered his principal work, the *Divinae institutiones*, as belonging primarily to the field of moral philosophy.

14 Jerome says] Ep 58:10 (CSEL 54:539)

15 Jerome brings] Ep 112:15 (CSEL 55:385)

16 Jerome writes] Ep 58:10 (CSEL 54:539)

17 Lactantius] *Divinae institutiones* 5.1.25 (CSEL 19:402)

18 *De doctrina christiana*] 4.21 (CC 32:151–7).

19 Quintilian] Eg 10.1.105, 12.1.22, 12.10.52

20 Jerome] Cf Epp 396 introduction, 844:132–276; C. Béné *Erasme et Saint Augustin* (Geneva 1969) 54–7.

21 heretic] Probably Bishop Stephen is intended; see Cyprian's Ep 75:25 (CSEL 3-2:826–7).

22 bedridden] Cyprian Ep 69:12–13 (CSEL 3-2:760–3)

23 one letter] The short treatise *Ad Donatium* (CSEL 3-1:3–16) was printed among the letters in Erasmus' edition (1520; 44–50). It was quoted and praised by Augustine in *De doctrina christiana* 4.14.31 (CC 32:138).

24 *Decretum*] *Corpus iuris canonici* Gratian, d 15 c 3 paragraph 2; ed E.L. Richter and E. Friedberg (Leipzig 1879–81) I 36

25 his view] In three councils held in 255–6 the African bishops supported Cyprian in requesting that those baptized by heretical Novatian priests must be rebaptized on admission to the church. This stand caused a serious dispute with the Roman pope, Stephen I (254–7).

26 acts of the Synod] The *Sententiae episcoporum* (1520; 339–48; CSEL 3-1:435–61)

27 Hilary] Erasmus here assumed that the Hilary mentioned in Jerome's *Dialogus contra Luciferianos* 21, 26 (PL 23:184, 189) was St Hilary, bishop of Poitiers (c 315–67/8). When editing St Hilary in 1523 he criticized Jerome for his sharp attack but admitted that he could not decide whether the Hilary concerned was St Hilary (cf Allen Ep 1334:563–6). When he re-edited Cyprian in 1525 he added here that Hilary was a deacon of the Roman church. By the time of the 1530 edition of Cyprian he had made up his mind that he was not St Hilary and changed the entire passage to line 151. Hilary was no longer mentioned, Cyprian's view was characterized as an understandable error and a precise reference was given for the orthodox arguments (line 143) stated by Augustine in *De baptismo contra Donatistas* 3, 6, and 7 (CSEL 51).

28 preferred to the accepted view] See above n27.

29 Lactantius] *Divinae institutiones* 5.1.27 (CSEL 19:403). Modern editors aggravate the charge by reading *Coprian* 'the dung-boy' rather than *Caprian* 'the goat-boy.'

30 Jerome elsewhere] In the 1530 edition of Cyprian the passage is identified. The reference is again to Ep 58:10 (CSEL 54:539).

31 we read] Jerome *De viris illustribus* 53 (PL 23:698)

32 prophet's curse] Isa 5:20

33 first place] See above lines 121–3.

34 preferred] Pucci was close to Pope Leo x (cf Pastor VIII 113) and actually lived
   in the Vatican palace; cf Ep 865:24–9.
35 Cyprian] The bishop of Carthage challenged Rome, as did the Carthaginian
   Hannibal.
36 Pope Cornelius] Cornelius (cf above n11) died 'gloriously' while being
   banished from Rome, whether as a martyr is uncertain. His feast day, which
   he shares with Cyprian, is 16 September.
37 Antonio Pucci] See Ep 860.

1001

1 Alamirus] He was a music scribe at the Netherlandish court and also a secret
   agent.
2 Aachen] It is now missing. Could it have been a prompt reply to Ep 993?
3 Mechelen] Evidently on the way to his second visit to Antwerp (cf Ep 999
   introduction). The specific date of this letter suggests that the approximate
   dates given for the two meetings with Alamirus are somewhat inaccurate.
4 Utrecht] Philip of Burgundy, bishop of the diocese in which Erasmus was a
   priest, was in fact at Mechelen on 7 August; see Allen's note.
5 Robbyns] See Ep 1046 introduction.
6 responsibility] Cf Virgil Aeneid 12.59.
7 College of the Three Tongues] The new college, inspired by Erasmus and
   founded in accordance with the will of Jérôme de Busleyden (cf Epp 691,
   934) continued its struggle for recognition by the university of Louvain; cf the
   preface.
8 The first] Ep 711, requesting a reply to Ep 501. Erasmus had received Ep 501
   (he had it copied into the Deventer Letter-book), but either could not remember its contents exactly or failed to realize that it was the letter Spalatinus
   meant. Imagining thus a letter written on behalf of the elector and the
   university reconfirmed his impression that Wittenberg was the seat of an
   enthusiastic literary society (cf below line 103 and Ep 1119) perhaps like
   those at Strasbourg and Erfurt; cf Epp 305, 870 introduction.
9 answered] Probably a reply to the elector's Ep 963 which was perhaps accompanied by a letter from Spalatinus, now missing, as are these answers by
   Erasmus
10 cinders] Cf Adagia I ix 30.
11 I opened] The three remaining letters mentioned by Erasmus are all missing.
   For Willibald Pirckheimer see Ep 1085; for the itinerant humanist and poet
   Riccardo Sbruglio, for a time attached to the court of Maximilian I, see Ep 1159.
12 Behaim] Georg Behaim of Nürnberg (c 1461–1520) is not otherwise mentioned
   as a correspondent of Erasmus. A graduate of Leipzig, he was given a
   canonry at Mainz and had been since 1513 provost of St Lorenz at Nürnberg.
   He was a brother of the colourful Lorenz Behaim (c 1457–1527), master of the
   papal artillery and later canon at Bamberg, who was a friend of Pirckheimer;
   see NDB.
13 Jonas] Justus Jonas and Kaspar Schalbe had visited Erasmus in May (cf Ep
   963:6n) and carried back Ep 978 for Spalatinus.
14 medal] A present from Frederick the Wise; see Epp 872:27n, 978:11–14, and cf
   Ep 1119:5–6.

15 Liège] Bishop Erard de la Marck had gone to Germany by the end of May as member of a high-powered delegation assigned the task of promoting the election of Charles v (cf below n19). Erasmus had an opportunity of meeting him at the court of Brussels on c 21 May (cf Ep 968 introduction). Immediately after the election the Netherlandish ambassadors met with several electors at the castle of Albert of Mainz at Höchst near Frankfurt (now part of the city). It is there that the English ambassador, Richard Pace (cf Ep 999 introduction; below line 58), was informed of the outcome of the election. Pace was invited to join the prince-bishop of Liège for the dangerous journey back to the Netherlands (cf below lines 73–6). They travelled together, protected by Erard's hundred horse; see Harsin *Erard de la Marck* 353–4; LP III 338, 363, 392.

16 physician] Perhaps Erard's; cf Ep 1038 n2.

17 Pace] See Ep 999 introduction; above n15.

18 refusal] See Ep 1030 n16.

19 Charles] He was elected emperor on 28 June 1519 at Frankfurt; cf the preface.

20 plague] Cf Ep 993 n11.

21 large force] After the defeat of Ulrich of Württemberg (cf Ep 986) some of the troops of the victorious Swabian League were recruited for Hapsburg and stationed at Höchst in the proximity of Frankfurt, where the atmosphere was rife with rumours. Strong forces of unknown identity were reported in the regions of Koblenz, Cologne, and Maastricht. Perhaps it was intended to waylay the French ambassadors. This news caused alarm among the returning Netherlandish ambassadors and Erard gathered a strong guard (cf above n15), although his fears proved in the end unfounded; see Kalkoff *Kaiserwahl* 277–8; Harsin *Erard de la Marck* 354–5; LP 363, 392.

22 Asperen] See Ep 643:32n.

23 scot-free] See Epp 825:5–9, 829:10–21.

24 traditional democracy] On the functioning of the States-General of the Netherlands see H.G. Koenigsberger *Estates and Revolution* (Ithaca 1971) 125–43. They were summoned with reasonable frequency as there remained some concern that they might renew their former claims for the right of free assembly without ducal summons. On 9 April 1519 Charles v wrote to his aunt Margaret of Austria: 'We wish and desire you expressly not to consent to the meeting of the said general assembly, so that no league or confederation may be formed to the detriment of our pre-eminence, nor cause resistance to our officers' (quoted by Koenigsberger 135). For the Netherlands at least Erasmus' pessimism was not fully justified at this time. His support of civil freedom is more fully stated in the *Institutio principis christiani*; see ASD IV-1 165–6; cf also Epp 999:88–90, 1039:39–41.

25 friendly letter] Ep 988; for his gift see Ep 999:334.

26 Cyprian] See Ep 1000.

27 prince] Frederick the Wise, elector of Saxony

28 society] See above n8.

29 'Take pains ... the day.'] Catullus 62.16

1002

1 whitewash] Cf *Adagia* III vi 23.

2 frequently] No previous letters by Erasmus are known to exist.

3 about dawn] Cf Ep 296:19–20 where Erasmus states that once awakened he could never go to sleep again for several hours.
4 do not aim] Erasmus replies to Ep 925:26–32. In view of Bérault's enthusiasm and the agitation of their common friend Wilhelm Nesen at Louvain (see Ep 1000A introduction and cf below lines 38–46), Erasmus thought it advisable to redefine his position with regard to Thomas Aquinas and other scholastic theologians as he had recently exposed it more fully in his *Apologia* against Latomus (LB IX 80–1); cf Ep 934, and for similar statements Ep 1125 introduction.
5 your letter] Obviously Ep 925, although its date is 16 March
6 brought by Nesen] Ep 994
7 letter to Grolier] Ep 831 of 24 April 1518, published in the *Auctarium*
8 proverbial] Cf *Adagia* I ix 15.
9 Grolier's reply] It is missing now, but there may be a trace of its existence in the manuscript letter-book of the Milanese printer Alessandro Minuziano in the Biblioteca Nazionale Braidense, Milan, MS AD XI 31 ff 148 verso–149 recto. On 7(?) May 1519 Minuziano wrote to Grolier that he had looked for and found the copy of a letter by Grolier to Erasmus written about two years earlier from Paris when Grolier had returned to France. The letter was copied once more and enclosed with Minuziano's to Grolier. Despite the discrepancy in dates, this is no doubt the same answer to Erasmus as is mentioned in a letter of Francesco Giulio Calvo (BRE Ep 120) which is probably to be dated from the summer of 1518. Calvo wrote that Grolier had been called back to Paris and suggested that his letter to Erasmus should be printed by Froben.
10 to Dorp] Cf Ep 1000A.
11 Herman] Haio Herman of Friesland, who had recently lodged at the College of the Lily (cf Ep 994 n1), had apparently brought Ep 989 (see below line 47–8 and cf Ep 1003:3–8) and also the letter to Dorp here mentioned, which had been sent before July (cf Ep 994:13). Erasmus now recommended Herman 'in reverse' (line 53) to his friends in Paris, as he was off for another visit to the French capital. Juan Luis Vives too recommended him to Guillaume Budé (cf Budé *Opera Omnia* I 289). From Paris Herman returned again to Louvain after the middle of August (cf Ep 1011 introduction). Since Budé knew of his arrival at Paris and expected that he would take Ep 1011 back with him to Louvain (cf Ep 1015 postscript) it seems logical to assume that he was the young man who delivered Ep 1004 (cf Ep 1011:10) and probably also Epp 1002–3; but cf Ep 1024 n6 for another possible carrier.
12 becoming more moderate] Cf Ep 1022.
13 letter] Ep 989; cf above n11.

1003
1 he says] Ep 989:12–15
2 Thersites] In Homer's *Iliad* and elsewhere the inadequate counterpart to the valiant Achilles. Achilles killed him, some say with a box on his ear, for having railed at him.
3 University of Paris] In comparison with the continuing clashes between humanists and scholastic theologians at Louvain (cf Epp 993, 1022), the atmosphere of Paris seemed harmonious to Erasmus (cf Epp 1104, 1111). While careful to voice his due respect for traditional theology (cf Ep 1002:11–13), he was also aware of royal support for the study of pure Latin and of Hebrew

(cf Ep 810:397–400, 489n), more recently also of Greek, as Janus Lascaris had been attracted to Paris; cf Epp 836 introduction.

4 only country] Cf Ep 1004 n30.

5 undermine ... liberty] Cf Ep 1001 n24.

6 important Williams] For Erasmus' obsession with this name cf Epp 534, 957:140n, 1184, Allen 1191:54, and for other examples of his faith in the maxim that *nomen est omen* see Epp 1005:17–20, 1091:44–50.

1004

1 Many people] Cf below n3 and Epp 935:8n, 992 introduction, 994 n1.

2 three times] Erasmus probably means Epp 915, 987, 992, but it is only in the postscript of Ep 992 that Budé wonders whether he will ever receive an answer to his Ep 915 (of which Erasmus here quotes the initial words).

3 Vives] For his recent visit with Budé see the beginning of Epp 987, 1015. In a letter to Budé written from Louvain, 7 March [1520], Vives withdrew his earlier reservations against Budé's Epp 810, 896, 915, then recently published in the *Farrago*, and emphasized Erasmus' satisfaction with these letters; see Melchior Goldast *Philologicarum epistolarum centuria una* (Frankfurt 1610) Ep 52.

4 your letter] Evidently Ep 915

5 saying] Cf *Adagia* II iv 57.

6 I had suggested] Ep 906:139–42

7 you twist] Ep 915:18–22

8 battle-ground] Cf *Adagia* I viii 82.

9 you challenge] Ep 915:31–9

10 jealous ... make trouble] Repeating Budé's own words in Ep 915:59

11 in the shade] Cf Ep 1107 n1.

12 Demonax' remark] Cf Lucian *Demonax* 28; *Adagia* I iii 51.

13 seven years] Cf Ep 915:69–70.

14 pouring out] Cf Epp 915:66–7, 935:33–5.

15 Jerome and the Areopagites] Cf Ep 915:86–92.

16 proverb] Cf *Adagia* I i 35, IV vi 67.

17 to say] Ep 915:96–100; line 99 there should read 'to Tunstall about you.'

18 to France] Cf Ep 994 n4.

19 you say] Ep 915:108–16. It is not clear that Budé said anything about dropping the project of bringing Erasmus to Paris, but in retrospect Erasmus may have given this interpretation to the conversations reported in Ep 568.

20 Davus] A character in Terence's *Andria*; cf *Adagia* I iii 36.

21 in a letter] Possibly a reference to a lost letter; cf Ep 744:13n.

22 shrew] Ep 915:115–29

23 you say] Ep 915:129–33; the reference is to Edward Lee.

24 Homer] *Odyssey* 17.66

25 Deloynes and Ruzé] Ep 915:137–46

26 misrepresenting you] Ep 915:149–56

27 one of your letters] Ep 987:27–9 or Ep 992:31–2

28 More and Richard Pace] Cf Ep 976:36–42.

29 Linacre] The court physician to Henry VIII was engaged in an ambitious project of translating Galen into Latin. Erasmus may now have seen the long-expected *Methodus medendi*, published in June 1519; see Ep 755:32n.

30 court like that] The unfavourable comparison (cf Ep 1028:3–6) of the court of
the Netherlands with the supposedly learned atmosphere at the courts of
England (cf Epp 969–70; 999:303–19, 1032:20–6) and France (cf above lines
148–61 and Ep 1005:35–9) shows that in Erasmus' eyes the invitations ex-
tended to him on behalf of Henry VIII (cf Epp 834 introduction; 1025 n4) and
Francis I (cf Ep 994 n4) merited further negotiations; cf also Epp 1065, 1073
introduction.
31 an answer] Ep 928

1005

1 heavenly bodies] Erasmus was not always so indifferent to astrological predic-
tions; cf Epp 755:32n, 936:60n, 993 n11, 1060:8–10.
2 Gillis] A very close friend and normally Erasmus' host when he visited Antwerp, as he did at that time. Erasmus thought it significant that he and
Zuutpene shared the same Christian name; cf Ep 1003 n6.
3 Pylades] The friend of Orestes, symbol of true friendship
4 courts of princes] Cf Ep 1004 n30.
5 Adolph] Adolph of Burgundy, lord of Veere, had been tutored by Erasmus'
old friend Jacob Batt.
6 son] Probably Philip of Burgundy, the eldest (b 1 October 1512), apparently a
child of weak health when he came to Louvain with his tutor in 1522. He
died about the end of 1526; see Epp 1321, 1787.
7 Borsele] Jan Becker of Borsele had recently escaped from tutorial duties to a
benefice at Veere (cf Ep 849:7n), but his escape was evidently incomplete.
8 Ferdinand] For recent negotiations about a suitable tutor for Prince Ferdinand
see Ep 917 introduction.
9 rich blockheads] Cf Ep 999 n47.

1006

1 your order] When Erasmus criticized individual Dominicans he was often at
pains to point out that his remarks concerned them as individuals, not as
Dominicans; see below line 142–4 and Epp 694:33–4, 808:11–14, 948:150–2,
993:86–9.
2 by what you write] In addition to Hoogstraten's style Erasmus had no doubt
noticed that in Hoogstraten's first *Apologia* against Giorgio Benigno (Cologne:
[sons of H. Quentel] February 1518) 1.8.6 and in his *Destructio cabalae* 4.18.2
his own New Testament was mentioned with approval and alleged to support
Hoogstraten's view on the points in question.
3 religious duty] Cf *Adagia* I i 47.
4 old saying] This is the hexametric translation of Hesiod *Works and Days* 266
given by Erasmus in *Adagia* I ii 14.
5 suffragan bishop] No doubt Theoderich Michwael (or Wichwael), an acquaintance of Erasmus (Ep 413:20n), who was apparently unaware of the
suffragan's recent death (before 3 March 1519)
6 Reuchlin's defence] See Ep 300:19–32, the letter to Reuchlin mentioned hereafter. It had been written before Erasmus met him in 1515.
7 the same regret] Cf Ep 636:33–5; for Erasmus' discreet efforts to restrain
Reuchlin's friends see Ep 694 introduction, and for a pacifying answer see Ep
747.

8 Pfefferkorn ... Arnold of Tongeren] Earlier letters reflect Erasmus' acquaintance with some of the polemical treatises of Johann Pfefferkorn (cf Ep 487:
22–4), Ortwinus Gratius (Epp 526:9–13, 622), and Arnold Luyd of Tongeren
(cf Ep 543:5–9).

9 report] No doubt the *Acta iudiciorum inter F. Jacobum Hochstraten Inquisitorem
Coloniensium et Johannem Reuchlin LL. Doc. ex registro publico, autentico et sigillato*
(Haguenau: T. Anshelm February 1518); cf Geiger *Reuchlin* 290–6.

10 your pamphlet] Hoogstraten's first *Apologia* against Benigno (see above, n2).
Benigno had published a *Defensio* of Reuchlin in 1517; cf Ep 680:28n.

11 that preface] In view of lines 162–4 below it seems clear that Erasmus refers to
Hoogstraten's *Apologia secunda* ([Cologne: sons of H. Quentel] 1519), which
is a point-by-point reply to Hermann von Neuenahr's *Epistolae trium illustrium
virorum* (cf n12). In the preface Reuchlin's defenders are colourfully compared to 'mad and rabid dogs barking at the moon.'

12 small book] *Epistolae trium illustrium virorum ad Hermannum comitem
Nuenarium* (Cologne: E. Cervicornus May 1518; cf Hutten *Opera* I 20*–21*). It
included the letters mentioned by Erasmus, Hoogstraten's attack on Reuchlin's
Augenspiegel, with Reuchlin's reply, and other attacks upon Hoogstraten.
In the subsequent quarrel with Erasmus Hutten strongly objected to the
following remarks, which he thought were insincere, whereas Neuenahr,
according to Erasmus, was not offended; see Hutten *Opera* II Ep 310.58–9;
Erasmus *Spongia*, ASD IX-1 134–6.

13 two pamphlets] *Destructio cabalae seu cabalisticae perfidiae ab Ioanne Reuchlin
Capnione iampridem in lucem editae* (Cologne: sons of H. Quentel April 1519)
and *Apologia secunda*; cf above n11 and Hutten *Operum supplementum* II
103–4. For Reuchlin's *De arte cabalistica* cf Ep 500:22–3.

14 Gratius] At the end of Hoogstraten's *Apologia secunda* there is a letter from
Ortwinus Gratius to Johann Ingenwinkel dated from Quentel's shop, 1
October 1518. Erasmus suggests that Gratius might have collaborated with
Hoogstraten (cf below line 323) much the same way as he had with Pfeffer-
korn cf Ep 526:10n.

15 title] Of the *Destructio cabalae*

16 fly at Celsus] Origen's eight books *Contra Celsum* were written shortly before
250. Celsus, a Platonic philosopher in Rome, had composed his work c 178,
but his arguments against Christianity still merited a careful reply.

17 not been condemned yet] Cf below n18.

18 before the judge] Reuchlin's case was investigated by a papal commission of
experts between June 1514 and July 1516, but its findings, favourable to
Reuchlin, were superseded when Leo x suspended the proceedings. Not until
June 1520 was a final decision handed down at Rome, and at this time it
amounted to a condemnation of Reuchlin; see Geiger *Reuchlin* 307–19, 451.

19 some pamphlet] Reuchlin's *Augenspiegel*; cf Ep 300:3n.

20 detest the Jews] Cf Ep 694 introduction.

21 shock the Paris theologians] While perhaps there were specific reasons to
render each of these three Dominicans objectionable in the eyes of some
Paris theologians it is doubtful whether Erasmus had any in mind. Agostino
Giustiniani's appointment as a royal lecturer in Hebrew (cf Epp 810:397n,
906:529n) may have antagonized the opponents of the three languages.

Tommaso de Vio, Cardinal Cajetanus, had defended papal authority against the Council of Pisa (cf Ep 256:40n, 49n) and against the conciliarist tradition of Paris. Prierias (cf Ep 872:19n) was a protégé of Cajetanus and, like him, a rigid Thomist who had attacked the Scotism popular at Paris (cf Renaudet *Préréforme* 659–60 and passim; F. Lauchert *Die italienischen literarischen Gegener Luthers*, Freiburg im Breisgau 1912, 8 and passim). At this time, however, Cajetanus and Prierias were universally known as exponents of the curial efforts to silence Luther, and Erasmus was probably thinking in terms of a general conflict between the critics and the supporters of Reuchlin, Luther, and his own Christian humanism, associating Cajetanus in Germany and Prierias at Rome with the belligerence of Hoogstraten and other Dominicans (cf Ep 1033:157–61). On the opposite side he had recently experienced hearty support from Paris for his own stand (cf Ep 1000A introduction) and may also have learned that Luther was popular with some theologians in the French capital (cf Luther w *Briefwechsel* I Ep 146), while the Dominicans there attacked Lefèvre for his defence of Reuchlin; cf Ep 1030:7–10.

22 preface] To the *Apologia secunda*; cf above n11.
23 criticize me] In his *Destructio cabalae* (2.5–12). In 2.5.1 Hoogstraten quoted Erasmus' annotation of Matt 19:8 and context in the New Testament of 1516 (*Annotationes* 276), without, however, mentioning his name. Erasmus had stated that Matthew's text was the sole basis for the church's rejection of divorce, a stand she stubbornly maintained in contrast to some other precepts of Christ, such as that of non-resistance, which now appeared to be abrogated by an *interpretatio commoda* (cf below lines 203–5, 226–7). Erasmus also questioned why the relief which Moses granted the Jews for their 'hardness of heart' was not admissible for Christians, as brothels apparently were. In the revised New Testament of 1518–19 this specific argument in much the same formulation was moved to a long disquisition on divorce added to 1 Cor 7:36–9 (*Annotationes* 325–34, especially 329) which expressed his views with greater care but no less vigour (cf below lines 213–16). See E.V. Telle *Erasme de Rotterdam et le septième sacrement* (Geneva 1954) 218, 228–30.
24 unmerciful] Cf Epp 967:79–80, 1033:42, 1160.
25 in another place] In the new disquisition on divorce, *Annotationes* (1518) 325; cf above n23.
26 according to your account] *Destructio cabalae* 2.5.3: only the words 'attack on the church as a whole' are cited verbatim, but Erasmus' repeated use of the word 'dogma' reflects Hoogstraten's emphasis.
27 a note] See above n23.
28 I had promised] In the preliminary pieces to the *Novum instrumentum* and on other occasions; cf Epp 809:70n, 1053:258–62, 1074:106–7.
29 to Basel] In the spring of 1518; cf Ep 843 introduction.
30 interpreting for the best] In his note on Matt 19:8 (cf above n23) Erasmus had used the term *commoda interpretatio* in the sense of 'convenient': the church suited herself in observing some of Christ's precepts rather than others, but here as in line 204 he implies a different meaning of the same term.
31 Christ (to give an example)] The following examples are derived from the Sermon on the Mount, which also forbids divorce; see Matt 5:22, 32, 34.
32 solemn vow] In Catholic theology certain vows are considered 'solemn vows,'

among them some monastic vows and the vow of chastity implicit in the reception of the subdiaconate. In the *Institutio christiani matrimonii* (LB V 634–7) Erasmus treated the matter at length as a legal device unduly favouring monasticism.

33 certain doctor] Erasmus, of course. The following citations are taken from the context indicated in n23 above.

34 fifth chapter] Matt 5:31–2, cf 19:8–9; see above n31.

35 he there ordains] In 1 Cor 7:10–16, treated in Erasmus' disquisition (cf above n23) as a most difficult passage

36 in this place] Matt 5:32, 19:9

37 laws] *Corpus iuris canonici*, Gratian causa 32 q 7 c 1–10; causa 33 q 2 c 1

38 you say] *Destructio cabalae* 2.6.1 (Erasmus summarizes); cf Deut 24:1.

39 other men write] See above n14.

40 rightly distinguish] *Apologia secunda* ff A ii–A iii (preface); *Destructio cabalae* 1.12.3

41 the French] The suggestion seems to be that they prefer to leave the fighting to mercenaries such as the Swiss; cf Ep 855:4n.

42 poisonous attacks] Cf Epp 948, 993, 1022, 1053 n62.

43 absurd stories] See for example Epp 948, 950.

44 Paul's words] Gal 5:15

45 Jethro] Moses' father-in-law; for his counsel see Exod 18:17–24. Hoogstraten matriculated at Louvain in 1479, and thus must have been older than Erasmus.

1007

1 recommended] With Ep 864

2 the name] Cf Epp 335:151–69, 1003 n6.

3 dedicated] With Ep 384

4 we owe even our belief in the Gospel] Echoing perhaps a line of Augustine in *Contra epistolam Manichaei quam vocant fundamenti* 1.5; cf Ep 347:248–9 and Allen Ep 1637:62–4.

5 changed their minds] So especially Maarten van Dorp; see Epp 347, 1000A; cf also Epp 993:64–6, 1002:44–5, 1022, and Allen Ep 1225:69–72.

6 outstanding judges] Cf Horace *Epistles* 1.17.35–6.

7 Seneca's] Allen gives a reference to page 640 of Erasmus' edition of 1515, which we were unable to confirm. Cf Publilius Syrus *Sententiae* 333 ed Giancotti (Turin 1968): 'loco ignominiae est apud indignos dignitas.'

8 poetry] Cf Ep 1110:17–19.

9 undue freedom] Erasmus had probably his *Moria* (cf Ep 967:198–9) in mind, especially the transparent critique of curial conduct under Julius II; see ASD IV-3 172–6; cf Ep 749:16–18.

10 blackened one hair] Cf *Adagia* I viii 4; similar assurances of innocence are frequently repeated in Erasmus' letters; see Epp 337:63–5, 950:14, 998:66–7, 1053 n57, n62, 1061:505–6.

11 poisoned pamphlets] Cf Ep 1053 n62.

12 eminent monarchs] Cf Epp 948:189–224, 1004 n30.

13 far away] Charles V still had not returned from Spain (cf Epp 596, 1106 introductions). This letter explains Erasmus' anxiety for his renewed presence

in the Netherlands; cf Epp 1030:73–4, 1070:15–16, 1079:11–12, 1081:9, 1094:39.
14 reconciled] For the London treaty of perpetual peace, October 1518, see Ep
964:39n.

1008
1 twice a year] For other rumours of Erasmus' death cf Epp 854:9n, 1142
introduction.
2 love] 1 John 4:8
3 unto the Lord] Rom 14:8

1009
1 your efforts especially] Albert and his brother Joachim, elector of Brandenburg, had at first pledged their support to Francis I (cf Ep 744:52n), but
Albert changed his mind earlier than others and well before the election emerged as a warm advocate of the Hapsburg cause. Erasmus' information came
no doubt from Richard Pace (cf Ep 1001 n15) who gives his assessment of the
rewards reaped by Albert in LP III 353; cf Ep 1030 n16. See also Kalkoff
Kaiserwahl 183–4, 221–5, 274–6.
2 emperor] Cf Ep 1001 n19.
3 perpetual peace] Cf Ep 1007 n14.
4 against the enemies] This is no doubt a tribute to Pope Leo x's untiring advo-
cacy of a crusade against the Turks; cf Epp 729:56n, 964:39n.
5 Hector's valour ... Aeneas' glory] Hector of Troy was defeated and killed by
Achilles (Homer *Iliad* 22) and Turnus, king of the Rutilians, by Aeneas
(Virgil *Aeneid* 12).
6 not sold] To secure electoral votes the Hapsburgs paid some 852,000 florins,
half of it in the form of bribes (Bruno Gebhardt *Handbuch der deutschen
Geschichte*, 8th ed, Stuttgart 1955, II 36). This sum is presumably expressed in
terms of the South German money-of-account based upon the Rhenish gold
florin of the Four Electors, and should not be confused with the Flemish
money-of-account frequently referred to elsewhere in this correspondence
(cf Ep 1046 n4; CWE 1 316–17, 338–9). In 1523 Jakob Fugger reminded Charles
V, 'It is well known and clear as day that your Imperial Majesty could not
have acquired the Roman crown without my help ... For if I had remained
aloof from the house of Austria and had served France, I would have
obtained much profit and money, which was then offered to me' (*The Portable
Renaissance Reader* ed J.B. Ross and M.M. McLaughlin, New York 1951,
180). For a frank expression of Erasmus' feelings cf Ep 927:10.
7 hearts of all kings] Prov 21:1
8 small book] The *Institutio principis christiani*; for its connections with Prince
Ferdinand, the brother of Charles v, see Epp 853, 917 introductions.
9 on his return] See Ep 999 introduction.
10 widow's mite] Cf Mark 12:42–4; Luke 21:2–4.
11 Hutten's sake as well] Hutten was still in Albert's service, a fact that
led Erasmus to believe that the cardinal shared many of his views; cf Ep
1033.
12 the man's] Beatus Rhenanus' mistake; see Ep 976:18n.
13 not yet arrived] Cf Ep 999:333–6.

1010

1 detractors] 'Zoili' in Latin (cf below n3), men such as Edward Lee. In his *Apologia invectivis Lei* Erasmus emphasized again that he had tried to prevent Martens' edition and had added this preface to warn the reader, not to oblige the printer; see *Opuscula* 273.

2 our own text] The Vulgate

3 Zoilus] A sophist who had dared to criticize Homer and earned proverbial disrepute; cf *Adagia* II v 8.

4 blindfold gladiators] Cf *Adagia* II iv 33.

5 pontiff] Leo x's brief, Ep 864, was reprinted in Marten's edition; cf Ep 1007 introduction.

1011

1 Longueil] A rising star among the younger men dedicated to humanistic studies, Longueil (cf Epp 914, 935) was then travelling in the company of a young gentleman, Lorenzo Bartolini, abbot of Entremont in Savoy (cf Ep 1187). On 12 August they were in Paris, and the visit in Marly here mentioned must have taken place some days after, for Budé told Longueil that Erasmus owed him a letter (cf Ep 1023:2–4) and on 19 August made the same complaint when writing to Vives (cf Budé *Opera omnia* I 252). Thus the day which brought Budé first Longueil's visit and later the arrival of Erasmus' Ep 1004 cannot have been before 20 August. From Marly Longueil and his companion went on to England and from there to Louvain, always carrying letters (cf Epp 1023, 1024), and afterwards to Lyon and Italy. At Louvain Longueil spent two or three days with Erasmus (c 15 October), bringing him the sad news of Colet's death; see Epp 1026, 1029. For their conversations see Ep 1706; cf P.A. Becker *Christophle de Longueil* (Bonn and Leipzig 1924) 35–6.

2 young man] Probably Haio Herman of Friesland; cf Ep 1002 n11.

3 you invite me] Ep 1004:137–41

4 amnesty] Cf Ep 1004 introduction.

5 you said] Ep 1004:14–15, 136–7

6 three letters] Epp 915, 987, 992, but most of Erasmus' Ep 1004 is written in answer to Ep 915 alone.

7 permanent attachment] Epp 906 salutation, 1004:5–8

8 comic play] Cf Aristophanes *Plutus* 600

9 Maimakterion] The fifth Attic month, deriving its name from the feast of Turbulent Zeus

1012

1 Karel] Karel van Hedenbault (c 1444–1527), Fevijn's paternal cousin, had served the dynasty of Burgundy from his boyhood. Perhaps from the turn of the century he was attached to the Prinsenhof, which was still visited occasionally by members of the Burgundian-Hapsburg family and also served as a meeting place for diplomatic gatherings; see de Vocht *Literae ad Craneveldium* xciii, 56–7.

2 Marcus] Marcus Laurinus (Lauwerijns), another canon of St Donatian's (cf Ep 651), was to be appointed dean of the chapter on 24 September 1519.

3 Robert] Robert Hellin (d 1527) came from a French family domiciled at Bruges and was married to Eleanor van Fevijn. He was a pensionary or legal advisor to the city of Bruges and also lived at the Prinsenhof; see de Vocht *Literae ad Craneveldium* 124.

4 precentor] Gisbert van Schoonhove (d 1524); see de Vocht CTL II 179.

5 Nicolaus Fistula] Probably Jan Pipe (Fistula), canon of St Donatian's 1505–7 and 1510–31; see de Vocht *Literae ad Craneveldium* 475.

1013

1 remedy] Pliny *Naturalis historia* 29.29.91; cf Ep 1212.

2 seek refreshment] Cf Ep 704:3–15.

3 travelled] See Ep 999 introduction.

4 intimacy] At Orléans in the autumn of 1500; see Epp 133:116, 147:52–3.

5 pagan writing] Cf the colloquy *Convivium religiosum* ASD I-3 251–2, and for Erasmus' complex view of Cicero see P.G. Bietenholz *History and Biography* 64–6.

6 Augustine] Cf perhaps *Enarrationes in Psalmos* 100:8; CC 39:1413 and also Erasmus' *Antibarbari* (CWE 23 95–8) summarizing a pertinent argument from Augustine's *De doctrina christiana*.

7 poetical] Cf Ep 1110:17–19.

8 dedicated] In 1501; cf introduction.

1013A

1 your brother] The Latin term used by Erasmus, 'fraterculus iste,' is unusual and ambiguous. It could refer to a younger brother of Gerardus, and a Bernardus Listrius of Rhenen, which was Gerardus' native town, did in fact matriculate in Louvain on 10 June 1523 (cf *Matricule de l'Université de Louvain* ed E. Reusens et al, Louvain 1903– , III-1 699). On the other hand, Erasmus' term could mean: 'that little friar' or 'novice.'

2 wife] Evidently the 'little Justina' of line 28. Erasmus' wishes suggest that the marriage was of recent date. In BRE Ep 193 [c March 1520] Listrius announces that his young wife Justina has just given birth to his first child, a daughter.

3 *Moria* ... into French] Probably the translation by Joris van Halewijn; cf Ep Epp 641:6n, 1115.

4 letters] The *Farrago*, to be followed in 1522 by the *Epistolae ad diversos* (cf Ep 1009 introduction). The *Farrago* was twice as large as the preceding collection of Erasmus' letters (cf CWE 3 349–50). In those years most Basel editions were launched at the Frankfurt book fairs.

5 Tilmannus] Unidentified; possibly Tielmannus Gravius (cf Ep 610:50), a friend of Erasmus living at Cologne where Listrius had studied (cf RE Ep 233). A letter to Cologne at this time might be carried by a messenger going to the Upper Rhine region; see Ep 1014.

6 *Enchiridion*] Listrius was the editor of an edition, without commentary (Zwolle: S. Corver 7 October 1519 [NK 2927]).

7 any weight] See below n10.

8 peace] See Ep 1022 introduction.

9 do not understand] Cf Ep 1007:58–9, 101.

10 Simon] No doubt the Zwolle printer, Simon Corver. Between 1519 and 1522 he published many writings by both Listrius and Erasmus. Those of Erasmus include the adages *Sileni Alcibiadis* and *Dulce bellum inexpertis*, both c 1520, which identify Listrius as the editor (NK 869, 2857), *De constructione*, September 1519 (NK 2897), *De copia*, 23 January 1520 (NK 2914) and again 1523 (NK 2916); also the *Enchiridion*; see above n6.

11 Mont] The Prior of St Agnietenberg near Zwolle, Gerard of Kloster (cf Epp 504, 1116). The reference to him in the next sentence appears to be an afterthought, recalling that the prior was then, it seems, at Louvain.

1015

1 Tunstall] Cf Ep 1004:70–75, referring to Ep 583, the letter from Budé to Tunstall.

2 Vives] Cf Ep 1004 n3; nothing is known about the letter Budé showed him.

3 Italian] Perhaps Giambattista Egnazio (cf Ep 588) who on 5 January 1519 wrote to Jean Grolier in Paris, venting his displeasure with Erasmus in view of Ep 648 and stating that he owed Budé a reply to the latter's letter of 27 November 1518. Therefore Egnazio's letter may well have been sent for Budé to see; cf Ep 648:58n; Budé *Opera omnia* 1 258–9.

4 replied in Greek] Ep 1011, answering Erasmus' Ep 1004

5 you let pass] Cf Ep 1004:121–2.

6 when I said] Ep 915 123–4

7 spiteful and odd] Ep 1004:69–70

8 swallowed] Cf Ep 810:361–2.

9 practice] Epp 915:126, 1004:104–8

10 longer letter] Ep 906

11 leaden-witted] Ep 1004:89

12 reopen wounds] Cf Ep 906:224–5; cf Cicero *De lege agraria* 3.2.4.

13 Williams] Guillaume Petit, the influential confessor to Francis I and from 1518 bishop of Troyes. Erasmus had first praised him among his many benefactors by the name of William (Ep 534:32–54; cf Ep 1003 n6), but later had accused him of insincerity in a letter (Ep 778:24–9) which he promptly published. Budé's remarks here are, again, in Greek, but like Erasmus he published them without delay.

14 the words] Ep 915:112–13

15 good news] Ep 1004:95

16 Deloynes] Cf Epp 1004:122–3 and 915:139.

17 Iliad] Meaning Ep 1004

18 amnesty] Cf Ep 1004 introduction.

19 'I forgive ... remarks'] Ep 1004:121

20 maintaining our unanimity] Ep 1004:9

21 deserted] Ep 1004:144–5

22 foray] Perhaps a reference to Budé's trip to Montpellier, where abortive negotiations with the representatives of the future Charles V took place in the spring of 1519 (cf Ep 924:19–21). The promised account in Greek was apparently never written; see Epp 1066:58–62, 1073:73–5.

23 Herman] See Ep 1011 introduction.

24 plague] See Ep 993 n11.

1016

1 commendator] A title given to officers in the military orders of St John, the Teutonic Knights, and of Spain, referring here to a man who has not been identified. Ep 1017 suggests that he was travelling to Rome via Paris.

2 weather] For similar complaints cf Epp 1025:22–3, 1038:3–4.

3 conspiracy] Cf Epp 993, 998, 1006–7, 1012.

4 peace] See Ep 1022 introduction.

5 Rochester] For John Fisher's controversy with Jacques Lefèvre d'Etaples see Ep 1030 n1, n2; for Poncher's part cf Ep 936:27n.

6 letters from Bérault] Cf Ep 994 n4.

7 prove the truth] Erasmus apparently considered dedicating one of his works to Poncher, but he never did.

8 Scodrensis] Marino Becichemo (c 1468–1526) of the Venetian town of Scutari (Shkodër in Albania) began to teach rhetoric at Padua in 1517. For his notes on the first book of Pliny *Naturalis historia* (which Erasmus here calls 'world history') see the introduction. It is not clear whether Erasmus had actually seen Bérault's edition, or part of it, in print.

9 complete] Several other works by Pliny the Elder were known to have existed, but they have never been found.

10 Cop] Guillaume Cop, the royal physician, by whose Ep 523 Francis I's invitation was relayed to Erasmus.

1017

1 dedicated] With Ep 710; but a copy of the printed book was sent only with Ep 835.

2 letter] It seems that Erasmus is referring once again (cf Ep 835 introduction) to the missing answer to his Ep 334 and that his further letter to Grimani, Ep 835, had also gone unanswered. Andrea Ammonio died in August 1517; see Ep 623 introduction.

3 Origen's commentary] Nothing is known about such a request by Archbishop William Warham, nor about Erasmus' project at this time. Not until 1527 did the Froben press publish fragments of Origen's commentary on Matthew in Erasmus' Latin translation. In 1536 Hieronymus Froben and Nicolaus Episcopius launched the first edition of Origen's collected *Opera* in Latin, which also claimed Erasmus as an editor. Other Latin editions of Origen were published in Paris in 1512 and in 1519; moreover at the time of his death in October 1519 (cf Ep 1084 n5) Bruno Amerbach was collecting material for an Origen edition by the Froben press, but Caspar Hedio (cf Ep 1459) hardly dared to hope for Erasmus' co-operation in this project; see Hedio's letter of 21 November 1519 in Zwingli *Werke* VII Ep 102.

4 commendator] See Ep 1016 n1.

1018

1 Arnold] He was probably in charge of the boy's household.

2 Goclenius] This was the name taken by Konrad Wackers of Mengeringhausen in Westphalia (c 1489–1539). After studying at Deventer and Cologne he came to Louvain in 1511 and from 1 December 1519 until his death held the Latin chair at the Collegium Trilingue; see Ep 1209.

1019

1 Lee] Edward Lee (cf Ep 998 introduction) had been a friend of both Erasmus and Lips. When he started to criticize Erasmus Lips attempted – with Erasmus' encouragement – to stay on good terms with him so as to get hold of his critical notes, which Lee tried to conceal from Erasmus; cf Epp 898A, 960 introduction.

2 suppress] Cf Epp 1026:17–20, 1029:12–16.

3 real lion] In Latin Lee (*Leus*) and lion (*leo*) sound very similar.

1020

1 misplaced modesty] Amerbach refers no doubt to his long silence (lines 25, 49); no earlier letter from him to Erasmus is extant.

2 immortality] This text is found in the *Anthologia Palatina* (7.327.4), the largest collection of Greek epigrams, rediscovered in 1606. Bonifacius Amerbach knew the text from his copy of an earlier collection: *Florilegium diversorum epigrammatum* (Venice: A. Manuzio 1503); see AK II Epp 556, 741.

3 Apelles or Pyrgoteles] Alexander the Great was said to have decreed that none but Apelles should paint him and none but Pyrgoteles engrave him; see Pliny *Naturalis historia* 7.125.

4 surpass them all] The reading of this sentence is uncertain.

5 plague] Cf Ep 993 n11.

6 Avignon] The celebrated professor of law, Andreas Alciati (cf Ep 1250) had been teaching there since the autumn of 1518. Bonifacius' older brother Bruno had recently renewed his acquaintance with him (cf Ep 1014; AK II Epp 588, 660, 673). Bonifacius, however, could not carry out his plan at once because of Bruno's death in the plague epidemic (cf Ep 1084:37–8, 44–6). He eventually arrived in Avignon on c 11 May 1520 and returned to Basel a year later; see AK II Epp 733, 739, 779–83.

7 works] Andrea Alciati *Paradoxa iuris civilis* (and other legal essays) Milan: A. Minuziano 1518. This work established Alicati's lasting reputation. Bonifacius was much involved in the printing of revised editions in Basel by Andreas Cratander (1523 and 1531); see AK II Ep 772; Bietenholz *Basle and France* 226, 254.

8 Zasius] Udalricus Zasius, professor of law at Freiburg and Bonifacius' former teacher

9 disputation] The famous Leipzig disputation between Eck, Karlstadt, and Luther was held in June–July 1519 (cf Ep 948 introduction). At the end of the debate Duke George of Saxony invited the theological faculties of Paris and Erfurt to hand down a judgment; but nothing came of it, as Erfurt declined and Paris demanded an exorbitant fee; see Boehmer *Luther* 289–93; cf below Ep 1033 n21. On 3 October Bonifacius Amerbach knew about the forthcoming publication of the proceedings (cf AK II Ep 686). Three editions were printed by Matthes Maler in Erfurt, 1519; see Luther W II 254–383; Benzing *Lutherbibliographie* 405–7.

10 'Great Zeus … of men!'] Aristophanes *Clouds* 153

11 Eck] Johann Maier of Eck, professor of theology at Ingolstadt

12 'I cannot … madder yet'] Cf *Anthologia Palatina* 11.127.3–4; cf above n2.

13 Melanchthon] Philippus Melanchthon had addressed a long letter to Johannes

Oecolampadius dated 21 July 1519 (*Melanchthons Briefwechsel* I Ep 59), reporting on the Leipzig disputation. He was highly critical of Eck, although he paid tribute to his sharp wit. Eck replied angrily with an *Excusatio*. In turn Melanchthon showed his 'horns' in a *Defensio* against Eck. All were published at once, and reprinted together through the efforts of Oecolampadius at Augsburg and at Basel by Froben (cf Ep 910:5n; Melanchthon *Werke in Auswahl* I 3–22). Amerbach's own views are confirmed by a contemporary statement in which he praises Erasmus and Luther as the twin reformers of theology; see AK II Ep 686:45–6.

1021

1 my letter] A missing letter answered by Erasmus with Ep 950
2 your death] See Ep 1008 introduction.
3 Nestor] Cf *Adagia* I vi 66; Homer stated that Nestor outlived three generations.
4 friends with like] Cf Ep 999 n6.
5 Apelles] Cf Ep 1020 n3.
6 Antisilenuses and Gnathos] 'Antisilenuses' refers to men who are the opposite of ancient statuettes of Silenus, which were plain on the outside, but beautifully crafted on the inside (cf *Adagia* III iii 1); Gnatho is the name of the parasite in Terence's *Eunuch*.
7 letter that killeth] 2 Cor 3:6
8 'breeds ... hate'] Terence *Andria* 68; *Adagia* II ix 53.
9 New Testament] See Ep 864 introduction.
10 Daedalus] The proverbial and ingenious craftsman; cf *Adagia* II iii 62, and for other admirers of Froben's books cf Ep 925:18–25.
11 Hercynian forest] A classical name for all wooded highlands north of the Danube
12 hydra] Cf *Adagia* I x 9.
13 Nicolaites] See Rev 2:6, 15; Erasmus understood the term to mean promiscuous men; see his answer, Ep 1039:50–2.
14 three sects] The following outline of the religious divisions and troubles in Bohemia and Moravia is quite sound. After the radical Taborites had been defeated (at Lipany in 1434 by the Catholics and Utraquists, and again at Mount Tabor in 1453 by the Utraquist regent George of Poděbrady), their movement split into many sects. The only one to achieve some prominence and prestige was the Czech Brethren, whose basic tenets are described fairly by Šlechta, although without the noticeable measure of sympathy revealed by Erasmus' answer; see F.G. Heymann *John Žižka and the Hussite Revolution* (Princeton 1955); by the same author *George of Bohemia, King of Heretics* (Princeton 1965).
15 Another sect] The Utraquists came to form a church on the basis of a tradition reaching back to Jan Hus and other Czech reformers. A *modus vivendi* with the Catholic subjects of Bohemia was found and strengthened in the course of much external warfare under the Utraquist king George of Poděbrady, 1458–71. Šlechta himself is proof of the continued vitality of this *modus vivendi*. Although a Catholic (line 176), he is clearly sympathetic to the Utraquist position.
16 Compacts] The Compacts present a compromise negotiated with the Council

of Basel which was accepted by the emperor Sigismund (1368–1437) and the Bohemian estates in 1436 and ratified by a bull issued by the council on 15 January 1437. Communion was to be given in one kind or in both, as the communicant chose and without prejudice, and similar compromises were reached on the issues of preaching by lay people, the authority of secular courts over the clergy, and the property of religious institutions.

17 in this form] See John 6:53; 1 Cor 10:16, 11:23–5; Pope Gelasius I in *Corpus iuris canonici*, Gratian *De consecratione* d 2 c 12 (Richter-Friedberg I 1318). The subsequent change in Catholic thought is discussed by Thomas Aquinas, who finally endorses the adequacy of communion without the chalice, in his *Summa theologiae* III questions 76.2, 79.1, 80.12.

18 Eugenius] Eugenius IV (1431–47), never passed specific judgment on the Compacts, but he first authorized and subsequently condemned the Council of Basel, which had ratified them. The Compacts were solemnly rejected by Pope Pius II in 1462.

19 expressly stated] The firmness of this assertion is all the more noteworthy as modern studies of patristic thought on the Eucharist offer no evidence to support it.

20 Pyghards] Some forty 'Pikart' refugees and their families, probably Beghards from Flanders rather than from adjacent Picardie, arrived at Prague in 1418. The name was later applied to a sect of the Taborite movement (cf above n14) which was destroyed in 1421. The Pyghards allegedly denied the real presence and practised promiscuity. The name was commonly transferred to the Czech or Bohemian Brethren, the pacifist successor movement to the militant Taborites, which seems indeed to have undergone certain Pyghard influences; see H. Kaminsky *A History of the Hussite Revolution* (Berkeley and Los Angeles 1967) 353–60.

21 Žyžka] Jan Žižka of Trocnov (d 1424), a Bohemian nobleman who led the Taborites to repeated victories over the armies of Emperor Sigismund.

22 Vladislav] Vladislav II Jagiełło, d 1516 as king of Bohemia and Hungary.

23 beast ... harlot] Cf Rev 13 and 17.

24 Apollo's shafts] In book I of Homer's *Iliad* Apollo shoots plague into the Greek camp with his arrows to avenge a slight to his priest. For the ravages of the plague at this time see Ep 993 n11.

25 Jodocus] Justus Jonas; see Ep 876.

1022

1 spiteful disputes] Cf Ep 1006 n8.

2 long letter] Ep 1006

1023

1 Longueil] For his recent visit with Budé before departing for England and the Netherlands see Ep 1011 n1.

2 last two letters] Epp 987, 992

3 my last letter] Ep 1004

4 letter to Vives] Dated 19 August 1519 (Budé *Opera omnia* I 252–4), it was clearly intended for Erasmus to read; cf Ep 1066:59–60.

5 died] On 16 September 1519; cf Ep 1025 introduction and n1.

1024

1 Longueil] See Ep 1011 n1.
2 hornets' nest] Cf *Adagia* I i 60; Bérault had evidently referred to the Louvain theologians.
3 letter of yours] To Dorp; see Ep 1000A introduction.
4 peace] See Ep 1022.
5 publishing a speech] See Ep 1044.
6 letter ... by Augustine] Possibly Ep 1002, or perhaps a subsequent short letter. The carrier was perhaps Augustijn Agge, a native of The Hague and a physician who had been in Paris in 1517; see Ep 511.
7 Du Ruel] Jean Du Ruel taught medicine at Paris and was physician to King Francis I.

1025

1 succeed him] As dean of St Paul's; the appointment dated from 25 October 1519.
2 your books] Apparently lost on his return from Italy in 1514. Among them was a manuscript draft for Erasmus' *Antibarbari*; cf Epp 706:38n, 1100.
3 Campeggi] The papal nuncio in England had been called back to Rome in June 1519 (cf Ep 995:77). He took leave of Henry VIII at Greenwich on 15 August and departed from London on the seventeenth. On the twenty-second he was at Dover, the twenty-fourth at Calais, departing for the court of Brussels on the twenty-sixth. On the way there he met Erasmus at Bruges (cf Ep 999 introduction). Next he visited the French court at Blois between 18 and 23 September, was at Lyon 1–3 October, at Bologna c 22 October to 14 November, and was officially received by Leo X on 28 November, having entered Rome on the preceding day; see *Calendar of State Papers, Venetian* ed R.L. Brown et al (London 1862–1940) II 1279, 1297; LP III 433–4, 439, 452, 454, 461, 533, and for Pace's efforts in promoting Erasmus' interest cf Ep 996:22–4.
4 to reply] No answers had been received from either Henry VIII or Cardinal Wolsey to Erasmus' Epp 964, 967. In spite of his usual ambiguity (cf Ep 1032:21–7) Erasmus was clearly interested in a definitive offer of preferment in England (cf Epp 1028 n2, 1031:3–6; see also Epp 994 n4, 1004 n30, 1012). Nothing, however, was to come of it; see Epp 1060:3–8, 1079, 1098 introductions.
5 inclement season] Cf Ep 1016 n2.
6 paraphrases] Cf Ep 1043 introduction.

1026

1 Longueil] Cf Ep 1011 n1. In the following Erasmus refers to Longueil's French patriotism (also expressed in his Ep 914) and to the fact that as the son of a French bishop and a girl from Mechelen he had spent his early youth with his mother and her family.
2 your friends] From common days in Paris; see Ep 994 n1.
3 puny friend] Edward Lee is intended. Lupset was one of several Englishmen acquainted both with their countryman Lee and with Erasmus who were either prepared to intervene in the dispute between them or were asked to do so. Others were Thomas More (cf Epp 999 n24, 1053 n21, 392, and 1090

introduction), bishops John Fisher and Richard Foxe (cf Ep 1099), Cuthbert
Tunstall (cf Epp 886, 1029), Hugh Latimer, John Colet, and Richard Pace.
Pace and Lupset had recently met with both opponents (cf Epp 999, 1026
introductions). By Lee's own admission, his critical notes had been available to More, Latimer (cf Ep 1061:72, 919), and above all to Fisher, to whom
Lee had sent them in March 1519 with Erasmus' consent (cf Ep 1061:73).
Fisher, with some assistance from More, apparently wrung from both protagonists a pledge that from there on they would keep the peace (Epp 936:99–
107, 1090:9–10). All along their common friends in England had counselled
moderation on both sides and pleaded with Lee to suppress rather than
publish his critical notes, but the conflict continued to escalate and eventually
Erasmus himself urged Lee to publish (cf Ep 1037 n1). For the time being,
however, as this letter shows, he continued his efforts of gaining access to the
notes behind Lee's back (Epp 998 n3, 1029–30). Fisher and More probably
had some reservations about Erasmus' tactics (cf Epp 1029:34–5, 1068:3–5, 1090),
but on the whole he was supported by his English friends with loyalty and
increasing determination (cf Epp 1083 introduction). In return, he did his best
to prevent the flood of abuse unleashed against Lee by himself and others
from reflecting unfavourably upon the English nation in general; see Epp 1083
introduction and n12, 1089, 1100 introduction, 1103:18–22.

1027
1 'Real tears … coin'] Juvenal 13.134
2 Christ his Master] Cf Allen Ep 1211:325, 329.
3 Gerard] Master William Garrard was Colet's steward and one of the executors
of his will.
4 peace] See Ep 1022 introduction.
5 If Christ] Cf Rom 8:31.

1028
1 your court] Cf Ep 1004 n30; and for the nabobs cf Ep 999 n47.
2 my letter] Probably Ep 965, which referred unobtrusively to the possibility of
Erasmus' moving to England (cf Ep 1025 n4). Mountjoy had relayed a royal
offer to Erasmus in April 1517; see Ep 694:11n.
3 never return] Cf Ep 1027:6 and 2 Sam 12:23.
4 peace] See Ep 1022 introduction.
5 single individual] Cf Ep 1029 n2.

1029
1 peace] See Ep 1022 introduction.
2 Noxus] Latinized form of Ate (Bane or Curse personified, cf below 338 n19), a
pun on the name of Jan Briart of Ath, or Atensis, the 'vice-chancellor' of the
University of Louvain (cf Ep 948:27n). Erasmus believed that he had secretly
encouraged such critics of his New Testament as Dorp and Lee (cf Epp
337:393n, 843:538n, 993 n9) and more recently Hoogstraten (cf Epp 1006 introduction, 1030:21–3, 1064). Briart had attacked him publicly only once, in
February 1519 (cf Ep 946), but on that occasion they had quickly been recon-

ciled (cf Ep 998 introduction). Erasmus himself acknowledges Briart's role in bringing about the recent accord with the Louvain theologians (lines 6–7; cf Ep 1028:23), but as he took a dim view of that agreement (cf Ep 1022 introduction), he distrusted Briart's motives. Three years after Briart's death on 8 January 1520, Erasmus chose his *Spongia* against Hutten to pay tribute to the fairness of the 'vice-chancellor,' even though he called him irritable and suggested that on occasion he had been egged on by the enemies of the new learning; see ASD IX-1 158–60; cf Allen I 22.

3 not to your taste] Perhaps Erasmus recalled Tunstall's admonition in Ep 663: 99–103. He may also be referring to other recent defences (cf Epp 934, 946), in particular to his published statements against Edward Lee (cf Epp 843, 998 introduction), who was evidently in touch with Tunstall; cf Epp 886, 1026 n3.
4 Dorp] See Ep 1044 introduction.
5 pickets will remain] See Ep 1074 introduction.
6 paraphrases] See Ep 1043.
7 Longueil] Cf Ep 1011 n1.
8 Campeggi] Cf Ep 1025 n3.
9 third edition] Of the New Testament; cf Ep 1030:28.
10 Rochester] John Fisher had counselled silence to Erasmus as well as Lee; cf Epp 936, 1026 n3, 1030:25–43.

1030

1 three books] Fisher's *De unica Magdalena libri tres*, Paris: Josse Bade 22 February 1519 (cf Ep 936:9n). This is the first of Fisher's three contributions (see n2 below) to an extensive controversy (cf Ep 936:27n), in the centre of which were Jacques Lefèvre's sound arguments against the traditional assumption that three different passages in the Gospels all referred to Mary Magdalen; see Ep 766:26n; Surtz *Fisher* 5–7, 157–60, 274–89; E.F. Rice ed *The Prefatory Epistles of Jacques Lefèvre d'Etaples and related texts* (New York 1972) Ep 124 introduction.

2 subsequent work] Fisher's *De unica Magdalena* was followed by his *Confutatio secundae disceptationis per Iacobum Fabrum Stapulensem habitae* (Paris: J. Bade 3 September 1519) and by an attack on Clichtove, who had rallied to the defence of Lefèvre, his teacher and colleague. Fisher's *Eversio munitionis quam Iodocus Clichtoveus erigere moliebatur adversus unicam Magdalenam* (Louvain: D. Martens [early 1519] and again in September; NK 943, 4509) was no doubt the publication that had involved Erasmus in negotiations with the printer (lines 12–15; cf Ep 936:92–3). Erasmus had not much sympathy for tradition-hallowed misinterpretations of Scripture or for Lefèvre's principal opponents, the conservative theologians of Paris, who had their faculty declare Lefèvre's views heretical on 9 November 1521. As he was not anxious to declare himself in the matter, assisting Fisher's publishing efforts had evidently made him unhappy, and he hoped that the bishop's zeal and perseverance would at long last be exhausted; cf Epp 1016:22–8, 1068.

3 supporter of Reuchlin] Cf Ep 1006 n18. As Fisher himself had shown continued interest in Reuchlin, the remark was probably calculated to soften his stand against Lefèvre.

4 surprisingly awkward] For other indications of Dirk Martens' religious lean-
ings cf Epp 849:32n, 1163.

5 Peace] See Ep 1022 introduction.

6 cauldrons of Dodona] Cf *Adagia* 1 i 7: cauldrons were hung close to one
another around the oracle of Jupiter at Dodona, so that one stroke would keep
them all sounding for a long time.

7 Hoogstraten] No doubt Erasmus knew more about the reasons for this visit
than he cared to tell Fisher. The Louvain theologians had repeatedly called
Luther to the attention of their colleagues at Cologne (cf Ep 938:5n). On 30
August 1519 the Cologne faculty condemned a collection of Luther's Latin
writings published by Froben (cf Ep 904:20n). Hoogstraten, a chief advocate of
the Cologne verdict, was then sent to Louvain and on 12 October formally
presented it to the Louvain faculty of theology, which in turn condemned
Luther's views on 7 November (cf Allen Epp 1670:3n, 2445; Luther w VI 175–8;
de Vocht CTL I 425–7). Erasmus was bound to be sensitive to Hoogstraten's
appearance (cf Epp 1006, 1022); in fact, the inquisitor brought with him
from Cologne Erasmus' Ep 980 to Luther, recently published without the
author's knowledge, which was now circulated as proof of his connivance
with the heretic (cf Epp 1033:28–35, 1038 introduction, 1040:3–6) and may
have led to another investigation of Erasmus' own works; cf the preface.

8 plague] Cf Ep 993 n11.

9 unpopularity] See Ep 877:18–35.

10 Lee] See Ep 1026 n3.

11 reprint] The revised edition was evidently selling well; cf Epp 864, 1174.

12 his master, Christ] Cf Ep 1027 n2.

13 has any force] Reminiscent of Virgil *Aeneid* 9.446–7, Ovid *Tristia* 1.6.35–6

14 two letters] Ep 963, and an earlier letter now missing; cf Ep 963:6n.

15 he says] A paraphrase of Ep 963:22–7

16 refused] As a last effort to prevent the election of Charles v (cf the preface),
Pope Leo x and his diplomats attempted to promote the candidacy of
Frederick the Wise. Highly regarded by his peers, he seemed in the course of
the actual election proceedings assured of a majority of votes. But in spite
of the papal promises he believed that his resources were inadequate to the
demands of effectual rule and he refused to be a candidate, urging instead
the election of Charles. Of all the electors only Frederick had long refused to
commit his vote against payments and promises. In the end he too negotiated
with the Hapsburg ambassadors at Höchst to secure some advantages in the
event of Charles' election (cf Kalkoff *Kaiserwahl* 49–50). According to the
Fugger accounts Electoral Saxony received 70,000 gold florins in total, as
against 184,100 for the Palatinate, 113,200 for Mainz, and 52,800 for Cologne;
see Brandi *Kaiser Karl v.* I 91, II 103. On these German florins, cf Ep 1009 n6
and CWE 1 316–17, 338–9.

17 Liège] Erard de la Marck; cf Epp 1001 n15, 1038 introduction.

18 resuming the war] Ulrich of Württemberg attempted to reconquer his lost
duchy with very inadequate means (cf Epp 986, 1001 n21). Stuttgart opened
the gates to him on 14 August 1519, but most other cities and most of the
nobility refused to obey his orders. He was decisively defeated in October
and Württemberg came under Hapsburg administration from 1520 to 1534.

19 return of Charles] See Ep 1106 introduction.

1031
1 letter] Ep 967; Erasmus hoped that Wolsey's reply would confirm the royal offer; cf Ep 1025 n4.
2 Campeggi] See Ep 1025 n3.
3 no court] Cf Epp 999:303–19, 1004 n30.

1032
1 English court] Cf Ep 1004 n30.
2 lady of Rhamnus] The goddess Nemesis, often equated with Fortuna, had a temple at Rhamnus in Attica.
3 invited me] Cf Epp 577, 1025 n4.
4 Mountjoy] See Ep 1028 n2.
5 deaf ears] Cf *Adagia* I iv 87.

1033
1 present] See Epp 986:40–8; 999:333–5, 1038:7–14.
2 earthenware] Erasmus uses the term 'Samian,' that being the commonest form of pottery in Roman times.
3 Croy] The young cardinal was continuing his studies at Louvain; cf Epp 957–9.
4 party] See Ep 1022 introduction; for Erasmus' abhorrence of drinking parties cf Epp 643:38n.
5 letter] Ep 980; see below lines 55–63 and Ep 1030 n7.
6 Reuchlin's business] See Ep 1006 introduction.
7 Cabbala and Talmud] Cf lines 147–8 and Epp 541:149–70n, 798:20–9, 1160.
8 know as little] Cf Ep 939:69n, and also Ep 933:15.
9 Peter Lombard] The twelfth-century 'Master of the Sentences,' model of scholasticism
10 prevent their publication] See Epp 904:20n, 1143.
11 Luther had written] Ep 933, answered by Ep 980
12 answerable] The Latin can also be translated :'nor am I myself on trial.' To remove the ambiguity, Erasmus substituted in the *Epistolae ad diversos* 'nor am I his judge,' a formula he also used in Ep 1041:39 and Allen Ep 1167:247.
13 prophet] Cf Isa 36:6, 42:3, quoted in Matt 12:20 and in Ep 939:121.
14 here] Cf Ep 1030 n7.
15 put in writing] In the *Sermo de poenitentia*, published in 1518; Luther w I 322. For Erasmus' analogous views and the reactions in Louvain see Allen Ep 1301:28–56.
16 Carmelite divine] In the *Epistolae ad diversos* Erasmus suppressed these two words. The Carmelite was Nicolaas Baechem of Egmond; he is identified in a repetition of this passage in Wilhelm Nesen's biting *Epistola de magistris nostris Lovaniensibus*, published in 1520 (repr in de Vocht CTL I 591). Baechem was not amused; see Allen Ep 1153:41–3.
17 Bernard and Augustine] Both St Augustine and St Bernard of Clairvaux are often mentioned with approval in Luther's Latin writings of this period (cf Ep 939:105n) and are quoted by him in the *Sermo de poenitentia*; see above n15.

18 largely mine] Cf the preface and below lines 224–31.

19 Augustine] Erasmus repeats this point at length in the *Supputatio* (LB IX 582D–E). His basis is Augustine's Ep 185 (CSEL 57:1–44).

20 and ... doubts] Omitted in the *Epistolae ad diversos*

21 Apostolic see ... universities] In his hearing before Cardinal Cajetanus on 14 October 1518 Luther had presented a written statement, subsequently printed, in which he promised to submit himself to the judgment of the church and, more specifically, the universities of Basel, Freiburg, Louvain, and Paris; see Luther W II 9; *Briefwechsel* I Ep 110:189–92; cf above Ep 1020 n9.

22 Jewish ceremonial] Cf above n7.

23 articles] See Ep 1030 n7.

24 three Dominicans] The reference to Alvarus is probably to the Franciscan Álvar Pelayo (d 1349) who had defended the powers of popes and cardinals in his work *De planctu ecclesiae*, recently published in Lyon and also considered for publication by Froben (cf Ep 575:37n). For Silvester Prierias, and Cajetanus, cardinal of San Sisto, see Ep 1006 n21. The three names are repeated in Nesen's *Epistola de magistris nostris Lovaniensibus*; see above n16 and de Vocht CTL I 587, 595.

25 Thomas] Luther made light of Thomas Aquinas in his hearing before Cajetanus; cf above n21.

26 confession] Cf above n15.

27 Virgil] *Georgics* 1.514

28 the ancient censors] It was their particular duty to revise the roll of senators and remove those whose conduct they judged to be unworthy.

29 Dominicans and Carmelites] For Erasmus' feuds with members of these orders cf CWE 5–8 indexes.

30 in the same parcel] Cf above lines 107–9 and n18.

31 Alvarus ... Prierias] Cf above n24.

32 Thomas] Aquinas; cf Allen Ep 1126:262n.

33 extreme penalty] Cf above n19 and *Supputatio*, LB IX 580F. The earliest imperial laws prescribing the death penalty for heretics date from the end of the fourth century.

34 those who mind] Inquisitors such as Jacob of Hoogstraten who had just accused Luther before the Louvain faculty; cf Ep 1030 n7.

35 Savoronella] Girolamo Savonarola of Ferrara (1452–98) was the prior of the Dominican house of San Marco, Florence, and a relentless critic of immorality at home and corruption at the papal court. He presented his prophetic visions in powerful sermons and for a time commanded great influence. When it waned he was convicted of heresy at the instigation of Pope Alexander VI and executed, together with two fellow Dominicans. While the German reformers were to see in him a victim of papal despotism, it is worth noting that he is presented here as an example of greed and fanaticism comparable to the scandalous friars of Bern.

36 outrage at Bern] Erasmus refers to the widely discussed affair of Johann Jetzer, a tailor and a novice in the Dominican house at Bern, 1507–9. Jetzer, claimed that in a series of apparitions the Virgin Mary had confirmed that the Dominicans were right in opposing the Franciscan tenet of her immaculate conception. When it was discovered that the apparitions and Jetzer's stigmata

were faked, the authorities concluded, incorrectly perhaps, that he had
been manipulated by the friars and executed four of them, including the prior,
whereas Jetzer was let off lightly. The Franciscan Thomas Murner (cf Ep
1397) exploited the scandal in two widely-read pamphlets; see Richard Feller
Geschichte Berns (Bern 1946–60) II 99–106.

37 Reuchlin's case] See Ep 1006 n17.
38 universities] Cf n21 above; also Ep 1020 n9.
39 *Methodus*] An enlarged edition of the *Ratio verae theologiae* was published by
   Johann Froben at Basel in February 1520. It was Froben's first edition to
   contain Ep 745 to Albert; cf BRE Epp 147, 153.

1037

1 after a whole year] Despite Erasmus' impulsive denials, which sparked a great
   deal of animated debate between the two protagonists (cf Epp 1053:2ff,
   1061:616ff, *Apologia invectivis Lei: Opuscula* 251–9), it is clear that Erasmus had
   initially laboured to prevent the publication of Lee's critical notes. Subsequently, when he had reason to believe that several manuscript copies were
   circulating among his opponents, he began to urge publication. The
   change in his stance cannot well have occurred before the end of October
   1518, when Jan Briart abandoned his efforts at arbitration (cf Ep 998 introduction). Lee's own account of the events leaves no doubt that by the time he
   was approaching the two Antwerp printers in the spring of 1519, Erasmus
   no longer aimed for the suppression of Lee's notes but rather for a delayed
   publication that would permit him to upstage Lee, as he had done on
   earlier occasions, by first issuing Ep 1053 and possibly other rejoinders (cf Ep
   1061:644–7, 735–47). This letter and also the close connections between the
   Paris publisher Konrad Resch (cf Ep 1083 n1) and the Basel press of Johann
   Froben, who was Erasmus' principal publisher, support the assumption
   that Lee's book was finally published with Erasmus' knowledge and consent.

1038

1 fog] Cf Ep 1016 n2.
2 physician] He may be the unidentified physician by the name of Master Adam
   who accompanied Erard on his travels in 1514–15 and is repeatedly mentioned by Girolamo Aleandro; see J. Hoyoux *Le carnet de voyage de Jérôme
   Aléandre en France et en Liège (1510–1516)* (Brussels 1969).
3 at close quarters] See Ep 1001 n15.
4 cup] See Epp 986:40–2, 1033:5–28.
5 common pottery] Cf Ep 1033 n2.
6 princes of Bergen] No doubt Jan, who was councillor to the regent, Margaret
   of Austria (cf Epp 1025 introduction; 1040:7–8) and probably Antoon, the abbot
   of St Bertin, of whose sympathies Erasmus could not be so sure; see Ep 739.
7 Hoogstraten] Antoine de Lalaing, count of Hoogstraten (1480–1540) was one
   of the most influential advisors to the regent and in 1522 was made governor of Holland and Zeeland.
8 made it up] On Erasmus' peace with the Louvain theologians see Ep 1022
   introduction.
9 one individual] Jan Briart of Ath; see Ep 1029 n2.

1039

1 brief answer] It turned out to be longer than Šlechta's letter.

2 reading my works] Cf Ep 1021:48–55.

3 brigandage] Cf Ep 1021:62–77.

4 the Swiss] From the origins of the Swiss confederacy security and maintenance of roads, such as the one across the Gotthard pass, were a major
economic concern, as witnessed by the 'Pfaffenbrief' of 1370. On 23 April 1523
the Strasbourg council recommended that for their safety and comfort a
diplomatic mission should travel on Swiss roads rather than on an alternative
route through Hapsburg territory; see *Handbuch der Schweizer Geschichte* ed
H. Helbling et al (Zürich 1972–   ) I 270, 400; cf Ep 1001 n24.

5 Charles] Cf Ep 1009:35–42.

6 divisions of faith] Cf Ep 1021:97–103.

7 Epicurus] Cf Ep 958:13–15.

8 Plato] See Ep 999 n41.

9 Pythagoras] See Diogenes Laertius 8.19.24, 34.

10 a nation] The Massagetae, according to Herodotus 1.216

11 St Augustine] *De haeresibus* 40 (CC 46:307), referring to a sect called Apostolici

12 to Judas] The Cainites, an early Gnostic sect; cf Irenaeus *Adversus haereses*
1.31.1 (PG 7:704).

13 Some chanted] Cf Augustine *De haeresibus* 57 (CC 46:326), referring to the
Euchitae.

14 three sects] Cf Ep 1021:103–85.

15 artificer] Cf below lines 210–34.

16 James] His Epistle, especially chapter 2, is noticeable for its emphasis on acts
of charity and honesty. Luther disliked it as it seemed to rate good works
above faith.

17 you mention first] The Catholic church, headed by the pope

18 Holy See] Cf below lines 211–27, where, however, the temporal power is
associated with the ecclesiastical one in their joint responsibility for peace
and justice. For a similar definition of the functions of the pope and the
prelates see Ep 288:91–7.

19 will not answer] Cf below line 128–30.

20 the apostle] 1 Pet 2:18

21 Eugenius] Cf Ep 1021 n18.

22 Pyghards] Cf Ep 1021:186–237.

23 Augustine's opinion] See eg *In Iohannis evangelium tractatus* (CC 36:53–6; cf PL
43:823).

24 St Nicholas] Pope Nicholas I (858–67). Erasmus' information was derived,
originally, from the *Liber pontificalis*; see PL 28:1357–8 (Nicholas' biography
is probably by Anastasius Bibliothecarius).

25 Ambrose] The appointment of Ambrose to the see of Milan with popular
support is further explained in Allen Ep 1855:75–83.

26 Milanese] The Milanese or Ambrosian rite of celebrating the liturgy continues
to be used in the archdiocese of Milan.

27 Jerome's generation] In his Ep 109 Jerome defends the cult of relics and
martyrs against a radical rejecter, but at the same time he emphasizes that the
veneration due to men must differ substantially from the adoration due to God.

28 laments of neighbouring regions] From the early fifteenth century the
grievances of the German nation against the Roman church had often been
voiced at diets and in tracts.

29 ten categories] A system of ten basic entities or classes such as quantity,
quality, place, and time, had been proposed by Aristotle in his *Categories*
and was adopted by the scholastics.

30 abstain from tyranny] Cf above lines 39–41, 117–24, 138–44 and Ep 872:20n.

31 Jonas] He was in fact elected rector for the summer term of 1519 while he was
visiting Erasmus; see Ep 963:6n and E. Kleineidam *Universitas studii Erffor-
densis* (Leipzig 1964–81) II 240.

1040

1 his suggestion] Possibly Edward Lee is intended.

2 in Brussels] This seems to suggest a personal visit, perhaps in early September
(cf Ep 999 introduction), or perhaps in late October when Erasmus intended
to go to Brussels; see Ep 1038.

3 Hoogstraten] He had been in Louvain from early October, if not earlier (cf Ep
1030 n7) and quite possibly had also gone to Brussels to promote his
causes.

4 I having published it] Ep 980 to Luther appeared in the *Farrago* of October
1519 and also in a separate printing by Michaël Hillen at Antwerp (cf Epp
1033 introduction, 1041 n7). The precise date of Hillen's edition cannot be
determined, but in view of his close relations with Erasmus in this period
(cf Ep 1061:679–741) it does not seem likely that it was undertaken against the
author's wishes.

5 He] Perhaps the person referred to in line 2, or possibly Hoogstraten

6 Bergen] See Ep 1038 n6.

7 heads together] Hoogstraten here appears in the company of Erasmus' old
adversaries Jean Briselot and Nicolaas Baechem (Egmondanus). The suffragan
bishop of Cambrai in succession to Briselot was another Carmelite, Adriaan
Aernout (or Arnoldi, d 1536). As a monk of the monastery of Bruges, he had
been sent in 1504 to Louvain for study and received a BA in theology there
in 1507.

8 new *Colloquia*] See Ep 1041.

1041

1 another point] In addition to those mentioned in Ep 909, the preface reprinted
in Marten's new edition of the *Familiarum colloquiorum formulae*; see the
introduction.

2 letters] A first collection of such letters had been published in 1514; enlarged
by a second book, it had been recently reissued as *Illustrium virorum epistolae ... ad Ioannem Reuchlin* (Haguenau: T. Anshelm May 1519). Among the new
letters were five from Erasmus – the only five prior to 1519 that are known
today – none of which had been published by Erasmus himself. The latest of
the five, Ep 713, was a particular source of embarrassment to him; cf Epp
300, 713 introductions.

3 'not ... Christian ape'] See Ep 713:4–5, where the Latin text has 'non chris-
tianus sed christianistes' in both of Allen's sources, whereas here Erasmus

writes 'christianista'; the meaning, however, is the same. It cannot now be ascertained whether he had used any such expression in the letter actually sent to Reuchlin, but it is reasonable to assume that he had and now could not, or would not, remember.

4 headings] On the title-page of the 1519 collection (cf above n2) occurs a reference to the 'army of Reuchlinists' to be listed on the next page, and that list is headed by the statement which Erasmus here paraphrases.

5 ordinary friendship] Cf Ep 967:80–3.

6 for the supreme judge] Cf Ep 1006 n18.

7 Liège was added] When Ep 980 was published in Leipzig a reference to Bishop Erard de la Marck was added to a statement about great men favouring Luther, or so Erasmus claims here. Presumably it would have been more to the point to say that this reference was deleted when Erasmus released the text of Ep 980 for publication in the *Farrago* at Basel (cf Epp 980, 1038 introductions). Whatever the bishop's private opinion on Luther, he was certainly unsympathetic to many of Luther's prominent opponents; for his litigation with the University of Louvain and his widely noted attack on the Roman curia during the diet of Augsburg in 1518 see Harsin *Erard de la Marck* 230ff, 241ff.

8 I know not who] Beatus Rhenanus, who had earlier edited Erasmus' correspondence for Froben (cf Ep 886:57n), was absent from Basel when the *Farrago* was being printed (cf Ep 1014). The text here is bound to create the impression that he was not responsible for the *Farrago* and the inclusion of Ep 980; but evidently he was and followed Erasmus' instructions; see Epp 1009 introduction, 1040:4–5; cf also Allen Ep 1143:47–8.

9 letter] Dated from Leipzig, 24 July 1519, it asks for Hoogstraten's assistance against Luther in the wake of the Leipzig disputation. A printed copy, *Epistola ... missa ex Lipsia ad Iacobum Hoogstratensem* [J. Rhau: Wittenberg 1519] (British Library 3906 f 52), mentions on the title page that it was proudly passed around by Hoogstraten and copied by other Dominicans. If critical remarks were suppressed, they most likely concerned the elector Frederick the Wise; see Boehmer *Luther* 291.

10 Brussels] Cf Epp 1038, 1040.

11 Cyprian ... Tertullian] Cf Ep 1000:165–70.

12 Lactantius ... Origen] Cf Epp 337:589–90, 843:435–8, 844:272–4. On views expressed by Cyprian, Lactantius, and Origen that were later judged heretical see Jerome Ep 82.2 (CSEL 55:121–2) and *De viris illustribus* 53 (PL 23:698).

13 especially assigned] Erasmus probably thought of Silvester Prierias, Cardinal Cajetanus, Karl von Miltitz (cf Ep 1188), and perhaps even the universities (cf Epp 1020 n9, 1033 n21), as opposed to such self-appointed critics as Eck and Hoogstraten.

14 smoking flax] Cf Ep 1033:76–7.

15 letter] Ep 980; cf Epp 1030 n7, 1033:28, 1042:13–14.

16 his last letter] It followed the exchange of Epp 939, 980 and is missing today. Erasmus answered it with Ep 1127A.

1042

1 peace] See Ep 1022 introduction.

2 two letters] The following lines suggest that they may have connected Erasmus with Luther. The reference was perhaps to Hillen's edition of Epp 1033 and 980 (cf Ep 1033 introduction), or to one of the other pamphlets combining Ep 980 with Ep 948 or Ep 1033; cf Epp 980 introduction; 1030 n7.

1043

1 saying] Cf *Adagia* I i 49.

1044

1 these people] Cf Epp 1022 introduction, 1040.
2 oration] See introduction. This introductory lecture had been given by Dorp in 1516 (cf Ep 438). At the time of its publication a dedicatory preface to Beatus Rhenanus was added; see BRE Ep 126; cf BRE Ep 143.
3 Nicholaas] Nicolaas Everaerts; see Ep 1092.
4 lecture rooms] Dorp gave an oration on the teaching of Christ's life before the Council of Holland; cf de Vocht MHL 218.
5 Assendelft] Probably Gerrit, heer van Assendelft and Heemskerk (1488–1558); cf Ep 1166 introduction. He matriculated at Orléans in 1505 and probably succeeded his father as a member of the Council of Holland, succeeding Everaerts (cf above n3) as its president in 1528. Erasmus was still connected with him in 1533; see Ep 2819; de Vocht MHL 95–8; NNBW. As an alternative, Hugo van Assendelft, canon of The Hague and ecclesiastical member of the Council of Holland could be intended.
6 warden] Probably Jan Bijl; cf Ep 749 introduction; de Vocht MHL 224.
7 Amandus] Amandus of Zierikzee, who died in 1524 or 1534 as a Franciscan Observant at Louvain. His uncommon learning is confirmed by the editor of his *Chronica mundi* (Antwerp 1534); see NNBW.
8 never mind who etc] It seems that the editor here suppressed some specific and evidently critical references.
9 'better turn ... ill-judged'] A line from a Greek comedy, quoted by Lucian, *Lucius or the Ass* 18, here given in Latin; cf Ep 659:23–4.
10 mention me] Erasmus certainly did. His short letter to Beatus Rhenanus (Ep 1063) may well be an example of others now missing. He also wrote to Oecolampadius (Ep 1064) and to Hutten. Beatus Rhenanus had already been approached by Dorp directly (BRE Ep 121). Bonifacius Amerbach sent Dorp's *Oratio* to Udalricus Zasius (cf AK II Ep 715) and also reassured Dorp in Zasius' name (cf Ep 1084:26–9; AK II Epp 731, 787). Dorp also received messages from Thomas More (Rogers Ep 82), Hutten (cf AK II Ep 738), Botzheim (cf Ep 1103), Paul Volz, Zwingli, Joachim Vadianus, Osvaldus Myconius, and no doubt others still; see de Vocht MHL 230–4; 376–84.
11 letters] Epp 304, 337, and 438 were already published; Epp 536 and 852 had recently been included in the *Farrago* (cf Ep 1009 introduction), which Dorp had not seen as yet.
12 abbot] Meynard Man; cf Ep 304:178n.
13 My father] Bartholomeus (Mees) Hendrikszoon van Dorp served abbot Meynard Man as steward of Egmond (cf above n12). He was a prosperous citizen and from 1510 an alderman of The Hague; see de Vocht MHL 293–5.
14 Arras] At Louvain; cf Ep 177 introduction.

15 Mauritszoon] An old acquaintance (cf Ep 176) who was appointed to the Council of Holland in 1514

16 Luther] The beginning of this letter may suggest that Dorp had now heard about the recent condemnation of Luther by the Louvain theologians (cf Ep 1030 n7). It seems that Froben's edition of Dorp's *Oratio*, with this letter appended, was sent to Luther from Antwerp and was welcomed as an expression of disapproval of the Louvain censure (see de Vocht MHL 234–8). Dorp's earlier letter to Erasmus is missing.

17 a man] Perhaps Cornelis Hoen, a lawyer attached to the Council of Holland (cf Ep 1358) and a friend who had gone to school with Dorp at Utrecht. Some time before 1521, Hoen wrote a much-noted letter rejecting transubstantiation.

18 Neve] Jan de Neve, regent of the College of the Lily; for past disagreements with Dorp see Ep 696 introduction.

19 Berselius and Rescius] Paschasius Berselius and Rutgerus Rescius; see Epp 674, 546.

20 Koolman] A Louvain MA in 1510, Jan Koolman was a secular priest and from c 1516 to his death in 1538 confessor of the nuns of St Agatha's in Delft. See de Vocht MHL 375.

1045

1 volume] The *Farrago* containing Ep 620, which must have reached Paris in December 1519; see Ep 1009 introduction.

2 your name] Brie plays on the meaning of 'Erasmus,' which is 'lovable,' and of 'Germanus,' which is 'brother.'

3 More] The name is spelled 'Mωrus' throughout this letter, suggesting the Greek word for 'fool,' as does the title of Erasmus' *Moria*.

4 Homer] *Odyssey* 9.506–35

5 *Apologia* against Lefèvre] See Ep 597:37n.

6 Isle of Never-never] Attempting to improve on More's use of Greek, Brie here put 'Udepotia' in preference to 'Utopia'; the meaning is the same. The alternative form of 'Udepotia' had earlier been suggested by Guillaume Budé; see Allen's note.

7 *pater patratus*] Brie uses the title of the chief of the board of *fetiales*, who had authority to sign treaties in the name of the Roman republic.

8 Patroclus] See Homer *Iliad* 16. Is the reference to Achilles intended to suggest Erasmus?

9 invitation] Cf Ep 994 n4.

10 Venice ... Padua] See Ep 212.

11 Maecenas ... Lucullan palaces] Lucius Licinius Lucullus (117–56 BC) and Gaius Maecenas (c 70–8 BC) both owned splendid palaces. They were also famous as patrons of literature and the arts. For Erasmus' well-known love of gardens cf eg the colloquy *Convivium religiosum* (1522; ASD I-3 231–66) and Allen Epp 1756:44, 2147:21–9. Perhaps Brie was thinking of Budé's two country houses 'in the Lucullan style'; see Epp 435:146–9, 480:165, 568: 14–15.

12 Homer] *Iliad* 1.602–4

13 my other letter] Ep 569, also published in Froben's *Farrago*

14 roses and wildflowers] Cf *Adagia* II vi 41.

1046

1 Paul] Cf Eph 3:1, 4:1, 2 Tim 1:8; Philem 1:9.

2 Rutgerus] Rutgerus Rescius, professor of Greek from September 1518; cf Ep 691:19n.

3 Bartholomeus] Bartholomeus van Vessem or Wessem (d 1539), had been Jérôme de Busleyden's chamberlain and trusted assistant and was among the executors of his will. Busleyden had secured for him a canonry at Aire. After his master's death he received, apparently through Robbyns, another canonry at St Rombaut's in Mechelen and moved to Louvain, where he supervised the construction of the new college building and other practical arrangements; see de Vocht CTL I 52–5, 471, 473.

4 salary] It was apparently paid half-yearly. The rate here stipulated by Erasmus, 18 florins or gulden or livres d'Artois (identical, silver-based moneys-of-account worth 40d gros; cf CWE 1 323, 347) was the sum actually paid to Rescius until August 1519. From 1 September his salary was raised to 48 florins (= £8 gros Flemish, or about £5 10s sterling) annually; see Ep 836:8n; de Vocht CTL I 294, 474.

5 Latin professor] Adrianus Cornelii Barlandus had recently resigned the Latin chair. In his place the trustees appointed Conradus Goclenius (cf Ep 1018:14) as of 1 December 1519. Erasmus had apparently supported another candidate, paying personally for his travel expenses between Germany and Louvain before he was reimbursed by the Trilingue. This candidate was probably Hermannus Buschius; see Epp 884, 1050–1, 1083 introductions; de Vocht CTL I 482.

6 Hebrew chair] The first professor of Hebrew, Matthaeus Adrianus (cf Ep 686:7n) had left abruptly by the end of July 1519, and was now negotiating for a position at Wittenberg, presenting himself as a victim of the Louvain theologians (cf de Vocht CTL I 371–5; Luther w *Briefwechsel* I Epp 217–18). He was succeeded on 1 August by Robert Wakefield, a young Cambridge scholar (cf Ep 674:30n) who resigned after four months and recommended as a successor his countryman Robert Shirwood of Coventry, who was apparently not well qualified and left after one month at the end of December, perhaps not having been appointed after a probationary term; see de Vocht CTL I 379–86, 500–1.

1047

1 seven months] This reply did not travel much faster; cf Allen Ep 1137:2–3.

2 phrase] Cf *Adagia* II ix 54.

3 my own skin] Cf *Adagia* I vi 92.

4 timepieces] On the beginnings of glass manufacture in Bohemia see J. Blau *Die Glasmacher im Böhmer-und Bayerwald* (Regensburg 1954–6); K. Hetteš *Glass in Czechoslovakia* (Prague 1958). On 18 October 1509 Bishop Thurzo issued a detailed charter to one Hans Fleissig for the establishment of a glass hut at Jungferndorf, Reichenstein; see E. von Czihak *Schlesische Gläser* (Wrocław 1891) 22–4; cf G. Agricola *Ausgewählte Werke* VIII 713–23.

5 within the jurisdiction] Within the episcopal territory of Neisse (Nysa, Poland) there were important gold mines at Reichenstein (Złoty Stok, Poland), Freiwaldau (Jeseník, Czechoslovakia), and elsewhere. The bishops of

Wrocław frequently resided at Neisse. While Reichenstein and Freiwaldau received charters as 'free mining towns' in 1491 and 1506 respectively, the mines were exploited primarily by the Fugger-Thurzo company. About 1513 Bishop Thurzo obtained from the emperor Maximilian I the privilege of striking gold coins. Hungarian ducats and Rhenish florins were minted at Reichenstein; see W.C. Hazlitt *The Coinage of the European Continent* (London 1893–7) 343, supplement 20; and references in G. Agricola's *Bermannus: Ausgewählte Werke* II 74, 102, 365–6. G. von Pölnitz *Anton Fugger* (Tübingen 1958–) I 371.

6 told you before] See Ep 850:48–52.

1048
1 Hebrew Old Testament] Probably the *Biblia rabbinica* (Venice: D. Bomberg 1518); cf Ep 456:103n.
2 what would you like done] Perhaps with a sum of money held in trust by Erasmus for book purchases; see Epp 934, 955.

1049
1 Hagius] Jan Fage (Fagie, Faets) of Kortenberg near Louvain who had made his profession as an Austin canon in 1491 and died in 1526; see de Vocht MHL 561–2.
2 son in years] Jerome's greeting to Augustine (Ep 105.5.2), already used by Erasmus in Ep 807.

1050
1 close their ranks] Cf *Adagia* I i 11; Ep 1046 introduction.

1051
1 executors] The executors of the will of Jérôme de Busleyden continued to act as trustees for the Collegium Trilingue, which was founded with his bequest. They were Adriaan Josel, Bartholomeus van Vessem (cf Ep 1046 n3), Nikolaas van Nispen, and Antoon Sucket (cf Ep 1331); see de Vocht CTL I 49–59.
2 twelve livres] Cf Ep 1046 n4.
3 abbot] Henry de Vocht suggested Meynard Man, abbot of Egmond, a relation of Alaard's (cf Ep 676:40) and normally sympathetic to Erasmus and the new learning; cf Ep 1044:61–3.

1052
1 Chrysostom] There was an edition of his complete works in Latin (Basel: J. Froben 1517; cf Ep 575:39n). For the Hebrew book cf Ep 1048:9.
2 Hagius] See Ep 1049 n1.
3 pamphlet ... slanderous] The Latin expression is 'libellus famosus'. Erasmus implies that the author could not be charged under Roman law (cf Ep 1053 n62) since he was a cleric.

1053
1 friend] Probably John Fisher; cf *Apologia invectivis Lei* (*Opuscula* 258–9).

2 threats] Cf Epp 998 n14, 1037 n1.
3 proverbial] Cf *Adagia* II x 19.
4 defective] Cf Horace *Epodes* 12.3.
5 'Sweet is ... turned.'] Cf *Adagia* IV iv 92, quoting Plutarch *Amatorius* 5 (752A).
6 old saying] Cf *Adagia* III vi 41.
7 Quintilian] 4.2.93
8 Dominicans or Carmelites] For Erasmus' misgivings cf indexes to CWE 5–8.
9 this business] The task of examining Erasmus' works with a view to finding theological errors; cf the preface.
10 licentiates] Cf Ep 946:4.
11 satirist] Juvenal 1.79
12 the last time we met] Lee and Erasmus seem to have met repeatedly in the spring of 1519. In March they agreed that Lee should send his notes to Bishop John Fisher (cf Ep 1061:800–1), and Fisher's reaction led in early April to peace overtures (cf Ep 936:99–103). At about the same time, between Lee's approaches to the Antwerp printers Thibault and Hillen respectively (cf below n19 and Ep 1061 n71, n75) they met at the church of St Peter's (cf Ep 1061:668–9 and below n14). Another contact took place in July (cf Ep 1061:802). Perhaps this is the meeting here mentioned, as by that time the second edition of Erasmus' New Testament would have been available to Lee for a number of weeks; cf Epp 955 introduction, 1061: 793–7.
13 always said the same thing] Cf Ep 1037 n1.
14 first meeting] St Peter's church was an obvious place for Lee and Erasmus to meet either by chance or on purpose (cf Ep 1061:215, 668–9). The meeting here mentioned must have taken place in c October 1518 and ended in an agreement to submit the issue to the arbitration of Jan Briart Atensis; cf Epp 998 introduction, 1061:769–72; *Apologia invectivis Lei* (*Opuscula* 245–9).
15 not yet published] The colophon date of the *Annotationes* is 23 August 1518, but the volume was not released until the text of the New Testament was ready in the following March; cf Ep 864 introduction.
16 read solely] Not quite; see below lines 124–5 and Ep 1026 n3.
17 at my own expense] Cf Ep 1037 n1.
18 Dirk of Aalst] Dirk Martens, the Louvain printer and friend of Erasmus
19 two printers in Antwerp] Michaël Hillen and probably the Frenchman Jean Thibault, according to Lee were the only ones to own Greek type. Both had recently worked for Erasmus (cf Epp 934, 1043 introductions). For Lee's version of these events see Ep 1061:126ff, 620ff; cf *Apologia invectivis Lei* (*Opuscula* 252–3).
20 Cologne] In Ep 1074:92 and in the *Apologia invectivis Lei* (*Opuscula* 257–8) Erasmus specifies Bonn rather than Cologne and alleges that the rumour was planted by Lee and his friends. For Lee's denial cf Ep 1061:786–7. One of the two friends Erasmus approached was probably Neuenahr; cf Ep 1078 introduction.
21 Wilfred] Very little is known about Lee's family except that his parents maintained friendly relations with those of More (cf below lines 393–5 and Ep 1097:10; More's long letter to Lee in Rogers Ep 75:102–4, 114–17). The presence in Louvain of one of Edward's brothers, Wilfred, is frequently mentioned at this time. It appears that he conveyed messages between Erasmus

and his brother, who were no longer on speaking terms, and generally attempted to mediate. Thus Wilfred is probably the brother remembered by Erasmus with friendship and gratitude in 1533 (cf Ep 2780). Wilfred was connected with Thomas Lupset, Thomas Paynell, and Thomas More; cf Froben's *Epistolae aliquot eruditorum virorum* 78–9 (below Ep 1083 introduction); Rogers Ep 75:1–3.

22 Michaël] Michaël Hillen (c 1476–1558) of Hoogstraten became a citizen of Antwerp in 1508–9. NK lists a first book with his imprint from 1506. In 1546 he handed his business over to his son-in-law, Jan Steels; cf above n19.

23 threats] The following paragraph is among Erasmus' shrewdest; cf Ep 998 introduction.

24 cudgel] Cf Epp 999:337, 1055.

25 to warn Lee] With Ep 998:80–1

26 defamatory libel] See below n62.

27 letter] Ep 998; it may be doubted, however, whether Lee thought he was being encouraged to publish his book; cf Ep 1061:3–4, 126ff.

28 his friends] Cf Ep 1026 n3.

29 intercepting] Cf Ep 998 n3.

30 youthful fire] Cf Ep 993 n3.

31 Erostratus] He sought and achieved immortality by burning the temple of Diana at Ephesus.

32 Horace's phrase] *Satires* 2.3.321; cf *Adagia* I ii 9.

33 Gratius] He had assisted Pfefferkorn in his attacks on Reuchlin and edited a rejoinder to the *Epistolae obscurorum virorum*; cf Epp 622, 1006:81.

34 Pindar's saying] *Pythian Odes* 2.115–21

35 proverb] Cf *Adagia* II ii 91.

36 Hesiod] *Works and Days* 289–91

37 Lucian's fluteplayer] Cf Lucian *Harmonides* 2 (853).

38 flying steed] Cf *Adagia* I ii 46.

39 'with swelling breath … fill'] Cf Horace *Satires* 2.5.98.

40 stated this myself] In the preliminary material to the New Testament of 1516 (cf below lines 274–5; Ep 809:70n). In the revised edition, 1518–19, a similar wish that others might carry on was expressed in the *Capita argumentorum*; cf LB VI f ***3 recto.

41 newly started] Cf Ep 998 n5.

42 in the Old] Cf Ep 1061 n101.

43 Pope Leo] Cf Ep 864.

44 *Apologia*] Cf above n40; LB VI f **2–3.

45 personally invite Lee] See Ep 765 introduction.

46 the man] Presumably Jan Briart of Ath; cf Epp 998:5–6, 1029 n2.

47 star] Cf Ep 1060:10–11.

48 Momus] The chronic fault-finder of classical literature; cf *Adagia* I v 74.

49 men] See Ep 1061 n103.

50 far away] At Basel to edit the revised New Testament; cf Ep 843 introduction.

51 scratched that sore] Cf *Adagia* I vi 79.

52 cauldrons of Dodona] Cf Ep 1030 n6.

53 I was dead] Cf Epp 867, 1008 introduction, 1061:887–96.

54 Thomas More access] Lee insisted that More had seen his notes (cf Ep 1061:72,

919). More confirmed that Lee had invited him to peruse the copy sent to
John Fisher and that he received, albeit not from Fisher, some notes, but of
these he was highly critical (cf Rogers Ep 75). More's name is not given in
the early editions of this letter; it was inserted, however, in the *Opus
epistolarum* of 1529.

55 Aesop's crow] Borrowing the peacock's feathers, cf *Adagia* i iv 6.
56 many men] Cf Epp 998:71–80, 1083 introduction.
57 blackened] See Ep 1007 n10. Lee protested this claim with good reason (cf Ep
   1061:362–440, 505–15). For additional departures from Erasmus' norm cf
   Epp 1074, 1083, 1195.
58 defamatory libel] Cf below n62.
59 Midas] Cf Ep 999 n47.
60 serpent] Cf Gen 3.
61 evangelical characters] Cf above lines 34–40; Ep 998:69–71.
62 Defamatory libel] For some time (cf Ep 785:41–5) Erasmus had been very concerned about the effects of libellous allegations frequently made in anonymous printed pamphlets, and about slander and innuendo (cf above lines
   423–35), which were even harder to answer than printed pamphlets. He
   believed that scholars in particular – Reuchlin, for example (cf Epp 694:81–
   107, 700:43–5, 701:34–5, 703:17–18) – needed and deserved to be protected
   by the authorities. He appealed to the pope for remedial legislation and raised
   the matter with a papal legate (cf Epp 858:454–60, 908, 936:34–8, 993:1–16,
   1007, 1052, 1062). Defamatory libel is a capital charge according to the *Codex
   Iustinianus* (9.36.2; cf 9.46.5–10; *Institutiones* 47.10.5; Tacitus *Annals* 1.72).
   The need for proper legislation was repeated in the *Lingua* of 1525 (ASD IV-1
   288, 328), but Erasmus himself had, in the short run at least, some difficulty
   in complying with the ethical norms he attempted to enunciate; see above n57
   and P.G. Bietenholz 'Ethics and Early Printing: Erasmus' Rules for the
   Proper Conduct of Authors' *The Humanities Association Review* 26 (1975) 180–
   95.
63 several emperors] For an example, cf Suetonius *Augustus* 55.
64 method of denial] Erasmus uses a rhetorical term (*status infitialis*); cf Quintilian
   3.6.15, 32.
65 excused by necessity] Erasmus was later attacked for this statement and had to
   explain himself more fully; see Allen Ep 1126:273–93.
66 Aeneas] Turnus, king of the Rutilians, had killed young Pallas, the son of
   Aeneas' friend Evander. When Aeneas defeated Turnus, the sight of Pallas'
   belt on his shoulder so incensed Aeneas that he killed him; see Virgil *Aeneid*
   12.939–52.
67 Alecto] One of the three Furies. Erasmus is suggesting that the recent pros-
   pects of enduring international peace (cf Ep 1007 n14) had turned them in a
   new direction.
68 the Gospel speaks] Cf Matt 6:22–3; Luke 11:34.
69 paraphrases] Cf Ep 1043 introduction.
70 myself and the Muses] Cf *Adagia* iii v 80.
71 Colet] Cf Epp 1023 n5; 1025 introduction.
72 without a fee] The point is repeated in Allen Ep 1211:282, 344. Erasmus had
   done likewise at Cambridge; cf Ep 296:141–3.

1054

1 a work] The *Collectanea antiquitatum in urbe atque agro Moguntino repertarum*, collected by Dietrich Gresemund and edited by Johann Huttich (Mainz: J. Schöffer 1520). This work contains (f c) an annotated sketch of the Eigelstein or Eichelstein outside Mainz, erected as a memorial for Nero Claudius Drusus, the Roman commander in Germany, after his death in 9 BC; see Pauly's *Realencyclopädie der classischen Altertumswissenschaft* new ed by G. Wissowa (Stuttgart 1893–) sv 'Mogontiacum.' Erasmus had given some assistance to the press of Johann Schöffer earlier in the year; see Ep 919.

2 Nicolaas] Nicolaas van Broeckhoven of 's Hertogenbosch; cf Epp 616:15n, 1061 n74.

1056

1 two of yours] Not known to exist

2 taverns] Cf Ep 1053:430.

3 friendly with Lee] Cf Ep 1019.

4 read the Fathers] For similar advice frequently given to Lips see Epp 750:4–5, 46–8, 807, 843:750–2, 901:27–8, 1048–9, 1174.

5 proverbs] Following the 1517–18 edition of the *Adagia* (cf Ep 783:29n), Froben would publish another in October 1520. It contained no more than 21 additional adages and stated on the title-page: 'who buys this new edition stands to make a gain; who is content with the preceding has nothing to lose.'

1057

1 Chancellor] Jeroen van der Noot (d 1541), chancellor of Brabant and a relative of Joost. Erasmus addressed him in Ep 1300.

2 'You're no consul … senator'] Crassus' words quoted by Cicero *De oratore* 3.1.4

3 letters] Very likely the *Farrago*; cf Epp 1009, 1056 introductions.

1059

1 Homer] Cf Homer *Iliad* 13.633–9, but cf also 19:221.

2 against my books] See the preface.

3 Atensis] Jan Briart Atensis died on 8 January 1520; cf Ep 1029 n2.

4 Elishas] Briart's eager followers; cf 1 Kings 19:19–21.

5 letters] The *Farrago* had not actually been published before 13 September, but the printer's copy had been sent off to Basel before that date; cf Ep 1009 introduction.

6 nothing to hurt] For one deletion to this effect see Ep 1041 n7; in other cases, though, identification was easy, at least for readers familiar with the Louvain scene; Epp 948:27, 998, 999:344–51; cf Ep 1053 n57.

1060

1 I had accepted] See Epp 834 introduction; 1025 n4.

2 the stars] Cf Epp 936:57–61, 1005 n1.

3 venomous the pamphlets] Cf Ep 1053 n62.

4 cabbage-patch] Cf Epp 1062:127–8, 1066:84.

5 profess poverty] The friars; cf Ep 1053:440–1.

6 all over the world] See eg Ep 1021:48–51.
7 a man] Henry Standish; cf Ep 1072 introduction.
8 Cyprian, Hilary, Jerome] These and other authorities are cited at length in the *Apologia de 'In principio erat sermo'* LB IX 115–18; cf LB VI 335–6.
9 Jerome] Ep 82.1 (CSEL 55:108)
10 Pelagius] This famous heretic (born c 354, probably in Britain and documented until 418) taught that man was born without sin and that his will was entirely free; thus divine grace and predestination, so important to Augustine, became insignificant.
11 support of liberal studies] Cf Ep 967:29n.
12 write to the pope] For other approaches to Leo x and other expressions of the same concern see Epp 1007, 1053 n62, 1062.
13 St Paul] Cf Gal 2:7.
14 written] Ep 1007
15 paraphrases] Cf Ep 1062 introduction.
16 set your name] The latest paraphrase was about to be dedicated to Cardinal Lorenzo Campeggi with Ep 1062. When Campeggi was in England Erasmus was well aware of the rivalry between the pope's special nuncio and Cardinal Wolsey (cf Ep 964:39n) and made a practice of treating both with similar distinctions (cf Ep 961 introduction). This practice is continued here with the pledge of a dedication to Wolsey, which was to be redeemed with Ep 1112.

1061
1 letter] Ep 998, published in the *Farrago* (cf Ep 1009 introduction). The following statement may suggest that the letter actually sent to Lee had afterwards been expanded for printing.
2 second edition] of the New Testament (cf Ep 864). For Briart's arbitration cf Epp 998 introduction, 1029 n2, 1053 n14.
3 you saw them all] Erasmus had seen some annotations, at any rate at the time of his departure for Basel in May 1518; cf Epp 765, 843.
4 *Apologia*] Prefaced to Lee's *Annotationes*; cf Ep 1037 introduction.
5 two exceptions] See below n23, n24.
6 More ... Rochester] See Ep 1026 n3.
7 squared up] Cf Plautus *Asinaria* 360.
8 in writing] Erasmus admitted that while they were still on friendly terms he had received some annotations from Lee and eventually returned them with his comments added on the margin; cf Ep 1074:35–47; *Apologia invectivis Lei* (*Opuscula* 242–3, 260–2).
9 answers] See Erasmus' angry Ep 843.
10 a man] Maarten Lips, who provided Erasmus with Lee's notes answered in Ep 843; cf *Apologia invectivis Lei* (*Opuscula* 262–3) and below lines 462–9. His letter to Erasmus described here as having fallen into Lee's hands appears to be lost; but cf Ep 960 for Erasmus' alarm concerning other documents Lee had recovered from Lips.
11 second edition] The claim that Erasmus had used some of Lee's early notes (cf below lines 154–6) cannot be checked. Erasmus' counter-claim was that in preparing his notes for publication Lee had cut out much material which the revised New Testament had rendered superfluous; cf Ep 1053:51–4.

12 Pharisees] Cf Matt 23:27.

13 Ananias] Acts 23:3

14 Polycarp] See Irenaeus *Adversus haereses* 3.3,4 (PG 7:851–3).

15 Paul] Cf 1 Tim 5:20.

16 hundreds of passages] The actual phrase used by Erasmus in Ep 998:22 and here repeated is 'six hundred passages.' Lee's denial refers to the literal meaning.

17 If thy brother ... to the church.] Matt 18:15–17

18 twice been prevented] For the following cf Ep 1053:126–51 and below lines 620ff.

19 paraphrase on Timothy] Printed by Michaël Hillen at Antwerp; see Ep 1043 introduction.

20 dialogue of ... Latomus] See Ep 934 introduction; Erasmus brushed off this charge in his *Apologia invectivis Lei* (*Opuscula* 286).

21 crows' eye] Cf *Adagia* I iii 75; the sense is: to outshine the recognized masters of a discipline.

22 Rochester] John Fisher

23 Winchcombe] Richard Kidderminster (c 1462–c 1532) was from 1488 abbot of the Benedictine house of Winchcombe, Gloucestershire. He was a patron of learning and an accomplished antiquarian; see Emden BRUO.

24 Overey] Bartholomew Linsted, also called Fowle, was from 1513 prior of St Mary Overey, a convent of the Austin friars at London of which the church survives as Southwark cathedral. He died after 1553.

25 Suffenus] This bad poet, blind to his own faults, was the target of Catullus' poem 22; cf *Adagia* II v 12.

26 play] Terence *Eunuchus* 252

27 St Peter's] Cf Ep 1053 n14.

28 one of them] Johann Reuchlin; Lee appears to be careful not to give Erasmus and his German supporters any grounds for associating him with Hoogstraten and other opponents of Reuchlin; cf Ep 1006.

29 the other] Wolfgang Capito; for his Hebrew grammar cf Ep 998 n6.

30 twice] This charge is repeated in the *Apologia* prefaced to Lee's *Annotationes* f cc verso (cf Ep 1037 introduction) with reference to the *Dialogus bilinguium ac trilinguium*, where Lee is twice lampooned unmistakably among the enemies of the Muses (see above 343:335–53). While Lee's *Apologia* does not connect Erasmus with the doubtful authorship of the *Dialogus*, the latter repeats in the same context Erasmus' pun on Lee as a 'Scotist,' which Lee must have noted twice in the *Farrago* (cf Epp 843:88–9, 993:22) and which he also noted (below lines 383–5) in the *Colloquia*. In what follows here (lines 245, 252–3) Lee also protests against being labelled 'sycophanta,' a term frequently applied by Erasmus to the conservative theologians, including Lee.

31 'how scant ... home'] Persius 4.52

32 confusedly and in a hurry] When reviewing, in a letter now published, the many problems that had beset the publication of the *Novum instrumentum* of 1516 Erasmus admitted to being 'already weary and well-nigh exhausted when I came to the annotations' (Ep 421:72–3). Since then, however, he had devoted a great deal of his energy and time to the revised second edition.

33 double status] As a theologian and a monk; cf above line 117.

34 immortal glory] See above lines 195–7.
35 four times] See the four books by Erasmus mentioned below lines 375, 586–9, or perhaps the *Auctarium*, including Ep 843.
36 friends in England] See Epp 886, 936, 973, 1026, 1029–30, 1053; but Lee evidently did likewise, cf below lines 522–4.
37 say somewhere] Ep 1053:163–6; cf n62.
38 *Colloquia*] The following quotation comes from Martens' recent edition of the *Colloquia* (NK 2869; f d 2 verso; cf Ep 1041 introduction and ASD I-3 18, 113–20, where the two passages in question are not reprinted). There can be no question that Lee was intended, although in his *Apologia invectivis Lei* (*Opuscula* 289–90) Erasmus blandly asserted that none but Lee had reason to think so. Martens' edition of the *Colloquia* was never reprinted and in his next revision (Basel: J. Froben March 1522) Erasmus suppressed the whole of this passage and most of the next (lines 422–30). The two speakers are normally identified as Augustinus Vincentius Caminadus and Christian Northoff.
39 Scotist] Cf above n30.
40 sardonic laugh] Cf *Adagia* III v 1.
41 thrasonical] Thraso is the braggart soldier in Terence's *Eunuchus*.
42 tail] A medieval tradition that the English had tails lived on as a joke and was repeated at Lee's expense here, in the *Dialogus bilinguium ac trilinguium* (see above 343; cf above n30), in the tract *Hochstratus ovans* (Hutten *Operum supplementum* I 485; cf Ep 1083 introduction), in Ep 1077:6, and in BRE Ep 162. Lee's complaints about the jest are repeated elsewhere in his *Annotationes* (f CC verso). In his *Apologia invectivis Lei* (*Opuscula* 290) Erasmus claimed that some one else must have inserted it in Martens' *Colloquia*. Literature on this curious medieval tradition is cited in Allen IV 168 and de Vocht CTL I 566–7.
43 scrap of difference] Cf Ep 1007 n10.
44 like this] The quotation is again taken from Marten's *Colloquia* and was for the most part removed in the subsequent revision; cf above n38.
45 rapscalleon] The Latin term 'ardelio' has been changed to 'ardeleo' (busybody, rapscallion) so as to reflect Lee's name and provide an easy clue to the identity of the man who is insulted here; cf below lines 477–8.
46 Christ] John 8:49
47 Paul ... path] Gal 2:11 (Peter being called Cephas)
48 someone I know] Evidently Lips; cf above n10.
49 to prove this] According to both Roman Law and English common law practice the proof of truth was admissible in actions of libel or slander used against a private person; see P.F. Carter-Ruck *Libel and Slander* (London 1972) 34–43; *Corpus iuris civilis, Institutiones* 47.10.18.
50 rapscalleon] Cf above n45.
51 in letters] Lee could read the expressions that follow in the *Farrago*; the two letters in question did not, however, identify him by name; see Epp 906:494, 498, 501, and 999:345–51; cf also *Dialogus bilinguium ac trilinguium* (above 343).
52 more stoutly built] For another impression of Erasmus' personal appearance cf Ep 999 n6.

53 Rochester] Ep 936:34–8; cf Ep 1053: 458–60.
54 favourite word] The Latin term is *sycophantiae*, which can mean both 'libel' and 'slander.'
55 another context] Cf Ep 1007 n10.
56 stands or falls] Rom 14:4
57 judge not] Cf Matt 7:1.
58 you say] Lee here resumes his rebuttal of Ep 998.
59 friends in England] Cf Ep 1026 n3 and above n36.
60 Erasmus] Lee here summarizes the end of Ep 998 with more freedom than he had used in his preceding quotations.
61 nothing ... bath] Cf *Adagia* I vi 44, assuming that baths are visited by those anxious to meddle in other people's affairs.
62 cudgels] Cf Ep 998 n14.
63 *Apologia*] See Epp 934, 998 introductions.
64 trilinguals] See above 329ff.
65 libellous posters] In his *Annotationes* (f cc²; cf Ep 1037 introduction) Lee specified that they were printed. Erasmus stated in his *Apologia invectivis Lei* (*Opuscula* 271) that he had hardly heard about them.
66 letters ... Froben] The *Farrago* (cf Ep 1009 introduction) included Ep 998 and other attacks; cf above n51.
67 letter to Lupset] Ep 1053
68 Paul] Cf 1 Cor 9:12.
69 letter to Lupset] Ep 1053
70 earlier letter] Ep 998
71 printer] Probably Jean Thibault (cf Epp 1053 n19; below line 679), approached by Lee c March 1519
72 your servant] Probably Pieter Meghen; cf below line 696.
73 St Peter's] Cf Ep 1053 n14.
74 a man] Possibly Nicolaas van Broeckhoven (cf Ep 1054), who took an active part in the negotiations with Michaël Hillen in Antwerp; see Erasmus' *Apologia invectivis Lei* (*Opuscula* 252–4).
75 Wednesday] Here and in the following lines Lee indicates specific weekdays for his first round of negotiations with Hillen at Antwerp. Allen concluded that this Wednesday was either 27 April or 1 June 1519. Lee suggests (line 701) that a letter from Thomas More caused him to desist for the time being before making a second attempt (line 706). We have one letter from More to Lee (Rogers Ep 75; cf Ep 1053 n54), which in fact judged the notes to be insignificant and urged their suppression. It is dated 1 May 1519 and provided it is the one here intended, it will support the conclusion that these negotiations took place between April and June. For Erasmus' presence at Antwerp in this period see Ep 964 introduction.
76 Pieter] Meghen; cf above line 624 and Ep 996 n5.
77 More's letter] Perhaps Rogers Ep 75; cf above n75.
78 paraphrases] See Ep 1043.
79 my agreement] The publishing contract between Hillen and Lee, apparently c 6 November.
80 this letter] Ep 1053, which Lee is now answering
81 my brother] Wilfred Lee (cf Ep 1053 n21) would have gone to Antwerp c 6 November.

82 precise day] 14 December according to line 727

83 Dirk's] Dirk Martens'

84 barred me] Cf Epp 1053 n20. Lee's remarks here are difficult to reconcile with his statements above lines 522–4 and below lines 786–7.

85 Dirk] Martens; answering Ep 1053:126–8

86 three hundred] Cf Ep 1053:85–6.

87 offers you made] In the meeting at St Peter's church of c October 1518; see Ep 1053:82–121.

88 subterfuge] See Ep 998 introduction. The confusion surrounding Briart's role is well illustrated by the contradictory remarks Lee made about the relations between the 'vice-chancellor' and Erasmus; see above lines 69–72 and 172–3.

89 as you say] Cf Ep 1053:122–3.

90 when you say] Cf Ep 1053:137–41.

91 skipped the prefaces] Cf Ep 1053:275.

92 cut out much] Cf Ep 1053:50–4.

93 slip of memory] Cf Ep 1053:64.

94 Rochester] John Fisher; cf Ep 1026 n3, and for Erasmus' version of this circumstance see *Apologia invectivis Lei* (*Opuscula* 267).

95 Dodona] Cf Epp 1030 n6, 1053:361.

96 thirst for glory] Cf Ep 1053:216–26, the passage discussed here down to line 860.

97 censor's rod] Cf Epp 898A:6, 899:3, 998:43–4.

98 befouled by heretics] Cf introduction; at the beginning of his second *Responsio* against Lee Erasmus lists some of the specific charges of heresy put forward by his opponent; cf Ep 1080 introduction; LB IX 123.

99 Arius] A leading priest of Alexandria, condemned at the Council of Nicaea in 325 for his teachings concerning Father and Son.

100 unloose the hatchet] John 1:27; cf *Adagia* I v 94.

101 volume of notes] Cf Ep 1053:298–300. The only other trace of the notes Lee gathered on the Old Testament is a statement by Roger Ascham, who believed that on his death Lee had left a manuscript commentary on the Pentateuch; see R. Ascham *The Whole Works* (London 1864; reprint 1965) I Ep 24.

102 saying] Cf Ep 1053:352–4.

103 order] The Dominicans or the Carmelites are meant; cf Epp 1040, 1053:36, 452.

104 libellous story] Cf Ep 1053:365–9.

105 Dirk] Dirk Martens (cf Ep 867:207–51); Matthaeus Adrianus was one of the physicians who treated Erasmus.

106 six hundred passages] Cf above n16 and lines 765–6.

107 Achates] The inseparable and proverbial friend of Aeneas

108 your saying] See Ep 1053:390–3; Lee read 'a certain person,' as More's name was not given in the early editions of this letter.

109 secretly let you see] Cf Ep 998 n3.

1062

1 Euripus] Cf *Adagia* I ix 62: the water in the narrow gulf between Boeotia and Euboea was said to rush in and out again seven times each day and night.

2 Philistines] Cf Gen 26:14–18; Ep 858:196–200.

3 break in like enemies] For recent examples of excessive zeal in favour of

humanistic studies see Epp 1000A, 1044, 1046 introductions, 1055; also above 335ff.
4 off the bridge] Cf *Adagia* I v 37.
5 pamphlets] See Ep 1053 n62.
6 corrects ... St John] As Erasmus had been accused of doing; cf Epp 948:108–19; 1072 introduction.
7 tares] Cf Matt 13:24–30.
8 salt] Cf Mark 9:50.
9 cultivate any garden] Cf Ep 1060 n4.
10 into agreement] Cf Ep 1007 n14.
11 *fidus Achates*] Aeneas' faithful friend, a model of friendship. For Henry VIII's and Cardinal Wolsey's support of the new learning cf Epp 948:203–24, 967:40n.
12 inscription] This reference was added in 1521. It is not clear to what inscription Erasmus is referring.
13 engages men] For Leo's patronage of learning, and especially a college of Greek studies founded in the first year of his pontificate and directed at first by Janus Lascaris, see Pastor VIII 258–80. The following lines appear to be alluding both to the Greek college and to Leo's hopes for a crusade; see Epp 729:56n, 785:22–41.
14 New Testament] For Leo's involvement see Epp 384, 835 introduction, 864.
15 genuine letters] In addition to the five new paraphrases (Ephesians, Philippians, Colossians, 1 and 2 Thessalonians; cf introduction) there remained Hebrews to be paraphrased at a later time (cf Ep 1181). The formulation here and in Ep 1060:62 shows Erasmus' reluctance to ascribe Hebrews to Paul; cf LB VI 1023–4.
16 generosity] Cf Ep 995 n9.
17 in writing] See Ep 996:62–4.
18 Bruges] Cf Epp 1025 n3, 1029:30.

1063
1 intrigues] Cf the preface.
2 Sapidus, Volz, Wimpfeling] Members of the humanist circle at Sélestat
3 Atensis] Jan Briart died on 8 January 1520.

1065
1 The man] Probably Paschasius Berselius (cf Ep 956:6). From the suspicion concerning him expressed in lines 8–9 it may be surmised that his relations with Erasmus had taken the turn for the worse from which they never recovered, despite Ep 1077 and Berselius' subsequent efforts to earn Erasmus' respect and gratitude. Henry de Vocht thought that the estrangement was linked to the recent competition for the chair of Latin at the Collegium Trilingue; see Ep 1051 introduction.
2 dedicating] See Ep 956.
3 king] Probably Charles V (cf introduction). For Erasmus' appointment as his councillor and for further offers of preferment see Epp 370:18n, 475:5–6; for Erasmus' desire to see him return from Spain see Ep 1007 n13.

1066

1 letter] Ep 1004; answered by Budé in Epp 1011 and 1015
2 forbidden me to answer] Cf Ep 1011:135–9.
3 overwhelmed] A frequent assertion. At this time Erasmus' exhaustion was due to Lee and his other critics in Louvain rather than to creative writing and scholarly work; see the preface.
4 bygones be bygones] Erasmus uses the Greek term 'amnesty'; cf Ep 1004 introduction.
5 St James] Cf James 5:16.
6 Milo] A wrestler from Croton who had won six times in the Olympic games; the proverbial champion
7 you say] Ep 1015:121–2
8 Greek letter] Ep 1004
9 letter to Tunstall] Cf Ep 1015:2–3, referring to Ep 583.
10 Italian] Possibly Giambattista Egnazio; cf Ep 1015 n3.
11 foray] Cf Ep 1015:188.
12 to Luis Vives] See Ep 1023 n4.
13 engaged in rhetoric] Erasmus uses the Latin term 'declamat'; this may refer to Vives' preparing his *Declamationes Syllanae*; cf Ep 1082 introduction and 28–9.
14 you promise] Cf Ep 1015 n22.
15 performance] Cf Epp 1042, 1046, 1057.
16 siege to the Capitol] After the disastrous defeat suffered by the Romans on the banks of the Allia, c 390 AD
17 cabbages] Cf Ep 1060 n4.
18 closing their ranks] Cf Ep 1050 n1.
19 your king] For the cultural policy of Francis I cf Epp 1004 n30, 1073 introduction.
20 Leo] Cf Ep 1062 n13.
21 king of England] For Henry VIII's support of the new learning at Oxford and Cambridge cf Epp 1004 n30, 1062 n11.
22 *Farrago*] Cf Ep 1009 introduction.
23 book] Edward Lee's *Annotationes*; see Ep 1037.

1067

1 I have suffered] In years past Wimpfeling had been engaged in a number of controversies. Quite recently, in a letter of 10 January 1520 (BRE Ep 144; Zwingli *Werke* Ep 114) Beatus Rhenanus related how Wimpfeling had been offended by the pro-Lutheran stance of Johannes Sapidus, a younger member of the Sélestat humanist circle, and had threatened to denounce him to the Inquisition. A few months later, however, it was said among the reformers that a god had spirited Wimpfeling away from the battlefield like the Homeric Aeneas; see C. Schmidt *Histoire littéraire de l'Alsace à la fin du xve et au commencement du xvie siècle* (Paris 1879) I 94–6; P. Kalkoff in *Zeitschrift für die Geschichte des Oberrheins* n s 13 (1898) 112–19.
2 *Enchiridion*] Cf Epp 164, 858.
3 *Compendium*] The *Ratio verae theologiae*; cf Ep 745.
4 Quinquagesima] The Latin text has 'Esto mihi,' the first words of the introit of

the mass for Quinquagesima, which is the last Sunday before Lent; cf Ep 1070 n4.

1068

1 suspects] Perhaps from Erasmus' remarks about Lefèvre at the beginning of Ep 1030; but cf Ep 936:66–7.
2 pamphlet] *De unica Magdalena;* cf Ep 936:9n.
3 In the second] Erasmus means a second pamphlet rather than a new issue of *De unica Magdalena.* After the latter Fisher continued to participate in the controversy with two more publications, the *Confutatio* against Lefèvre and the *Eversio* against Josse Clichtove (cf Ep 1030 n2). The latter was clearly known to Erasmus and may be intended here. Lefèvre is not its main target and it seems much more carefully written than the *Confutatio.* See the analysis of both works in Surtz *Fisher* 280–9; for charges of Lefèvre's lack of loyalty to the church in *De unica Magdalena* see John Fisher *Opera* (Würzburg 1697; repr 1967) 1395, 1397, 1407, 1446, 1459.
4 'The mountain ... the mouse'] Horace *Ars poetica* 139; cf *Adagia* I ix 14.
5 soon happen] See Ep 1037 introduction.
6 peace] Erasmus assumed at first that he would not be answering Lee; see Ep 1069.

1069

1 N] Perhaps Nicolaas Baechem; cf Epp 1064, 1072 introduction.
2 no lack of others] See Ep 1083 introduction.

1070

1 Luther] Cf Ep 1030 n7; the *Condemnatio doctrinalis ... Lutheri* by the universities of Cologne and Louvain was published in February 1520 by Dirk Martens at Louvain (NK 7) and answered by Luther in the second half of March; cf Luther w VI 170–95, and below Ep 1113:38–9.
2 your present lot] It appears that Lips – not for the first time (cf Ep 901 introduction) – had expressed some dissatisfaction with his life in the Augustinian monastery of Louvain. Presumably in this matter as in others he set before himself the example of Erasmus, who had escaped from the routine of another Augustinian house to the service of Bishop Hendrik van Bergen; cf Ep 1075.
3 overwork] Cf Ep 1066 n3.
4 Lent] 22 February – 7 April 1520; cf Ep 1079 n1.
5 king's arrival] Cf Ep 1106 introduction.
6 Luxembourg] See Ep 1071.

1071

1 cardinal] Probably Guillaume de Croy; cf Ep 1033:17–20.

1072

1 answer] The *Apologia invectivis Lei,* answering Lee's Ep 1061, to be followed by two replies to Lee's *Annotationes* (cf Ep 1080 introduction). As on similar occasions Erasmus probably underestimated the time taken up by answering his critics.

2 more time on the clock] According to the practice of ancient Athens; cf *Adagia* I
iv 73.

1073

1 fast days] Cf Ep 1070 n4.
2 headache] Cf Ep 435:133–5.
3 courier] Presumably a trusted servant of Erasmus (cf introduction), possibly
Lieven Algoet; see Ep 1091 introduction.
4 Bérault] As he had not been greeted in Erasmus' Ep 1066 but was now evidently sending Erasmus a letter, perhaps Bérault was answering a letter
from Erasmus sent along with Ep 1066. A similar exchange could have taken
place with Brie, who was also trying to attract Erasmus to Paris (cf Ep
1117:4–6). But no such letters seem to exist now.
5 amnesty] Cf Ep 1004 introduction.
6 what you say] Ep 1066:45–54
7 wash ... vinegar] Persius 5.86; this was supposedly a cure for deafness, cf
Celsus 6.7.
8 ill-tempered] Ep 1066:3
9 brine and saltiness] Cf Horace *Satires* 2.8.53.
10 you yield] Cf Ep 1066:24–5.
11 once write] The citation has not been traced. Perhaps it came from a missing
letter to a friend at Paris who showed it to Budé.
12 tell me] Ep 1066:70–4, 99–100
13 prelate] Jérôme de Busleyden
14 in this city] Paris
15 letters] On 21 February Budé had received letters from Jacopo Sadoleto at
Rome (sent by way of Venice) and Pietro Bembo and Christophe de Longueil at Venice; likewise a letter from Adolf Eichholz at Cologne. He answered
them all on 22–24 February; see Budé *Opera omnia* I 269–75.
16 project] Intended is no doubt *De contemptu rerum fortuitarum* (Paris: J. Bade,
n d), to which Budé's letters of this period keep referring. By January 1521 it
was in print; cf L. Delaruelle *Répertoire ... de la correspondance de Guillaume Budé*
(Toulouse and Paris 1907) Epp 43, 48, 50, 60–2, 82–3.
17 feast-day] 26 February 1520 was the first Sunday in Lent; cf Ep 1070 n4.
18 the first February ... following day] On the second, actually; Budé *Opera omnia*
I 250–2

1074

1 the Carthusians, the Minorites] Erasmus accuses Lee of attempting to ingrati-
ate himself with these orders, which were often seen as rivals of Lee's
regular supporters, the Dominicans and the Carmelites. For Erasmus' own
connections with Minorites and Carthusians of Epp 1174 n5, 1196 n58.
2 moved to Louvain] Lee matriculated in August 1516 (cf Ep 765 introduction);
Erasmus' residence dates from July 1517 (cf Ep 596 introduction). For another account of their early relations see Erasmus' *Apologia invectivis Lei* (*Opuscula* 241–3).
3 Greek] Cf Ep 607:16–17.
4 Matthew first] Cf Epp 750:9n, 17n, 1061 n8.

5 'Remember ... so are you'] Cf Ep 1039:119–20.
6 to Basel] In May 1518; cf Ep 843 introduction.
7 through England] Cf Ep 1026 n3.
8 return] In September 1518; cf Ep 867 introduction.
9 his letter] Ep 1061; for Erasmus' meeting with Lee see Ep 1053 n14.
10 Atensis] Jan Briart of Ath; cf Ep 998 introduction.
11 abbot] See Ep 1061:175.
12 disliked it] Cf Epp 1026 n3, 1053 n54, 1089–90.
13 Pace] See Ep 999 introduction.
14 labouring mountains ... mouse] See Ep 1068 n4.
15 bitter attack] Perhaps Nesen's *Dialogus bilinguium ac trilinguium* (cf Epp 998 introduction and 329–47 above) or an anonymous placard posted on Lee's door (see Ep 1077 n3).
16 Bonn] Cf Ep 1053 n20.
17 Gourmont] Gilles de Gourmont; see Epp 263:11n; 1037 introduction.
18 brother] Wilfred Lee; see Ep 1053 n21.
19 new annotations] Cf Ep 1037 introduction.
20 promised to do] Cf Ep 1006 n28.
21 Antwerp ... Brussels ... Bruges] From summer 1516 to summer 1517; cf *Apologia invectivis Lei* (*Opuscula* 238–41).
22 traitor] Maarten Lips; cf Ep 1061 n10.
23 a long life] Cf Ep 1061:893–6.
24 menace] Cf Ep 1061 introduction.
25 six times] Cf Ep 1061:69–73, 156–8, *Apologia invectivis* Lei (*Opuscula* 249–50)
26 twice that quantity] Cf above line 52 and Ep 1061 n16.
27 last invective] Ep 1061
28 crow ... feathers] Cf Ep 1053 n55.
29 Orestes] He avenged his father Agamemnon by slaying his mother. Hunted by the Erinyes, he wandered around stark mad until cleansed by Apollo; cf *Adagia* IV i 48.

1075
1 Oecolampadius] See Ep 1095 postscript. It may be noted that in two letters to Oecolampadius (Epp 1102:3–4, 1158) Erasmus expresses a longing for retirement similar to what he says above in lines 4–6.
2 Wimpfeling] Cf Ep 1067:5–6.
3 Colet] He died on 16 September 1519; cf Ep 1025 introduction.
4 Satan] Edward Lee
5 to save him] For the ambiguity of his efforts cf Epp 1061:526–62, 1074 introduction.
6 says mass] Since Erasmus and Lee were both priests, each could repeatedly charge the other with behaviour unworthy of the priesthood; cf for instance Ep 1061:436–40.

1076
1 friendly fashion] Cf Ep 1061:821–4. For some other examples of Erasmus' willingness to accept friendly criticism see Epp 180, 811, 1140.
2 vast sea of historical material] Allen assumed that 'mare historiarum' indicated

that Gruntgen probably corrected a passage in Erasmus' edition of either
Suetonius and the *Historiae augustae scriptores* (cf Ep 586) or Quintus Curtius
(cf Ep 704), but he failed to find any correction ascribed to Gruntgen. In fact
the reference could be to almost any work Erasmus had edited so far.

1077

1 a letter] This text has not been identified.

2 Dirk] Dirk Martens (NK 0393); no copy is known today.

3 more than ten places] Probably on the church doors. It appears that Lee had
earlier been attacked in the same fashion (cf Ep 1061:587) and also in an
anonymous placard attached to his own door, which, according to Erasmus'
Apologia invectivis Lei, proved particularly provocative; see *Opuscula* 252; cf
Ep 1074:86.

4 long-tailed] Cf Ep 1061 n42.

5 virulent poison] Cf Horace *Satires* 1.7.1.

6 whole story] Or 'another story' ('tragediam non illepidam'). Henry de Vocht
(CTL I 498) suggests that a 'lepidum facinus' mentioned by Wilhelm Nesen
could be meant. It concerned a German who defiled a copy of Lee's *Annotationes* in the library of the Louvain Franciscans.

7 what you are doing] Erasmus wrote parts of his various defences against Lee
when he was in Antwerp; cf Ep 1080 introduction.

1078

1 ass of Cumae] Cf *Adagia* I iii 66, I vii 12: a runaway donkey, trying to elude his
masters by concealing himself in a lion's skin.

2 This Lee] The entire sentence is given in Greek.

3 men in black] For the close collaboration between the theologians, especially
the Dominicans, in Louvain and Cologne cf below line 58 and Epp 1030 n7,
1070 n1; and for possible traces of a connection between Lee and the latter cf
Ep 1053 n20.

4 Lee's *Annotationes*] See Ep 1037.

5 Gerhard] Gerhard von Enschringen; see Ep 1082 n16.

6 sound and fury without sense] Cf Virgil *Aeneid* 10.640.

7 of robbers] Perhaps a reminiscence of the parable of the good Samaritan, Luke
10:30–6.

8 Reuchlin] Cf Ep 1006 n18; for a related attack on Neuenahr and Erasmus cf Ep
1006:163–5.

9 my self-restraint] Erasmus deplored Neuenahr's earlier intervention in the
Reuchlin controversy; see Epp 680:28n, 703.

10 lately] Probably in the missing letter; see introduction.

11 beggarly jackdaws and black-beetles] Cf above n3 and Ep 1082:16; *Adagia* I vii
22.

12 'no plough ... fern'] Persius 4.41

13 in the fable] See *Adagia* I v 41: the monkeys make fun of the ass with impunity
because it lacks their agility.

14 *Apologia*] Cf Ep 1080 introduction.

15 arrival] There are several indications that amid various plans for a trip or
even a permanent relocation (cf Ep 1079 introduction), Erasmus considered

travelling to Germany (cf Epp 1085:13–14, 1101:3–4, 1102:12, 1119:26–7, 1123). He was expected to arrive in Basel in May (cf BRE Epp 162, 166, 176), and throughout the spring humanists elsewhere in Switzerland were preparing to meet him there (cf Zwingli *Werke* VII Epp 131, 133, 140, 142, 145). But the expected return of Charles V held him in the Netherlands (cf Ep 1106 introduction) and in the end he went only as far as Cologne in October – November; see Ep 1155 introduction.

16 no plague] An important consideration for Erasmus' travelling plans; cf Epp 770 introduction; 993 n11, 1085 n5, 1095 n18.

17 Bedburg] For an earlier visit to Neuenahr's castle west of Cologne see Ep 867:8on.

18 our prince] Hermann von Wied was elected archbishop of Cologne in 1515, but his solemn entry did not take place until 15 July 1522. He was one of four brothers. The eldest was Johann, count of Wied; Friedrich, the youngest, matriculated together with Hermann in the University of Cologne and succeeded him as archbishop; see C. Varrentrapp *Hermann von Wied* (Leipzig 1878) I 35–8; NDB.

19 my brother] Wilhelm von Neuenahr, who in 1519 married Anna, daughter of Count Wilhelm von Wied, the remaining brother (cf above n18) of Archbishop Hermann; see Varrentrapp I 68; *Annalen des historischen Vereins für den Niederrhein* 128 (1936) 148.

1079

1 diploma] Probably a document issued in the name of Leo X permitting Erasmus to eat meat in Lent. A draft of it was perhaps sent at this time, with the original to follow if he expressed satisfaction (cf Epp 1080:4–5, 1353). In view of Ep 1081 it seems very likely that Lorenzo Campeggi had also assisted Erasmus in this matter. In 1525 he issued in his capacity as papal legate to Germany a formal dispensation in the name of Clement VII (Ep 1542). As this would have replaced the diploma here mentioned, it is understandable that Erasmus discarded the latter, and kept only the subsequent dispensation among his papers.

2 return of Charles] See Ep 1106 introduction.

3 bear witness] He did; see Ep 1181.

1080

1 diploma] See Ep 1079 n1.

1081

1 a book] See Ep 1062.

2 return] Cf Ep 1106 introduction.

1082

1 favouring wind and tide] Homer *Odyssey* 3.300

2 castle] The Bedburg; cf Ep 1078 n17.

3 Pliny] *Epistulae* 1.6

4 Delia] Artemis, born on the island of Delos

5 *Ptochotyrannophilomousomachia*] The battle between the beggar-bullies (or

mendicant friars) and the friends of the Muses waged at Louvain; cf the preface.

6 monster] Edward Lee; for the books published on both sides of the controversy see Epp 1037 and 1080 introductions.

7 Dorp] Cf Ep 1044 introduction and n10.

8 rant] A play on words: while others 'clamant,' Vives 'declamat,' ie produces his *Declamationes*.

9 precedents of Antiquity] Cf Ep 917:27–34.

10 identity of name] Vives was a native of Valencia. Ῥώμη (here identical with *Roma*) means strength, and *valens*, from which *Valentia* is derived, means strong.

11 such skill] Cf Ep 917:28–30.

12 art] Cf Ep 917:32–4.

13 against the clock] Cf Ep 1072 n2.

14 generation] Cf Ep 917:25–6.

15 Croy] Guillaume de Croy; for his connections with Vives and Erasmus cf Epp 957 introduction, 1071:7.

16 Episcopus] While Erasmus' Latin rendering of the name is unusual, the reference is clearly to Gerhard von Enschringen, who accompanied Neuenahr to Bologna in 1509 and remained in his service after their return, gradually becoming his confidential secretary and chaplain. After Neuenahr's death in 1532 he became a fiscal officer at Trier and married. He shared Neuenahr's scholarly interests and was fondly remembered by Johann Sturm, the famous master of the Strasbourg school, as one of his earliest teachers; see G.C. Knod *Deutsche Studenten in Bologna* (Berlin 1899; repr 1970) 115–16, 672; O. Brunfels ed *Herbarium* (Strasbourg: J. Schott 1530–6) II 2, 116; J. Sturm *Classicae epistolae* ed J. Rott (Strasbourg 1938) 24.

1083

1 Konrad] Konrad Resch, publisher and master of the bookstore 'à l'écu de Bâle' in Paris, travelled frequently to Basel and was perhaps a distant relative of Froben; see Bietenholz *Basle and France* 29–30, 33, 37; and for his edition of Lee's *Annotationes* see Ep 1037 introduction and n1.

2 Minerva] Cf *Adagia* I i 40–1.

3 flash in the pan] Cf *Adagia* II vii 90.

4 *Annotationes*] On the New Testament (cf Ep 864), where Erasmus sometimes paid tribute to friends and helpers; cf Ep 1074:41–2.

5 Erostratus] Cf Ep 1053 n31.

6 praise] See Ep 1061:228–38, where Reuchlin too is paid some compliments. The following reference to Hutten has not been traced; but cf Ep 1055.

7 crow ... borrowed plumes] Cf Ep 1053 n55.

8 Hutten's pen] See his letter to Lee in Hillen's *Appendix* and Froben's *Epistolae aliquot eruditorum virorum*, dated from Mainz, 20 May [1520] (Hutten *Opera* I Ep 166); the lampoon *Hochstratus ovans* too was sometimes attributed to Hutten. See Allen 1165:22n.

9 Oecolampadius] Although he is not known to have participated in the campaign against Lee, he is said to have done so (together with Melanchthon, Petrus Mosellanus, Euricius Cordus, Justus Jonas, Eobanus, and others) in an

undated letter from Johannes Sapidus to Lee, published in Froben's *Epistolae aliquot eruditorum virorum* 169.

10 Zasius] Cf Ep 1084:78–102.

11 twice already] Cf Ep 1074 introduction.

12 spare his countrymen] Erasmus had endeavoured quite successfully to muster support against Lee among his English friends while at the same time he cautioned his German admirers not to injure English national pride in their attacks on Lee; cf Epp 1026 n3, 1058, 1088–9, 1097–9, 1129. The majority of the letters published in Hillen's *Epistolae aliquot eruditorum* came from England.

13 my work] Cf Ep 1074 introduction.

14 Rhenanus] Erasmus relied on Beatus Rhenanus for editions of his correspondence and other matters requiring discretion.

15 Frankfurt] Where the spring book fair was about to open. It was regularly attended by printers and booksellers from Basel as well as the Netherlands and thus offered opportunities for the expeditious conveyance of this letter.

1084

1 Greek saying] Cf Thucydides 2.40.3.

2 anxious fears] Cf Ovid *Heroides* 1.12.

3 Maarten van Dorp] Cf Ep 1044 n10.

4 I wrote] Amerbach's letter to Dorp (AK II Ep 731, de Vocht MHL 376–81), dated 19 March, was evidently sent with this letter to Erasmus. Despite the artificial formality displayed elsewhere in this letter, Amerbach's reluctance is genuine. On 31 January 1520 he had accused Dorp of having attacked Erasmus under the pseudonym of Latomus (cf Ep 934) and as recently as 19 March some people at Basel believed that Dorp had guided the pen of Lee; see AK II Ep 715; BRE Ep 159; cf below Ep 1121:33–5.

5 Bruno] He died on 21 or 22 October 1519; cf AK II Ep 695. For the plague which had been afflicting Basel since August, see Ep 993 n11 and BRE Epp 124–5, 128–9, 133–4. Erasmus' epitaph for Bruno is Reedijk poem 108.

6 Avignon] See Ep 1020 n6.

7 certain princes] Zasius had recently written to Amerbach that he was hard pressed preparing legal opinions for several princes and for the Swabian League (cf AK II Ep 727); for one intervention on behalf of minor princes see Ep 1120.

8 name and nature] Lee's name is spelled in Greek, Λαιός, which means 'queer.'

9 Apollonius] Philostratus *Vita Apollonii* 1.34

10 elephant] Cf *Adagia* III i 27.

11 write to Zasius] The letter is missing.

12 full reply] AK II Ep 729, which shows, incidentally, that Amerbach had sent Zasius a rough copy of this letter to Erasmus and that he followed one of Zasius' suggestions for changes before he sent it to Louvain.

1085

1 young man] Pirckheimer confirmed in his answer (Ep 1095:3–5) that a kinsman of his had visited Erasmus and suggested that he could henceforward facilitate the exchange of letters. It seems likely that the relative had frequent commercial ties with Antwerp or even planned to reside there for some

time. Therefore he was probably not Pirckheimer's only brother-in-law, Martin Geuder of Heroldsberg, burgomaster of Nürnberg, who had married Juliana Pirckheimer in July 1495 and was indeed no longer a young man. Erasmus' term 'husband' may be mistaken. Rather a son of Geuder could be intended or a member of the Imhof family. A 'gener' (son-in-law or brother-in-law) of Pirckheimer was on his way home from Holland in June 1520 (Hutten *Opera* I Ep 174.1); perhaps he was Hans Imhof (d 1524), the husband of Felicitas Pirckheimer; see W.P. Eckert and C. von Imhoff *Willibald Pirckheimer* (Cologne 1971) 58–63. For the frequent connections of the Imhof and Geuder families with Antwerp see Albrecht Dürer *Diary of his Journey to the Netherlands, 1520–1521,* ed J.-A. Goris and G. Maurier (Greenwich, Connecticut 1971) 58, 65, and passim. Another son-in-law, Hans Straub, the husband of Barbara Pirckheimer, also maintained commercial contacts with Antwerp and collaborated after Pirckheimer's death with Erasmus in producing a posthumous edition of Pirckheimer's translation of the *Orationes* of Gregory of Nazianzus (Basel: H. Froben 1531); see H. Haller von Hallerstein *Beiträge zur Wirtschaftsgeschichte Nürnbergs* ed Staatsarchiv Nürnberg (Nürnberg 1967) 144; Niklas Holzberg *Willibald Pirckheimer* (Munich 1981) 352– 61.

2 Edward Lee's book] See Ep 1037.
3 Hoogstraten and Pfefferkorn] For Pirckheimer's opposition to the adversaries of Reuchlin see Epp 685, 747.
4 monster] Edward Lee
5 Germany] Cf Ep 1078 n15.

1086

1 Carmelite] He is not identified; cf the index to this volume.
2 Nazianzen] In number 39 of his *Annotationes* (cf Ep 1037) Lee had cited Gregory of Nazianzus *De Christi genealogia,* lines 30–2 (PG 37 483–4) to the effect that Joseph had two fathers, as here stated. The context is a controversy over Luke's genealogy of Christ which reached back to 1518 (cf Epp 784:54n; 886:82n). In his first *Responsio* to Lee (cf Ep 1080 introduction) Erasmus merely remarked that Gregory Nazianzen lacked authority; see LB IX 157F.

1087

1 Phormio] The proverbial parasite; the hero of Terence's comedy bearing his name
2 two or three epigrams] More's *Epigrammata* (first published with *Utopia;* Basel: J. Froben 1518) include ten epigrams dealing with Brie; in Froben's new edition of December 1520, four more were added in response to the *Antimorus;* see More Y III-2 nos 188–95, 209, 266–9. In four instances some of Brie's verses are printed with the epigram to show More's point.
3 peace ... concord] Cf Ep 964:39n and below lines 230–1.
4 *Chordigera*] *Chordigerae navis conflagratio* (Paris: J. Bade 13 January 1513), a poem of 350 hexameters (ed and tr in More Y III-2 429–65). It commemorated the French ship *La Cordelière,* which burnt and sank in the Atlantic off Brest on 10 August 1512 together with the English flagship. In particular Brie celebrated the allegedly heroic death of the French captain, Hervé de Portzmoguer, a Breton. The poem was dedicated to Queen Anne of Britanny, who

employed Brie as her secretary and had also equipped the *Cordelière* and had inspected her personally; see M.M. de la Garanderie in J.-C. Margolin ed *Colloquia Erasmiana Turonensia* (Paris and Toronto 1972) I 365–8.

5 the saying] Cf *Adagia* I ix 89.
6 letter] Ep 620; More refers primarily to lines 34–45.
7 accepts it] Cf Ep 1045:11–22; this letter was published with Brie's *Antimorus*.
8 claiming] Cf Ep 1045:82–3.
9 breaking treaties ... perjured] *Chordigera* lines 18–21 in More Y III-2.
10 Polyphemus] Cf Ep 1045:39–46.
11 Abingdon] Henry Abingdon (d 1497) was a prominent member of the king's chapel. In his *Antimorus* More Y III-2 508–11 Brie took issue with one of More's epigrams (no 160 in More Y III-2) which was a cenotaph rewritten in medieval rhymes and unclassical Latin to satisfy the taste of Abingdon's heir. Brie chose to ignore the explanation of this mockery given in the following epigram, no 161; cf below n34.
12 collection] The *Antimorus*; cf Ep 1045 introduction.
13 Valeria Proba] Proba, wife of the prefect Adelphus of Rome, composed in hexameters a cento or patchwork of borrowed lines on the subject of sacred history, especially as contained in the Gospels.
14 execrations and curses] Cf Ep 1045:49.
15 one of my epigrams] In epigram 189 in More Y III-2
16 Martial's remark] Martial 11.93.3–4
17 many parasangs distant] A proverbial expression referring to an ancient measure of length comparable to our miles; cf *Adagia* II iii 82.
18 nine others] Cf above n2.
19 Hervé] Cf above n4 and More's epigrams 190–2 in More Y III-2. For Hervé's speech see *Chordigerae navis conflagratio*, More Y III-2 456–9.
20 Hervé's cenotaph] An appendix to the *Chordigerae navis conflagratio* (More Y III-2 464–5), ridiculed in More's epigram 194 in More Y III-2.
21 I never published] See Ep 1093 n16.
22 what steps I took] There is no trace of this in More's surviving correspondence; cf Ep 1093 n16.
23 an epigram ... countryman] No 95 in More Y III-2
24 in another passage] In epigram 271 (More Y III-2) on James IV of Scotland, which was withdrawn in the 1520 edition. France and her allies were laid under an interdict following the schismatic Council of Pisa in 1511.
25 ties of hospitality] See Ep 1106 introduction.
26 prince's father] Epigram 19 in More Y III-2 is an ode on the coronation day of Henry VIII. More does not mention Henry VII, but praises the young king as the restorer of freedom and justice after an age of lawlessness and excessive taxation. In his *Antimorus* (More Y III-2 492–3) Brie had accused More of slandering the memory of Henry VII.
27 laughter of Ajax] Cf *Adagia* II vii 46.
28 Coroebus or Margites] Cf *Adagia* II iii 71, II ii 64.
29 his boast] Cf Ep 1045:36–9.
30 his idiot *Antimoros*] Latin *moricus eius Antimoros* 'his idiot anti-fool'; cf Ep 1045 n3.
31 camel dancing] Cf *Adagia* II vii 66.

32 Aesop's donkey] *Fables* 21 (Thiele)
33 marginal note] Such marginal notes as 'ironice' are provided for emphasis on a
   number of pages of the *Antimorus* (given as footnotes in More y iii-2).
34 one place] In his verse treatment of More's epigram on Abingdon (cf above
   n11) Brie praised More's mastery of this peculiar genre, but in the prose
   commentary following the metric part of *Antimorus* he calls this epigram ridiculous, speaking elsewhere of More's inexcusable offences against the metre,
   solecisms, barbarisms and so on; see *Antimorus*, More y iii-2 514–47, especially
   547.
35 makes fun] *Antimorus* (More y iii-2 534–5), referring to More's *Utopia* book 1;
   see More y iv 80–5.
36 in name alone] See Ep 1045 n3.
37 Punic] The language of Carthage; cf Plautus *Poenulus* 982–1029.
38 'as soars ... heaven'] Virgil *Aeneid* 6.579
39 Beatus Rhenanus] See *Antimorus* (More y iii-2 542–3), where Beatus is censured for his 'adulation,' although his name is not given. He had written a
   dedicatory preface (addressed to Willibald Pirckheimer) for Froben's edition of
   More's epigrams (cf Epp 634, 845); see bre Ep 72; More y iii-2 72–7.
40 Aeschines] This Athenian orator and partisan of King Philip of Macedon
   attacked his rival Demosthenes in public and also attacked Ctesiphon, who
   had prepared special honours for Demosthenes (336, 330 bc), but in the end
   was himself exiled.
41 commended to Willibald] Pirckheimer; cf above n39.
42 gnat ... elephant] Cf Ep 1084 n10.
43 one mule ... back] Cf *Adagia* i vii 96.
44 praised in print] Pieter Gillis, Jérôme de Busleyden, Jean Desmarez, Gerard
   Geldenhouwer of Nijmegen, and Cornelius Grapheus had all made complimentary contributions to the first edition of *Utopia*, Guillaume Budé to the second
   (see More y iv 4–37). For Hutten's praise of More cf Ep 999 n1; for Udalricus
   Zasius' see the preface of his *Lucubrationes* (1518; cf Ep 862). Vives' testimony
   seems to be missing; for his connections with More cf Ep 1106 introduction.
   Cornelius Grapheus (Schrijver) of Aalst (c 1482–1558) was secretary of the
   town of Antwerp and thus a colleague of Pieter Gillis, More's good friend.
   Himself a highly respected humanist and poet, he counted among his friends
   many humanists and artists such as Albrecht Dürer, who received from him
   a copy of Luther's *De captivitate Babylonica*. In 1522 he was tried for heresy
   and, after a public abjuration, was kept for many months at Brussels, first in
   jail and subsequently in confinement; see de Vocht *Literae ad Craneveldium*
   484–6.
45 takes it hard] See above n39.
46 Marullus and Pontano] Michael Marullus, a native Greek, and Giovanni
   Pontano were authors of well-known collections of Latin epigrams. In his
   preface (cf above n39) Beatus Rhenanus suggested that their jokes were un-
   suited to Christian ears.
47 'In mist ... muttonheads'] Juvenal 10.50
48 Aleandro] A complimentary letter by Girolamo Aleandro prefixed to Brie's
   Chordigera praises the poem and the dedication to Queen Anne of Britanny;
   see More y iii-2 440–3.

49 he says] Cf Ep 1045:56–60.

50 those verses] *Antimorus*, More Y III-2 508–9

51 he says] Ep 1045:36; cf *Antimorus*, More Y III-2 536–9.

52 eleven-syllable lines] 'Ad lectorem,' *Antimorus*, More Y III-2 512–13

53 wolf] Allen cites *Adagia* II i 86, where the wolf is a symbol of ingratitude. Cf Macrobius *Saturnalia* 1.20.14–15, where the wolf symbolizes loss of memory about the past, and also Aesop *Fables* 40 (Thiele). The symbolic use here is without a clear parallel in classical literature.

54 that place] Cf Ep 1045:22–7.

55 letter of warning] Ep 620

56 his own words] Ep 1045:121–7

57 not willing] When repeating this point in Ep 1096:18–34, More added that his information came from reliable sources at Paris, but it is not confirmed elsewhere. In the *Antimorus* (More Y III-2 502–3) Brie stated that previously (*olim*) he used to submit his verses to the judgment of friends like Budé, Deloynes, and Lascaris before publication.

58 cardinal] Antoine Bohier (c 1460–27 November 1519), archbishop of Bourges from 1515 and cardinal from 1517. A member of his household was the young poet Jean Salmon Macrin, who contributed some preliminary verses to Brie's *Antimorus* and is addressed by Brie in an answering poem; More Y III-2 482–5.

59 goodness of heart] Cf Ep 1045:15–22.

60 Lefèvre] Cf Ep 1045:66–9.

61 your defense] The *Apologia ad Fabrum*; cf Ep 597:37n.

62 he does say] Cf Ep 1045:71–3.

63 he puts it] For this entire paragraph cf Ep 1045:85–98.

64 epimonê] The rhetorical figure of 'dwelling on a subject'

65 palm] In the introductory verses 'Ad lectorem' of the *Antimorus* Brie used the image of the resilient palm tree; cf *Adagia* I iii 4.

66 Homer] The *Batrachomyomachia* (Battle of Frogs and Mice), a parody of an epic poem, was in antiquity ascribed to Homer. Zeus intervened in the battle, but his thunderbolts failed to achieve their purpose.

67 you say] Cf Ep 620:35–7.

68 'of such ... call unworthy I'] Virgil *Aeneid* 1.335

69 an answer] See the introduction.

70 Ovid's line] *Tristia* 3.11.21

71 horse] Cf *Adagia* I viii 82.

72 Hercules] Cf *Adagia* IV i 95.

73 I shall never write] More may be referring to Brie's tetrastichon, *Antimorus*, More Y III-2 544–5.

74 he says] Ep 1045:94

75 pale ... mask] Cf Juvenal 3.175.

76 those lines] *Antimorus*, More Y III-2 510–11

77 Morychus] Cf *Adagia* II ix 1. Morychus, the epitome of foolish behaviour, provides another allusion to More's name; cf Ep 1045 n3.

78 Patroclus, or Thersites] For Patroclus cf Ep 1045:97. Thersites is a foul-tongued soldier, silenced by Odysseus with blows; see Homer *Iliad* 2.212–70.

79 'wrath ... unworthy'] Cf Ovid *Metamorphoses* 1.166.

80 Strepsiades] Reacting in this manner in Aristophanes *Clouds* 293
81 Cacus] In legend, a brigand who terrorized his neighbourhood and was slain by Hercules. More is alluding to the similarity between the name and the verb *cacare*, to defecate.
82 'to piss … right'] Juvenal 1.131
83 Calais] See Ep 1106 introduction.
84 Lupset] See Ep 1026 introduction.
85 Clement] Formerly a tutor in More's house and later the husband of his adopted daughter, John Clement had preceded Lupset as Wolsey's reader in the humanities at Oxford (cf Ep 907). The study of medicine which he had now undertaken would eventually lead him to Louvain; cf Allen Ep 1256: 121–4.

1088

1 letter] None of Jonas' letters to Erasmus is known to exist.
2 I have replied] See Ep 1080 introduction.
3 praise] Cf Ep 1083 n12.
4 Nesen] Here is an indication that Nesen, the editor of Hillen's *Epistolae aliquot eruditorum* (cf Ep 1083 introduction) had been sent on a mission to Germany in order to organize the campaign against Lee. By 20 April he had returned to Louvain (cf Froben's *Epistolae aliquot eruditorum virorum* 54), but a few weeks later he left the Netherlands for good; cf Ep 1126 n49.
5 I have been] Cf Epp 872, 1038 introduction, 1127A. For the Dominicans cf Ep 1092:9–14.
6 Atensis] Cf Ep 1029 n2.
7 Baechem] Cf Ep 1072 introduction. He is also called 'blear-eyed' in the *Dialogus bilinguium ac trilinguium*; see below 342 n46.
8 Latomus] Cf Ep 1059 introduction; there are many references to his disability; see Ep 1123; Allen Epp 1256:24, 1804:211; de Vocht CTL I 347, 567, 569.

1089

1 defences] See Epp 1037 introduction; 1080 introduction.

1090

1 advice] See Ep 1026 n3 and More's affectionate, but severe letter to Lee after reading some of his notes in manuscript (1 May 1519; Rogers Ep 75); cf Ep 1053 n54. More's argument here is repeated in Rogers Ep 85:8–12.
2 should be allowed] Cf Ep 1037 n1.
3 the book] Lee's *Annotationes* (cf Ep 1037 introduction). For More's acquaintance with them in manuscript see above n1.

1091

1 Terence] *Eunuchus* 600; *Adelphi* 69–71, 72–3, lines spoken by Micio
2 Menander's tag] Quoted in 1 Cor 15:33, this line from Menander's *Thais* had become proverbial by the time it was used by the Apostle.
3 Carinus] Cf Ep 994 n1.
4 Laurinus] Cf Ep 1012 n2.
5 deity] Cf Ep 1003 n6.

1092

1 visit Holland] Cf Epp 1079 introduction; 1094:9–10. In view of the sequence of letters dated from Louvain throughout the summer it would seem that the intention was not carried out.

2 Erasmus in lead] This is the earliest reference, soon followed by others (cf Epp 1101:8–9, 1119:8, 1122) to the famous medal of Erasmus attributed to Quinten Metsys (cf Epp 616:10n, 1408, 1452, 1985). It shows the date of 1519 under Erasmus' profile and on the reverse the god Terminus with his motto 'Concedo nulli,' both already depicted on Erasmus' seal (cf Ep 712:40n). For the medal and its derivatives see A. Gerlo *Erasme et ses portraitistes* (2nd edition, Nieuwkoop 1969) 18–27; L. Smolderen in *Scrinium Erasmianum* ed J. Coppens (Leiden 1969) II 513–25. Everaerts' son, known as Johannes Secundus, later became an outstanding medallist, producing medals of Erasmus and many of his friends; see J. Simonis *L'Art du médailleur en Belgique* (Brussels 1900) 83 and passim.

3 two little books] Evidently the *Apologia invectivis Lei* and the first of the two *Responsiones*; the second now being in the press; cf below line 15, Ep 1080 introduction.

4 Dominicans] Cf Ep 1088:14–15 and the index to this volume.

5 your son] No doubt the oldest, Pieter Jeroen Everaerts better known as Petrus Hieronymus Nicolai, who was promoted doctor of civil and canon law at Louvain on 22 May 1520. He had entered the Premonstratensian order at Middleburg and was thus wearing the white habit of his order. Later he became the parish priest of Flushing; see NNBW; de Vocht CTL II 431.

6 Sasbout] Joost Sasbout, heer van Spalant (1487–1546), was doctor of law and from 1515 a member of the Council of Holland. He ended his career as chancellor of Gelderland. He was a friend of Dorp and a supporter of the new learning, later sending his son to study in the Collegium Trilingue; see Epp 2645, 2844; NNBW; de Vocht CTL II 199–200.

7 Carolus] He is not identified.

8 Mauritszoon] Jacob Mauritszoon was another member of the Council of Holland; cf Ep 176.

9 Bernard] Bernard Bucho van Aytta, member of the Council of Holland and dean of The Hague; see Ep 1237.

10 Nassau] Henry III of Nassau was governor of Holland and Zeeland. It is not known why Erasmus was indebted to him; cf Ep 829:14n.

11 Veere] Adolph of Burgundy, heer van Veere; cf Ep 93.

1093

1 my letter] Ep 620, which Brie claimed did not reach him until his *Antimorus* was already being printed; see Ep 1045:25–9.

2 epigrams] See Ep 1087 n2.

3 shoulder to shoulder] Cf Juvenal 2.46.

4 you of all people] Cf Ep 999:254–6.

5 difficulty] Having just answered Lee; cf Epp 1080 introduction, 1092.

6 not you] Cf Ep 1087:173–6 and below n16.

7 copyist's ... printer's] Cf Ep 1087:237–9.

8 *Chordigera*] Cf Ep 1087 n4.

9 Abingdon] Cf Ep 1087 n11.
10 prince] Henry VIII; cf Ep 1087 n26.
11 they say] Cf *Adagia* I iv 70.
12 charm] The Latin term, *suavitas*, is a key word in Erasmus' description of More; see Allen Ep 999:20, 111, 301.
13 a book] See Ep 1087 introduction, 588–90. Erasmus may have found it inexpedient to admit that he knew from Ep 1087 that More's rejoinder was already printed; cf the introduction.
14 to suppress] Ep 620:30–45
15 Brie's letter] Ep 1045:4–7, 22–5
16 too late] This sentence echoes More's remarks in Ep 1087:173–6. We do not know when More had requested that the pieces regarding Brie be removed from the publisher's copy of his epigrams. In September 1516 he had left it explicitly to the judgment of Erasmus whether or not to include the epigrams against Brie (cf Ep 461:22–7). In May 1517 Erasmus had sent More's manuscript to Froben, evidently without removing them, but Froben did not publish until March 1518. Whatever the timing of More's further action, Erasmus had a share in the decision to print the epigrams, but More was probably too considerate to state this openly (cf Epp 1087:181–3, 1096:142–5).
17 omitted in future] They were not; rather, more were added; see Epp 1087 n2, 1096:135–54.
18 confusion] Of publishing his replies to Lee; cf Ep 1080 introduction.

1094
1 synod] Of rural deans; see below line 20–1.
2 Wednesday] 11 April 1520; the letter is missing.
3 blank form] Referring to his travel plans (cf Ep 1079 introduction), Erasmus had asked politely for a prepayment of his annuity. The half-yearly payment of 65 Rhenish florins (ie the silver-based Flemish money-of-account, and thus a sum worth £10 16s 8d gros Flemish or about £7 10s sterling; cf CWE 1 323, 340–1, 347) was not due until 24 June, St John Baptist's day, but Jan de Hondt had complied in the past with similar requests for an advance payment (cf Epp 794:5n, 913:2). To facilitate the transaction, Erasmus may have sent a signed receipt, leaving it for he Hondt to fill in the particulars about the time and mode of payment in proper form. Or, as in Ep 913:9–12, he may have requested the canon to return the completed document for himself to sign upon receipt of the money. The quarter-days were those days on which payments of rents, debts, bills, taxes, etc, usually but not necessarily quarterly payments, were due. The customary days varied by country. In England, they were Lady Day (25 March), Midsummer or St John Baptist's day (24 June), Michaelmas (29 September), and Christmas (25 December); in Scotland, Candlemas (2 February), Whitsun (Pentecost, the seventh Sunday after Easter, around 15 May), Lammas (1 August), and Martinmas (11 November); in the Low Countries of 1520, the central days of the great Brabant fairs: Easter, Whitsun (Pentecost or 'Pinxter'), St Bavo's day (Bamis, 1 October), and Martinmas (11 November). The text would suggest the English quarter-day of St John the Baptist, despite the locale and the money-of-account mentioned in the letter.

4 Michael] Unidentified; conceivably he was Michael Bentinus, mentioned at the beginning of Erasmus' Ep 1433 to Jan de Hondt.

5 stuivers] The Flemish silver coin worth 2d, ie the double gros, formerly called the patard, briquet, plaque, and botdragher (cf cwe 1 323, 327, 331, 340–1, 347). Note that the stuiver also served as the shilling in the Flemish money-of-account system based on the notional 'florin' worth 40d gros (a system used by the Flemish and Dutch until the French Revolution).

6 Barbier] Pierre Barbier (cf Ep 443), now in Spain with the court of Charles v, evidently had a say together with Erasmus and de Hondt in the financial and legal transactions referred to rather obscurely in the following lines. At the beginning of 1517 Erasmus apparently resigned to Barbier all the benefices belonging to the canonry at Courtrai to which he had himself just been named. In turn it seems that Barbier resigned most of them to de Hondt, who was to reside at Courtrai, to pay Erasmus' annuity, and also to administer some benefices still held in Barbier's name. It seems that Erasmus' consent was needed when Barbier now attempted to convert the latter into an annuity (below lines 35–7). On the other hand it seems that Barbier's letter of *significamus* (in the diocese of Tournai a letter attesting non-resident status) was required every year to ensure the validity of the substitution arrangements and the income on which Erasmus' annuity was based. Cf Ep 2404 and P. Gorissen 'Het Kortrijkse pensioen van Erasmus' *De Leiegouw* 13 (1971) 131–2, 143–4.

7 bishop of Tournai] Louis Guillard; see Epp 360:20n, 1212.

8 St Gillis-Waas] Between Antwerp and Ghent; St Niklaas is five kilometres to the south of St Gillis. Jan de Hondt was himself a native of the Waas district.

9 Chièvres] Guillaume de Croy (cf Ep 532:30n); his second chaplain is not identified, but was conceivably to return with Charles v's court and to take charge of Barbier's benefices; see above n6.

10 long hoped for] Cf Epp 1007 n13, 1106 introduction.

11 Thielt] Jacob van Thielt of Wervik in Flanders (c 1475–1541 or 1543) was precentor of the Courtrai chapter and subsequently vicar-general to the bishop. In November 1517 he and de Hondt had shared a house.

12 Johannes Soti] Despite the discrepancy in the Christian names, this young man was probably identical with Jacobus Scoti of Courtrai, who registered at the University of Louvain on 28 August 1520 as a student of the College of the Lily, and the Jacob Soti who was a protégé of Jacob van Thielt and later chaplain and choirmaster at Courtrai. Aardenburg is 18 kilometres north-east of Bruges.

13 regent] Jan de Neve, a friend of Erasmus

1095

1 kinsman] See Ep 1085 n1.

2 *Farrago*] It was published late in 1519 (cf Ep 1009 introduction) and contained Pirckheimer's Ep 747 and Erasmus' reply, Ep 856. Pirckheimer's other recent letters are now missing, but one of them had actually been received, although very late (through the fault of Petrus Alamirus; cf the following note).

3 Alamirus] See Ep 1001 lines 34–5 and n1; Pirckheimer had read Ep 1001 in the *Farrago*.

4 attack] See Ep 1037 introduction.

5 *Apologia*] The *Apologia invectivis Lei* (cf Ep 1080 introduction) which announces Erasmus' *Responsiones*; see *Opuscula* 302–3.

6 fewer cheeses] See Epp 877:18–35; 1030:22–3. The malicious story of Hoog-straten's expulsion from Cologne had evidently reached Pirckheimer, who was like many others inclined to think that Lee and Hoogstraten were in collusion, perhaps on account of the *Hochstratus ovans*; cf Epp 1078 n3, 1083 introduction and n8.

7 another man's play] Cf Ep 998 introduction.

8 your pamphlet] Cf Ep 993:40–3; it did not mention Lee by name.

9 recognized his picture] See Ep 1061:585–6.

10 turn to roses] Cf Persius 2.38.

11 Lefèvre] From Pirckheimer's rough draft (cf introduction) it is clear that he was thinking of the controversy over the Magdalens. Pirckheimer himself wrote a short *Dissertatio ... de Maria Magdalena*, reiterating Lefèvre's argu-ments (first printed in his *Opera*, Frankfurt 1610, repr 1969, 220–3); cf Anselm Hufstader 'Lefèvre d'Etaples and the Magdalen' *Studies in the Renais-sance* 16 (1969) 31–60, especially 39. He may have assumed that John Fisher and other English divines supported Lee as well as attacking Lefèvre; cf Epp 1030 n2, 1099 n4.

12 Luther] Cf Epp 1030 n7; 1070 n1.

13 heresy] Cf Ep 1182 n2.

14 theologian] In line 136 it is claimed that he had met Erasmus at Basel. No identification can be offered; Pirckheimer seems to have invented the epi-sode (cf lines 150–1) in imitation of stories told by Erasmus; see eg Ep 948, printed in the *Farrago* and also in pamphlets published in Germany.

15 croaking] Cf Persius 5.12.

16 story] Cf *Adagia* I vii 87, an adage about wishful thinking. As an example Erasmus quotes Theocritus 9.16–17 on the dreams of a shepherd.

17 a little credit] The German humanists collectively are commended in Lee's *Annotationes* f cc² recto (cf Ep 1037).

18 plague] Cf Ep 1078 n16; *Christoph Scheurl's Briefbuch* (Potsdam 1867–72) II Ep 213, page 107.

19 Charles' arrival] See Ep 1106 introduction. In the Golden Bull of 1356 Nürn-berg had been stipulated as the location of the first diet in each reign. On his election Charles v had promised to abide by this rule and the Nürnberg city fathers had sent a delegation to Spain mostly to complain about mar-grave Casimir of Brandenburg, but also to remind him of his promise. It in-cluded Christoph Scheurl, who wrote a lengthy report of their mission in the form of a letter to Otto Beckmann, 27 March 1520; see *Scheurl's Briefbuch* Ep 213; J. Müller 'Nürnbergs Botschaft nach Spanien zu Kaiser Karl v. im Jahre 1519' *Historische Zeitschrift* 98 (1907) 302–28.

20 Oecolampadius] In response to Luther's teachings Oecolampadius felt com-pelled to subject his own religious views to a painful process of reassess-ment. It became difficult for him to carry out his duties as a preacher, a fact that may be reflected in his repeated relocations (cf Ep 1064 introduction).

He went to Altomünster in hopes that monastic life would give him ample time for study and prove compatible with his new understanding of the Gospel. Pirckheimer had just learned of his decision from a letter by Bernhard Adelmann of 24 April. Adelmann was close to Oecolampadius but failed to grasp the nature of his inner struggle; see E. Staehelin *Das theologische Lebenswerk J. Oekolampads* (Leipzig 1939) 111–15; for Erasmus' reactions see Epp 1102, 1139.

21 monastery] Altomünster, between Augsburg and Freising, belonged to the Brigittine order and since 1497 had accommodated nuns and monks in separate communities.

1096

1 wondering] Cf Ep 1093 introduction.

2 nearly two years] So More's first premonitions would have followed the publication of his *Epigrammata* in March 1518; cf Epp 550, 620 introductions. This remark may cast some doubt on the date preferred for Ep 620.

3 no persuasion from his friends] Cf Ep 1087 n57.

4 Cardinal] Antoine Bohier; cf Ep 1087 n58.

5 John] He is not identified.

6 *Chordigera*] Cf Ep 1087 n4.

7 Morychus] Cf Ep 1087 n77. More uses a hyperbolic play on words: madder even than the madman (who, he thinks, I am).

8 old saw] Cf *Adagia* I ix 30.

9 Empedocles] According to a classical legend the philosopher from Agrigentum (fifth century BC) had jumped into the crater, hoping his disappearance would be taken for an apotheosis.

10 a single book] Initially More considered reprinting the preceding controversial exchanges together with his *Epistola ad Germanum Brixium* (cf Ep 1087 introduction). Erasmus' remarks in Ep 1117:43–8, 120–3 suggest that the first part of the project was subsequently abandoned.

11 Bérault and Budé in the box] Cf Ep 1045:27–31.

12 'one witness … but ears'] Cf *Adagia* II vi 54.

13 'Whom saw I … nightfall?'] Terence *Andria* 768–70. Canthara was seen entering the house 'with something bundled up under her dress' that turns out to be a baby. Brie resembles her in his endeavour to conceal the true facts.

14 more than eight] Allen counted nine. Brie had stated that 'a great part' was set in type (Ep 1045:27); More infers that it was not half finished.

15 so he writes] Ep 1045:123–4.

16 the printer] Richard Pynson (d 1530), was a Norman by birth who began printing in London by 1490 and was appointed printer to the king in 1508. In this capacity he printed Henry VIII's *Assertio* of the seven sacraments against Luther.

17 keep them shut up] Permanently, it would seem, to judge from the rarity of the book. Erasmus apparently thought that More's reply might now be considered as not published, but it did reach Paris; see Epp 1117:123–4, 1131, 1184.

18 reprinted] Cf Ep 1087 n2.

19 appeal for you] Cf Ep 1093 n16.

20 as ill-matched oxen … awry] Ovid *Heroides* 9.29
21 Calais] Cf Ep 1106 introduction.
22 queen] Claude de France (October 1499–July 1524) was the daughter of Louis
   XII and Anne of Brittany. In May 1514 she married the future Francis I. Brie
   had been her mother's secretary. It is not known whether he attended the
   Calais meeting.

1097
1 you were promoting] The plural form in the Latin text shows that Erasmus was
   not referring to More alone (cf Ep 1026 n3, 1090:3–9). Not until line 32 does
   Erasmus address More individually in the second person singular.
2 in his society] Cf Ep 1053 n21.
3 Pace … returning] Cf Ep 999 introduction.
4 abbots] Cf Ep 1061 n23, n24.
5 helpers] Cf Ep 998 introduction.
6 part of the work] It is difficult to reconcile this statement with Erasmus' remark
   on 17 April that the third (and last) part of his answer to Lee was then
   being printed (cf Epp 1080 introduction, 1092:15). In fact, the latter parts were
   reprinted at Basel in the course of May (cf Ep 1100) and the book sent to
   Henry VIII (cf Ep 1098:27–8) was most likely the complete reply, already suitably bound. Barring an inaccurate statement, this letter could have been
   delayed and dated only when a messenger was available; cf Ep 1090
   introduction.

1098
1 pope himself] See Ep 864.
2 conspired] Cf the preface.
3 not an Englishman] Cf Ep 1083 n12.
4 a book] See Ep 1097 n6.
5 forty days] Cf Ep 1080 introduction.
6 Exaltation] No doubt Erasmus intended to write 'Finding of the Holy Cross,'
   which is 3 May, rather than 'Exaltation,' which would have been 14 September. By the latter date the quarrel with Lee was settled.

1099
1 abuse] Answered with the *Apologia invectivis Lei*; cf Ep 1080 introduction.
2 arguments] Answered with the two *Responsiones*; cf Ep 1080 introduction.
3 another book] There are no other references confirming this rumour which
   Erasmus may have heard on his return to Louvain.
4 Batmanson] The Carthusian John Batmanson (d 16 November 1531) rose to be
   prior of the Charterhouses at Hinton (Somerset) in 1523 and London in
   1529. It seems that he supported Lee's attack on Erasmus as well as John
   Fisher's attack on Jacques Lefèvre d'Etaples (cf Ep 1030) in the question of
   the Magdalens; see Ep 1113:9–12; Emden BRUC 44–5.

1100
1 personal attack] The *Apologia* to the students of Louvain and Ep 1061, which
   in Lee's volume (cf Ep 1037 introduction) preceded and followed the *Annota-*

tiones. As a quid pro quo Erasmus made sure that his own personal attacks, Ep 1053 and the *Apologia invectivis Lei*, were also excluded from Froben's volume; but cf the introduction.

2 English circles] CF Ep 1026 n3.

1101

1 Charles] For the return of Charles v and the following meetings of the three monarchs see Ep 1106 introduction.
2 reflection] Evidently the portrait medal by Quinten Metsys; cf Ep 1092 n2.
3 in my books] Cf Ep 995 n2.

1102

1 index] Perhaps unknown to Erasmus, it was published at just this time; *Index in tomos omnes operum divi Hieronymi cum interpretatione nominum Graecorum et Hebraeorum per Ioan. Oecolampadium theologum in ordinem digestus* (Basel: J. Froben May 1520), with a preface by Wolfgang Capito, dated 18 April. With it Oecolampadius brought to conclusion the great edition of Jerome (cf Ep 396) which had caused Erasmus and Oecolampadius to become friends and collaborators.
2 fortune] Allen's note gathers a large number of references as evidence of Erasmus' conception of himself as habitually unfortunate; cf Epp 1103:6–7, 1104:2–4.
3 Germany] Cf Ep 1078 n15.
4 conference of kings] Cf Ep 1106 introduction.
5 archbishop of Canterbury] William Warham
6 a friend of yours] Erasmus means himself; see Ep 1113:16–22.
7 three pamphlets] CF Ep 1080 introduction; for the other steps cf Epp 1074, 1083 introductions, and for Oecolampadius' own role cf Ep 1083 n9.
8 paraphrase] Cf Ep 1112.
9 Pharisees ... publican] Cf Luke 18:10–14.

1103

1 Urbanus] Urbanus Rhegius, an admirer of Erasmus, was born near Constance and had probably met Botzheim when on his way to Basel where he was to obtain a degree in theology in the autumn.
2 Abstemius] This name was adopted by Botzheim after his return from Italy, perhaps in honour of the Italian humanist Laurentius Abstemius (Astemio, c 1440–c 1505), whose edition of Sextus Aurelius Victor's *De vitis Caesarum* Botzheim arranged to have reprinted (Strasbourg: J. Prüss senior 1505).
3 against Pace] It was thought that he had written slightingly of Constance in his *De fructu* (cf Ep 887:7n). A printed defence is not known to exist; nor was Pace's book reprinted until 1967.
4 at my expense] See Ep 776:4n.
5 as faithful a friend] Cf Epp 1026 n3, 1089.
6 lately succeeded] See Ep 1025 n1.
7 Dorp] Cf introduction; neither Botzheim's letter nor a reply by Dorp is known to exist.
8 Oecolampadius] See Ep 1102 introduction.

9 Fabri] He was the vicar of the bishop of Constance and in September 1518 had
   been the host of Urbanus Rhegius; cf Ep 386.

1104

1 speaking ill] Vives had attacked the Paris professors in his *In pseudodialecticos*;
   see Ep 1106 n5.
2 certain monks] Cf below n8.
3 to better things] Cf Epp 618, 1108:217–21.
4 Fausto] Fausto Andrelini, the light-hearted friend of Erasmus' days at Paris,
   held none the less a degree in canon law; he died on 25 February 1518.
5 College of the Three Tongues] Cf the preface.
6 University of Paris] Cf Ep 1003 n3.
7 Nesen] Cf Epp 1046, 1057, 1111 n9.
8 two or three people] Cf above lines 7–9, Epp 1029 n2, 1040 n7, 1072
   introduction.
9 Camillus] Marcus Furius Camillus was the saviour of Rome at the time of the
   catastrophic Gallic invasion in the early fourth century BC.
10 say of Budé] See Epp 1004 n3, 1108:108–216.
11 Lucullus ... Diogenes] Diogenes had nothing; Lucullus had everything. Erasmus' answer to Vives is as frugal as Diogenes' hospitality.

1105

1 Zasius ... Amerbach] Could this letter be contemporary with Ep 1084 written
   by Bonifacius Amerbach both in his own name and that of Zasius? In Ep
   1084:50–1 Amerbach had mentioned that Zasius was going to write to both
   Dorp and Erasmus by the next messenger. While nothing is known of the
   existence of a letter to Dorp, Zasius wrote to Erasmus in July (Ep 1121). In
   Froben's *Epistolae aliquot eruditorum virorum* Engelbrecht's present letter is
   followed by one from Zasius to Beatus Rhenanus, in part on the subject of
   Lee, dated from 5 June 1520; see BRE Ep 168; cf Ep 164.
2 my exile] Engelbrecht had gone to Constance on account of the plague (cf Ep
   993 n11). By 5 March 1520, if not a month earlier, he had returned to
   Freiburg; cf Zwingli *Werke* VII Ep 123; AK II Ep 717:45.
3 literary society] The Latin term is 'senatus literarius.' While it is open to question to what kind of decision Engelbrecht is referring, the severity of the
   plague at Freiburg can be gathered from the numbers of matriculating students
   listed in the university register: 53 in the summer term of 1518; 34 in the
   winter term 1518–19; 7 in the summer term of 1519 (when the rector himself
   died) and another 13 after the plague had forced the evacuation of the
   university; then, following the return to Freiburg, 26 from January to April
   1520 and 100 from May to October 1520; cf *Die Matrikel der Universität
   Freiburg im Breisgau von 1460–1656* ed H. Mayer (Freiburg 1907–10; repr 1976)
   I-1 236–47. For later evidence of discussions in Freiburg whether it was
   legitimate to flee before the plague see Ludwig Baer's *Responsio* to this question, published as an appendix to his *De praeparatione ad mortem* (Basel: J.
   Oporinus November 1551).
4 'of rarest spirit he'] Ennius, quoted by Cicero *Tusculanae disputationes* 1.9.18.
   Edward Lee is intended.

5 Bactrian camel] An amazing beast; cf Apuleius *The Golden Ass* 7.14 implying that it has an enormous appetite, Pliny *Naturalis historia* 8.26 mentioning its prodigious age.
6 last letter] Ep 998
7 Greek and Hebrew] Cf Ep 998 n5.
8 a leaden straight-edge ... Lesbos] Cf *Adagia* I v 93: bending the rule to suit the facts.
9 elephant] Cf *Adagia* I ix 11.
10 Marsyas] A satyr who preposterously challenged Apollo to a contest in music
11 this class of men] The friars
12 'some massy theme ... match'] Persius 1.14
13 Hercules] It was nothing new for Erasmus to be called a Hercules on account of his literary labours (cf Epp 494:37, 1020:6), but the reference here, Hercules putting an end to the monsters in the cowl, forecasts the famous image of Luther as the German Hercules; see the well-known cartoon attributed to Hans Holbein, c 1522, in R.H. Bainton *Here I Stand* (New York: Mentor Books 1955) 93–4. For comparable expressions of loyalty to Erasmus as leader of the German humanists and reformers at this time see Allen's note to Ep 1105:27; Bietenholz in *The Sixteenth Century Journal* 8 supplement (1977) 69–70.
14 Anton] Anton Engelbrecht of Engen (d 1558) studied at Basel from 1517 and in 1518 was appointed chaplain to the cathedral. On 6 June 1520 he received a doctorate in theology and four days later, in the cathedral of Basel, he was consecrated bishop to become suffragan to George, count Palatine, bishop of Speyer (cf Ep 1109 n3). With this appointment he obtained the parish of Bruchsal. Subsequently he became a Protestant preacher at Strasbourg, but by 1544 had returned to the Catholic faith and settled in Cologne; see Werner Bellardi in *Archiv für Reformationsgeschichte* 64 (1973) 183–206.

1106

1 young man] We learn that he had written to Thomas More, who was able, it seems, to discuss the matter with the boy's father in person. Perhaps he was one of several English students in Louvain at this time. Among them was Thomas Winter, natural son of Cardinal Wolsey. Winter was in touch with both Erasmus and Vives (cf Vives' references to Maurice Birchinshaw, Winter's tutor, in Epp 1256, 1303, and de Vocht MHL 15–16), but More's remarks suggest a man of rather modest social standing, perhaps a businessman, who had summoned his son to return.
2 schoolmaster] Possibly Adrianus Aelius Barlandus (cf Ep 1025 introduction) whose renewed presence in the Netherlands is not documented before 1526, when he was made a member of the academic senate of the University of Louvain; see de Vocht CTL I 260.
3 you tell me] Ep 1082:60
4 *Declamationes*] The *Declamationes Syllanae*; cf Ep 1082 introduction, and for Erasmus' appraisal, lines 28–59.
5 *In pseudodialecticos*] Published together with *Aedes legum* in a collection of Vives' *Opuscula varia* (Louvain: D. Martens, n d; NK 2172). Together with Vives' *Pompeius fugiens* it was reprinted by Lazarus Schürer (Sélestat June

1520) and has now been critically edited and translated by Charles Fantazzi (Leiden 1979) and Rita Guerlac (Dordrecht-Boston-London 1979).

6 almost the same words] In her critical edition of *In pseudodialecticos* (cf above n5) Rita Guerlac reprints and translates this letter in Appendix I. In the same appendix she also includes four lengthy passages from Thomas More's letter to Maarten van Dorp (21 October [1515]; Rogers Ep 15). She notes the closeness of More's 'opinions, arguments, and phrasing' to some specific passages of Vives' treatise (page 158).

7 cardinal] Guillaume de Croy

8 *Aedes legum*] See above n5; for the *Somnium* see Ep 1108 n28.

9 *Declamationes*] See above n4.

1107

1 Erasmus in the shade] Erasmus expressed himself in similar fashion with regard to other young scholars: Philippus Melanchthon (Ep 605:37), Adrianus Cornelii Barlandus (Ep 646:13), Henricus Glareanus (Ep 903:12), Christophe de Longueil (Ep 905:23–4), Johannes Alexander Brassicanus (Ep 1146).

2 break ... the sophists] Cf Ep 1108 n3.

3 health] See Ep 1112 introduction.

1108

1 Croy] Guillaume de Croy; Vives was his tutor.

2 old acquaintances] Vives had studied at the Collège de Montaigu c 1509–12 and revisited Paris more than once.

3 pseudologicians] *In pseudodialecticos* (cf Ep 1106 n5), a short treatise in the form of a letter to Johannes Fortis (below n4), dated Louvain, 13 February 1519 (probably old style, ie 1520).

4 Fortis] Johannes Fortis came from Aragon and is documented as a student at Paris in 1510. Like Vives, he was an inmate of the Collège de Montaigu (above n2). In 1514 Vives dedicated an edition of Hyginus to him and introduced him as one of the speakers in his *Christi Iesu triumphus*; cf above n3.

5 Población] Juan Martín Población acquired a reputation as mathematician and physician. He moved in imperial court circles, was in 1529 physician to Alonso Manrique, archbishop of Seville and by 1531 to Eleanor, queen of France and sister of Charles V.

6 Melo] A Portuguese noble (1490–1536) who became a noted mathematician and representative of Erasmian humanism in Portugal. On his return from Paris he was appointed tutor to the king's sons, and he was the rector of the University of Lisbon, 1529–33.

7 Aquilinus] Aquilinus matriculated on 17 September 1520 at the University of Montpellier, where Poblición had registered in 1506; Fortis was to do likewise in 1523; see *Matricule de l'Université de Médecine de Montpellier (1503–1599)* ed Marcel Gouron (Geneva 1957) 10, 41, 44.

8 Enzinas] Perhaps Fernando de Enzinas of Valladolid (d by 1528), author of many works on logic which appeared in Paris between 1518 and 1526 with dedications dated from the Collège de Beauvais. It is possible, however, that there was also a Juan de Enzinas; see CEBR I 433–4.

9 Dom Martinho] An illegitimate son of Dom Afonso and a grandson of King Manuel I. Martinho was the Portuguese ambassador to Rome (1525–36) and later bishop and archbishop of Funchal on Madeira. Known as an admirer of Erasmus, he died in 1547.

10 king] Manuel I (1469–1521), king from 1495.

11 Jerome] For the publications of Erasmus mentioned in this paragraph see Epp 326, 373, 864, 126, 260, 222.

12 Suisset's] Richard of Swineshead or Swyneshed (fl 1340–54), a fellow of Merton College, Oxford, is mentioned by Vives in his In pseudodialecticos (ed Fantazzi 76–7) among other mediaeval scholars who 'were not grammarians, but philosophers and theologians, and therefore the logicians do not understand them'; see Emden BRUO.

13 syncategorema] A term of logic designating a word which cannot be used as a term by itself.

14 Etruscan soothsayer] The Etruscans, an ancient people of Italy, were famous for their methods of divination.

15 Budé, now mine too] After a recent change of heart on Vives' part; see Ep 1004 n3.

16 Greeks themselves] Such as Johannes Lascaris and others; cf Ep 1096:21, 32.

17 De asse] A work on the as and other ancient coins, with many digressions; cf Ep 346:12n.

18 Annotationes in Pandectas] Cf Ep 307:49n.

19 all your Ermolaos ... Vallas] Ermolao Barbaro, Giovanni Pico della Mirandola, Angelo Poliziano, Theodorus Gaza, and Lorenzo Valla; all leading Italian humanists.

20 Tunstall] See Ep 571:105–7.

21 'To cavil ... to copy it'] These words, In Greek, appear on the title-page of the second edition of Budé's De asse (Paris: J. Bade 14 October 1516).

22 light-hearted letters] See for instance Epp 810, 896, published in the Farrago of October 1519; cf CWE 6 preface.

23 moderation] Cf Horace Satires 1.1.106.

24 Cicero] Pro Sexto Roscio Amerino 21.58

25 Apologia] Cf Ep 597:37n.

26 Atticus and Brutus] Titus Pomponius Atticus and Marcus Iunius Brutus (who helped murder Caesar) were close friends of Cicero's and recipients of many of his letters.

27 Alecto's] One of the three Erinyes or Furies; cf Ep 1087:646.

28 dream] Vives chose to lecture on a topic which had been the subject of his recent publication, Somnium quae est praefatio ad Somnium Scipionis Ciceroniani, followed by another essay related to Cicero's Somnium Scipionis and the text of the latter (Antwerp: J. Thibault, with a dedicatory preface to Erard de La Marck, dated from Louvain, 28 March 1520; NK 4065). Vives' own Somnium is addressed to the students of Louvain (cf Ep 1111 n9). Thomas More saw the volume in May (cf Ep 1106:107) and it was reprinted by Froben in March 1521.

29 Trinity Sunday] 3 June 1520

1109

1 Basel] At the height of the controversy with Lee Erasmus had evidently dis-

patched a man to carry letters and printer's copy (perhaps including Epp 1100, 1102–3, 1110) as far as Basel and deliver other messages on his way (including perhaps Ep 1101).

2 defence] See below n6.

3 Speyer] Apparently then Buschius' home (line 26). Later in the year he was in Basel and, in addition to helping with Froben's *Epistolae aliquot eruditorum virorum*, published there a poem at the occasion of the solemn entry into Speyer of Bishop George, count Palatine: *Hypanticon* (Basel: A. Cratander 1520). For another connection between Speyer and Basel see Ep 1105 n14.

4 his name] The pun is based on the similarity between Leus and 'levis,' light.

5 beetle] Cf *Adagia* III vii 1.

6 two previous books] Perhaps the *Apologia invectivis Lei* and the first of the two *Responsiones* (cf Ep 1080 introduction). Erasmus' gift (above line 4) probably included all three pieces.

7 most worthless ... animals] Apuleius *The Golden Ass* 4.10

8 Hattstein] Hattstein (1489–1522) was a kinsman of Hutten and a Paris graduate. Since 1509 he had been a canon at Mainz. In 1521 he welcomed Erasmus at Mainz and helped him on his way to Basel (cf Ep 1342); see NDB.

9 now I know] See Ep 1044 n10.

1110

1 'poetry'] Nicolaas Baechem is named as a representative for this attitude in Allen Ep 1153:215; cf also Epp 1007:57, 1013:79. In Latin the term 'poetria' is very awkward.

2 no man by name] Cf Ep 1053 n57, n62.

3 Glaucon] A principal speaker in Plato's *Republic*. Erasmus was probably thinking of his speech in *Republic* 2.358–67; cf Ep 26:15–16.

4 Pace] At Ferrara in the winter 1508–9; cf Ep 211:53n.

5 *Vallum humanitatis*] Published in Cologne (N. Caesar 12 April 1518); the title means 'bulwark of the humanities.'

6 a work on letter-writing] *De conscribendis epistolis*, another early draft soon to be published without Erasmus' permission; cf Epp 71 introduction, 1193 n2.

7 our native Germany] For the strength of Erasmus' German patriotism at this time see the prefaces of CWE 6 and 7.

1111

1 rather weary] Perhaps because of his incipient illness; cf Ep 1112 introduction.

2 Sorbonne] A college of the University of Paris, founded in 1257 and famous for its tradition of scholastic scholarship. In the sixteenth century its name came to stand for the university as a whole. For Erasmus' current view of the University of Paris cf Ep 1003 n3.

3 Cinthius, and Cyllenius] Poetic names for Apollo and Mercury

4 John, bishop of Rochester] Erasmus had paid a brief visit to John Fisher in April 1517; cf Ep 592, but 'three years ago' is probably not meant to be taken exactly. This passage may recall conversations with Fisher at Rochester that took place some nine months earlier; cf Ep 456:253–70, 315, and for Fisher's connections with Cambridge cf Ep 229 introduction.

5 Oxford University ... blessing] Cf Epp 948:190–200, 965, 967:40n.
6 Alcalá] Founded in 1508 by Cardinal Jiménez de Cisneros, Alcalá was comparable with Cambridge in that it was intended to be a university city rather
than a city university. Jiménez' aim was a better formation for the Castilian
clergy, but he recognized that the new learning was important in order to
meet this goal. In 1527 Erasmus was invited to Alcalá; see Epp 1813–14.
7 Nebrija] Nebrija (1444–1522) was the leading philological scholar of Spain in
his generation.
8 open to anyone] Professors were appointed by the city council; cf Ep 722:17–
20; for Erasmus' general view of the University of Cologne cf Epp 821:19n,
1053 n20, 1078 n3.
9 ancient regulation] The regulations invoked to stop the irregular lectures of
Wilhelm Nesen (below lines 70–1; cf Epp 1046, 1057) were not actually
new, but may have been enforced more regularly from the time of Nesen's
case, as all lecturers were subjected to regular matriculation and annual
renewal of the 'venia legendi.' But the first rule was apparently waived in the
case of Vives himself who was granted the 'venia legendi' on 3 March 1520,
and the second rule was finally waived in the case of professors of the Collegium Trilingue. The prolonged negotiations had involved the full academic
senate as well as the Council of Brabant, and also Cardinal Guillaume de
Croy, whose support of the Trilingue had evidently been encouraged by
his tutor Vives; see de Vocht CTL I 445–64, 526–32, II 3–4.
10 Fausto] Fausto Andrelini; cf Ep 1104 n4.
11 the *Priapeia*] A collection of obscene poems in honour of Priapus, the Roman
god of fertility
12 Rome itself, Milan] Janus Lascaris, who had headed the Greek college at
Rome, was called to Milan in 1520 to head a similar institution founded by
Francis I; cf Ep 836 introduction.
13 Horace's] *Odes* 4.4.57; when their branches have been chopped off the oaks
on the Algidus mountains bud with renewed vigour.
14 munificent proposals] Cf Epp 994 n4, 1434.
15 indigestion] See Ep 1108:225–6.

1112
1 any of my works] After dedicating to Wolsey a translation from Plutarch; cf
Epp 284, 297.
2 genuine] Cf Ep 1062 n15.
3 take up arms] Cf Epp 1080 introduction, 1083 introduction.
4 be restored] A hint at Wolsey's reformation of monasteries and patronage of
academic study; cf Ep 967:25–38. In offering this flattering comparison Erasmus can hardly have been unaware of Wolsey's ambitions to obtain the
papacy.
5 always towards the worse] Cf Epp 384:27–9, 586:76–80; Bietenholz *History and
Biography* 28.
6 *Glossa ordinaria*] A Bible commentary based on the works of the Fathers, including the Venerable Bede (d 735), compiled under the direction of Anselm of Laon (d 1117).
7 first Epistle] 1 Pet 3:19–20, 4:6. In the paraphrase (LB VII 1096c) the second

passage is related to those buried in sin rather than to the deceased. As for
the first, Erasmus' note in the New Testament (LB VI 1051D) likewise refers to
Bede.

8 the second] 2 Pet 2:4, 11. Bede is criticized in the New Testament note on the
first passage (LB VI 1062D), but not mentioned in those on the second.
However, in the paraphrase of 2:11 (LB VII 1106B) Erasmus intends the fallen
angels who, unlike men, will not rebel to the point of blaspheming God.
The parenthetical clause was added, evidently by Erasmus, when Froben
reprinted the paraphrase and this letter in March 1521.

9 the earth consisting ... fire] 2 Pet 3:5, 10. *Condita* can be translated 'consisting
of' or 'brought forth.' The first meaning is given in the Latin translation of
the New Testament (LB VI 1066B, E) with a note explaining that Bede admits
both but that the second is closer to the Greek text. Accordingly the paraphrase (LB VI 1108A) prefers the second translation and refers to the second
day of creation.

10 Jude] Jude 9 and 14–15. In a note in the New Testament (LB VI 1090E–F)
Erasmus first refers to Jerome, who had associated Jude 9 with the book of
Enoch. Secondly he refers to Origen *De principiis* 3 [2.1] where the passage is
attributed to *De ascensione Mosis*. Both are Jewish apocrypha of the period
100 BC to 100 AD. The passage in *De ascensione Mosis* is now missing. Erasmus
evidently doubted that any written text could go back to Enoch, the father
of Methuselah (Gen 5:18–21).

11 surprising agreement] It is widely accepted today that much of Jude is incor-
porated into 2 Pet 2.

12 the Lord's transfiguration] 2 Pet 1:16–18; cf Matt 17:1–2.

13 Paul] Titus 1:12; cf LB VI 968C–D.

14 Sylvanus] 1 Pet 5:12

15 saying] 2 Pet 3:1

16 they suppose] In a long note on 1 Pet 5:13 (LB VI 1056–7) Erasmus mentions the
sources, including Jerome, but rejects the identification of Babylon with
Rome which was a convenient proof for Peter's presence in Rome; cf John
Fisher *Opera* (Würzburg 1697, repr 1967) 1345, 1351.

17 approval] In Latin *candida calcula*; Erasmus elegantly refers to the white pebble
cast as a vote for acquittal.

18 your generous auspices] Cf Epp 967:40n, 1111:38–41.

1113

1 health] Cf Ep 947 postscript.

2 conspiracy] See the preface.

3 abbots] Cf Ep 1061 n23, n24.

4 Standish] Henry Standish, bishop of St Asaph from 1518, was mocked by
Erasmus in *Adagia* II v 98. For his alleged connection with Lee cf Epp 1072
introduction.

5 Carthusian] John Batmanson; cf Ep 1099 n4.

6 Orestes] Cf Ep 967:132n.

7 Briart] Cf Ep 1029 n2.

8 Latomus] Cf Epp 934, 1059 introductions.

9 people connect] See the preface.

10 burnt in England] The following statements expand on an earlier remark in a letter published by Erasmus (Ep 1102:15–16). Luther's books had been burnt in Rome as early as the spring of 1519 (Luther w *Briefwechsel* I Ep 182) and elsewhere, including Cambridge, in 1520 (cf Ep 1141 n11). A solemn burning followed at London on 12 May 1521 'with all the pageantry of which Wolsey was capable.' John Fisher preached an English sermon which was translated into Latin by Richard Pace; see Surtz *Fisher* 8, 405–6; Fisher *Opera* (Würzburg 1697, repr 1967) 1372–92. By contrast there is apparently no further evidence of a burning planned at this time or of Erasmus' action to prevent it. Wolsey, however, was presumably present when Henry VIII raised the subject of Luther during Erasmus' audience at Calais (cf Ep 1106 introduction) and that the cardinal was no friend to Standish is shown by LP II 4074, 4083, 4089. In fact when he was first urged by Rome to proceed with the burning he refused for lack of requisite powers (LP III 1210), but later, under pressure, he complied (LP III 1234).

11 denial] For such denials, albeit qualified, see Luther's *Resolutiones disputationum de indulgentiarum virtute* (1518), and more recently the Leipzig disputation and following it the *Resolutiones Lutherianae* (1519); see Luther w I 567–70, 574–84, II 397–400.

12 towards civil strife] A premonition repeated in Epp 1127A, 1128, 1143 n5.

13 if must needs ... offences come] Cf Matt 18:7; Luke 17:1.

14 in indifferent health] Cf Ep 1112 introduction.

15 answer of Luther's] *Responsio ad condemnationem doctrinalem per Lovanienses et Colonienses factam*; six editions are known from 1520, including one by Claes de Grave, Antwerp (Luther w VI 172, 181–95; Benzing *Lutherbibliographie* 627–32; cf above Ep 1070 n1). Among those attacked by the conservative theologians Luther mentions (w VI 184) Lefèvre d'Etaples and 'Erasmus, that ram with his horns entangled in a thornbush'; cf Allen Ep 1186:13–14.

16 Hutten] See Ep 1114 introduction.

17 beggar-bullies] The friars; cf Ep 1082 n5.

1114

1 Le Sauvage] The chancellor had died on 7 June 1518; cf Epp 852–3.

2 Barbier] Pierre Barbier remained in Spain when Charles V left (cf Ep 1106 introduction), as he was now serving Charles' regent, Cardinal Adriaan of Utrecht. Marliano and Barbier were good friends (cf lines 16–17, but the letter there mentioned is now missing).

3 *Apologia*] See Ep 1072.

4 advice] To refrain from further controversies; see Ep 1198.

5 health] Cf Epp 1112, 1117 introductions.

1115

1 the passage ... *Moria*] The passage (ASD IV-3 190) mentions as a view commonly held by Christians and Platonists that the fetters of the body prevent the soul from contemplating things as they really exist. It is followed by a reference to the myth of the cave in Plato's *Republic* 7.514–16.

2 *Metaphysics*] It is not clear of what section Erasmus is thinking.

3 Paul] 2 Cor 4:18

4 remembers] Cf Ep 854:34n.
5 method of learning Latin] Halewijn expressed his view that grammar was too much emphasized in the study of Latin (below lines 45–6) in a treatise which, although composed in 1508, was not published until later: *Restauratio linguae latinae* (Antwerp: S. Cocus June 1533; NK 4238). For the danger Erasmus perceived in the excessive reliance on the reading of texts, cf his remarks about John Colet, Allen Ep 1211:519–25.
6 polygraph] Probably a reference to a treatise by Johannes Trithemius (1462–1516), abbot of Sponheim, *Polygraphiae libri sex* ([Basel: A. Petri] for J. Haselberg 1518), dealing with unusual scripts, various forms of cipher, and their application to magic. It is based on the many manuscripts the abbot had been collecting on this topic.
7 snake in the grass] Cf Virgil *Eclogues* 3.93.
8 Hutten] See Ep 1114 introduction.
9 illness] Cf Epp 1112, 1117 introductions.

1116
1 Canon] It seemed to Allen that Lips had added this word later in a space left at first copying; hence it may be inaccurate.
2 book] The paraphrase on Peter and Jude; see Ep 1112.

1117
1 Englishman] Cf Ep 1118 introduction.
2 the third] Of the earlier letters one was probably Ep 1045, the two others are missing; cf Ep 1073 n4.
3 visit] See below n12.
4 written to Bérault] The letter is missing; Erasmus refers to it again in lines 41, 80 and in Ep 1131. It may have been contemporary with Ep 1066; cf Ep 1073 introduction.
5 return their affection] A favourite formula of Erasmus; cf Epp 786:9–10, 873: 3–4.
6 than Budé] Cf Ep 1111:95–7; no answer to Budé's Ep 1073 is known.
7 Paolo Emilio] Author of a humanistic history of France
8 Cyprianus] Cyprianus Taleus; see Ep 768:5n.
9 business of Lee] Cf Ep 1080 introduction.
10 return of ... Charles] Cf Ep 1106 introduction.
11 business connected with Spain] For possible clues cf Epp 1094 n6, 1174. One could also think of Erasmus' old hopes for a major benefice, now renewed with the return of Charles' court; cf Epp 475:5n, 1141.
12 promise to come] See Epp 1073, 1179 introductions.
13 written to More] Ep 1093
14 letter to Bérault] Cf above n4.
15 arranged to have it printed] Only one edition of the *Antimorus* is known, which is Brie's (cf Ep 1045 introduction). For More's project of a reprint cf Ep 1096 n10.
16 your French friends] Cf Ep 1087:487–8.
17 a wicked attempt] See Ep 1087 n26.
18 to Bérault] Cf above n4.

19 Greek] In his careful account of More's studies (Ep 999:149–67) Erasmus does not mention Linacre and Grocyn. More himself confirms that he studied Aristotle with Linacre (Rogers Ep 15:1319–21). His acquaintance with Grocyn, and perhaps with the first rudiments of Greek, presumably occurred at Oxford (c 1492–4); cf Rogers Epp 2:14, 3:66; Reynolds *More* 15.

20 word-play] See Ep 1045 n3.

21 preface] See the preface to Brie's *Poematia duo* (Paris: N. de la Barre 2 June 1520). The relevant section repeating Brie's principal charges against More is reprinted in More y III-2 567.

22 paraphrase] Cf Ep 1112.

1118

1 promotion] To be dean of St Paul's; cf Epp 1025 n1, 1103:23–4.

2 business] Perhaps preventing a fresh attack by Lee; cf Ep 1099:4–6, 14–15.

3 fresh ruse] Cf Epp 1111 n9, 1113:4–5.

4 More's letter] Probably a now missing letter to More, either sent together with this note, or more likely already in More's possession, perhaps at Calais.

1119

1 Alexander] He is not identified. Allen tentatively suggested Alexander Schweiss (see Ep 1192) or Johann Alexander Brassicanus (cf Ep 1146).

2 letter] It is now missing. Perhaps it answered Ep 1001, and the medals of Frederick the Wise were sent along with it to make up for the loss described in Ep 1001:46–57.

3 talent] The same figure of speech, based on Athens' standard weight of gold, is used in Allen Ep 1125:52.

4 my own image in bronze] Cf Ep 1092 n2.

5 despised the empire] Cf Epp 1001:62–4, 1030:60–2.

6 new university] The University of Wittenberg was founded by the elector Frederick the Wise in 1502 and was intended to rival the neighbouring University of Leipzig, situated in the territory of Duke George, his cousin. While some professorships were tied to benefices within the gift of the Wittenberg chapter, others were endowed by the elector or filled with members of Wittenberg's two monastic communities, such as Staupitz and Luther. Humanistic studies were greatly strengthened with the appointment of Philippus Melanchthon as professor of Greek in 1518.

7 in Germany] Cf Epp 1078 n15, 1155 introduction.

8 I wrote] Ep 1113

9 Hutten] See Ep 1114 introduction; cf Ep 636:29n.

10 the truth] The following statement is significant as an early formulation of a concept that soon came to have considerable attraction for Erasmus, and through him for many others; cf Allen Ep 1167:164–7 and cwe 8 preface.

1120

1 friend] This salutation is found at the bottom of Zasius' rough draft.

2 bearer of this] See below n3.

3 Salzmann's] Johann Salzmann or Salius (d 1530) was a native of Steyr, Upper Austria, and was registered at the University of Vienna in 1497. On 19 June

1507 he dedicated to the city fathers of Annaberg in the Erz mountains a poem in praise of their town. In his preface he stated that a year earlier Maximilian I had crowned him with the poet's laurel as a reward for his verse on the duchy of Carinthia. The poem on Annaberg is published in Michael Barth *Annaberga* (Basel: J. Oporinus 1557). By 1510 Salzmann was town physician at Sibiu (Hermannstadt) in Transylvania and published a treatise about the plague. Subsequently he became physician at the court of Ferdinand I. He evidently delivered this letter and Ep 1121 to Erasmus; cf Ep 1129 introduction and ASD IX-1 144–5.

4 Geroldseck] A noble family with branches on both sides of the Upper Rhine. Gangolf I (d 1523) was a captain in the service of the Hapsburgs. In 1510 he regained possession of Hohengeroldseck near Lahr, from where his family had been driven in 1486. One of his sons, Gangolf II (d 1543) was a Hapsburg colonel and 'Landvogt' of the Hapsburg territory in Alsace. In 1519 he regained temporarily the lordship Sulz on the Neckar. His brother Diebold (c 1490–1531) was a Benedictine at Einsiedeln and from 1513 coadjutor of the aged abbot. His clerical vocation notwithstanding, he fought in defence of Sulz (1525), joined the reformers, and died like Zwingli in the battle of Kappel. He admired, and perhaps corresponded with, Erasmus at about this time and encouraged Leo Jud (Ep 1737) to undertake his German translation of the *Institutio principis christiani* (Zürich 1521, dedicated to Gangolf II); see NDB; J. Kindler von Knobloch *Badisches Geschlechterbuch* (Heidelberg 1898–1906) I 435; Zwingli *Werke* VII Epp 114, 156; *Zwingliana* 2 (1905–12) 164.

1121

1 Paul the jurist] Julius Paulus (fl 210 AD), a jurist frequently quoted in the *Corpus juris civilis* and the author of *Libri quinque sententiarum*, printed repeatedly in the sixteenth century. Zasius' reference has not been traced.

2 Caligula] Reported in Suetonius' *Caligula* 30

3 Mucius Scaevola] A Roman of the earliest days of the republic who showed heroism of legendary proportions in the struggle against an Etruscan chief, whom the Roman annalists call Porsena. Mucius' fellow conspirators are mentioned in Livy 2.13.2.

4 eagle ... flies] Cf *Adagia* III ii 65.

5 the Lord] Cf Prov 3:26.

6 What about Dorp?] Cf Ep 1044 n10. The following statements show that Zasius shared, and perhaps even inspired, Bonifacius Amerbach's reluctance to believe Dorp's conversion; cf Ep 1084 n4.

7 Budé] After the publication of Zasius' *Lucubrationes* (containing the treatise *De origine iuris*; cf Ep 862) Budé wrote to Zasius on 25 July [1519], reacting disagreeably to a gift copy of the work and an accompanying letter. Budé's letter caused a modest stir, and although Zasius refrained from publishing his answer of 1 September (cf *Udalrici Zasii epistolae* ed J.A. Riegger, Ulm 1774, II 466–78), neither he nor Bonifacius Amerbach were able to forgive Budé easily; see AK II Epp 674–5, 680, 703; Bietenholz *Basle and France* 188–92.

8 our king] Charles V; cf Ep 1065:20.

9 regency] The *Regentia* or *Regenz* was the governing council of the university. On 5 December 1520 Zasius was excused from attending its meetings hence-

forward on grounds of his age, merits, and recent marriage (to his former maid). It seems, however, that the dispensation was only temporary and limited to the duration of an extra lecture course on rhetoric which he began to teach in January 1521; cf Universitätsarchiv Freiburg, Senatsprotokolle xi 680 (information kindly supplied by Professor Steven Rowan); *Udalrici Zasii epistolae* (above n7) i 63–4; AK ii Ep 744.

THE DIALOGUE OF THE TWO-TONGUED AND THE TRILINGUALS / *DIALOGUS BILINGUIUM AC TRILINGUIUM*

Introductory note
330
1 Cf Ep 999 introduction, Allen Ep 1061:505n, below n26.
2 Cf BRE Ep 121.
3 Cf BRE Ep 128; AK ii Ep 680.
4 Cf *Vadianische Briefsammlung* ed E. Arbenz and H. Wartmann (St Gallen 1890–1908) ii Ep 170.
5 Cf *Opuscula* 197–8.
6 Cf BRE Ep 132.
7 Cf *Opuscula* 197.
8 Cf Epp 328–9, 462.
9 Cf Ep 925 introduction.
10 Cf Ep 994 n1.

331
11 Cf Ep 930:10–13.
12 Cf below n42, n43.
13 Cf Epp 696 introduction, 838.
14 Cf Ep 1000A.
15 Cf Ep 1084 n4, 1121 n6.
16 Cf Ep 1044 n10.
17 Cf BRE Ep 121.
18 Cf Ep 1044 introduction.
19 Cf Ep 1022 introduction.
20 Cf Ep 1053 n62.

332
21 Cf below n32.
22 Allen Ep 1225:108–9; cf Ep 636:21.
23 Cf Hutten *Opera* i Ep 143, *Opuscula* 199.
24 Cf AK ii Ep 680.
25 Zwingli *Werke* vii Ep 113
26 See Pace's letter in Froben's *Epistolae aliquot eruditorum virorum*; cf Ep 1083 introduction.
27 Cf BRE Ep 132.

28 Hutten *Opera* IV 535.
29 See Ep 1061:528–9, 585–9 and Lee's *Apologia* published with his *Annotationes* f CC verso; cf Ep 1037.
30 Cf *Opuscula* 269.
31 Cf Allen Ep 2615:168–70.
32 Cf Epp 1057, 1083 introduction, 1088 n4.
33 Cf Ep 1030 n7.
34 Like the third edition of the *Dialogus bilinguium ac trilinguium* it was printed by Lazarus Schürer (Sélestat 1520); cf Ep 1165 n17, de Vocht CTL I 575–602, Zwingli *Werke* VII Ep 111.

Title and dedicatory letter

334
1 Two-tongued] The Latin term 'bilinguis' means 'of two languages' as well as 'double-tongued, hypocritical.' At 344–5 above the second meaning is emphasized. Erasmus used the term in Epp 761:69–70, 794:82, perhaps ambiguously implying both meanings.
2 Calliope] One of the nine Muses; the patroness of epic poetry, and here evidently of the humanists
3 Lent] In 1519 Lent began on Ash Wednesday, 9 March; Easter Sunday was 24 April.
4 literary amusements] Cf Epp 636:16n, 961:41–50.
5 25 February] See introduction.

The Dialogue of the Two-tongued and the Trilinguals

335
1 Speakers] Aside from Mercury, the trickster, messenger, god of property, of roads, and of travel, no obvious reason suggests itself for the names chosen for the interlocutors in the dialogue. Pomponius is perhaps intended to bring to mind Cicero's Hellenophile friend and correspondent, Titus Pomponius Atticus. This association could account for the name Titus as well.
2 Hail, all hail!] This and some subsequent short exclamations used by Baramia are in transliterated Hebrew in the original text. The following line spoken by Titus is given in Greek, and Greek words and phrases appear in the text throughout.
3 half-black, half-white] The term points primarily to the Dominicans, who wear a black mantle over a white cowl; but cf below n47, n74, and 346 above.
4 impart all things to all] Latin *omnibus impartire omnia*; cf 1 Cor 9:22; Allen Ep 1233:84–5, 93–4; Bietenholz *History and Biography* 86–9, 93.
5 Crassus] Marcus Licinius Crassus, called 'the Rich' was consul in 70 BC, together with Pompey, and was killed by the Parthians in 53. According to Dio Cassius (40.27.3) they executed him by pouring molten gold into his mouth.
6 sesterce ... talent] A small coin and a very large sum of money, respectively
7 pigs in marjoram] Cf *Adagia* I iv 38.

8 snakes] This is a translation of the extremely rare word *excetrae* in the original. The word is used metaphorically for an evil woman in Plautus (*Casina* 644, *Pseudolus* 218); also in Livy 39.11.2.

336

9 Frankfurt] The Frankfurt trade fair, held both in the spring and autumn, was known in humanist circles mostly because of its great importance for the book trade. In March 1518 Erasmus had jestingly referred to Frankfurt as 'that sink of human vileness' (Ep 797:3–4). Nesen, who was a native of the same region, was to be appointed rector of a Frankfurt school in September 1520.
10 moles and Tiresiases] Cf *Adagia* I iii 55, 57.
11 Homer] Cf *Iliad* 5.454–5.
12 To the devil with them!] Literally, to the ravens; cf *Adagia* II i 96.
13 gods and goddesses] Cf Ep 967:129–32.
14 Veiovis] A Roman underworld deity whose name was taken to mean 'the counterpart (or antithesis) of Jupiter.' Antijove would almost serve as a translation.

337

15 Greek proverb] Cf *Adagia* IV vii 4. Mercury was the god of treasure-trove; with the words 'Mercury to share' one could claim part of something of value found by another.

338

16 pretext] Cf Epp 1007:52–4, 1033:252–64.
17 judge ... defendant] The text as translated is that of Schürer; the text of other editions is garbled. Defendant (*reus*) is perhaps here to be taken, somewhat awkwardly, in the sense of defence counsel; or it may represent a bit of hyperbole; cf Ep 1033:63–4.
18 in Homer ... by brother] Actually this is far from being a prominent theme in Homeric epic. De Vocht cites numerous references in his note on the passage, but erroneously; they deal with an entirely unrelated subject. However the point can be vaguely substantiated by, eg, *Iliad* 8.266 (Ajax and Teucer) or 4.148 (Agamemnon and Menelaus), and a number of other passages.
19 Ate] Here and in the next several lines, there is a protracted pun which it appears hopeless (and pointless) to attempt to translate. Mercury refers to the Greek goddess Ate (Ruin), but is understood by Pomponius to be saying the Latin words *a te* 'from you.' Ate clearly represents Jan Briart of Ath, 'vice-chancellor' of the University of Louvain; cf Epp 948:27n, 1029 n2.
20 that Ate] The one described by Homer; see *Iliad* 9.504–5, 19.91–5, 126–31.

339

21 Homer] See n20.
22 Lucian] *Tragopodagra* 184 identifies Podagra (gout) with Ate. That Briart suffered from the gout is confirmed in an unedited life by Gerard Morinck (cf Ep 1994), preserved with other writings by Morinck in a manuscript formerly of the abbey of St Truiden, now in Brussels, Archives Générales du Royaume; see de Vocht CTL I 555, 607, 621.

23 blear-eyed] Morinck (cf n22) described Briart's eyes as 'a little protruding, rather bleary; he used to almost close one whenever he thought about something intently'; see de Vocht CTL I 556.

24 'Like sighting ... one eye.'] The original here translated is a verbatim quotation of Persius 1.66.

25 pygmy] According to Morinck (cf n22) Briart was a little short of growth.

26 seps] The seps is one of a long list of deadly serpents, real and imaginary, in a gruesome passage of Lucan's *Pharsalia* (9.764). The venom of the seps was supposed to cause flesh to liquefy.

27 Tisiphone] See below note 30.

28 *merde*] The familiar French vulgarism is used here in an attempt to reproduce the striking effect of the coined word in the original, *stronton*. *Stront* is a coarse Dutch word corresponding in meaning to *merde*. It is here provided with a Greek ending, to produce, in the original, a rather feeble pun with *oncon* (tumor) of the preceding line.

340

29 spectacles] Cf above 336 and Ep 798:8n.

30 Megaera] Megaera, Alecto, and Tisiphone were the three Erinyes or Furies.

31 Cacus] A legendary monster who lived on what was to become the site of Rome. He was killed by Hercules. The association with Tisiphone is original here. Cf Virgil *Aeneid* 8.218ff.

32 Chole] In Greek χολή means 'gall, bile, hatred.' One person who logically could have been said to dominate and control Briart was Cardinal Adrian of Utrecht, subsequently Pope Adrian VI. In his absence his duties as the chancellor of the University of Louvain were exercised by Briart, his friend. In 1517–19 Erasmus' passing references to Adrian were critical (cf Epp 608, 713, 969). In contrast to this passage, Erasmus claimed in July 1520 (and repeatedly afterwards) that it was Jacobus Latomus (cf below n65), who was 'solely responsible for stirring up Noxus' (Ep 1123).

33 Chiragra ... Glossagra] Chiragra (arthritis; *chir-* 'hand'), Cephalagra (migraine; *cephal-* 'head'), and Glossagra (linguitis; *gloss-* 'tongue') are coined on the analogy of Podagra (gout; *pod-* 'foot').

34 associated with ... the court] From about 1490 to 1503 Briart belonged to the court of Margaret of York, widow of Duke Charles the Rash of Burgundy.

35 Salmacis] A water nymph who fell in love with Hermaphroditus. When he bathed in her fountain, she merged with his body in such a way that they then combined both sexes in one. Cf Ovid *Metamorphoses* 4.285ff.

341

36 Priapus] Originally a fertility deity associated with gardens. He was often represented with a grotesquely oversized phallus, and so came to be a symbol of lewdness.

37 Throw ... out] Cf *Adagia* III i 70.

38 epomis] Epomis is the Greek for Hebrew *ephod*, a priestly mantle, here used for the distinctive garment of the Magistri Nostri (see following note).

39 Magister Noster] This was a traditional title for professors, used by the humanists for the theologians of Louvain, Paris, Cologne, etc.

40 There are ... who plough.] Cf *Adagia* I vii 9.

41 hardly even alive] According to Morinck (cf above n22) Briart was plagued
with several disabilities in addition to his gout and severely ill for some
time before his death on 8 January 1520; cf de Vocht CTL I 558 and below n73.

42 Phenacus] Phenacus (Trickster), the patron god of cheats, is clearly to be identified with Maarten van Dorp (cf introduction). That Dorp was cross-eyed
(341 above) is confirmed by Gerard Morinck in his life of Dorp: 'He had quite
large eyes and a rather forbidding glance; one of his eyes stared forth with
less mobility than the other, and this marred his appearance somewhat' (de
Vocht CTL I 560 and MHL 262). The omission of this revealing detail in
Schürer's edition may be intentional. If it is indeed an indirect reflection
of Erasmus' many efforts to rehabilitate Dorp (cf Ep 1044:57–9, n10), the
concession is minimal. Dorp fared better in the lampoon *Eccius deodolatus*,
attributed to Pirckheimer. Whereas Briart, Baechem, Lee, and Latomus are
all matched with the names given to them in the *Dialogus bilinguium ac trilinguium*, Phenacus is merely said to be someone who had since acknowl-
edged his error (cf Hutten *Opera* IV 535). Dorp was also recognized as the
object of this passage in BRE Ep 143 as well as by Adelmann in the manuscript
notes of his copy (cf introduction) and likewise by Bonifacius Amerbach in
his copy (Öffentliche Bibliothek of the University of Basel, D.B. VI 4 number 5).
Adelmann and Amerbach also identified Briart, Baechem, Lee, and Latomus as targets of the dialogue. That Dorp is intended here is also accepted by Ferguson, de Vocht, and Jozef IJsewijn (in CEBR).

43 octopus] See *Adagia* II iii 91, where the octopus is associated with dullness,
stubborn greed, and conformism, changing its colour when it is opportune
to do so. Apparently this was thought to match Dorp's record, who from
friend to Erasmus had turned to critic (cf Epp 304, 347) but was now again
willing to defend Erasmus and the new learning (cf above 346). This passage
clearly suggests that Dorp's most recent conversion was insincere and
temporary.

44 Litae] The Greek word for prayers, here personified

342

45 Arami ... diuara] Evidently magicians' gibberish, like hocus pocus and abraca-
dabra, but with an appropriately Hebrew sound

46 headless Philip] A pun involving the Latin term *lippus* 'blear-eyed' used in the
following line. The reference is to the Carmelite Nicolaas Baechem called
Egmondanus; cf Ep 1088:17 and above n42.

47 patchwork cloak] Carmelites wear a white mantle over a brown cowl; cf above
n3.

48 Elijah] In the period of the Crusades the earliest Carmelites lived on Mount
Carmel near the 'fountain of Elijah'; hence the legend, here ridiculed, that
Elijah had founded the order.

49 Momides] A patronymic formed from the Greek Μῶμος, Latin *Momus*, Blame
personified; hence son (or descendant) of Blame

50 Corebus] Cf *Adagia* II ix 64; Corebus counted the waves of the sea.

51 Midas] Midas had tried in vain to conceal the donkey's ears Apollo had given
him; cf *Adagia* I iii 67.

343

52 Philautia] 'Self-Love,' the sister or attendant of 'Folly'; cf *Moria*, ASD IV-3 78, 96, 128, etc; Ep 1061:388–9.

53 Camelites] Erasmus used this pun with reference to Baechem rather than the Carmelite order as a whole; cf eg *Colloquia*, ASD I-3 267–8.

54 cousin of Philautia] In view of the Latin term *cacabus* 'pot' in the following description de Vocht suggested that Nicolas Coppin was intended. He was the regent of the College of the Falcon, formerly known as College of the Pot. In 1520 he succeeded Cardinal Adrian of Utrecht as dean of St Peter's and chancellor of the university. Subsequently he was an outspoken critic of Erasmus.

55 Vertumnus] An obscure god whose name was connected with the Latin *vertere* 'to change,' and who consequently served as a symbol of changeability.

56 pale and skinny] Cf Ep 906:494.

57 sardonic smile] The same term was used by Erasmus when he satirized Lee in Martens' re-edition of the *Colloquia* late in 1519; cf Ep 1061 n38, n40.

58 Smooth-lee as a hedgehog.] Titus here speaks in Greek, using the Greek term λεῖος [*leios*] 'smooth,' to refer to Edward Lee (cf Ep 1061:386–7). The whole sentence is also a pun on the Greek proverbial expression, λεῖος ὥσπερ ἐγχέλυς 'smooth as an eel,' with ἐχῖνος [*echinos*] 'hedgehog,' replacing ἐγχέλυς [*enchelys*] 'eel.'

59 Phthonides] A patronymic formed from the Greek word φθόνος [*phthonos*] 'envy,' here personified; hence son (or descendant) of Envy

60 long tail] Cf Ep 1061 n42.

61 almost free] Added in the revised Sélestat edition, this sentence presents another instance of deference to a well-known concern of Erasmus, who feared that his friends in exposing Lee to abuse and ridicule might offend the national pride of other Englishmen; cf Ep 1083 n12.

62 Scotland] Cf Epp 993:22, 1061:384–5.

63 nothing] Cf *Adagia* I viii 4.

64 herd of pigs] Evidently the students of Jacobus Latomus (cf below n65) are intended. According to de Vocht (CTL I 325, 568) Latomus had been teaching at the College of the Pig; cf above 346.

65 Gryllus] One of Plutarch's moral essays, *Gryllus*, represents a dialogue between Odysseus and Gryllus, a philosopher turned pig, at the court of the enchantress Circe. Intended is the theologian Jacobus Latomus; cf above n42.

344

66 speaks French] Probably francophone by descent, Latomus first studied at Paris in the Collège de Montaigu.

67 limping] Cf Epp 1088:17 and above 346.

68 Thee, god ... to speak] The text of the swine-chorus as here translated is that of Schürer. The earlier editions present an entirely different and somewhat inferior version:
Now we carry to the tomb
One Muse, and this seems fine to us,
As she is the biggest reason
That sophistry is now called very evil.
And that's why Magistri Nostri want to bury her

And not hear any defence of her.
The reason they call her a heretic
Is that she spurns Peripatetic theology,
Which those modernists are beginning now actually to scorn,
Even though it is the only way to confound the more stubborn heretics.

345
69 one of them] The first of the two laymen has not been identified. Henry de
   Vocht suggested Ruard Tapper, but Tapper was a priest and became doctor
   of divinity on 16 August 1519.
70 Carian ... Paphlagonia] Carians represent worthlessness, Paphlagonians re-
   moteness and stupidity.
71 But ... descent] In Schürer's edition, the only one that includes this line, the
   change of speaker has been inadvertently omitted.
72 that Bacchus] Cf *Adagia* II ix 1 on Bacchus, whose statue was placed outside
   the temple. The saying refers to those who attend to remote problems and
   neglect the immediate ones.
73 the other] Probably the physician Jan van Winckele; cf Ep 1042.
74 magpies in reverse] Perhaps Dominicans or Carmelites are intended; cf above
   n3, n47.
75 Silenus within] Cf Ep 1021 n6.
76 Cloacina] The goddess of the sewer, from *cloaca* 'sewer.' Such a goddess was
   actually worshipped in Rome at a shrine in the Forum, because of the
   importance of the drainage system that rendered the area usable.

346
77 more brutish] Cf Ep 980:39–40.
78 not lame] Cf above n67.
79 Marsyas] Marsyas was a satyr who had challenged Apollo to a contest of
   music. He was defeated by the god and flayed alive; cf Epp 998 n14, 1055.
80 Momides] Cf above 342.
81 Phenacus] Cf above n42.
82 helmet] Cf above 343.

TABLE OF CORRESPONDENTS

WORKS FREQUENTLY CITED

SHORT-TITLE FORMS

INDEX

TABLE OF CORRESPONDENTS

WORKS FREQUENTLY CITED

This list provides bibliographical information for works referred to in short-title form in the headnotes and footnotes to Epp 993–1121. For Erasmus' writings see the short-title list, pages 444–7. Editions of his letters are included in the list below.

AK	Alfred Hartmann and B.R. Jenny eds *Die Amerbach-korrespondenz* (Basel 1942–)
Allen	P.S. Allen, H.M. Allen, and H.W. Garrod eds *Opus epistolarum Des. Erasmi Roterodami* (Oxford 1906–58) 11 vols and index
ASD	*Opera omnia Desiderii Erasmi Roterodami* (Amsterdam 1969–)
Auctarium	*Auctarium selectarum aliquot epistolarum Erasmi Roterodami ad eruditos et eorum ad illum* (Basel: Froben August 1518)
Benzing *Lutherbibliographie*	Josef Benzing *Lutherbibliographie* (Baden-Baden 1966)
Bietenholz *Basle and France*	P.G. Bietenholz *Basle and France in the Sixteenth Century* (Geneva-Toronto 1971)
Bietenholz *History and Biography*	P.G. Bietenholz *History and Biography in the Work of Erasmus of Rotterdam* (Geneva 1966)
Boehmer *Luther*	Heinrich Boehmer *Martin Luther: Road to Reformation* (New York: Meridian Books 1957)
Brandi	Karl Brandi *Kaiser Karl v.* new ed (Darmstadt 1959–67)
BRE	A. Horawitz and K. Hartfelder eds *Briefwechsel des Beatus Rhenanus* (Leipzig 1886, repr 1966)
Budé *Opera omnia*	Guillaume Budé *Opera omnia* (Basel 1557; repr 1966) 3 vols
CC	*Corpus Christianorum: series Latina* (Turnhout 1953–)
CEBR	*Contemporaries of Erasmus: A Biographical Register of the Renaissance and Reformation* ed P.G. Bietenholz and T.B. Deutscher (Toronto 1985–7) 3 vols
CSEL	*Corpus scriptorum ecclesiasticorum latinorum* (Vienna-Leipzig 1866–)
CWE	*Collected Works of Erasmus* (Toronto 1974–)
DHGE	*Dictionnaire d'histoire et de géographie ecclésiastiques* ed A. Baudrillart et al (Paris 1912–)
Emden BRUC	A.B. Emden *Biographical Register of the University of Cambridge to AD 1500* (Cambridge 1963)
Emden BRUO	A.B. Emden *Biographical Register of the University of Oxford to AD 1500* (Oxford 1957–9) 3 vols; *Biographical Register of the University of Oxford, AD 1501 to 1540* (Oxford 1974)
Epistolae ad diversos	*Epistolae D. Erasmi Roterodami ad diversos et aliquot aliorum ad illum* (Basel: J. Froben 31 August 1521)
Farrago	*Farrago nova epistolarum Des. Erasmi Roterodami ad alios et aliorum ad hunc: admixtis quibusdam quas scripsit etiam adolescens* (Basel: J. Froben October 1519)

Geiger *Reuchlin*   Ludwig Geiger *Johann Reuchlin. Sein Leben und seine Werke* (Leipzig 1871; repr 1964)

Harsin *Erard de la Marck*   Paul Harsin *Etude critique sur l'histoire de la principauté de Liège II: Le règne d'Erard de la Marck 1505–1538* (Liège 1955)

Hutten *Opera*   E. Böcking ed *Ulrichi Hutteni opera* (Leipzig 1859–61; repr 1963) 5 vols

Hutten *Operum supplementum*   *Ulrichi Hutteni equitis Germani operum supplementum* ed E. Böcking (Leipzig 1869–71; repr 1966) 2 vols

Kalkoff *Kaiserwahl*   Paul Kalkoff *Die Kaiserwahl Friedrichs IV. und Karls V.* (Weimar 1925)

LB   J. Leclerc ed *Desiderii Erasmi Roterodami opera omnia* (Leiden 1703–6) 10 vols

LP   *Letters and Papers, Foreign and Domestic, of the Reign of Henry VIII* ed J.S. Brewer, J. Gairdner, R.H. Brodie (London 1862–1932) 36 vols

Luther w   *D. Martin Luthers Werke: Kritische Gesamtausgabe* (Weimar 1883–)

Melanchthons Briefwechsel   *Melanchthons Briefwechsel: Kritische und kommentierte Gesamtausgabe* ed Heinz Scheible (Stuttgart-Bad Cannstatt 1977–)

Melanchthon *Werke in Auswahl*   *Melanchthons Werke in Auswahl* ed R. Stupperich et al (Gütersloh 1951–)

More Y   *The Yale Edition of the Complete Works of St Thomas More* (New Haven-London 1961–)

NDB   *Neue Deutsche Biographie* ed Historische Kommission bei der Bayerischen Akademie der Wissenschaften (Berlin 1953–)

NK   W. Nijhoff and M.E. Kronenberg eds *Nederlandsche Bibliographie van 1500 tot 1540* (The Hague 1923–71)

NNBW   *Nieuw Nederlandsch Biografisch Woordenboek* ed P.C. Molhuysen et al, 2nd ed (Amsterdam 1974) 10 vols and Register

Opuscula   W.K. Ferguson ed *Erasmi opuscula: A Supplement to the Opera omnia* (The Hague 1933)

Opus epistolarum   *Opus epistolarum Des. Erasmi Roterodami per autorem diligenter recognitum et adjectis innumeris novis fere ad trientem auctum* (Basel: J. Froben, J. Herwagen, and N. Episcopius 1529)

Pastor   Ludwig von Pastor *The History of the Popes from the Close of the Middle Ages* ed and trans R.F. Kerr et al, 3rd ed (London 1938–53) 40 vols

PG   J.P. Migne ed *Patrologiae cursus completus ... series graeca* (Paris 1857–1912) 162 vols

PL   J.P. Migne ed *Patrologiae cursus completus ... series latina* (Paris 1844–1902) 221 vols

RE   L. Geiger ed *Johann Reuchlins Briefwechsel* (Stuttgart 1875; repr 1962)

Reedijk	C. Reedijk ed *The Poems of Desiderius Erasmus* (Leiden 1956)
Renaudet *Préréforme*	Augustin Renaudet *Préréforme et humanisme à Paris pendant les premières guerres d'Italie (1494–1517)* 2nd ed (Paris 1953)
Reynolds *More*	E.E. Reynolds *St. Thomas More* (Garden City, NY: Image Books 1958)
Rogers	Elizabeth Frances Rogers ed *The Correspondence of Sir Thomas More* (Princeton 1947)
Surtz *Fisher*	Edward Surtz *The Works and Days of John Fisher* (Cambridge, Mass 1967)
Vives *Opera*	Juan Luis Vives *Opera omnia* ed G. Mayáns y Siscar (Valencia 1782–90; repr 1964)
de Vocht *Busleyden*	Henry de Vocht *Jérôme de Busleyden* Humanistica lovaniensia 9 (Turnhout 1950)
de Vocht CTL	Henry de Vocht *History of the Foundation and the Rise of the Collegium Trilingue Lovaniense 1517–15ʒ0* Humanistica lovaniensia 10–13 (Louvain 1951–5) 4 vols
de Vocht *Literae ad Craneveldium*	*Literae virorum eruditorum ad Franciscum Craneveldium, 1522–1528* ed H. de Vocht (Louvain 1928)
de Vocht MHL	Henry de Vocht *Monumenta Humanistica Lovaniensia. Texts and Studies about Louvain Humanists in the First Half of the xvith Century* (Louvain 1934)
Zwingli *Werke*	*Huldreich Zwinglis Sämtliche Werke* ed E. Egli et al, Corpus Reformatorum vols 88–101 (Berlin-Zürich 1905– ; repr 1981)

SHORT-TITLE FORMS FOR ERASMUS' WORKS

Titles following colons are longer versions of the same, or are alternative titles. Items entirely enclosed in square brackets are of doubtful authorship. For abbreviations, see Works Frequently Cited.

Adagia: Adagiorum chiliades 1508, etc (Adagiorum collectanea for the primitive form, when required) LB II / ASD II-5, 6 / CWE 30-36

Admonitio adversus mendacium: Admonitio adversus mendacium et obtrectationem LB X

Annotationes in Novum Testamentum LB VI

Antibarbari LB X / ASD I-1 / CWE 23

Apologia ad Fabrum: Apologia ad Iacobum Fabrum Stapulensem LB IX

Apologia ad Caranzam: Apologia ad Sanctium Caranzam, or Apologia de tribus locis, or Responsio ad annotationem Stunicae ... a Sanctio Caranzam defensam LB IX

Apologia ad viginti et quattuor libros A. Pii LB IX

Apologia adversus Petrum Sutorem: Apologia adversus debacchationes Petri Sutoris LB IX

Apologia adversus monachos: Apologia adversus monachos quosdam hispanos LB IX

Apologia adversus rhapsodias Alberti Pii LB IX

Apologia contra Latomi dialogum: Apologia contra Iacobi Latomi dialogum de tribus linguis LB IX

Apologiae contra Stunicam: Apologiae contra Lopidem Stunicam LB IX / ASD IX-2

Apologia de 'In principio erat sermo' LB IX

Apologia de laude matrimonii: Apologia pro declamatione de laude matrimonii LB IX

Apologia de loco 'Omnes quidem': Apologia de loco 'Omnes quidem resurgemus' LB IX

Apologia invectivis Lei: Apologia qua respondet duabus invectivis Eduardi Lei Opuscula

Apophthegmata LB IV

Appendix respondens ad Sutorem LB IX

Argumenta: Argumenta in omnes epistolas apostolicas nova (with Paraphrases)

Axiomata pro causa Lutheri: Axiomata pro causa Martini Lutheri Opuscula

Carmina varia LB VIII

Catalogus lucubrationum LB I

Christiani hominis institutum, carmen LB V

Ciceronianus: Dialogus Ciceronianus LB I / ASD I-2 / CWE 28

Colloquia LB I / ASD I-3

Compendium vitae Allen I / CWE 4

[Consilium: Consilium cuiusdam ex animo cupientis esse consultum] Opuscula

De bello turcico: Consultatio de bello turcico LB V

De civilitate: De civilitate morum puerilium LB I / CWE 25

De concordia: De sarcienda ecclesiae concordia LB V

De conscribendis epistolis LB I / ASD I-2 / CWE 25

De constructione: De constructione octo partium orationis, or Syntaxis LB I / ASD I-4

De contemptu mundi: Epistola de contemptu mundi LB V / ASD V-1

De copia: De duplici copia verborum ac rerum LB I / CWE 24

De immensa Dei misericordia: Concio de immensa Dei misericordia LB V .

De libero arbitrio: De libero arbitrio diatribe LB IX

De praeparatione: De praeparatione ad mortem LB V / ASD V-1

De pueris instituendis: De pueris statim ac liberaliter instituendis LB I / ASD I-2 / CWE 26

De puero Iesu: Concio de puero Iesu LB V

De ratione studii LB I / ASD I-2 / CWE 24

De recta pronuntiatione: De recta latini graecique sermonis pronuntiatione LB I / ASD I-4 / CWE 26

De tedio Iesu: Disputatiuncula de tedio, pavore, tristicia Iesu LB V

De virtute amplectenda: Oratio de virtute amplectenda LB V

Declamatio de morte LB IV

Declamatiuncula LB IV

Declarationes ad censuras Lutetiae vulgatas: Declarationes ad censuras Lutetiae vulgatas sub nomine facultatis theologiae Parisiensis LB IX

Detectio praestigiarum: Detectio praestigiarum cuiusdam libelli germanice scripti LB X / ASD IX-1

[Dialogus bilinguium ac trilinguium: Chonradi Nastadiensis dialogus bilinguium ac trilinguium] *Opuscula* / CWE 7

Dilutio: Dilutio eorum quae Iodocus Clithoveus scripsit adversus declamationem suasoriam matrimonii

Divinationes ad notata Bedae LB IX

Ecclesiastes: Ecclesiastes sive de ratione concionandi LB V

Elenchus in N. Bedae censuras LB IX

Enchiridion: Enchiridion militis christiani LB V

Encomium matrimonii (in De conscribendis epistolis)

Encomium medicinae: Declamatio in laudem artis medicae LB I / ASD I-4

Epigrammata LB I

Epistola ad Dorpium LB IX / CWE 3

Epistola ad fratres Inferioris Germaniae: Responsio ad fratres Germaniae Inferioris ad epistolam apologeticam incerto autore proditam LB X

Epistola ad graculos: Epistola ad quosdam imprudentissimos graculos LB X

Epistola apologetica de Termino LB X

Epistola consolatoria: Epistola consolatoria virginibus sacris LB V

Epistola contra pseudevangelicos: Epistola contra quosdam qui se falso iactant evangelicos LB X / ASD IX-1

Epistola de esu carnium: Epistola apologetica ad Christophorum episcopum Basiliensem de interdicto esu carnium LB IX / ASD IX-1

Exomologesis: Exomologesis sive modus confitendi LB V

Explanatio symboli: Explanatio symboli apostolorum sive catechismus LB V / ASD V-1

Expostulatio Iesu LB V

Formula: Conficiendarum epistolarum formula (see De conscribendis epistolis)

Hymni varii LB V
Hyperaspistes LB X

Institutio christiani matrimonii LB V
Institutio principis christiani LB IV / ASD IV-1 / CWE 27

[Julius exclusus: Dialogus Julius exclusus e coelis] *Opuscula* / CWE 27

Lingua LB IV / ASD IV-1
Liturgia Virginis Matris: Virginis Matris apud Lauretum cultae liturgia LB V / ASD V-1

Methodus: Ratio verae theologiae LB V
Modus orandi Deum LB V / ASD V-1
Moria: Moriae encomium LB IV / ASD IV-3 / CWE 27

Novum Testamentum: Novum Testamentum 1519 and later (Novum instrumentum
    for the first edition, 1516, when required) LB VI

Obsecratio ad Virginem Mariam: Obsecratio sive oratio ad Virginem Mariam in
    rebus adversis LB V
Oratio de pace: Oratio de pace et discordia LB VIII
Oratio funebris: Oratio funebris Berthae de Heyen LB VIII

Paean Virgini Matri: Paean Virgini Matri dicendus LB V
Panegyricus: Panegyricus ad Philippum Austriae ducem LB IV / ASD IV-1 / CWE 27
Parabolae: Parabolae sive similia LB I / ASD I-5 / CWE 23
Paraclesis LB V, VI
Paraphrasis in Elegantias Vallae: Paraphrasis in Elegantias Laurentii Vallae LB I /
    ASD I-4
Paraphrasis in Matthaeum, etc (in Paraphrasis in Novum Testamentum)
Paraphrasis in Novum Testamentum LB VII / CWE 42-50
Peregrinatio apostolorum: Peregrinatio apostolorum Petri et Pauli LB VI, VII
Precatio ad Virginis filium Iesum (in Precatio pro pace)
Precatio dominica LB V
Precationes LB V
Precatio pro pace ecclesiae: Precatio ad Iesum pro pace ecclesiae LB IV, V
Progymnasmata: Progymnasmata quaedam primae adolescentiae Erasmi LB VIII
Psalmi: Psalmi, or Enarrationes sive commentarii in psalmos LB V / ASD V-2
Purgatio adversus epistolam Lutheri: Purgatio adversus epistolam non sobriam
    Lutheri LB IX

Querela pacis LB IV / ASD IV-2 / CWE 27

Ratio verae theologiae: Methodus LB V
Responsio ad annotationes Lei: Liber quo respondet annotationibus Lei LB IX
Responsio ad collationes: Responsio ad collationes cuiusdam iuvenis gerontodidas-
    cali LB IX

Responsio ad disputationem de divortio: Responsio ad disputationem cuiusdam Phimostomi de divortio LB IX

Responsio ad epistolam Pii: Responsio ad epistolam paraeneticam Alberti Pii, or Responsio ad exhortationem Pii LB IX

Responsio ad notulas Bedaicas LB X

Responsio ad Petri Cursii defensionem: Epistola de apologia Cursii LB X

Responsio adversus febricitantis libellum: Apologia monasticae religionis LB X

Spongia: Spongia adversus aspergines Hutteni LB X / ASD IX-1

Supputatio: Supputatio calumniarum Natalis Bedae LB IX

Vidua christiana LB V

Virginis et martyris comparatio LB V

Vita Hieronymi: Vita divi Hieronymi Stridonensis *Opuscula*

Index